California Natural History Guides: 56

A NATURAL HISTORY
OF CALIFORNIA

Allan A. Schoenherr

University of California Press

Berkeley • Los Angeles • London

CALIFORNIA NATURAL HISTORY GUIDES
Phyllis Faber and Bruce M. Pavlik, *General Editors*

University of California Press
Berkeley and Los Angeles, California
University of California Press, Ltd.
London, England

Copyright © 1992 by
The Regents of the University of California

First Paperback Printing 1995

Library of Congress Cataloging-in-Publication Data

Schoenherr, Allan, A.
    A natural history of California / Allan A. Schoenherr.
      p. cm.—(California natural history guides ; 56)
    Includes bibliographical references and index.
    ISBN 978-0-520-06922-0 pbk.
    1. Natural history—California. I. Title. II. Series.
    QH105.C2S36   1992
    508.794—dc20   91-42759

Printed in the United States of America
17 16 15 14 13 12 11 10 09
13 12 11 10 9 8 7 6

A NATURAL HISTORY
OF CALIFORNIA

A CENTENNIAL BOOK

One hundred books
published between 1990 and 1995
bear this special imprint of
the University of California Press.
We have chosen each Centennial Book
as an example of the Press's finest
publishing and bookmaking traditions
as we celebrate the beginning of
our second century.

UNIVERSITY OF CALIFORNIA PRESS

Founded in 1893

Contents

Acknowledgments

For fear of forgetting someone, I am tempted not to acknowledge anyone's help on this book. However, with a project of this size, it is obvious that quite a few people had something to do with the outcome. With this in mind, I hope that the friends, colleagues, and acquaintances that were inadvertently overlooked will understand how much I appreciate their help.

For starters, I am indebted to the administration of Fullerton College for providing me with a sabbatical leave, during which time I wrote the first draft. Second, Debbie Horrocks and Amy Gigliotti converted the typewritten first draft to word-processed versions. I am also deeply indebted to Fullerton College computer wizards such as Kent Gordon, Co Ho, Vinh Ho, Geoff Clifton, and Bill Dalphy, who tirelessly gave of their time to jury-rig equipment and write programs enabling me to incorporate numerous revisions with minimal effort and convert all my computer files to a single format.

Unless otherwise noted, all photographs are mine. For contributions of art, I appreciate the work of Karlin Grunau Marsh, Phil Lingle, Geoff Smith of Fullerton College, Pat Brame of Eaton Canyon Nature Center, and Philip Brown of the Southwestern Herpetologists Association. Further thanks go to those many persons cited in text who gave me permission to use work from previously published materials.

For their sage advice and comments on writing style, I am deeply appreciative to the following persons: Diana Cosand from California State University at Fullerton and Chuck Leavell of Fullerton College, for their help with the sections on basic ecology; Peter Tresselt of Fullerton College and N. King Huber of the United States Geologic Survey, for their help with the sections on geology; Alan Romspert of the California State University Desert Studies Consortium and Lenny Vincent of Fullerton College, for help with chapter 9, on deserts; Dana Seagars of the National Marine Fisheries Service, for his thoughtful review of the section on marine animals in chapter 12; and Phil Pister of the California Department of Fish and Game for his extremely helpful review of chapter 11, on inland waters.

Finally, I am indebted to Art Smith and Ernest Callenbach, editors from the University of California Press, who provided invaluable assistance and encouragement at all stages in the development of this project.

Introduction

A natural history is an account of natural phenomena. Over 300 years before Christ was born, Aristotle wrote his *Historia Animalium,* a series of nine books on the anatomy and habits of many animals native to Greece. In A.D. 77, Pliny the Elder, a Roman, wrote the 37-volume *Natural History* in an attempt to compile an encyclopedia of all known natural phenomena. For over 1500 years this work served as the basic reference for information about "nature." Ever since then, the expression "natural history" has been used to refer to a description of living organisms, their habits, and how they relate to the environment.

A more modern term used to describe organisms and their relationships with the environment is "ecology." The literal meaning of this word is "study of the house." In this context, "house" means the environment. This book easily could have been entitled *The Ecology of California,* because it is about the creatures and the environment in the state of California. In recent years, however, ecology has become a highly theoretical and technical science, and it does not encompass a study of rocks and geologic history. This book includes a description of organisms, rocks, and the environment, and an attempt to explain what factors through time created what we see today. The facts behind the concepts that are stressed in this book have been drawn from ecology, zoology, botany, biogeography, climatology, paleontology, and geology. Therefore it seems best to call it a natural history.

California is a highly complex geographic unit. There is more climatic and topographic variation in California than in any other region of comparable size in the United States. The highest and lowest points in the lower 48 states are less than 100 miles (160 km) from each other in eastern California. Mount Whitney, located on the crest of the Sierra Nevada, at an elevation of 14,496 feet (4418 m), is only 80 miles (128 km) west of Bad Water in Death Valley, which is 282 feet (87 m) below sea level.

California also has a great range of climates. The *Sunset Western Garden Book* (Lane Publishing Co.) describes 24 different climatic zones within the state. Outside of California, few states have more than four zones, and most have only one.

Total precipitation per year can exceed 120 inches (300 cm) in the northwestern forests, although the official record for annual precipitation, 161 inches (403 cm), occurred in the Santa Lucia Mountains of the southern Coast Ranges. In the southwestern deserts it is not uncommon for some locations to go several years without measurable precipitation. Bagdad, a now-deserted community on old Route 66 in the Mojave Desert, was reported to be the driest place in the United States. No measurable precipitation was recorded for 25 months.

The range of temperatures in California is also extreme. Subzero temperatures may continue for many days at high elevations in the mountains; and Furnace Creek in Death Valley, at 134°F (57°C), holds the record for the highest official air temperature ever recorded in the Western Hemisphere.

The geologic picture of California is also very complex. Most of the state is composed of a melange of rock units from different sources, and of different ages, that became attached to its western border as North America slid westward over the floor of the Pacific Ocean. Tremendous forces have stretched and warped the land, so that California today is a mixture of mountains and valleys of diverse origin cut through by major fault systems. Lands west of the San Andreas fault, for example, have slid to their present position from a point adjacent to mainland Mexico, perhaps as much as 300 miles (480 km) to the south.

The great variety of rock materials degrade to form a corresponding variety of soils. Soils of different mineral content and texture have a profound influence on plants and animals. A particular soil type may have its own specially adapted community of organisms.

The combination of diverse climate and diverse soil is responsible for the development of a diversity of habitats. The total number of habitat types varies, depending on whether the classifier is a splitter or a lumper. For example, the California Natural Heritage Section recognizes about 300 natural communities, and the California Department of Fish and Game recognizes 178 major habitat types. This book shall consider about 35 terrestrial communities based on the system developed by Munz and Keck in 1959. Furthermore, about 15 different aquatic communities will be discussed.

Many specialized plants and animals are found in California. There are more endemic species in California than in any area of equivalent size in North America. There are more than 5000 native plants in California, and at least a third of them occur naturally nowhere else on earth. Among vertebrate animals, there are nearly 1000 native species. Depending on how a person classifies the species, that number includes about 540 birds, 214 mammals, 77 reptiles, 47 amphibians, and 83 freshwater fishes. Of these, 65 species are considered to be endemic. Among animals as a whole, including insects and other invertebrates, at least 50 percent of the species and subspecies are confined within the borders of the state.

The reason for writing a book of this type is to familiarize readers with this special place called California. After reading it, a person should be able to describe the climate, rocks, soil, plants, animals, and biogeography of any area in California. The reader should be able to explain how those things got there and the ways in which they relate to each other.

Another, no less important reason for writing a book of this type is to foster appreciation for California's natural diversity. Much of California's nature is threatened. The Nature Conservancy has reported that about 25 percent of the state can no longer support its original communities of plants and animals. Since 1900, 65 percent of the state's coastal wetlands have been dredged, filled, or drained. Riparian forests of the Great Central Valley, which once covered hundreds of square miles, are nearly gone, and some specialized communities, such as Southern Coastal Dune Scrub, have been reduced to only a few hundred acres. Not only does California have the greatest number of unique organisms in the continental United States, but it also has the highest number of threatened species, many of which are among the unique or endemic ones. Some 608 kinds of plants are listed as threatened with extinction.

This book is organized around geographic regions using, as a starting point, the 12 geomorphic provinces described by the California Division of Mines and Geology. Superimposed on these regions are the natural biotic provinces based on climate and living organisms. The result is a sequence of chapters in which various regions of the state are characterized with respect to climate, geology, and biotic communities. Animals and plants are discussed using recent standardized common and scientific names wherever possible. Standardized vocabulary is also used for geologic formations.

In no part of this book is the treatment of plants, animals, and geologic units meant to be exhaustive. In each region the emphasis is on those things that are conspicuous, distinctive, and/or interesting. In cases where an organism, a community, or a rock unit occurs in more than one geographic area, it is discussed in the context in which it seems to be most significant.

Every attempt has been made to ensure that facts and concepts presented here are based on the most up-to-date references. However, there is a good deal of disagreement among experts, particularly about evolutionary relationships, biogeography, and geologic history. If errors or discrepancies seem to occur, or if more information is desired, the reader is encouraged to consult the references at the back of the book.

I

California's Natural Regions

The California Division of Mines and Geology has divided the state into 12 geomorphic provinces based on rock type and topography (fig. 1.1). The words *topography* and *geomorphic* refer to the shape of the land: *Topography* means "place picture," and *geomorphic* means "earth form." These geomorphic provinces represent natural units within which the boundaries of landforms are remarkably consistent with those of biological communities. That is, the shape of the earth influences climate, and climate influences the distribution of plants and animals. These provinces, with some modifications, shall provide the framework of organization for this book (fig. 1.2). A brief overview of these regions is the subject of this chapter.

SIERRA NEVADA

The Sierra Nevada is the most conspicuous geographic feature of the state of California. Essentially a single mountain range approximately 400 miles (640 km) long and 50 miles (80 km) wide, it is one of the largest of its kind in the world. In Spanish, *sierra* means "saw" or "jagged range," and *nevada* means "frozen" or "snowed upon." The plural form, *sierras*, is a common but incorrect reference to this single large range of mountains.

The Sierra is a large block of granitic rocks known as a batholith. According to many authorities, uplift of this granite has taken place during the past 10 to 12 million years, most of it during the last 3 million. Most of the uplift occurred along a deep fissure known as the Sierra Nevada fault zone, which lies along the base of the steep eastern wall of the range. In 1872, in the vicinity of Lone Pine, one of the largest earthquakes in history took place on this fault. Scarps as high as 20 feet (6.5 m) are visible in this area. A common grave north of town contains the remains of 23 persons, most of the population living there at the time. The recentness of this earthquake testifies that the Sierra is youthful and still actively rising. Its jagged appearance is because there has not been very much time for it to wear down.

By virtue of its geologic history, the Sierra Nevada is unique among mountain ranges of the world. It is a large, jagged, glacier-carved mass of granite. Its distinctive scenery has captured the minds and hearts of naturalists and photographers such as John Muir and Ansel Adams, whose writing and photography have made the landscape of the Sierra Nevada familiar all over the world.

Because uplift has taken place mostly on the eastern edge of the Sierra, the western slope is, in fact, the top of a large rock mass. This mass angles gradually westward (about 2°) to pass beneath sediments that form the floor of the Great Central Valley. The eastern slope, a high scarp that runs on a north-south line along the western border of Owens Valley, may be seen as the edge of the rock mass. From the tops

FIGURE 1.1   Geomorphic provinces. (From M. Hill. *California Landscape*. Berkeley: University of California Press, 1984.)

of high peaks along the crest of the Sierra, 13 of which are higher than 14,000 feet (4268 m), the eastern slope drops nearly 2 vertical miles into Owens Valley. At 14,496 feet (4418 m), Mount Whitney, west of Lone Pine, is the highest mountain in the contiguous 48 states.

There are faults along the western slope of the Sierra too. Uplift along these faults has not been great, but crystallization of precious minerals at the edge of the granitic rocks has been a major source of gold and silver. In fact, the Gold Rush that began in 1849 and brought a huge wave of humans to California was caused (at least indirectly) by the special geologic processes that go along with the formation of granitic rocks. The rich gold-mining district along the western edge of the Sierra is still known as the Mother Lode country, and the associated fault system is called the Mother Lode fault.

LANDFORMS AND NATURAL REGIONS OF CALIFORNIA
 1. SIERRA NEVADA
 2. KLAMATH MOUNTAINS ⎫ PACIFIC
 3. CASCADE RANGE ⎰ NORTHWEST
 4. COAST RANGES
 5. TRANVERSE RANGES ⎫ CISMONTANE
 6. PENINSULAR RANGES ⎰ SOUTHERN CALIFORNIA
 7. GREAT BASIN DESERT ⎫
 8. MOJAVE DESERT ⎬ DESERTS
 9. COLORADO DESERT ⎰
10. GREAT CENTRAL VALLEY

FIGURE 1.2   Landforms and natural regions of California. (Courtesy of California Insect Survey, Department of Entomology and Parasitology, University of California.)

As air masses move off the Pacific Ocean, they must rise if they are to cross the Sierra Nevada. As the air rises, it becomes cooled and water vapor condenses. The western slope of the Sierra therefore receives abundant precipitation. During an average year in the Red Fir forest at middle elevations, over 80 inches (200 cm) of precipitation may fall. The steep eastern slope is, however, considerably drier. To the east of the Sierra is Owens Valley, a desert land that lies in the Sierran "rain shadow." Owens Valley is the westernmost part of a vast desert region known as the Great Basin, which extends eastward all the way to the Rocky Mountains.

Large rivers flow down the western slope of the Sierra Nevada. For the most part, these rivers have been impounded to provide a water supply for massive agricultural enterprises of the Great Central Valley and for the San Francisco Bay area. By means of the Sacramento River and the California Aqueduct, some of this water is carried from its source in the northern Sierra over 500 miles (800 km) to southern California. Most of the water in rivers that cascade down the steep eastern slope of the Sierra is diverted into the Los Angeles Aqueduct and transported to the city of Los Angeles. The Sierra Nevada and its water are responsible not only for great scenic beauty but also for the wealth of California as a whole and the crowding of southern California in particular. California is the most populous state in the union, and the Los Angeles area is the most densely populated area of its size in the United States. Agriculture and industry are California's economic base, and they depend on the water that comes from the Sierra Nevada.

The heavy precipitation that falls on the western slope of the Sierra supports a dense coniferous forest. Included among many species of cone-bearing trees are the economically important Ponderosa Pine, White Fir, and Red Fir. Many of these trees become very large. The tallest pines in the world, Sugar Pines, occur here, and the largest organisms that have ever lived, Sierra Redwoods, occur nowhere else in the world.

The ruggedness of the Sierra has made large portions of the range inaccessible to motor vehicles. To allow people to experience the extraordinary beauty of the Sierra Nevada, the federal government has set aside large tracts of land as wilderness areas that may be visited only by foot or on horseback. These areas today are divided among three national parks—Yosemite, Sequoia, and Kings Canyon—as well as national forest wilderness areas such as those named for John Muir and Ansel Adams. Altogether, these wilderness areas represent the largest roadless area in the contiguous 48 states.

Along the crest of the Sierra is the 170-mile (270-km) stretch of alpine wilderness known to hikers and packers as the "high Sierra," or simply "the high country." From Sonora Pass on State Highway 108 southward to the road up Ninemile Canyon to Kennedy Meadows, the Sierra is traversed by only one road, the road through Yosemite National Park. It crosses Tioga Pass at 9941 feet (3031 m) elevation. This spectacular region of alpine meadows, sculpted rock, twisted trees, and thousands of alpine lakes is the home of Bighorn Sheep, ground squirrels, marmots, pikas, and a unique species of salamander. The high lakes of this country are legendary for their beauty and their trout fishing. It is interesting to note, however, that all species of trout but one were introduced by humans. The unique Golden Trout, native to the Kern Plateau of the southern Sierra, is the state freshwater fish. This highly colored descendant of the Rainbow Trout is the only true high-country fish, and its distribution was limited originally to those southern Sierra streams that escaped glaciation.

KLAMATH MOUNTAINS

In the northwest corner of California is one of the least accessible and least known mountain regions in the state. This region is a rocky upland about 5000 to 7000 feet (1500–2100 m) in elevation. It has been cut deeply by three river systems, the Smith, Klamath, and Trinity rivers. The highest peak is Thompson Peak at 8936 feet (2725 m). Heavy precipitation occurs here. In the wettest part of the area, the Douglas Fir forest of the Siskiyou Mountains, average precipitation is reported to be about 140 inches (450 cm) per year. Runoff from this rain is the cause of the large river systems.

The geological picture of the Klamath Mountains is similar to that of the Sierra Nevada. Apparently, rocks of the Klamath Mountains were once continuous with the northern Sierra Nevada. About 130 million years ago the Klamath region became separated from the Sierra and was carried about 60 miles (100 km) to the northwest. An intervening sea apparently lay in the rift until volcanism of the Cascade system filled the area between the two regions with numerous lava flows.

The heavy precipitation, abundant fog, and comparatively mild temperatures associated with a coastal position contributed to the formation of a dense forest similar to that which occurs along the coast of Alaska and western Canada. In fact, the southernmost distribution of such Alaskan species as Alaskan Cedar and Silver Fir bears witness to the wetness of this area. Other members of this northern rain forest also extend southward into the northern Coast Ranges. These include Red Cedar, Western Hemlock, and Sitka Spruce. At higher elevations are a few species, such as Subalpine Fir, also found in the Rocky Mountains. The presence here of Foxtail Pine, which grows primarily in the southern Sierra Nevada at about 11,000 feet (3300 m) in elevation, is an interesting enigma. Foxtail Pines are closely related to Bristlecone Pines, which grow on mountaintops throughout the Great Basin. Of primary economic importance are dense stands of Douglas Fir, the major source of construction lumber. The little access that exists in the Klamath Mountains is on logging roads that have been cut into steep slopes to carry out timber.

Subunits of the Klamath Mountains are formed by deep incisions that have been made by large rivers. The northernmost region, which lies astride the California-Oregon border, is known as the Siskiyou Mountains. The main drainage to the west of the Siskiyous is the Smith River. To the south, the main gorge of the Klamath River separates the Siskiyous from the Salmon and Marble Mountains. These are drained by the Salmon River, a tributary of the Klamath. South of the Salmon River, the highest peaks of the area rise in the Trinity Alps. The Trinity River, which drains the Trinity Alps, is also quite large. It enters the Klamath just before that river dumps into the Pacific Ocean. Although the uppermost reaches of the Klamath and Trinity rivers have been dammed, the lower reaches still flow freely. These rivers of the Pacific Northwest are the last such free-flowing rivers in California. Because of this they are the last places in California where salmon and steelhead are able to swim unimpeded upstream to their ancestral spawning grounds. Recognizing the economic and esthetic value of these rivers, the federal government has assigned wild and scenic status to them. This designation means that no human activities will be allowed to reduce their flow. In California, the wild and scenic rivers include the Smith, Klamath, and Eel rivers of the Pacific Northwest as well as parts of the American, Tuolumne, Kings, and Kern rivers of the western Sierra Nevada.

CASCADE MOUNTAINS

The Cascade Mountains in northern California represent the southern end of a long range of volcanic mountains that lies on a north-south axis through Washington, Oregon, and northern California. Like the Sierra Nevada, the Cascades present a major barrier to the flow of moist air. In fact this "great stone wall" formed by the Cascades and the Sierra Nevada is responsible for the rain shadow that has caused the Great Basin Desert.

In California only two major peaks are associated with the Cascades: Mount Lassen at 10,457 feet (3187 m) and Mount Shasta at 14,162 feet (4317 m), one of California's 15 peaks higher than 14,000 feet (4268 m). Sutter Buttes, a volcanic outcrop in the Sacramento Valley near Marysville, rises over 2000 feet (300 m) from the valley sediments. This pile of volcanic rocks, the only structure of its type in the Great Central Valley, is probably the southernmost of the Cascade volcanoes.

Mount Lassen and Mount Shasta loom spectacularly above the surrounding countryside. Each of these large, treeless peaks can be seen from the other, as is typical in most of the Cascade topography. The peaks are surrounded by a coniferous forest dominated by Ponderosa Pine, which is of prime importance for wood products. This forest is distributed widely over rounded foothills of lower aspect. These hills represent numerous episodes of volcanism.

From a geological point of view, the entire Cascade Range is young. Its oldest portion may be no older than about 5 million years. Many of its peaks are much younger: Mount Lassen probably appeared only 10,000 years ago. Recent eruptions of Mount Saint Helens in Washington attest to the fact that some of the Cascade volcanoes are still capable of significant activity. Mount Shasta last erupted in 1786, a mere 200 years ago, and Mount Lassen, the last known active volcano in California, most recently erupted repeatedly from 1914 to 1921.

Precipitation on the western side of the California portion of the Cascades averages about 80 inches (200 cm) per year. Abundant snow often caps Lassen and Shasta all year long. Mount Shasta is nearly always white-topped, and its glacier field is perhaps the most spectacular in the state. The Cascades are drained by the Pit River, which comes from the Modoc Plateau to the east. The Pit River formerly ran into the Sacramento River, but it now drains into Shasta Reservoir, a part of the massive State Water Project that includes the California Aqueduct.

COAST RANGES

California's Coast Ranges extend over 500 miles (800 km) from near the Oregon border southward to the Santa Barbara area. Here they meet the Santa Ynez Mountains of the Transverse Ranges. The Coast Ranges rise abruptly from the sea to nearly 6000 feet (2000 m) in elevation. On the east they dip beneath the sediments of the Great Central Valley. In general, they consist of a series of northwest-to-southeast–trending ridges and valleys associated with faulting and folding. Many of the rivers of the Coast Ranges flow northward to empty into the Pacific Ocean many miles from their source. In the northern Coast Ranges, the Eel River dumps into the ocean south of Eureka, approximately 150 miles (240 km) north of its source. In the southern Coast Ranges, the Salinas River does likewise to empty into Monterey Bay. The northern and southern Coast Ranges are separated from each other by San Francisco Bay.

Geologically, the Coast Ranges are extremely diverse, although for the most part the rocks are ocean sediments in various stages of alteration. One interesting assemblage is known as the Franciscan Formation, in honor of the city of San Francisco. Included among the Franciscan rocks is a waxy green rock known as serpentine, or serpentinite, which has been designated the state rock. It has a unique combination of minerals that degrade into a specialized impoverished soil. In turn, this soil supports a unique assortment of plant species. These *serpentine endemics* are an important part of California's species diversity.

The southern Coast Range has a granitic core that extends northward to terminate at the Farallon Islands. Formed at the same time as the Sierra and Southern California batholiths, this granitic material originally lay in place south of the present Sierra Nevada. It has since been carried to its present position by northward displacement along the San Andreas fault and is now bounded on the east by the San Andreas fault and on the west by the Nacimiento fault.

An interesting feature of the coastal side of these ranges is the presence of coastal terraces, old wave-cut benches that have been elevated to their present positions by rising of the land. A combination of variable sea-level and tectonic forces has produced the steplike appearance of the land. Seventeen such terraces are visible in the Ventura area. Vegetation on these terraces varies in accordance with age and differences in climate.

On the coastal side of the ranges, the climate is heavily influenced by the presence of comparatively cold water offshore. As a result, heavy fog often cloaks the coastal slopes. An interesting assemblage of plants that water themselves with fog drip is characteristic of this region. To the north, particularly on the second terrace above the sea, the towering Coast Redwoods depend on this fog drip. Unlike Sierra Redwoods, Coast Redwoods are an important lumber crop. Fortunately, large tracts of Coast Redwoods (the state tree) have been preserved within a series of state parks and a national park that are showcases of natural beauty in northern California.

Also scattered in pockets up and down the coast, particularly on impoverished soils, are specialized species of closed-cone pines. These trees, such as Bishop, Monterey, and Knobcone pines, require periodic fires to open their cones and promote seed dispersal. They also require fog drip. This set of specialized conditions is responsible for extremely localized distribution of these pines. Their natural ranges are among the smallest in the world.

An important component of the vegetation in the southern Coast Range is chaparral, which dominates on hot south-facing slopes. Cooler north-facing slopes tend to be occupied by evergreen oak woodland. This distinctive patterning of vegetation in association with slope effect is one of the characteristic features of the southern Coast Ranges. It is accentuated by the long, dry summers associated with the area's Mediterranean climate.

To the interior of the Coast Ranges is a woodland of Blue Oaks and Digger Pines that encircles the Great Central Valley. The Foothill Woodland of the lower slopes of the western Sierra Nevada is actually this same community. This picturesque woodland is characterized by large, well-spaced trees with a grassy understory. It is a region of many cattle ranches, beef being a major industry in California. Interior valleys of the Coast Ranges, formerly grasslands, have for the most part been converted to pastures or agriculture. In southern valleys corn, sugar beets, and various garden crops are grown. To the north the valleys are important for grapes. Napa Valley, north of San Francisco, for example, is known worldwide for its excellent wines.

TRANSVERSE RANGES

Unlike most mountain ranges in North America, the Transverse Ranges lie on an east-west axis. Uplift of these ranges has taken place along a series of faults that are part of the San Andreas fault system. Similar to the Sierra Nevada, most of the uplift seems to have occurred during the last 3 million years. These mountains are geologically complex. They have a large granitic component that is part of the Southern California batholith, which formed about the same time as the Sierra batholith. Large amounts of older rock materials overlie the granitics. These older components were once also in place on top of the Sierra Nevada, but they were eroded away by heavy precipitation. The reduced amount of erosion in the Transverse Ranges is due in large part to much smaller amounts of precipitation at this southern California latitude. In addition, there was a near absence of glaciation, a major erosional force.

The Transverse Ranges form the northern border of the Los Angeles Basin and provide the scenic snow-capped backdrop that millions of people see every New Year's Day when the television camera on top of the Rose Bowl pans the horizon. In spite of their apparent end-to-end orientation, these ranges are not all related to one another geologically. Rather, they are separated by active faults. Their present alignment may be quite temporary in terms of geologic time.

From west to east, the prominent ranges visible from the Los Angeles Basin are the Santa Monica, San Gabriel, and San Bernardino mountains. Apparent extensions of the Santa Monica Mountains are the Channel Islands. These are mountaintops that project above the surface of the ocean and lie on an east-west line directly to the west of the Santa Monica Mountains. Another prominent range is the Santa Ynez Range, which parallels the coastline from Santa Barbara to Ventura. It is separated from the Channel Islands to the south by a drowned valley known as the Santa Barbara Channel.

The San Bernardino Mountains lie to the east of the San Andreas fault and resemble mountains that lie farther east in the Mojave Desert. Mount San Gorgonio is in the San Bernardino range. At 11,502 feet (3506 m), it is the highest peak in southern California. It is also the southernmost point in California that shows signs of glaciation. Other landmarks in the San Bernardino Range are Lakes Arrowhead and Big Bear.

To the west of the San Bernardino Mountains, across the San Andreas fault, are the San Gabriel Mountains. Cajon Pass is the prominent gap between the two ranges.

The San Gabriel Range forms the dominant backdrop on the north side of the Los Angeles Basin. The highest peak in this range, and the third highest peak in southern California, is Mount San Antonio (Mount Baldy) at 10,064 feet (3068 m). The San Gabriels also contain some of the oldest rocks in North America, at 1.7 billion years of age. Another prominent feature of the range is Mount Wilson, upon which Los Angeles has placed its major television transmitters. The major earthquake that occurred in 1971 was on the Sierra Madre fault at the western edge of the San Gabriel Mountains.

The Transverse Ranges are ecologically unique. The side of these ranges that gets the greatest amount of precipitation is covered with drought-tolerant scrub vegetation known as chaparral. These scrub-covered slopes face southward and therefore receive direct sunlight. Even though these slopes get 30 to 40 inches (100 cm) of precipitation per year, the amount of evaporation is so high that moisture-loving plants cannot survive. This phenomenon, known as slope effect, is accentuated by the long, hot summers associated with southern California's Mediterranean climate. On the slopes that face northward, a coniferous forest extends nearly to the desert floor. This side of the Transverse Ranges actually gets about half the precipitation of the south-facing side—about 15 to 20 inches (50 cm) per year—for the same reason that the eastern side of the Sierra Nevada is dry: It is in the rain shadow. Yet on this north-facing side of the Transverse Ranges, evaporation rates are lower and snow melts more slowly, so it is actually the moister side of the mountains. Such is the profound influence of slope effect.

Dry brushland is well known to southern Californians because it is a habitat that seems to burst into flame at the slightest provocation. Actually, most evidence indicates that periodic fires are necessary for chaparral plants and animals and that fire suppression is unhealthful for the entire community. It is unfortunate when homes are built in this fire-prone community. Fire is almost a certainty, and the expense that goes along with trying to put out a major blaze is horrendous. Unfortunately, as southern California becomes more populous, its residents are forced to use building sites that truly are not appropriate for homes—not only chaparral-covered hillsides, but floodplains and geologically unstable slopes such as those on fault systems or on geologic formations subject to slippage.

PENINSULAR RANGES

The Peninsular Ranges are so named because they form the northern end of the long peninsula known as Baja California. The area lies west of the San Andreas fault. Approximately 25 million years ago, and perhaps as recently as 5 million years ago, all of this country was part of what is now mainland Mexico, and there was no Gulf of California. Since that time, the entire peninsula has been dragged about 200 miles (320 km) northward along the San Andreas fault. This action opened up the Gulf of California and formed the low basin known as the Colorado Desert or Salton Trough that lies in the rain shadow east of the Peninsular Ranges.

The coastal side of these ranges, along with that of the Transverse Ranges, form what is known as *cismontane* (this side of the mountains) southern California, an area that includes the Los Angeles Basin. Many people equate the term *southern California* with this area. The desert slopes of the Transverse and Peninsular ranges are called *transmontane* (the other side of the mountains), which to many southern Californians is simply the rest of the United States.

From north to south along the main ridge of the Peninsular Ranges are the San Jacinto Mountains, Santa Rosa Mountains, and Laguna Mountains. These mountains are separated from the Santa Ana Range, to the west, by a broad plain that includes the Hemet and Elsinore valleys. To the south of this plain, the Santa Ana Range connects by means of smaller ranges such as the Agua Tibia Mountains to the Laguna Mountains. Mount San Jacinto, at 10,805 feet (3293 m), is the second highest peak in southern California. It lies west of the city of Palm Springs, where it forms a towering backdrop. Palm Springs, in the Colorado Desert, is near sea level; therefore, the nearly 2-mile-high escarpment above that city is one of the highest in North America. A popular tourist attraction is the aerial tramway from the desert floor to Mount San Jacinto. In the Agua Tibia Mountains of San Diego County, Palomar Mountain, at 5202 feet (1586 m), is the home of the famous 200-inch (450-cm) telescope that was built there to take advantage of clear skies and the absence of urban light pollution.

West of the San Andreas fault is a series of parallel faults including the San Jacinto, Whittier-Elsinore, and Newport-Inglewood faults. The Peninsular Ranges, as well as Santa Catalina and San Clemente islands, have been uplifted along these faults. The numerous earthquakes that occur in southern California attest to the continuing geological activity of these faults. A major earthquake occurred in 1987 near the town of Whittier on the Whittier-Elsinore fault. Many hot springs, well-known tourist attractions, are located along these faults.

The Santa Ana Range, uplifted along the Whittier-Elsinore fault, is a prominent feature of the skyline between Orange and Riverside counties. The highest point at 5678 feet (1733 m) is Santiago Peak. This peak and its near neighbor, Modjeska Peak, form a saddle-shaped prominence known all over southern California as Saddleback.

The Peninsular Ranges resemble the Sierra Nevada in shape. The eastern scarp is steeper than the western, and vegetation of the western slopes is more moisture-dependent. As in the Transverse Ranges, old rocks overlie the granitics of the Southern California batholith. Before the encroachment of human activities, a type of low brushland known as Coastal Sage Scrub covered the terrain from the lower slopes all the way to the coast. This brightly flowering, odorous community is now nearly gone as a result of overgrazing, agriculture, and urban sprawl.

The Los Angeles Basin is considered part of the Peninsular Range Province, although the basin itself is merely a lowland filled with sediments. These sediments were deposited by runoff from the the Transverse and Peninsular ranges. The main rivers that drain the San Gabriel and Santa Monica mountains are the San Gabriel and Los Angeles rivers. The river that drains the San Bernardino, San Jacinto, and Santa Ana mountains is the Santa Ana River. All these rivers have been dammed and channelized to protect the urban populace from flooding. Before human activities were undertaken to prepare the area for "development," most of the basin was a marshy grassland. Underlying the basin sediments is the series of parallel faults, mentioned previously, that make the Los Angeles Basin "earthquake country."

Climate in the Los Angeles Basin always has been subject to fog and haze as a result of cold air that becomes trapped by the surrounding mountains. Cold air is heavy. It "puddles up" in basins, creating an air shed where there is very little natural ventilation. Today, this area also traps pollutants, including the by-products of fuel combustion, which react with direct sunlight to produce photochemical smog.

GREAT BASIN DESERT

Deserts are regions that receive less than 10 inches (25 cm) of precipitation per year. There are three main desert regions in California lying east of the great chain of mountains formed by the Cascades, Sierra Nevada, Transverse, and Peninsular ranges. The Great Central Valley is also a desert at its southern end, and it is generally dry throughout. Arid lands therefore make up a large portion of California.

The northernmost of the three eastern deserts is the Great Basin. Although this is the largest desert in North America, it enters California only along its eastern border. Two geomorphic provinces are included in the Great Basin: the Modoc Plateau and the Basin-Range Province. The Modoc Plateau of northeastern California is an undulating flatland east of the Cascades. It averages 4000 to 5000 feet (1200–1500 m) in elevation and is drained by the Pit River. This river flows southwestward between Mount Shasta and Mount Lassen, after which it dumps into Shasta Reservoir at the head of the Sacramento River. The path of the Pit River is significant to biogeographers. It has been speculated that during times of heavy precipitation associated with the Ice Ages (Pleistocene), the Pit River could have been an important avenue of dispersal for fishes and other aquatic creatures between the Sacramento River and the Great Basin.

Although there is some disagreement about age, the Modoc Plateau was formed by a series of lava flows dating back about 25 million years. Most of these eruptions took place about the time the Cascades were forming, about 5 million years ago. Actually, this plateau is no more than the southwestern corner of a large volcanic tableland that covers the northern Great Basin, including eastern Oregon, eastern Washington, southern Idaho, northern Nevada, northern Utah, and western Wyoming.

The Basin-Range Province lies south and east of the Modoc Plateau. It is composed of a series of north-south–trending valleys and mountain ranges associated with faulting and stretching of the terrain. This province occupies a large portion of the Great Basin, including Nevada, western Utah, northern Arizona, and eastern California. In California, it includes mountain ranges along the eastern border of the state. From north to south these ranges include the Warner Mountains, Sweetwater Mountains, Inyo-White Mountains, and the Panamint Range on the western border of Death Valley. Rocks within these ranges are mostly altered ocean-floor sediments that are now exposed as a series of distinctive bands on the faulted sides of the ranges.

The Warner Mountains, on the eastern edge of the Modoc Plateau, rise to 9722 feet (3015 m) at Eagle Peak. From a geologic perspective, this area is noted for its colorful mahogany obsidian. Subalpine trees such as stunted Whitebark Pines adorn the crests of its high peaks. With their aspen groves and pine forests, the Warner Mountains seem as if they were a part of the Rockies, out of place in California. The Washoe Pine, a high-elevation relative of Ponderosa Pine, forms a fine forest above 8000 feet (2500 m) in elevation. This is the only known location for the species in California. Indeed, with the exception of two small sites in nearby Nevada, this is its only known location in the world.

To the south, the Basin-Range Province can be appreciated best by looking eastward from the crest of the southern Sierra Nevada. Directly east of Owens Valley are the Inyo-White Mountains. Beyond are Saline Valley and Panamint Valley, then Death Valley, with the Panamint Range rising in between. On a clear day one may be able to see Charleston Peak rising to 11,919 feet (3644 m) in the Spring Mountains near Las Vegas.

Some of the highest mountains in California are in the ranges of the Great Basin. Telescope Peak in the Panamint Range is at 11,049 feet (3368 m). In the White Mountains, White Mountain Peak rises to 14,246 feet (4342 m). There is a tale widely told in the Owens Valley that White Mountain Peak is actually higher than Mount Whitney, which would make it the tallest in the contiguous 48 states. According to the tale, that information has been suppressed by the United States Forest Service because it doesn't want to deal with all the visitors it would create. According to official record, however, White Mountain is the third highest in the state, behind the Sierra Nevada's Mount Whitney, at 14,496 feet (4418 m), and Mount Williamson, at 14,375 feet (4382 m). Owens Valley is the trough between the Sierra Nevada and the White Mountains. As such, the peaks tower about 2 vertical miles on either side of the valley.

The climate of the Great Basin differs from that of other California deserts because a large proportion of its precipitation falls as snow. As the snow melts, the water percolates deep into the soil. Growth of desert vegetation in the Great Basin is delayed until spring, whereas the growth period in warm deserts occurs primarily during the winter when most of the precipitation falls.

The most common shrub in the Great Basin is Great Basin Sagebrush. One ecologist has calculated that all the sagebrush in the Great Basin outweighs the total mass of Sierra Redwoods, the largest living things. At lower elevations, in desert basins, a variety of saltbushes are found. Above the sagebrush, or often mixed with it, are pinyon pines and junipers that may form an open forest. At high elevations, near the tops of the mountains, are found subalpine trees such as Limber and Bristlecone pines. Several specimens of Bristlecone Pine from the White Mountains have been determined to be older than 4000 years. The oldest, known as Methuselah, is over 4600 years of age. Here, in one of the harshest climates of the United States, suffering drought, freezing, and gale-force winds, a forest of small trees has lived continuously since 2500 years B.C. These trees are considered the oldest living things.

Throughout the Great Basin, humans have made their mark in many ways. Ghost towns, such as Bodie, attest to mineral riches that were once there for the taking. Also, large patches of green vegetation demonstrate that with imported water, or water mined from deep underlying strata, the desert is capable of supporting various kinds of agriculture. This is particularly true on the Modoc Plateau. But overgrazing, more than any other activity, has altered the area. Cattle and sheep consume, in a few years, the above-ground portions of shrubs that have taken many years to grow. The feet of cattle compact the soil, which causes increased runoff of water that formerly was allowed to percolate deep into the ground. The increased runoff is evidenced by deep, steep-sided arroyos that were unknown before the advent of humans and their domesticated beasts. Even if proper land management practices were introduced all over the Great Basin, no one knows how long it would take for the desert to recover or whether it could recover within our lifetimes. Scars on the land from long-abandoned mines are graphic examples of how slowly desert lands heal.

MOJAVE DESERT

As a geomorphic province, the Mojave Desert may be described as a wedge-shaped area lying between the San Andreas and Garlock faults. The area extends eastward to southern Nevada and northwestern Arizona. On the west, the two faults intersect at about a 60° angle just north of the town of Gorman on Interstate 5. The Garlock fault runs northeastward along the uplifted beds of Red Rock Canyon and the southern edge of the Sierra Nevada to disappear in the southern end of the Basin-Range Province near Death Valley. The southern boundary, the San Andreas fault, lies along the northern edge of the San Gabriel Mountains. To the east of the San Gabriels, the southern border of the Mojave is formed by the San Bernardino, Little San Bernardino, and Eagle mountains. The geologic boundaries are so conspicuous that the Mojave is outlined boldly on relief maps and satellite photographs.

The average elevation of the Mojave is about 3500 feet (1200 m); therefore, in southern California it is often referred to as the "high desert." From a climatic perspective, however, the Mojave extends into Death Valley, which contains the lowest point in the United States.

Many large mountain ranges project from the gravels and alluvium of the Mojave. Ranges such as the Clark, Providence, and New York mountains are high enough to get considerable snowfall. The upper slopes of these ranges often bear forests of pinyon pines, the seeds of which are known as pine nuts or piñones. These seeds, which were an important staple for Indians, are still available in ethnic grocery stores. White Firs of Rocky Mountain affinities occur on the highest peaks.

Precipitation in this desert falls mostly in the winter, and at higher elevations snow is not uncommon. On upper gravel slopes, where snow often occurs, there are large, treelike yuccas known as Joshua Trees. Distribution of these trees fairly well outlines the Mojave Desert; they occur naturally nowhere else.

The deep, low valleys of the southern Basin-Range Province typically contain Mojavean plants and animals. This is one region where geological boundaries are not similar to biological boundaries. Low elevation and warm temperatures allow typical Mojavean vegetation to extend many miles north of the Garlock fault on the floors of the Owens, Panamint, and Death valleys.

At lower elevations the most common shrub is Creosote Bush, so named for its characteristic odor. This is the dominant shrub of warm deserts all over North America and probably the most common shrub in California. Recent studies of Creosote Bush in the Mojave Desert reveal that some shrubs may be quite old, a fact that was not discovered until it was realized that circular rings of shrubs are actually one very old bush. The oldest ring, dated at 11,700 years, may actually be the oldest living thing, having germinated about the end of the last Ice Age.

Creosote Bush is not snow-tolerant; it is therefore replaced to the north by Great Basin Sagebrush. Similarly, the northward distribution of cacti is limited by cold weather. Cacti are common in southern deserts; some species occur in the Mojave, and very few occur in the Great Basin.

The Mojave is not known to everyone for its scenic beauty, yet two of the largest units administered by the National Park Service are located in this desert. These two monuments may be elevated to national park status, and another national park in the Mojave Desert has also been proposed. Joshua Tree National Monument is a park in the high Mojave near Twenty-nine Palms. It includes some of the most spectacular scenery of the high desert. Campgrounds are nestled among huge granitic boulders, and roads wind among acres of Joshua Trees. Park boundaries also include a portion of the Colorado Desert to the south. The transition between the two deserts may be viewed in a few hours by driving southward through the monument.

Death Valley National Monument lies in the northern Mojave, although it is technically in the Basin-Range Province. In addition to its many acres of Mojavean vegetation, this large portion of desert terrain includes some of the most spectacular geologic formations in North America.

Between the two national monuments is a large tract of seldom-visited land, which lies roughly between Interstate 15 and Interstate 40 and is bounded on the east by the Colorado River. It has been proposed that the area be incorporated into an Eastern Mojave National Park. Included within its boundaries are some of the larger mountain ranges of the Mojave, such as the Providence and New York mountains. The Providence Mountains with their limestone caverns, known as Mitchell Caverns, are already included in a state park. The area also includes Kelso Dunes, one of the highest fields of sand dunes in North America.

COLORADO DESERT

In California the Colorado Desert area is called the "low desert" because a large portion of it occupies what geologists call the Salton Trough, a long, deep valley that is 274 feet (88 m) below sea level. At its lowest point is a large body of alkaline water known as the Salton Sea. Before 1905, the Salton Sea did not exist. It began to fill when an irrigation canal burst along the Mexican border. The accident created the New River, which still flows northward to the Salton Sea. After the ruptured canal was repaired, irrigation runoff from extensive agricultural operations in the Imperial and Coachella valleys has caused the Salton Sea to continue growing. At present it is the largest inland body of water in the state.

The Colorado Desert is so named because at the southern end of the Salton Trough, the delta of the Colorado River separates the area from the Gulf of California. Sands and gravels have been deposited in this area over millions of years as the Colorado River meandered back and forth near its mouth.

The Salton Trough and the Gulf of California owe their existence to the northward displacement of lands west of the San Andreas fault. On the east side of the Salton Trough the trace of the San Andreas fault is conspicuous where it offset stream channels and tilted and warped old lake beds. The many springs that occur along this fault are particularly visible from the air. Along this row of springs, groves of California Fan Palms stand out in stark contrast to the surrounding desert terrain.

The Salton Trough has frequently been inundated, sometimes by salt water and sometimes by fresh. This fact is evidenced by extensive badlands composed of highly eroded, colorful layers of clay and silt. Painted Canyon near Indio and Painted Gorge near El Centro are examples of deeply eroded lake-bed formations. A conspicuous waterline is visible at the foot of the Santa Rosa Mountains on the northwest side of the Salton Sea. This line, about 200 feet (65 m) above the present Salton Sea, was formed by freshwater algae in shallow water at the edge of Lake Cahuilla. That lake dried about 500 years ago, when the Colorado River turned southward and ceased to drain into it. In Fossil Canyon, near Ocotillo, abundant marine fossils indicate that the area was once a shallow lagoon filled with salt water.

From a biological perspective, the Colorado Desert is a subdivision of a much larger unit known as the Sonoran Desert, which surrounds most of the Gulf of California, including the coastal foothills of northwestern Mexico (Sonora), most of the Baja California peninsula, and the lowlands of southwestern Arizona. This desert is characterized by numerous cacti and trees of the legume family (Fabaceae). Distribution of the Smoke Tree, a grayish, leafless legume, fairly well outlines the Colorado Desert. Distribution of Ocotillo, a large, stalklike shrub with long, spiny, whiplike branches, outlines the Sonoran Desert.

The Colorado Desert is California's warmest desert. Most of the precipitation falls during winter, but it seldom snows. Summer thunderstorms are locally common. Indeed, the Colorado Desert gets more summer precipitation than any other of California's desert regions. As in the Mojave, the most common shrub of the lower slopes and flats is Creosote Bush. Unlike the Mojave, however, the upper slopes are occupied by a mixture of drought-deciduous shrubs and succulent plants that occur in a community known as Cactus Scrub.

A prime example of Colorado Desert is located in Anza-Borrego Desert State Park. This is California's largest state park, and it is only a few hours by automobile from metropolitan Los Angeles or San Diego. Perhaps it is best known for spectacular displays of spring wildflowers.

GREAT CENTRAL VALLEY

Lying between the Coast Ranges and the Sierra Nevada is California's Great Central Valley. This large valley is approximately 500 miles (800 km) long and 40 miles (64 km) wide. The valley floor is composed of thousands of feet of sediments deposited by runoff from the surrounding mountains. Below these sediments lie important petroleum and natural gas deposits. In an area near Bakersfield, oil wells dot the landscape for many miles.

Much of the valley is near sea level, although it is slightly higher on the edges. The northern portion, drained by the Sacramento River, is known as the Sacramento Valley. From the south, the San Joaquin Valley is drained by the San Joaquin River. The San Joaquin River flows northward to join the southward-flowing Sacramento River before it enters San Francisco Bay. The confluence of these two rivers has formed a 750-square-mile (1900-km^2) delta that has been drained and converted to a rich agricultural region. Groundwater from the delta is pumped into the California Aqueduct and pushed southward (uphill) all the way to southern California. So much water is pumped by this system that the State Water Project is the largest user of electricity in the state. Irrigation water is also provided by the Central Valley Project, which captures streams of the western Sierra Nevada. By virtue of all this water, the arid San Joaquin Valley has been altered from its native grassland to one of the nation's richest agricultural areas. Cotton is the number 1 export crop for California, but the area is also famous for rice, alfalfa, almonds, olives, and raisins. Crops in California's Great Central Valley bring in over $14 billion a year.

The climate of the Great Central Valley is a product of the surrounding mountains, which intercept precipitation and prevent the drainage of cold air. In spite of abundant fog throughout most of the San Joaquin Valley, measurable precipitation is low, averaging less than 10 inches (25 cm) per year. As such, the Great Central Valley may be classified as a desert. To the north, the Sacramento Valley gets more rain, but it too is dry compared to the surrounding mountains. At night, cold air drains off the uplands and puddles up in the valley. This air might drain out to sea through the gap in the Coast Ranges at San Francisco were the prevailing airflow not in the opposite direction. During winter, this cold air forms a dense, ground-hugging fog that is notorious for its effect on motor traffic. In the summer, this cool air is responsible for an ever-present haze. In the vicinity of metropolitan areas and oil fields, sunlight converts products of combustion to photochemical smog, just as it does in the Los Angeles Basin. On nearly any summer day, from a high vantage point in the Sierra Nevada, a person looking westward is struck by the appearance of a flat-topped, brownish mass of air lying across the Great Central Valley.

The conversion of California's arid lands to pastures and farmland has been an economic gold mine, but it has had ecological costs. Symptoms of desertification are widespread. Overgrazing has compacted the soil and promoted erosion. Native vegetation has been replaced by weed species, many of Mediterranean origin. Most exotic weeds were inadvertently introduced as domesticated animals were imported— with seeds in their hair, their digestive tracts, and their food. Groundwater pumping and the damming of rivers have dried former wetlands. Irrigation has caused salts to accumulate in the soil and runoff water, and the runoff has carried pesticides and toxic minerals into sloughs and marshes and contaminated bodies of water such as

San Francisco Bay, the Colorado River, and the Salton Sea. These toxins, such as selenium, have been implicated in the appearance of embryonic defects in waterfowl. Alarmed by possible dangers to humans, health departments have posted warnings about human consumption of aquatic organisms such as fish. Large grazing animals such as the Pronghorn and Tule Wapiti or Tule Elk have been eliminated except in protected situations, and the California Condor, as well as many lesser-known animals, is on the verge of extinction. Loss of habitat is the culprit. A day of reckoning is near, when California will be faced with the reality that its agricultural practices could lead to its own destruction.

2

Basic Ecology

To fully appreciate the special place called California, one must first understand the basic principles and processes of ecology, meteorology, and geology as they relate to natural systems. It is also necessary to become familiar with the vocabulary that scientists use to describe natural phenomena. This chapter and the next, on basic geology, provide the background information needed for a better understanding of California.

ECOSYSTEMS

An ecosystem is an interacting unit in nature made up of living and nonliving components. In a healthy ecosystem, matter is recycled over and over. Living organisms are in a balance with nature, and they do not use up their resources. It is traditional to divide organisms into three categories: producers, consumers, and decomposers (fig. 2.1). Producers are usually green plants, which convert light energy to food energy by means of photosynthesis. Because green plants produce the food for the ecosystem, they are known as producers. The amount of photosynthesis per unit of time is known as primary production. Animals are the consumers in the system. Herbivores are primary consumers because they are the first to consume food. Carnivores are secondary consumers because they eat the animals that eat the plants. Omnivores are able to function as either primary or secondary consumers, an important adaptation if food is scarce. Decomposers include bacteria, fungi, or other micro-organisms that break down detritus, the remains of other organisms. These products of decay are, in turn, used by green plants to carry on more photosynthesis. In this way, matter in nature is recycled.

Although it is convenient, and generally correct, to employ these three categories, there are many exceptions. For example, some special ecosystems contain micro-organisms that produce food without relying on photosynthesis. Instead, they use a process that is sometimes called chemosynthesis. These organisms may live in mud, in caves, in hot-water vents of the deep ocean, or in salt flats. Conspicuous examples are red bacteria that are so numerous on salt flats that they make the salt appear red. This phenomenon occurs in various salt pans in southwestern deserts, but the most visible example is Owens Lake on the eastern side of the Sierra Nevada. The red color of these bacteria is created by a pigment similar to the light-sensitive pigment in the human eye. This pigment enables the bacteria to convert light to food in the absence of chlorophyll. Although chemosynthesis is not as efficient as photosynthesis, the bacteria that use it are, indeed, producers rather than decomposers.

Other exceptions to the three simple categories of organisms are scavengers or detritus eaters. For example, it seems logical to consider vultures as carnivores even

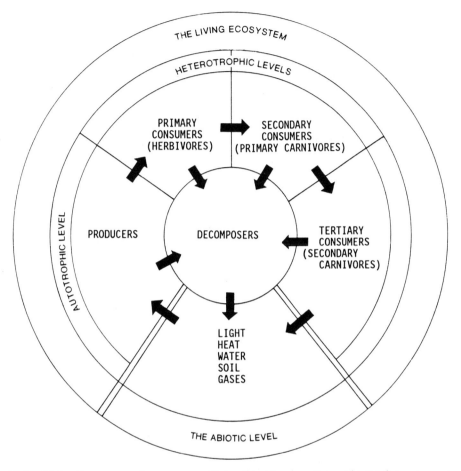

FIGURE 2.1   Components of an ecosystem. Living (biotic) and nonliving (abiotic) factors interact to form ecosystems. The source of the light and heat is the sun. Arrows indicate the flow of energy and materials through an ecosystem. The presence of tertiary consumers, as indicated here, is rare in terrestrial ecosystems. (After M. W. Parratt and M. E. Parratt. *A Spaceship Called Earth: Our Living Environment.* Dubuque: Kendall/Hunt, 1985.)

though, like bacteria, they consume carrion. Likewise, it seems logical to consider mushrooms as decomposers even though they are not micro-organisms.

Actually, it is simplest to view the organisms of an ecosystem in terms of two rather than three categories. The first category, called *autotrophic* (self-nourishing), contains organisms that produce their own food. The second, called *heterotrophic,* contains organisms that do not produce their own food. As far as an ecosystem is concerned, there is little difference between consumers and decomposers. They all eat one another. In fact, they compete with one another for a fair share of the same food. When humans put food into a freezer, they are putting their share where micro-organisms can't get to it. Micro-organisms, on the other hand, get their share by producing foul odors or toxins that discourage humans from eating the food.

A simple ecosystem might have only two kinds of organisms. A sewer outflow, for example, might have only algae (autotrophic) and bacteria (heterotrophic). The important thing is that one organism makes the food, and the other recycles matter by consuming it.

The nonliving components of an ecosystem include matter that is cycled and the energy that powers it. Energy in an ecosystem is represented by heat and light, the ultimate source of which is the sun. Fluctuations of these two energy forms have a profound influence on the system. The matter in a system may be thought of in terms of pure elements such as carbon, hydrogen, oxygen, nitrogen, and phosphorus. These elements may combine to form various materials such as water (H_2O), carbon dioxide (CO_2), carbohydrate (CH_2O), nitrate (NO_3), and phosphate (PO_4). A simple way to describe the nonliving components of an ecosystem is to lump all these factors into five categories: light, heat, air, water, and soil (minerals). If one factor is deficient, it becomes ecologically limiting and exerts a powerful influence on the ecosystem. This phenomenon is described by the *law of the minimum*: that is, whichever factor occurs at a minimum becomes limiting, and the entire ecosystem must adapt to it. Light is limiting on the ocean floor, water is limiting in the desert, heat is limiting on a mountaintop, and so forth. Matter can also be limiting. We therefore refer to nitrate, phosphate, carbon dioxide, water, and carbohydrates as nutrients: plants and animals cannot live without them.

The Flow of Energy and Nutrients

A characteristic of ecosystems is that energy and matter (nutrients) seem to flow through them (fig. 2.1). It is important to realize, however, that materials cycle, whereas energy flows through the system in one direction. Matter is used over and over, but energy dissipates.

Energy powers all life; all ecosystems therefore depend on a constant transfer of energy. At its simplest, we can think of energy transfer as a three-step process:

1. The sun is the source. Nuclear activity causes the sun to emit solar radiation, upon which life on earth depends.
2. Green plants convert light energy to chemical energy (food). In other words, the process of photosynthesis converts solar radiation to the energy locked up in food molecules. This step may be symbolized in this way:

$$CO_2 + H_2O \xrightarrow[\text{chlorophyll}]{\text{light}} CH_2O + O_2$$

More specifically, the chlorophyll in green plants absorbs light energy and uses it to rearrange molecules of carbon dioxide gas from the air and water from the soil to form energy-rich carbohydrate molecules. The chemical notation for carbohydrate is CH_2O, which indicates that it is composed of carbon and water. The specific carbohydrate produced is glucose, a sugar that is symbolized as $C_6H_{12}O_6$.

3. Consumers, through cellular respiration (metabolism), convert the energy in carbohydrate to the energy that makes them move, grow, or think. This step may be symbolized this way:

$$CH_2O + O_2 \longrightarrow CO_2 + H_2O + energy$$

The cyclical nature of this sequence of steps should be obvious. The end products of photosynthesis are the raw materials for cellular respiration, and the end products of cellular respiration are the raw materials for photosynthesis.

The raw materials for cellular respiration are easy to remember. You eat to obtain carbohydrate (glucose), the source of energy. You breath to obtain oxygen. It's also easy to remember the end products of cellular respiration. You exhale carbon dioxide, and you exhale water, which appears in the form of a small cloud when you breathe out in cold air. All living organisms, including bacteria, depend on cellular respiration as a source of energy. Some micro-organisms are able to carry on metabolism without oxygen, but they still depend on glucose as their energy source. Likewise, green plants carry on cellular respiration, but they produce more glucose and oxygen than they use. The oxygen is excreted, and the carbohydrate is stored.

In summary, then, energy is transferred from solar radiation to green plants, and then to animals and micro-organisms. Without this transfer there would be virtually no life on earth.

Laws of Thermodynamics

The transfer of energy through organisms in an ecosystem is not very efficient. An ecosystem will therefore support only a limited number or mass of organisms. Not all organisms are equally efficient, but they are similar enough that we may generalize. Autotrophic (photosynthetic) organisms are about 1% efficient. Heterotrophic organisms are about 10% efficient. This means that only 1% of the solar radiation that falls on a green plant is converted to food and only 10% of that energy is incorporated into the animal that eats it. Simply stated, this means that 100 pounds of vegetation will support only 10 pounds of herbivore, which will in turn support a mere 1 pound of carnivore (fig. 2.2).

This limitation exists because two "laws" of nature dictate energy relationships: the first and second laws of thermodynamics. *Thermodynamics* means "heat power," and heat, of course, is a form of energy. Because energy may be converted from one form to another, it has become convenient to discuss energy relationships in terms of heat. For example, a calorie is a unit to measure heat energy. To express the energy available in a given food item, we assign it a value in Calories. A food Calorie is spelled with a capital C. The Calories used to express food values in human nutrition are the same as the kilocalories used by scientists. A Calorie (kilocalorie) will raise the temperature of 1 liter (1.06 qt) of water 1°C (1.8°F). This means that 1 ounce

(28.35 g) of milk chocolate has enough energy in it to raise the temperature of 147 liters (more than 25 gallons) of water 1°C.

The first law, loosely translated, states that the total amount of energy in the universe is constant, and we cannot add to it or take away from it. Perhaps even more loosely translated, the second law states that energy can be converted from one form to another, but transformations are never completely efficient. Disorder (entropy) tends to occur during energy transformations; therefore to create order or put things in a precise arrangement, requires more energy than can be reclaimed later. This is the reason that energy transfers in ecosystems (that is, from producers to consumers) are so inefficient. Nature tends to move toward randomness or disorder. If humans try to fight that tendency by putting things in order, we expend a great deal of energy that we can not reclaim. For example, planting crops in rows requires effort, and weeding them, which is fighting randomness, also requires effort. By the time the crop is harvested, processed, and transported to our homes, we have expended more total energy than we can hope to reclaim by eating the food. You can't break the laws of nature!

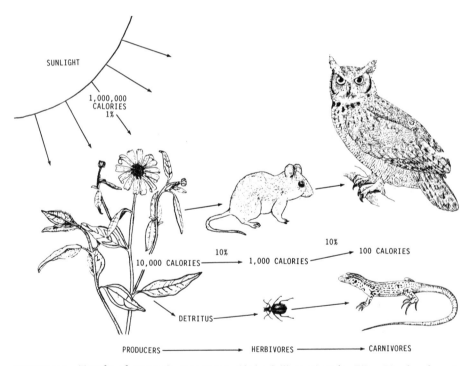

FIGURE 2.2   Transfer of energy in ecosystems. (Animal illustrations by Ellen Blonder, from J. Verner and A. S. Boss. *California Wildlife and Their Habitats: Western Sierra Nevada,* Gen. Tech. Rep. PSW-37, Berkeley: Pacific Southwest Range Exp. Stn., Forest Service, USDA, 1980. Plant illustration by Karlin Grunau Marsh.)

Food Pyramids

A food chain is the sequence by which energy is transferred from sunlight, to green plant, to herbivore, to carnivore. The total amount of energy that flows along a food chain in an ecosystem can be graphically depicted as a food pyramid, sometimes called an Eltonian pyramid after Charles Elton, an English ecologist. Food pyramids are simple applications of the laws of thermodynamics: In any given ecosystem, plants are more common than herbivores, and herbivores are more common than carnivores.

Pyramids can be based on three types of data: numbers of individuals, amount of energy, or total weight (biomass) (fig. 2.3). A pyramid of numbers is a simple expression of what a person sees on a walk in the forest. There are more plants than squirrels, and more squirrels than Coyotes. A more quantitative pyramid is based on energy. Given the efficiencies previously described, 100,000 calories of light will support 1000 calories of vegetation because photosynthesis is only 1% efficient. That vegetation in turn will support 100 calories of herbivores, which will support about 10 calories of carnivores. A biomass pyramid would show the same pattern, with

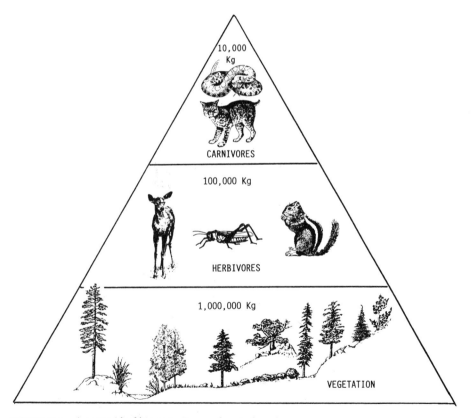

FIGURE 2.3   A pyramid of biomass. Energy flow is from bottom to top.

only one-tenth the mass at each successive level. It should be obvious that it takes a tremendous biomass of vegetation to support a large population of carnivores.

Because these pyramids are based on who eats whom, the steps are called *trophic* (nourishment) levels. Sometimes, food pyramids consist of four trophic levels, including two levels of carnivores. However, it would take an extremely large ecosystem, such as the ocean, to support such a scheme. For example, a tuna eats sardines, which eat krill, and krill eat diatoms. Most terrestrial ecosystems are unable to support a tertiary (third-level) consumer because only a small amount of energy or mass would be available to feed an animal that routinely feeds four steps removed from sunlight. For the same reason, in food-poor ecosystems, such as desert or chaparral, very few animals are exclusively carnivorous. Animals such as foxes and Coyotes, which have reputations for being fierce predators, are actually omnivores that survive primarily on plant material. It is also noteworthy that in nations where human populations have become too large, people are obliged to be vegetarians. Ten times as many humans can be fed by the same food if the calories are not pushed through animals first. This explains why the largest animal that has ever lived, the Great Blue Whale (*Balaenoptera musculus*), eats plankton. It also explains why "big, fierce, animals" are scarce in nature.

Food Webs

A diagram of who eats whom is known as a food web because it illustrates the interweaving of many different food chains. For example, a simple food web may be superimposed upon a food pyramid to illustrate that, no matter how many species occur at a given trophic level, the biomass of those species cannot exceed the limits imposed by the laws of thermodynamics.

Stability as a Function of Complexity

Although there are exceptions, the population sizes of complex ecosystems, with many species on each trophic level, tend to be more stable than those of simple systems. Suppose that a given area has 100,000 pounds of vegetation. It will support 10,000 pounds of herbivorous species and 1000 pounds of carnivores. Suppose there are five kinds of carnivores. If one species were eliminated, the remaining four probably would increase in number until they reached a total of 1000 pounds. If four species were eliminated, the remaining population would increase in size dramatically until it reached the limit of 1000 pounds. The temporary surplus of food created by the elimination of four species would, however, stimulate reproduction to the degree that more offspring would be produced than could be sustained over a long period. As a result, the population might become too large for long-term existence, in which case a number of the animals would have to either die or emigrate. If this occurs, we say that the population has overshot carrying capacity. These sorts of population fluctuations have a minor effect on the ecosystem when there are many kinds of animals on each trophic level, but they tend to have extreme effects in simple ecosystems.

Humans have a tendency to cause simplification of ecosystems and thus produce unstable ecosystems. Agriculture, for example, creates a simple ecosystem that is not only energetically inefficient because of the laws of thermodynamics, but unstable as well. Suppose a logging company clears and replants a forest. This is an example of agriculture because frequently only the economically important species is replanted. The crop is then weeded and sprayed with pesticides to keep out other species. In the end, it would take an outbreak of only one resistant pest species to wipe out the whole crop. A managed forest is therefore not very stable and takes considerable effort to maintain.

Sometimes, in an attempt to make a natural ecosystem "better" for a certain species, humans wind up doing more damage than if they had left it alone. For example, humans have declared war on predators (varmints) that might attack livestock. The California Grizzly Bear (*Ursus arctos*) was exterminated by a state-supported program of hunting, poisoning, and trapping. The bounty for a grizzly was $10. By 1922 they were gone. The California Grizzly Bear is still the state mammal, and its image adorns the state flag. California is the only state in the union that has as its symbol an animal that humans forced to extinction.

A controversial war on the Coyote (*Canis latrans*) continues, in spite of evidence showing that coyotes eat mostly vegetable material, not livestock. They eat an abundance of meat only when small mammals such as mice and rabbits become too numerous. When rabbits become too common, they eat crops. Coyotes thus serve as a natural control mechanism. A similar controversy rages over protection of the Mountain Lion (*Felis concolor*).

Wildlife managers have discovered that the genetic diversity of individual species is also important because of its role in the protection and management of endangered species. Even if a species returns from the brink of extinction, the new population may be fostered by too few parents, and therefore all its members would be very much alike. This could be a problem with the present herds of Tule Elk (*Cervus elaphus nannoides*), numbering about 2500, all of which are descended from as few as 2 individuals. This lack of diversity in the gene pool could mean that a single environmental change or disease would wipe them all out. The greater its diversity, the more likely a species is to survive a crisis. The reason that all California Condors (*Gymnogyps californianus*) were removed from the wild was to increase the number of individuals, and hence the genetic diversity, in the captive breeding program. When a population of proper size and diversity was achieved, captive California Condors were released into the wild.

Productivity

In ecosystems, productivity refers to the production of food. The first step is photosynthesis, so the amount of food produced by green plants is known as primary production. The total amount, or gross primary production, however, is not all available for herbivores to use because cellular respiration and other processes in plants use some of the energy. Net primary production is the amount of energy available for herbivores. That amount, measured over a certain period of time, is called net primary productivity. It may be measured by weight (mass) or by energy (calories) and is often expressed in proportion to a square meter of surface per unit of time. For example, primary productivity in a typical desert region, the least productive of all ecosystems, can be expressed as approximately 100 g/m²/yr or 400 Cal/m²/yr. The reason that the caloric value is usually about four times the mass is that the product, carbohydrate, yields 4 Calories (Cal) per gram.

Because values of productivity vary considerably from one study to another, they must be considered estimates. But, as in many forms of ecological research, tendencies are more important than precise numbers. To put the value for desert productivity in perspective, compare it to that of other ecosystems (table 2.1). The most productive terrestrial ecosystem is a tropical forest, at 5000 g/m²/yr. Ecosystems with comparable productivity include marshes and estuaries. The most productive ecosystem on earth seems to be the intertidal kelp community. Causes for this remarkable productivity are discussed in chapter 12. Ecosystems with low productivity include deserts, mountains, lakes, and open ocean.

Cycles of Matter

Energy flows through an ecosystem and is dissipated, but matter is continually recycled. In order to appreciate the role of all the organisms in a food web, we must examine the cycling of nutrients such as carbon, nitrogen, and phosphorous.

TABLE 2.1   A Comparison of Primary Productivity in Selected Communities

	C, g/m²/yr	C, lb/acre/yr
Oligotrophic lake	25	222
Eutrophic lake	250	2,225
Intertidal kelp	14,600	129,940
Upwelling	6,000	53,400
Open ocean	200	1,780
Estuary	3,200	28,480
Salt marsh	3,000	26,700
Tropical forest	5,000	44,500
Coniferous forest	1,400	12,460
Chaparral	1,056	9,400
Coastal sage scrub	335	2,980
Coastal grassland	527	4,690
Alpine	140	1,250
Desert	100	890

NOTE: Primary productivity refers to the amount of carbon (C) that is added to a plant each year through the process of photosynthesis. There is a high degree of variability for these communities, so the numbers should be considered as rough estimates only.

Carbon Cycle. The carbon cycle (fig. 2.4) exemplifies the cycles of matter in nature. Carbon flows through producers, consumers, and decomposers in the form of organic compounds. A major reservoir for carbon is the inorganic compound CO_2 (carbon dioxide), which makes up less than 0.1% of the atmosphere. Green plants absorb CO_2 through photosynthesis and produce organic compounds, all of which contain carbon. Consumers and decomposers, all heterotrophs, metabolize these organic compounds and excrete CO_2.

The largest reservoir of carbon on the earth is limestone or calcium carbonate ($CaCO_3$). Carbonates dissolve in water. Various animals take up this carbonate from water and use it to form skeletal parts such as bones and shells. Limestones are formed either by this activity in living organisms or by precipitation in certain specialized aquatic environments. By far the most common source of limestone rock is organic activity. More than 99% of the carbon on earth is bound up in carbonate rock. This carbon is recycled through the weathering of rocks, as rainwater runs over limestone in the mountains. This carbonate then becomes the source of inorganic carbon for animals that live in water. Volcanoes also recycle carbon by adding tons of CO_2 to the air.

Fossil fuels are another reservoir of organic carbon. They consist of carbon compounds that have accumulated over millions of years because the organisms from which they were derived became trapped in special environments where they did not decompose readily. Environments that are too cold or too acidic or that lack oxygen are hostile to decomposer organisms. Coal, gas, and oil are organic compounds that,

FIGURE 2.4 The carbon cycle. (From R. J. Putnam and S. D. Wratten, *Principles of Ecology.* Berkeley: University of California Press, 1984.)

when burned, yield energy. The process resembles cellular respiration. Oxygen is required, and CO_2 and H_2O are produced.

Before humans became abundant, the amount of combustion on earth was minimal. Since the Industrial Revolution in the early 1800s, we have increased combustion rates to the point that the fossil fuel reservoir is nearly depleted. Using 1980 standards of consumption, scientists have calculated that there are only about 35 years' worth of oil left. Severe depletion seems likely by the year 2000. In the United States we import about 50% of the oil we use. If we had to depend on our own resources, we would use up the reserves in our known Alaskan oil fields in 2 years. The oil that is trapped in ocean sediments off California, deemed so necessary to exploit, would only last about 40 days at our present rate of consumption. Californians must make some important decisions regarding the true value of offshore drilling.

Excessive combustion has two important effects on the carbon cycle. It depletes the fossil fuel reserve, and it causes an increase in atmospheric CO_2. The global increase in CO_2 has been documented by continuous monitoring devices that have been in place for many years. Similar trends have been recorded in localities as far apart as the Hawaiian Islands and the Antarctic. The problem with increasing the amount of CO_2 is that it tends to trap heat like the glass in a greenhouse. (On a small scale, you can experience the greenhouse effect by sitting in your car with the windows rolled up.) It has been projected that the amount of atmospheric carbon will double by the middle of the next century, increasing global temperatures by about 2.5°C (over 4°F). This is equivalent to the amount of warming that has occurred since the height of the last Ice Age, about 18,000 years ago. Such a temperature increase would warm the earth's oceans, causing the seawater to expand. This expansion would be associated with a rise in sea level. Actual warming is greater at the poles, so we could witness the melting of a significant portion of polar ice and increased precipitation at higher latitudes. It is difficult to predict precisely the outcome of these changes, but authorities agree that sea level would rise 20 to 30 feet (7–10 m). In California, this would flood most coastal cities, greatly decreasing the habitable terrain within the Los Angeles Basin and the Great Central Valley. Climate would change, and California might become unsuitable for agriculture, because western deserts would expand considerably. The relative sea level over time also varies with factors such as tectonic uplift or subsidence. Most reports indicate that during the last century, sea level has risen about a foot (30 cm) on the Atlantic coast and, due to simultaneous uplift of the land, only 4 inches (10 cm) on the Pacific coast.

It appears that an increase of atmospheric CO_2 could increase the amount of photosynthesis on the planet. Theoretically, this could increase agricultural production of certain crops such as rice, wheat, and soybeans, although they would be grown considerably farther north. Could the increase in atmospheric CO_2 be offset by an increase in photosynthesis? This is not likely, because humans are removing forests from the land at a prodigious rate. There is 20 times more photosynthesis in a tropical forest than there is in the equivalent area of a typical agricultural crop or pasture, yet areas of tropical forest half the size of California are denuded each year. Although about 70% of the photosynthesis on earth takes place in plankton in the ocean, the conversion of forest to agricultural land and pasture causes a significant increase in the amount of atmospheric CO_2. An increase of forested land could help solve the problem of the greenhouse effect, but rapid deforestation has become a contributing cause.

A cycle in nature depends on the synchrony of all of its parts. No single part can move faster than any other because all parts are linked. The structure is not as rigid as that of a bicycle wheel, where you can't move one spoke at a time, but it is similar. A cycle in nature can be stretched because it's flexible, but if one part fails, the cycle ceases to function.

How far out of balance is our rate of combustion? In the United States today, 41% more fossil fuel is burned each year than the total amount of biomass produced by photosynthesis; we use 141 calories for every 100 we produce. We are squandering our savings. In other words, the fossil fuel that has accumulated over millions of years represents a savings account that we have been overdrawing since the Industrial Revolution and squandering since the rise of the internal combustion engine in the early 1900s.

California contributes to the problem. It is an oil-producing state, but its people are also the greatest consumers of oil in the world. They add CO_2 to the air because of combustion, and they clear-cut their forests. Because California is a significant part of the problem, its people will have to face a significant part of the consequences.

Nitrogen Cycle.   Nitrogen is the most abundant gas in the air, accounting for 78% of the total. It is also a component of amino acids that are the building blocks of proteins. Proteins have three uses in living organisms: (1) to form structures (skin, hair, muscle), (2) to provide energy (4 Cal/g), and (3) to act as enzymes that regulate chemical reactions. The conversion of nitrogen gas to amino acids is known as nitrogen fixation. Unfortunately, most organisms in the ecosystem are unable to carry out this process. To them, nitrogen gas is inert. Some micro-organisms, such as certain soil bacteria and blue-green algae (Cyanobacteria), have the ability to fix atmospheric nitrogen. Entire ecosystems therefore depend on these unsung heroes for their protein (fig. 2.5).

Nitrogen-fixing bacteria often inhabit the roots of certain plants in terrestrial ecosystems. Air spaces in the soil provide the atmospheric nitrogen, and the continued growth of roots provides the bacteria with a constant supply of fresh air. This is an example of mutualism, a type of symbiosis. The plants depend on bacteria in their roots for amino acids, and the bacteria depend on the plants to continue penetrating the soil to provide new air space.

Because they have nitrogen-fixing bacteria in their roots, one family of green plants, the legumes (Fabaceae), are well known for their ability to provide protein in human nutrition. For this reason, beans and peas are a staple in diets all over the world. All natural ecosystems require plants with nitrogen-fixing bacteria for the same reason. Not all these plants are legumes, however. In forest ecosystems, for example, alders have nitrogen fixers in their roots, and in chaparral, California lilacs (*Ceanothus* spp.) and mountain mahoganies (*Cercocarpus* spp.) do the job.

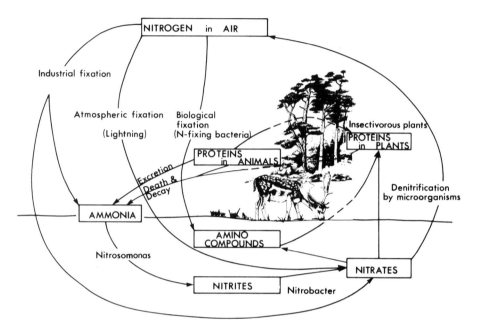

FIGURE 2.5   The nitrogen cycle. (From R. J. Putnam and S. D. Wratten. *Principles of Ecology*. Berkeley: University of California Press, 1984.)

In aquatic ecosystems, blue-green algae (Cyanobacteria) are the nitrogen fixers. These are the first algae to cloud our waters when they warm up in the spring. Blue-green algae also live in the soil of many ecosystems and are sometimes a component of lichens that form colorful crusts on rocks and tree trunks. A lichen is another example of mutualism. An alga provides food, and a fungus provides attachment. The two species live together in a tangle of filaments as if they were one organism. Photosynthesis is carried on by the algal species, which derives both CO_2 and H_2O from the air.

In an ecosystem, protein is passed between organisms as they eat one another. In the nitrogen cycle, the role of decomposers seems disproportionately important because there are so many decomposition steps. It must be remembered, however, that in a cycle no single step is more important than another. The steps are interdependent, just as the spokes in a bicycle wheel are interdependent.

There is often a predictable succession of species that reinhabit the terrain of a disturbed ecosystem—that is, one from which vegetation has been removed. A disturbance could be caused by a natural phenomenon such as a fire, flood, or landslide. Or it may be caused by humans, as in logging, road building, and agriculture. It should not be surprising that among the first species to appear in a disturbed area (the pioneers) are often plants equipped with nitrogen-fixing bacteria in their roots. Sometimes we call these weeds, because the disturbed area may be a newly seeded lawn. But at other times we appreciate them because in the spring they provide a splash of color to a vacant lot or the roadside. That is when we call them wildflowers. It is also not surprising that many of these pioneer species, such as lupines and clover, are legumes.

Agriculture is an example of a disturbed ecosystem that is far from natural. Through much effort, the farmer maintains a single-species system (monoculture), eliminating weeds (competitors) and animals (pests) and applying nitrogen-rich fertilizers. In natural systems, animals (including insects) are part of the cycle because they are able to convert amino acids to glucose and use them as a source of energy. To make this conversion, animals remove the amino part from the amino acid. This is the part of the molecule that contains the nitrogen. Animals then excrete the nitrogen as some form of waste. Ultimately this nitrogenous waste is acted upon by a series of decomposer organisms to produce the nitrates (NO_3), which are absorbed by the roots of the plants. Plants that do not have nitrogen-fixing bacteria in their roots must rely on nitrates that are the products of the decomposing bacteria. If soil is deficient in nitrates, plants cannot make proteins to act as enzymes. A deficiency of enzymes causes plants to grow and reproduce poorly. Thus an agricultural system without animals has to be fertilized artificially with nitrates.

In agriculture, we can help to duplicate nature through crop rotation. This is the practice of alternating a non-nitrogen-fixing crop such as cotton, corn, or tobacco with a nitrogen fixer, a legume, such as beans or alfalfa. Crop rotation may completely eliminate the need for fertilizers, which are merely nitrate-rich applications absorbed by plants along with water. In agriculture, fertilizers may be unnecessary for the first year or so after a natural ecosystem has become disturbed by plowing and weeding. Soon, however, natural nitrates are removed from the soil, and they must be applied as chemical fertilizers. Alternating crops with a legume can make it unnecessary. When a clear-cut forest has been replanted, alders, the nitrogen fixers, are not included because they are less valuable as timber. The cost of fertilizer and weeding must therefore be added to the cost of the next crop. It takes energy to keep the system simple.

Organic farming is merely the use of the nitrogen cycle in an attempt to duplicate nature more closely. Organic fertilizers such as manure or mulch are added to the soil. These materials are cycled by decomposer bacteria to form nitrates, which are then absorbed by the plants. Truly, the plants have no way of knowing where the nitrates came from, and they are no healthier if the source was organic. However, the organic gardener who refuses to use pesticides, weeds by hand, and practices crop rotation, should be able to produce a high-quality product with less expense. When this type of farming has been practiced on a large scale, it has proved economically worthwhile. The yield may be lower, because of some loss to pests, but the money saved by not applying pesticides and fertilizer more than compensates.

Large-scale agriculture in California is practiced in the San Joaquin Valley and the Imperial Valley south of the Salton Sea. In these areas, the use of fertilizers and pesticides is still widespread. This expensive practice has been made possible by an abundance of cheap land and water. It is an artificial situation created, most likely temporarily, by government-subsidized long-distance water transport systems such as the California Aqueduct, the Colorado Aqueduct, and the All American Canal, which have enabled farmers to develop lands that are normally not suitable for growing crops. Several factors may change in the near future as Arizona continues to lay claim to its share of the Colorado River. Furthermore, increasing problems with salt buildup and the accumulation of toxins may take land out of productive agricultural use.

Other Cycles. Phosphate (PO_4) is a component of animal skeletons. it is necessary for all living organisms as a component of lipids in membranes and minerals in skeletons, and as an integral part of the DNA and RNA mechanism by which amino acids are put together to form proteins. It is also a part of the molecule known as ATP (adenosine triphosphate), which is involved in transfers of metabolic energy such as photosynthesis and cellular respiration. An ecosystem that is deficient in phosphate is severely limited, which is the reason that chemical fertilizers include not only nitrates, but phosphates as well. In fact, in an attempt to cover all possible deficiencies, trace minerals such as potassium are also included in most fertilizers.

Because it occurs naturally in small concentrations, phosphate is a major limiting factor on algal growth in lakes. This is particularly true of clear mountain lakes in granite basins. In recent years, water in Lake Tahoe has become greener as a result of the nitrates and phosphates washed in from the surrounding terrestrial environment. An increase in runoff is associated with the disturbance that goes along with the construction of houses, condos, casinos, and other forms of development. In an attempt to slow this process, development in Tahoe Basin has been curtailed and put under strict control. Furthermore, with support from the Environmental Protection Agency, an expensive sewage treatment plant was built at South Lake Tahoe. This plant processes water more thoroughly than most because it employs an extra step, known as tertiary treatment. This process involves the removal of both phosphates and nitrates from the sewer water. Lake Tahoe is one of the few places in the world where sewer water receives tertiary treatment.

Probably the most variable factor in ecosystems is water. Its cycle is similar to that of carbon: It is a requirement for photosynthesis and a waste product of cellular respiration. The nonbiological part of the cycle consists of evaporation from the surface of the earth to form water vapor in the air. When the air is chilled, water condenses and falls as precipitation. Once on the land, it percolates into the ground to form aquifers or groundwater; that which does not percolate into the ground becomes the runoff that forms rivers. A large amount of water passes through plants to be evaporated from leaves in a process known as transpiration. Far more water is transpired by a plant than is used in photosynthesis. For example, an acre of corn transpires the equivalent of 11 inches (28 cm) per year. A deficiency of water therefore severely limits ecosystems.

In California, 85% of the water is used by agriculture. Agriculture does best where it is sunny, but where there is abundant sunlight, it doesn't rain much. Therefore, California's agriculture depends on imported water. In the San Joaquin Valley, most of the water is supplied by groundwater pumping, which is akin to mining water.

Groundwater overdraft occurs when more water is mined than is restored by runoff and precipitation. As in the case of fossil fuels, this is similar to withdrawing more from a savings account than has been earned. In the San Joaquin Valley, groundwater overdraft has caused widespread subsidence. That is, the land actually is sinking. Springs, lakes, and streams have dried up as the water table is lowered. Wells have to be drilled deeper, and many dry up.

It seemed for a while that the answer to the problem was a massive aqueduct system to carry water from parts of the state where it is abundant to those areas where it is needed for agriculture, industry, and metropolitan uses. Four such aqueduct systems have been built. They all carry water to southern California, where high evaporation rates are leading to increased problems with salt accumulation. These disturbances of the natural water cycle could have disastrous effects. Groundwater overdraft, salt buildup in the soil, abandoned fields, and wind erosion are all part of a phenomenon known as desertification, which could become California's most serious environmental problem.

Summary

Ecosystems are composed of living and nonliving components. The living components include producers (green plants), consumers (animals), and decomposers (microorganisms). The nonliving components include light, heat, air, water, and soil (minerals). The source of all energy in ecosystems is sunlight. Energy flows through ecosystems in one direction. Its transfer is not very efficient, as dictated by the first and second laws of thermodynamics. Matter and materials cycle through the ecosystem. Because these materials are parts of cycles, no single part can function without influencing all other parts. Any factor that becomes deficient in an ecosystem becomes limiting, and the entire ecosystem must adapt to that limit or perish. Humans have a tendency to simplify ecosystems, which usually requires a large input of energy and causes the system to become unstable.

CLIMATE AND WEATHER

The study of climate and weather is known as meteorology. *Climate* refers to the overall combination of temperature, precipitation, winds, and so forth, that any region may experience. *Weather* refers to daily variations in these phenomena. Changes in temperature and precipitation are functions of many variables. As the earth rotates, light strikes its surface at different angles in different latitudes, and these angles change with the seasons. These differences cause uneven heating, which is expressed as wind. Winds carry water vapor, the amount of which is influenced by differing rates of evaporation and precipitation, depending on the temperature. Furthermore, wind circulation patterns are influenced by the earth's rotation on its axis and differences in local topography. All this translates into major generalizations about what causes climate for a specific geographic region.

Major Movement of Air Masses

Near the equator, sunlight hits the earth directly. It is summer in the northern hemisphere when the direct rays of the sun strike north of the equator. On the first day of spring, or the first day of autumn, the sun is directly over the equator. Wherever the sun shines straight down, there will be a greater degree of warming than anywhere else. Air will rise at that point. Air on the surface of the earth will move toward the point of rising air from the north and south. As the air rises, it becomes less dense and thus cooler. This is called adiabatic cooling. When the air is cooled, water vapor condenses and falls in the form of rain. As a result, it rains every day, usually in the afternoon, in a belt around the earth between the Tropic of Cancer on the north and the Tropic of Capricorn on the south. The climate in this region between the tropics is therefore said to be tropical. The precise amount of cooling varies with the amount of water vapor in the air, but on the average it is about 3° to 5°F per 1000 feet (1°C/100 m). A drop in temperature of 20°F (11°C) will decrease the amount of water held by the air by one-half.

When air descends to the earth, the procedure reverses. Descending air becomes compressed and heats at about the same rate as it cools when rising. This process causes the air to absorb water vapor. Descending air therefore tends to be dry and causes liquid water to evaporate from the environment. This dry air descends in two belts around the earth, approximately 30° north and south of the equator, just outside the tropics. A quick glance at a world map will show that a belt of deserts lies along this line. When it is summer in the northern hemisphere, this belt of dry, descending air is pushed farther north. It therefore seldom rains in southern California in the summer. Los Angeles lies at about 35° north latitude.

It is not really accurate to use the terms *warm* and *cool* with respect to air masses. What actually causes air to rise or descend is a change in density. Warm air is less dense, so it will rise. Cool air is comparatively dense, so it will sink. As it sinks and becomes warmed by compression, it gets even denser. Even though it has become warmed, it will continue to descend. It is best, therefore, to compare air masses in terms of density. Dense air pushes downward with greater pressure; thus it is said to represent a region of high pressure. Conversely, rising air represents a low-pressure region. Meteorologists explain changes in weather as changes in pressure, which are measured by a barometer. They translate predicted changes of pressure into a weather forecast. A reduction in air pressure might imply that a storm, or a mass of rising air, is approaching.

The Influence of Ocean Currents

Ocean water swirls clockwise in the northern hemisphere and counterclockwise in the southern hemisphere (fig. 2.6). This swirling, a product of the earth's rotation, is known as the coriolis effect. The earth turns in an easterly direction. That is why the sun appears to rise in the east and set in the west. The effect of this eastward motion is that the water at the equator appears to flow westward. As the water moves westward

FIGURE 2.6 Pacific Ocean currents. (From M. Caughman and J. S. Ginsberg. *California Coastal Resource Guide*. Berkeley: University of California Press, 1987.)

relative to the earth's surface, it begins to turn toward the right in the northern hemisphere and toward the left in the southern hemisphere. This phenomenon occurs because the earth's motion is fastest at the equator, where the circumference of the earth is greatest. To make one complete rotation, the land at the equator has to travel farther than at any other place on earth. Because the surface of the earth moves more slowly north or south of the equator, the increased drag makes flowing water turn to the right in the northern hemisphere and to the left in the southern hemisphere.

As the water moves westward at the equator, it picks up heat because this is the region of direct sunlight. Currents of water that come from the equator are comparatively warm, and they flow northward along the eastern edge of a continent in the northern hemisphere. As this water flows through the arctic region, it cools considerably. When the water flows southward again, toward the equator, it flows along the western edge of a continent. A cold current of this type flows southward along the coast of California.

In the southern hemisphere, ocean water swirls counterclockwise, always turning toward the left. Warm currents from the equator flow southward on the eastern edge of a continent. Cold currents from the Antarctic flow northward along the western edge of continents. One bit of consistency to emerge from all this is that water off the east coast of any continent is comparatively warm regardless of the hemisphere and water off the west coast of any continent is comparatively cold.

A climate dominated by the influence of the ocean is known as a maritime climate. On a daily basis, water temperature fluctuates very little. Therefore, air temperature on the land nearby also fluctuates very little. When the water offshore is comparatively cold, as it is on the west coast, fog forms over the water and land nearly every day, a condition that is accentuated as you go farther north. Rain is typically confined to the ocean and a short distance inland. For rain to occur farther inland, the land itself must be significantly cooler than the air. When the offshore current is comparatively warm, as it is on the east coast, it rains frequently on the land, and fog seldom forms.

Air masses tend to follow the ocean currents because they are also under the influence of the coriolis force. The circles of flow, however, are interrupted by the descending air at latitudes about 30° north and south. Where air is descending, very little wind flows transversely across the surface of the earth. Years ago, seamen in wooden sailing ships would have to row when they got becalmed in this part of the ocean, so they would throw over some of the cargo to lighten the load. So many horses from the old world were floating "belly up" that this part of the ocean became known as the Horse Latitudes. A comparable area of little wind, known as the Doldrums, occurs at the equator. Here, the air is rising. In the northern hemisphere, air flowing toward the earth at the 30th parallel turns to the right, forming a clockwise flow. The effect is that air south of the 30th parallel tends to flow southwestward, forming what is known as the Trade Winds, so named because sailing ships could use these winds to carry goods across the Atlantic to the new world. North of the 30th parallel, winds tend to flow from west to east. These winds are known as the Prevailing Westerlies.

Storms develop as low-pressure areas over the ocean. Air rises, carrying with it evaporated water. Wind on the surface of the earth therefore blows toward a low-pressure cell. In the northern hemisphere, air moving across the surface to replace the rising air of a low-pressure cell must turn to the right, which gives the mass a counterclockwise spin. This spinning mass is similar to a spinning top. It moves randomly unless other forces give it a direction. Prevailing winds provide this direction. Storms generated in the tropics tend to be blown westward by the Trade Winds, and storms generated over the northern part of the ocean tend to be blown eastward. In North America, major winter storm tracks come from the north Pacific and flow southeastward. They spin counterclockwise as they travel down the coast, so they continue to pull moisture off the ocean and dump it on the land. As one moves from north to south, the land warms faster than the water because air changes temperature more rapidly. During summer, when the land in southern California is considerably warmer than the water, the storm fizzles because water vapor won't condense. During winter, storm after storm makes its way down the coast. Some of the storms cause precipitation in southern California, but more rain falls in northern California. This is the basic reason that the northern half of the state gets two-thirds of California's precipitation. Very few storms continue as far as the center of Baja California because they are deflected by the descending air (high pressure) near the 30th parallel. Baja California still has cold water offshore, but the land seldom experiences measurable precipitation. The coast of Baja California is frequently foggy. Plants water themselves with fog drip but cannot depend on rainfall to provide adequate water. In Baja California, therefore, the desert occurs on the coastline.

In the summer it seldom rains in southern California (fig. 2.7C). The sun has moved northward so that it shines straight down on the Tropic of Cancer. That is where the belt of rising air generates tropical storms. Because the rising air is farther north at this time, so is the descending air, that keeps southern California dry in the summer. During late August or September occasional tropical storms move into southern California from the south. These storms are usually carried westward toward Hawaii, but some of them move into the belt of descending air where there is no surface wind to give them a westward push. These storms can spin erratically (like a top) and may move over the land, dumping a considerable amount of water in a short time. These sporadic storms, known in Baja California as *chubascos,* are able to move up the Gulf of California on the east side of the Peninsular Ranges. Such thunderstorms over the Colorado Desert and Peninsular Ranges may cause intense local flooding. Some 5 to 10 inches (12–25 cm) of rain may fall in a few hours, representing a large portion of the annual share of precipitation. Some of these tropical storms also come all the way from the Gulf of Mexico (fig. 2.7A).

The moist forests of the Pacific Northwest contain a variety of relict species that depend on the relatively predictable supply of summer rain from the tail end of Alaskan storms. Summer rain in southern California, however, may not occur every year. Nevertheless, certain plant species, such as different populations of relict cypress (Cupressaceae), to some degree owe their existence to summer rain.

On the east coast of North America, a current of warm water from the equator flows northward. This current, known as the Gulf Stream, is part of what makes Florida famous for its winter climate. During winter, descending dry air keeps Miami Beach dry and sunny. In the summer, however, one thunderstorm after another moves across the Florida peninsula. The southern tip of Florida is near the Tropic of Cancer. During summer the belt of rising air and the zone of heavy precipitation are just offshore to the south.

Summer rain is a feature of the entire Atlantic seaboard. As the Gulf Stream moves northward, the water cools slowly. The land cools comparatively faster than the water all the way up the coast, and this difference tends to promote summer rain. From the Carolinas northward there is also a significant amount of winter snow. The overall effect is that along the Atlantic coast some form of measurable precipitation occurs every month of the year. There is no true dry season.

The center of the North American continent tends to be dry because it is a long way from the ocean, the main source of water. Pacific storms, during summer, are deflected over the Midwest by the southern belt of high pressure. In winter, strong storm systems carry precipitation all the way to the interior (fig. 2.7A). Furthermore, during summer, thunderstorms from the southern storm belt carry northward across the Gulf of Mexico all the way to the plains states (fig. 2.7B). They may carry as far as California's Colorado Desert. In late August these storms often reach as far as Arizona, where locally heavy precipitation is common. The Arizona portion of the Sonoran Desert experiences considerable summer precipitation. This rain falls during the hottest time of the year, however, so that evaporation rates are very high and the

FIGURE 2.7   Rivers of air. *A.* The typical winter air flow depicted here for the United States may bring an onshore flow of warm air to coastal California.

FIGURE 2.7(*continued*)   Rivers of air. *B.* On occasion, polar air flows southward west of the Rocky Mountains. This flow brings clear, cold air to the western deserts and may cause an offshore flow of air (a Santa Ana condition) in the Los Angeles Basin.

FIGURE 2.7*(continued)*   Rivers of air. *C*. Most of California's precipitation is associated with the southeasterly flow of polar Pacific air. The position of the Pacific high determines how far south the storms will travel. During winter, when the Pacific high is farther south, many storms are able to reach southern California. During summer, as depicted here, the storms are deflected toward the Pacific Northwest. (From H. Gilliam. *Weather of the San Francisco Bay Region*. Berkeley: University of California Press, 1962.)

water does not sink very far into the ground. The area around Tucson is a desert, whereas the area around Los Angeles is not. Both areas receive approximately the same amount of precipitation each year.

In summary, major storm tracks and ocean currents influence weather in North America. On the west coast winter storms come from the north Pacific and travel southward, gradually producing less precipitation (fig. 2.8). Central Baja California seldom gets winter rain. During summer, high pressure over southern California deflects storms northward. Summer rain is common from Alaska to northern California. It seldom rains in summer from about San Francisco southward. Cold water offshore keeps the coastal area foggy, particularly toward the north. In southern California, intense summer sunlight "burns off" the fog by about noon on most days.

On the east coast, summer storms spin northward from the low-pressure zone near the Tropic of Cancer. Florida experiences considerable summer rain in a pattern known as a monsoon climate. The amount of summer rain diminishes to the north, but warm water offshore contributes to summer precipitation over the entire Atlantic coast. Winter snowstorms are also common along the Atlantic coast, particularly at higher elevations and toward the north. Florida is sunny and dry in the winter. In the center of North America, the plains states get reduced amounts of precipitation, although they receive some winter precipitation from the north, which may be snow, and they also get summer thunderstorms from the south.

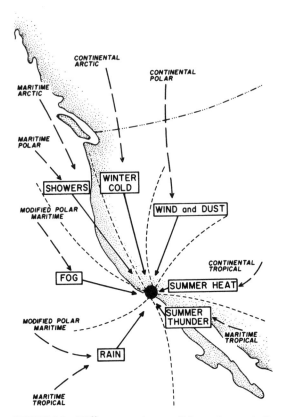

FIGURE 2.8   Different weather conditions. Arrows indicate the direction and source of different weather conditions and seasons for the southern part of California. (From
H. P. Bailey. *Weather of Southern California*. Berkeley: University of California Press, 1966.)

   The pattern of storm systems and ocean currents for North America is similar to
that of any other continent in the world. Northwestern Europe (Norway) is similar to northwestern North America (Alaska). Southwestern Europe is similar to the
southwestern United States. Spain, Portugal, southern France, and Italy are on the
Mediterranean Sea, where the climate is similar to that of southern California. Wherever the climate is characterized by winter precipitation and long, hot, dry summers,
it is known as a Mediterranean climate. Drought-tolerant scrub vegetation is characteristic of such a region no matter where in the world it may occur. To continue the
comparisons, Russia is similar to Canada, China is similar to the Atlantic states, and
Southeast Asia is similar to Florida. The type of climate where heavy rains occur in
the summer, but the winter is dry, is known as a monsoon climate. It is typical of
the southeast corner of a continent in the northern hemisphere.

In the southern hemisphere climatic relationships are reversed, but as in the north, the west coast of a continent has cold water and the east coast has warm water. Ocean currents swirl counterclockwise as flowing water tends to turn to the left. Low-pressure cells cause storms to swirl clockwise. Air flow is a mirror image of that in the northern hemisphere. A journey up the west coast of South America from Tierra del Fuego to Peru is similar to a journey along the west coast of North America from Alaska to Mexico. There is a zone of Mediterranean climate at about 35° south latitude near Santiago, Chile, and there is a coastal desert similar to the coast of Baja California from Chile to Peru. Similarly, there is a monsoon climate in South America on the northeast side. Mediterranean and monsoon climates in Australia are also located at predictable regions.

The Influence of Local Topography

Rain-Shadow Effect.   Mountain ranges have a profound influence on climate. Figure 2.9 is an exaggerated cross section through the state of California at about the latitude of Fresno. It shows how the Sierra Nevada intercepts precipitation on its western slope. This phenomenon is known as the rain-shadow effect. As moisture-laden air flows inland from the ocean, it passes eastward, rising over the Sierra Nevada. Air is chilled adiabatically as it reaches higher elevations, like rising air at the equator. This chilling causes precipitation on the side of the mountain toward the coast. As the air descends from the mountain into Owens Valley, on the eastern side of the Sierra, it becomes heated. This causes an environment of evaporation—a desert, specifically the Great Basin Desert. Owens Valley is thus in the rain shadow of the Sierra Nevada.

This drying effect is similar to that which occurs at the 30th parallel, both north and south, where air descends in a belt around the world. On the western side of the Sierra Nevada, the influence of elevation is similar to that of changes in latitude. As air moves up the western slope of the Sierra, its temperature decreases adiabatically by about 3° to 5°F per 1000 feet (1°C/100 m), which is roughly equivalent to moving about 300 miles (480 km) northward. Precipitation increases accordingly, and the form of precipitation switches to snow. Climate above 11,000 feet (370 m) is roughly equivalent to that of the Arctic. A mountain is thus a microcosm of many types of climate.

FIGURE 2.9   The influence of local topography on climate and weather, as indicated by an exaggerated cross section of California at about the latitude of Fresno.

Temperature Inversion Layers.   Valleys also affect climate. Dense air flows downhill like water, a phenomenon known as cold air drainage. Also like water, cold air collects in low spots that have limited or no drainage, such as the Great Central Valley of California. Cold air flows from the mountains at night and collects in the valley, filling it to the brim. In this case, the brim is the top of the Coast Ranges. Sometimes this cold air is so dense that winds are unable to disturb it as they pass over the top. These circumstances produce dense fog that may remain in the valley for many days. In the Great Central Valley this is known as a tule fog. Episodes of tule fog are famous for causing massive traffic jams and huge chain-reaction collisions. What is unique about these puddles of cold air is that normal temperature relationships seem to be inverted. It is supposed to become gradually cooler as one goes higher in an air mass, but when cold air masses are trapped in a valley, it becomes suddenly warmer at the top. This paradoxical phenomenon is known as a temperature inversion layer.

The same kind of temperature inversion occurs in the Los Angeles Basin, where air is trapped by the Transverse and Peninsular ranges (pl. 6C). Cool marine air, which flows inland from the ocean and joins cool air flowing off the mountains, is held in the basin by the onshore flow of marine air.

A serious consequence of an inversion layer is that exhaust gases or other pollutants rise until they reach a layer of equal density. The difference in density is so great at the inversion layer that pollutants are unable to rise above it. Below the inversion layer, sunlight effects a chemical change on these materials, causing photochemical smog, a mixture of haze and oxidized chemical vapors. Smog is not restricted to the Los Angeles Basin, but it is especially bad there because of the amount of industry and vehicular traffic, which produce the vapors. On nearly any summer day, from a position in the mountains above the inversion layer of the Great Central Valley or the Los Angeles Basin, one can see the flat top of a yellowish brown mass of air trapped in the valley below.

In the Los Angeles Basin the only relief from the inversion layer occurs when the prevailing air flow is offshore rather than onshore. The flow of air is commonly onshore, however, because inland air heats up more quickly than air over the ocean. This creates a low-pressure cell, and air flows toward a low. The inland air rises and draws the marine air onshore, where it becomes trapped by the mountains. Occasionally, though, when air becomes cooler or denser in the Great Basin and the Mojave, a high-pressure cell is formed. Air flows away from a high, so a flow toward the coast can occur (fig 2.7B). To escape from the desert, air must travel through Cajon Pass, one of the few gaps in the surrounding mountains. Situated between the San Gabriel and San Bernardino mountains, Cajon Pass allows air to flow from the high desert at 3500 feet (1200 m) elevation downhill toward the coast, where the Los Angeles Basin lies just above sea level. This flow occurs at irregular intervals, during autumn and winter when the air in the desert is cooler than it is in the basin. At the extreme, a strong wind from the desert blows through Cajon Pass and becomes heated by compression as it descends to the Los Angeles Basin. This is known as a Santa Ana wind because air follows the course of the Santa Ana River as it pushes pollutants out to sea.

Unlike the Los Angeles Basin, the Great Central Valley has little chance to be cleared out by a wind: It is too thoroughly surrounded by mountains. The only gap is where San Francisco Bay has formed an opening in the Coast Ranges. Air usually flows onshore through that gap, and when it flows toward the coast, it tends to flow over the dense air of the Great Central Valley.

Seasons in California

People who were raised in the east find seasons in California to be confusing. The pattern of the east has been popularized for years by romantic poets, novelists, and songwriters. Winter snow is followed by a spring awakening. Green summer forests are followed by autumn color. This pattern, associated with eastern deciduous forests, is caused by a climate in which some form of precipitation can be expected at any time of year. Water is seldom scarce, and the vegetation responds to marked seasonal change in temperature. A person from the east who yearns to see that sort of change in California must visit a community where vegetation borders a permanent stream. This is called a riparian (riverside) community. Canyons all over the mountains of California experience seasonal change similar to that of the eastern United States. Water is always present, and temperature fluctuates markedly. Autumn color in aspen groves on the eastern side of the Sierra Nevada provides a scene of great beauty that may be reached by driving Highway 395 northward from Mammoth Lakes (pl. 8A). In southern California, autumn color is provided by sycamores and cottonwoods in canyons bordering the Los Angeles Basin.

The claim that southern California has no seasons is simply untrue. In southern California, the most significant variable component of the climate is precipitation rather than temperature. In lowlands the "awakening" season is winter, when hillsides and valleys turn green as vegetation responds to winter precipitation. If precipitation has been heavy enough, spring wildflowers may cover many acres, even in the desert. Summer is the season of warm, sunny days. It is the time to visit the beach or go hiking in the mountains. Autumn brings the Santa Ana winds. Clear skies and warm days extend into October. In winter, rainstorms alternate with clear, warm days associated with mild Santa Ana conditions. Football games, viewed by fans in summer clothing, are played in stadiums surrounded by snow-capped peaks—all on national television! Spring may seem to be the least spectacular of southern California's seasons because of many foggy days along the coast (pl. 6B). A short trip inland or to the mountains, however, may reveal carpets of wildflowers, a reward for any Californian willing to drive one hour from the coast. Critics of southern California's climate emphasize the worst: spring fog followed by summer smog, autumn fires followed by winter floods. Nevertheless, seasons are distinct. If you are willing to travel, you can find examples of any sort of climate somewhere in the state.

A series of satellite photos (fig. 2.10) illustrates the four seasons. Satellite photos have improved meteorologists' attempts to forecast the weather. They also show how different parts of the state may experience completely different weather on any given day.

FIGURE 2.10   Seasons and weather conditions in California. *A*. Winter: The Santa Ana condition in southern California, fog in the Great Central Valley, and clouds over the Sierra Nevada and mountains of the Great Basin.

FIGURE 2.10 (*continued*)   Seasons and weather conditions in California. *B*. Winter: Storm approaching the northern California coast. If the Santa Ana condition in the southern part of the state weakens, this storm should reach southern California in the next day or two.

FIGURE 2.10 (*continued*) Seasons and weather conditions in California. *C*. Late spring: Northern California is overcast, and the Los Angeles Basin is outlined by heavy fog.

FIGURE 2.10 (*continued*) Seasons and Weather Conditions in California. *D*. Autumn: A major storm in the north Pacific and a cold front west of California are indicated by a swirl of puffy clouds. Note the tropical storm off Baja California. If this storm moves north to mix with the cold front, it could bring significant precipitation to southern California. (Satellite photographs courtesy of the National Oceanic and Atmospheric Administration, Satellite Data Services Division.)

Northern California may experience precipitation any time of year, although it is heaviest in winter. Along the coast, fog is frequent as a result of persistently cold water offshore. The influence of a maritime climate is felt over the entire coastline, but it seems to be stronger in northern California because of the persistent fog. Coast Redwoods, which require a great deal of moisture, do not do well beyond the influence of maritime climate. Heavy winter precipitation is followed by persistent summer fog, which condenses on the foliage and continues to wet the soil by dripping.

A chain of mountains formed by the Cascades, Sierra Nevada, Transverse Ranges, and Peninsular Ranges forms a rain shadow, east of which lies a vast desert area. In California the Great Basin desert covers the Modoc Plateau and extends southward to Owens Valley. The Great Basin is a region of winter precipitation, mostly snow. South of the Great Basin, the Mojave Desert gets snow at higher elevations. Still farther south, the Colorado Desert rarely gets snow, but it does get summer rain in the form of thunderstorms that move northward from the Gulf of California.

California has a surplus of water in the north and in the mountains. Toward the south, evaporation and transpiration rates exceed precipitation, creating a net deficit of water. Two-thirds of the water is in the north, but two-thirds of the people live in the south. California's massive water transport systems are an attempt to solve this discrepancy.

CLASSIFICATIONS OF BIOTIC COMMUNITIES

It has been recognized for many years that different vegetation is associated with different types of climate. Various classifications of vegetation, based on climatic data, have pervaded scientific and lay literature. Table 2.2 compares three such systems that apply to California's flora.

One of the earliest attempts was the life zone system of C. Hart Merriam. This system, published in 1892, was based primarily on temperature. The zones were named for geographic areas that had temperature regimes similar to that which Merriam observed in Arizona as he traveled from the floor of the Grand Canyon to the summit of nearby San Francisco Peaks. Merriam worked for the United States government, and his system became entrenched in government communications. It is still used by many naturalists who are employed by various federal and state agencies. The correlation between elevation and latitude has merit, but the fact that the system is based on temperature and infers precipitation makes it truly applicable only to the southwestern United States.

Two ecologists, Clements and Shelford, popularized the biome concept. Biomes are large ecosystems in which variations in temperature and precipitation have created a characteristic assemblage of plants and animals. On a broad scale this system is appropriate, and its vocabulary is in widespread use.

In 1947, L. R. Holdridge proposed a scheme for classifying world plant formations based on evapotranspiration ratios. It is an eloquent system that applies raw climatic data more precisely than the biome system. The Holdridge scheme, however, lacks simplicity and has not gained widespread use.

TABLE 2.2   A Comparison of Three Systems of Community Classification

Biome	California Community	Life Zone
Grassland	Valley Grassland	
Desert	Cactus Scrub	
	Sagebrush Scrub	
	Creosote Bush Scrub	
	Shadscale Scrub	Lower Sonoran
	Alkali Sink	
	Blackbrush Scrub	
	Joshua Tree Woodland	
Scrub	Coastal Sage Scrub	
	Lower Chaparral	
	Upper Chaparral	Upper Sonoran
	Desert Chaparral	
	Oak Woodland	
Coniferous Forest	Pinyon-Juniper Woodland	
	Yellow Pine Forest	Transition
	Lodgepole–Red Fir Forest	Canadian
	Subalpine Forest	Hudsonian
Temperate Rain Forest	Coast Redwood Forest	—
	Mixed Evergreen Forest	
Tundra	Alpine	Arctic-Alpine
Temperate Deciduous Forest	Riparian	—

NOTE: The California communities listed here are modified from those described in 1959 by Munz and Keck in *A California Flora*.

In California the range of climate is so extreme and the vegetation so diverse that broad classification schemes involving variables such as world plant formations cr biomes have proved inadequate. Instead, a system of plant communities, published by Phillip Munz and David Keck in 1959, has become the system of choice used by many ecologists in California. This system is based on the dominant plant species that occupy each area. It is broad enough that there are not too many categories to remember, and it is precise enough that its categories encompass meaningful units. A new system published by the U.S. Forest Service in 1983 may not gain wide acceptance among lay people because there are so many categories that it is difficult to remember what each one means. Throughout this book, the Munz and Keck system of communities, with some modification, will provide the basic frame of reference.

3

Basic Geology

Geology is the study of the earth—more specifically, it is the study of rocks, the nonliving components of the earth. Scientists have divided matter into 102 pure inorganic substances known as elements. Living organisms consist primarily of four elements: hydrogen (H), oxygen (O), nitrogen (N), and carbon (C). Ninety-nine percent of all rocks are composed of some combination of eight elements: silicon (Si), oxygen (O), aluminum (Al), iron (Fe), calcium (Ca), sodium (Na), potassium (K), and magnesium (Mg). All the other elements are present in the earth in small amounts. The earth is composed of these elements, either alone or in a myriad of combinations called compounds.

A mineral is composed of a single element or compound. By definition, a mineral is a naturally occurring inorganic substance with a definite chemical composition and ordered atomic structure. Table salt, for example, is a mineral called sodium chloride (NaCl). Its ordered structure is apparent because it occurs in crystals shaped like small cubes. Another common mineral is quartz, or silicon dioxide (SiO_2). Its crystals have a specific hexagonal shape. Gold (Au) and silver (Ag) are minerals composed of a single element. Coal is a mineral composed entirely of carbon, originally trapped by living organisms through the process of photosynthesis. The carbon in coal is therefore of organic origin, which leads some authorities to object to the definition of a mineral as an inorganic substance. The controversy over the true definition of a mineral, however, is beyond the scope of this book.

Rocks are usually composed of several minerals. Granite is a rock with a speckled appearance caused by different minerals in crystal form, such as quartz, mica, and feldspar. Limestone is a rock composed of a single mineral, calcium carbonate ($CaCO_3$). On the basis of their origin on earth, rocks may be divided into three primary categories: igneous, sedimentary, and metamorphic.

IGNEOUS ROCKS

Igneous rocks are formed from cooling and solidification of molten rock. The term *igneous* refers to fire; it comes from the same root as *ignite*. The high internal core temperature of the earth causes convection of heat energy, which melts rock to produce magma. Upon cooling, magma becomes igneous rock. The length of time magma takes to cool determines the size of the crystals of each mineral. The texture of the rock is an indication of the length of time it took to cool. If it remains deep in the earth, it will cool slowly, and the crystals will have a long time to form. These rocks will be coarse-grained; the individual mineral crystals will be visible to the naked eye. Granite is the most common of these coarse-grained rocks. If magma comes to the surface and cools rapidly, as in a volcano, it will be fine-grained because there has been too little time for large crystals to form. The most common fine-grained igneous rock is basalt, a heavy, black volcanic rock. Rocks that have been cooled slowly, deep beneath the earth, are called intrusive or plutonic rocks. Rocks that have been formed by molten material that flowed out upon the surface are called extrusive or volcanic rocks.

Igneous rocks also differ in color and composition. Some minerals, such as quartz and feldspar, are light-colored. Minerals that include iron and magnesium are dark-colored and are called ferromagnesian minerals. The relative proportions of quartz and feldspar and of ferromagnesian minerals are responsible for the principal color of the rock. Table 3.1 is a list of minerals found in igneous rocks. On the basis of relative proportions of orthoclase feldspar, plagioclase feldspar, and quartz, geologists have named 15 different kinds of plutonic rocks alone, which is beyond the scope of this book. For purposes of simplicity, six main types of igneous rocks based on chemical composition (color) and texture (table 3.2) will be considered here.

In California, granite and diorite are the common rocks that make up much of the Sierra Nevada. A large intrusive block such as that of the Sierra Nevada is known as a *batholith* (deep rock) in reference to its origin deep beneath the surface. Granite, associated with the Southern California batholith, is found in the Transverse Ranges, the Peninsular Ranges, and some of the ranges in the Mojave Desert. Gabbro is a dark-colored plutonic (intrusive) rock. It is found in the Peninsular Ranges in San Diego County and the foothills of the sierra Nevada in El Dorado County, where it has degraded into a dark, iron-rich soil upon which many specialized (endemic) plants live.

TABLE 3.1   Common Minerals Found in Igneous Rocks

Mineral	Chemical Composition	Appearance
Quartz	Silicon dioxide	Glassy, clear, cloudy, white, gray, pink
Feldspar		
Plagioclase	Calcium or sodium aluminum silicate	Blocky, dark gray to white
Orthoclase	Potassium aluminum silicate	Blocky, pink
Mica		
Biotite	Complex iron silicates	Thin, shiny black sheets
Muscovite	Complex potassium silicates	Thin, shiny clear sheets
Ferromagnesian minerals		
Pyroxenes	Complex iron, magnesium silicates	Short, stubby crystals, green to black
Amphiboles	Complex iron, magnesium silicates	Grains or long crystals, light green to black
Olivine	Complex iron, magnesium silicates	Glassy to grainy, light green

TABLE 3.2   Types of Igneous Rocks

Texture	Color		
Fine-grained (volcanic)	Rhyolite (light)	Andesite (medium)	Basalt (dark)
Coarse-grained (plutonic)	Granite (light)	Diorite (medium)	Gabbro (dark)

NOTE: Darker rocks indicate increased amounts of ferromagnesian materials and decreased amounts of quartz.

Of the volcanic (extrusive) rocks, basalt is highest in ferromagnesian minerals. It is the dark black rock that forms large flows on the eastern side of the Sierra Nevada, for example, in Devil's Postpile, near Mammoth Mountain. Basalt is most common, however, as the main component of oceanic islands such as the Hawaiian Islands. Andesite, lighter in color than basalt, is the primary volcanic rock found on the borders of continents. The name comes from the Andes, the large mountain range on the western border of South America. In North America, the Cascades are composed primarily of andesite. Rhyolite, the extrusive rock with the lightest color, has approximately the same chemical composition as granite, but differs because it cooled quickly as it flowed out upon the surface. In California, rhyolite is found in the Mojave Desert, where it forms layered mesas, flat-topped buttes that project hundreds of feet above the desert floor. Rhyolite is viscous or sticky when it flows: therefore, it often has many stones imbedded in it, and when it cools it can trap large bubbles of gas. One popular campground in the Mojave, called Hole-in-the-Wall, gets its name from large holes formed by trapped gas in the rhyolite.

Of the extrusive rocks, obsidian has the smoothest surface. It is noncrystalline, similar to glass. It lacks ordered atomic structure: therefore, by definition, there are no minerals in obsidian. It is an amorphous mixture of the same elements found in granite or rhyolite, but, due to rapid cooling, atoms did not have time to become arranged in an ordered structure. Black obsidian cooled in the absence of oxygen. Its color is due to nonoxidized (reduced) iron.

Large deposits of obsidian are found east of the Sierra Nevada north of the town of Bishop. A large mountain, prominent on the horizon there, is known as Glass Mountain, and a large butte, known as Obsidian Dome, is found north of Mammoth Lakes. Obsidian is also found on two buttes south of the Salton Sea. Obsidian was of great importance to early California Indians, who carried it great distances in order to make their tools. It was used to make knives, arrowheads, and spear points. It is not uncommon to find large numbers of obsidian flakes high in the Sierra Nevada many miles from the nearest source.

Mahogany obsidian is brown because its iron is oxidized. Large amounts of high-quality mahogany obsidian are found in the Warner Mountains, on the eastern edge of the Modoc Plateau. Although mahogany obsidian is found in limited amounts at other localities, Modoc Indians must have traded obsidian with peoples farther south because flakes of high-quality mahogany obsidian are found in chipping sites as far south as the Kern Plateau of the southern Sierra Nevada.

Obsidian commonly is found with pumice, a lightweight volcanic "froth." The gray-colored soil that extends for miles in the Mammoth Lakes area is composed of pumice. The rock is so light that the wind is able to pick up pea-sized pieces of gravel. If the gravel lands upon a lake, it floats because of all the air trapped in it.

SEDIMENTARY ROCKS

Sedimentary rocks make up only 5% of the earth's crust, but they make up 75% of the rocks on the surface. Usually they are formed by the consolidation of particles transported from another source. The formation of sedimentary rocks is a significant part of what is known as the rock cycle (fig. 3.1). Mechanical and chemical weathering causes rock materials to break up into smaller particles. These particles are transported from their source by forces of erosion such as wind, water, and glaciers. (These processes are discussed in more detail in chapter 4.) When particles come to rest, they represent a sediment that in time may become cemented or consolidated into rock.

Most sedimentary rock is clastic, that is, composed of clasts or particles. These rocks are named according to the size of the particle that makes up more than 50% of its framework (table 3.3). If the sediment is composed of fine particles (i.e., clay), the rock is called shale. Silt makes siltstone, and sand makes sandstone. If the particles are gravel-sized (2 mm) or larger, the consolidated stone is known as a conglomerate. If the rocks imbedded in the conglomerate are sharp or angular, the rock is known as a breccia.

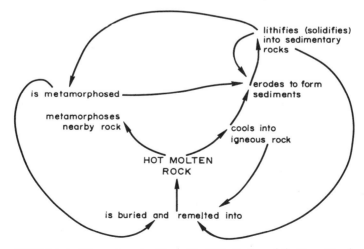

FIGURE 3.1 The rock cycle. (From M. Hill. *Geology of the Sierra Nevada.* Berkeley: University of California Press, 1975.)

TABLE 3.3   A Classification of Sediments
Based on Particle Size

Sediment	Particle Size (mm)
Gravel	Larger than 2.0
Very coarse sand	2.0 − 1.0
Coarse sand	1.0 − 0.5
Medium sand	0.5 − 0.25
Fine sand	0.25− 0.10
Very fine sand	0.10− 0.05
Silt	0.05− 0.002
Clay	Less than 0.002

NOTE: Classification based on United States Department of Agriculture classification of soil textures.

For many millions of years the area we now call California was covered by seawater, and during that time sediments accumulated at the bottom of the ocean. Today those sediments are above sea level, many having been uplifted thousands of feet by mountain-forming processes. Mountains composed of sedimentary rock have a distinctive banded appearance. Often the bands are of different colors. Mountains of this type are found throughout the Basin-Range Province, extending from the eastern side of Owens Valley and the Modoc Plateau all the way to the Rocky Mountains. Formerly, the Sierra Nevada also was covered with sedimentary rock, but erosional forces have carried almost all of it away. Small remnants of the overlying sediment, called roof pendants, are still found along the crest of the Sierra Nevada in the area near Bishop. Most of the sediments have been redeposited as sand and gravel thousands of feet deep on the floor of the Great Central Valley. The rain shadow provided by the Sierra Nevada has been a major factor in the preservation of all the old ocean sediments we now see exposed throughout the deserts: there has not been enough precipitation to carry those materials away.

The size of the particles in the sediment depends on the amount of energy in the water at the time of deposition. Fast-moving water is capable of carrying most small particles in suspension. The size of the particles left behind, those that settle out, is directly proportional to the motion of the water. As water slows down, finer particles settle out. Conglomerates indicate a high-energy environment of deposition, such as a river bottom or beach. A sand bottom indicates slow-moving water, and a mud bottom is deposited in still water. Marine sediments are deposited under seawater. The nature of the sediment is a good indicator of the depth of the ocean at the time of deposition. Sandstone was deposited close to the shoreline. Shale was deposited in deeper water, indicative of a mud bottom. Trilobite fossils may be found in shales as old as 600 million years. These creeping crablike creatures, apparently among the most common organisms in these ancient seas, have been extinct for nearly 300 million years.

Sedimentary rocks also may have a chemical or biological origin. Those rocks with a chemical origin are produced by the precipitation of minerals from solution. Precipitation occurs because the solution is saturated; it holds all it possibly can, and the extra material precipitates. Evaporation of water also causes minerals to precipitate from solution. Four common sedimentary rocks have a chemical origin; limestone (calcium carbonate), gypsum (calcium sulfate), halite (sodium chloride), and chert (silicon dioxide).

Salt flats in California deserts are produced by evaporation, and the minerals are known as evaporites. Certain locally common minerals are valuable. Some of the lakes have very rare minerals or minerals of economic importance. Trona is a town in the Mojave that gets its name from a rare mineral mined from Searles Dry Lake. Potash, a potassium mineral also mined from the salt of Searles Lake, is the primary source of potassium for commercial fertilizers.

Borates are also important minerals found in Searles Lake. Boron is used as an additive in jet fuel, and some borates are used in detergents. Boron became infused into lake water by volcanic gas emissions that occurred millions of years ago, when huge lakes filled many basins in the desert. Due to evaporation, crystalline borate minerals are also found among the salts of some lake beds. Other lake deposits with borate minerals are found in the Mojave Desert. In Death Valley are borate minerals known as colemanite and ulexite, and near the town of Boron is a large mine where borate minerals such as ulexite, colemanite, and kernite are profitably mined.

Plaster of Paris is gypsum, an evaporite composed of calcium sulfate ($CaSO_4$). It is an important component of the various kinds of plasterboard used in construction. Plaster City, in the Colorado Desert, is a location where gypsum is mined. During the Renaissance, a solid form of gypsum known as alabaster was a common material used in the carving of statuary.

Halite is the same substance as common table salt, or sodium chloride (NaCl). It has been mined from Bristol Dry Lake in the Mojave Desert, and it is also extracted by evaporation from seawater. Up until the 1950s, table salt evaporation ponds could often be found at the upper ends of estuaries such as Newport Bay and San Francisco Bay.

Chert is a form of silicon dioxide (SiO_2), or quartz. It occurs in many colors. Depending on its color and the mechanism by which it was formed, chert might be called flint, jasper, agate, or petrified wood. Geodes are nearly spherical deposits of this material in which quartz crystals have grown inward to a hollow cavity. Well-known geode localities occur in the Colorado Desert south of Blythe.

Sedimentary rocks of biological origin are also common. Most limestone is produced this way. Many organisms extract calcium carbonate from water and use it to form shells or other skeletal parts. Among the organisms with this ability are molluscs, corals, sponges, and micro-organisms such as foraminifera and blue-green algae (cyanobacteria). Many of these creatures live in clear, shallow, warm seawater. Most limestone in the desert area was formed in this environment. These desert limestones commonly contain fossils including crinoids, corals, brachiopods, and molluscs.

Foraminifera are ameba-like micro-organisms that are extremely important preda-tors at midwater depths in the ocean. They produce calcium carbonate "shells" that accumulate in great abundance in fairly deep water. In some parts of the world there are limestones 250 to 350 million years old made up of great numbers of foraminifera. For example, the pyramids near Cairo, Egypt, are composed of solidified foraminifera skeletons. In California, these deep-water limestones are now uplifted in the Coast Ranges.

Some organisms are able to extract silicon dioxide from seawater to make skeletons of glass. Among these organisms are certain sponges, microscopic amebas known as radiolaria, and photosynthetic planktonic algae known as diatoms. Diatoms are among the most abundant organisms in the world. Their contribution to photosynthesis is unrivaled, and they probably contribute more oxygen to the atmosphere than any other living organism. Their microscopic glass skeletons may accumulate in great numbers in deep water forming a sedimentary rock known as diatomite. Below 18,000 feet (6000 m) extreme pressure causes all calcium carbonate to dissolve, and thus diatoms form pure deposits. These deep-water deposits of diatomite are now displaced above sea level in various regions along the coast of California. One deposit near Lompoc is reported to be 700 feet (230 m) thick.

Calcium phosphate is incorporated into the skeletons of some organisms, including modern crabs, lobsters, and shrimps, as well as many extinct organisms. Where calcium phosphate accumulates, it forms a mineral known as apatite. Apatite deposits are not widespread, but where they occur, they are mined as a source of phosphate for fertilizers. In the United States such deposits occur in Wyoming, Florida, and Georgia. The largest apatite deposit occurs in Morocco. This is one of the most important sources of the world's fertilizer.

Coal is also a sedimentary rock of biological origin. It is composed of carbon material produced by vegetation that accumulated in an environment with very slow decay rates. Such an environment is warm, acidic water, as in bogs or swamps. These environments were common in North America about 350 million years ago, at which time the continent was located in an equatorial position on the earth. As a result, abundant coal resources are now found in the United States, particularly in Appalachia. The eastern Rocky Mountain deposits are the result of a similar climate of deposition that occurred on the fringes of an inland sea about 100 million years ago.

The western part of North America was submerged by sea water for about 400 million years, during which time the ocean level fluctuated and successive layers of sediment were deposited. The result was an accumulation of about 23,000 feet of limestones, shales,and sandstones, which are now exposed in mountain ranges of the Great Basin. A similar series of sediments is exposed in the Grand Canyon, Arizona, where the Colorado River has cut through to basement rocks more than a billion years of age.

Lake sediments are also found throughout California's deserts. Many of these silts and clays were deposited during periods of heavy precipitation. Remains of these large fresh-water lakes are testimony to the changes in climate and topography that took place over millions of years in western North America. One fascinating area is in northeastern Arizona, where preserved in lake sediments are the remains of a forest that existed some 100 million years ago. This area is now known as Petrified Forest National Park. In these lake sediments, entire trees have been turned to chert by mineral replacement of wood. These logs are so well preserved that even the cell structure is visible under a microscope. Trees similar to these still live today in the Andes, but they are no longer native in the Northern Hemisphere. California has no fresh-water lake beds that are this old, but in the beds uplifted in the Red Rock Canyon area of the northern Mojave are preserved important vertebrate fossils over 60 million years of age. This fossil assemblage is important because that epoch, known as the Paleocene, has a very poor record in the west.

METAMORPHIC ROCKS

Rocks that have been altered from their original form by heat and pressure are called metamorphic. The term means "after-form," in reference to its altered form. Table 3.4 lists some common metamorphic rocks, indicating also the rock from which each was derived.

Heat and pressure are generated as large blocks of land, known as plates, move around on the surface of the earth. These phenomena associated with plate movements are known as plate tectonics. Movement of plates also produces the force that causes rock to become molten. In the case of metamorphic rock, enough force is supplied to cause the rock to become "plastic" but not molten. As a result, some characteristics of the parent rock remain after the deformation.

Many of the oldest rocks on the continent are metamorphic, and some of these are found in California. In the San Gabriel Mountains are metamorphic rocks that have been dated in excess of a billion years. Included among these rocks are gneisses at 1.05

TABLE 3.4 A Partial List of Metamorphic Rocks

Metamorphic Rock	Appearance	Original Rock
Slate	Fine grain, laminar, splits easily	Shale
Quartzite	Tough, visible grains, many colors	Quartz sandstone
Schist	Splits easily, many fine layers, often rich in mica	Slate
Gneiss	Thick banding, resembles granite	Granite
Marble	Many colors, variously banded, fizzes with acid	Limestone
Serpentinite	Green to black, waxy surface	Basalt, gabbro

billion and 1.7 billion years of age. There is also a schist known as the Pelona schist that formerly was assigned an age of 1.1 billion years, but new evidence indicates that it may not be older than 130 million years. Another place in California where corresponding rocks occur is 100 miles (160 km) south, on the other side of the San Andreas fault. This site is in the Orocopia Mountains, east of Indio, in the Colorado Desert. This displacement is important evidence that land west of the San Andreas fault has been displaced considerably northward since its time of origin. Other ancient metamorphic rocks well represented in the Mojave Desert are exposed in the Newberry-Ord Mountains, Old Woman Mountains, and Marble Mountains, all of which may be visited by traveling on Interstate 40 east of Barstow.

Another ancient schist that is of interest lies at the bottom of the Grand Canyon. It has been dated at 1.1 billion years. Overlying it are thousands of feet of sedimentary rock—limestones, shales, and sandstones, with the oldest at the bottom, on top of the schist. This layering illustrates a geological principle known as the law of superposition, which simply states that unless the land is deformed by mountain-building processes, the youngest rocks are on top. If the schist is 1.1 billion years of age and the oldest sedimentary layer is about 600 million years of age, this means that there is nearly a half-billion-year period of time for which the record is missing. Such an absence of rock layers is called an unconformity. It is assumed to represent a period of erosion, during which materials were carried away. It is interesting that rocks representing this time period are missing all over the West. It has been proposed that much of the material is represented by sediments thousands of feet thick that lie in the Nopah Mountains of the eastern Mojave Desert.

GEOLOGIC TIME SCALE

Figure 3.2 shows a geologic time scale. The dates and terminology used here are those agreed upon in 1983 by a coalition of geologists, and it may not jibe exactly with other published versions. A geologic time scale combines absolute age determinations, in years, with relative age based on sequences of rock strata. Estimations of absolute age are derived by combining known rates of sedimentation and erosion with decay rates of radioactive minerals, the latter being much more reliable. A complete sequence of rock strata is not found at any single locality, although the Grand Canyon is one of the best places in the world to observe repeated layers of sediments representing hundreds of millions of years of absolute time.

Certain fossil organisms are associated with certain time periods. If these index fossils are found in an area of unknown age, fairly reliable age estimations can be made even though a complete fossil assemblage is not present. The law of superposition dictates that fossils found in deeper rock layers are older than those found in layers above. This layering of fossils is the basis for relative age determinations. Many different techniques have been discovered for making estimations of absolute age and relative age. These techniques can be combined to produce a picture of events that have occurred during the earth's history. Unfortunately, there is considerable disagreement among geologists about the absolute ages of certain events, particularly since the

RELATIVE TIME			ATOMIC TIME (in millions of years)
Era	Period	Epoch	
Cenozoic	Quaternary	Holocene	0.2
		Pleistocene	2–3
	Tertiary	Pliocene	5
		Miocene	24
		Oligocene	37
		Eocene	53–54
		Paleocene	65
Mesozoic	Cretaceous		145
	Jurassic		210
	Triassic		245
Paleozoic	Permian		280
	Carboniferous Systems	Pennsylvanian	
		Mississippian	380
	Devonian		410
	Silurian		430–440
	Ordovician		500
	Cambrian		570
	Ediacarian		700
Precambrian	Proterozoic		4600

FIGURE 3.2 Geologic time scale.

beginning of the Miocene, about 24 million years ago. In this book, every attempt has been made to use the most recent interpretation, or at least the most commonly held belief, for these ages.

The different time subdivisions are named for life-forms and localities where certain rocks are found. For example, the terms *Proterozoic, Paleozoic, Mesozoic,* and *Cenozoic* respectively mean "first animals," "ancient animals," "middle animals," and "recent or new animals." Many of the periods are named for localities; for example, *Cambria* is the Roman name for Wales, *Mississippian* refers to the Mississippi Valley, and so on. Within the Cenozoic Era, epochs are named for their relative age. Paleocene is the oldest epoch; the word means "ancient-recent," or "oldest of the new." *Pleistocene* means "most recent."

The geologic history of California may be explained in part by reference to the geologic time scale. Proterozoic (Precambrian) rocks in California include the billion-year-old metamorphic rocks of the San Gabriel Mountains and desert ranges. Paleozoic rocks are represented by the sedimentary rocks of the Mojave and Basin-Range complex. Mesozoic rocks include plutonic rocks (granitics) in the Sierra Nevada, the Transverse Ranges, and the Peninsular Ranges. Cenozoic rocks include mostly sediments, but many volcanic rocks are also recent, including those of the Cascades and Modoc Plateau. In order to understand why certain rocks are associated with these different eras, it is necessary to understand what was happening in California during each of these major periods of time. To this end it is necessary to recreate the processes of rock formation in relative time and to study the forces responsible for these phenomena.

PLATE TECTONICS

No other concept in geology is as important to understanding how California came to be so diverse than that of plate tectonics, plates sliding about on the surface of the earth. Two or more plates interact on continental margins, but the type of interaction is not always the same. Two plates may converge on each other, but the speed of convergence may differ. On the other hand, two plates may diverge from each other. Each of these types of relative motion produces a different topography.

Figure 3.3 illustrates four types of plate boundaries along with a summary of geologic events in California. California is on the western margin of the North American plate. At first, California was underwater as part of a diverging margin similar to that which is present today on the Atlantic side of North America. About 400 million years ago (Devonian), that motion reversed, and California became a converging margin. The floor of the Pacific Ocean began to slide under the advancing edge of the North American plate in a manner known as subduction. Heat and pressure caused by the subducting Pacific plate caused an offshore series of volcanic islands. At this time the shoreline ran from about southern Idaho southward, cutting across what is now eastern California. One or more island arcs occurred offshore about where the Klamath Mountains lie today. The topography of the continental margin at that time resembled the present-day east coast of Asia in the vicinity of Japan. As the Pacific plate continued to slide beneath North America, the rocks of the island arcs became attached (accreted) to the western margin of the continent. By means of these accreted terranes the continent began to grow westward. More island arcs would form, and portions of the western margin would break and thrust eastward along thrust faults over the top of the land. Mountains were uplifted in this way.

About 210 million years ago (Jurassic) the speed of convergence on the west coast increased rapidly, presumably as North America collided with Europe, obliterating what may have been a former Atlantic Ocean. In the west, episodes of continental accretion accelerated and subduction rates increased as the Pacific plate was shoved rapidly, often obliquely, beneath the North American plate. The heat generated as the ocean floor squeezed beneath the land caused the rock to melt, forming a deep pool of magma that, upon cooling, would become the granites, diorites, and gabbros of the batholiths that now make up much of the Sierra Nevada and southern California mountains. A deep trench formed offshore west of the zone of subduction. Sediments from this trench, including shale, diatomite, and serpentinite, are now uplifted and exposed in the Coast Ranges. During this period of maximal subduction, the topography resembled what is found today on the west coast of South America. There was a large mountain range similar to the Andes, the proto-Sierra Nevada (nongranitic). A narrow continental shelf extended steeply to a deep submarine trench.

Beginning about 65 million years ago, with the onset of the Cenozoic Era, roughly 40 million years of erosion from the highlands and deposition westward occurred. Deposition covered most of the western half of the state. The Klamath Province, which broke away from the northern Sierra, moved to its present position about 60 miles (100 km) northwestward, where it sat as a large island. The Great Central Valley was underwater, and the ocean extended northward to cover what is now the Cascades and Modoc Plateau. Volcanism continued in the areas now occupied by deserts and the Coast Ranges.

California as we know it today originated about 25 million years ago, about the beginning of the Miocene. The relative motion of the two plates changed from head-on convergence to a sideways motion known as a transform system. Deep cracks or faults formed in the earth's crust. Motion began to take place along these faults as some blocks sank and others rose. Some blocks were carried sideways. The western part of the United States began to be stretched in a manner known as extension.

Earthquakes occur when these blocks move. If most of the motion is up or down along a fault, it is called dip-slip. If most of the motion is sideways, it is called strike-slip. Most of the time, motion along a fault is oblique, but the major direction will be either dip-slip or strike-slip. The modern Sierra Nevada, Transverse Ranges, and Peninsular Ranges were uplifted along dip-slip faults and are known as fault-block mountains. Other fault-block mountains are those of the Basin-Range Province. In California, conspicuous examples include the Warner Mountains, Inyo-White Mountains, and Panamint Mountains, but the topography of alternating basins and ranges continues all the way across Nevada to the Rocky Mountains.

Prior to 25 million years ago, everything west of the San Andreas fault was a good deal farther south, some authorities contend—as much as 300 miles (480 km).

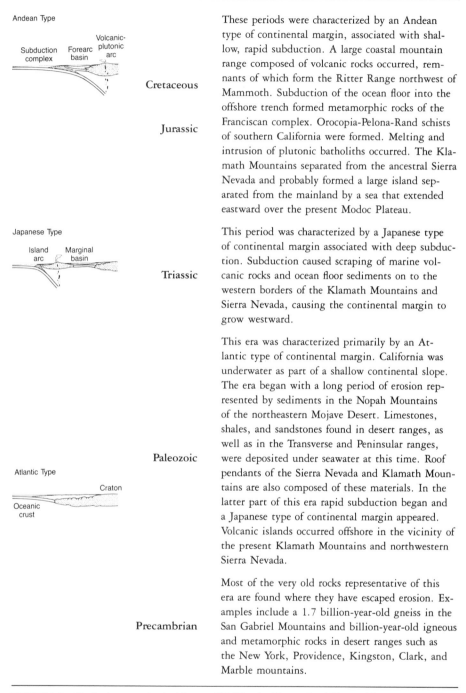

Andean Type

Subduction complex | Forearc basin | Volcanic-plutonic arc

Cretaceous

Jurassic

These periods were characterized by an Andean type of continental margin, associated with shallow, rapid subduction. A large coastal mountain range composed of volcanic rocks occurred, remnants of which form the Ritter Range northwest of Mammoth. Subduction of the ocean floor into the offshore trench formed metamorphic rocks of the Franciscan complex. Orocopia-Pelona-Rand schists of southern California were formed. Melting and intrusion of plutonic batholiths occurred. The Klamath Mountains separated from the ancestral Sierra Nevada and probably formed a large island separated from the mainland by a sea that extended eastward over the present Modoc Plateau.

Japanese Type

Island arc | Marginal basin

Triassic

This period was characterized by a Japanese type of continental margin associated with deep subduction. Subduction caused scraping of marine volcanic rocks and ocean floor sediments on to the western borders of the Klamath Mountains and Sierra Nevada, causing the continental margin to grow westward.

Paleozoic

Atlantic Type

Oceanic crust | Craton

This era was characterized primarily by an Atlantic type of continental margin. California was underwater as part of a shallow continental slope. The era began with a long period of erosion represented by sediments in the Nopah Mountains of the northeastern Mojave Desert. Limestones, shales, and sandstones found in desert ranges, as well as in the Transverse and Peninsular ranges, were deposited under seawater at this time. Roof pendants of the Sierra Nevada and Klamath Mountains are also composed of these materials. In the latter part of this era rapid subduction began and a Japanese type of continental margin appeared. Volcanic islands occurred offshore in the vicinity of the present Klamath Mountains and northwestern Sierra Nevada.

Precambrian

Most of the very old rocks representative of this era are found where they have escaped erosion. Examples include a 1.7 billion-year-old gneiss in the San Gabriel Mountains and billion-year-old igneous and metamorphic rocks in desert ranges such as the New York, Providence, Kingston, Clark, and Marble mountains.

FIGURE 3.3   Geologic events in the history of California. Figure should be read by paragraphs from bottom to top starting with the Precambrian. (Four types of plate boundaries after W. G. Ernst. "California and Plate Tectonics," *California Geology* 32(9): 187, September 1979.)

| Holocene | This epoch was characterized by continued motion along fault lines associated with earthquakes and volcanism. Rain-shadow effects continued with increased drying of deserts. |

Holocene

This epoch was characterized by continued motion along fault lines associated with earthquakes and volcanism. Rain-shadow effects continued with increased drying of deserts.

Pleistocene

This, the "Ice Age," was characterized by repeated glacial episodes in the mountains and heavy rains elsewhere. Sedimentation occurred in coastal and desert basins, and in the Great Central Valley. Formation of the Cascade volcanoes occurred. Uplift of southern Coast Ranges closed direct access from the sea to the San Joaquin Valley. Major uplift and rotation of fault-block mountains occurred in association with northward translocation along the San Andreas fault system. Coastal terraces formed by uplift and changing sea level.

Californian Type

Rifted borderland

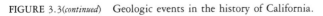

Pliocene

Sedimentation occurred in the Great Central Valley, and marine sandstones continued to be uplifted along the coast. Early Cascade and Modoc Plateau volcanism occurred, and Sutter Buttes erupted.

Miocene

This epoch was characterized by a Californian type of continental margin as the San Andreas fault system began to move. In the early parts of the epoch, coastal southern California was located many miles to the south. Large islands occurred offshore composed of uplifted Franciscan rocks. A large inland sea covered most of the present coastal plain. Northern Coast Ranges began to be uplifted. Volcanism was widespread, including the first basalt flows of the Modoc Plateau and andesite flows that formed mesas in the southwest deserts. A period of heavy erosion transformed the ancestral Sierra Nevada to a gentle rising plain. Red Rock Canyon exhibits 6100 ft of sediments deposited at this time. The climate was warm and moist.

Oligocene

Eocene

Paleocene

These epochs were characterized by long periods of erosion. The only terrestrial Paleocene fossil record in California is in the El Paso Mountains along the Garlock fault. Freshwater sediments of the Peninsular Ranges were deposited at this time. Seawater covered most of the present coastal plain.

FIGURE 3.3(*continued*) Geologic events in the history of California.

Most authorities agree on at least 200 miles (320 km) of displacement. This translocated region includes most of the Coast Ranges south of San Francisco, the Transverse Ranges (except the San Bernardino Mountains), and the Peninsular Ranges. The plutonic rocks (e.g., granite) of these ranges were formed by subduction along the continental margin, but the entire unit was south of the Sierra Nevada, forming one long sequence of batholithic igneous rocks. The Salton Trough and the Gulf of California did not exist prior to 25 million years ago because the entire Peninsular Ranges sequence including Baja California was actually the west coast of what is now mainland Mexico. However, some authorities place the formation of the Gulf of California as recently as 5 to 10 million years ago.

EARTHQUAKES AND FAULTS

The San Andreas is but one of many faults in California (fig. 3.4). Motion on the San Andreas fault is right-lateral strike-slip. That means that the land is moving primarily sideways, and if a person stood on either side of the fault during an earthquake and watched the other side, the land would move to the right. The Garlock fault along the north side of the Mojave Desert is a left-lateral strike-slip fault. During an earthquake on the Garlock fault, the relative motion of the land would be to the left. Total displacement on the Garlock fault has been calculated at 40 miles (64 km).

The type of continental margin found in California today has no modern counterpart in the world. It is known as a rifted borderland. Right-lateral motion on the San Andreas is responsible for much of the rifting, but not all of it. Considered in total, it is known as the San Andreas Transform System.

Parts of the San Andreas fault move at different rates, expressed by different degrees of displacement at various points along the fault. Some of this discrepancy may be explained by major motion along one part of the system shifting to a parallel but different fault. For example, the San Gabriel fault, on the south side of the San Gabriel Mountains, used to be the major fault. It has been inactive for some time, and now the major fault is on the north side of the mountains.

Another discrepancy is that some parts of the system experience many small earthquakes each year, whereas others go many years between quakes. Areas where there are many quakes may move 2 inches (5 cm) a year, but there is seldom a serious earthquake. Regions such as these are known as active areas or creep zones. For example, the town of Hollister, about 100 miles (160 km) south of San Francisco, is bisected by the Calaveras fault, just east of the San Andreas. In Hollister, fences bend, sidewalks buckle, foundations on buildings crack, and streets become displaced as the western part of the town is carried slightly farther northward each year.

In contrast to creep zones are locked zones. These areas are bounded by hard rock materials such as granite, so they do not move often. When they do move, a large earthquake is the result. Apparently, tension or strain in a creep zone is released a little at a time, but in a locked zone it builds up for many years. When the earth finally does move, a tremendous amount of energy is released all at once, causing severe damage to buildings and reshaping the surrounding terrain. In California,

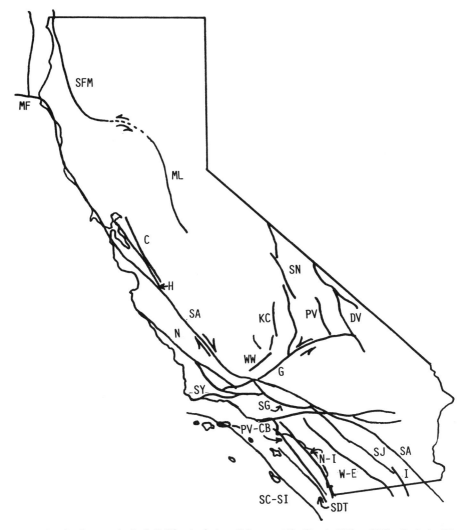

FIGURE 3.4   Some principal California faults: Calaveras (C), Death Valley (DV), Garlock (G), Hayward (H), Imperial (I), Kern Canyon (KC), Mendocino Fracture (MF), Mother Lode (ML), Nacimiento (N), Newport-Inglewood (N-I), Palos Verdes–Coronado Bank (PV-CB), Panamint Valley (PV), San Andreas (SA), San Clemente–San Isidro (SC-SI), San Diego Trough (SDT), San Gabriel (SG), San Jacinto (SJ), Santa Ynez (SY), Sierra Nevada (SN), South Fork Mountain (SFM), White Wolf (WW), Whittier-Elsinore (W-E).

the most famous such earthquake took place in 1906 in the locked zone north of San Francisco. It resulted in 21 feet of right-lateral displacement, most of which took place in a sparsely inhabited area near Point Reyes. The effect of that earthquake may be seen today at Point Reyes National Seashore. In this area, the National Park Service maintains a trail along the fault trace with signs and markers at appropriate points of interest. Damage to buildings in San Francisco was widespread, largely because many of them were constructed of brick (nonreinforced brick buildings suffer the most damage in an earthquake), and damage to water delivery systems was so severe that citizens were helpless to put out fires. What the earthquake didn't topple, fire burned to the ground.

In 1857 a break took place in another locked zone at Fort Tejon, near the present town of Gorman, about 50 miles (80 km) north of Los Angeles. The amount of right-lateral slip from that earthquake has been measured at 35 feet (12 m), and the line of disturbance was visible along the San Andreas fault for 225 miles (360 km).

An elevated face occurring along a fault is known as a scarp. Some fault scarps are visible for many years; others become buried by sediment. By digging a trench across the San Andreas fault near Pallett Creek on the north side of the San Gabriel Mountains, scientists were able to locate the 1857 fault scarp as well as 11 others dating back to A.D. 260. Estimation of the intervals between earthquakes at Pallett Creek indicated that in that part of the locked zone, breaks occurred on the average every 140 years: some had occurred as close together as 57 years, and some were as far apart as 275 years.

Research such as that on the fault scarps of Pallett Creek is necessary if we are to attempt to develop a system for predicting earthquakes. Another technique is to measure tension or strain in rocks along a fault. Regions of high strain are likely candidates for an earthquake. Recent evidence indicates that a region of high strain occurs along the San Andreas fault just north of the Salton Sea. By combining several techniques, scientists have concluded that the locked zones on the San Andreas might be expected to move about every 100 to 140 years, and that movement in these zones has averaged 2 inches (5 cm) per year over the last 25 million years. Consensus among scientists is that there is a 50% probability of an earthquake of major magnitude in the next 20 years, and it probably will occur near San Bernardino.

In the northern locked zone, there was an earthquake in 1865, another in 1906 (only 41 years later), and another in 1989, 83 years later. Another earthquake could occur at any time, although using the 100–140-year average, one might expect the next major quake to occur sometime after the year 2100. Strain in the rocks near San Juan Bautista, near Monterey Bay, has accumulated to such a degree that scientists are predicting an earthquake to occur there at any time.

The first earthquake for which there is a recorded witness took place in southern California in 1769. Gaspar de Portola, a Spanish explorer, witnessed what must have been a major quake in the Santa Ana Narrows of the Santa Ana Canyon. His account describes the Santa Ana River changing direction.

Earthquakes do not always occur on faults with a recent history of activity. In 1952 one of the largest earthquakes in California history took place on the White Wolf fault near the town of Tehachapi, in southern Kern County. This fault was presumed to be inactive. Its total length was mapped at only 34 miles (55 km), and it had never been known to move. Yet the earthquake ranks as the largest in southern California since 1857. Crustal shortening near Bealville was measured at 10 feet (3.3 m). Similarly, in 1987 near the town of Whittier, in Los Angeles County, a damaging earthquake took place on a virtually unknown extension of the Whittier-Elsinore fault.

The largest earthquake in California during recorded history took place in 1872 on the Sierra Nevada fault near the town of Lone Pine in Owens Valley. Earth movements were enormous: 23 feet of vertical displacement and 20 feet of right-lateral shifting were recorded. There are reports by native peoples of a major quake in the same area in the 1790s. The validity of these reports is subject to question, but if a 100-year interval is assumed, that fault is also due to move at any time.

If a major earthquake were to occur today near a major population center, the probable damage and loss of life would be immense. Collapsing structures is one problem, but all major utilities cross faults. Imagine gas lines, power lines, and water lines bursting. All the major aqueducts that deliver water to southern California cross the San Andreas fault, and the California Aqueduct crosses it several times. Ever since 1933, when an earthquake on the Newport-Inglewood fault caused severe damage in Long Beach, building codes have required that new structures be built to resist earthquakes of certain magnitude. A great deal of progress has been made also on developing plans to deal with large-scale emergencies. Nevertheless, the spectre of the next big quake is a fear with which all Californians must live.

There are two ways to measure the size of an earthquake. The Richter scale is a mathematic measure of magnitude based on a logarithmic scale. Each number on the scale indicates an increase in magnitude by a factor of 10. A magnitude 8 earthquake is 100 times more severe than one with a magnitude of 6. An instrument known as a seismograph measures vibrations in the earth. Data from many seismographs are

TABLE 3.5   A Comparison of Magnitude and Intensity

Magnitude	Intensity	Effect
1	I	Only observed instrumentally
2	II	Is barely felt near epicenter
4.5	VII	Slight damage at epicenter, felt 20 miles (36 km) away
6+	VIII	Moderately destructive
7+	IX	Considerable damage—a major earthquake
8+	X+	All buildings suffer some damage, panic is general—a great earthquake

NOTE: The Richter scale measures the magnitude of an earthquake at its source. The Modified Mercalli Scale measures the intensity of an earthquake where a person feels it. Intensity varies with the type of ground (bedrock vs. sand) and the degree of saturation by water. The two scales therefore are difficult to equate.

TABLE 3.6   A Partial List of Major Earthquakes in California

Date	Location	Magnitude	Intensity
1769	Santa Ana Canyon	8.0	XI
1812	San Juan Capistrano	7.0	X
1836	Hayward	7.0	X
1838	San Francisco	7.0	X
1857	Fort Tejon	7.7	X
1861	Livermore	7.0	VII
1872	Lone Pine	8.3	XI
1906	San Francisco	8.3	X
1918	San Jacinto	6.8	IX
1925	Lompoc	7.5	X
1929	Whittier	6.8	XI
1933	Long Beach	6.3	IX
1940	Imperial Valley	7.1	X
1952	Tehachapi	7.7	XI
1971	San Fernando	6.6	XI
1979	Imperial Valley	6.4	IX
1980	Eureka	7.0	VII
1983	Coalinga	6.7	VIII
1986	Palm Springs	6.0	VII
1987	Whittier	5.9	VIII
1987	Imperial Valley	6.3	IX
1989	Loma Prieta (Santa Cruz Mts.)	7.1	X

NOTE: Magnitude figures are based on Richter scale, and intensity figures are based on Modified Mercalli Scale.

coordinated to locate the epicenter of a quake. Based on the amounts of vibration at various distances from the epicenter, a magnitude value is assigned to the quake.

Because logarithmic scales are difficult to understand by laymen, intensity values are assigned to earthquakes as well. Intensity scales are based on the amount of damage caused by the earthquake or its effect on people. Intensity scales are subjective, but they are intended to be understood more easily by people with limited mathematic skills. The most popular intensity scale is known as the Modified Mercalli Scale. Table 3.5 is a comparison of the two scales. The levels of magnitude and intensity of early earthquakes has to be inferred, but a list of major California earthquakes with magnitude and intensity values is presented in Table 3.6. The largest conceivable earthquake is one of magnitude 8.8. If such a quake were to occur, damage would be total, and it would be assigned the highest intensity value, XII.

GEOLOGIC MAP OF CALIFORNIA

The geologic map depicted in figure 3.5 could be color-coded to illustrate rocks of different age and origin, making California appear to be a patchwork quilt. Such

FIGURE 3.5 Generalized geology of California, indicating units of various ages and some major faults. (From W. G. Ernst. "California and Plate Tectonics," *California Geology* 32(9): 188, September 1979.)

illustrations are invaluable in demonstrating that California is one of the most diverse areas in the world. Superimpose on this picture a diversity of soils and climate, and it becomes possible to understand why California has more endemic species of plants and animals than any region of equivalent size in the United States.

SUMMARY

There are three kind of rocks: igneous, sedimentary, and metamorphic. Igneous rocks are formed by the cooling of magma. If the cooling takes place deep in the earth, the resulting rocks are said to be plutonic or intrusive. Plutonic rocks are coarse-grained because minerals have had a long time to accumulate into visible crystals. The most common plutonic rock is granite, a light-colored form that is rich in silica but low in iron and magnesium. Volcanic rocks that have cooled on the surface are said to be extrusive. The most common extrusive rock is a dark, heavy form known as basalt. The glassy variety of extrusive rock is known as obsidian. Volcanic rocks are fine-grained due to rapid cooling.

The great diversity of rocks in California is due to the area's long history as a continental borderland. During most of the Paleozoic Era, California was the trailing edge of a land mass moving eastward. During this time thousands of feet of marine sediments were laid down over what is now California. These sediments are now visible in mountain ranges uplifted in the southwest deserts. During the Mesozoic Era subduction of the Pacific Ocean floor caused a pool of magma to form; this is now represented by the Sierra Nevada and Southern California batholiths. Volcanics that were built up as offshore island arcs became accreted to the western border of North America as the sea floor slid beneath the continental margin. Volcanic rocks and sediments from an offshore deep marine trench are now uplifted in the Coast Ranges.

During the Cenozoic Era a long period of erosion and sedimentation was followed by evolution of the San Andreas Transform System. California became a rifted borderland crossed by many faults, most of which are dip-slip and some of which are strike-slip. Right-lateral displacement has carried everything west of the San Andreas fault northward from its position prior to the Miocene (24 million years ago), which was at the western edge of what is now the Mexican mainland. Fault-block uplift of the Sierra Nevada, the Transverse Ranges, the Peninsular Ranges, and the Basin-Range Province took place during the last 10 to 12 million years, but the greatest amount of uplift probably took place during the last 3 million years.

4

Sierra Nevada

The primary topographic feature of the state of California is the Sierra Nevada, a tilted fault block approximately 400 miles (640 km) long and 50 miles (80 km) miles wide (fig. 4.1). Its spectacular glacier-carved scenery is frequently the subject of photographs or artwork that depicts California's natural beauty (fig. 4.2). The eastern face of the Sierra Nevada is a fault scarp that has been uplifted 11,000 feet (3600 m) above the floor of Owens Valley (pl. 8D). Uplift at the southern end has been greater. From Bishop south to Olancha, several peaks make up the jagged crest that towers over Owens Valley. The high country at the southern end of the range is bisected by the Kern River, which flows southward along a fault. At the southern end, therefore, there are two high divides: the main divide, just mentioned, and the western divide, which extends from Sequoia National Park southward. Many peaks of the western divide exceed 13,000 feet (3900 m) in elevation. Along the northern two-thirds of the range, the terrain slopes gradually westward from the main divide to merge with the Central Valley.

CLIMATE

Because of a profound rain-shadow effect, the western slope receives much more precipitation than the eastern slope, that borders the Great Basin. In the Yosemite area at 5500 feet (1800 m) elevation, the western slope receives approximately 75 inches (188 cm) of precipitation annually, whereas the eastern slope receives only 20 inches (50 cm). There is also a decline in precipitation from north to south. At 5000 feet (1600 m) in the north, average annual precipitation is 90 inches (225 cm), whereas at that elevation in the Yosemite area, it is 55 inches (138 cm). Farther south, in Kern County, the average annual precipitation at that elevation is only 30 inches (75 cm).

A person ascending a mountain will observe certain trends in climate. On the west side of the central Sierra, precipitation increases from about 10 inches (25 cm) in the Great Central Valley to a high of 90 inches (225 cm) at about 8000 feet (2400 m). There are no official weather stations above that elevation, but precipitation generally declines above 9000 feet (3000 m).

The lower snow line is at about 3000 feet (1000 m). Above this point, the proportion of precipitation that falls as snow increases with elevation to as much as 90% of the total. The snowfall and the resulting snowpack in the Sierra Nevada is the highest in the state. Although there is considerable variation from year to year, during the winter of 1982–1983 there was a snowpack of 86 feet (29 m) on Donner Pass. Ten inches (25 cm) of snow is equivalent to about 1 inch (2.5 cm) of rain; thus 80 feet of snow roughly equates to 8 feet or 96 inches (240 cm) of rain.

Over half of Sierra precipitation falls during January, February, and March. Less than 3% is received in summer. Even though summer thunderstorms seem to dump

FIGURE 4.1 The Sierra Nevada.

a lot of water, precipitation is patchy, and the contribution to the yearly total is not great. Precipitation decreases abruptly below about 3000 feet (1000 m), which is the average elevation of the crest of the Coast Ranges. The rain shadow formed by the Coast Ranges influences precipitation across the Great Central Valley and into the foothills of the Sierra Nevada.

FIGURE 4.2 Pioneer Basin, a subalpine basin in the John Muir Wilderness, Sierra National Forest. (Drawing by Geoff Smith.)

Temperature also is influenced by elevation. Due to adiabatic cooling, the air temperature tends to drop 3–5°F per 1000 feet (ca. 1°C/100 m). The combination of lower temperature and greater amounts of snowfall reduces the length of the growing season at higher elevations in the alpine zone to about 6–8 weeks during the summer. Conversely, at lower elevations, particularly on the desert side, the growing season is reduced by summer drought. The shift from a winter growing season to a summer period of growth occurs at about the lower snow line.

Air becomes drier at higher elevations. Adiabatic cooling causes condensation and a loss of water vapor, but also, air at higher elevations has a lowered capacity to hold water because it has fewer molecules per unit volume. This is the reason that humans experience difficulty breathing at high elevation. There are fewer oxygen molecules, too. This dry air at high elevation changes temperature rapidly, which creates strong winds. Furthermore, the wind travels at a greater rate as it moves over peaks and passes, a phenomenon known as the venturi effect. Air passing through a narrow place, or a constriction, must increase in speed for all of its molecules to go through in the same length of time. This windy, dry air tends to increase evaporation rates, which makes it even drier for plants in exposed places and increases the effect of evaporative cooling. In total, at high elevation wind causes drying, chilling, and abrasion.

The prevailing wind in the Sierra Nevada blows from west to east (fig. 2.9). Air tends to heat more rapidly in the desert, and the rising desert air draws air from the coast over the top of the Sierra Nevada. Coupled with adiabatic cooling, this flow causes heavy precipitation on western slopes and comparatively little on the east.

During summer months, the intensity of this wind is increased, particularly in the afternoon. As air in the Great Central Valley is heated, it begins to rise. This rising air is caught by the eastward flow over the mountains and is drawn up the canyons of the western slope. Because canyons become narrower near the top, this wind moves faster as it ascends. This phenomenon is known as the chimney effect, but it is merely an expression of the venturi effect. This air increases in speed as it moves over passes and ridges, and it descends into the Owens Valley, becoming heated by compression. The result of this daily air flow is a predictable afternoon period of wind, uphill on the west and downhill on the east.

When temperatures become equalized at night, a gentle downhill flow of cool air prevails on both sides of the Sierra. It is this cold-air drainage that contributes to the inversion layer, which characterizes the Great Central Valley year-round. It is also the reason that nighttime temperatures are considerably colder in canyons and valleys. Campers who enjoy sleeping next to streams in the high country soon learn to place their sleeping bags with the foot toward the cold airflow. If the air is too cold, moving away from the stream to slightly higher ground can increase the temperature by several degrees.

Large lake basins in the Sierra are also subject to the inversion layer phenomenon. Lake Tahoe (fig. 11.4), for example, has an inversion layer complicated with smog, which is caused by the enormous number of automobiles carrying tourists to and from casinos and other resorts. The photochemical production of ozone has caused a loss of chlorophyll (chlorotic decline) in pine trees around the shoreline of Lake Tahoe. Another place where chlorotic decline is evident, for the same reason, is in Ponderosa Pines in Yosemite Valley. Chlorotic decline can also be observed in any number of canyons on the western slope, where chimney effect during summer draws smoggy air up the canyons on a daily basis from the Great Central Valley.

Another effect of thin air at high elevations is an increase in ultraviolet radiation, high-energy light that is invisible to the naked eye. Its short wavelength gives it penetrating power beyond that of other forms of light, which makes it especially harmful to the tissues of plants and animals. Ultraviolet light causes chromosome breakage and mutations in irradiated tissue. Alpine organisms therefore have special adaptations to protect them from this potentially harmful radiation.

Changes in soil are also apparent during the ascent of a mountain. On any slope, the soil tends to become coarser toward the top, so water-holding capacity is greater at the bottom. Soil also is influenced by a variety of parent rock types, such as serpentine and limestone. The effect is a mosaic of soil types, some of which are notable for specialized vegetation. This mosaic is particularly evident in the western foothills.

At higher elevations almost all soil is decomposed granite. Mountain climate results in podzolization of soils. These soils, known as spodosols, become increasingly acidic at higher elevations. Alpine soil with a pH reading of 4 is not uncommon. In boggy areas the soil is even more acidic.

These spodosols (podzols) also tend to be nutrient-deficient, which poses several problems for plants in mountain environments. Symbiotic relationships between nitrogen-fixing bacteria and members of the legume family (Fabaceae) have developed in response to the problem. Species of lupine and vetch are common legumes in all communities in the mountain environment. In forests, members of the genus *Ceanothus*, often known as California lilacs, have nitrogen-fixing bacteria in their roots. Along streams these bacteria are found in the roots of alders.

Conifers have a symbiotic relationship with fungal filaments known as mycorrhizae. These filaments originate as part of the absorptive structure of a number of mushroom species, but they become intimately associated with the root system of the conifers. The fungus improves the absorption of nutrients by the tree, and the tree produces excess carbohydrates for the fungus. Ultimately, the mycorrhizal filaments connect the root systems of the trees with each other, allowing them to share various chemicals, including those that may discourage herbivores.

At high elevations, soil is coarse and thin. In low places the soil tends to become water-logged because percolation is prevented by bedrock or permafrost. In the Sierra, bedrock is usually the complicating element. Soggy soil slips on slopes, and it freezes solid in cold temperatures. This type of soil is a poor substratum for most plant species and is not a good place for burrowing animals to build a home.

GEOLOGY

Rocks of the Sierra Nevada (fig. 4.3) can be divided into three groups: batholithic, prebatholithic, and postbatholithic. The Sierra is made up primarily of granitic rocks of the Sierra batholith. These rocks were formed during the Mesozoic Era, which ended about 65 million years ago. The batholith resulted as subduction of the ocean crust beneath the North American plate caused formation of a pool of magma about 10 miles (16 km) beneath the surface (fig. 4.4). This process of magma formation must have lasted more than 100 million years, during which time numerous major subunits (plutons) developed. These plutons are north–south-trending units of homogeneous material that grow gradually younger toward the east. This age relationship is interpreted as a result of the North American plate moving gradually westward over the Pacific plate during the time of magma formation.

Uplift of the batholith probably began about 80 million years ago. The overlying prebatholithic rocks were old ocean-floor sediments. As these sediments were raised a proto-Sierra began to form, and erosion carried rock materials westward, gradually thinning the 10-mile (16 km) layer of materials overlying the granitics. The actual height to which the sediments were raised has been the subject of considerable debate, but by 40 million years ago, near the close of Eocene, the Sierra Nevada consisted of a relatively flat terrain of low, rolling granitic hills and broad valleys.

From about 20 million to 5 million years ago there was extensive volcanism along the northern crest of the Sierra. These volcanoes were most likely the southern extension of the Cascade Range. Examination of these lava flows shows that they covered an essentially level terrain. Fossil remains to the east show no evidence of a

FIGURE 4.3   Sierra Nevada geology. (From S. Whitney. *A Sierra Club Naturalist's Guide to the Sierra Nevada.* San Francisco: Sierra Club Books, 1979. Reprinted by permission.)

rain shadow until some 10 to 12 million years ago. Fossil plants show a drying trend at about that time to the east of the Sierra, implying that uplift and rain-shadow activity had begun. Drainage was still primarily to the west, adding more sediments to what is now the Great Central Valley. Major uplift and tilting westward of the Sierra batholith began about 3 million years ago and is still continuing. Uplift was recorded as recently as 1872, when an earthquake in the vicinity of Lone Pine raised the eastern front of the Sierra 23 feet (8 m).

Erosion is believed to have removed about 1.5 feet (46 cm) of earth every thousand years. Thus, nearly all of the overlying sediments were removed, exposing to modern-day weathering the granitics of the batholith. Also, based on comparison of erosion

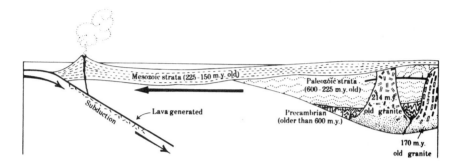

A. LATE PALEOZOIC

FIGURE 4.4   A summary of geologic events leading to the formation of the Sierra Nevada. *A.* Toward the end of the Paleozoic Era, about 250 million years ago, subduction of the Pacific plate beneath the North American plate had begun. At this time there was a Japanese type of continental margin with island arc volcanoes that spewed a vast amount of volcanic debris into an inland sea. This debris mixed with the material eroding from the continent to form sediments that are found today as roof pendants in some parts of the Sierra Nevada.

B. EARLY MESOZOIC

FIGURE 4.4 (*continued*)   A summary of geologic events leading to the formation of the Sierra Nevada. *B.* During the early parts of the Mesozoic Era, over 200 million years ago, subduction deepened, and an Andean type of continental margin formed. At this time magma was generated beneath the surface, and this would ultimately become the granite of the Sierra Batholith. Also at this time, in an event known as the Nevadan orogeny, a "proto–Sierra Nevada" of faulted, folded mountains was formed. Large amounts of volcanic rock were also deposited along the continental margin. Metamorphosed remains of the old mountains are still found as roof pendants at various points along the Sierran crest.

C. PRESENT

FIGURE 4.4 (*continued*)   A summary of geologic events leading to the formation of the Sierra Nevada. *C*. By the end of the Mesozoic Era, over 60 million years ago, a long period of erosion had removed most of the volcanic rocks, and the granite batholith was becoming exposed. By middle Cenozoic, some 30 million years ago, the ancestral Sierra Nevada was eroded to a range probably no more than a few thousand feet high. By early Miocene, about 25 million years ago, the Californian type of margin with its rifted borderland evolved. The San Andreas fault, with its lateral motion, created a set of stresses causing major uplift of the Sierran batholith that is still occurring today. During late Miocene, particularly north of Yosemite, there was a new period of volcanism associated with the formation of the Cascade Range. This volcanism, which terminated about 5 million years ago, covered the range north of Yosemite with a variety of lava flows and formations, most of which have since been eroded. Now, after more than 150 million years of erosion, the Sierra Nevada stands as a range over 14,000 feet (4230 m) high, composed mostly of granite that was formerly buried by 5 to 10 miles (8–16 km) of rock. That eroded material now makes up the 5000 to 10,000 feet (1800–3000 m) of sediment in the Great Central Valley. (Illustrations from R. C. Bateman. "Model for the Origin of Sierran Granites." *California Geology* 27 (1): 1–5.)

rates to rates of uplift, it appears that the Sierra will one day be considerably higher than it is now.

Westward tilting of the Sierra is evident because uplift along the eastern flank was considerably greater than it was on the west. Likewise, uplift in the south was greater than it was in the north. A consequence of higher elevation was the stripping of nearly all old rock sediments from the southern part of the range. As the Sierra rose, it pushed aside a portion of the prebatholithic rocks. On the east side of the Sierra, south of Bishop, all of that metamorphic rock has been carried away. In that area today, the east face of the Sierra is composed of a series of staggered parallel fault scarps exposed to further weathering. Granitics rise sharply from the floor of Owens Valley to form the highest peaks of the Sierra, 13 of which are higher than 14,000 feet (4230 m). This great granitic wall represents one of the most abrupt elevational gradients in the world, rising about 2 miles (3.5 km) above the valley floor (pl. 8D).

Prebatholithic rocks in the Sierra today are mostly metamorphic rocks that lie on the eastern and western flanks of the range north of the San Joaquin drainage. Folding and metamorphism of the prebatholithic sediments is closely tied to the forceful emplacement of the plutons, at depths where high pressures and temperatures would allow plastic deformation of the sediments. Throughout the high country are isolated outcrops of prebatholithic rock perched on top of the granite. These outcrops, known as roof pendants (fig. 4.5), represent portions of prebatholithic rock that have not

FIGURE 4.5   View of the east side of the Sierra Nevada from Sherwin Grade north of Bishop. Note the metamorphic roof pendant on Mount Tom and the staggered fault scarps on the eastern face of the range to right of center.

yet been eroded. Roof pendants are highly visible because the uppermost portion of the peak is a darkly colored mass of rock, distinctly different from the underlying granitics. A number of high peaks north of Mt. Whitney have roof pendants.

Many prebatholithic outcrops are composed of metasediments (altered sedimentary rock). Sandstones become quartzite, limestones become marble, and shales become slate and schist. These metasediments are of Paleozoic age. They are visible as deep red or chocolate brown rocks on top of grayish granitics. On the east side of the Sierra from Convict Lake, north of Bishop, nearly to Bridgeport, these red and brown rocks are conspicuous (fig. 4.6). Entering the high country by any of the canyons in this portion of the Sierra, a person cannot help but be struck by the marvel of colors and folding in the rocks. Mount Banner, Mount Ritter, and the Minarets, near Mammoth, are composed of these old metamorphic rocks, too.

Metavolcanics are also included in this prebatholithic assemblage, although these are considerably younger than the metasediments. The metavolcanics are of Mesozoic age and may have been established in place by magma coming to the surface explosively, or they may have been island arc volcanics scraped off the ocean floor as subduction proceeded to consume the Pacific plate. Mount Dana and the Ritter Range in eastern Yosemite are chiefly metavolcanic rocks of explosive origin. Roof pendants composed of volcanics are often black. The Kaweah Ridge (fig. 4.7) is a series of metavolcanics located on the western divide in Sequoia National Park. It is visible from all over the southern Sierra as a ridge of dark-colored peaks.

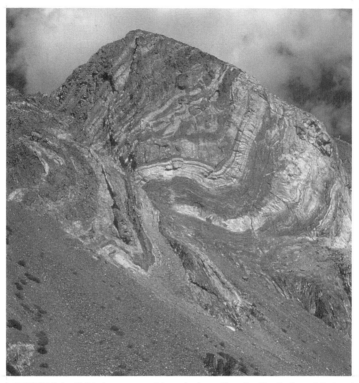

FIGURE 4.6   Folded metamorphic rock along Convict Creek, Inyo National Forest.

FIGURE 4.7   Kaweah Ridge from Little Five Lakes, Sequoia National Park.

The largest sequence of metasediments and metavolcanics occurs along the western foothills on the northern flank of the range. These long belts of metamorphic rock are oldest to the east and become progressively younger westward. Interbedded with these Paleozoic metasediments are slices of Mesozoic rocks similar to those known as the Franciscan Formation in the Coast Ranges. Conspicuous among the Franciscan rocks are the serpentines and sandstones that form specialized soils with specialized plants. It is assumed that these metasediments and Franciscan rocks were deposited by accretion against the western edge of the North American continent as the sea floor slipped beneath. Many of these ancient sediments became folded and compressed as they were layered onto the the western margin of the continent. In the foothills east of Merced is a "tombstone pastureland," where thin layers of metavolcanic rock stand vertically amid grasses and livestock.

At the point of contact between the metamorphic rocks and the granites are important mineral-bearing rocks. Where sedimentary rocks are intruded by large masses of granite, deposits of metals such as gold and platinum may be present. At the time of intrusion, hot water driven to the surface by the heat of magma carried gold and quartz in solution. Where the silica solutions cooled in cracks of the overlying rocks, veins formed, and erosion carried minerals from these deposits out to the valley floor. It was in the American River near Sutter's Mill that gold was discovered in the gravel, initiating the Gold Rush. Miners moved into the foothills and dug out the quartz veins hoping to find the source of the gold that had washed out into the rivers. This dream discovery, known as the "mother lode," was never realized, nor was it likely. The action of rivers carrying away light materials concentrates heavy minerals such as gold in the gravel left behind. Searching through gravel is known as placer mining, and this technique has proved to be the most fruitful. A drive on Highway 49 along the foothills through the mother lode country is a drive back into history. Along the way, town names such as Placerville bear witness to the days of the forty-niners.

Although gold is the most valuable metal that has been mined in the Sierra Nevada, other metals have accumulated along these contact zones, and their occurrence is not limited to the western foothills. On the east side of the Sierra, north of Bishop, is a similar contact zone between the intrusive granite and the old metamorphic rocks where one of the largest tungsten-processing mills in the United States is located. This mill, in Pine Creek, a few miles northwest of Bishop, gets its ore from a series of mines located between 9500 and 12,000 feet (2800 and 3650 m) near the headwaters of Pine Creek. This mill is large enough that layoffs of personnel influence the economy of Bishop. There are also many tungsten mines in the low range known as the Tungsten Hills just north of Bishop Creek.

Postbatholithic rocks of the Sierra are sedimentary and volcanic. Sediments washed westward as the proto-Sierra was eroded, and this sedimentation has continued to the present day. About 20 million years ago, there began a major period of volcanism that spilled lava over the top of the northern Sierra Nevada and filled valleys of the undulating lowland. Volcanic rocks of the Modoc Plateau were formed at that time, too. Most of that volcanic material has since eroded away from the Sierra Nevada, but a few peaks north of Yosemite, such as Mount Rose, Squaw Peak, Sonora Peak, and Dardanelles Cone, are remnants of that period. The uplift of the Sierra and accumulation of sediment in the Great Central Valley during that period pushed back the sea on the west.

Recent volcanism of the Sierra occurred along the eastern flank, where lava flows and cinder cones dot the landscape. A major volcanic field lies in the area from Mammoth Mountain to Mono Lake (pl. 1B). Major eruptions in this area have occurred in the last million years, and the activity along the Sierra Nevada fault system during this time caused a major portion of the uplift of the Sierra Nevada range.

A long, steep grade on Highway 395 north of Bishop is known as Sherwin Grade. It progresses up a large deposit of rhyolite and volcanic ash known as the Bishop tuff. The tuff is represented by 30 to 40 cubic miles (126–168 km^3) of material that resulted from a massive volcanic eruption about 700,000 years ago. Ash from this eruption is found in sediments as far east as Kansas and Nebraska. This eruption formed a huge crater that covered about 75 square miles (195 km^2). That crater today, known as the Long Valley caldera, extends from about the summit of Sherwin Grade, near Tom's Place, to Glass Mountain Ridge, east of Mammoth Lakes, a town that lies along the southwestern edge of the caldera. This valley is a collapsed block or caldera that was formed by subsidence when the material that became the Bishop tuff was forceably evacuated from beneath. During glacial times, this caldera was filled by a huge lake about 300 feet (90 m) deep. Today in the bottom of the caldera is Lake Crowley, a reservoir on the Los Angeles Aqueduct. The Long Valley caldera represents the headwaters of the Owens River. The river formerly cut a gorge in the rim of the caldera to drain south, ultimately all the way to China Lake, near the present town of Ridgecrest in the Mojave Desert.

Mammoth Mountain is a quiescent volcano that formed about 370,000 years ago. It is 11,053 feet (3370 m) high. From the top of Mammoth Mountain a person looking toward the northeast can see a chain of volcanic peaks that lies in a straight line for about 40 miles (64 km). Beneath these features is a major fault or fissure that is part of the Sierra Nevada system. Obsidian Dome lies along this line, as do the Inyo and Mono craters. Ages of the Mono Craters are from 6000 to 6500 years. Inyo Craters are 600 to 850 years old. The islands in Mono Lake are the northernmost points of this volcanic system. Steam eruptions were recorded in Mono Lake as recently as the early 1900s.

Less than 100,000 years ago a basalt flow occurred southwest of Mammoth Mountain. As the basalt cooled, it cracked into long hexagonal columns. A glacier smoothed off the top, and the result is what is known as Devils Postpile (fig. 4.8). It is now managed by the National Park Service as a National Monument.

Recent earthquakes in the Mammoth area indicate that this area is still active. In May 1980, four earthquakes within 48 hours, registering about 6 on the Richter scale, jolted Mammoth Lakes. Tremors of lesser magnitude continued through the summer of 1983. Geologists studying the area since 1975 have found that in the two-year period following the 1980 earthquakes, the magma pool beneath the Mammoth area rose from a depth of 6 miles (10 km) to about 2 miles (3.2 km). Steam vents and

FIGURE 4.8   Devil's Postpile National Monument, Mono County.

hot springs became realigned. It also was discovered that the terrain within the Long Valley caldera northeast of Mammoth Lakes had risen about 12 inches (30 cm). In 1982 the U.S. Geologic Survey issued a "notice of potential hazard" to warn people of the imminent threat of eruption. The Mammoth Lakes–Long Valley area became the greatest threat of volcanic activity in the lower 48 states.

The volcano notice sent the local chamber of commerce into a frenzy. They predicted that skiers and other tourists would stay away in droves, and they feared that all the newly built condominiums would lie vacant and unsold. The chamber of commerce was critical of the U.S. Geologic Survey, who pointed out that they had accurately predicted the Mount Saint Helens eruptions, and that it would be criminal to keep such a threat a secret for the sake of business. Instruments in the area will continue to monitor potential threat, in the hope that if an eruption appears certain, there will be adequate time for evacuation.

The presence of active volcanism on the east side of the Sierra Nevada has spawned a controversy of a different kind. In association with the effort to establish alternate forms of generating electricity, a number of geothermal facilities have been proposed. The largest, associated with Coso Hot Springs in Inyo County, was begun in 1987. Because that area is not frequented by large numbers of tourists, and because the project generates tax dollars for Inyo County, it has been the source of little controversy. On the other hand, a number of proposals for similar facilities in the Long Valley area have been the subjects of heated debate. In particular, proposed plants near Hot Creek (fig. 4.9), are viewed as possibly disruptive to a popular swimming area, a fish hatchery, and one of California's most popular trout streams. The issue is one of tourism versus industry, with possible implications for the economy of Mono County and the city of Mammoth Lakes.

The appearance of the Sierra today is largely a function of geologic processes. It is unique among major mountain ranges because it is composed almost entirely of granitics. It is also geologically young and therefore characterized by steep, jagged landforms. Domes are also a typical feature of granitic landforms.

Certain characteristics of granite influence weathering processes. Granite is very hard, and it weathers slowly. But fissures develop in granite along points of structural weakness. These fissures, known as joints, tend to run parallel to the north-south axis of the range and also perpendicular to that axis. Granite thus has a tendency to break up into large cubes. Furthermore, granite appears to expand from the inside, which causes domes to form, within which there are more horizontal fractures. The cause of this expansion is not fully understood, but the present theory is that as the overlying sedimentary rock was peeled away by erosion, it relieved pressure from the underlying

FIGURE 4.9 Hot Creek, Mono County. An area of hot springs east of Mammoth Mountain.

granite. Loss of this overburden allowed the granite to expand from within, causing it to crack in a spherical or onion-peel pattern. Intersections of joints and horizontal cracks have caused the granite to break into large cubes. Freezing of water or growth of roots, forces of mechanical weathering, expand these cracks. Gravity and other erosive forces cause portions of each of these layers to fall away in a process known as exfoliation. These processes—expansion, cracking, weathering, and erosion—have caused the dome shape so characteristic of granitic landforms (fig. 4.10).

Tree roots and frost wedging are not the only sources of mechanical weathering. Fires, by causing expansion and contraction, also break up rocks. In arid areas, growth of salt crystals in cracks can hasten the breakup of rock materials. In general, these processes work more rapidly on sedimentary and metamorphic rocks.

Chemical weathering is more subtle than mechanical weathering. The dark color on the surface of granitics in desert areas is a consequence of the oxidation of metals such as iron and manganese. Water dissolves some minerals and leaves others behind. In granite, the feldspars tend to be more water-soluble; the quartz minerals have low solubility in water. Water dissolves limestone, forming grooves and creases on the surface. If subterranean water saturates a layer of limestone, it can form caverns. Large caverns such as those near Carlsbad, New Mexico, were formed in this way. The western slope of the Sierra Nevada has a few limestone outcrops that contain caverns, including Boyden Cave, in Kings Canyon, and Crystal Cave, in Sequoia National Park.

FIGURE 4.10   Granitic landforms. View eastward from Glacier Point, Yosemite National Park.

Another form of chemical weathering is the action of weak acids, such as carbonic acid (H_2CO_3). This can produce small pits on flat granite surfaces, in which organic debris and water may accumulate. As bacteria decompose the organic material, they excrete carbon dioxide, as do all heterotrophic organisms. The carbon dioxide combines with the water to produce carbonic acid. Over millions of years the pits become larger as this weak acid eats away at the rock. The tops of many Sierra peaks are flattened, and on these flat surfaces are many such pits, most of which are fist-sized or slightly larger. Such pits occurring along streams were used for thousands of years as ready-made *morteros*. Using a rounded stone, Indians would grind acorns and buckeyes to a mush in these pits.

Another way in which carbonic acid is produced is by the fungus component of lichens. Lichens growing on the surface of rocks are called crustose lichens because they seem to form a colorful crust on the rocks. These lichens adhere to the surface by microscopic fungal filaments, which excrete carbon dioxide (the fungus is a heterotrophic organism). The weak carbonic acid formed helps to break up the rock, and it also provides small cracks and fissures to aid attachment of the lichen to the rock surface.

Mechanical and chemical weathering break up the rocks into smaller and smaller particles. Erosion carries away the rock fragments and exposes new surfaces to weathering. The forces of erosion include gravity, wind, water, and glaciers. They transport rock materials from their source and deposit them somewhere else.

Gravity is an important force on all steep slopes. Rock falls, landslides, and avalanches are gravity-driven as are streams, waterfalls, and glaciers. The rubble at the base of a cliff, known as talus, is the result of weathering processes, which loosen the materials on the cliff face, and gravity, which does the rest.

Wind is an important factor in the alpine zone. Strong winds loaded with sediment produce the sand-blasted look on the sides of high-elevation trees. In the winter, the wind picks up ice particles, which have the same effect. This abrasion not only works on vegetation, but on rock surfaces as well. Hollows on the sides of otherwise smooth rock can be the product of this abrasion, although it is less likely to be seen on high-country granite than it is in the desert, and it is less likely to be seen in granite than in softer materials such as sandstone or limestone.

Water is the primary erosive force in the Sierra today. It carries away rock materials before they have a chance to show the strong color change associated with surface oxidation. The granitics of the high country are blue-gray, but they are of the same chemical composition as those in the Alabama Hills near Lone Pine (fig. 4.11). There, in the rain shadow of the Sierra, granitics are coarse and brown on the surface, showing the effects of thousands of years of chemical weathering by oxidation, with limited influence by water or snow.

The granitics of the Alabama Hills are noteworthy for other reasons as well. The rounded boulders are a product of chemical weathering of the large cubes produced by jointing. Because there is proportionately more surface at the corners of a cube than there is in the center of each side, oxidation works on the corners more rapidly. Over the course of thousands of years the cubes become rounded.

FIGURE 4.11   Granitic landforms in the Alabama Hills near Lone Pine, Inyo County. Mount Whitney is in the background. Note that Sierran granite has a lighter color due to weathering by ice and water rather than oxidation by sunlight.

It is also interesting that the Alabama Hills lie on a small down-dropped block located between two parts of the Sierra Nevada fault system. Most of the Sierra uplift has taken place to the west of the Alabama Hills, but the 1872 earthquake took place on the eastern side. Nevertheless, the crest of the Sierra and the top of the Alabama Hills were formerly at the same elevation. The Alabama Hills and the rest of the Owens Valley have been dropping, while the mountains on both sides have been rising. This type of valley is called a *graben*, which means "grave" in German.

The major force responsible for the appearance of the Sierra today is glaciation. It has carved and shaped the terrain and removed most of the soil. During the Pleistocene, the Ice Age, there were many periods when glaciers covered large portions of the high country. Four of these major intervals correspond to periods of continental glaciation in the Midwest. The oldest episode was about 3 million years ago. Other major episodes can be dated to 1 million, 75,000, 20,000, and 4,000 years ago. Also, a short period of glacial advance, a little ice age, was recorded about 600 years ago. The present 60 to 70 glaciers of the Sierra Nevada date back to that time. The Palisades Glacier near Big Pine (fig. 4.12) is the largest of these glaciers today, only about 1 square mile (2.6 km^2) in surface area.

A glacier (fig. 4.13) occurs when snow accumulates faster than it melts. As the snowpack becomes thicker, it becomes compressed into ice by its own weight. The ice then flows slowly downhill, often in a canyon, to a point at a lower elevation

FIGURE 4.12   Palisades Glacier and Fourth Lake, Big Pine Creek, Inyo National Forest.

FIGURE 4.13   Diagrammatic representation of a valley glacier.

where the ice melts. If snowfall at the upper end is greater than the melt at the lower end, the glacier advances. If snowfall is less than the amount of melt, the front retreats. Rocks that fall on the surface of the ice gradually sink to the bottom of the glacier. As the glacier slides downhill, the rocks trapped at its lower surface grind against the bedrock. This grinding shapes the canyon into a U-shaped trough, unlike canyons cut by water, which are V-shaped. The grinding of rock on rock also produces a fine powder that remains suspended in the water flowing from the toe of the glacier. Rivers and lakes fed by glacier melt have an azure color due to this suspended rock material.

When a glacier retreats, it leaves behind a ridge of rubble known as a moraine. The moraine left at the toe of the glacier is a terminal moraine, and those left along the sides of the glacier are lateral moraines. Sometimes, isolated boulders are left stranded upon a surface that has been smoothed by a glacier. Boulders of different composition from the rock upon which they lie are known as erratics (fig. 4.14). The enormous size of some erratics bears witness to the erosive power of glaciers.

The upper end of a glacier freezes into cracks and fissures, a process that causes more rocks to break off. Sliding of the glacier away from its upper wall of rock carries off the quarried material, making room for more ice. This process causes the glacier to "eat" its way into the rock at its upper end, and the result is a basin with a circular cliff wall. This type of basin, resembling an ampitheater, is known as a cirque (fig. 4.15).

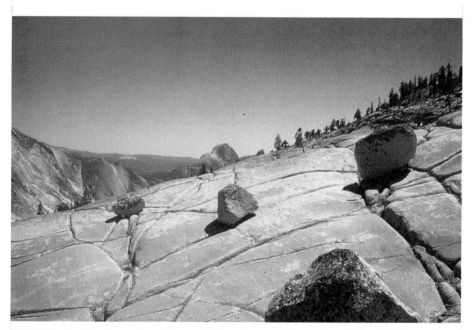

FIGURE 4.14   Glacial erratics at Olmstead Point, Yosemite National Park. Note Half Dome in the background.

FIGURE 4.15   A cirque lake in Fourth Recess, upper
Mono Creek, Sierra National Forest.

Many lakes and meadows in the Sierra today lie in such basins. Often these cirque
lakes occur in a series, one above the other in a canyon. These series are known as
paternosters (pl. 10A). *Paternoster* means "Lord's prayer"; the term refers to a string
of lakes as if they were a string of beads in a rosary.

The mechanism by which paternosters form is subject to some debate. One theory
is based on the fact that all rock is not of equal hardness. As the glacier slides
downhill in the canyon, it cuts more deeply in some areas than in others, and the
low spots become the cirques. Another theory implicates waves in the ice. A third
theory assumes that a glacier forms only one cirque at a time, and that a series
of cirques is formed by different glaciers, each occurring during a different glacial
episode. Uplift of the mountain range between glacial episodes carries the older
cirques upward, so the lowest cirque would be the youngest. Two bits of evidence
support this theory. First, there are often 4 or 5 lakes in a Sierra paternoster, each
presumably corresponding to a major glacial episode. Second, glaciers form best at a
single elevation, at the zone of heaviest precipitation. The tops of the high peaks in
the Sierra were never glaciated. They emerged above the glacial ice, like islands.

Large glacial systems flow down canyons like rivers of ice and are joined by ice from side canyons or tributaries. Since these side canyons have less ice in them, the main glacier cuts into the rock to a depth that is below the side canyons. Ice from the side therefore tends to flow out on top of the larger mass. After the ice melts, a deep canyon remains where the major ice flow was, but the side canyons, which were not cut as deeply, appear as valleys high up on the wall of the main canyon. These side tributaries are known as hanging valleys. When hanging valleys contain flowing water, they dump into the larger canyon as waterfalls. The high waterfalls of Yosemite Valley are examples of this phenomenon. The Yosemite Falls plunge in two steps from a hanging valley. The total drop is 2565 feet (782 m), making it one of the highest waterfalls in the world.

The process of a glacier eating backward into the rock can produce other landforms besides cirques. If two glaciers work toward each other back to back, the result could be a high, thin ridge known as an arête. An arête can lie between two cirques, or it may be a ridge formed by two glaciers that flowed parallel to each other. If two back-to-back glaciers eroding headward merge across a mountain divide, they will carve a low saddle known as a col. The major east-west passes across the Sierra, such as Donner and Tioga, were formed by this process. When three glaciers move toward each other, they can leave a pyramid-shaped peak known as a horn. The Matterhorn of the European Alps is the most famous such horn. In the Sierra, the Palisades, the Minarets, and the Kaweahs are large arêtes. In the Yosemite area, Clark Peak, Cathedral Peak, and Unicorn Peak are horns. Figure 4.16 shows a single location featuring both horns and an arête.

The surface over which a glacier slid also shows distinctive features. Grooves and striations show where rocks were dragged. Some surfaces have been polished to a high shine, and this glacial polish can be dangerous to walk on when wet. Walking over polished surfaces should never be attempted next to a cliff, a rapids, or a waterfall.

Maximum glaciation occurred in the Sierra about 60,000 years ago. An ice cap about 275 miles (445 km) long and 40 miles (64 km) wide stretched across the high country, with tall peaks protruding above the ice. The longest glaciers flowed through what are now Yosemite and Hetch Hetchy valleys. The glacier of Hetch Hetchy followed the course of the Tuolumne River for a distance of 60 miles (100 km). At its thickest, it filled a 4000-foot (1300-m) gorge with ice. On the east side of the Sierra the glaciers were much shorter due to steeper terrain and less precipitation. The large moraines from these glaciers are found at the mouths of numerous canyons from Big Pine northward. Some of these moraines are hundreds of feet high.

John Muir first entered the Sierra Nevada in the 1860s, and he shocked the geologists of the time by suggesting that the landforms of the Sierra were the result of repeated glaciations. It was many years before his ideas were verified. Yosemite Valley, John Muir's home, is the ultimate glacial landscape (pl. 1A). The floor of Yosemite Valley is not U-shaped today because it is filled with sediment, but other glacial features, such as hanging valleys, cirques, moraines, and erratics, are all evident. Yosemite Valley is estimated to have about 2000 feet (650 m) of sediment in its

FIGURE 4.16   Glacial landforms: horns and an arête near Lost Lake, Kings Canyon National Park.

bottom. That means that the glacier there about 60,000 years ago was at least 4000 feet (1300 m) deep.

At the valley's eastern end, Half Dome and Cloud's Rest stood above the glacial ice. Half Dome (see figs. 4.10 and 4.14) was once a typical dome, but its northern half was probably heavily jointed, and the ice flowing down Tenaya Creek carried away the rocks of the dome's northern half. Tenaya Creek joins the Merced River at the eastern end of the valley. At the juncture is a medial moraine that still separates the flow of the two rivers for over a half-mile (1 km).

Largely because of its glacier-scoured beauty, Yosemite was established as a state park in 1866. It was not until 1890 that it and Sequoia were established as national parks. With the addition of Kings Canyon National Park in 1940, the largest region of glaciated mountain terrain in the lower 48 states was set aside to remain unspoiled forever (pl. 2A).

The southernmost glacier in the Sierra flowed southward along the Kern Canyon. The Kern River today flows nearly due south for about 50 miles (80 km), following the course of a right-lateral strike-slip fault that is the longest fault in the Sierra. Offset on this fault up to 8 miles (13 km) has been measured. The fragmented nature of the rock in the fault zone represents a "soft" spot along which the ice could gouge and water could cause erosion. At its upper end the Kern Gorge is a long, straight, U-shaped valley (fig. 4.17). At its lower end, south of the influence of glaciation, it is V-shaped. The gorge and its adjacent plateaus bisect the Sierra high country into

FIGURE 4.17   View southward along Kern Canyon, a U-shaped valley, Sequoia National Park.

two long ridges known as the western divide, at 13,000 feet (3900 m), and the main divide, at 14,000 feet (4230 m).

The plateaus on each side of the Kern Gorge are believed to be erosion surfaces that predate the glaciers. The oldest surfaces are represented by slanting, flat peaks such as Mt. Whitney and Mt. Langley, both of which are higher than 14,000 feet (4230 m). These surfaces were eroded by events over 12 million years ago that predate most of the Sierra uplift. Alternating phases of uplift and erosion formed other tablelands at later intervals. These plateaus were presumably formed at successively lower elevations as cycles of erosive forces stripped away the rock in between periods of uplift. South of Mt. Langley is Cirque Peak at 12,863 feet (3828 m), which could represent the next oldest period of erosion, the next period of quiescence. Flat-topped Diamond Mesa, near Forester Pass, probably formed at the same time. Following this, uplift occurred again, followed by another period of quiescence during which the Boreal Plateau, near Rocky Basin, was formed. This plateau, at 11,000 feet (3300 m), roughly matches a plateau on the west side of the Kern Gorge near the Kaweahs. Other plateaus occur at the same elevation all around the Kern Basin. To the north, these include Siberian Flat, Guyot Flat, Sandy Meadow, and Bighorn Plateau, landmarks along the Pacific Crest Trail.

Uplift then took place again, perhaps amounting to a gain in elevation of 2500 feet (760 m). The following erosional period formed the 9000-foot (2750-m) Chagoopa Plateau, on the western side of the Kern Gorge. The Kern Basin lava flow partially covers this plateau. These volcanics have been dated at 3.5 million years of age, making the Chagoopa surface Pliocene in age. Following this, the glacial episodes of the Pleistocene, coincident with the bulk of the Sierran uplift, raised the mountains to their present elevation. Glaciers sliding along the Kern fault cut the U-shaped Kern Gorge a full 2000 feet (600 m) deeper into the surface of the Chagoopa Plateau. From the west a small glacier cut a 1000-foot (300-m) gorge known as Big Arroyo. At the confluence of Big Arroyo and the Kern Gorge there is a spectacular hanging valley and waterfall.

BIOTIC ZONATION

The distribution of communities in the Sierra Nevada (fig. 4.18) is influenced by elevation, latitude, rain-shadow effect, and slope effect. Complex interactions of living and nonliving factors provide an environment that is called the habitat. Among the nonliving (abiotic) factors of the environment are variations in light, heat, water, and soil. The biotic factors include all the organisms and their interactions. A habitat, therefore, is where organisms live.

Changes in environment that are associated with elevation are superimposed upon the differences in latitude between the northern and southern parts of the Sierra. As one moves to the north, precipitation increases and temperature decreases. Three hundred miles (480 km) of latitude is roughly equivalent to 1000 feet (300 m) of elevation. The trend, therefore, is for biotic zones to be displaced downward as a person goes northward. Upper timberline is about 1000 feet (300 m) lower at the northern end of the Sierra than at the southern end.

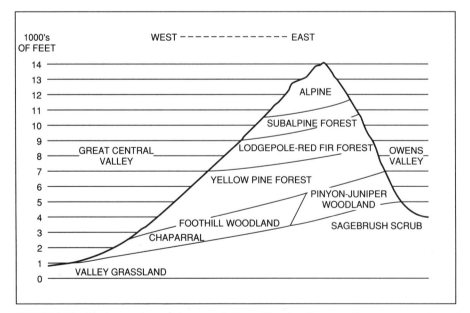

FIGURE 4.18   Biotic zonation of the central Sierra Nevada. Corresponding zones are elevated toward the south and on the east side of the Sierra Nevada.

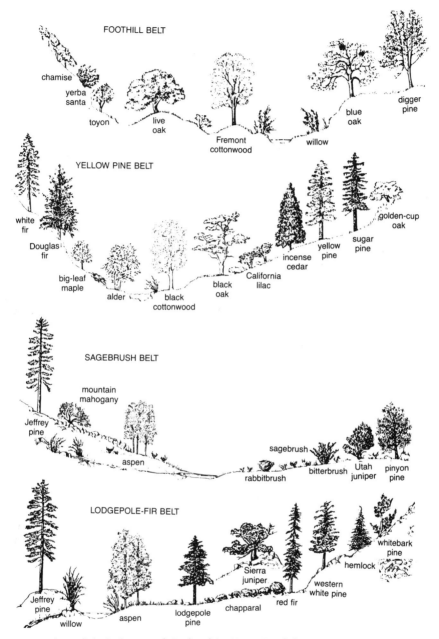

FIGURE 4.19   Principal trees and shrubs of the Sierra Nevada biotic zones. (From T. I. Storer and R. L. Usinger. *Sierra Nevada Natural History.* Berkeley: University of California Press, 1963.)

The eastern slopes are drier than the west because of the rain-shadow effect. The result is that zones tend to occur at higher elevations on the east side of the range. It is cooler at higher elevations, and cooler temperature means less evaporation; therefore, the water goes farther. Near the crest of the Sierra, east-west relationships are reduced because precipitation and temperature are similar. The effect on east-side biotic zonation is that each zone is displaced to a higher elevation but also confined to a narrower belt of distribution.

The influence of temperature on evaporation is called slope effect. South-facing slopes are hotter and drier. Slope effect is more pronounced at lower elevations, and also toward the south because that is where the growing season is limited by summer drought. On the west side in the vicinity of Three Rivers, at about 3000 feet (1000 m) elevation, slope effect is pronounced. Drought-tolerant scrub vegetation appears brown on south-facing slopes during the summer, and oaks appear green on north-facing slopes. The result is a conspicuous color mosaic illustrating slope effect. On the southeastern side of the Sierra, in the vicinity of Olancha, a similar color mosaic is obvious at about 9000 feet (3000 m) in elevation (pl. 3B). North-facing slopes are covered by pinyon pines, drought-tolerant evergreen trees. South-facing slopes are covered by desert vegetation, blue-gray Great Basin Sagebrush. Principal trees and shrubs of the Sierra Nevada biotic zones are depicted in figure 4.19.

Valley Grassland

The Valley Grassland community, which will be discussed in more detail in the chapter on the Great Central Valley, is a highly disturbed ecosystem characterized by introduced Mediterranean grasses and weeds. Of primary significance to the Sierra Nevada is that these introduced species have invaded the Foothill Woodland as well.

Grassland is a community associated with deep alluvial soils. Sands and gravels thousands of feet thick have washed out of the mountains and lie in the valley. Water percolates too deeply to supply root systems, so these plants tend to die out every summer. They resprout from seed or dormant root systems with each new surge of winter precipitation. Approaching the perimeter of the Great Central Valley, soils become thinner, and water is closer to the surface. At this point, deep-rooted oak trees become scattered among the grasses. This mixture of trees and grasses often is referred to as a savannah. This is where the Valley Grassland meshes with the Foothill Woodland.

Foothill Woodland

The Foothill Woodland surrounds the Great Central Valley. Also known as Oak Woodland, this is one of California's most widely distributed communities. Excluding brushy habitat such as Chaparral, Oak Woodland covers about 10 million acres (4,000,000 ha) of California's foothill or low mountain terrain. Foothill Woodland is composed of a mixture of drought-tolerant species that are truly Californian in distribution. The two predominant trees found throughout this belt are Digger Pine,

Pinus sabiniana, and Blue Oak, *Quercus douglasii* (fig. 4.20). The discussion of pines and oaks in California may begin here, for no two groups of conspicuous woody plants more clearly illustrate the diversity of habitats that occur in California. Although the total number of species and/or subspecies varies with the person doing the classifying, there are at least 20 species of pines and 16 species of oaks in California. The greater portion of these species are truly Californian in distribution, and many occur nowhere else. Oaks and pines will be mentioned as indicator species as each biogeographic province and its communities are discussed. Pines are more widely distributed in mountain communities, but oaks are more common in communities associated with summer drought. Because many oaks and pines are relatively easy to identify, and because they are conspicuous, attention will be directed to their appearance and characteristics of their distribution.

The first pine encountered by a person driving into the Sierra Nevada from the Great Central Valley is the Digger Pine. Some authorities object to this name because "Digger" was a derogatory term used for the Miwok Indians, who ate the seeds of these pines. These Indians also ate various bulbs and tubers they dug from the soils; hence they became known as "Digger Indians." An alternative name that has been proposed is Gray Pine, in reference to its distinctly gray-green foliage.

The Digger Pine is characterized by long needles that occur in clumps (fascicles) of three. They are 7 to 13 inches (18–33 cm) in length. The grayish foliage is sparse enough that the tree is nearly transparent. Because the trees seldom grow in a crowded forest situation, the crown is seldom composed of a single trunk from which other branches grow outward. Rather, the crown tends to be rounded, and commonly there are several main branches growing upward. Cones are quite large, ranging from softball to volleyball size. Scales making up the base of the cone have large hooks on the outer edge. At the base of each of these scales are found large seeds, about the size of kidney beans. These are the seeds that were gathered by the Indians. In fact, these seeds, along with acorns from a variety of oaks, are an important food for many foothill animals.

An unexplained gap occurs in Digger Pine distribution. It should be an associate of Blue Oak all around the Great Central Valley. However, it is missing from the Kaweah drainage near Three Rivers, at the southern entrance to Sequoia National Park. Otherwise, components of Foothill Woodland in this region appear typical.

Blue Oak is a member of a subgroup known as white oaks. It is winter-deciduous. Its leaves are about 3 inches long (7.5 cm), and the margin of the leaf is often composed of seven large lobes, but this is highly variable (fig. 4.20). Some leaves seem to have only undulations. These slow-growing trees mature to rugged, stately specimens.

Acorns of Blue Oaks are among the most palatable of all the oaks. They are eaten by a variety of birds and mammals and formerly were a staple for Indians. The predator extermination program imposed by humans has caused an unnatural abundance of acorn-eating animals such as gophers, mice, ground squirrels, rabbits, and deer. Cattle grazing also has taken its toll. The consequence of this imbalance is that throughout much of the Foothill Woodland, in the Sierra Nevada and the Coast

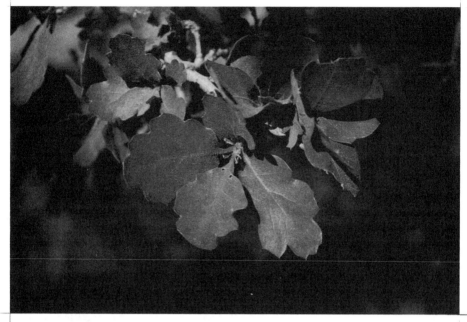

FIGURE 4.20   Blue Oak, *Quercus douglasii*, the dominant species of oak in the Foothill Woodland of the eastern Sierra Nevada and Coast Ranges.

Ranges, Blue Oaks are not regenerating. Acorns and seedlings are being eaten out of existence, which ultimately could cause Blue Oaks to disappear.

Plants that are fed upon heavily by animals seem to have developed chemicals (phytotoxins) that discourage herbivores. Tannins in acorns discourage herbivory by binding to protein molecules such as digestive enzymes. This action interferes significantly with chemical digestion in animals, such as cattle, that are unaccustomed to acorns as natural food. On the other hand, native foothill animals, such as squirrels and Mule Deer, have enzymes in their saliva that bind to the tannins before they are swallowed, enabling digestive enzymes farther along in the digestive tract to function correctly. Indians solved the problem by making a mush of the acorns and leaching out the water-soluble tannins with running water.

Other large oaks found in Foothill Woodland include Valley Oak, *Quercus lobata* (fig. 10.13), and Interior Live Oak, *Quercus wislizenii*. Valley Oak is another white oak. It differs from Blue Oak by having larger, greener leaves, with 9 to 11 lobes, and long, narrow acorns. The largest of our western oaks, it is often the first oak to invade the grassland, but it requires deep soil. Its distribution therefore is localized. This stately oak was a major component of the savannahs and gallery forests that were formerly widespread on deep soils throughout the Great Central Valley. They fell victim to the damming of water courses and drying of lowland habitats, activities associated with agriculture. Large numbers of these trees also have been cut down for firewood and, to promote cattle and sheep grazing, with the mistaken notion that the amount of grass would be increased if oaks were removed. Recent research shows that certain species of grass grow taller, are more nutritious, and last longer into the dry season under the large canopy of the aged oaks.

Valley Oaks are also winter-deciduous. Like Blue Oaks, they drop their leaves in response to cold. Their huge root systems reach deeply to tap underground water supplies to enable them to remain active during the long, hot summer. Blue Oak is more drought-tolerant than Valley Oak. Blue Oak forms savannahs, but it also occurs in association with Digger Pine on slopes, close together, in a community known as a woodland rather than a savannah.

Interior Live Oak does not drop its leaves in the winter. It is an evergreen oak, with dark-green leaves that are smooth and hairless on the underside. Leaf margins may be smooth or spine-tipped. Interior Live Oak commonly occurs with Blue Oak and Digger Pine, but it tends to occupy rocky outcrops where its roots tap deeply into cracks and fissures that hold water. Interior Live Oak is more common at higher elevation, where it is responsible for the green canopy on north-facing slopes. Interior Live Oak is sometimes confused with Canyon Live Oak (Golden-cup Oak), *Quercus chrysolepis* (pl. 7A), which grows primarily in canyons where the soil remains wet near the surface. Canyon Live Oak, one of the most widely distributed oaks in the state, is more of a riparian or streamside species and occurs at middle elevations. The underside of its leaves is gray with golden fuzz.

At slightly higher elevations than Blue Oak, California Buckeyes and Redbuds become common on north-facing slopes. These are small, shrub-like trees. California Buckeye, *Aesculus californica* (fig. 4.21A) is the only member of the horsechestnut family (Hippocastanaceae) native to California. This is not a large family of plants, but buckeyes are widely distributed in the Northern Hemisphere. Another species, the Ohio Buckeye, *Aesculus glabra*, is the state tree of Ohio. California Buckeye is distinctive in the spring because of long, 4–6-inch (10–15-cm) clusters of white flowers (fig. 4.21B). Unique among foothill trees, it is drought-deciduous, dropping its leaves in the summer. These trees are easily spotted in early summer, because as their leaves turn brown they appear to be dying. In late summer and fall they are further distinctive because they bear large, pearlike seed pods on naked stems. From these pods come the buckeyes or "horsechestnuts," an important food for some animals. In addition, they were formerly harvested by Indians, who treated them by leaching, as they did for acorns. Without leaching, they would be toxic to humans. It also is interesting that the nectar is poisonous to nonnative Honey Bees (*Apis mellifera*), whereas native bees are not affected.

At scattered localities in the foothills there are Redbuds, *Cercis occidentalis*. They are particularly conspicuous along the Merced River west of Yosemite National Park. During late winter and early spring these shrublike trees are covered with small, reddish pink flowers. They are winter-deciduous, so there are no leaves on them when the flowers appear. The flowers are quite small and give the appearance that the tree is covered with small, reddish buds. Close inspection, however, reveals that

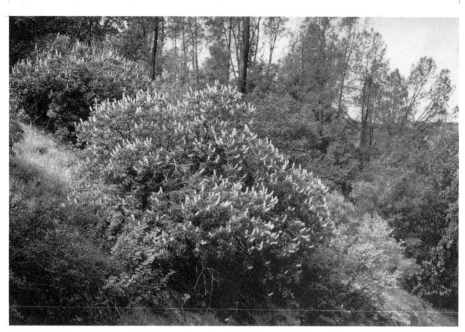

FIGURE 4.21   *A*. California Buckeye, *Aesculus californica*, with Digger Pines in the background.

FIGURE 4.21 (*continued*)   *B*. Flowers and foliage of California Buckeye.

the flower has the distinctive appearance of a member of the legume or pea family (Fabaceae). A pair of small, fused petals, the banner, projects upward as an attractant for pollinators. The other petals are variously modified to enclose the stamens and pistil, the reproductive parts. An insect pollinator must pry open the flower to expose these parts, at which time they spring upward to dust its lower abdomen with pollen; the insect at the same time transfers pollen from the previously visited flower to the pistil of this flower. Large, heart-shaped leaves remain on the tree through the summer, and large, brown beanpods persist into the next winter. These beanpods are also an important source of food, particularly protein. Nitrogen-fixing bacteria inhabit the roots of these plants.

Oak woodlands also include a large component of ephemeral or annual plants that grow vigorously and bloom after winter rains (pl. 3C). Some of California's most attractive wildflowers, such as Owl Clover, *Orthocarpus purpurascens* (pl. 16H), and Harlequin Lupine, *Lupinus stiversii* (pl. 16C), are found here also. Unfortunately, many of these are being eliminated by livestock grazing and the invasion of Mediterranean weeds.

Chaparral

There are several kinds of scrub or shrub communities that go by the name of chaparral. These variations will be discussed in detail in the chapter on cismontane southern California, where scrub communities dominate. In the northern part of the Sierra Nevada, chaparral is an important component of the foothill community only on impoverished soils. South of Yosemite, however, it becomes increasingly abundant on south-facing slopes, which, due to heat and evaporation, have a shortened growing season. Most of the shrubs keep their leaves all year, but the leaves are variously adapted to resist water loss. Leaves are often small and coated with resinous or waxy secretions. They typically bear fine hairs, and they roll when they dry out. Many species bear berries. All species are fire-adapted. Chamise, *Adenostoma fasciculatum* (fig. 8.17), is the dominant species. Several species of California lilac, *Ceanothus* spp., occur here. Two varieties of Scrub Oak also occur here; California Scrub Oak, *Quercus berberidifolia* (= *Quercus dumosa*) (fig. 8.20), and a scrub form of Interior Live Oak, *Quercus wislizenii.*

One of the most spectacular plants in Sierran Chaparral is Flannel Bush, *Fremonto-dendron californica* (fig. 4.22), so named because its leaves are covered with a myriad of fine hairs. They are known also by the name of the former genus, Fremontia. In spring, these large shrubs produce showy yellow flowers in great abundance. Along the Kern River, in the southern Sierra, entire hillsides appear yellow because of the abundance of these shrubs. The shrub was named in honor of John C. Fremont, the explorer–army officer who became one of California's first politicians. The journal of the California Native Plant Society is called *Fremontia* in honor of the plant. A peculiarity of its distribution is that, in addition to its occurrence on the western side of the Sierra, it occurs as a component of Desert Chaparral on the north side of the Transverse Ranges.

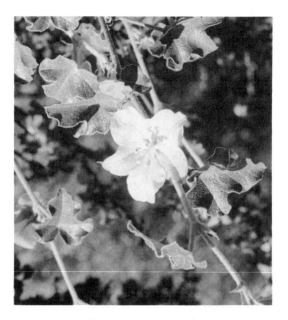

FIGURE 4.22   Flannel Bush, *Fremontodendron californica*.

Edaphic Communities

Edaphic communities occur where soil is the principal factor to which the community must adapt. The western foothills from about Yosemite northward include a belt of metamorphic and sedimentary rocks more typical of the Coast Ranges. Patches of soil, such as serpentines, with peculiar mineral composition and texture form ecologic islands in the Sierra Nevada and Coast Ranges upon which specialized plants have evolved (figs. 7.10 and 7.11). Ecologic islands are isolated habitats around which different ecologic conditions present a different environment. Plants and animals of these islands tend to be specialized or unique, and they are often relicts of a former time when the climate was different.

A total of 215 species and varieties of plants are restricted to (endemic on) serpentine soils in California. (There is some confusion between the terms *serpentine* and *serpentinite*. Serpentine is the official state rock of California. It is composed of several minerals, yet some authorities contend that the group of minerals is called serpentine, and the rock composed of those minerals is serpentinite. Historically, however, the term *serpentine* has been used to refer to both the mineral group and the rock. Because of its common usage, the term *serpentine* will be used here.) Serpentine soils are high in magnesium and low in calcium, and they contain heavy metals such as cobalt, nickel, and iron. They are often claylike and low in nutrients. Chamise is not endemic, but it is able to tolerate serpentine soils and thus is an indication that these soils represent a dry substrate for plants.

Included among the serpentine endemics are Interior Silk Tassel, *Garrya congdonii*, and a special scrub oak known as Leather Oak, *Quercus durata*, which differs from other scrub oaks in that the leaves are distinctly curled or convex. Often they are quite hairy on both surfaces as well. Knobcone Pine, *Pinus attenuata* (fig. 8.55), is also typical of serpentine soils, although it is more common in the Coast Ranges. It is one of the closed-cone pines that requires fire to open its cones. Its distribution in the northern Sierra is patchy, as it is along the coast, where it waters itself with fog drip.

Serpentine endemism is not restricted to plants. No one knows how many insect species are restricted to these areas, but at least nine species and subspecies of butterflies are associated with serpentine endemic plants.

Pine Hill in El Dorado County has a soil derived from gabbro, a dark plutonic rock. This soil is also high in magnesium. It is interesting to note that Leather Oak occurs here also. An endemic species, occurring nowhere else in the world, is Pine Hill Flannel Bush, *Fremontodendron decumbens*. Near the town of Ione, in Amador County, there is a localized patch of oxisol, a red clay laterite formed in the Eocene during a period of tropical climate. Among the peculiarities of the soil here is its acidic pH, less than 4.0. Ione Buckwheat, *Eriogonum apricum*, and Ione Manzanita, *Arctostaphylos myrtifolia*, are found nowhere else in the world. The few other chaparral shrubs that occur in this region are dwarfed, indicative of the nutrient-poor nature of this soil.

Patches of limestone and marble also occur in the western Sierra. Limestone endemics are not as common in the Sierra as they are in desert ranges; one notable exception is on the east side of the Sierra along Convict Creek. Here, in a mixed situation of Desert Chaparral, Sagebrush Scrub, and riparian vegetation, is a cluster of Rocky Mountain and Great Basin species that are found nowhere else in California. Included are a manzanita, *Arctostaphylos uva-ursi*, a willow, *Salix brachycarpa*, and a sedge, *Scirpus rollandi*. A lousewort (Scrophulariaceae), *Pedicularis crenulata*, is an herbaceous species that grows along the stream here and nowhere else in California.

Foothill Animals

The foothill community is drought-adapted. Deep-rooted species such as oaks are able to remain active during seasons lacking in precipitation. Consequently, a greater mass of animals can be supported in a foothill community than might be expected based on raw climatic data. The bulk of these animals, as in the desert or scrub communities, are ectothermic and of small size. There are many kinds of insects and reptiles, whose low metabolic rates means that they require less food, and whose long periods of dormancy enable them to endure the long, hot summer or cold winter. Dormancy during a cold period is called hibernation, and dormancy during a warm or dry period is called estivation; however, there is little difference physiologically. The strategy is for the animal to lower its metabolic rate, which significantly reduces its requirement for food. It then lives on organic molecules, such as fat stored within its body.

The great variety of foothill insects and reptiles will be discussed thoroughly in the chapter on southern California communities. Likewise, a host of nocturnal, seed-eating rodents are associated with Foothill Woodland, and they will be discussed more thoroughly in the section on southern California chaparral communities. In this chapter, attention will be on conspicuous mammals and birds that cope with their harsh habitat through one of two basic strategies. Either they harvest resources when they are abundant, storing some for future periods of scarcity, or they change diet with the seasons, feeding on what is abundant.

Another concept to be introduced here is that of niche partitioning. An ecologic niche refers to the "space" in a particular ecosystem occupied by a species. A niche refers to the role played by a particular species as it interacts with all the other species of an ecosystem. Ecologic and evolutionary theories predict that an ecologic niche can be occupied by only one species at a time. A broad ecologic niche occupied by two similar species may become divided or partitioned so the species avoid head-to-head competition for the same resources. An alternative to niche partitioning is extirpation of the species that is more poorly adapted. A combination of niche partitioning and extirpation leads to an assemblage of plants and animals best suited to the vagaries of climate and/or resources at a particular locality.

A consequence of niche partitioning, well illustrated by communities in the Sierra Nevada, is that as one moves up in elevation, an orderly replacement of similar

Community	Ground Squirrels	Tree Squirrels	Jay-Crow Family	Finch Family
Valley Grassland	California Ground Squirrel		Crow	House Finch
Foothill Woodland	California Ground Squirrel	Gray Squirrel	Yellow-billed Magpie (north)	House Finch
Yellow Pine Forest		Gray Squirrel	Steller's Jay	Purple Finch
Lodgepole–Red Fir Forest	Golden-mantled Ground Squirrel	Chickaree	Steller's Jay	Cassin's Finch
Subalpine	Golden-mantled Ground Squirrel	Chickaree	Clark's Nutcracker	Cassin's Finch
Alpine	Belding's Ground Squirrel			Gray-Crowned Rosy Finch
Pinyon Pine Woodland	White-tailed Antelope Squirrel		Pinyon Jay	House Finch
Great-Basin Sagebrush	White-tailed Antelope Squirrel		Raven, Black-billed Magpie	House Finch

FIGURE 4.23   Distribution of related species according to communities.

species seems to take place (fig. 4.23). This replacement is particularly evident in conspicuous families, such as squirrels (Sciuridae). Among birds, members of the crow-jay family (Corvidae) and members of the finch-sparrow family (Fringillidae) also show this replacement. The effect is that similar ecologic niches at different elevations seem to be occupied by different but related forms. Thus, for a biotic zone, animals as well as conspicuous plants can be listed among indicator species.

A more subtle form of niche partitioning is illustrated by groups of similar species that inhabit the same community but utilize it in slightly different ways. Examples of this type of partitioning are found within a number of bird families, such as the wood warblers (Parulidae) and woodpeckers (Picidae).

Birds.   Foothill Woodland is the home for large variety of bird species for which oaks, in particular, are important for food and shelter. Daytime retreats for Great Horned Owls, *Bubo virginianus* (fig. 8.42), and California Quail, *Callipepla californica* (pl. 13A), are provided by the canopy. Owls hunt for small rodents at night, and they rest in the trees in the daytime. Quail escape the heat of the day by remaining in the trees, emerging to search for seeds and insects when it cools off.

Cavities in oak trees are homes for a variety of animals. Gray Squirrels and owls use large cavities. Woodpeckers, Western Bluebirds (*Sialia mexicana*) (pl. 13D), and the White-breasted Nuthatch (*Sitta carolinensis*) use smaller holes for homes. The Western Bluebird is a characteristic bird of the foothills on a year-round basis. They make their homes in the oaks, but they forage daily into adjacent communities for food. These small birds are blue on the back and have buff-colored sides. They are conspicuous on fenceposts or high perches, where they wait for flying insects. The White-breasted Nuthatch is a small, acrobatic bird that walks head-first up and down tree trunks. It uses its long bill to snap up insects found on the surfaces of bark, a foraging technique known as gleaning.

Most birds of the foothills are omnivores. It is a disadvantage to be too specialized, because favored food is not always abundant. For example, acorns are not available year-round, nor are they common every year. When the acorn store has been exhausted, as in the summer, animals turn to other forms of food—particularly insects, which are the most abundant animals in the foothills.

Acorns are probably the most important food in the foothills. The problem with predation by a host of small mammals on acorns and seedlings of Blue Oak was mentioned earlier. Several bird species conspicuous in the foothills also depend heavily on acorns for food. Acorns are fed upon by Band-tailed Pigeons, *Columba fasciata*; Western Scrub Jays, *Aphelocoma californica* (pl. 13F); and Acorn Woodpeckers, *Melanerpes formicivorus* (fig. 7.28). Band-tailed Pigeons and Scrub Jays feed heavily upon acorns when they are abundant, but they switch to other foods, such as berries and insects, when the acorns are gone. Scrub Jays and Acorn Woodpeckers store the acorns and eat them later in the season, when the source on trees is gone. Scrub Jays bury their acorns, and in so doing help to plant oak trees.

Acorn Woodpeckers place acorns in holes they have drilled into dead or dying tree trunks. It is noteworthy that they also store the large seeds of Digger Pines in these holes. They return sometime later to eat the stored food. Spaniards referred to them as *carpintero* in reference to their wood-working activity, which can appear destructive. They put holes in cabin walls, and they can make a telephone pole look like Swiss cheese. The soft wood of a telephone pole is a favored place to store acorns, and utility companies have taken to painting them with a green-colored woodpecker repellant, which works only temporarily.

The Acorn Woodpecker has been the subject of considerable behavioral research, which will be discussed in chapter 7, on the Coast Ranges. They are conspicuous, gregarious birds that are easy to watch. They are dark with a white chin and a small red cap. When they fly they display a conspicuous white rump and white patches in the wings. Typical of woodpeckers, they flap their wings a few times and then glide a short distance. This pattern makes them seem to move up and down as they fly. They also attract attention because they make considerable noise. Their call is an easily recognized "wack-a, wack-a."

Niche partitioning among similar species is particularly true among birds that feed upon the abundant insects in foothill areas. In particular, woodpeckers are specialized to avoid competition by partitioning food resources in space and time. Acorn Woodpeckers apparently do not eat insects that invade their stored acorns, but when the acorns are gone they behave as though they were flycatchers: they perch on a high branch and catch flying insects in midair. The Northern Flicker, *Colaptes auratus* (fig. 4.24), is also a woodpecker. It prefers ants and termites, but it also eats berries. In agricultural areas, much to the dismay of farmers, Northern Flickers are known to hollow out fruit while it's still on the tree. Nuttall's Woodpecker, *Picoides nuttallii*, eats insects that bore in bark, avoiding surface insects, which are eaten by White-breasted Nuthatches. Downy Woodpeckers, *Picoides pubescens*, eat the same way as Nuttall's Woodpecker, but they prefer to feed on the bark of riparian trees such as alders and sycamores. The Lewis Woodpecker, *Melanerpes lewis*, is a vagrant; it doesn't remain in an area long unless food is abundant. It eats acorns when they are available, but it seems to prefer feeding on beetle larvae in areas that have been burned. Sapsuckers (*Sphyrapicus* spp.) drill parallel holes in the bark of trees, usually in the riparian community. They return to feed on sap, soft wood, and small insects in the holes.

Flying insects are an abundant food source, but mostly in the summer. The Black Phoebe, *Sayornis nigricans* (fig. 4.25), is a year-round resident of foothill communities. In the winter, it is one of the few species that continues to rely on flying insects. In the summer, however, a number of migratory insect eaters appear on the scene in order to share the wealth. Several species of flycatchers, including the Western Kingbird, *Tyrannus verticalis*, hunt from a perch. Swallows and swifts catch insects high in the air by continuously flying. Nighthawks (*Chordeiles* spp.) are large-mouthed birds that appear at dusk, catching insects on the wing when other insect eaters are at rest. The peculiar, slow wingbeat and jerky flight of the nighthawks make them appear batlike as they move among the insects in midair. Bats avoid the competition of nighthawks by feeding after dark and locating insects with sonar, inaudible squeaks that bounce off objects in the air. The acute hearing of bats enables them to locate

FIGURE 4.24   Northern Flicker, *Colaptes auratus*. (Photo by Richard L. Bellomy.)

FIGURE 4.25   Black Phoebe, *Sayornis nigricans*, a flycatcher.

insects and accurately judge distance by the length of time it takes for the sound to return to their ears.

In addition to the White-breasted Nuthatch, there are numerous other gleaners. Gleaners among the foliage include the Plain Titmouse, *Parus inornatus*, a small, gray bird with a crest, which is conspicuous in outer foliage. Other gleaners include bushtits, vireos, and warblers, each of which avoids competition by feeding in a different part of the foliage.

A number of migratory birds are conspicuous at different times of year. In winter, red-breasted American Robins, *Turdus migratorius*, feed on worms and grubs in the soil. With their acute hearing, they apparently are able to hear the digging noises of the subterranean burrowers. In autumn, beautiful Cedar Waxwings, *Bombycilla cedrorum*, move through in large flocks, feeding on berries. The summer visitors that feed on insects were mentioned previously.

It may seem that for a "food-poor" ecosystem there is an inordinate number of animals sharing oak trees. The number, however, is minimal compared to an eastern deciduous forest, where there may be hundreds of species of birds sharing the canopy. In an eastern forest there may be 10 to 20 species of warblers sharing the food resources of a single tree.

Mammals. A conspicuous member of the Grassland and Foothill Woodland communities is the California Ground Squirrel, *Spermophilus beecheyi* (pl. 12A). Their natural range extends from coastal bluffs to the foothills. These grizzled-looking squirrels typically dwell in hillsides, where they build complicated burrows. The burrows include many dead ends and blind alleys that presumably are to confuse potential predators, but may also form homes for many other species. Where food is too scarce in summer, they estivate. In areas where it is cold, ground squirrels hibernate in winter.

In agricultural areas humans have warred against ground squirrels, shooting and poisoning them. In cultivated areas, their numbers have become considerably reduced. Where squirrels are not preyed upon by humans, or where their natural predators are controlled, their numbers have increased, encouraged by an abundant seed crop associated with introduced Mediterranean weeds. Ground squirrels have moved to considerably higher elevations by invading road cuts, a vacant niche created by humans. In areas such as Yosemite Valley, where visitors insist on sharing their junk food, California Ground Squirrels have become tame and conspicuous. They make burrows along roads and trails and subsist on an unnatural diet of potato chips, corn chips, and cheese puffs. In their natural habitat, their diet consists of seeds, herbaceous vegetation, and acorns gathered from the ground. This appetite for acorns, coupled with their increase in numbers, is considered to be one of the contributing factors leading to the decline in the number of oak seedlings.

In areas where oaks are close together, typically at upper elevations in the Foothill Woodland, Western Gray Squirrels, *Sciurus griseus* (pl. 12B), harvest acorns by climbing in the trees. The Gray Squirrel is typically a tree squirrel. In the absence of Gray Squirrels, California Ground Squirrels are also known to climb trees and harvest acorns.

An entire community of animals is associated with California Ground Squirrels. These squirrels are preyed upon heavily by Red-tailed Hawks, *Buteo jamaicensis*, that swoop down upon them as they venture from their burrows. Badgers, *Taxidea taxus*, dig them out from their burrows and also make homes out of enlarged, abandoned ground squirrel burrows. Another inhabitant of abandoned burrows is the Burrowing Owl, *Athene cunicularia* (fig. 4.26), which raises its young in underground nests. These quail-sized owls decorate the burrow entrance with the dung of livestock, apparently to disguise their odor. In this way, the predators, including Badgers, seem not to recognize the burrows as being occupied. An interesting instinct in juvenile Burrowing Owls helps to further protect them from potential predators. If an intruder is heard entering the burrow, young owls clack their bills together, which collectively makes a sound that resembles the rattling of a rattlesnake. Rattlesnakes do use these burrows for refuge, and they also enter burrows in search of food. A mammal usually makes a hasty retreat upon hearing the warning of the rattlesnake.

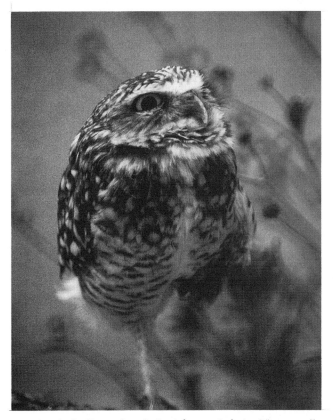

FIGURE 4.26 Burrowing Owl, *Athene cunicularia*. These small, long-legged owls often inhabit abandoned ground squirrel burrows.

Ground squirrels have a warning system that not only alerts each other, but every other animal in the vicinity as well. A member of the squirrel community, upon noticing danger, emits a shrill squeak, and all potential prey species duck for cover. It is interesting that the alarmist, by attracting attention to itself, is often the only squirrel that is captured. It seems, however, that the alarmist is usually one of the oldest squirrels in the colony and, as such, already has reproduced. By sounding an alarm, it protects its offspring. In so doing, it accomplishes what it set out to do by reproduction; it contributes a genetic endowment to the squirrel population.

Yellow Pine Forest

Different authorities refer to the Yellow Pine Forest by different names. In the old life zone system, this community was known as the Transition Zone. Modern biologists also call it Mixed Coniferous Forest or Lower Montane Forest. The terms *mixed coniferous* and *transition* refer to a mixture of coniferous and winter-deciduous trees. The name Western Yellow Pine refers specifically to Ponderosa Pine, *Pinus ponderosa*, but *yellow pine* is used also in a general sense to refer to a closely related species, the Jeffrey Pine, *Pinus jeffreyi*. Throughout this book the term *Yellow Pine Forest* shall be used for a forest in which either Ponderosa Pine or Jeffrey Pine is a major component.

Yellow Pine Forest is one of the most widely distributed communities in California, occurring in every mountainous region with sufficient elevation and climates (pls. 1A, 1B, 4A, 6A, 8C). Authorities differ in their estimates of total coverage, partly because of the controversy in naming the community, but it is probably safe to say that there are around 14 million acres (5,700,000 ha) of Yellow Pine Forest in California.

Yellow Pine Forest occurs on both east and west slopes of the Sierra Nevada. It is composed principally of coniferous trees requiring at least 25 inches (63 cm) of precipitation, much of which falls as snow. Adapted to a summer growing season, the community requires sufficient groundwater remaining from snowmelt and winter rains. From about 2000 feet (600 m) in the north and 5000 feet (1500 m) in the south, the Foothill Woodland grades into Yellow Pine Forest. Average precipitation in the Yellow Pine Forest is 40 inches (100 cm) per year, twice that of the foothills. On the east side of the Sierra, the lower elevation reached by this forest is about 4000 feet (1300 m) to the north, and about 10,000 feet (3300 m) to the south.

Depending upon which species predominate, Yellow Pine Forest has been divided further by various authorities into subgroups, which overlap across broad regions. Separation of the subgroups occurs in nature primarily in association with changes in available soil moisture, although temperature plays a role as well. In this book we shall distinguish two subgroups, dry Yellow Pine Forest and moist Yellow Pine Forest. At most elevations, the distinction between the two groups is as simple as the difference between north-facing and south-facing slopes. On the east side of the Sierra, dry Yellow Pine Forest prevails.

Members of the dry Yellow Pine Forest include Ponderosa and Jeffrey pines, as well as California Black Oak, *Quercus kelloggii* (fig. 4.27), and Incense Cedar, *Calocedrus*

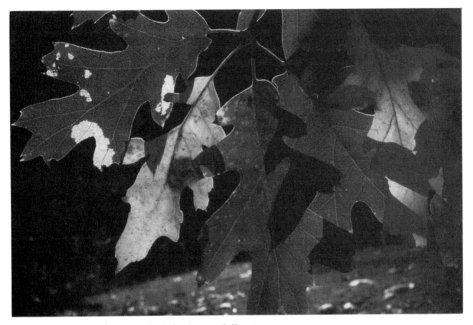

FIGURE 4.27   California Black Oak, *Quercus kelloggii*.

decurrens. Black Oak replaces Blue Oak above the foothills, and like Blue Oak or Valley Oak, it is winter-deciduous. It differs from them by having larger leaves with seven pointed lobes. It is characteristic on open slopes and dry ridges, where it often grows in clumps. This clumping may result from unclaimed acorns left behind by Gray Squirrels, who bury them in sizable caches for winter sustenance. Black Oaks also are able to resprout after a fire, which can give a single tree the appearance of multiple trunks.

Instead of needles, Incense Cedar has flattened, scale-like leaves arranged in branching chains (fig. 4.28). Its color is bright yellow-green, which is particularly visible in winter. The bark is reddish and fibrous, resembling the bark of giant Sierra Redwoods, and many people confuse large old cedars with redwoods. One important difference, however, is that redwood bark is fireproof. Bark of Incense Cedar, when shredded, makes excellent tinder for starting fires. It was favored by Indians for that purpose.

It is not easy for most people to tell Ponderosa Pine from Jeffrey Pine. The needles of both pines occur in clusters of three and are yellow-green. They differ from those of Digger Pine by being darker and shorter, 5–10 inches (12.5–25 cm) in length. They also differ from Digger Pines by having a single vertical trunk in the crown. The bark of Ponderosa and Jeffrey pines is similar, particularly on young trees. In older trees, Ponderosa bark tends to be a brownish yellow, whereas Jeffrey bark tends to be a brownish pink. Jeffrey bark tends to consist of a series of narrow ridges, whereas Ponderosa bark is often composed of large, flat plates. The odors of the bark

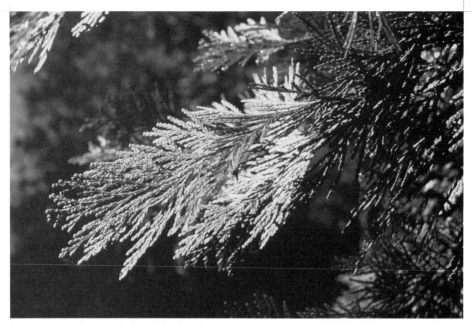

FIGURE 4.28   Incense Cedar, *Calocedrus decurrens*.

are markedly different. Jeffrey Pine is noted for its pleasant vanilla or butterscotch odor; Ponderosa bark has no distinctive odor. Cones of the two trees are similar in shape, but Jeffrey cones are usually much larger. Ponderosa cones are seldom longer than 5 inches (12.5 cm), whereas Jeffrey cones can be as long as 10 inches (25 cm). An important distinguishing feature is that a Ponderosa cone has small spines that stick out of the ends of each scale. On Jeffrey cones the spines are turned under. A person who rolls a Ponderosa cone between his or her hands will be pricked by the spines (prickly Ponderosa!); spines of the Jeffrey cone do not prick (gentle Jeffrey!).

Ponderosa and Jeffrey Pines can grow to a very large size. In Plumas there is a Ponderosa Pine that stands 223 feet (69.7 m) high. It is almost 8 feet (2.4 m) in diameter, and the crown has a 68-foot (21-m) spread. The largest Jeffrey Pine is on Sonora Pass. Standing 175 feet (54.6 m) high, it is almost 8 feet (2.4 m) in diameter, but the spread of its canopy is a mighty 87 feet (27 m).

Digger Pine, Ponderosa Pine, and Jeffrey Pine are similar in appearance, and they may grow together. What range of tolerances and requirements can be outlined to explain their differences in distribution? One important factor is the ratio between photosynthesis and cellular respiration, which is not the same for all plants. Temperatures above or below the optimum tend to decrease photosynthetic rate, and the rate of cellular respiration tends to increase as temperature increases. This increase continues beyond the temperature for optimal photosynthesis, and the result is that cellular respiration requires more carbohydrate than can be produced by photosynthesis. In this way, a lower elevational limit or a limit in southward distribution of any species could be controlled by temperature. Ponderosa Pine might be subject to such limitation. It seems not to occur where average January temperature is below 30°F (−1°C). It occurs below 3000 feet (1000 m) only in northern latitudes, but it is widespread throughout the west from the Pacific coast to the Rockies, to the exclusion of Digger Pine or Jeffrey Pine. In California, Ponderosa Pine has only limited distribution south of Riverside County, but it reaches its southern limit in the Peninsular Ranges of San Diego County. Specimens previously reported from Baja California apparently were misidentified.

Photosynthesis also requires water; therefore, precipitation could limit photosynthetic rate. The distribution of Ponderosa pine seems to coincide roughly with those areas that get more than 25 inches (62.5 cm) of precipitation, most of which is snow.

Jeffrey Pine (fig. 4.29) of the western Sierra tends to be restricted to rocky outcrops at higher elevations than Ponderosa Pine. It also grows on serpentine soils at lower elevations. The implication is that it can tolerate more cold and less water. Distribution of Jeffrey Pine has been correlated with areas where the average temperature in January is no warmer than 30°F (−1°C). Its tolerance for dry conditions is substantiated by its widespread distribution along the eastern side of the Sierra to the exclusion of Ponderosa Pine. A nearly pure stand of Jeffrey Pine occurs over many acres on pumice soil just north of Mammoth (pl. 1B). Jeffrey Pine also extends along the Peninsular Ranges into Baja California far south of the southernmost Ponderosa Pines. North of the Sierra, however, in areas east of the Cascades that seem to resemble the eastern Sierra, Ponderosa Pine occurs to the exclusion of Jeffrey Pine. In the Warner Mountains, in the northeastern corner of the state, Ponderosa Pine occurs at higher elevations than Jeffrey Pine (pl. 8C). This is exactly reversed from the elevational relationship on the western side of the Sierra. This distribution seems to imply that water is more limiting to the distribution of Ponderosa Pine than it is to Jeffrey Pine. Jeffrey Pine has a more extensive root system than Ponderosa Pine. Perhaps this feature, related to water absorption capability, is what separates the species in nature.

Another theory is that Jeffrey Pine is more able to survive lightning strikes, which are more likely at higher elevation. Jeffrey Pine in southern California commonly survives lightning, maybe due to its open crown. Perhaps the structure of its thick bark enables the tree to tolerate lightning without shattering, or the unique chemical nature of Jeffrey Pine bark may provide the answer. It has been reported that about 80% of Ponderosa Pines are killed by bark beetles after being struck by lightning, whereas a much smaller fraction of Jeffrey Pines are so afflicted. Jeffrey is the only pine whose bark contains paraffinlike compounds and aldehydes rather than terpenes. This different chemical nature may provide a resistance to bark beetles, or it may influence the way lightning is conducted by the tree. A logical question, of course, is how do other species of high-elevation conifers survive lightning?

What is it that prevents Digger Pines from moving upslope into the realm of Yellow Pine Forest? Could it be the photosynthesis-respiration ratio as a function of temperature? Perhaps it is simply a function of how deeply roots are able to penetrate. Digger Pines and Jeffrey Pines are known to have elaborate root systems. If the answer simply is drought tolerance, why does not Digger Pine occur farther south or more abundantly along the eastern Sierra in conjunction with Jeffrey pine? Tolerance for drought or heat certainly is demonstrated by the intermingling of Digger Pines and Pinyon Pines, a desert species. In the southern Sierra, from the Kern River drainage eastward to the Owens Valley, there is an intermingling of Digger Pine, Pinyon Pine, and Jeffrey Pine. In this area, Jeffrey Pine clearly occupies the moister sites.

The question of whether temperature or water, or a combination of the two, limits the respective distributions of these pines has not been answered, but microclimate differences do occur, as illustrated in localities where several species grow in close proximity. Such an area occurs in the southern Sierra on the western side of the Kern River, in the vicinity of Peppermint Creek. This area at 6400 feet (2100 m) elevation has nice groves of Ponderosa Pine on relatively flat, sandy alluvium along the stream. On slopes and rocky outcrops above the stream are Jeffrey Pines. On exposed south-facing slopes and the tops of granite domes are Digger Pines. The total distance of this gradient is about 1/4 mile (400 m). Approximately 1/2 mile to the east on a dry,

FIGURE 4.29   Jeffrey Pine, *Pinus jeffreyi*, on rock outcrop along Mono Creek, Sierra National Forest.

exposed, south-facing slope, there are also a few Pinyon Pines. Separation of species along a cool–moist to warm–dry gradient is clearly evident in this area.

Yellow pines are known to be associated with a wide variety of insects. Over 200 species have been catalogued that may, on occasion, become pests. Bark beetles (Scolytidae) are important, but they seem to attack primarily weak or old trees. One of the most common and best-known pests is the larva of a butterfly known as the Pine White, *Neophasia menapia*. The adults of this species are about 2 inches (5 cm) across. They are white, with heavy black markings around the tips of the front wings. They are difficult to see close up because they spend most of their time fluttering high in the trees. During rare outbreaks, the caterpillars of this species can completely defoliate a variety of conifers.

An interesting pest that attacks in alternate years is the Pandora Moth, *Coloradia pandora* (fig. 4.30B). The adult is one of the silk moths (Saturniidae). It is a heavy-bodied moth with a wingspan of about 2 inches (10 cm). It has a drab, brownish color and a single black spot on each wing. It is the larvae that do the damage. These caterpillars are a greenish color with six broad, interrupted longitudinal stripes. They eat pine needles, and although their cyclical infestations seem to create a lot of damage, they are an important part of the forest ecosystem. They recycle nutrients by converting pine needles, which normally decay slowly, to fertilizer that is easily available from the forest floor. They also provide a short-term abundant food supply for birds and other wildlife. Indians also ate the caterpillars, particularly in the Jeffrey

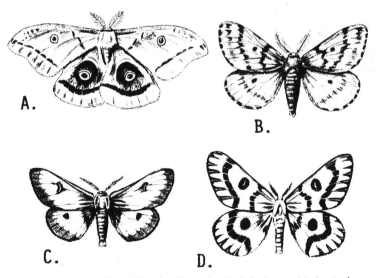

FIGURE 4.30   Some Sierra Nevada silk moths: *A.* Polyphemus Moth, *Antheraea polyphemus. B.* Pandora Moth, *Coloradia pandora. C.* Nevada Buck Moth, *Hemileuca nevadensis. D.* Sheep Moth, *Hemileuca eglanterina.* (From J. A. Powell and C. L. Hogue. *California Insects.* Berkeley: University of California Press, 1979.)

Pine forests of the eastern Sierra Nevada. As late as the early 1900s, Indians in the Mono and Modoc areas gathered the larvae by digging trenches, which trapped them beneath the trees as they crawled down. They were baked in hot soil and dried out for later consumption.

In the Warner Mountains, in extreme northeastern California, there is a third member of the yellow pine group. At high elevations, usually above 8000 feet (2600 m), are found Washoe Pines, *Pinus washoensis* (fig. 4.31). These unique pines are found only in a few localities, at high elevations on the western edge of the Great Basin in California and Nevada. In the Warner Mountains, Jeffrey Pines are found on the lower slopes, typical of the tree's distribution bordering desert areas. Above that, and more commonly toward the north, are the Ponderosa Pines. Washoe Pines grow above the Ponderosas.

Washoe Pine is probably of hybrid origin. It appears that hybridization between Ponderosa and Jeffrey pines has led to the Washoe Pine. This large pine has needles in clusters of three, similar to the other two species. The cone is intermediate in appearance. Washoe Pine cones have the spines turned inward, similar to those of Jeffrey Pine, but the cones are smaller than either of the parental species. They look like small versions of Jeffrey Pine cones and are about 3 inches (7.5 cm) in length.

Washoe Pines in the Warner Mountains grow in a woodland that includes Quaking Aspen, *Populus tremuloides* (pl. 8A). This community more nearly resembles what a person would expect to find in the Rocky Mountains. In California, aspens tend to occur as a riparian species, highly dependent upon abundant soil moisture. Their presence in a woodland setting in the Warner Mountains seems to indicate a reasonably moist habitat, and it is probably dependent on a good supply of summer rain. This implies that the Washoe Pine also requires a good supply of moisture. This beautiful forested area is also the location for abundant deposits of high-quality mahogany obsidian, which was so useful to Indians. The entire area is included in the Warner Mountains Wilderness, probably the least-visited wilderness area in the state.

The moist Yellow Pine Forest occurs on north-facing slopes and at higher elevations than the dry Yellow Pine Forest. The moist forest is dominated by White Fir, *Abies concolor* (fig. 4.32), and Sugar Pine, *Pinus lambertiana* (fig. 4.33), although Ponderosa Pine is not uncommon. White Fir has stiff, blunt needles distributed evenly along the stem. On the parts of the tree where needles are exposed to abundant sunlight, particularly near the top, they grow upward on the stem. Small firs are popular, expensive Christmas trees. Any of a number of firs that grow in western states can be sold as Christmas trees, but they often are sold as "Silver Tips," the implication being that the Christmas tree comes from the top, or tip, of a Silver Fir, *Abies amabilis*, a species of the Cascades. Red Firs, *Abies magnifica*, because they actually may have a silver tip, is perhaps the most common of the firs sold as a "Silver Tip."

In contrast, inexpensive Christmas trees are Douglas Firs, *Pseudotsuga menziesii*. Although they are not common in most of the Yellow Pine Forest, they do occur in moist locations, particularly on the west slope of the Sierra north of Yosemite

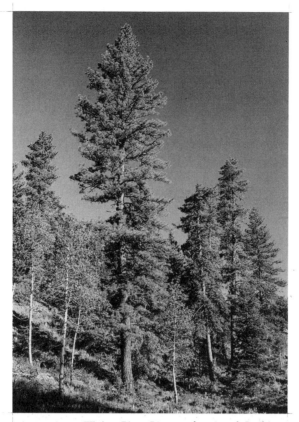

FIGURE 4.31   Washoe Pine, *Pinus washoensis* and Quaking Aspen, *Populus tremuloides*, in the Warner Mountains, Modoc National Forest.

Valley. Douglas Fir is darker green and has long, hanging side branches. If cones are visible, the firs are easy to tell apart. White Fir cones grow upward on the tips of the branches, and Douglas Fir cones grow downward. Furthermore, White Fir cones are composed of tightly layered scales that are deciduous; the cones come apart when they dry out. Douglas Fir is an important component of coastal forests from northern California to Washington, but overall, its presence is minor in the Sierra. They occur no farther south than the San Joaquin River drainage, and only on the western slope of the Sierra Nevada.

Sugar Pine is the tallest and largest of all pine species in the world. The largest known living specimen is on the western slope of the Sierra in Tuolumne County. It is 216 feet (64.8 m) high and 10 feet (3 m) in diameter. Cones of Sugar Pines dangle from the tips of long, horizontal branches. The cones are usually over a foot (30 cm) in length and often reach lengths of 18 inches (45 cm). Large Sugar Pine cones are often prized as table decorations. Needles are 3 to 4 inches (33–45 cm) long, much

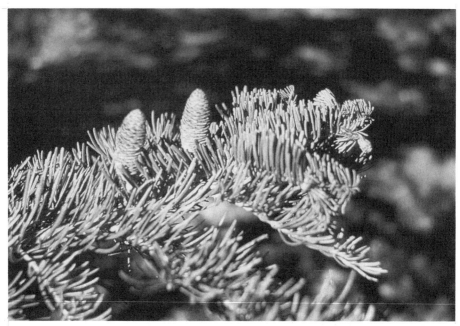

FIGURE 4.32 White Fir, *Abies concolor*.

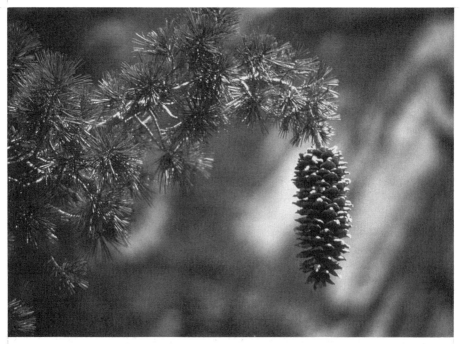

FIGURE 4.33 Sugar Pine, *Pinus lambertiana*.

shorter than those of other pines of the Yellow Pine forest, and occur in clumps of five. When viewed against the horizon, Sugar Pines are a majestic sight. They seem to be rather flat-topped, with the long branches extending horizontally away from the trunk. The short needles give the branches a "furry" appearance, like huge spider arms.

In general, five-needle pines are common at high elevations, but Sugar Pine occurs at lower elevations and requires more water than the other five-needle species. It is moderately shade-tolerant; has thick, fire-proof bark; and may exceed 500 years of age. If the bark is cut, it exudes a thick, sweet sap. John Muir is reported to have preferred Sugar Pine sap over that from the Sugar Maple. Indians ate the sugary pitch and used it as a laxative. They also harvested and ate the seeds.

Giant Sierra Redwoods or Giant Sequoias, *Sequoiadendron giganteum* (fig. 4.34), are the most moisture-demanding of all the species in the Yellow Pine Forest; hence they are absent from the east side of the Sierra as well as most of the west side. They require year-round soil moisture of at least 15 to 20%. In the southern Sierra Nevada, soil moisture is maintained at this level by runoff from higher elevations. The contribution of summer thundershowers is particularly important. Runoff accumulates in granite basins or where bedrock is near the surface, and the patchy distribution of these basins means that favorable sites for redwoods are limited. Redwoods therefore tend to occur in groves in basins and on north-facing slopes. There are 75 such groves scattered along the western slope of the Sierra Nevada. Unlike the groves toward the south, however, northern groves tend to occur on south-facing slopes. Toward the north, precipitation is heavier so water is less limiting, and trees grow on south-facing slopes, where light is more intense.

The combination of light and moisture required by these trees exemplifies the climate that was formerly widespread on the west coast of North America; hence these groves are only relics of a former widespread distribution in the Northern Hemisphere. Historical factors such as glaciation may also have influenced present-day distribution. In the western United States, fossil redwoods are known from as far east as Colorado, Wyoming, and Nevada, and as far south as the Santa Monica Mountains. Studies of pollen 30 feet down in meadows indicate that Sierra Redwoods did not grow at their present localities until 4500 years ago. On the other hand, mummified remains associated with woodrat nests in caves indicate that 10,000 to 35,000 years ago, during the height of glaciation, Sierra Redwoods occurred as low as 3000 feet (900 m) in elevation. Apparently, they moved upslope to their present localities as warming and drying occurred following the end of Pleistocene.

Because the distribution of climatic features required by Sierra Redwoods is so localized, it may be stated that they grow in ecological islands, like the foothill plants mentioned previously that are restricted to certain soils. Plants and animals of ecologic islands are often unique, or they are relics, which is the case for redwoods. In either situation, distribution is limited, and endemism is the result. There are over 1500 endemic plant species in California representing over 30% of the total number of species. Ecological islands therefore are an important feature that makes California a special place.

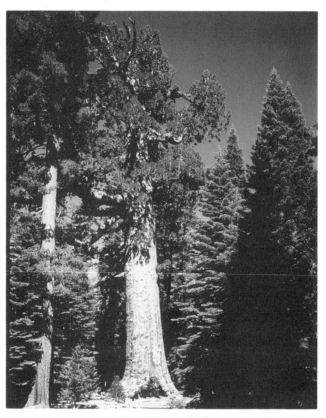

FIGURE 4.34   Sierra Redwood, *Sequoiadendron giganteum*. The Grizzly Giant, Wawona Grove, Yosemite National Park.

Redwood bark is resistant to fire. The wood will burn, but it is impregnated with tannins that are toxic to termites and other wood-consuming organisms. This resistance to both fire and insects allows the trees to reach great age, with many surpassing 2000 years. The oldest is considered to be the *Grizzly Giant* in the Wawona Grove of Yosemite National Park (fig. 4.34). Given abundant moisture, the trees grow rapidly. It has been said that Sierra Redwood is the fastest-growing tree in the United States.

Rapid growth and old age lead to great size. Sierra Redwoods are the largest living things in the world. General Sherman, the largest of the redwoods, is 273 feet (83 m) tall and 36.5 feet (11.1 m) thick at its base. If it were a useful lumber tree, it would contain the equivalent of 175 miles (280 km) of 2-by-4 (inch) planks, enough wood to build 40 five-room houses. Its lower branches are individually larger than any single tree east of the Mississippi River. General Sherman grows in a grove at Giant Forest in Sequoia National Park. A few miles to the north in Kings Canyon

National Park is the second largest living thing, General Grant, another redwood in another grove. General Grant is 268 feet (81.5 m) high and 40.3 feet (12.3 m) thick at its base.

The practice of naming these giants after generals began at the turn of the century with the establishment of the first national parks. Military heroes were honored by naming trees after them. Up until that time, General Sherman was known as the Karl Marx tree, named after a hero of another sort by a group of Communists that had established a cooperative colony in the area now known as Sequoia National Park. The Friedrich Engels tree stood nearby.

The name *Sequoia* also is of historical interest. Sequoyah was an Indian who established an alphabet, consisting of 86 characters, for the Cherokee language, making it possible to write in that language. Redwood trees were named for this native American, and the park was named for the trees. It was later determined that the Sierra Redwoods were different enough from Coast Redwoods to warrant their own genus. The name *Sequoia* was retained for Coast Redwoods, because they were named first, and the name for the Sierra Redwoods was changed to *Sequoiadendron*, which means "sequoia tree." The common name for the Sierra Redwood, "Giant Sequoia," became inappropriate with the new genus name, but neither it nor the name of the park were changed. Would it make it any less spectacular if the park were called Sequoiadendron National Park?

A great deal is understood about Sierra Redwood ecology. They are conspicuous, inspirational trees that have long been studied and eulogized. One of the most significant discoveries about Sierra Redwoods did not emerge until the early 1960s, although it had been known for some time by scientists. Redwoods require fire if they are to perpetuate. Ground fires do not burn through redwood bark, but the rising heat opens the cones, which remain on the trees up to 20 years. When the cones open, the seeds fall on the soft, recently burned earth. When it rains, these seeds germinate in sunlight that shines to the ground, uninhibited by an overstory of vegetation.

In the past, fires were started by lightning or by natives who knew the value of such fires to the economy of the forest ecosystem. These frequent fires would burn off litter and duff, open the canopy to allow light to enter, and open the cones. Fires would loosen and soften the soil and release nutrients to it. In contrast, fire suppression allowed a long accumulation of flammable materials that could produce a very hot conflagration if a fire did start.

There is also evidence that long periods of fire suppression enabled a deadly fungus to invade the root systems of the conifers, particularly Ponderosa and Jeffrey pines. This disease, known as root-rot or Annosus root disease, is killing an inordinate number of trees in Yosemite Valley.

A fungus that seems to be a fire follower is the morel, *Morchella angusticeps*, a conical mushroom with deeply pitted cross veins between gray to black vertical ridges. This edible fungus is most common on recently burned soils, where it usually appears as soon as the snow melts. It is particularly common in areas of Yellow Pine Forest where California lilacs, *Ceanothus* spp. (fig. 4.35), have become established.

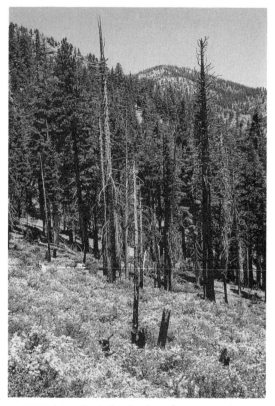

FIGURE 4.35   Buck Brush, *Ceanothus cuneatus*, in a recently burned area.

Morels are highly prized for their flavor and may cost $250 a pound in gourmet food stores.

By suppressing fire, the National Park Service and the U.S. Forest Service were "loving their trees to death." White Firs began to encroach upon the redwood groves, posing a problem because they shade out redwood seedlings and they are flammable from top to bottom. A fire in tall White Firs can carry flames to the foliage of the redwoods, high above the forest floor, and large, hot crown fires can kill the redwoods, too. In 1955, a 13,000-acre (5,200-ha) fire threatened Grant Grove. In 1963, the A. Starker Leopold report indicated that downed wood and other fuels could cause a holocaust if they became ignited. In the late 1960s and early 1970s the National Park Service began to view fire as a natural component of the ecosystem. Fires at elevations above 8000 feet (2650 m) were allowed to burn themselves out. In redwood groves, small prescribed burns were initiated to reduce fuel buildup, burn White Firs, kill root-rot, and otherwise simulate more natural conditions. For a variety of reasons, the U.S. Forest Service has been slow to recognize the value of fire. Mountain cabins and resorts occur in national forests, and timber is a marketable resource. Suppressing forest fires helps to preserve these outside interests. Because national parks and national forests are adjacent to each other, at the present time it is possible literally to move in one step from a philosophy of prescribed burning to a philosophy of fire suppression.

During the summer of 1987 there were an inordinate number of fires in California. In less than a month, more than 12,000 lightning strikes ignited fires that burned for 50 days. By the time the fires were put out, a total of 775,000 acres (315,000 ha) had burned. About 90% of the affected land was managed by the U.S. Forest Service. During the same period of time, lightning-caused fires also occurred in the national parks. Where there was no danger to people or structures, these fires were allowed to burn themselves out. The U.S. Forest Service viewed the fires as a disaster, even in areas a great distance from the nearest roads or habitations. The National Park Service, while justifiably concerned, considered the fires as part of the natural scheme of things. Some authorities contend that one of the reasons the damage was more severe in the national forests is that too much fuel had accumulated over too long a period of time, and the consequence was predictable. It has been determined that humus alone accumulates at the rate of about 1000 pounds per acre (185 kg/ha) per year.

Nevertheless, the U.S. Forest Service has calculated that 1.4 billion board feet of marketable timber was damaged. This is the equivalent of 140,000 three-bedroom homes, with a market value of $140 million. On the other hand, 84% of the burned timber was salvageable. Furthermore, 155 miles (248 km) of Riparian Woodland was burned, 274 miles (438 km) of trails were destroyed, and 100,000 acres (40,000 ha) of designated wilderness was burned. The U.S. Forest Service will have to rebuild the trails, relocate campgrounds, and plant about 100 million seedlings to revegetate the most seriously burned land. Some environmentalists fear that the amount of true damage was overestimated, and that the U.S. Forest Service will use the salvageable lumber as an excuse to put roads into formerly roadless, wilderness-quality areas.

In August 1969 four redwood trees fell over in the Hazelwood picnic area of Sequoia National Park, one killing a 60-year-old lady who was eating her lunch. A hierarchy of park supervisors began to worry about liability, and the resultant flurry of research uncovered another interesting fact about redwood groves. Giant Carpenter Ants, *Camponotus laevigatus*, make nests in redwood trees by hollowing them out, a phenomenon that weakens the structure of the trees. One investigator discovered a nighttime trail of these ants 2 inches (5 cm) wide. These ants passed by, 200 of them per minute, on their way to consume honeydew, an exudate of aphids that live in the White Firs. The reason that Giant Carpenter Ants were so common is that there were too many White Firs, and the reason there were too many White Firs is that fire had been suppressed for nearly 50 years.

In December 1973 during the night a large lower branch fell off General Sherman. Had it fallen at midday in July, untold numbers of people might have been killed. It is hoped that the program of prescribed burning will reduce the number of Giant Carpenter Ants so that such catastrophes will not occur again.

Redwood trees have few enemies. In addition to Giant Carpenter Ants, there are Spruce Budworms, Bark Beetles, fungi, and Dwarf Mistletoe. Periodic fires reduce the fuel at the same time they reduce the pests. Pests are typically associated with weak or sickly trees. It has been estimated that over 140 species of insects live in the crown of a redwood grove without harming the trees. Of particular importance are green lacewings (*Chrysopa* spp.) which feed upon aphids. Of course, there is also a variety of organisms that feed on the lacewings.

A long-horned beetle, *Phymatodes nitidus* (Cerambycidae), helps cones release their seeds. An average Sierra Redwood produces about 1500 cones per year, with about 200 seeds per cone. The cones remain unopened on the tree for about 20 years, or until some mechanism such as heat from a fire or sunlight causes them to open. The larvae of the long-horned beetles chew into food-conducting channels in the stems of the living cones, which causes the cones to die. The cones dry out when they die, and the seeds are released. Heat, however, remains the major mechanism for opening cones. Among mammals that are considered beneficial to redwoods are Chickarees, *Tamiasciurus douglasii* (pl. 12C), also known as Douglas Squirrels or Red Squirrels. They feed on 2–5-year-old redwood cones, but as they feed, many tiny seeds are released. This mechanism also contributes to the seed bank that could become future Sierra Redwoods.

Under appropriate conditions, seedlings grow from 6 inches (15 cm) to 2 feet (60 cm) per year. If litter or duff on the ground is thicker than $1/2$ inch (12.5 mm), seeds will not be able to reach bare mineral soil. Stored carbohydrate in the tiny seeds is not adequate to sustain root growth beyond that distance, and the seedling dies. After germination and for 600 to 700 years, the trees retain a spire shape that is typical of many species adapted to shed snow. After that, the uppermost branches reach the canopy of the forest about 250 feet (80 m) from the ground. Old trees have rounded tops, and all their branches are near the top. These tall trees are often the victims of lightning strikes, but they often survive the strike with various degrees of damage to the crown. Flaming branches from a lightning strike land on the ground and roll downhill. If a flaming log rests against the trunk of another Sierra Redwood, by continuously burning it may "eat away" the bark. Without its protection of bark, the wood is able to ignite, and the fire may actually hollow out the tree. The resulting loss of wood tissue reduces the ability of the tree to transport water to its crown, and the uppermost branches begin to die, also rounding the top. Lightning thus causes the rounding directly and indirectly. Drying winds also play a role in shaping the crown of an old tree.

Another effect of rolling, burning logs is that the upper sides of many old trees become burned. The root system of redwoods is remarkably shallow: approximately 95% of the trees have root systems no deeper than 3 feet (1 m). On the other hand, the base of an old redwood is a good deal larger than the upper portion of the trunk, and this "buttresses" the tree to help it remain standing in spite of its shallow root system. The buttresses at the bases of many old trees are burned off on the uphill side, which is why these trees often fall uphill when they do go over. Another pattern is for trees to fall into meadows because they lean toward spongy ground. Where Sierra Redwoods grow, the easiest way across a meadow is often by walking along one of these fallen trees. Because these trees are so resistant to decay, some of them have been used as bridges for hundreds of years.

The first national park was Yellowstone National Park in Wyoming, established in 1872. The second and third oldest parks are Yosemite and Sequoia, which were established in 1890. Kings Canyon was added in 1940. The effort to preserve Sierra Redwoods in these national parks of the Sierra Nevada is largely attributed to the legendary John Muir, who popularized these trees and the Yosemite Valley in numerous writings that appeared in the late 1870s. Of the huge redwoods he exclaimed, "God has cared for these trees . . . but He cannot save them from fools. Only Uncle Sam can do that." John Muir and the Sierra Club can be thanked for preserving many of these ancient treasures for posterity. The 150th anniversary of John Muir's birthday was celebrated throughout the National Park Service on April 21, 1988.

Sierra Redwood does not make good lumber. Huge Sierra Redwoods tend to break up when they are felled, as if they are brittle. Nevertheless, the ancient giants were threatened by logging in the 1870s; the wood was used principally for fenceposts and shake shingles. The new logging threat is that, in some national forests, all trees *but* the redwoods are logged, leaving them to stand as silent sentinals without the benefit of the forest ecosystem.

Photochemical smog is having an influence on the composition of Yellow Pine Forest. Ozone causes loss of chlorophyll and early death for needles on some species. This degradation, known as chlorotic decline, particularly affects Ponderosa Pines and White Firs. When trees become weakened by ozone, particularly during periods of drought such as occurred during the mid-1970s and late 1980s, bark beetles (Scolytidae) invade, forming channels beneath the bark. This invasion may kill the trees. During the droughts of the 1970s and 1980s, many dead trees of the Sierra Nevada bore witness to the insidious effect of the photochemical smog produced in the San Joaquin Valley. Nearly every afternoon, prevailing wind drew the smog up the slopes. Selective destruction of one or two species can alter significantly the makeup of an ecosystem.

There is also a shrub component in Yellow Pine Forest. Several species of manzanita (*Arctostaphylos*) grow on sunny sites. In Spanish, *manzanita* means "little apple" in reference to the plant's berries, which are an important food for forest animals. Manzanitas are in the heath family (Ericaceae) and are characterized by shiny red bark, urn-shaped flowers, and oval leaves (fig. 4.36).

Another common shrub on dry sites, particularly south-facing slopes, is Kit-kit-dizze, *Chamaebatia foliolosa*, a member of the rose family (Rosaceae). In spring the shrubs are covered with small white flowers resembling those that appear on fruit trees of the rose family, such as apricots, peaches, plums, and apples. Kit-kit-dizze is the name given to this fernlike resinous shrub by the Indians, who made a tea from the leaves and used it for a variety of maladies. Old-timers, particularly those that rode horses, referred to it as Mountain Misery; apparently, the resin irritated the

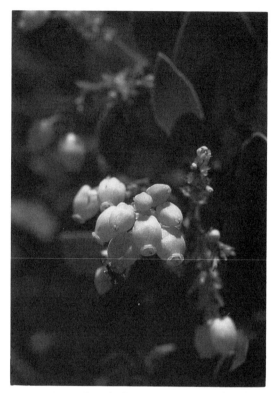

FIGURE 4.36   Greenleaf Manzanita, *Arctostaphylos patula*.

horses when they walked through it. It is also known as Bear Clover. It is believed that bears roll in it to help prevent ticks from attaching to them, and people who work with bears in Yosemite National Park say that the odor of Kit-kit-dizze reminds them of the odor of bears. Perhaps the horses become irritable because the odor makes them think a bear is in the area!

Various kinds of wild currants (*Ribes* spp.) also occur in shady areas. In autumn these shrubs produce sweet berries that are an important food for animals and are particularly relished by bears. The spiny-fruited members of the group are called gooseberries, the flowers of which resemble small fuchsias (fig. 4.37). They are among the most attractive of all forest shrubs.

In moist places, either along streams or in redwood groves, Western Azalea, *Rhododendron occidentale*, is conspicuous. Showy white blossoms cover the shrubs in late spring and early summer. The foliage is poisonous, another example of a plant equipped with phytotoxins to discourage herbivory.

In areas that have experienced a recent fire, various members of the California lilac group (*Ceanothus* spp.) occur in thick stands (fig. 4.35). This shrub has nitrogen-

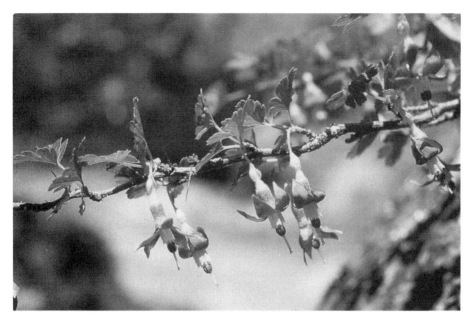

FIGURE 4.37   Sierra Gooseberry, *Ribes roezlii*. A. Flowers.

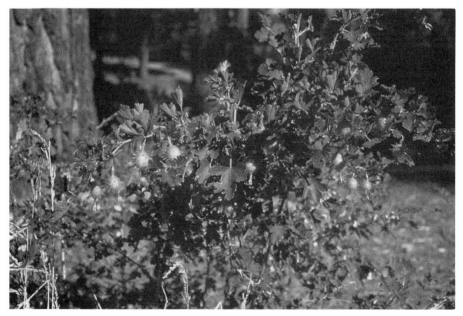

FIGURE 4.37 (*continued*)   Sierra Gooseberry, *Ribes roezlii*. B. Fruit and foliage.

fixing bacteria in its roots and is an important browse for deer. Hence the names of certain members of the group, such as Buck Brush, *Ceanothus cuneatus*, and Deer Brush, *Ceanothus integerrimus*, reflect this dietary association. In spring they produce small, fragrant white flowers in clumps that resemble miniature lilacs.

Animals of the Yellow Pine Forest.   At the elevational level where Foothill Woodland grades into Yellow Pine Forest, there is a major environmental change. Snow becomes a significant part of the precipitation. Along with the change in vegetation, many animals shift from a period of winter activity to a period of summer activity. Some animals store food to make it through the winter; others become dormant. Many animals migrate south or to the foothills in the winter. Ectothermic animals, such as amphibians, reptiles, and insects, are far more common in Foothill Woodland than they are in areas where low winter temperatures restrict activity.

Amphibians.   Amphibians are neither conspicuous nor common above the foothill belt, or away from water. Amphibians include salamanders, toads, and frogs. Among salamanders, that which occurs farthest from water is the Sierra Nevada Salamander, *Ensatina eschscholtzii platensis* (fig. 4.38), which may be found under rocks and logs in moist places. Depending on moisture conditions, these salamanders may remain active all summer. If they estivate during summer months, it is in holes or under woodrat nests. They are brownish with large orange spots on their backs.

At the southern end of the range, the Sierra Nevada Salamander is replaced by the Yellow-blotched Salamander, *Ensatina eschscholtzii croceator*. It occurs from the Kern River Canyon south to Mount Pinos. On this form, the spots may be $^1/8$ to $^1/4$ inch (0.5 cm) across. At the northern end of the range for this species, as in the Klamath Mountains, the spots are smaller—in some cases mere speckles. In the Coast Ranges these salamanders have no spots at all, and they are known as Monterey Salamanders, *Ensatina eschscholtzii eschscholtzii* (fig. 8.32). They are common in the Foothill Woodland of the Coast Ranges, and in southern California they range up into Yellow Pine Forest. The solid-colored form has limited distribution in the Sierra foothills east of Sacramento; otherwise it is missing from the Sierra Nevada. Distribution of this highly variable species is interesting from a geographic perspective. The fact that both the spotted and the solid-colored forms may be collected at the same locality in southern California makes it a fascinating subject for biogeographic and evolutionary studies. The story of this salamander and its peculiar distribution will be discussed in the section on the Peninsular Ranges (fig. 8.31). Most of the other amphibians will be discussed in the sections on Oak Woodland and Riparian communities.

Reptiles.   The most common snakes and lizards of the Yellow Pine Forest are also found in the foothills. As typical chaparral dwellers, they will be discussed in a later chapter. One lizard of the Yellow Pine Forest is particularly interesting—Gilbert's Skink, *Eumeces gilberti* (pl. 15A). As a juvenile, its tail is an iridescent blue. If a predator goes for the lizard, the tail breaks off very easily. The bright blue tail then quivers and bounces, distracting the predator and allowing the lizard to escape. The lizard is subsequently able to grow a new tail. As an adult the lizard loses the blue color, and its head takes on an orange-red color. Gilbert's Skink may be 8 inches (20

FIGURE 4.38   Some salamanders of the *Ensatina* complex. From top to bottom: Painted Salamander, *Ensatina eschscholtzii picta*, from the Klamath Mountains; Sierra Nevada Salamander, *Ensatina eschscholtzii platensis*; and Large-blotched Salamander, *Ensatina eschscholtzii croceator*, from the Sierra Nevada. For range map and complete discussion of this group, see chapter 8 (fig. 8.31). (From R. C. Stebbins. *California Amphibians and Reptiles.* Berkeley: University of California Press, 1972.)

cm) in total length, and when it moves it appears to be a snake. It uses its small legs for locomotion primarily when it moves slowly, stalking insects on the forest floor. Most often it is nocturnal, spending daylight hours beneath logs or rocks.

The Western Skink, *Eumeces skiltonianus*, has a relict population on the Kern Plateau. Juveniles have the bright blue tail of Gilbert's Skink, with which it easily can be confused. In fact, in old collections, specimens of the Western Skink were frequently misidentified because they were not expected to occur in the Sierra Nevada. In general, where the ranges might overlap, as in the southern Sierra Nevada, Gilbert's Skink occurs in Foothill Woodland, and the Western Skink occurs in the pine forests. The southern Sierran form of the Western Skink is markedly smaller than forms from the Coast Ranges or southern California. Where ranges of the two species overlap in southern California, such as the Oak Woodland near Gorman, juvenile Gilbert's Skinks have red tails.

There are also two kinds of alligator lizards in the Yellow Pine Forest. The Northern Alligator Lizard, *Elgaria coerulea* (= *Gerrhonotus coeruleus*), is a northern species that occurs throughout the forest belt of the Sierra Nevada. It is replaced to the south, and to some degree in the foothills, by the Southern Alligator Lizard, *Elgaria multicarinata* (= *Gerrhonotus multicarinatus*) (fig. 7.27). On the southeastern part of the Kern Plateau and in canyons on the east side of the Sierra, the Southern Alligator Lizard occurs to the exclusion of the northern form. Along the west slope of the Sierra, ranges of the two species overlap. In canyons in the lower parts of the Yellow Pine Forest both species can be found within a few feet of each other.

Alligator lizards are among the most sedentary of lizards. They prefer not to bask in the sun, seeming to prefer the shade of the forest. Unlike many lizards, they avoid temperatures above 86°F (30°C). They seem to prefer temperatures around 72°F (22°C) and are able to maintain digestive efficiency and other physiologic activities at this low body temperature. Apparently, they are ambush foragers, lying in wait for insects and other small prey items.

Two interesting snakes may be visible in the daytime, although neither is common. The California Mountain Kingsnake, *Lampropeltis zonata* (pl. 15C), and the Rubber Boa, *Charina bottae*, are more common in the Yellow Pine Forest than in the foothills. Both snakes occur particularly where there are large rock outcrops that serve as retreats and/or sites in which to hibernate.

The kingsnake gets its name from the fact that it will eat other snakes, including rattlesnakes. Most often it eats lizards—skinks and fence lizards in particular. The California Mountain Kingsnake is threatened because of its beauty. It is colorful, with red, white, and black bands. It is illegal to collect and sell native reptiles, but the lucrative income therefrom leads a number of unscrupulous persons to continue collecting them in spite of the threat of being caught and fined. Another threat to these docile reptiles comes from people who mistake them for venomous coral snakes, which do not naturally occur in California. However, even venomous snakes, such as rattlesnakes, are protected in national parks, and it is illegal to collect or kill them.

The Rubber Boa has a habitat similar to that of the California Mountain King Snake. It is yellowish below and greenish above. Its head and tail are similarly rounded, so it appears to be a large worm. It feeds on insects, salamanders, lizards, and small mammals. When molested, it rolls into a ball and wiggles its tail, seemingly to perplex a predator who would attempt to bite it and swallow it head first. Its tail is often scarred, and some authorities contend that the scars are from the bites of predators. Other authorities point out that the Rubber Boa crawls into the burrows of mice and feeds on the babies, and they believe the scars are mouse bites. These snakes are very docile. Their greatest threat also appears to be snake collectors.

The Rubber Boa of the Sierra Nevada is the Pacific Rubber Boa, *Charina bottae bottae*. In the San Bernardino and San Jacinto Mountains there occurs a smaller subspecies, the Southern Rubber Boa, *Charina bottae umbratica*. Because of habitat reduction in southern California, the state of California lists this subspecies as threatened. The two subspecies seem to intergrade in the Mount Pinos area, but neither is present in the region between Mount Pinos and the San Bernardino Mountains, even though appropriate habitat seems to be present. This unexplained disjunct pattern of distribution seems to apply to other animals as well, such as the spotted salamanders (*Ensatina*) discussed earlier.

Birds.   Among Sierran birds (fig. 4.39), there are no known hibernators at higher elevations. Most birds migrate in the winter, but some, such as Steller's Jay, *Cyanositta stelleri*, remain active in the winter, living on stored food. Steller's Jay gathers and stores acorns and pine seeds. Similar to the Western Scrub Jay, *Aphelocoma californica* (pl. 13F), of the foothills, Stellar's Jay is the alarmist. It is a brightly colored bird with a loud, raucous call, which it uses to alert the entire forest community when there is danger. Stellar's Jay differs in appearance from the Scrub Jay by having a large, dark crest on its head. It is the only crested jay in the west. Scrub Jays and Steller's Jays eat acorns, but both are omnivorous, feeding also on available insects.

Why do their ranges not overlap to a greater degree? Scrub Jays can tolerate higher temperatures, and they can survive without liquid water as long as they eat insects or berries. Steller's Jays must drink water. Comparative tests of the two jays, in chambers where the temperature is gradually raised, show that Scrub Jays are able to keep a constant body temperature of 107°F (42°C) if they remain in the shade, even if the air temperature is raised from 50° to 90°F (10–32°C). Apparently, Scrub Jays are better able than the Steller's Jays to lose heat by radiation from the unfeathered portions of their feet.

Perhaps the most common bird of the Yellow Pine Forest is the Dark-eyed Junco, *Junco hyemalis*. This is a small gray bird with a dark head. The name *junco* refers to the medieval executioner who wore a black hood. A seed eater, the junco in winter moves downslope below the snowline, where it continues to forage for seeds. In summer it nests on the ground among sedges or grasses. When threatened, it does a broken-wing act, leading a potential predator away from its nest.

Another common bird of the Yellow Pine Forest is the Mountain Chickadee, *Parus gambeli* (fig. 4.40). It is a gleaner, eating small insects on bark. In this niche, it replaces the White-breasted Nuthatch above the foothills. The Mountain Chickadee is not often seen, but it is often heard. Its call is the mournful sound of the Yellow Pine Forest. It utters three slow notes — two high tones and one somewhat lower. They are small birds with gray bodies and black and white stripes on their heads. Their chins are black, and the sides of their heads are white.

The jolly or rollicking sound of the Yellow Pine Forest is that of the Black-headed Grosbeak, *Pheucticus melanocephalus*. This large finch has a very thick bill, implying that it is a seed eater, but it also eats buds and insects in the upper canopy of trees. This bird migrates to Mexico in the winter, but in spring and summer its melodic song of rising and falling notes is one of the common sounds of the forest. This bird has a rusty-colored body with a black head and black and white wings. It is replaced at higher elevations by Evening Grosbeaks, *Coccothraustes vespertinus*, and Pine Grosbeaks, *Pinicola enucleator*.

A list of summer visitants is long, but two conspicuous birds are worth mentioning: the Western Tanager, *Piranga ludoviciana*, and the American Robin. Both have songs that resemble that of the Black-headed Grosbeak. The Western Tanager is a gleaner

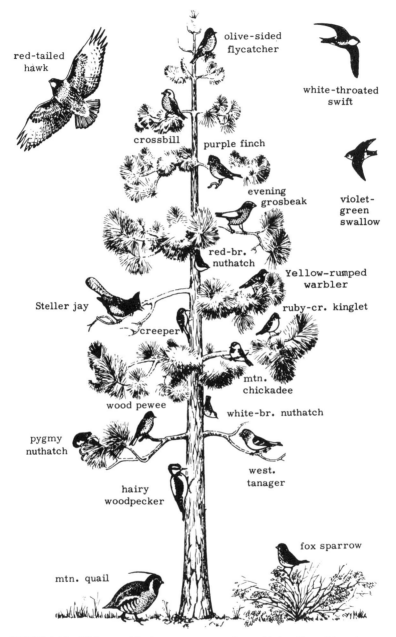

FIGURE 4.39 Niche partitioning among some forest birds. (From T. I. Storer and R. L. Usinger. *Sierra Nevada Natural History.* Berkeley: University of California Press, 1963.)

FIGURE 4.40   Mountain Chickadee, *Parus gambeli*.

in foliage. Its bright yellow body and red head are sure to attract attention. The American Robin is a conspicuous ground feeder in the foothills and the forest. It has a brownish back and an orange breast, and it feeds on worms and grubs that it locates by sound.

An assortment of woodpeckers is also characteristic of the Yellow Pine Forest. As in the foothills, they are partitioned according to food habits. The Northern Flicker (fig. 4.24) ranges from the foothills to the forest. Other woodpeckers fill niches similar to related forms of the foothills. The Downy Woodpecker of the foothills is replaced by a larger cousin, the Hairy Woodpecker, *Picoides villosus*, in the forest. Nuttall's Woodpecker is replaced by the White-headed Woodpecker, *Picoides albolarvatus*, the most commonly seen woodpecker in the Yellow Pine Forest. It often works the bark of the lower portions of the trees in search of insects.

The most spectacular woodpecker is the Pileated Woodpecker, *Dryocopus pileatus*. This crow-sized bird is black with a bright red, pointed crest on its head. It seems to prefer feeding on White Firs, although it is found on pines and oaks as well. The Pileated Woodpecker can be heard seemingly for miles, hammering on dead or diseased trees. They feed mainly on Giant Carpenter Ants and large beetle larvae (grubs). For a time it was thought that these spectacular woodpeckers were on the decline in the Sierra, but numerous sightings in recent years, particularly in the Yosemite area, indicate that they are still with us.

Niche partitioning among warblers and sparrows is also evident, if one takes the time to attempt positive identification. These busy little creatures spend most of their time out of sight in the foliage. Warblers are all gleaners. As many as 10 different species can be identified at certain times in the Yosemite area. Because most warblers are yellow to some degree, they are often called wild canaries. Different seasonal population and foraging habits prevent these birds from competing with each other.

Perhaps 15 different kinds of sparrows may be sighted at various elevations in the Sierra Nevada, most of them lowland or foothill species. In the Yellow Pine Forest or above, one is likely to see only 4 kinds. The sparrow that typically hangs around campgrounds is the Chipping Sparrow, *Spizella passerina*. In the summer it has a distinctive reddish crown. In willows along water, the incessant chipping noise that one hears is usually the call of the White-crowned Sparrow, *Zonotrichia leucophrys* (fig. 4.41), which can be identified by three white stripes outlined in black on its head. Often joining the White-crowned Sparrow in the willows is a more typical-looking brown sparrow, the Lincoln's Sparrow, *Melospiza lincolnii*. Another common-looking brown sparrow is the Fox Sparrow, *Passerella iliaca*, which forages in shrubs located away from water. Sparrows feed primarily on seeds, but many of them rely heavily on insects when seeds become scarce.

Mammals. Among mammals, the most conspicuous is the Western Gray Squirrel, *Sciurus griseus* (pl. 12B). Subsisting largely on acorns, gray squirrels inhabit oaks in the upper foothill belt and in the Yellow Pine Forest, where they occur in association with California Black Oaks. Black oaks are a component of the dry Yellow Pine Forest; therefore gray squirrels are more common there. In moist Yellow Pine

FIGURE 4.41 White-crowned Sparrow, *Zonotrichia leucophrys*.

Forest they eat seeds from Sugar Pine and White Fir, but where snow becomes deeper, gray squirrels are replaced by Chickarees, *Tamiasciurus douglasii* (pl. 12C).

Western Gray Squirrels remain active through the winter and find shelter in cavities, particularly in oaks. They bury caches of acorns or pine seeds in many places on the forest floor, and during the winter they dig through the snow to retrieve their stored food. Apparently, they locate the caches through a combination of odor and memory. If a squirrel dies, or for some other reason fails to dig up its cache, the seeds may germinate. It is in this way that oak trees become dispersed uphill, and it also explains why they may grow in clumps (fig. 4.42). Another reason for clumped oaks may be regeneration of sprouts from a single trunk after a fire.

In areas where snow lies deeply on the ground for a long time, gray squirrels are absent. Presumably, the energy required to dig through deep snow would not be rewarded by the calories supplied by a small cache of food. On the other hand, the Chickaree stores its food in a few large caches, mostly above ground near its home, or at the base of a tree where it is able to defend the stores. In digging through

FIGURE 4.42   California Black Oaks growing in a clump.

deep snow, the energy expended is replaced by the much larger amount of food in the cache. Chickarees replace gray squirrels in redwood groves and at higher elevations in the Lodgepole–Red Fir Forest.

In Yosemite Valley, at least three squirrel species seem to coexist. These include the California Ground Squirrel, the Western Gray Squirrel, and the Chickaree. It is also possible that, under certain circumstances, the Golden-mantled Ground Squirrel, *Spermophilus lateralis* (pl. 12D), may join the group.

Most of the floor of Yosemite Valley would be characterized as dry Yellow Pine Forest. Dominant trees include Ponderosa Pine, California Black Oak, and Incense Cedar. The Merced River meanders broadly through Yosemite Valley. On its banks, and in shady localities, are trees of riparian affinity that also are sources of food and shelter. Among these are Canyon Live Oak, *Quercus chrysolepis* (pl. 7A), California Laurel, *Umbellularia californica* (fig. 7.9), Pacific Dogwood, *Cornus nuttallii*, and Bigleaf Maple, *Acer macrophyllum* (fig. 6.9). Even so, in other areas where this assemblage of trees occurs, there does not seem to be the overlap of squirrels that occurs in Yosemite.

Perhaps the situation is a consequence of humans. A great deal of food is available, either directly from handouts, from untended picnic tables, or from trash. In campgrounds, predator species are normally wary and may be reduced in abundance. Coyotes in Yosemite Valley also depend heavily on handouts and may be well fed without having to rely on prey species. Furthermore, the numerous roads and trails have provided abundant open, clifflike habitats for ground squirrel burrows. It seems that the parklike environment of Yosemite Valley, with all its human trappings, is responsible for this atypical assemblage of squirrel species.

The Yosemite area also provides a setting for the discussion of Mule Deer and Black Bears. The history and present distribution of these two large mammals is deeply rooted in the story of human impact on natural habitats.

The history of the Mule Deer, *Odocoileus hemionus* (fig. 4.43), on the west side of the Sierra can be explained by describing the changes in the Jawbone deer herd recorded since the days of the forty-niners. Prior to disturbance by humans, a mosaic of formerly burned and recently burned chaparral vegetation provided adequate food, so that deer did not occur abundantly in forest communities. They were also controlled by predators, such as Mountain Lions and Gray Wolves. During the first few years following a fire, annuals and herbaceous perennials are common. From 4 to 10 years after a fire, California lilacs, *Ceanothus* spp., and mountain mahoganies, *Cercocarpus* spp., are choice browse. New growth on these common shrubs contains about 14% protein and an abundant supply of calcium, which is necessary for bones and antlers.

Gold was discovered in 1849, and the Gold Rush was on. Thus began a 50-year decline in the deer herd. Deer were hunted for food and hides; in 1880 one firm in San Francisco marketed 35,000 deer hides. The amount of winter forage, one of the most significant limiting factors on the size of deer herds, was severely reduced by the introduction of sheep and cattle. By 1876, 6 million sheep were reportedly grazing in the Sierra foothills. If hunting and competition were not enough, between

FIGURE 4.43   Mule Deer, *Odocoileus hemionus*.

1879 and 1907 a series of hard winters further reduced the amount of winter forage in the foothills, and the remaining deer were pushed lower into the valleys. By the first decade of the 1900s, deer were considered scarce in the Sierra foothills.

The decline of the Jawbone deer herd was not unnoticed. In the late 1800s a new environmental awareness became significant. National parks were established in Yosemite and Sequoia. John Muir and the newly formed Sierra Club fought for regulations to control the killing of big game. Parks were to be refuges for plants and animals alike. In 1883 the "buck law" was born: does were not to be hunted. In 1893 the buck season was reduced to six weeks. In 1901 the concept of limits was begun: no more than three bucks could be taken during a single hunting season. In 1905 the legal kill was reduced to two. In 1907 the state of California began two programs that were to have a profound effect for many years to come. A hunting license became required, and this not only generated revenue, but it enabled the state to enforce hunting laws. Also during 1907 a bounty on Mountain Lions, *Felis concolor*, was initiated and was to remain in effect, at least locally, until 1964.

The influence of government control in the early 1900s had a profound effect, and the deer herd began to recover. By 1940 the deer range was fully stocked, but a new pattern of deer behavior began to emerge. Fire suppression in the foothills had allowed a thick vegetative cover to develop, and without fire, the primary food for deer became more and more scarce. In order to find adequate food, and because wading through snow is energetically expensive, greater numbers of deer began migrating into the forest communities in spring and moving back to the foothills and valleys with the onset of winter.

By the 1950s the Jawbone deer herd had reached 6000 animals. In the summer they were feeding in Yosemite National Park, where there were over 250 square miles (625 km^2) of range available to them. In contrast, there were only about 40 square miles (100 km^2) of winter feeding grounds in the foothills. A pattern began to emerge in which there was a sizable die-off of fawns, nursing does, and aged animals each winter. A 20% winter die-off was not atypical, and in a harsh winter 40% of the animals would starve to death. The overabundance of deer also impacted the summer range. In 1951 and 1952 studies in the national parks showed that wildflowers and seedling oaks were being heavily browsed. Juvenile California Black Oaks had disappeared, leaving only mature trees. Meadows that formerly abounded with spring wildflowers were becoming dominated by noxious species, such as milkweed and thistles, not fed upon by deer.

Overpopulation by deer in the Jawbone herd had created a problem similar to the famous episode documented for the Kaibab deer herd in Arizona. Human tampering with population dynamics once again proved to cause more harm than good. In the 1960s a series of corrective measures was begun in an attempt to restore deer herds to a more realistic size, one regulated by more natural environmental phenomena. In 1963 national parks began translocating thousands of deer to other localities. In 1964 special doe hunts and late season hunts were initiated. Also in 1964 the last bounty for a Mountain Lion was paid. In 1968 grazing fees for cattle in national forests were raised. Reduced grazing could increase the available food for deer and restore winter range to a more normal condition. In 1970 Mountain Lions were declared game animals, so that a season and a limit could be established if they became too abundant; however, as of 1991, no hunts have been authorized.

According to state records, during the 56 years that a bounty on Mountain Lions was in effect, 12,461 lion bounties were paid. According to some authorities, there were fewer than 600 Mountain Lions left in California at the time the bounty was dropped. Year after year since 1964, the moratorium on lion hunting was renewed over the objection of ranchers and sheep herders, even though lions that harm livestock may legally be killed. The moratorium remained until 1987, when, under pressure from hunters and ranchers, a limited lion hunt was approved. Environmentalists, however, initiated a series of legal blocks to the lion hunt. As of this writing that lion hunt has never taken place. To this day very little clear-cut evidence has been presented that the government expense in controlling predators has been rewarded with equal value in livestock saved. On the contrary, a healthy herd of deer kept in check by a healthy number of predators has repeatedly proved to be a more stable, cost-efficient program. The balance of approximately 200 deer per 200 acres (80 ha) in association with one Mountain Lion is a figure that seems to prevail throughout the west.

The lessons learned from the Jawbone and Kaibab deer herds are part of the basis for game management principles applied on a nationwide scale. Game management involves not only protection for a single species; it must involve entire ecosystems. Species do not occur in isolation.

The story of the Black Bear, *Ursus americanus*, is also closely related to game management practice in Yosemite National Park. Grizzly Bears are no longer found in California; all Sierra bears are Black Bears. They are smaller and less ferocious than Grizzlies, although people tend to overestimate their size. Large males may exceed 400 pounds (190 kg), but most Black Bears spotted in the Sierra Nevada are about the size of a Saint Bernard dog. They are omnivorous, but they rely heavily on vegetable matter as a staple in their diet and eat a large amount of grass. For protein, they rely mostly on ants and termites. In season they feed heavily on berries.

Black Bears are shy, retiring creatures that seldom interact with humans. In national parks, however, campers who are careless with their food have caused bears to become dependent on human sources of food. It's almost as if the bears have become junk-food addicts. High-calorie food has become a motive for the animals to dump ice chests and break into cars. Humans are not harmed by Black Bears unless they try to take their food back. To protect foolish campers from possible harm, the National Park Service has developed a practice of capturing errant bears (fig. 4.44), tagging them, and translocating them to a portion of the park where natural food is abundant. If the bear returns to pester campers, it is moved again. It will be moved several times before drastic action is taken. Unfortunately for the bear, if it returns several times to steal food or break into cars, or if it develops a pattern of bluff-charging humans, it will be killed. Although this killing is justified in order to protect campers, ironically, the campers who feed bears are actually leading the bear to its death.

Bears are able to travel long distances in search of food. If a bear raids a camp in the back country, it is for the same reason it raids a camp in a popular car-camping area. Aggression or competition for food can cause subdominant bears to be forced out of major campgrounds to fend for themselves in the back country.

If a tagged bear appears outside of national park boundaries, it does not mean that the National Park Service carried the bear by helicopter and dropped it off in the hopes of being rid of it. Helicopter flying time is expensive and is never used to transport Black Bears. Bears are released in remote parts of the park deliberately to avoid human interactions. They are transported in a trailer, towed by a pickup truck.

During the winter, Black Bears go into a state of hibernation. Some authorities contend that Black Bears do not really hibernate, because their body temperatures do not drop as low as that of the environment, and they do not produce high-calorie brown fat. It is unlikely, however, that a mammal of such large body size would lower its body temperature as much as a small mammal. Black Bears lower their body temperature about 12°F (7°C) during winter torpor. They remain at about 88°F (31°C) for most of the winter, which lowers their heart rate and metabolic rate to about one-half. Most small mammals that hibernate waken every few days, burning brown fat to raise their body temperatures, so that they can move around and urinate. Some eat and defecate. Black Bears seldom waken, they do not urinate, and they do not defecate. They recycle nitrogenous wastes to form amino acids, and they live on stored fat during their dormancy.

FIGURE 4.44   Tranquilized Black Bear, *Ursus americanus.* Note radio collar and tag in ear.

Black Bear cubs do not hibernate. They are born in the den during January while the mother is hibernating. Cubs weigh about a pound at birth. They sleep against the mother's warm, sparsely haired underside and suckle while she remains dormant. From time to time the mother arouses and eats the cubs' feces.

In spring the mother and cubs emerge from the den. The cub at this time weighs about 4 pounds, having increased its weight about fourfold since birth. The mother has lost from 15% to 30% of her body weight during winter, and she is ready to eat. Bears mate in the spring after they emerge from hibernation, but the fertilized egg does not implant in the uterus until fall. Whether or not it does implant depends on how much food the female has eaten during the summer; in lean years the egg is reabsorbed. When food is abundant, twins or triplets may be born. In national parks, where campground food has added calories to the diet, bears often have multiple births, which acts to further increase the number of bears in the campgrounds.

The problems of human and Black Bear interaction are exacerbated by ignorant humans. Black Bears' "addiction" to human food is not a natural situation. The National Park Service is charged with the responsibility of protecting wildlife, and rigid enforcement of no-feeding laws is a means to that end. Fortunately for Californians, these are not Grizzly Bears that crave high-calorie food.

Lodgepole–Red Fir Forest

The Lodgepole–Red Fir Forest is the snow forest of the Sierra Nevada (pls. 1C, 3A). Trees here are spire-shaped in order to shed snow. Precipitation in this forest, most of which is snow, is the heaviest in the range, averaging from 35 to 65 inches (90–165 cm) per year. It is not uncommon for snowfall of 50 feet (13 m) to fall in a given year. Within the Lodgepole–Red Fir Forest of the western Sierra, the greatest amount of precipitation occurs in the central portion of the range, east of Sacramento. More precipitation falls here because at this latitude there is a "window" in the rain shadow of the Coast Range. The opening in the Coast Ranges is where San Francisco Bay is located. Air masses that flow through this gap are allowed to carry their moisture all the way to the Sierra before adiabatic cooling causes precipitation.

In the Merriam system of classification, this forest community was known as the Canadian Life Zone. It is also called the Upper Montane Forest. Some authorities insist on separating the community into two realms, the Lodgepole Pine Forest and Red Fir Forest.

On the west side of the Sierra, from Yosemite National Park northward to the latitude of Lake Tahoe, there is a magnificent forest composed of nearly pure stands of Red Fir, *Abies magnifica* (fig. 4.45). As mentioned earlier, Red Firs are among the species sold as Christmas trees under the name "Silver Tip." These are moisture-loving trees. Depth of the winter snow averages 10 to 30 feet (3–10 m), as evidenced by the lower level of lichen growth on the trunks. These lichens (*Letharia* spp.) are known as staghorn lichens in reference to their branched appearance. They are of a variety known as fruticose lichens, in reference to their cup-shaped fruiting bodies. These lichens are active all year long, deriving their moisture entirely from the air. Because these lichens require light, the lowest point on a trunk where they can grow is dictated by snow depth.

Red Fir requires deep, moist but well-drained mature soil. It can tolerate cold temperature as well as any conifer, but availability of soil moisture is an important limiting factor. For this reason, Red Firs are scarce on the eastern slope of the Sierra, and south of Mammoth they are absent on the east slope. On the other hand, water-logged soil near a meadow also cannot be tolerated. Red Firs are not fire-tolerant. Lightning commonly kills old Red Firs, but fires are seldom large due to the moist nature of litter beneath the forest canopy. Nevertheless, these small fires are important for opening the forest canopy and allowing germination of new trees. Decay at maturity also provides openings. The resulting mosaic of trees of different ages provides a variety of habitats for animals as well. This is a major reason for preservation of old-growth forests.

Red Firs grow at higher elevations than White Firs, and there is a zone of overlap, although the two species are not known to hybridize. They are difficult to tell apart without practice. Red Firs usually have redder bark, but unless the trees are large and old the color difference may be difficult to discern. Cones are visible at the tops of trees in late summer and autumn. If cones are apparent, the trees are easy to identify. Red Fir and White Fir cones both grow upward on the stem, but Red Fir cones are twice as large. They are fatter, and they are 4 to 8 inches (10–20 cm) long. If no cones are available, it is difficult to distinguish a Red Fir from a White Fir, and it requires close inspection of the needles. Needles of Red Fir are shorter than those of White Fir, but on both species they grow upward on the stem when there is abundant

FIGURE 4.45   Red Fir, *Abies magnifica*.

light. White Fir needles are flattened and have a quarter turn, or slight twist at the base. Red Fir needles are round in cross section and have no such twist.

The most common species of tree in this forest is the Lodgepole Pine, *Pinus contorta murrayana* (fig. 4.46). Where conditions are appropriate, other associated tree species may include Mountain Hemlock, *Tsuga mertensiana*, Western White Pine, *Pinus monticola*, and Sierra Juniper, *Juniperus occidentalis*. Lodgepole Pine is easy to identify. It is the only native two-needle pine of the high mountains. Its bark is whitish and scaly. It appears as if hundreds of corn flakes are stuck to the bark.

Lodgepole Pine is a pioneer tree species. At higher elevations, it is the first tree to move into an area denuded by fire, flooding, or avalanche. This is a rapidly growing species, but it is not long-lived. Large specimens over 3 feet (1 m) in diameter are often less than 300 years of age. The largest Lodgepole Pine in the Sierra Nevada is found in the Emigrant Basin Wilderness. It is 7 feet (2.2 m) in diameter, it is 91 feet (28.4 m) tall, and its canopy covers 36 feet (12 m). A Lodgepole Pine of similar size also occurs near Big Bear Lake, in the San Bernardino Mountains of southern California. This tree is 110 feet (34.3 m) high, but it is slightly smaller in diameter.

In the Sierra Nevada, Lodgepoles occur in small, even-aged clumps. These clumps are seldom larger than 900 square feet (80 m^2). The primary sites for regeneration are

FIGURE 4.46   Lodgepole Pine, *Pinus contorta murrayana*.

areas of treefall, usually associated with winds or avalanches. In contrast, in the Rocky Mountains, where summer lightning is more common, crown fires may occur that wipe out extensive stands. The Rockies therefore contain large stands of Lodgepole Pine trees of similar size and age.

Over a period of thousands of years, Lodgepole Pines gradually invade and replace high-country meadows. Their roots can tolerate water-logged soil, so they probably aid in the drying of this wet soil. As soil and humus accumulate and the soil becomes better drained, Red Firs gradually replace Lodgepoles. Because the Sierra Nevada is geologically young, Lodgepole Pine is abundant and widespread throughout higher elevations. In many areas it occurs all the way up to treeline. Back-country hikers and backpackers are familiar with Lodgepole Pines. The needles are everywhere on the ground, and the small, sharp cones always lie in great abundance exactly where you want to lay out your tent or sleeping bag.

The shape and density of Lodgepole Pines are highly variable. The name refers to its use by Indians for the structural support of their homes. In locations where the trees grow close together, the trunks are straight and thin—exactly what an Indian would want. In exposed sites, old trees are short—less than 30 feet (10 m) tall—and the trunk may be 2 feet (60 cm) thick (fig. 5.4). Commonly, old trees are twisted and may show the effect of lightning. On the east side of the Sierra many lakes are rimmed by pure stands of Lodgepoles (pl. 10B). These rather widely spaced trees form an open forest approximately 30 feet (10 m) high. In contrast, on the west side of the Sierra there are many acres of Lodgepoles where the trees grow close together and reach heights of 50 to 80 feet (15–25 m) (pls. 1C, 3A; fig. 11.1). The difference between these two types of forest is simply the amount of moisture. Of all pine species studied, Lodgepole Pine has the most remarkable ability to regulate its internal water balance over a wide range of soil moisture.

During the last 30 years or so, many acres of Lodgepoles have been defoliated by a small moth larva known as the Lodgepole Needle Miner, *Coleotechnites milleri*. These defoliated trees are particularly conspicuous in Yosemite National Park along the Tioga Pass Road through Tuolumne Meadows. Every other year, during August, millions of tiny white moths hatch from their pupae. They mate and lay their tiny yellow eggs on the needles of mature Lodgepoles. During this time, millions of the moths may be in flight at any time, giving the air the appearance of being filled with blowing ashes. When the eggs hatch, a tiny caterpillar bores into the needles and hollows them out. They go dormant in the winter, but otherwise they continue to feed until the spring of their second year of life, after which they metamorphose into moths, and the cycle is repeated. Normally, they are kept under control by heavy predation from gleaning birds such as the Mountain Chickadee. There are also many species of parasitic wasps and other insects that feed on the Needle Miner larvae. However, for some unknown reason, there are occasional population explosions, and the moths become extremely abundant. At first the National Park Service, in an attempt to save thousands of acres of Lodgepoles, used DDT and malathion to kill the moths. The experiment was a disaster, because the insecticides killed many of the moth's natural enemies, including birds. Furthermore, the DDT began to appear in tissues of trout living in high-country lakes and streams. Today, the National Park Service regards Lodgepole Needle Miner infestations as a natural phenomenon. Educational exhibits along the Tioga Pass Road explain how defoliation of Lodgepole Pines by Needle Miner larvae is a part of the grand scheme of things.

In regions where there is slightly more moisture and the soil is cold, Lodgepole Pines are joined by Mountain Hemlocks. This is particularly true for the west-slope forest from Yosemite northward (pl. 1C). Southernmost Mountain Hemlocks are located near Silliman Lake in Sequoia National Park. Toward the south and on the east side of the Sierra, Mountain Hemlocks become a part of the upper forest community, the Subalpine Forest, where the trees grow in clumps in moist, cold pockets (fig. 5.3). In exposed sites they appear shrublike. Most often, Mountain Hemlocks occur in even-aged stands, and they seem to die all at the same time, usually in association with a root fungus.

Hemlocks resemble firs by having needles all along the branches. They differ from firs in that the needles project outward from all sides of the branches. Cones grow downward from the tips of the branches and superficially resemble those of Douglas Fir. In fact, the scientific name for Douglas Fir, *Pseudotsuga*, means "false hemlock." Mountain Hemlock is not as large a tree as Douglas Fir, but the largest specimen, near Tyron Meadows in Alpine County, is a healthy 113 feet (35.3 m) tall. It is over 7 feet (2.2 m) in diameter, and its crown spreads to 44 feet (14 m).

Foliage on Mountain Hemlocks is flexible and droops downward, giving the tree a beautiful, graceful appearance. Often the top nods over, making the tree easy to recognize from a viewpoint overlooking the forest canopy. In his first book, *The Mountains of California* (1894), John Muir raved about Mountain Hemlocks, calling them "the most singularly beautiful of all the California coniferae."

Western White Pine, also known as Silver Pine (fig. 4.47), replaces Sugar Pine at higher elevations. It is a five-needle pine with needles about 2 to 4 inches (5–10 cm) long, and it has the same sort of appearance as Sugar Pine, with long horizontal branches that resemble spider arms. However, White Pine branches tend to grow upward at the outer end, sort of like a candelabra. Cones of Western White Pine resemble those of Sugar Pine, but they are only one-quarter to one-half the size; they are seldom over 8 inches (20 cm) in length. The bark of Western White Pine is easy to recognize because it breaks up into squarish plates 2 to 4 inches (5–10 cm) across. On dry sites such as slopes with coarse soil, where water percolates rapidly, there may be pure stands of Western White Pine. In this respect they resemble a

FIGURE 4.47   Western White Pine, *Pinus monticola*.

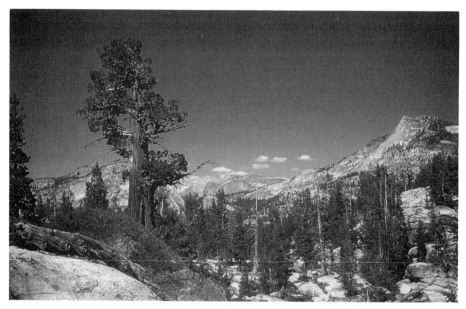

FIGURE 4.48   Sierra Juniper, *Juniperus occidentalis australis*.

high-elevation version of Jeffrey Pine. Large, old trees may stand in solitary splendor on rocky outcrops.

Sierra Juniper, *Juniperus occidentalis australis* (fig. 4.48), grows in the most exposed sites of the Lodgepole–Red Fir Forest and is the tree most commonly associated with rocky outcrops here. Most species of juniper in California are shrubs, but this is a true tree. Old trees on exposed sites have a distinctive appearance. The trunk is very thick in proportion to the height of the tree, and it is often twisted and contorted by wind and lightning. Many a photographer has used the twisted shape of a Sierra Juniper to accent a picture of the Sierra Nevada. The largest known juniper in the world is a Sierra Juniper that grows near Sonora Pass. This tree, known as the Bennet juniper, is estimated to be at least 3000 years old. It is nearly 14 feet (3.5 m) in diameter and 87 feet (28 m) in height. As in the other junipers, the cone is fleshy and berrylike. These cones are an important autumn food for many birds and mammals in spite of their turpentine flavor.

On the east side of the Sierra Nevada, Sierra Junipers are common on south-facing slopes in canyons at elevations lower than the forest belts. This distribution applies particularly from Lee Vining southward to Lone Pine. They also grow in isolated localities as far south as the Transverse Ranges.

To the north of the Sierra Nevada, Western Junipers, *Juniperus occidentalis occidentalis* (fig. 6.13), are common on upper slopes of the Great Basin, where they grow amongst Great Basin Sagebrush. These close relatives of Sierra Juniper are particularly common on the east side of the Cascades in Northern California, Oregon, and Washington.

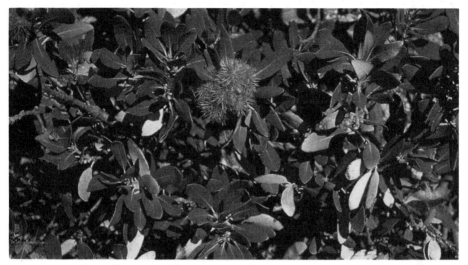

FIGURE 4.49   Bush Chinquapin, *Chrysolepis sempervirens*.

There is not much of a shrub component in Lodgepole–Red Fir Forest. Deep shade precludes low-growing vegetation in many areas, and deep snow makes it difficult in others. When there is a shrub component, it is likely to be dominated by Bush Chinquapin, *Chrysolepis sempervirens* (fig. 4.49), a member of the beech and oak family (Fagaceae). The fruit has a spiny husk enclosing three bitter nuts. Humans seldom get a chance to taste these nuts because they are harvested by squirrels and bears as soon as they are ripe. On dry slopes in the forest there may be thickets of one or more species of manzanita. Of particular note is a prostrate (ground-covering) species known as Pinemat Manzanita, *Arctostaphylos nevadensis*.

The deep shade of the Lodgepole–Red Fir Forest makes it difficult for understory plants in general. Some plants, however, have developed a strategy of deriving most if not all of their nutrition not from photosynthesis, but from decay of humus. These plants are known as saprophytes. Many fungi, such as mushrooms and puffballs, live this way.

A number of members of the heath family (Ericaceae) possess little or no chlorophyll. These plants have solved the problem of limited light by tapping into the mycorrhizal fungi that thrive in the forest soil and deriving nutrition and water in this way. The beneficial association of the roots of conifers with mycorrhizal fungi was mentioned previously, but these saprohytic plants survive with little or no photosynthetic activity. The degree to which the saprophytes are associated with or depend upon the fungi is variable. Shinleaf or White-veined Wintergreen, *Pyrola picta*, contains some chlorophyll, but its preference for deep shade dictates that it rely to some degree on nutrition from the mycorrhizae.

Snow Plant, *Sarcodes sanguinea* (fig. 4.50), is perhaps the most spectacular of the saprophytes. It is a bright red, thick-stemmed plant that appears early in the spring.

FIGURE 4.50   Snow Plant, *Sarcodes sanguinea*.

Its name refers to the fact that it erupts mushroomlike from the forest floor when there is still a good deal of snow on the ground. It often occurs in clusters about a foot (30 cm) high. These plants do not possess chlorophyll, but their roots are associated with mycorrhizal fungi. Later in the spring a cluster of red flowers appears at the tip of each stem. It is not uncommon to see hummingbirds or butterflies drawing nectar from these flowers.

Pinedrops, *Pterospora andromedea*, looks like a tall, skinny Snow Plant. Some authorities prefer to call this plant a parasite because it has no root system or fungi of its own. Instead, it draws its nutrition from the mycorrhizae that are associated with adjacent plants.

The coral roots (*Corallorhiza* spp.) are members of the orchid family (Orchidaceae) and are also dependent for nutrition on symbiotic fungi. The name refers to the coral-like appearance of the reduced root system. These are thin-stemmed plants that usually grow individually from humus or a rotting log. The color of the stems ranges from pale red or yellow to brown or purple. At blooming time, close inspection will reveal a long cluster (raceme) of up to 40 orchid-shaped flowers, each of which is about $^1/_4$ inch (6–8 mm) across.

Phantom Orchid, *Eburophyton austinae*, so called because it may appear to be an all-white plant, is a saprophytic orchid that arises from a branched, creeping rootstock. Its flowers, which may be tinged with yellow, are about twice the size of those of the coral roots; therefore it is more easily recognized as a flowering plant.

Animals of the Lodgepole–Red Fir Forest

Birds.   Many bird species of the Lodgepole–Red Fir Forest are shared with Yellow Pine Forest. However, some good examples of replacement within similar species are found within the finches (Fringillidae) (fig. 4.23). In particular, there are three species of finches in which the male has a red head and brown streaking on the breast; the females all resemble sparrows but can be distinguished because they have thicker bills. At lower elevations, in the western foothills and the Great Basin on the east, the House Finch or Linnet, *Carpodacus mexicanus*, is a common bird seen in foliage on the outer edge of trees. Males defend their territories and court females with a loud warbling song. They eat buds, seeds, and small insects. In the Yellow Pine Forest, the same niche is occupied by the Purple Finch, *Carpodacus purpureus*. It forages similarly and sounds the same. It also looks like a House Finch, but streaking on the breast is less distinct. In the Lodgepole–Red Fir Forest Cassin's Finch, *Carpodacus cassinii*, occurs in this niche. It also looks and sounds similar. It takes considerable skill to tell these birds apart by sight. Most amateurs identify them according to elevation and assume they are correct. Designation by elevation is helped by the fact that these finches tend to remain resident in each zone regardless of season, although a bit of downslope movement in winter tends to confuse the issue somewhat.

Another source of confusion is that the male Pine Grosbeak also looks and sounds like the other three finches. However, the Pine Grosbeak is much larger. The small red-headed finches are seldom over 6 inches (15 cm) long, whereas the Pine Grosbeak is about 8 inches (20 cm) long. The female Pine Grosbeak is yellow and is so different in appearance from the male that it's difficult to believe they are related. More confusion can occur if Evening Grosbeaks are in the area. Both male and female Evening Grosbeaks are yellow, and, in contrast with the female Pine Grosbeak, they have larger, light-colored beaks and distinctive white wing patches. Evening Grosbeaks are not good singers. The Black-headed Grosbeak is the large, brightly colored singer of the Yellow Pine Forest. Large finches, the grosbeaks feed and act similarly to the smaller red-headed finches. Grosbeaks are also somewhat separated by elevation, but the boundaries are less distinct. The Black-headed Grosbeak occurs in the foothills and the Yellow Pine Forest, Evening Grosbeaks tend to be most common in White Fir forests, and the Pine Grosbeak is a component of the Lodgepole–Red Fir Forest. These six finches are separated by elevation and, to some degree, the size of their food. Grosbeaks are much more dependent on pine seeds as a source of food, but they also eat buds and insects. Habitat partitioning keeps these species from competing severely with each other.

Large finchlike birds observed in nervous flocks are probably Red Crossbills, *Loxia curvirostra*. Males are red, and females are yellow, like the Pine Grosbeaks. Furthermore, Red Crossbills are grosbeak-sized. Careful inspection, however, will reveal the large crossed bill tip that is used to pry seeds from unopened Lodgepole Pine cones. These birds are year-round residents of the Lodgepole forests, but they are not always common. They migrate in large flocks, congregating where food is abundant.

If the Mountain Chickadee is the mournful voice of the Yellow Pine Forest, the Hermit Thrush, *Catharus guttatus* (fig. 4.51), may be its equivalent in the Lodgepole–

FIGURE 4.51   Hermit Thrush, *Catharus guttatus*.

Red Fir Forest. Its clear, liquid whistle of alternating long low and short high notes is common from May through July. Similar to other thrushes, such as the American Robin, it feeds on the ground. It is a solitary bird, and its brown plumage and reddish tail make it difficult to spot. Seldom seen but often heard, the Hermit Thrush is one of the most common summer visitors of this forest zone. During winter it migrates to Mexico.

A large bird that remains resident year-round is the Sierra or Blue Grouse, *Dendragapus obscurus* (fig. 4.52). Even though these birds are 20 inches (50 cm) long, they are difficult to see. Their bluish, mottled appearance is a perfect disguise as they walk slowly or poise motionless in filtered light on the forest floor. They feed primarily on needles of pines and firs, although they take some berries and insects as well. Apparently, the diet of conifer needles has provided a distinct flavor to the meat. Those that have tasted the flesh of a Blue Grouse indicate that the meat tastes like turpentine. Perhaps this combination of a food that few others eat and its residue in the flesh is what makes the grouse so common. They are well concealed, but they move slowly. It seems that they would be a favored prey species.

The sound of the courting male grouse, a deep-throated booming noise that carries for a mile or so, is familiar to hikers. A female moving along slowly, herding and clucking quietly to her brood of six or seven small grouse, may be a surprise sight along a trail. In the summer the birds are dispersed widely in the upper forests. In winter, they become concentrated at the lower fringe of the forest among Red Firs on the west side of the Sierra. There are also reports of large winter flocks of grouse in the Yellow Pine belt of canyons on the eastern side of the Sierra.

The primary predator of the Lodgepole–Red Fir Forest is the Marten, which preys on Chickarees and other small mammals. There are also predatory birds such as hawks

FIGURE 4.52   Sierra Grouse, *Dendragapus obscurus*.

and owls. Although these birds may nest or take refuge in deep forest, it seems they prefer to hunt in meadows.

In general, owls are nocturnal and hawks are diurnal. There are at least nine different kinds of owls and seven kinds of hawks that range through Sierran forests. Owls hunt at night, using their excellent vision and hearing to locate their prey. An owl's eyes are about 100 times more sensitive than a human's; therefore owls are able to spot their prey in very dim light. Furthermore, the large ring of feathers around each eye gathers sound in the same way as the external ear of a mammal. By having a sound-gathering device around each eye, an owl is able to locate its prey very accurately even if it is pitch dark. The most common owl is the Great Horned Owl (fig. 8.42). It ranges through a variety of habitats from the desert to the mountains, wherever there are trees for nests and daytime refuge. Hooting of this large owl from dusk to dawn is a familiar sound to campers.

Perhaps the most spectacular Sierran owl is the Great Gray Owl, *Strix nebulosa*. The largest of all the Sierran species, it has a wingspan of 4 1/2 feet (1.5 m). Unlike most owls, it tends to be diurnal, although the sounds produced by prey are still important for hunting. In fact, they can locate pocket gophers (*Thomomys* spp.), which are among their favorite prey, by sound alone while they move underground. A Great Gray Owl can swoop down and take a hapless gopher from its burrow by grasping it with its talons while it is still beneath the surface. Great Gray Owls are not common in California, although they range throughout Arctic forests of the Northern Hemisphere. In California there are probably no more than 30 pairs,

FIGURE 4.53   Northern Goshawk, *Accipiter gentilis*.

and these are concentrated in the Central Sierra Nevada, particularly in the Yosemite area.

Forest-dwelling hawks are not common either, but the Northern Goshawk *Accipiter gentilis* (fig. 4.53), is a year-round inhabitant of the forests. It resembles a Red-tailed Hawk in size, but it does not soar like a Red-tail, and it has a narrow, black-and-white–banded tail. A Northern Goshawk may circle a few times, but it tends to pursue prey through the trees with uncanny speed and agility, sometimes crashing through branches to make a capture. It feeds on squirrels, chipmunks, and birds, including grouse. Birds are plucked before they are eaten, leaving a tell-tale pile of feathers as evidence of the capture.

Mammals.   In this forest, deep snow is the most important feature to which mammals must adapt. Squirrels are the most conspicuous mammals here. They cope with deep snow either by hibernating or by relying on stored food. The most common squirrel is the Golden-mantled Ground Squirrel, *Spermophilus lateralis* (pl. 12D). Why it seldom ventures into the Yellow Pine Forest is an unanswered question. Perhaps it is a matter of competition from nocturnal rodents, which are more common in the lower forest belt. Unlike those of the chipmunk, this squirrel's stripes do not extend up to the head and face. The head is a solid bronze color. Although most predators see only black and white, a Golden-mantled Ground Squirrel is difficult to see among patches of light and dark on the forest floor. Many hikers unknowingly call these squirrels chipmunks because of the stripes, but chipmunks are much smaller and spend much of their time in trees. Golden-mantled Ground squirrels seldom climb trees.

These are familiar squirrels to backpackers because they boldly search for food in campgrounds. In areas where there are many visitors, the squirrels have become very tame as they beg for handouts. These squirrels have learned that plastic bags contain food, and when given the chance, they will gnaw a hole in anything wrapped in plastic expecting to find it edible. Many a backpacker has neglected to tie down the top flap on the pack or to close a zipper, only to find that a Golden-mantled Ground Squirrel has crawled inside and gnawed holes in everything plastic, including the bag that contains dirty clothes.

Normal food for these ground squirrels includes grasses, sedges, bulbs, and berries. They seem to eat the greens early in the season, and later, during the time they are nursing young, they vigorously search for fungi. They are particularly fond of a variety of underground mushrooms known as truffles. The spores of these fungi pass undigested through the digestive tracts of the squirrels. The squirrels therefore are very important in dispersing the fungi, which add considerably to the mycorrhizae that help the forest trees absorb nutrients. The squirrels also eat some insects, an important source of protein.

In autumn the Golden-mantled Ground Squirrel retreats to its burrow under a rock or log and curls up to hibernate for the winter. When autumn days become too cold or snow becomes too deep, it would be energetically too expensive to keep foraging for food. The squirrel allows its body temperature to drop considerably, during which time its lower rate of metabolism enables it to continue on the energy provided by stored high-calorie brown fat. Every few days the squirrel becomes aroused, and urinates and perhaps nibbles on a bit of stored food. When snow melts in the spring and daytime temperatures warm up, the squirrel comes out of hibernation and begins to forage, eagerly awaiting the arrival of the first backpackers.

The tree squirrel of the Lodgepole–Red Fir Forest is the Chickaree, *Tamiasciurus douglasii* (pl. 12C). Its principal food is seeds from pines, firs, and redwoods. It gathers cones and seeds in great numbers and stores them at the base of trees or in hollows near its home. Chickarees are noisy squirrels, and make a considerable racket in the early morning, particularly as they chase each other in circles, up and down the trunks of trees. Even when they are not seen, they are frequently heard. They make a rapid series of high-pitched, birdlike chirps, each series lasting 2 or 3 seconds.

Except in places such as Yosemite Valley, where there is an abundance of food, Chickarees seldom venture into the realm of the Gray Squirrel. Apparently, Gray Squirrels must have their acorn supply. Other limitations to distribution of Gray Squirrels into the realm of the Chickaree include deep snow and the predatory Marten. As mentioned earlier, Gray Squirrels bury small caches in many locations. The Chickaree, however, makes a few large caches near its home, which it defends vigorously. In deep snow there is more reward for digging out a larger cache of food.

The Marten, *Martes americana*, is a large weasel, up to 20 inches (50 cm) from nose to rump. It is an agile predator that hunts on the ground and in the trees. Its prey is largely squirrels and chipmunks. Small Chickarees frequently escape from the Marten, but presumably the large Gray Squirrel is no match for it. Why the Marten does not go down the mountain in search of plump, succulent Gray Squirrels is a question that has not been answered, but two hypotheses are worth considering. First, perhaps competition from other predators such as Bobcats, *Lynx rufus* (fig. 8.49), and Coyotes (Fig. 8.47) excludes them. Second, it is suspected that the thick fur of the Marten would cause it to overheat during times of maximum energy expenditure, such as when it is running down its prey.

Martens are seldom seen. They hunt at night and early morning. When they are seen, they are usually running, probably across a snowfield. Their short legs and long bodies give them a very distinctive appearance when they run. The only animal with which it might be confused is the Fisher, *Martes pennanti*, which is rare in the Sierra.

Martens remain active during winter. They grow additional hair on their feet to aid locomotion on soft snow, and they feed on winter-active mammals such as pocket gophers, Pikas, and mice. They dive and/or dig rapidly in the snow to chase their prey. It is said that they will dive under the snow and attack Porcupines from beneath, thus avoiding the quills.

Chipmunks (*Tamius* spp.) are small squirrels, seldom exceeding 6 inches (15 cm) from nose to rump. There are eight different species in the Sierra, and they all look alike. As in the case of woodpeckers and warblers, each has its own ecologic niche. They are separated by behavioral interactions, elevation, latitude, and slope exposure. Some remain in trees, some seldom climb trees, and others prefer rocks and fallen timber.

The complex of factors responsible for separation of chipmunks into different eco-logic niches can be illustrated with three species that occur in Lee Vining Canyon, on the eastern slope of the Sierra Nevada, in the Yosemite area. The Lodgepole Chip-munk, *Tamius speciosus*, primarily inhabits Lodgepole Pine forests. It is restricted to forested sites because it is vulnerable to heat stress. It excludes other chipmunks by aggression. The Yellow-pine Chipmunk, *Tamius amoenus* (pl. 12F), occurs in the Jeffrey Pine and Pinyon Pine forests. It is more tolerant of heat stress than the Lodgepole Chipmunk. The Least Chipmunk, *Tamius minimus*, occupies open Sagebrush Scrub habitats. Throughout the Great Basin, the Least Chipmunk occurs in all habitats that are available in the eastern Sierra Nevada. In the Sierra it is kept from entering adjacent forested habitat by aggression from the Yellow-pine Chipmunk, but it is able to inhabit hot, dry habitat because it possesses thermoregulatory adaptations absent in other species. For example, the Least Chipmunk can tolerate a body temperature of 109°F (43°C) and a range of 13°F (7°C). So, in general, dispersal up the mountain is restricted by aggression, and movements down the mountain are restricted by physiological adaptations to heat stress.

Chipmunks are conspicuous and abundant. They feed mostly on small seeds, which they store in small holes in the ground. They also eat a surprising number of insects, including grasshoppers. One of the important controls on the abundance of termites seems to be predation by chipmunks, particularly when termites in winged form are dispersing. Chipmunks hibernate during winter, but unlike Golden-mantled Ground Squirrels, they are unable to rely on stored brown fat. Chipmunks become aroused frequently, during which time they urinate and eat. They dig through the snow to their food caches, which they locate by memory and odor.

Northern Flying Squirrels, *Glaucomys sabrinus*, are not common. They occur mostly in moist forests from Yosemite northward on the west side of the Sierra, but they are locally abundant on the east side of the Sierra as well. One interesting population occurs at Sagehen Basin north of Truckee, and residents of Mammoth, south of Yosemite, report that Northern Flying Squirrels beg for food in residential areas. These are small squirrels, about the size of chipmunks. They have a large web of loose skin between their forelimbs and hindlimbs, which they use to glide from tree to tree. They are nocturnal, and perhaps this is why they seem more scarce than they really are. Apparently, they are omnivorous, as many of them have been caught in meat-baited traps set for carnivores.

Riparian Woodland

Riparian communities occur along watercourses. Abundant water and cold-air drainage provide a cold, moist climate that is unique in California, where hot, dry summers dictate the nature of most communities. Characterized primarily by small trees and large shrubs, this community is often called a woodland. At higher elevations, however, the vegetation is typically all shrubs. At lower elevations, the trees are so large and dense that the community may be referred to as Riparian Forest. Discussion here will emphasize elevational differences in the community. Where it is relevant, a comparison will be made with riparian communities in other parts of the state.

The density and diversity of species in a riparian community are greater than in any other community in California. This occurs for two reasons. First, a riparian community is very productive. Lots of food means lots of animals. Second, the riparian community is a transitional community between water and land. The zone where two communities overlap, called an ecotone, shares characteristics of both communities and therefore is diverse. That is, the edge of a community is more diversified than its center, a phenomenon also known as "edge effect."

Trees and shrubs that grow along a watercourse are highly water-dependent. Abundant water on a year-round basis dictates that many species of plants will be broad-leaved. Because there are seasonal fluctuations in temperature, and winter is particularly cool due to cold-air drainage, most of these species are winter-deciduous. Unlike conifers, broad-leaved plants are particularly sensitive to low temperature. Photosynthesis in these plants during winter is unable to keep up with cellular respiration. The net effect is that, rather than use up carbohydrate stores during the winter, the plants respond by dropping their leaves and becoming dormant. This is the strategy followed by forests of hardwoods in the eastern United States.

Another characteristic of riparian species is that they are often wind-pollinated and wind-dispersed. Wind dispersal is an effective way for a riparian plant to get its seed from one body of water to another. To enhance dispersal by wind, fruits or seeds may bear wings or plumes. Also, some riparian species have floatation devices or fleshy fruits to encourage animal dispersal. Flowers are usually small, borne in dense clusters that hang down, and many are wind-pollinated. Flowers often occur in catkins, a name that refers to the resemblance of the clusters to a cat's tail. Common woody plants are willows, poplars, alders, maples, ashes, and dogwoods.

Notable among riparian species are members of the willow family (Salicaceae), which includes willows (*Salix*) and poplars (*Populus*). Willows are distributed throughout the state from the alpine zone to the coast, invariably along water. California has 31 species, most of which are shrubs, and many of which have very localized distribution. They can be recognized by their simple, elongate leaves. Flowers are in unisexual catkins borne on different plants. The fruit is a furry capsule with many hairy seeds.

In the high country, growing season is short, and soil is thin. Riparian plants at high elevation therefore are deciduous shrubs, not trees. Willows appear where water first appears. At high elevation, along streams leading away from snowbanks, Alpine Willow, *Salix petrophila*, may be found. The scientific name means "rock-loving." This common species occurs as a carpetlike shrub from Mount Lassen to Mount Whitney. Of limited distribution in similar habitat are Snow Willow, *Salix nivalis*, and Mono Willow, *Salix monica*. Snow Willow is found only on metamorphic rock on the east side of the Sierra Nevada between Koip Peak and Mount Dana. Mono Willow is found in the same general region, but only on the west side of the ridges.

Going down the mountains along watercourses, one observes a regular replacement of species. At lower elevations the shrubs are taller, and in the valleys, willows are trees. Throughout the state, from about 10,000 feet to 5000 feet (3000–1500 m) a common species is Lemmon Willow, *Salix lemmonii*. Common between 10,000 and 8,000 feet (3000 and 2400 m) is Eastwood Willow, *Salix eastwoodiae*. Lemmon Willow has narrow, lance-shaped leaves about 3 inches (7.5 cm) long, whereas Eastwood willow has shorter, broader leaves. Of limited distribution at the same elevation in the Sierra Nevada are species such as Jepson Willow, *Salix jepsonii*; Grayleaf Sierra Willow, *Salix orestera*; Yellow Willow, *Salix lutea*; and Bryant Willow, *Salix caudata*. Grayleaf Sierra Willow occurs in the northern Sierra, and Jepson Willow occurs in the northern Sierra and the Pacific Northwest. Bryant Willow and Yellow Willow occur from the San Bernardino Mountains northward on the east side of the Sierra to the Warner Mountains. Common below 5000 feet (1500 m) is Arroyo Willow, *Salix lasiolepis*, and common below 3000 feet (900 m) is Sandbar Willow, *Salix hindsiana*, both of which reach tree size, 20 to 30 feet (7–10 m) in height.

Tree species of willow do not occur higher than about 8000 feet (2400 m). Pacific Willow, *Salix lasiandra* (fig. 10.8) occurs from the foothills to about that elevation. Pacific Willow is often called Yellow Willow, but that name is more appropriate for the shrub mentioned above, the scientific name for which, *Salix lutea*, means "yellow willow." In the foothills and Great Central Valley, common willows are Black Willow, *Salix gooddingii*, and Red Willow, *Salix laevigata*. Red Willow may occur as high as 5000 feet (1500 m).

A very interesting phenomenon associated with various species of willows is that they produce a plant toxin known as salicin, a name derived from the name of the genus, *Salix*. This chemical is similar in some ways to aspirin, or acetylsalicylic acid, also named for the willow genus. Salicin is apparently produced by willows to discourage herbivores from eating them. In harsher climates, such as high elevation, the plants appear to produce greater concentrations of the chemical. An interesting side effect of this production is that some insects have developed an immunity to the toxin and have taken deliberately to eating willow leaves in order to use the toxin for their own protection. Similarly, larvae of the Monarch Butterfly consume milkweed to make themselves distasteful. In the case of willows, the insect involved is the larva of a leaf beetle, *Chrysomela aenicollis*. Studies of Grayleaf Sierra Willow between 8000 feet (2400 m) and 9500 feet (2950 m) along Big Pine Creek of the eastern Sierra showed that the plants with more salicin were more heavily preyed upon by beetle larvae. Furthermore, beetles on those willows suffered less predation. In this case, it appears that the production of the toxin has backfired, as it has encouraged predation by the beetle larvae.

Trees called poplars include cottonwoods and aspens, and they occur all across North America, Europe, and Asia. They are moisture-loving trees occurring in forests in some areas. In California, they are primarily riparian species, nicely segregated by elevation. At lower elevation, from the coast to about 2500 feet (750 m), there is Fremont Cottonwood, *Populus fremontii* (fig. 8.54). On the desert side of mountain ranges, it occurs in canyons up to 6500 feet (2000 m) in elevation. This is the common cottonwood with serrated, heart-shaped leaves that are bright green on both surfaces, turning yellow in autumn. When female catkins come into fruit, long white hairs produce cottony masses that give the tree its name. Black Cottonwood, *Populus trichocarpa* (fig. 4.54), occurs at higher elevation, up to about 9000 feet (2700 m), and along streams in forests along the coast. This cottonwood differs from Fremont Cottonwood by having finely serrated leaves that are dark green above and rusty or silvery beneath. At higher elevations, leaves become more lance-shaped than heart-shaped. This is the largest of all native poplars, up to 160 feet (50 m) in height. A third species of cottonwood, Narrowleaf Cottonwood, *Populus angustifolia*, occurs in a few small groves at about 6000 feet (1800 m) on the eastern slope of the Sierra near Lone Pine and Independence. This species is more common to the east, into the Rockies. It is a small, slender tree with lance-shaped leaves.

Quaking Aspen, *Populus tremuloides*, has the widest distribution of any tree species in North America. This tree gets its name from the fact that its leaves tremble because they have a flattened, flexible stem (petiole). Even the slightest breeze sets the pendulous leaves quivering. This characteristic is shared by many cottonwoods as well, but it seems more pronounced in Quaking Aspens. Leaves differ from cottonwoods by being smaller, about the size of a half-dollar. They are light green on top and silvery

FIGURE 4.54   Leaves of Black Cottonwood, *Populus trichocarpa*, and Quaking Aspen, *Populus tremuloides*. Most species of riparian trees are winter-deciduous.

underneath. Quaking Aspen shoots, rich in calcium, are a very important browse for Mule Deer and Bighorn Sheep.

Throughout most of its range, Quaking Aspen is considered a successional species. It is an aggressive pioneer, one of the first species to return after a disturbance. Sprouts return from an extensive root system.

In California, Quaking Aspens are usually a high-elevation, riparian species. They occur in groves bordering streams at elevations higher than Black Cottonwoods. At lower reaches of their distribution they occur as good-sized trees, up to 80 feet (25 m) tall. These large trees are easily recognized by their white bark, which becomes broken up into black, warty bands. At the upper reaches of their distribution, at about 10,000 feet (3000 m), trees are much shorter, sometimes shrublike. Young trees often have greenish bark.

In the northern Sierra Nevada, at upper elevations in the Great Basin, and in the White Mountains, Quaking Aspen groves are not restricted to riparian sites. They may occur in sunny places where soil remains wet, such as at the foot of talus slopes. In the Warner Mountains, above 8000 feet (2400 m), they occur in groves along with Washoe Pines and are not riparian trees in this setting (fig. 4.31). The situation in the Warner Mountains resembles that of the Rocky Mountains, where summer precipitation keeps the soil moist throughout the year.

The most vivid displays of autumn color that occur in California are associated with Quaking Aspens (pl. 8A). Leaves range from yellow to gold, orange, and red.

Because of the sprouting behavior of this species, groves are often clones of the same color. Because all clones do not enter dormancy at the same time, some groves remain green while others have turned. This obvious difference in behavior for different clones has led scientists to study the mechanism that initiates dormancy. The stimulus to turn color is not the first hard frost of the winter, as is often thought. Rather, the change is a hereditary response to day length, to shortening of the photoperiod as winter approaches. The most spectacular displays of autumn color in these Quaking Aspen groves are on the eastern side of the Sierra Nevada and the Glass Mountain area north of Bishop. Here the groves occur at lower elevation, and their brilliant colors stand out in bold relief against the surrounding terrain covered with sparse Great Basin vegetation. An early October drive up Highway 395 through the June Lake Loop to Lee Vining will reward the motorist with some of the most beautiful scenery in California.

There is some evidence to support the contention that Quaking Aspen never goes fully dormant during winter. Bark tissues contain a high chlorophyll content, which may allow photosynthesis to continue on sunny winter days. Furthermore, it has been determined that Quaking Aspen's killing temperature of $-100°F$ ($-80°C$) represents the lowest such temperature among winter-deciduous trees.

Quaking Aspen wood is light and brittle. Dry snags of Quaking Aspen are easy to break, and they form an ideal wood for a campfire. The wood burns hot and without smoke. An unfortunate characteristic of Quaking Aspen (as well as some other poplars) is that it also burns when it is green. People hard up for firewood will cut down green Quaking Aspens. These are the same people who complain that Quaking Aspen wood burns with a foul odor. It serves them right.

Other winter-deciduous species grow along streams with willows and cottonwoods. At lower elevations from the foothills to the coast, Western Sycamore or California Sycamore, *Platanus racemosa*, is a common species (pl. 7C). This is California's only native member of the plane tree family (Platanaceae). It is essentially a California species, but it extends into Baja California on the coastal side of the Peninsular Ranges. In California, its distribution occurs along the coast from the southern Coast Ranges southward through the Transverse and Peninsular ranges. To the interior it occurs along the southwestern side of the Sierra Nevada and along the Sacramento and San Joaquin rivers of the Great Central Valley, where it ascends the main tributaries to low elevations in the Sierran foothills. In the Sierra Nevada foothills it is more common in the south, but it occurs northward as far as Tehama County.

Sycamores are characterized by large, palmate leaves and whitish, scaly bark. Often they do not grow straight but twist back and forth, giving the trunk a gnarled appearance. These are long-lived trees that may become quite large, up to 100 feet (30 m) in height.

Alders are in the birch family (Betulaceae). There are four species in California. They play an important role wherever they occur, because they are equipped with nitrogen-fixing bacteria in their roots. The White Alder, *Alnus rhombifolia* (fig. 4.55) has the most extensive distribution, but they are all similar in appearance. Their leaves, elmlike, are oval and serrated, up to 5 inches (12 cm) in length. Flowers are borne in catkins, but male and female catkins occur on the same tree.

FIGURE 4.55   White Alder, *Alnus rhombifolia*, with female cones.

After the seed is set, the remains of a dry, hard fruit that resembles a small redwood cone stays on the tree.

White Alders occur throughout California in Riparian Woodland. They are easy to distinguish by their straight, grayish trunks. A dark, downturned mark appears on the trunk just above each branch. Where old branches have fallen off, the dark marks remain, giving the tree trunk the appearance of having many mustaches.

On wet slopes and along streams between 5000 and 8000 feet (1500 and 2500 m) in elevation, from Tulare County north, there is a shrublike alder known as Mountain Alder, *Alnus tenuifolia*. It replaces White Alder at higher elevations. These small trees have leaves similar to other alders, but the serrations are of two sizes. Fine teeth along the margin are superimposed on larger sawlike teeth.

On the eastern slope of the Sierra Nevada from about 5000 to 9000 feet (1500–2700 m) there is another member of the birch family: Water Birch, *Betula occidentalis*. It looks very much like Mountain Alder, but its leaves lack the large sawtooth serrations. Furthermore, its distribution is patchy. It is conspicuous along Lone Pine Creek and Big Pine Creek, in Inyo County, and it also occurs on Mount Shasta and westward through the Klamath Province to the interior of the northern Coast Ranges. A disjunct distribution of this sort is similar to distributions of some of the subalpine plants, such as the Foxtail Pine, which will be discussed in the chapter on mountaintops. Although Water Birch is essentially a Great Basin species, it also occurs along watercourses in the mountains of the western Mojave Desert.

Big-leaf Maple, *Acer macrophyllum* (fig. 6.9) is California's largest member of the maple family (Aceraceae). Like the sycamores, maples have large, palmate leaves, but the leaves are arranged opposite to each other on the stem. In spring, they produce small, greenish yellow flowers in hanging clusters. The flowers are large enough that five small petals can be seen. The fruit is the type known as a samara. Fruits are winged and, when dry, fall from the tree like little helicopters.

In the northwest, Big-leaf Maple is a forest species, growing with Douglas Fir and Coast Redwood. Its range extends southward along the western Sierra Nevada and down the coast on the western side of the Transverse and Peninsular ranges. In the southern part of its range, it is a riparian species growing at middle elevations along with White Alders. Big-leaf Maple is one of California's commercially valuable hardwoods.

At lower elevations in the Sierra Nevada, Big-leaf Maples are replaced by another member of the maple family that occurs in California: the California Box Elder, *Acer negundo californicum*. It occurs frequently in association with Western Sycamores and Fremont Cottonwoods. It is not present in all streams, but where it occurs it may be common. The species is widespread in the United States, but California has its own endemic subspecies. Box Elders resemble maples, but the leaves are compound, composed of three palmately veined leaflets, giving the appearance of a maple with small leaves.

Often co-occurring with White Alders and Big-leaf Maples is one of California's most beautiful native trees, Pacific or Mountain Dogwood, *Cornus nuttallii* (fig. 4.56). This is the only member of the dogwood family (Cornaceae) that is a tree in California. Because its distribution is not limited to mountains, closely paralleling that of Big-leaf Maple, it seems best to refer to this species as Pacific Dogwood. In moist forests, such as in association with Sierra Redwoods, it becomes an understory tree growing in deep shade. It rarely grows in full sun, and maximum photosynthesis in this species occurs at only one-third the intensity of full sun.

During spring, Pacific Dogwoods are most conspicuous when leafless branches become laden with white flowers up to 6 inches (15 cm) across. Close inspection of the blossoms will reveal that what are thought to be petals are actually large white bracts, and what appears to be the center of a single large flower is a cluster of small flowers. There are usually five to six of these white bracts, whereas the eastern Flowering Dogwood, *Cornus florida*, has only four. The eastern variety often has reddish notches at the end of each bract, leading to the story that dogwood was used to build Christ's cross. Lest we forget, cross-shaped flowers with blood spots remind us of that event. Although the dogwood family does occur in Europe, the genus *Cornus* does not, and the eastern Flowering Dogwood is the only species with four showy bracts.

Leaves of dogwoods resemble alder leaves in shape, but they are not serrated. They are opposite on the stem, and the veins of the leaf turn and run parallel to the midrib. If a dogwood leaf is torn, elastic threads within the veins remain intact, often holding the torn parts of the leaf together.

If the beautiful flowers are not enough, the autumn display provided by Pacific Dogwood leaves is spectacular. The color ranges from orange to scarlet. Bright red berries may also be seen on the tree at this time. They are quite bitter, but Band-tailed Pigeons are reported to feast upon them every autumn.

FIGURE 4.56   Pacific Dogwood, *Cornus nuttallii*.

A shrubby dogwood of the Sierra Nevada and northern forests is known as Creek Dogwood or Red-osier Dogwood, *Cornus stolonifera*. (The term *osier* refers to pliable twigs used in basket making.) This shrub often grows in association with alders and willows. The leaves have the same type of venation as the other dogwoods, but the flowers do not have large, showy bracts. Instead, small white flowers grow in clusters at the tips of the stems. The fruits are whitish and are relished by many species of birds. The most distinctive feature of this shrub is its bright red bark. Presumably, Indians scraped, dried, and smoked the inner lining of this bark, which is reported to have hallucinatory properties. Perhaps this helped them weave the pliable branches into the intricate patterns found in their baskets.

Perhaps the most beautiful of the riparian shrubs is Western Azalea, *Rhododendron occidentale*. These shrubs occur in similar locations as Pacific Dogwoods, although they are absent from the southern Coast Ranges and Transverse Ranges. Among members of the heath family (Ericaceae) these are unique by being winter-deciduous and having large flowers. Manzanitas and Madrone are also in this family, but they are characterized by their small, urn-shaped flowers. Western Azaleas, in contrast, have large, white, funnel-shaped flowers, fully 2 inches (5 cm) long. During spring, when Pacific Dogwoods and Western Azaleas are in full bloom, a person cannot help but admire the beauty of these plants. In moist localities within the forest, these shrubs also become a part of the understory. When they are not flowering, they are more easily overlooked among willows and other riparian species of shrubs. Azaleas may be recognized by their thin, light green, lance-shaped leaves, up to 3 inches (8 cm) in length, which grow in whorls on the stem. Of special interest is that they are poisonous, particularly to domestic livestock.

One more group of deciduous trees occurs in the Riparian Woodland. These are the ashes, deciduous members of the olive family (Oleaceae). These small, shrublike trees are usually characterized by pinnately compound leaves, with about five to seven lance-shaped leaflets. The most common is Flowering or Foothill Ash, *Fraxinus dipetala*. The name *dipetala* refers to the branched clusters of white flowers that each bear two petals. Fruits of these ashes are single-winged samaras. This species occurs throughout the foothill areas of the state along streams or on north-facing slopes. Its range extends outside of California into appropriate habitat in Baja California.

California's only large treelike ash is Oregon Ash, *Fraxinus latifolia*. This is a species found on rich alluvial soils. It occurs along the big rivers in the Great Central Valley and into the Sierra Nevada foothills along with willows and Fremont Cottonwood.

The Mixed Evergreen Forest of northwestern California includes broadleaf evergreen species, relicts of southern affinities that also occur to various degrees in riparian situations. The presence of permanent water compensates for the long, dry summer. Included among these species are broad-leaved trees such as California Laurel, *Umbellularia californica* (fig. 7.9), and Madrone, *Arbutus menziesii* (fig. 6.7).

The odoriferous laurel, also known locally as Pepperwood, is common in canyons as far south as the Laguna Mountains in San Diego County. In the Sierra Nevada, it occurs primarily below 5000 feet (1500 m), particularly where streams cut through chaparral. Shrubby forms of this species may be associated with moist serpentine soils in the northern Sierra Nevada foothills.

Madrone occurs in the northern Sierra Nevada primarily between Butte and Calaveras Counties, where it also becomes a component of Yellow Pine Forest, particularly in association with White Firs. As a broad-leaved tree with a twisted trunk, it stands in stark contrast to the conifers.

Among the conifers of Mixed Evergreen Forest that occur in riparian communities are Douglas Fir, *Pseudotsuga menziesii*, and California Nutmeg, *Torreya californica*, both of which occur in canyons of the western Sierra Nevada. Particularly striking are the large Douglas Firs that occur along the famous Mist Trail to Vernal and Nevada falls in Yosemite National Park. This is also one of the localities where California Laurel is viewed by millions of people each year.

In summary, so many dominant species are found over such a wide elevational range that it is difficult to get a picture of species assemblages within the riparian communities. On an elevational basis we may think of four assemblages. Along larger streams in the valleys and foothills, Western Sycamore, California Box Elder, Fremont Cottonwood, and one or more of the tree-sized willows are dominant species. Up through the Yellow Pine Forest are Riparian Woodlands that include species also found in the northern forests and Coast Ranges. For example, Big-leaf Maple, Pacific Dogwood, California Laurel, and Black Cottonwood occur along the coast and reappear along streams in the mountains where they are joined by White Alder. In the Lodgepole–Red Fir Forest and on the eastern side of the Sierra, Quaking Aspen dominates. At high elevations, into the alpine zone, riparian vegetation becomes shrubby. Various species of willow dominate this community.

Animals of Riparian Woodland. The diversity of animals is very great in Riparian Woodland. Most of the animals come to the streams to find water or food or to escape the heat. These animals are discussed in other parts of the book. The aquatic animals will be discussed in chapter 11, on inland waters. In this section emphasis will be on conspicuous butterflies and birds.

Butterflies. Butterflies often occur along watercourses because they commonly feed on riparian plants. For many butterflies the larvae are restricted to a single plant species. Adults seem to be less specialized but may be associated with certain species as well. Adult butterflies rely entirely on liquid food, usually nectar obtained from flowers by means of a long, hollow proboscis.

In foothill canyons, as in the valleys, the most common butterflies are admirals and swallowtails. Some of them, such as Lorquin's Admiral, *Basilarchia lorquini*, and the Western Tiger Swallowtail, *Papilio rutulus*, are discussed in the chapter on the Great Central Valley (fig. 10.14). Also common in the foothills are two powerful fliers: the Two-tailed Tiger Swallowtail, *Papilio multicaudatus*, and the Pale Swallowtail, *Papilio eurymedon*. The Two-tailed Tiger Swallowtail has two tails on each wing and is the largest western butterfly. The Pale Swallowtail looks like the Western Tiger Swallowtail, but its background color is whitish rather than bright yellow.

The larvae of these butterflies are bright green with a yellow line on each side. They have two black-bordered yellow spots that resemble eyes on each side of the body. When at rest, they tuck their heads under so that the segment with the large spots looks like a large head with big eyes. Larvae of the Western Tiger Swallowtail feed on a variety of riparian plants such as willows, cottonwoods, alders, and sycamores. Larvae of the Pale Swallowtail feed on chaparral plants that border the Riparian Woodland, such as Coffee Berry (*Rhamnus californica*), California lilacs (*Ceanothus* spp.), and Holly-leaved Cherry (*Prunus ilicifolia*). Larvae of the Two-tailed Swallowtail feed on ash, serviceberry (*Amelanchier* spp.), and Hop Tree (*Ptelea baldwini*).

One of the most common and distinctive spring butterflies is the Sara Orange-tip, *Anthocharis sara*. This is a small butterfly with a wingspan of about 2 inches (5 cm). Its wings are white with orange tips. The adults fly up and down canyons, usually close to the ground. The larvae are green with wide yellow stripes on each side. They feed on members of the mustard family (Brassicaceae).

The Sonora Blue Butterfly, *Philotes sonoriensis*, is one of California's most beautiful butterflies. It occurs in local colonies in rocky canyons of the Sierra Nevada foothills from Placer County southward to the desert margins, and in the Coast Ranges from Santa Clara County southward to Baja California. The wingspan on this butterfly is barely over an inch (26 mm). Males are metallic blue with a bright orange spot on the forewing. Females have the orange spot on both wings. Adults fly close to rocky cliffs and steep canyon walls. Larvae of these butterflies are variable in color, from pale green to mottled rose, and they feed on various live-forevers (*Dudleya* spp.).

During late spring a common butterfly in foothill canyons is the Common Checkerspot or Chalcedon, *Euphydryas chalcedona*. The adult of this butterfly is frequently seen on wildflowers. It has a wingspan slightly over 2 inches (6 cm), and its wings are marked by numerous yellowish and red spots on a background of black. The larvae are black with branched spines and have a row of red-orange spots along the back. They feed on various members of the figwort or monkeyflower family (Scrophulareaceae).

Associated with willows in canyon bottoms are small butterflies known as hairstreaks. The Sylvan Hairstreak, *Satyrium sylvinus*, is a small gray butterfly with a pale blue cast. It is a reddish brown near its tail. The caterpillars are green with cream-colored side lines. Larvae appear to be restricted to willows, but adults will visit other flowers, such as milkweeds, for nectar.

Higher in the mountains, where streams wind through coniferous forests, you may see the Zephyr Anglewing, *Polygonia zephyrus*. The adults have a 2-inch (5-cm) wingspan. The ragged-looking wings are orangish with a brown border interrupted by large tawny crescents. They flit about as if they were propelled by little spurts of wind, or zephyrs. Adults feed on streamside wildflowers; the larvae feed on various wild currants and gooseberries (*Ribes* spp.). The larvae are black with reddish spines in front and white spines in back.

Birds.   Birds are the most conspicuous animals of riparian communities. Many species of small birds coexist in Riparian Woodland through mechanisms of niche partitioning. However, because they spend so much time among the leaves, they are seldom seen. Included here are flycatchers, vireos, goldfinches, warblers, and sparrows. They partition the resources by feeding on different plants and nesting in different places. The greatest threat to them is habitat destruction associated with drying and diversion of water.

Another threat that is becoming increasingly more serious is the invasion of introduced species. Such species are common in areas of habitation, but they also invade woodlands, particularly Oak Woodland and Riparian Woodland. For example, House Sparrows or English Sparrows, *Passer domesticus*, compete with native birds for food, nesting materials, and nesting sites. The more House Sparrows that occur in an area, the fewer other birds that can coexist. Starlings, *Sturnus vulgaris*, first appeared in California in 1942. Since that time they have become common near habitation and have invaded many woodland habitats. Both House Sparrows and Starlings have moved into woodlands in the Sierra Nevada, particularly in the vicinity of the national parks. Both species are examples of birds introduced from Europe that have been able to expand their ranges because they have no natural enemies here.

Starlings resemble blackbirds, but they are short-necked and short-tailed and have yellow bills. They are very aggressive, displacing all sorts of birds that nest in tree cavities. Cavity-nesting birds that are being replaced include woodpeckers, bluebirds, and small owls. The aggressive Starlings move into the nests and physically remove the juveniles.

A problem that is a bit more subtle than that of introduced European birds is what has happened with Brown-headed Cowbirds, *Molothrus ater*. These birds are in the blackbird family and look like Brewer's Blackbirds, *Euphagus cyanocephalus*, with stubby bills. The male cowbird is the same color as a male blackbird, but its head is brown and it does not have yellow eyes. Female cowbirds differ from female blackbirds by being browner and by often having a streaked breast. It is sometimes difficult to tell these birds apart, particularly because the two species occur in mixed flocks.

Cowbirds get their name from their frequent association with livestock. Prior to the introduction of domesticated livestock, they were "Buffalo-birds," accompanying herds of bison on the prairies. They then followed humans and their domesticated animals to California. They eat seeds and other edible items found in droppings, and they may be seen feeding in pastures, corrals, and feed lots.

The problem with Brown-headed Cowbirds is that they are nest parasites. Female cowbirds remove the eggs of native riparian birds from their nests and replace them with their own. The native birds then incubate the eggs and raise young cowbirds instead of their own offspring.

Recent studies of Brown-headed Cowbirds in the Sierra Nevada have revealed an interesting pattern of daily migration. Cowbirds spend the night in the mountains roosting in riparian vegetation. In the morning, the birds are solitary, and females do their nest robbing. Usually each female lays a single egg per day in another bird's nest. Then the cowbirds make their way down the mountain to pastures or pack stations, where they spend the day feeding in flocks. In the evening, they fly back up mountain to repeat the procedure, a round trip that may cover 15 miles (20 km). This is a very large home range for a songbird, which typically has a range measured in meters, not miles. Cowbirds must expend an incredible amount of energy on their long daily migrations, and such energy expenditure is possible only if the food is rich enough to make it worthwhile. It does not seem logical that the long trips would be worth it, but one cannot argue with success. Cowbirds continue to expand their ranges to the detriment of native songbirds. They have even invaded Catalina Island, where they feed in association with the bison herd there.

A question arises: Why do Brown-headed Cowbirds parasitize the nests of some birds but not others? The answer seems to lie in the color of the eggs. Species that lay blue eggs, such as the American Robin or the Hermit Thrush, easily recognize cowbird eggs and remove them from the nest. It is thus apparent that the true value of specific colors and/or patterns on eggs is parental recognition. Nest parasites such as Brown-headed Cowbirds must depend on their eggs bearing some resemblance to those of the host species. Those birds that invest a bit of energy in producing uniquely colored eggs enjoy the benefit of not being parasitized.

Another blackbird associated with wetland habitats is the Red-winged Blackbird, *Agelaius phoeniceus* (pl. 13E). This bird and its close relative, the Tricolored Blackbird, *Agelaius tricolor*, are conspicuous in marshy habitats from the coast to forest-bordered meadows. Males have a conspicuous red patch on their shoulders and defend their territories by calling from a perch as high as possible in shrubs or tules. Their distinctive call is not pretty, resembling the sound made by a squeaking, rusty gate.

Experiments with Red-winged Blackbirds have revealed an interesting thing about the roles of color and sound in the defense of territories. If the red patch is covered, birds in forest habitats are able to defend territories with their calls, but birds in open habitats, such as marshes, are not. On the other hand, if the birds are made mute, those in open habitats are still able to defend territories, but forest birds are not. The conclusion is that in habitats where birds may be concealed by heavy vegetation, sounds are more important signals. In habitats where visibility is not a problem, color is more important. These experiments tend to verify the oft-quoted hypothesis that shrubland and forest birds need not be colorful, but they commonly are equipped with distinctive voices.

Typical of cavity-nesting birds that inhabit streamside woodlands, and particularly susceptible to invasions of nonnative birds is the House Wren, *Troglodytes aedon* (fig. 4.57). In the Sierra Nevada, this bird is particularly associated with Quaking Aspens and cottonwoods, where nests are often found in abandoned woodpecker holes. It is especially common on the east side of the mountains and the western foothills. As its name implies, a House Wren also may nest in or around houses and barns. In the spring or summer the bubbling song of a male from a prominent perch is one of the familiar sounds of east-side aspen groves. Males and females forage for insects in adjacent brushy habitat. Sierran birds migrate south to a warmer climate for the winter, but southern California birds may remain resident.

Perhaps the most strictly riparian bird is the American Dipper or Water Ouzel, *Cinclus mexicanus*. These small, gray, stubby-tailed birds inhabit mountain streams throughout the state and never leave the company of water. They fly up and down the stream course, following every bend. Once they mate, each pair will maintain a territory of about 150 feet (50 m) along the stream. They build nests, often of moss, right next to the water, and sometimes behind waterfalls. Imagine this little bird flying kamikaze-like into a waterfall.

Dippers get their name from their habit of standing on a boulder near a stream and bobbing up and down. It is believed that the bobbing helps them see beneath the glare of surface water. They feed on aquatic insects and larvae, which they gather

FIGURE 4.57   House Wren, *Troglodytes aedon*.

by entering the water. They swim well, and they can walk on the bottom of a stream. They do this by holding their wings partway open; turbulence pressing on the wings helps to hold them down. They have been observed to go as deep as 20 feet (6 m) and to remain under for as long as a minute.

Dippers are year-round residents of forest streams. As long as the water remains unfrozen, they continue to feed there. During winter, they sometimes become more common in lower reaches of the streams on the western slopes of the Sierra Nevada. This tendency implies a downslope migration. The highest elevation at which they have been recorded during the winter is 7500 feet (2250 m), an observation made by John Muir at the turn of the century.

The Belted Kingfisher, *Ceryle alcyon* (pl. 13G), is also an obligate waterside bird. Unlike the Dipper, Belted Kingfishers also frequent estuaries and lagoons, especially in winter. They are more common along lower reaches of streams, where they hunt for small fish from a streamside perch, usually an overhanging tree branch. When the water becomes murky, they rely mostly on crayfish as a food source. Kingfishers are rarely seen above 7000 feet (2300 m) elevation. They do move into desert areas where permanent water occurs.

The call of a Belted Kingfisher is a well-known sound along streams. It is a loud, screeching rattle. During breeding season males pursue females up and down the stream, calling loudly, and females battle for good nesting sites. These are large birds, up to 13 inches (33 cm) in length. Their heads appear to be extra large; its size is accentuated by a large, ragged, often double-pointed crest and by the bird's very small feet, which are a clue that these large fish eaters are actually somewhat related to hummingbirds.

Belted Kingfishers are blue-gray above and white beneath. Both males and females have a blue-gray band across the upper breast; the female also has a rust-colored band across the lower breast. The additional color present on females is rare among birds: the female is more colorful! When this is the case, as in phalaropes, there is a reversal of sex roles: the female defends the territory. This seems to be the case with Belted Kingfishers, although it is not as extreme as in the case of a phalarope.

The birds are solitary except during breeding season. They construct a nest in a stream bank, consisting of a tunnel that may go back 6 feet (2 m). At this time the sex-role reversal becomes evident: males do most of the nest building. The advantage of the male doing most of the digging is that it allows the female to conserve her energy for laying eggs. Five to eight young are raised in the tunnel, and feeding the young keeps both parents busy. In open habitats they hunt from a hovering position, similar to a kite or kestrel. Once they grasp a fish, they return to a perch, where they thump the fish repeatedly on a branch until it stops squirming. Only then will they swallow it, head first.

Another advantage to conservation of energy for the female is that these nests may be wiped out by flooding. If this occurs, the female must have enough stored energy to lay another clutch of eggs. The point is that to maximize the number of offspring he produces, the male should do more than his share of nest building and caring for the young in order to keep his mate healthy.

5

Mountaintops

Mountaintops are isolated from each other by regions of low elevation and different climate (fig. 5.1). Just like regions of specialized soil, mountaintops are ecologic islands. On mountaintops, therefore, relicts and endemics are found. Species may be remnants of former widespread distribution, or they may be products of evolution during a long period of isolation. Similar, closely related species are found on adjacent mountaintops, just as they are on adjacent oceanic islands.

Mountaintop climate is similar in every mountain range throughout the state of California. Plants and animals have evolved similar strategies for these communities, regardless of their location. The climatic trends that one observes upon ascending a mountain reach their extremes on the mountaintop. Here is the coldest climate, the most intense sunlight, and the strongest wind. Precipitation is reduced from that of the Lodgepole–Red Fir Forest, and, with the exception of an occasional thunderstorm, nearly all precipitation falls as snow; only 3% of total precipitation in the Sierra Nevada comes from summer rainfall. Snow is late to melt, and the summer growing season may be less than seven weeks. Frost can occur at any time of year. Soil is shallow, nutrient-poor, and coarse, and it has an acidic pH.

BIOTIC ZONATION

The Sierra Nevada has the greatest abundance of alpine and subalpine communities, but other areas in the state also are of sufficient elevation to support these types of communities. Subalpine and alpine communities occur in the Klamath Province, the Cascades, the Great Basin, the Transverse Ranges, and the Peninsular Ranges.

Pinyon-Juniper Woodlands are also mountaintop ecologic islands. This is a community that is both drought-tolerant and snow-tolerant. Although these woodlands represent desert communities to some authorities, their localized distribution and evolutionary history qualify them as mountaintop communities.

Subalpine Forest

The subalpine zone is the region referred to by C. Hart Merriam as the Hudsonian life zone. It is the upper limit for trees. The term *alpine* is in reference to the Alps, a European mountain range; it does not mean "all pines." The alpine zone has no trees. Precipitation, falling almost entirely as snow, measures from 30 inches (75 cm) to 50 inches (125 cm) per year. On the average, precipitation is 10 inches (25 cm) per year less than that which falls in the Lodgepole–Red Fir Forest, at lower elevation.

At upper timberline, trees are bent and twisted by the wind. This twisted form is known as a *krummholz*, which means "bent wood" in German (fig. 5.2). The height to which these trees grow is closely correlated with snow depth and wind intensity.

FIGURE 5.1   Mount Whitney at dawn. (Photograph by Geoff Smith.)

Three winter phenomena shape these trees: snow loading, blowing ice particles, and dehydration. Snow loading refers to heavy snow that can break and bend vegetation. Many trees have "snow knees," bent-over portions of the trunk that heal, followed by new erect growth.

During winter, branches that protrude above the snow are subjected to ice blast and drying by the wind. The abrasion from wind-blown ice particles damages the outer, waterproof cuticle of conifer needles and the resultant water loss causes death of the tissue. Furthermore, ice from chilled water vapor may form on needles exposed to fog or clouds. The intensity of the wind may be so great that it causes ice to change to water vapor without ever entering a liquid phase. This extremely rapid rate of evaporation causes an extreme drop in temperature, which kills tissue by supercooling.

Most conifers protect themselves from cold weather by withdrawing water from cells in twigs and stems. In most cases it is the formation of ice crystals within plant tissues that does the damage. There are two theories of what causes cell death when ice crystals form. The oldest theory implies mechanical damage to membranes from freezing of water inside the cells. The alternative explanation, known as the vital-water hypothesis, implies that all water is pulled from the cells except that which

FIGURE 5.2   Jeffrey Pine, *Pinus jeffreyi*, on top of Sentinel Dome, Yosemite National Park.

is mechanically bound to structural molecules, such as those in membranes. With a continued decrease in temperature, particularly in association with supercooling, the membrane proteins become altered, allowing irreversible dehydration of cells and/or the accumulation of toxic dissolved materials inside the cells. In cases of supercooling, even withdrawal of water cannot protect tissues. Compounded by desiccation and abrasion, supercooling damages new foliage projecting above the snow level. If several years of deep snow occur, new foliage might be able to reach a height where the action of wind is less severe. Therefore such trees may have one or two tall branches with all the needles near the top, with the remainder of the needles forming a flat "skirt" of foliage near the ground.

The upper elevation achievable by any tree species seems to be dictated by temperature. It is true that lack of soil may be limiting, but the upper tree limit seems to be correlated with a line where the temperature may drop to $-40°F$ ($-40°C$). This is the temperature at which pure water freezes instantly. This particular line, known as the $-40°$ isotherm, seems especially important in limiting northward distribution of trees in the Arctic where soil or moisture conditions seem to be adequate. Whatever is the cause of upper treeline, it follows that photosynthesis is limited by cold temperatures. Where the annual rate of photosynthesis is so slow that cellular respiration would use all the plant's carbohydrates, growth is unable to occur. A tree cannot long endure under these circumstances.

Intuitively, a person would expect that photosynthesis cannot occur as long as snow is present, but this may not be the case. Experiments show that as long as the ground is not frozen, water transport and photosynthesis may begin in spring long before the snow is melted. Furthermore, it has been demonstrated that blue wavelengths of light required for photosynthesis may penetrate snow to a depth of over 30 inches (80 cm). The observation means that some plants may be able to carry on photosynthesis under the snowpack!

Under the best of conditions at treeline, however, photosynthesis barely exceeds cellular respiration, and growth rate is slow. John Muir counted the tree rings of a Whitebark Pine that was only 6 inches (15 cm) in diameter, and he found the tree to be 426 years old. One of its twigs, about 1/8 inch (3 mm) in diameter, was 75 years old.

In California, most of the trees of the subalpine zone are five-needle pines that occur in single-species stands. In some areas of the northern Sierra, however, Mountain Hemlock, *Tsuga mertensiana,* is the most common species (fig. 5.3). A member of the pine family (Pinaceae), Mountain Hemlock looks like a fir, but its needles are blunter and stick out all around the branchlets. It is distributed in cold climates throughout northwestern North America from Alaska to California. In California it is the most common subalpine tree in the Klamath Province (pl. 4C) and the northern Sierra Nevada as far south as Yosemite National Park. In the Cascade Province it is most common on Mount Shasta. Where it is common in the subalpine zone, soil is thick enough and remains moist enough to support these cold-tolerant but moisture-requiring trees. South of Yosemite it is restricted to pockets of moist soil at high elevation. At its southernmost locality, near Silliman Lake, it is localized on a spring-fed, rocky slope.

Two species of juniper also occur in the subalpine zone. Junipers are in the cypress family (Cupressaceae). Their leaves are not needle-like, as are those of the pines, but are small, flat scales that adhere tightly to the branches. The cones are berrylike and provide an important food for subalpine animals. In the central portion of the Sierra Nevada, high-elevation pines may be joined by Sierra Juniper, *Juniperus occidentalis australis* (fig. 4.48), although this species is more common on dry, exposed sites. This tree is discussed in chapter 4 as a component of Lodgepole–Red Fir Forest.

The true subalpine juniper is known as Pygmy Juniper, *Juniperus communis.* It occurs at scattered localities from Mono Pass, in Yosemite, to Mount Shasta. In California this juniper is rather rare, although its distribution is circumpolar, including Alaska, Canada, Greenland, and Eurasia. In more favorable localities, outside the harsh subalpine zone, this species may occur as a small tree; in these locations it is known as Common Juniper. Similar to Western Hemlock, this common northern species reaches its southernmost distribution at high elevation in the Sierra Nevada.

The two subalpine junipers, Sierra Juniper and Pygmy Juniper, clearly are relicts. Both species enjoy widespread distribution to the north, where they may grow in extensive stands (fig. 6.13). Their patchy distribution in California may be due partly to the apparent requirement that in order to germinate, their seeds first must be passed through the digestive tract of an animal. This provides an acid treatment known as scarification. It is a requirement in other plants as well, and will be mentioned later.

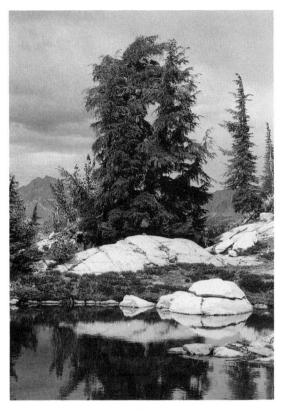

FIGURE 5.3 Mountain Hemlock, *Tsuga mertensiana*, in Subalpine Forest near Anne Lake, Sierra National Forest.

It is noteworthy that in the Rocky Mountains, a bird known as the Bohemian Waxwing, *Bombycilla garrulus*, was observed to pass 900 juniper berries through its digestive tract in a period of five hours!

The most characteristic pines of the subalpine zone are the five-needle pines. These trees dominate the Subalpine Forest throughout most of the state, including Mount Shasta, the Warner Mountains, the Sierra Nevada from Yosemite south, the Transverse and Peninsular ranges, and mountaintops in the Great Basin. These trees have short needles, less than 3 inches (8 cm) in length, that occur in clumps of five. There are four species of these pines in the subalpine zone of California. True to the ecologic-island concept, their ranges barely overlap. Each species usually occurs in a pure stand.

The four species of subalpine pines may be divided into two subgroups composed of closely related species. One subgroup includes Whitebark Pine, *Pinus albicaulis*, and Limber Pine, *Pinus flexilis*. The other includes Foxtail Pine, *Pinus balfouriana*, and Bristlecone Pine, *Pinus longaeva*. The two groups may be distinguished by the appearance of the needles. Trees in the latter group are characterized by short needles, seldom longer than 1 1/2 inches (4 cm) that grow for a considerable distance along each stem. The former group has needles up to 2 1/2 inches (8 cm) in length, and they occur mostly on the terminal portions of the stems, giving each stem the appearance of a bottle brush.

Other pines that sometimes occur in the subalpine zone are Lodgepole Pines and Western White Pines, both typical components of Lodgepole–Red Fir Forest, at lower elevation. Lodgepole Pine (figs. 4.46, 5.4) may look very much like Whitebark or Limber Pine. All three species have the same "cornflake" bark, and needles are concentrated on the tips of the stems. Inspection of the needles will distinguish the Lodgepole Pine, whose needles occur in clumps of two. Western White Pine (fig. 4.47) has needles in clumps of five, but the tree is not likely to appear dwarfed or krummholzed. Western White Pine cones are large, up to 8 inches (20 cm) in length, and the bark is usually distinctly checkered.

Limber Pines and Whitebark Pines are nearly identical in appearance. In their zone of overlap, the only sure way to tell them apart is by examining the cones. Cones of Limber Pines are small versions of the cones on Sugar Pines and Western White Pines, except that they have thick scales, and they seldom exceed 6 inches (15 cm) in length. Cones of Whitebark Pines are seldom seen because they are deciduous when dry; they fall apart. Furthermore, most Whitebark Pine cones are consumed while they are green by squirrels and birds, as will be discussed later. A five-needle pine occurring near timberline with no evidence of cones is usually a Whitebark Pine. If it looks like a Whitebark Pine, but cones are visible on the tree, it usually is a Limber Pine.

Whitebark Pine (fig. 5.5) is probably the most common subalpine pine. These trees frequently grow in clumps at or near treeline (pl. 2C). Distances between clumps vary with the terrain, but 20 to 30 feet (6–10 m) is common. Whitebarks grow in open woodland with very little understory. They often are found growing on coarse, bare soil at the edge of a meadow. At lower elevation, or in protected sites, they are capable of growing straight and tall, up to 50 feet (15 m) in height. In the Whitebark's most common location, in areas where glacial scour has removed most of the soil, the trees are seldom over 10 to 15 feet (3–5 m) tall. At timberline they are often krummholzed. At high elevation they may reach great age, although they do not reach the age of the other subalpine pines. The oldest Whitebark Pine recorded in the Sierra Nevada was a full 1000 years of age.

Few Whitebark cones escape being consumed by squirrels or birds (fig. 5.6). The ones that do, and that do not fall apart, will be observed to be small and circular with very thick scales. Golden-mantled Ground Squirrels, *Spermophilus lateralis* (pl. 12D), climb the trees and gnaw on the green cones as if they were apples. Often the central core is all that is not eaten. Birds such as Clark's Nutcrackers, *Nucifraga columbiana*, tend to peck large holes in the cones, nearly hollowing them out as they gather the seeds. These high-elevation members of the jay family bury the seeds

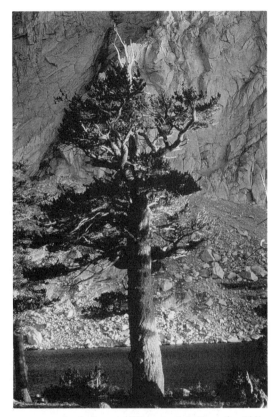

FIGURE 5.4   Lodgepole Pine on shoreline of middle
Crabtree Lake, Sequoia National Park. Old specimens of
Lodgepole Pine in the Subalpine Forest exhibit a growth
pattern of thick trunk and short branches, which is typical of other subalpine tree species.

and retrieve them the following spring. Seeds that are not retrieved may germinate,
which appears to be one of the reasons that Whitebark Pines often grow in clumps.

Limber Pines have only limited distribution in the Sierra Nevada. They grow
mostly in small groves on dry sites in association with Lodgepole Pines. These sites
are most common in steep eastern-slope canyons south of Mammoth. Limber Pines
seem to grow by default at high, dry locations where nothing else will grow—
analogous, perhaps, to Whitebark Pines growing on cold, dry localities with very
little soil.

Limber Pine is widely distributed throughout desert ranges in the Great Basin,
where they may be the only tree species in the subalpine zone. In southern California,
groves of Limber Pines occur at patchy localities on high peaks in the Transverse and
Peninsular ranges. The southernmost trees apparently occur on Toro Peak in the Santa

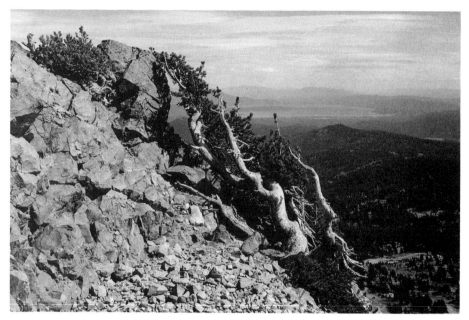

FIGURE 5.5   Krummholzed Whitebark Pine, *Pinus albicaulis*, on an exposed site near the summit of Mount Lassen.

FIGURE 5.6   Whitebark Pine cone partly consumed while still on the tree.

Rosa Mountains. Two localities where hikers are apt to see them are on Mount San Gorgonio, in the San Bernardino Mountains, and on Mount Baden-Powell, in the San Gabriel Mountains. One of the most spectacular Limber Pines is on the ridge near the summit of Mount Baden-Powell (fig. 5.7). Erosion by the wind had carried away most of the coarse soil, leaving its root system elevated. Approaching the tree from below, one observes blue sky between the ground and the root system. This tree has been dated in excess of 1200 years. The oldest recorded Limber Pine was a 2500-year-old specimen near Robinson Lake, in the Onion Valley area of the eastern Sierra Nevada, and a 2300-year-old specimen has been found on Mount San Jacinto. Most specimens, however, are no older than 250 years.

In the White Mountains and the southern Sierra Nevada, Limber Pines occur in the Subalpine Forest in association with Bristlecone Pines. Southwest of Lone Pine they occur in association with Foxtail and Lodgepole pines on the eastern slopes near Cottonwood Creek, and on Siretta Peak. Farther north, in Onion Valley, for example, Limber Pines may occur with lower populations of Whitebark Pines. On the west slope of the Sierra near Mount Whitney there is a region near Crabtree Meadow where Limber Pines, Whitebark Pines, and Foxtail Pines grow in close proximity. Here, Foxtails are on deep, coarse soils, and Limber Pines are on south-facing slopes with less soil. Limber Pines are not common.

The other subgroup of subalpine five-needle pines includes Foxtail and Bristlecone pines. If these trees grew together, they would be difficult to tell apart. Their distribution, however, never overlaps. In California, Bristlecone Pines are common only in the White Mountains on the east side of Owens Valley. Foxtail Pines are five-needle pines of the southern Sierra Nevada and Klamath Province. Both species have needles that are very stiff and short, seldom longer than $1\frac{1}{2}$ inches (4 cm). The needles remain on the tree for many years, which gives it a firlike appearance because the needles are not restricted to tufts on the ends of stems. The advantage of retaining needles for many years is that photosynthetic tissue is retained in adequate supply to provide food even though the amount of new growth for any year might be quite small. On Foxtail Pines needles have been reported to remain on trees up to 30 years. On Bristlecone Pines needles are reported to remain on the trees up to 45 years.

Foxtail Pines differ in appearance from other trees they may grow with (fig. 5.8). Needles grow all along the branchlets, and the weight of these needles may cause the branchlets to droop. It is the droopy branchlet, resembling fox's tail, that is the source of the tree's name. The bark of these trees differs from the "cornflake" bark of other subalpine trees. Resembling most closely the bark of Western White Pines, Foxtail bark breaks up into squares that are usually about 1 to $1\frac{1}{2}$ inches (2.5–4 cm) across, smaller than those of Western White Pine.

Unlike other subalpine species, Foxtail Pines seldom become krummholzed (pl. 2B). In particularly exposed sites on ridgetops, however, they may assume prostrate forms. Krummholzed Foxtail Pines may be viewed on the ridge above Rocky Basin Lakes in the Golden Trout Wilderness. In spite of the harsh climate and fierce wind,

FIGURE 5.7   Limber Pine, *Pinus flexilis*, on Mount Baden-Powell, San Gabriel Mountains, Angeles National Forest.

these trees usually remain erect, with a single stout trunk. The effect of the wind is that branches may all grow out of one side of the tree, a phenomenon known as flagging (fig. 5.9). Another effect of abrasive wind is that all the bark containing the living tissue needed to nourish a few living branches remains on the leeward side of the trunk. This sometimes causes what are known as "piggyback" trunks, a phenomenon that occurs when a branch on the leeward side of the trunk begins to grow erect. After many years, perhaps hundreds, this branch may form a new trunk. These trees have few enemies other than the climate and may be the oldest trees in the Sierra. The oldest specimen, aged at 3300 years, occurs on the south side of Split Mountain, near the northern end of its distribution in the Sierra. In the Sierra Nevada, only giant Sierra Redwoods are known to rival Foxtail Pines in age.

In spite of their great age, Foxtail Pines never reach the size of Sierra Redwoods. However, they are quite large for subalpine species. The largest Foxtail Pine is located at about 10,000 feet (3000 m) on a ridge above Timber Gap, in Sequoia National

FIGURE 5.8   Foxtail Pines, *Pinus balfouriana*, near Chickenspring Lake, Inyo National Forest.

FIGURE 5.9   Foxtail Pine flagged by the wind.
Nine Lakes Basin, Sequoia National Park.

Park. The diameter of the trunk is 8 1/2 feet (2.5 m), and it is over 70 feet (23 m) tall.

Most of the very old Foxtail Pines are only partly living (fig. 5.10). They inhabit the most exposed sites, where the wind has denuded most of the bark. In more protected localities they grow straight and tall and are conspicuous only because of their drooping, needle-covered side branches.

Their distribution is most common on coarse well-drained soils. On south-facing slopes they form pure stands of thick-trunked trees up to 30 feet (10 m) in height. Foxtails have a well-developed root system. Roots are widespread and penetrate deeply in order to absorb water from the well-drained soil. It may be this requirement for relatively deep soil that keeps these trees from expanding their distribution northward into the region occupied mainly by Whitebark Pines, where repeated glacial scouring has removed most of the soil.

The distribution of Foxtail Pines is the enigma of subalpine vegetation. Foxtails do not occur outside the state of California, and within the state there is a 300-mile (480-km) disjunction in their distribution between the Klamath Province and the southern Sierra Nevada. In the Klamath Province they occur at scattered localities, but the bulk of the population is in the upper Trinity Alps on south-facing, serpentine soils.

The disjunct distribution of Foxtail Pines is typical of a number of plant species, but the ecologic features responsible are not understood. One hypothesis associates these disjunctions with the distribution of summer rain. This may be true for Foxtails on southern exposures in the Kern and Cottonwood basins, but summer rain seems unlikely to be an important feature for populations on the west slope of the Sierra in the upper Kings River drainage. Summer rain may be a factor in the Trinities, but Foxtails grow there in the rain shadow, in drier localities.

A second hypothesis relates to light and/or temperature. Foxtails grow best on south-facing slopes with deep soil. These slopes are desertlike in terms of sunlight and dryness. The presence of deep, penetrating roots is a desertlike adaptation not shared by other subalpine trees. Long retention of needles probably enables the Foxtail to optimize intense light in order to shift the photosynthesis-metabolism balance in its favor while its deep roots tap the meager water supply.

Perhaps the critical factor in Foxtail distribution involves seed germination or seedling survival. Seed germination may require more heat, which would be optimized on these southern exposures. Once seedlings begin to appear, the intense light could favor root growth with a minimum of foliage, another desertlike adaptation. The similarity between Foxtail and Bristlecone Pines attests to drought tolerance, and the Foxtail's frequent association with other Great Basin species supports the concept that adaptations to a cold, desertlike environment are important.

In California, Bristlecone Pines, *Pinus longaeva*, occur only in a few localities (fig. 5.11). They are common in the subalpine zone of the White Mountains and at high elevations in the Inyo Mountains, the Last Chance Mountains, and the Panamint Mountains, in the southern Basin-Range Province. In Nevada and Utah they occur at

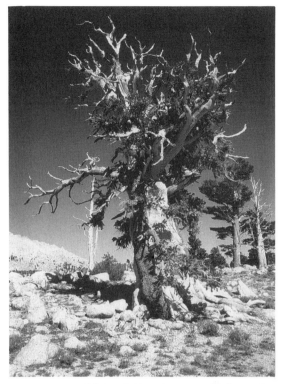

FIGURE 5.10   Old Foxtail Pine, Cottonwood Lakes Basin, Inyo National Forest.

scattered high-elevation localities. In Colorado and New Mexico, in suitable subalpine sites, the species is replaced by the Rocky Mountain Bristlecone Pine, *Pinus aristata*.

Bristlecone Pines are distinctive because their cones bear sharp spines on the end of each scale. Otherwise they resemble Foxtail Pines. The nearest the two species come to each other is 20 airline miles (32 km), across Owens Valley. In the White Mountains, Bristlecones grow in groves. A few Limber Pines grow with them, at lower elevations. Limber Pines are easily distinguished by their longer needles, clustered in tufts at the ends of the stems.

In California, Bristlecone Pines are notable because of their great age. Several specimens have been dated at more than 4000 years. The oldest standing tree, dated at 4600 years, has been named Methuselah and is billed as the oldest living thing. The oldest Bristlecone ever dated was 4900 years of age. Because its size was not appropriate for its great age, it inadvertently was cut down in order to date it. The usual dating technique is to remove a narrow core from the trunk that represents a cross section of the tree rings. On Bristlecone or Foxtail Pines, however, the core may not represent a true cross section of tree rings because new tissue is laid down only under healthy bark, and only a fraction of the outer trunk may be covered with bark.

FIGURE 5.11 Bristlecone Pine, *Pinus longaeva*, in the White Mountains, Inyo County.

Bristlecone Pines are notable for other reasons. They grow in one of the harshest climates possible. The White Mountains lie in the rain shadow of the Sierra Nevada, and where Bristlecone Pines grow, precipitation averages only about 12 inches (30 cm) per year. Snow makes up 99% of the precipitation; therefore growth is delayed until spring, and the growing season is rarely more than a few weeks. Bristlecones grow on the summit of the range, where wind is extreme. Furthermore, they grow on nutrient-poor alkaline soil derived from dolomite, a type of limestone. At the same elevation, on different soil, there is a scrub forest of Curl-leaf Mountain Mahogany, *Cercocarpus ledifolius*, and Great Basin Sagebrush, *Artemisia tridentata*.

In the White Mountains, Bristlecone Pines usually are not krummholzed. In exposed sites they may be short in stature, but they do not exhibit prostrate form. In eastern Nevada, on Mount Washington in the Snake Range, they are krummholzed at timberline. It is speculated that better drought resistance occurs in the White Mountains populations because growth of new needles occurs during summer drought. Because the eastern populations grow where there is summer rain, new needles are not produced during a time of drought stress. When winter wind desiccates the needles, they are poorly prepared and become damaged, forming a typical krummholz growth form.

Growth of these trees is so gradual that tree rings must be counted with a microscope. This slow production of new tissue also makes the wood very dense. At this elevation, decay rates of this wood are very slow, and fallen wood lies around for thousands of years. By overlapping known sequences of narrow and wide tree rings between standing and fallen wood, researchers have identified an absolute sequence of tree rings dating back about 8000 years. Because ring width is an indicator of climate, an estimation of each year's precipitation has been obtained.

An interesting side effect of this 8000-year record is that it has provided a means of checking the accuracy of the carbon-14 dating system. Carbon-14 is formed in the atmosphere by cosmic radiation and is then distributed randomly. The proportion of carbon-14 present in the atmosphere should also appear in plants, because photosynthesis absorbs CO_2 without discriminating against the radioactive form. The same proportion should also be present in the animals that eat the plants. When the plant or animal dies, the amount of carbon-14 within the organism gradually disappears. By measuring the amount of carbon-14 left in a specimen, one can estimate how many years ago the plant or animal died. It had been claimed that organic material can be so dated with reasonable accuracy to ages of 40,000 years. This claim is based on two assumptions. First, the rate of carbon-14 decay must remain consistent through time. Second, the amount of carbon-14 in the atmosphere must remain constant.

When tree rings from Bristlecone Pines were dated using the carbon-14 method, a surprising result occurred: Carbon-14 dating consistently underestimated the age of material older than 2500 years. Tree rings actually 7000 years old were dated radiometrically at only 6000 years of age. Carbon-14 ages were 1000 years too young! Of the two assumptions regarding carbon-14 dating, one of them must be wrong. Either decay rate is not consistent, or the amount of carbon-14 in the atmosphere has not been constant. The rate of decay does not alter: the half-life of carbon-14 is a consistent 5800 years. This means that, no matter how much carbon-14 is present at any given time, it will lose half of its radioactivity in 5800 years. Therefore the second assumption, that the amount of radioactive carbon in the atmosphere has always been the same, must be in error. Evidence from other sources has confirmed this conclusion. The amount of cosmic radiation that forms carbon-14 varies with changes in the composition of the earth's magnetic field and with alterations in sunspot activity.

An important facet of this discovery was that it allowed European artifacts to be dated correctly. Evidence of ancient man in Europe is older than was formerly thought. The oldest evidence of ancient civilization is in western Europe, not the Tigris-Euphrates Valley, as previously assumed. Western European structures such as Stonehenge were redated, and their construction was determined to have begun around 2600 B.C., a full 800 years earlier than was supposed. This means that Stonehenge-type structures were constructed far too early to have been influenced or copied from structures in the Middle East. Likewise, clay tablets from the Balkans were found to be nearly 7000 years old—a full 2000 years older than the oldest known form of writing in ancient Mesopotamia. What all this means is that because

Bristlecone Pines grow in California, in the rain shadow of the Sierra Nevada, we now have a better idea of how ancient civilization developed in Europe!

History of Subalpine Vegetation. The distribution of Subalpine Forest vegetation in the Sierra Nevada can be summarized as follows. Whitebark Pine is the most widely distributed, occupying the central Sierra on glacier-scoured terrain with little soil. North of Yosemite, Whitebark Pine is replaced by Mountain Hemlock. The northern Sierra is not as high as the rest of the range, so subalpine vegetation here occurs at lower elevation, where soil is more abundant. Mountain Hemlock is cold-tolerant but thrives in moist soil, so it is common in the north. The subalpine tree of the southern Sierra is the Foxtail Pine. This deep-rooted species occupies coarse, well-drained slopes with southern exposure and seems to require more soil than Whitebark Pines. In the Sierra, Limber Pines grow in dry canyons on the eastern slope, where they occur in groves among Lodgepole Pines. Their distribution seems to be limited primarily by moisture. Apparently, these dry sites resemble conditions on mountaintops in the Great Basin and in southern California, where Limber Pine is the distinctive subalpine tree. Its present discontinuous distribution is probably relict. They formerly occurred more commonly with lower-elevation species that were widespread about 10,000 years ago, during the moister conditions of the late Pleistocene.

Both Whitebark and Foxtail Pines have disjunct distributions between the Sierra Nevada and areas to the northwest. To the north of the Sierra, Whitebark Pine appears in the Warner Mountains and in the Cascade and Klamath provinces. Because of the northerly distribution, the elevation of the subalpine zone is remarkably low. On ridge crests and summits above 6700 feet (2200 m), particularly on nonglaciated southwestern exposures, there are dwarfed forests of Whitebark Pines. In the Cascades, only Mount Lassen and Mount Shasta have a subalpine zone. Krummholzed Whitebark Pines occupy southwestern exposures on these volcanic peaks (fig. 5.5). In these northern provinces, subalpine sites are not numerous and seem to be characterized by soil and exposure rather than high elevation.

Subalpine vegetation has not always been distributed in an islandlike mosaic. During the Miocene, 10 to 12 million years ago, the Sierra began to rise. Regions to the east began to get drier as the rain shadow increased, and, for other reasons, summer precipitation began to decrease. From pollen records and fossils of certain moisture-loving plants, it can be inferred that abundant summer precipitation continued throughout the Sierra and into southern California until about 1.5 million years ago. Up to that time, subalpine vegetation must have been distributed widely across the western United States.

During periods of extensive glaciation, from about 1 million to 10,000 years ago, ice sheets scoured terrains now occupied by subalpine vegetation. Fossils from the Pleistocene, the Ice Age, indicate that forest belts occurred at considerably lower elevation during that time. Extensive glaciers covered much of the Sierra, but they also were present in the Trinity Alps of the Klamath Province, on Mount Shasta and Mount Lassen in the Cascade Province, in the White Mountains, and as far south as Mount San Gorgonio in the San Bernardino Mountains. Following the end of the Pleistocene, about 10,000 years ago, subalpine vegetation presumably reinvaded the high country from low-elevation refugia. For long-lived plants such as subalpine pines, 10,000 years is not enough time for much speciation to occur. Only four to five generations of Foxtail and Limber pines may have occurred since the end of the Pleistocene. It is possible that there have been only three generations of Bristlecone Pines in the White Mountains since the retreat of the glaciers.

Foxtail and Bristlecone pines have been experimentally hybridized, indicating they are very closely related. In fact, evolution of the two species probably resulted from the forest separating into two populations as the Owens Valley sank and the Sierra Nevada and the White Mountains rose on each side. This geologic event and the coincident speciation probably began about 10 to 12 million years ago.

Studies of Whitebark and Limber pines indicate that they do not hybridize even though they may grow together, as they do in several localities at the lower fringe of Whitebark pine distribution in the central Sierra. This lack of hybridization implies that the speciation event occurred a long time ago. Whitebark Pine probably is a northern species, and Limber Pine is a Rocky Mountain, or southern, form accustomed to more summer precipitation.

These pines must be considered relicts. Perhaps their continued existence is threatened by increasing dryness since the end of the Pleistocene. Studies of fallen wood from Bristlecone Pines show that in the last 1000 years, upper treeline has been lowered by nearly 3000 feet (1000 m), perhaps in association with a change in summer temperature or a decrease in annual precipitation. In eastern Nevada, it has been speculated that a similar lowering of upper treeline may be due to an increase in summer precipitation over the last 4000 years. This trend certainly seems not to apply in the White Mountains.

Fossil evidence shows that until about 12 million years ago, the widespread Subalpine Forest was composed of many species. It was a diversified forest that has gradually become impoverished. Today in the eastern Great Basin there may be up to four species of subalpine trees in a mixed forest. This is where summer precipitation is still significant. In California, however, an area of Subalpine Forest seldom contains more than two dominant species. Single-species stands are most common. Furthermore, in California each of the four species of subalpine five-needle pines has a different, barely overlapping geographic distribution. Perhaps extensive Pleistocene glaciation in California reduced the former forest to localized pockets of trees in single-species stands. Different species must have been isolated in different localities. Reinvasion of specialized high-country habitats from low-elevation refugia occurred opportunistically by whatever species was nearby.

Refugia may have been extensive. Fossil evidence shows that during the Pleistocene, Foxtail and Bristlecone pines occurred at considerably lower elevations. Fossil Foxtail cones are found in Pleistocene deposits at Clear Lake, in the northern Coast Range. This locality is 5000 feet (1600 m) below and 65 miles (100 km) south of the nearest presently growing population in the Klamath Mountains. All over the Great Basin there is evidence of Bristlecone Pines that grew more than 2000 feet (700 m) lower than they do today. It must have been a species with widespread distribution during the Pleistocene.

It also could be argued that each island of subalpine climate is uniquely harsh, and that from a refugium of several species only one had the ability to tolerate the unique combination of ecological circumstances in a particular locality. In effect, each subalpine species today occurs in its locality by default; nothing else can tolerate the specific mix of conditions. This hypothesis seems simpler and therefore more believable, but it leads to the search for a suite of similarities and tolerances to explain apparent disjunctions in distribution. For example, it is difficult to imagine what elements of the climate could be similar between the southern Sierra Nevada and the Klamath Province of northwestern California. Foxtail Pines grow in both places, but nowhere in between.

Changes in montane vegetation during and since the Pleistocene can be analyzed by studying pollen, needle, and cone assemblages found in lake sediments. Similar climatic changes from the deserts can be analyzed by studying organic material fossilized in woodrat middens, which are piles of vegetational debris preserved by rat urine in rock crevices and other dry places. For example, we can infer that a coniferous forest of Rocky Mountain affinities was once more extensive in what is now the eastern Mojave Desert because a woodrat midden on Clark Mountain revealed that Rocky Mountain White Fir, *Abies concolor concolor*, has existed there continuously for 28,000 years. Distribution of Rocky Mountain White Fir in the area today is restricted to north-facing slopes above 6000 feet (1900 m) in the Clark Mountains, Kingston Mountains, New York Mountains, and Charleston Mountains north of Las Vegas. Species analyses in the Sierra Nevada suggest a drying trend following the retreat of glaciers about 10,000 years ago. Then, about 6000 years ago, a moist period including summer precipitation became apparent. At this time there was an increase of Mountain Hemlock, firs, and Limber Pine in the Sierra Nevada. At the same time in the Great Basin, there was an increase in the two-needle version of pinyon pine, indicating a similar trend. This was followed by another dry period, interrupted by a short glacial episode about 600 years ago. Apparently, the glaciers that remain in California today date back to that "little ice age."

Animals of the Subalpine Zone. In general, mammals of the subalpine zone are shared with the Lodgepole–Red Fir Forest or the alpine zone. Unlike plants of the subalpine zone, endemism or restricted distribution of subalpine mammals seems not to occur frequently. Golden-mantled Ground Squirrels, *Spermophilus lateralis* (pl. 12D), are perhaps the most conspicuous. They feed on pine seeds and the cones of Whitebark Pines, and in the spring they eat various fungi, such as truffles. Chipmunks, such as the Alpine Chipmunk, *Tamias alpinus*, also occur here, feeding on seeds, buds, and insects.

Certain birds of the subalpine zone exhibit some interesting behavior. Perhaps the most conspicuous member of the Subalpine Forest is Clark's Nutcracker, *Nucifraga columbiana* (fig. 5.12), the high-elevation member of the jay family (Corvidae). Resembling the Gray Jay, *Perisoreus canadensis*, of the Rockies, it is a large gray bird

FIGURE 5.12   Clark's Nutcracker, *Nucifraga columbiana*.

with black wings and white wing bars. These birds are uncommonly noisy. Their raucus sounds attract attention throughout the subalpine zone.

In winter, Clark's Nutcrackers migrate to lower elevations, usually to the pinyon pine zone. Nutcrackers gather seeds of Whitebark, Limber, Bristlecone, Foxtail, pinyon, and Jeffrey pines, and they store them in caches for the following winter and spring. Research shows that one Clark's Nutcracker may store up to 38,000 pine seeds in a single season, and it has been demonstrated that they locate these caches by memory. Birds are known to lack a well-developed sense of smell. Nutcrackers remember patterns of rocks and trees in the vicinity where they bury their seeds, and relocation of rocks can cause them to dig for them in the wrong place. Many stored seeds are never recovered and subsequently sprout. The clumping pattern commonly associated with Whitebark Pines has been attributed to this phenomenon, as has clumping of Limber and Bristlecone pines. These pines do not have winged seeds; hence Clark's Nutcracker is probably the major mode of dispersal.

Nutcrackers store seeds in two ways. They disperse them in forested areas and at lower elevations, particularly in the pinyon pine zone. Seeds are also concentrated in a communal cache on a slope of at least 20° to 30°. Nutcrackers have a pouch in the throat—the crop—where they can carry many seeds. It has been demonstrated that they will bury up to 15 seeds in a cache. Do Clark's Nutcrackers know how to count, or is the number of seeds dictated by the size of the crop? Although the answer has not been determined, the strategy of burying seeds in small caches is to make it energetically foolish for other animals to search randomly for them; more than 15 seeds per cache would be a reward worth searching for. Likewise, the energy expended in searching for seeds on a steep slope would not be rewarded unless the animal knew where to look.

In late August and September, Clark's Nutcrackers become concentrated in the Foxtail Pines of the southern Sierra. The young have fledged and are able to fly, but they are still being fed by the adults. Much of the racket associated with groups of Clark's Nutcrackers is from young birds begging for food. As winter sets in, they move downslope, particularly on the east side, to overwinter at lower elevations in the pinyon pines.

About 30 species of birds can be identified as typical of the subalpine zone. Most of them migrate to escape the rigors of winter. Some of them, such as the Hermit Thrush (fig. 4.51), go to Mexico. Others, such as American Robins, move into the western foothills. Clark's Nutcrackers and White-crowned Sparrows (fig. 4.41) move down the east side of the Sierra. Mountain Bluebirds, *Sialia currucoides*, congregate in large flocks and move to the Central Valley or to the Great Basin for the winter.

Mountain Bluebirds are conspicuous cavity-nesting birds of the subalpine zone. They nest in abandoned woodpecker holes and feed in nearby meadows. They are conspicuous by virtue of their bright blue feathers and their habit of hovering in open space while searching for insects on the ground. They are frequently observed perching on a high open snag, from which they are able to dart out and grab insects on the fly.

The reproductive behavior of these birds has been used as an example of how natural selection favors species that produce the greatest number of offspring. Once a pair-bond is established between a male and a female, they take turns tending the nest. If a male returns to the nest and finds another male attentive to his mate, he will drive away the intruder. He will drive away the mate as well, but not until he has pulled out some of her feathers. If, however, the female already has laid a clutch of eggs, for which he is the father, he will pay little attention to either the intruding male or his mate. The implication is that the important thing is for the bird to pass on his genetic material to the next generation. If he already has mated and his mate is tending a clutch of eggs, it would be counterproductive to drive her away, because he would be left to attend the nest himself. On the other hand, if he finds that another male has been attentive to his mate before the eggs are laid, it is possible that he would be expending energy to rear another male's offspring. To prevent that, he drives away both the male and female, maims her to make her less attractive, and proceeds to court and mate with another female. In this way he optimizes the production of his own offspring.

Pinyon-Juniper Woodland

Pinyon-Juniper Woodland is the lowest of the mountain communities, or it may be considered the uppermost desert community. Because the community often becomes isolated as ecologic islands on the tops of desert ranges, it will be discussed here.

Pinyon pines occur in the most hostile of habitats, experiencing snow and cold in the winter, followed by heat and drought in summer. The trees grow on rocky, exposed ridges where wind is often intense. Nevertheless, this is one of the most attractive landscapes of desert mountains. Pinyon pines are the nut pines. Their large

FIGURE 5.13   Single-needle Pinyon Pine, *Pinus monophylla*.

seeds, known as piñones (pine nuts), which were a staple for Indians, still may be purchased in specialty stores.

The Single-needle Pinyon Pine, *Pinus monophylla* (fig. 5.13), occurs at upper-elevation localities on mountain ranges of the Basin-Range Province, and southward along the eastern side of Sierra Nevada.

There are three other kinds of pinyon pines in California. Another single-needle type, *Pinus californiarum californiarum*, formerly considered synonymous with *Pinus monophylla*, occurs in the mountains of the eastern Mojave Desert and the eastern side of the Peninsular Ranges southward into Baja California. A two-needle form, *Pinus californiarum fallux* (= *Pinus edulis*), occurs at high elevation in the eastern Mojave, in the New York Mountains and the Mid Hills area to the southeast (fig. 5.14). The Four-needle Pinyon Pine, *Pinus quadrifolia*, occurs in patches in the Peninsular Ranges from Garner Valley in the Santa Rosa Mountains south to the northern part of Baja California. At some localities, Single-needle Pinyon Pine overlaps with one of the other types. Hybridization occurs in these overlap areas.

Differences in appearance and microhabitat are apparent among these different kinds of pinyon pine. In the New York Mountains where the two-needle and single-needle types occur together, the two-needle form occurs at higher elevation. At the summit it occurs with a few Rocky Mountain White Firs. Both White Firs and pinyon pines enjoy widespread distribution throughout the Great Basin eastward to the Rocky Mountains. The pinyon pine's occurrence in the New York Mountains represents its

FIGURE 5.14   Two-needle Pinyon Pine, *Pinus californiarum fallux*, in the New York Mountains, San Bernardino County.

westernmost extreme in distribution. Ongoing studies of the two types of pinyon pine here seem to indicate that there is a broad range of intergradation between the upper-elevation two-needle form and the lower-elevation one-needle form. Intergrade characteristics include variations in color, anatomy, and number of needles, as well as differences in the cones.

Where the Single-needle Pinyon Pine overlaps with the four-needle species in the Peninsular Ranges, the four-needle type occurs farther from the desert. Its habitat is on gravel flats and slopes associated with Great Basin Sagebrush and Jeffrey Pine. The Single-needle Pinyon occurs to the east, on ridges bordering the desert. In an area east of Tecate, just south of the border in Baja California, there appears to be a hybrid swarm between the two species (fig. 5.15). Pure Four-needle Pinyon Pines tend to be broadly pyramidal in shape, and the foliage is blue-green. Pure Single-needle Pinyon Pines have a sprawling, rounded shape, and the needles are yellow-green. The apparent hybrids show both color and shape variations, and the needles occur in clusters of one, two, three, four, and five!

These four-needle pines were probably carried to their present latitude by drift along the San Andreas fault. When the Baja California peninsula was farther south, these trees would have been adjacent to the range of the three-needle Mexican Pinyon

FIGURE 5.15   Pinyon pine hybridization near Tecate, Baja California. Single-needle Pinyon Pine, *Pinus californiarum californiarum*, to the left; Four-needle Pinyon Pine, *Pinus quadrifolia*, to the right; and a hybrid in between.

Pine, *Pinus cembroides*. It is possible that the four-needle type was derived from the three-needle species since Baja California began to move away from the mainland.

Throughout their range, Single-needle Pinyon Pines are associated with various species of juniper. On the eastern side of the Sierra, from the Bridgeport area north to the Nevada state line, pinyon pines are associated with Sierra Juniper, *Juniperus occidentalis australis* (fig 4.48). Eastward, throughout the Great Basin and Mojave, pinyon pines are associated with Utah Juniper, *Juniperus osteosperma*. In southern California and northward to the southern Sierra Nevada, Single-needle Pinyon Pine is associated with California Juniper, *Juniperus californica*. Ranges of California Juniper and Utah Juniper overlap on the north side of the Transverse Ranges, where Utah Juniper has spotty distribution. All three species of juniper are found on the north side of the San Bernardino Mountains.

Pinyon pines tend to occur on rocky slopes and ridges. Junipers tend to occur on coarse soils of the upper slopes. Because of these habitat preferences, it is not uncommon for junipers and pinyon pines to occur in the absence of each other. California Juniper occurs to the exclusion of Single-needle Pinyon Pine in southern California in the Elsinore Valley near Perris, between the Santa Ana and San Jacinto Ranges. It also occurs in similar habitat on the eastern side of the Coast Ranges, bordering the Great Central Valley.

Other associated plants of Pinyon-Juniper Woodland include various members of other drought- and snow-tolerant communities, such as Sagebrush Scrub, Blackbrush

Scrub, and Desert Chaparral. Included among these species are various manzanitas (*Arctostaphylos* spp.), mountain mahoganies (*Cercocarpus* spp.), and scrub oaks (*Quercus* spp.). Surprisingly, two snow-tolerant species of prickly pear cactus (*Opuntia* spp.) reach the upper-elevation limit of their distribution in the Pinyon-Juniper Woodland. These species are characterized by rather long spines, which may form a sort of fur coat that helps insulate the cacti.

Animals of the Pinyon-Juniper Woodland tend to be transient species. Food for these animals is surprisingly abundant and includes pine seeds (piñones), acorns, and juniper berries. Browse is available in the form of shoots and young twigs on Antelope Brush and mountain mahoganies. Indians also found abundant food in the pinyon zone, spending summer and autumn months at higher elevation and winter in the desert or at the coast.

During summer months, desert animal species move up into the Pinyon-Juniper Woodland to escape the heat. This group includes a variety of birds and large Mammals, such as Desert Bighorn Sheep, *Ovis canadensis nelsoni*. On the western borders of the desert where the mountains are high, numerous alpine and subalpine species migrate down the mountain to the Pinyon-Juniper Woodland in winter. These also include the California Bighorn Sheep, *O. c. californiana*, and various bird species, such as Clark's Nutcracker and Steller's Jay.

One bird that is identified particularly with Pinyon-Juniper Woodland is the Pinyon Jay, *Gymnorhinus cyanocephalus*. This jay differs from others by its uniform blue color and lack of a crest. These jays feed in large, noisy flocks that move incessantly from tree to tree. In the Peninsular Ranges, Pinyon Jays are also associated with Jeffrey Pines.

The importance of these birds for seed dispersal has been well documented. Clark's Nutcrackers and Pinyon Jays have been observed to cache seeds as far as 14 miles (22 km) from the parent trees. One study documented a flock of 150 Clark's Nutcrackers that succeeded in caching between 3.3 and 5 million seeds in a single season.

Alpine Zone

The alpine zone is the land above the trees. It was named in honor of the European Alps, but C. Hart Merriam called it the Arctic-Alpine zone, referring to the similarity of Alpine Tundra to Arctic Tundra. It is common for various authors to refer to the alpine zone as tundra, as if there were only one kind of community above treeline. At the other extreme are authors who find up to 31 different categories of alpine vegetation. This book will use six categories, broadly delineated according to soil characteristics and available moisture (table 5.1).

In a general sense, the alpine climate is one of intense light, temperature extremes, extreme wind, and short growing season. The important difference between arctic and alpine climates is that in the Arctic, day length in the summer is very long. One of the critical limiting factors for plants in the alpine zone is cold nights.

In the alpine zone of the Sierra Nevada, the precipitation of 35 to 40 inches (87–100 cm) per year is virtually all snow. Summer thunderstorms contribute patchy

TABLE 5.1   A Summary of Alpine Communities

1. Alpine pioneer zones
   · Rock faces, talus slopes
   · Little or no soil
   · Plant indicators: crustose lichens, Sky Pilot, Alpine Gold
   · Animals: Pika, Yellow-bellied Marmot

2. Alpine fellfields
   · Rocky gravel flats and slopes, patterned ground
   · Rapid percolation, strong wind, needle ice
   · Plant indicators: cushion plants
   · Animals: White-tailed Jack Rabbit, California Bighorn Sheep

3. Alpine heath
   · Open shrubland
   · Upper edges of meadows and lake shores
   · Plant indicators: heathers, willows
   · Animals: sparrows, warblers

4. Dry meadows
   · Well-drained acidic soil
   · Higher parts of meadows below the shrub zone
   · Plant indicators: mat-forming grasses, bunchgrasses, sedges, wildflowers
   · Animals: gophers, voles, Mule Deer

5. Wet meadows
   · Organic waterlogged soil, hummocks, peat
   · Lower parts of meadows; may border streams, lakes, or bogs
   · Plant indicators: sod-forming sedges and grasses

6. Snowfields
   · Areas where snow remains most of year
   · North-facing slopes, protected ridges
   · Plant indicators: "snow algae"
   · Animals: nematodes, rotifers, ice crawlers

precipitation that may be locally heavy. To the north, total annual precipitation is greater, but due to the lower elevations, alpine regions are less common there.

The greatest expanse of alpine terrain occurs from Lake Tahoe southward. From Sonora Pass south to the Cottonwood Basin it forms a discontinuous belt, broken broadly by the headwaters of the San Joaquin River near Mammoth Lakes. Near Lake Tahoe, alpine zones occur above 9900 feet (3000 m). To the south, the elevation of alpine terrain gradually increases to 11,000 feet (3300 m). In the southern Sierra Nevada, alpine communities are divided by the Kern River gorge. Along the western divide they extend southward to the Mineral King area. The Cottonwood Lakes area is the southernmost alpine region of any size along the main divide. Southward, distribution is patchy.

In southern California, due to drier conditions, the alpine zone occurs above 10,000 feet (3050 m). It is well represented only on three peaks: Mount San Antonio (Baldy), Mount San Gorgonio, and Mount San Jacinto. Other high peaks such as Mount Baden-Powell and Cucamonga Peak have small areas of alpine vegetation. Some authors contend that these southern California peaks do not have true alpine vegetation, that the alpine appearance is a consequence of strong winds and poor soil. There is a strong resemblance to the alpine vegetation of the Great Basin.

North of the Sierra Nevada, alpine vegetation occurs on Mount Lassen, Mount Shasta, and several localities in the Klamath Province, where the elevation of the alpine zone drops to about 8000 feet (2400 m). The alpine zone of the Klamath Province is a good deal wetter than it is in the Sierra. In this respect it resembles what one might find in the Pacific Northwest. Inclusion of some Sierran and Great Basin elements makes it unique.

In the California portion of the Great Basin, alpine vegetation is well established only in the White Mountains above 11,400 feet (3400 m), where it is divisible based on several distinct soil types. Similarly, in the Inyo Mountains to the south, there is a strong edaphic influence. The only other area of the Great Basin in California that supports alpine vegetation is Eagle Peak above 9000 feet (2700 m), in the Warner Mountains. Here the terrain is volcanic. What makes the alpine zone of the Great Basin unique is its intense solar radiation. It has been claimed that the solar radiation in the White Mountains is more intense, for this latitude, than anywhere else on the planet.

In California, the alpine zone is notable for occurring in a region of Mediterranean climate. Throughout the rest of North America, high mountains occur in regions where there is abundant summer precipitation. In the Rocky Mountains or in mountain ranges to the north of California there is commonly cloud cover and frequent rain in the alpine zone during summer months. In California, with the possible exception of the Klamath Province, summer days are clear.

Most alpine plants are drought-adapted perennials. It is interesting that many alpine plants have near relatives that are desert plants, including buckwheats, lupines, grasses, and many members of the sunflower family. The Sierra Nevada is further unique by having alpine plants that complete their entire life cycle in one season. These are known as ephemeral or annual plants. During a single growing season, they germinate from seeds and complete their growth and flowering in time to set seed, which is also a strategy of many desert plants. Accomplishing an entire life cycle in less than one year requires abundant sunlight. No other mountain range has a significant number of annual plants because no other mountain range has enough light in the summer. There is only one ephemeral species in the Rocky Mountains, for example.

The close relationship between Sierran alpine plants and desert plants might be expected for two reasons. First, the climate is similar: both are regions of drought and high light intensity. Second, the desert is nearby, which means that winds, birds, or other dispersal agents can carry seeds from one location to the other in a short period of time. Alpine and desert areas could share a reservoir of similar species.

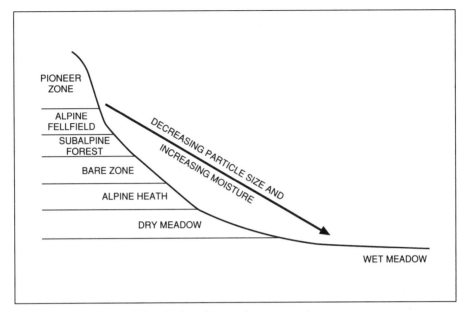

FIGURE 5.16 Generalized distribution of mountaintop vegetation.

In the Sierra Nevada, alpine communities are found south of Lake Tahoe. Here soil has a strong influence on the distribution of plant communities. Soil particle size influences water-holding capacity and drainage. Soil is also important because of the specific chemical composition associated with the rock from which it was weathered. North of Bishop there is a good deal of metamorphic rock in the high country. Sandstone, limestone, volcanic rocks, and schist weather into soils of different consistency and chemistry. In the Carson Pass area, a thorough study of alpine vegetation found that distribution of vegetation types was related positively to parameters such as snow depth, soil moisture, and parent rock material, with the last factor judged to be highly significant. Likewise, in the White Mountains, where many rock types are present, the alpine vegetation has been classified according to soil type based on parent rock material.

In the southern Sierra Nevada most parent rock material is granitic. Here the distribution of vegetation is clearly a function of water availability based on particle size of the soil. Progressing from steep cliff faces, where there is virtually no soil, to the center of meadows, soil particle size gradually gets smaller, and available soil moisture gradually increases. Along this gradient are distributed most of the alpine communities (fig. 5.16). Exposure to wind and sun and duration of snowpack are other locally important variables.

Alpine Pioneer Zones. Pioneer vegetation is the first to inhabit a bare area. Pioneer zones occur on cliff faces and talus slopes, where soil is so scarce that there is not enough substratum for typical plants to take root. Most of the vegetation here is made up of crustose lichens that occur in colorful patches on bare rock surfaces. These organisms derive their moisture from the air or from that which condenses on the rock. The fungal component of the lichen anchors it to the rock, and the algal component provides the photosynthesis. The weak acid produced by the fungus as it metabolizes is a primary force that gradually breaks up the rock into particles of soil.

Angular boulders break off of cliff faces to form rubble piles known as talus slopes. Lichens continue to adhere to these boulders where possible. Soil accumulates in cracks and low places between these boulders. In this habitat some of the most spectacular alpine wildflowers are found. Sky Pilot, *Polemonium eximium*, grows in rock crevices at higher elevation than any other Sierra plant. It can be found near the summit of Mount Whitney. This small plant, with bright blue flowers occurring in a globular head, is a source of mixed fragrances. The sweet odor of the flowers is extremely pleasant, but the resin-covered foliage has a very unappealing odor, something like that of urine. Here we see various adaptations to this harsh climate. First, the air is very dry at high elevations, and interpretation of odor requires moisture. Therefore most alpine plants rely on large, showy flowers rather than odor to attract pollinators. Sky Pilot compensates for the dry air by producing a very strong odor, and it is also brightly colored. However, the foliage has a noxious odor, perhaps to discourage herbivores. The resin coating of the foliage and the tight clustering of leaves about the stem are also desert adaptations that inhibit evaporation.

Another typical plant of these rocky crevices is Alpine Gold, *Hulsea algida*. This member of the sunflower family (Asteraceae) shows typical alpine adaptations. The flower head is very large, up to 2 inches (5 cm) across, whereas the whole plant is seldom taller than 8 inches (20 cm). The blossom is brilliant yellow and has no odor. As is true of many members of the sunflower family, the blossom faces the sun at all times of day. This action, known as sun tracking, enables direct rays of sunlight to warm reproductive parts, which accelerates their rates of development. The foliage is covered with a myriad of fine silvery hairs that reflect light and trap air, which acts as an insulation. Light-colored, hairy foliage is a common characteristic of alpine and desert plants.

In addition to anatomical adaptations, certain physiological processes are commonly associated with these plants. Most of them are long-lived perennials. This means that they grow for many years, during which time they establish an elaborate root system. The bulk of most alpine plants is in the roots. Also, because the growing season is short, it is common for plants to produce flower buds during the year prior to their blooming. Energy of the plant is thus conserved, and it will not break its dormancy too early. Most of these plants are capable of photosynthesis at remarkably low temperatures, but they will not begin to function until soil temperature is high enough and day length long enough. If they came out of dormancy too early, they could be damaged by an unexpected cold snap or snowfall.

Alpine Fellfields.   The term *fell* refers to a stony field. A fellfield is an area, usually flat or slightly sloped, that is composed mostly of gravel and rocks (fig. 5.17). Water percolates rapidly through fellfield soils, so they do not retain moisture for long.

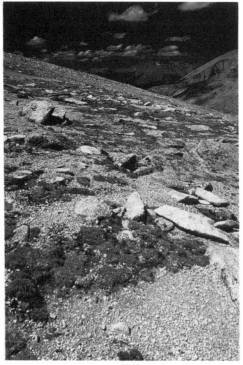

FIGURE 5.17   Alpine Fellfield, New Army Pass,
Sequoia National Park.

Strong winds sweep across these flat areas and carry away many fine soil particles,
so these areas remain coarse for many years. Many botanists who classify alpine
vegetation object to calling these communities *fellfields*, apparently because the term
describes the rocks and not the plants. The expression was originally used to describe
European rocky tundra, and there is some concern that it is inappropriate to use it
for a North American alpine zone composed of non-European plant species. Some
botanists refer to this and the Pioneer zone as Alpine Steppe, and others classify
each region according to dominant plant species. The term *Fellfield* will be used here
because it is widely used in the literature, and it aptly describes the high, flat, rocky
areas of the California high country.

   Plants of the Fellfield are known as cushion plants. These are long-lived perennials
with a deep taproot. All the foliage grows close to the ground in a small mound
about the size of a pincushion. By growing close to the ground, the foliage remains
out of the wind and takes advantage of the warmer temperatures near the ground.
Another advantage of a low, cushion-like growth form is that the plant traps its own
soil and organic matter. As wind blows over the cushion, friction causes the wind to
lose some of its energy. Fine dust particles, bits of leaf debris, and other matter fall

directly into the cushion. There is far more soil and organic matter within the leaves of the cushion than out in the open between plants.

Plants that form cushions usually have foliage covered with silvery hairs. Unlike plants in rocky crevices, these plants typically have many small flowers. The entire upper surface of the plant becomes covered with blooms, the strategy being to attract pollinators by sheer abundance rather than by size. Most common among the cushion plants are lupines and buckwheats. Lupines are in the legume family (Fabaceae) and have nitrogen-fixing bacteria in their roots, which helps to fertilize the entire ecosystem. When they blossom, the entire upper surface becomes covered with tiny blue flowers.

The buckwheat family (Polygonaceae) has many members in mountain and desert environments. Buckwheat cushion plants produce a myriad of yellow blossoms. As the flowers become older, the petals become reddish. This color change ensures that pollinators continue to visit flowers that are unpollinated. Pollinators are attracted to the yellow color but tend not to visit the red ones. In this way, foraging energy is optimized for both the pollinator and the plant. By retaining the older red flowers, however, the plant apparently maximizes its total color display, which is helpful for long-distance attraction of pollinators.

Another characteristic of Fellfields is that the rocks may form conspicuous patterns indicative of stream channels, even though water does not flow among them today. These patterns were formed many years ago during times of heavy precipitation, apparently when rocks were forced to the surface by freezing of water-logged soil. The rocks then slid or were blown by the wind to the lowest adjacent area, which must have been a small stream channel. Later, the wind blew away the soil between the rocks, so that they remain elevated in the pattern taken by the former stream channel. This process takes thousands of years. Because the Sierra is a young mountain range, such patterned ground is not as common as it is in the Rockies. Furthermore, soil in the Rockies is more likely to remain water-logged for long periods of time.

In the western Sierra foothills, at about 400 feet (130 m) elevation, are regions of "rock stripes." These are lines of fragmented rocks, 60 to 100 feet (20–30 m) apart, separated by alluvial soils. This phenomenon has been interpreted as a form of patterned ground that apparently dates back to the time of maximum glaciation during the Pleistocene. Intense frost-wedging broke up the rocks of uphill outcrops. Aided by snow and ice, the rocks were carried to their present positions in rows. Rock stripes are further evidence of the profound impact of glaciation on the topography of the Sierra Nevada.

In some areas of the alpine zone are gravel flats of rather uniform particle size. These areas are noteworthy because they support very limited plant cover. These barren zones may be 10 to 20 feet (3–6 m) wide at the edge of a meadow, below the tree zone, or they can cover many acres. One such large bare area, known as Guyot Flat, lies on a plateau at 11,000 feet (3300 m) on the eastern side of the Kern River gorge. This plateau probably formed during the same erosional interval as many of the other sandy plateaus, such as Siberian Flat, Sandy Meadow, and Bighorn Plateau, well-known landmarks along the Pacific Crest Trail. The surface was flattened by

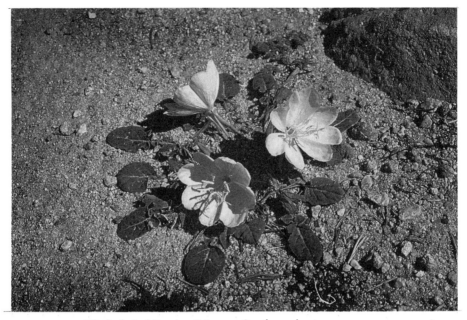

FIGURE 5.18   Woody-fruited Evening Primrose, *Oenothera xylocarpa.*

erosion and subsequently covered by deposits of gravel. Guyot Flat gravels have been measured to a depth of over 100 feet (30 m). The reason these zones are bare is not certain. One hypothesis is that needle ice forms during winter and kills the roots of trees. Another suggestion relates to the water-holding capacity of the soil during the growing season. When snow melts, water sinks rapidly through this gravel and is available to plants for such a short period of time that nearly nothing is able to grow.

One conspicuous plant ekes out a living on these gravel benches and bare zones, particularly in the southern Sierra. This is the Woody-fruited Evening Primrose, *Oenothera xylocarpa* (fig. 5.18). Its flowers have four large, bright yellow petals, up to 1 1/2 inches (3 cm) long. Similar to flowers of rock crevices, the blossom is disproportionately large. There may be one to four blossoms on a plant, clearly exceeding the leafy portion in size. The petals arc upward to form a large disc that captures light in the same way a satellite disc captures radio waves. Capturing light in this way increases the temperature of the reproductive structures and accelerates development. Insects have discovered that it is warm in these flowers, and many of them rest there for long periods of time, particularly in the morning.

The leaves on this plant show another alpine and desert adaptation. They occur in a circular rosette that lies flat on the ground, a growth habit that makes the most efficient use of heat and light while keeping the foliage out of the wind. When the snow melts, new leaves are produced. Leaves and flowers grow rapidly in order to accomplish their life cycle during the short growing season. The root of this plant is a thick, vertical, carrotlike structure that stores carbohydrate. The root probably is

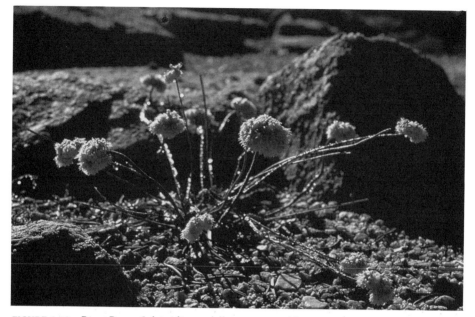

FIGURE 5.19   Pussy Paws, *Calyptridium umbellatum*, sun tracking.

a succulent water source that enables the plant to continue growing after soil water has percolated away. As is true of many high Sierra plants, the nearest relatives of this alpine species are desert plants.

Pussy Paws, *Calyptridium umbellatum*, is a common, widespread plant that grows on bare, sandy flats from the Yellow Pine Forest to the alpine zone. This is another desert-related species. Similar to the Evening Primrose, its leaves lie prostrate on the ground in a basal rosette. Unlike the Evening Primrose, the flowers are small and borne in fuzzy clusters on the ends of long, wiry stems. During most of the day these flower stalks lie on the ground, gathering heat and light. In the early morning, however, when the sun is low in the sky and the ground is cold, these stalks curl upward, lifting the flowers 2 to 3 inches (5–8 cm) above the ground (fig. 5.19). This enables solar radiation to warm the flower parts, accelerating their development. This form of sun tracking is the way Pussy Paws tries to cope with cold alpine nights.

Alpine Heath.   In Great Britain there are many acres of low, open brushland known as heaths. Many of the shrubs there are also known as heaths or heathers. In North American mountains there is an alpine shrubland also known as a Heath. Many of the shrubs in this community are either in the heath family (Ericaceae) or in the willow family (Salicaceae).

In the Sierra Nevada, members of the heath family are common in areas where snow provides most of the precipitation and soils tend to be acidic. These plants range upward in the mountains from Upper or Cold Chaparral, through conifer forests, to

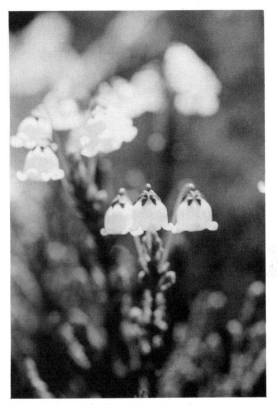

FIGURE 5.20   White Heather, *Cassiope mertensiana.*

the Alpine Heath. Manzanitas of Upper Chaparral are in this family, as are azaleas and rhododendrons of the forest communities. In the alpine zone is Red Mountain Heather, *Phyllodoce breweri*; White Heather, *Cassiope mertensiana* (fig. 5.20); Alpine Laurel, *Kalmia polifolia*; Blueberry, *Vaccinium occidentale*; and Dwarf Bilberry, *Vaccinium nivictum*. Flowers of the heath family are colorful and urn-shaped. On manzanitas, bilberries, and White Heather, the open end of the urn is tipped downward; on others, the flower opens upward, in a cup shape.

Water seems to be an important limiting factor for distribution of Alpine Heath. Quite often the shrubs are found ringing a lake or bordering a stream. Of equal importance, however, is well-aerated soil. This combination of moisture and soil conditions is not widespread in the Sierra. Consequently, Heath zones are not as conspicuous or as widespread as they are in the Rockies or the mountains of Oregon and Washington. Heath zones cover certain areas in the northern Sierra, but in California one must travel to the Klamath Province to see the Heath community at its best. Even there, its distribution is more localized than in areas that receive abundant summer precipitation.

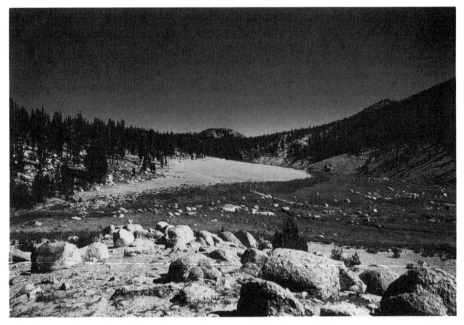

FIGURE 5.21   Zonation of Horseshoe Meadow, a southern Sierran meadow, Inyo National Forest.

In the southern Sierra, Heath shrubland commonly forms a fringe around meadows, but the shrubs do not occur in the wettest soil in the center of the meadows (fig. 5.21). Apparently, long roots of the shrubs are able to reach water deep in the ground, and more drought-tolerant vegetation may occur between the shrubs and the wet part of the meadows. It is common for Heath shrubs to form a transition between the bare zone of coarse soil and the actual meadow.

Alpine Meadows.   There are two kinds of meadows in the Sierra: Dry Meadows and Wet Meadows. Most meadows of the Sierra Nevada would be described best as Dry Meadows, although in the center of many meadows, at the lowest point, where soil is finest, there is true Wet Meadow.

Dry Meadow is characterized by mat-forming grasses (*Calamogrostis* spp. and *Poa* spp.), bunchgrasses (*Festuca* spp.), and various sedges (*Carex* spp.) that resemble grasses. Close inspection of the stems of sedges will reveal that they are triangular in shape. Various species of wildflowers are also common in these meadows. Conspicuous among them are various phloxes (*Phlox* spp.), paintbrushes (*Castilleja* spp.) (pl. 16A), lupines (*Lupinus* spp.), elephant's heads (*Pedicularis* spp.), and a number of members of the sunflower family (Asteraceae).

An interesting wildflower of these meadows is Scarlet Gilia, *Ipomopsis aggregata* (pl. 16B). In early summer those plants have many brilliant red, tubular flowers. When they are abundant it is truly a spectacular sight. They are fairly tall for wild-flowers, up to 4 feet (1.3 m) high. In early summer they are pollinated primarily by hummingbirds, who favor red, tubular flowers. Later in summer, however, hummingbirds tend to migrate to lower elevations. At this time, flower colors change to pink or white, attracting sphinx moths (Sphingidae), which pollinate at night. The shift in flower production from red to light colors is clearly an adaptation that makes these flowers more visible at night. No one is certain, however, how the plants "know" when to change color. It also has been demonstrated that during years when pollinators are scarce, the plants produce auxiliary vegetative growth that can produce flowers in a subsequent year.

Scarlet Gilia is often eaten by Mule Deer. An interesting study on Scarlet Gilia in the Rocky Mountains showed that once plants had been nipped off, they responded by growing larger roots, more stems, more flowers, and more fruits. This study showed that partial browsing actually increased the vigor of the plants. Therefore both Mule Deer and Scarlet Gilia benefit by partial browsing.

Soil in Dry Meadows tends to be thin and sandy. Duration of snowpack varies with exposure and season. At its upper edge, a Dry Meadow grades into a gravel flat or Alpine Heath zone. At its lower end it grades into a Wet Meadow. As snow melts, soil becomes exposed to light. In some areas snow becomes deflated, or is blown away by wind, exposing soil to sunlight during winter months. If plants began to sprout at that time, they would surely be killed by cold winter temperatures. Breaking of dormancy requires exposure of soil by melting of snow or wind deflation followed by warm soil or proper summer photoperiod. Combinations of proper moisture and appropriate temperature cause flowers to appear in a mosaic in the alpine zone. A common pattern is for flowers to appear first on the upper edge of a meadow, and as the season progresses, a belt of blooming plants moves toward the center. The outer edge of the meadow, where soil is coarsest, drains and warms first.

Wet Meadows are characterized by sod-forming sedges and grasses. These plants tend to reproduce by means of underground stems, or rhizomes. Soil tends to be fine, acidic, and rich in organic matter. The thick mat of rhizomes and black soil is known as sod. At its extreme, it decays to carbon-rich organic material known as peat. Where water never drains, this community is commonly known as a Peat Bog.

Freezing of waterlogged soil can damage plants. The most conspicuous effect of freezing is that expansion of the ice causes the earth to heave up in mounds, or hummocks (fig 5.22). These hummocks cause the center or wet part of a meadow to have a very lumpy surface that is difficult to walk on. Sometimes these hummocks are bare on top. What happens is that the earth, in rising, uproots the vegetation, which usually consists of sedges. When the uprooted plants die, wind scours the top of the hummock, blowing away dead parts of the plant and much of the soil. The long-term effect is that the sedges appear to grow in circles. The appearance of these circular growths is particularly striking in those areas that are water-logged during winter but drain rapidly in summer, so that very little else seems to grow there.

Where water-logged soil is present on slopes, sliding may occur. This is known as solifluction (fig. 5.23). As a result, the soil may pull the sod apart in a corduroy pattern, leaving alternating strips of vegetation and bare ground.

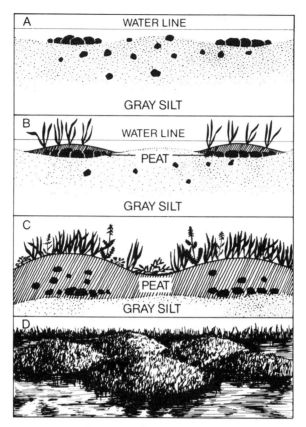

FIGURE 5.22 Formation of peat hummocks. *A*. During the winter, freezing churns the soil, heaving buried rocks to the surface, where they roll to the perimeters of the raised mounds to form rock polygons. *B*. Continued churning prevents plants from invading the centers of the polygons, but moisture-loving sedges may become established among the submerged rocks of the perimeter. *C*. The sedges contribute organic matter, initiating the formation of peat hummocks, which eventually protrude above the water surface. As the mounds increase in height, they become somewhat less soggy so that Wet Meadow plants such as elephant's heads and Alpine Willow can become established. *D*. Mature peat hummocks appear as groups of low, grassy mounds in moist meadows. (From S. Whitney. *A Sierra Club Naturalist's Guide to the Sierra Nevada*. San Francisco: Sierra Club Books, 1979. Reprinted by permission.)

FIGURE 5.23   The effect of waterlogged soil on steep
slopes. A. The soil begins to creep downslope in response
to gravity because the particles are lubricated by abundant moisture and no longer adhere to one another. B.
Small terraces form where the soil piles up. C. Eventually, moisture-loving sedges and grasses may invade the
slope, inhibiting further creep. Tiny ponds impounded
behind solifluction terraces are common features of moist
alpine meadows. (From S. Whitney. *A Sierra Club Naturalist's Guide to the Sierra Nevada*. San Francisco: Sierra Club
Books, 1979. Reprinted by permission.)

Some authors consider Wet Meadows to be the only true alpine meadows. To them,
alpine means a Wet Meadow, and nothing else. This interpretation is based on the
similarity of Alpine Wet Meadows to Arctic Tundra, zones with many plant species
in common. Plants of the Arctic Tundra are said to be circumpolar in distribution.
In the Rocky Mountains, about 40% of the alpine plants are circumpolar, that is,
shared with the Arctic. In the Sierra, however, only about 20% of the plants are
circumpolar in distribution. This is a testimony to the limited distribution there of
Wet Meadow and the scarcity of summer rain.

Due to the lower elevation north of Lake Tahoe, there is limited distribution of
Alpine Wet Meadow vegetation in the Sierra Nevada. Likewise, on Mount Shasta and
Mount Lassen, coarse volcanic soil limits alpine vegetation to the Pioneer and Fellfield
categories. In the Klamath Province, however, there are Wet Meadows more closely
resembling those of the north. Although Rocky Mountain elements are present, the
bulk of the plants in the meadows of the Klamath Province are of northwestern affinities. In southern California, the alpine zone consists primarily of gravel and Fellfields,
and the plants are associated primarily with the Great Basin. These communities are
probably associated primarily with soil and wind as overriding ecological factors.

So far no attempt has been made to distinguish meadows at different elevations. As meadows, these communities possess more similarities than differences. They are open, wind-blown habitats with low-lying vegetation, consisting mostly of turf-forming sedges and grasses. They are subject to cold air drainage; frost can occur any time of year. In general, these are habitats where moisture is abundant in the top few inches of soil during at least part of each year. It is this persistence of moisture that seems to exclude the invasion of shrubs or trees even within forest belts.

In wetter sites a common meadow plant is the Corn Lily, *Veratrum californicum*. It is sometimes called Skunk Cabbage, which it resembles only by having large leaf blades. On the other hand, it is suspected to share with Skunk Cabbage the ability to produce heat and cause early melting of snow. A common sight in early spring is young shoots of Corn Lily growing up through holes in the snow. Corn Lily is further notable because it is avoided by deer as a browse. It is one of the most poisonous plants in the Sierra, and Indians reportedly ate the root in order to commit suicide.

Meadows occur today where formerly there were lakes. These were low spots in glacially scoured terrain. As sediment accumulated in the bottom of the lakes, soil accumulated around the edges, and meadows gradually replaced the lakes (fig. 5.24). Many meadows still have a lake in the center. At the edges of the meadows, where soil is deeper and better drained, the shrubs of the Heath community begin to encroach. In areas below timberline, trees move into the areas behind the shrubs, most commonly Lodgepole Pines. Transpiration of the trees helps to dry the meadow, and this drying makes the habitat appropriate for the Alpine Heath community; therefore the shrubs often grow in rings around the bases of Lodgepoles.

At lower elevations, meadows are destined to be eventually replaced by forests. At upper elevations, meadows may avoid forest encroachment for thousands of years. As they accumulate soil, they become more like tundra of the north. Deeper soils remain wet for longer periods of time, and Wet Meadows become more common.

In the Sierra today the largest meadows are fringed by Subalpine Forest. Tuolumne Meadows in Yosemite National Park is the largest complex of meadows in the Sierra, and it is ringed by Lodgepole forest. Nearby are other large meadow areas, such as Dana Meadows near Tioga Pass, which has Lodgepole and Whitebark pines on its border. Most of the large Sierran meadows are in the Yosemite area, where glaciation has scoured vast flat areas that are now accumulating soil. Very few large meadows occur on the east side of the Sierra because not enough time has passed in this area of reduced precipitation. It takes thousands of years for the soil accumulation required for meadow succession.

In the southern Sierra, on the Kern Plateau, there is another large grouping of meadows. In this area, extensive glaciation was avoided, and longer periods of time have elapsed since major scouring of the landscape occurred. Some of these areas, such as Kennedy Meadows, are not true high-country meadows but are composed of Sagebrush Scrub and annual grasses, which are more typical of regions at lower elevation. In the Golden Trout Wilderness there are some true mountain meadows (fig. 5.25), but most of the research on high-country meadows has been to the north—

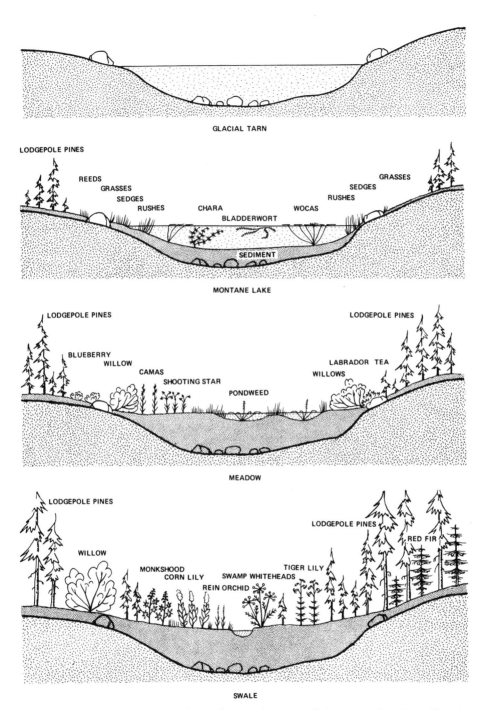

GLACIAL TARN

LODGEPOLE PINES

REEDS
GRASSES
SEDGES
RUSHES   CHARA
                BLADDERWORT
SEDIMENT

GRASSES
SEDGES
RUSHES
WOCAS

MONTANE LAKE

LODGEPOLE PINES   LODGEPOLE PINES

BLUEBERRY
WILLOW
CAMAS
SHOOTING STAR
PONDWEED

LABRADOR TEA
WILLOWS

MEADOW

LODGEPOLE PINES

WILLOW
MONKSHOOD
CORN LILY
REIN ORCHID
SWAMP WHITEHEADS
TIGER LILY

LODGEPOLE PINES
RED FIR

SWALE

FIGURE 5.24   Stages in succession from lake to Lodgepole–Red Fir Forest. (From E. Bakker. *An Island Called California*. Berkeley: University of California Press, 1984.)

FIGURE 5.25   Big Whitney Meadow, Inyo National
Forest.

at Carson Pass, Yosemite National Park, Sequoia National Park, Humphreys Basin, and Convict Basin. Very little is known ecologically about the meadows of the Kern Plateau, perhaps because they have been disturbed by cattle and sheep grazing since the 1800s. What research has been done on these meadows relates to the impact of grazing. It has been determined that the trampling alters the wet zone near the streams and encourages encroachment by sagebrush. Apparently, in Templeton and Ramshaw meadows at least half of the sagebrush zone used to be occupied by perennial sod-forming vegetation.

The Kern Plateau is home to numerous plants and animals with limited, endemic distribution. Foxtail Pine was discussed earlier. The Kern Plateau is also the home of the state fish, the Golden Trout, *Oncorhynchus* (= *Salmo) aguabonita*, as well as several undescribed species of sedentary slender salamanders, *Batrachoseps* spp. It is also the only Sierra Nevada location for the Western Skink, *Eumeces skiltonianus*, and three species of whipsnakes (racers), *Masticophus* spp.

Why has the Kern Plateau been the site of evolution for several endemic animals and plants? Presumably it was because ecological islands of favorable habitat endured throughout the Ice age, during which time relicts were preserved and specializations evolved. Furthermore, the near absence of organic material in the soil indicates that the Kern Plateau has been an arid region for a long time.

Snowfields.   In the Sierra Nevada, Snowfields persist on high passes, mountaintops, and north-facing slopes throughout most of the year. Likewise, Snowfields persist throughout the year on Mount Shasta, Mount Lassen, and protected locations in the Klamath Province. In southern California, Snowfields rarely persist on a yearly basis.

Snowfields have a surprising number of organisms associated with them. Food for the entire system is produced by micro-organisms variously called snow algae, snow protozoa, and snow protists. For the most part these are single-celled, photosynthetic organisms (*Chlamydomonas* spp. and *Chloromonas* spp.) that bear a pair of flagella. They are autotrophic and motile (i.e., bearing a combination of plantlike and animal-like characteristics), which has been the problem with giving them a common name. Botanists still think of them as algae, but zoologists think of them as protozoa. The debate over their classification is pointless.

These micro-organisms are circumpolar in distribution. They are distributed mostly by the wind. They overwinter in spore form. In the spring, when the surface layer of snow melts, they change to their motile, flagellated form and are able to swim in the few millimeters of water on the surface of a Snowfield. They absorb windblown nutrients associated with dust particles and organic debris. As the summer progresses, they become more abundant and are further concentrated as the Snowfields decrease in size due to melting. Each of these tiny organisms contains a small amount of red pigment in addition to its chlorophyll. By the end of summer they are so concentrated that the snow takes on a reddish hue. Stepping on the snow concentrates the organisms even more, and each footprint may be decidedly red in appearance.

Feeding upon the photosynthetic micro-organisms are various small herbivores, such as nematode worms, protozoa, and rotifers, common semiaquatic invertebrates in many habitats. The carnivores in this ecosystem are mostly insects, including ants, springtails, and ladybird beetles. Spiders feed on the insects and birds feed on all organisms that are large enough to see.

Most remarkable of the insects are cricketlike forms known as ice crawlers, *Grylloblatta* spp. (fig. 5.26). These are wingless, nocturnal, high-elevation forms that are most active during the cold seasons. Their optimal temperature range is around freezing, and they die quickly above $59°F$ ($15°C$). They live deep in crevasses under snow or glaciers and feed on soft-bodied insects or plant materials.

The mechanisms by which insects tolerate this cold climate are fascinating. Apparently, many arctic and alpine insects can tolerate solid freezing. One insect survival mechanism is to avoid freezing by producing natural antifreeze such as glycerol or even ethylene glycol, the same stuff used in automobile antifreeze. Other insects actually are freeze-tolerant. They reduce the proportion of body water locked up in ice by using a chemical such as glycerol as a "cryoprotectant." Similar to plants, their key to survival is to prevent dehydration and ice formation inside cells while ice slowly fills the rest of the body.

FIGURE 5.26 Ice crawler, *Grylloblatta*. (From J. A. Powell and C. L. Hogue. *California Insects*. Berkeley: University of California Press, 1979.)

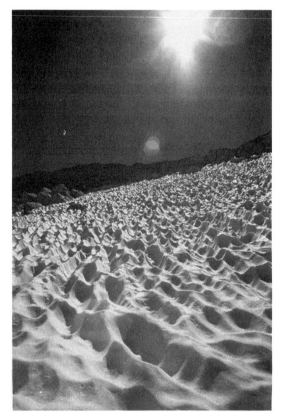

FIGURE 5.27 Suncups on Mono Pass, Inyo National Forest.

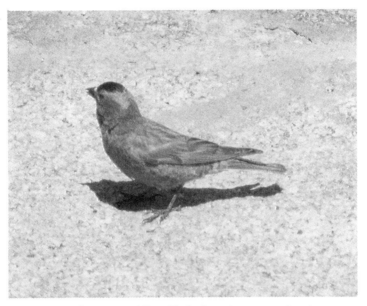

FIGURE 5.28   Gray-crowned Rosy Finch, *Leucosticte arctoa tephrocotis*.

Another problem with high elevation is high-intensity light. Insects and spiders living at these elevations are known to have high densities of wax on their outer surface. This wax probably helps to intercept damaging ultraviolet light. It also may serve to repel water in this environment, which is frequently wet.

Snowfields remain in place throughout the summer on north-facing slopes and in depressions that are free of wind. Their surfaces often become pitted with "suncups" (fig. 5.27), pits formed by small particles of windblown debris. A combination of gravity and heat absorption by these dark particles causes them to sink gradually into the snow until the surface looks like an enlarged egg crate. Each pit serves as a trap to capture more windblown debris and nutrients.

The toe of a snowfield melts, or retreats, at a surprising rate. To an unobservant visitor, the Snowfields seem not to change much, but on a typical summer day the edge of the snow will retreat 3 to 6 feet (1–2 m). This melting creates new snow-free habitat every day, where insects hatch and seeds germinate. This habitat at the edge of the snow is a rich feeding ground for alpine birds such as the Gray-crowned Rosy Finch, *Leucosticte arctoa tephrocotis* (fig. 5.28).

Animals of the Alpine Zone.   Most of the conspicuous animals of the alpine zone are birds and mammals that occur in other montane communities as well. On a yearly basis, the alpine zone becomes too cold for ectothermic species, and there is a coincident decrease in the numbers of species at higher elevations. There are not many reptiles, but there are some remarkable salamanders, as will be discussed later.

One of the interesting phenomena documented for mountaintops in general is that they seem to attract certain kinds of insects. Monarch Butterflies, *Danaus plexippus* (fig. 7.23), which will be discussed in the chapter on the Coast Ranges, are migratory. Thus they commonly occur in the high country in the course of their migration. What is difficult to understand is why so many other species of insects become concentrated on mountaintops, a phenomenon known as hilltopping. Swarms on the summits of ridges, hills, and mountains have been documented many times. One study in San Diego County documented 45 species of hilltopping butterflies alone. Several alternative hypotheses have been proposed to explain it, but it seems to be related to mating behavior. Most hilltopping butterflies are males, and females seem not to remain there long. Furthermore, the males on the hilltops engage in territorial patrolling behavior.

The California Tortoise-shell, *Nymphalis californica* (fig. 5.29), is an example of a butterfly that undergoes mass emigration in association with population outbreaks. These mass movements may be observed in early summer in the Cascades, the Sierra Nevada, the Santa Cruz Mountains of the southern Coast Ranges, and the San Bernardino Mountains of the Transverse Ranges. The species is particularly renowned for its massive outbreaks on Mount Shasta, where millions may appear in favorable years. Adults fly in such numbers that one collector gathered 50 of them with a single sweep of his net. Great numbers of dead Tortoise-shells may be seen on the snowfields in some years. The adult looks like a large anglewing, but it is less tattered in appearance. It has a 2-inch (5-cm) wingspan, and the centers of the wings are orange. Larvae of these butterflies are velvet black with a broken yellow line along the back. Each segment bears five branching spines supported on blue tubercles. The caterpillars feed on various species of *Ceanothus*, which they readily defoliate during their unpredictable population explosions.

There are three common but inconspicuous butterflies that characterize the alpine region of the Sierra Nevada. Riding's Satyr, *Neominois ridingsii*, occurs from Inyo County north to Carson Pass, and across the Owens Valley to the White Mountains. This "waif of the mountains" is gray with an irregular light band across the wings and two black spots. It is mothlike in appearance, relying on its coloration to conceal it when at rest. It flushes from underfoot when approached.

The Ivallda Arctic, *Oeneis ivallda*, occurs from Inyo County north to Donner Pass, where it flits about cliffs and summits. Its dull yellow-brown color enables it to blend with the granite rocks upon which it rests with open wings, perhaps to increase the absorption of solar radiation.

The Small Apollo or Phoebus Parnassian, *Parnassius phoebus*, is in the same family as the swallowtails (Papilionidae), although it lacks tails. It occurs in the alpine zone of the Siskiyou Mountains and the Sierra Nevada from the Mount Whitney area north to Plumas County. This butterfly is cream to snow white with black and red spots on its wings. It occurs on rocky summits and has been observed flying in snowstorms. Larvae feed on various stonecrops (*Sedum* spp.), small succulent plants that occur on exposed rock outcrops.

FIGURE 5.29   California Tortoise-shell, *Nymphalis californica*. (From J. A. Powell and C. L. Hogue. *California Insects*. Berkeley: University of California Press, 1979.)

One of the strangest examples of an alpine animal is the Mount Lyell Salamander, *Hydromantes platycephalus* (fig. 5.30). Its scientific name, *platycephalus*, means "flat-head," in reference to its body form, which is specialized for living in cracks and under rock flakes. This is another one of the lungless salamanders (Plethodontidae). The origin of lunglessness is an interesting theory. It is believed to be an adaption for living underwater in mountain brooks. Whereas air-filled lungs would cause an animal to float, lungless species can walk on the bottom and absorb oxygen directly through their skin. This mode of breathing functions particularly well in cool, well-aerated stream water. This is the type of habitat where lungless salamanders are found today in Appalachia, which is believed to be the center of origin for the family. The fact that western members of the family are nearly all terrestrial is incidental. As long as they remain cool and moist, they can absorb all the oxygen they need through their skin and throat membranes.

In general, ectothermic animals are not typical of cold climates, but this salamander seems to be associated with open rock habitats that are wet by water from snowmelt or spray from waterfalls. Its distribution in the Sierra is primarily in high-elevation bare habitats from Silliman Pass, in Sequoia National Park, to Sonora Pass. It was originally discovered on the east side of Mount Lyell at 10,800 feet (3214 m), and it also occurs in cracks near the large waterfalls in Yosemite Valley. One isolated population occurs at relatively low elevation, just above the floor of Owens Valley, in a canyon on the east side of Mount Baxter. The greatest number of observations for this salamander has been recorded on the top of Half Dome at 8852 feet (2634 m), in Yosemite National Park. This is a granite surface with no humus; the only soil is decomposed granite. Here the salamander spends daylight hours under rocks, particularly in the areas of snowmelt, and forages at night for spiders and insects.

In late summer, when habitats become dry, these salamanders slip into fissures and cracks, where they become dormant. This state of estivation grades into hibernation with the onset of winter. They remain dormant, living off of stored fat until the snow melts the following spring. Lifespan for these interesting salamanders averages eight to nine years.

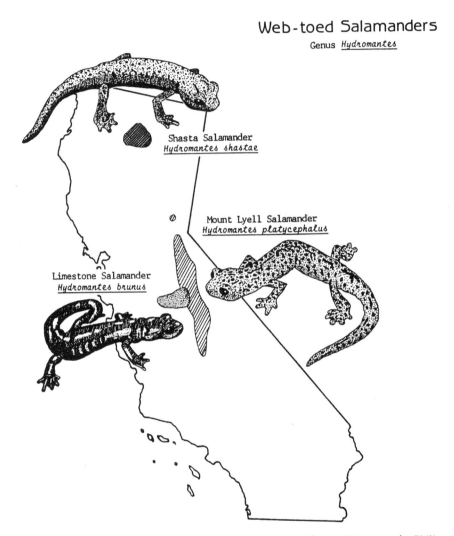

Web-toed Salamanders

Genus *Hydromantes*

Shasta Salamander
Hydromantes shastae

Mount Lyell Salamander
Hydromantes platycephalus

Limestone Salamander
Hydromantes brunus

FIGURE 5.30   Distribution of the web-toed salamanders in California. (Illustration by Philip R. Brown, from J. Gorman. "The Effects of the Evolution and Ecology of *Hydromantes* on their Conservation." In H. F. De Lisle et al. *Proceedings of the Conference on California Herpetology.* Southwestern Herpetologists Society Special Publication no. 4, pp. 39–42. Reprinted by permission.)

The distribution of this salamander and its relatives is an enigma. Not only is it strange for a delicate animal such as this to be localized in harsh, isolated places at high elevations, but its nearest relatives are also part of a strange pattern. These are the web-toed salamanders (Hemidactylinae), a group with five recognized species, although there is some controversy over whether each member deserves species status. Most of the species are restricted to limestone. Two are found in limestone caves in western Europe, and two others are found on limestone in California. One of these, the Limestone Salamander, *Hydromantes brunus*, occurs only along the Merced River in the foothills of the Sierra at about 2000 feet (600 m). The other, the Shasta Salamander, *Hydromantes shastae*, occurs at the same elevation, only in the vicinity of the McCloud River in Shasta County.

It is difficult to reconstruct a history to explain this pattern of distribution— western Europe and western North America. These are sedentary animals; over their entire lives they probably move no more than a few meters. It defies logic to think of them walking long distances in order to become established at such isolated locations. To consider them relicts of a former widespread distribution is more logical, but this means they would have had to be distributed nearly worldwide at one time, perhaps as long ago as the Cretaceous Period (80–90 million years ago). It is thought that at this time, salamander evolution was explosive, occurring very rapidly. The center of evolution for the family (Plethodontidae) was in Appalachia, in eastern North America. At the time of that evolution, North America was still attached to Europe in a giant continent known as Laurasia; the Atlantic Ocean was not yet formed. If the group is old enough, it could have occupied a wide range of distribution from eastern North America to western Europe. As Europe and North America separated and the Atlantic Ocean widened, the salamanders simply remained in place and slid with the continents as if they were passengers on a giant, slowly moving ferry.

Getting the salamanders from eastern North America to western North America is another problem. Web-toed salamanders no longer occur in eastern North America, but more evolved relatives do. One hypothesis has the web-toed salamanders dispersing westward from Appalachia through belts of coniferous forest to the newly uplifted Rocky Mountains. This migration would have had to have taken place after the retreat of an interior Cretaceous seaway that bisected North America into eastern and western halves, but it would have had to occur before drying of the interior of the continent took place. Once the salamanders reached the west, they were free to occupy new habitat as land above sea level grew westward. Presumably, salamanders were well established in the west at the time of initial uplift of the proto-Sierra, approximately 80 million years ago. As the old ocean-floor sediments were eroded away, the two foothill species survived in stable microhabitats, possibly limestone caves. The Mount Lyell Salamander, after all prebatholithic rock was stripped away, became associated with fissures and cracks in granite. Elevation of the Sierra to its present height took place during the last 1 to 3 million years. Several periods of glaciation scoured the high country, destroying salamander habitat. Mount Lyell, Half Dome, and other high peaks remained above the glaciers, and it is believed that the salamanders survived in places above the glaciers and exist there today as relicts. Dispersal to lower-elevation sites could have occurred by various gravity-aided means, such as sliding on ice or being carried by water or rocks.

There are sophisticated means by which scientists can determine how many years ago closely related species diverged. Application of these techniques to the five species of web-toed salamanders puts their age of divergence no earlier than Oligocene, 37 million years ago. If that is true, it would not have been possible for them to have occurred continuously from Appalachia to Europe. By that time, the continents had spread well apart, and the Atlantic was a sizable barrier. In this case, it would have been necessary for salamanders to walk from western North America across the Bering Strait to eastern Asia. From there they would have made their way westward to Europe without leaving any descendents behind in Asia.

Because all this walking seems unlikely for a sedentary salamander, scientists have been searching for an alternative explanation for such a peculiar pattern of distribution. One hypothesis is associated with plate tectonics. The salamanders rode, as if they were cargo, on moving pieces of land known as microplates or terranes. To explain the distribution of web-toed salamanders using this theory, we must first assume that their lineage is older than 37 million years. The disjunction between Appalachia and Europe could be explained by a population that extended across the area before the separation of Europe and North America. Distribution to western North America took place by a surprisingly devious route. Evidence supports the contention that the southern part of Mexico, a region known as the Maya Terrane, was formerly adjacent to southern Appalachia. This piece of land could have rifted away from eastern North America, carrying with it a cargo of salamanders. After that, pieces of western Mexico were carried northward and, during subduction, become attached to the western border of the continent in the vicinity of the developing proto-Sierra.

This is an attractive hypothesis because it provides a mechanism for delivering animals and plants to their present locations without involving them in some form of long-distance dispersal. The hypothesis is also supported by similar distributions of other plants and animals with poor dispersal ability. For example, the slender salamanders mentioned earlier also fit this pattern. This distributional range includes eastern North America, western North America, Mexico, and Central America. Furthermore, long-distance transport of the accreted terranes of western North America has been substantiated.

A weakness to this hypothesis is that to support proper "hitchhiking," the terranes would have to remain above sea level, and they would have to include portions of land that were translocated from one part of the continental margin to another. Most of the terranes are clearly of sea-floor origin or are island-arc volcanics formed by eruption out at sea. A variation of the hypothesis proposes that the organisms were carried by some form of rafting, such as floating on trees, from mainland Mexico to distant islands, which were then translocated northward and accreted to the western border of what is now the northern part of North America. Whatever explanation finally provides the solution to this peculiar distribution, it merely will add more interest to this remarkable group of salamanders.

Very few animals stay in the alpine zone year-round. Of the birds that occur there on occasion, none is more truly alpine than the Gray-crowned Rosy Finch, *Leucosticte arctoa tephrocotis* (fig. 5.28). It is the only bird known to nest above timberline. Usually it makes its nest among rocks, out of the wind, but it also has been reported to nest in the bergschrund at the top of a glacier. As is often the case in harsh habitats, these birds cannot afford to be too specialized in their food habits. They eat a wide variety of seeds and insects, commonly feeding on or near the edge of Snowfields. When insects such as mayflies emerge from mountain lakes, the birds feed voraciously in flocks, catching them on the water and in midair. On the tops of popular peaks such as Mount Whitney or Half Dome, these birds have become quite tame. They approach closely to feed on whatever scraps or handouts are offered. During winter these birds remain in the high country unless the weather is unduly harsh, in which case they will fly down the east side of the Sierra to feed as low in elevation as the sagebrush belt.

There are three ecological rules or principles, based on surface-volume ratio and color, that relate to temperature regulation, body form, and distribution among endothermic animals. These rules are based on minimizing heat lost or gained by radiation. Bergmann's rule states that within a given species, body size tends to increase in colder climates. Allen's rule states that within a given species, limbs tend to become longer in warmer climates. Gloger's rule states that within a given species, organisms tend to be darker in tropical (warm, moist) climates. In accordance with these rules, mammals of alpine zones should be expected to have large body mass and short limbs and to be light-colored, especially if they overwinter in the high mountains.

Among mammals of the alpine zone there are three basic strategies for dealing with harsh winter. Animals can migrate, they can hibernate, or they can remain active by storing food or somehow making use of available food.

Mountain or California Bighorn Sheep, *Ovis canadensis californiana*, spend summers in the high country. This is the subspecies that occurs in the Sierra Nevada and the Warner Mountains. During summer in the mountains, males gather in herds separated from ewes and lambs. In years past the Sierra Nevada herds would migrate down the east side of the range to overwinter in the pinyon pine and sagebrush belt of the Sierra Nevada, Owens Valley, and the White Mountains. They have declined in number seriously. As of 1988, it was estimated that there were only about 350 members of this high-mountain subspecies left in the state. Their decline is due to many factors, including diseases, hunting, and competition from cattle and domestic sheep. Some of the diseases were introduced from the domesticated animals. A particularly serious disease for the Bighorns is a virulent pneumonia. In 1988, for example, 11 out of a herd of 49 were found dead in the Warner Mountains. These outbreaks can be very serious. In Oregon in 1987, one outbreak of pneumonia killed 85 Rocky Mountain Bighorn Sheep out of a herd of 120.

Another serious problem for the herds in the Sierra Nevada was their inability to cross Owens Valley to the White Mountains because of the highway and the Los Angeles Aqueduct. Restricted to meager winter habitat on the steep east face of the Sierra, their numbers declined steadily. Various government agencies then stepped in to help them out. Areas in the vicinity of Mount Williamson and Baxter Pass were closed to entry during late summer and early winter. It was hoped that by restricting human entry to the high country during the time that sheep band together to breed, the disturbance would be reduced to a minimum.

Apparently, learned behavior is very important for sheep. Younger individuals must follow older sheep in order to learn where to step as they traverse steep cliff faces. Trying to cross these routes in panic causes them to fall. Although adults have been observed with well-healed broken limbs, it has been reported that a major cause of death of young sheep is starvation after suffering a broken leg caused by an untimely fall. As long as sheep remain away from well-traveled routes in the summer, frightening by humans should be minimal.

Since adoption of the closures, the Baxter herd has done well and is maintained at about 200 sheep. For some reason the Williamson herd has not fared as well; its number remains at around 30. Expansion of the Baxter herd has provided a source of sheep to be transported to other localities of the Sierra within their former range. Sheep have been transferred to the Mount Langley area, to Wheeler Crest, and to Lee Vining Canyon, in Yosemite National Park. A major problem with these translocations is that sheep apparently also learn their migratory routes and, when translocated to a new area, they must learn these routes without help from sheep that have traversed the area before. Translocations therefore must include a few old sheep that remember to migrate. Apparently, these old-timers lead the way as a new route is learned. It has been reported that without the old sheep to lead them, a group of young translocated sheep will attempt to overwinter in the high country, much to their discomfort.

The Peninsular Bighorn Sheep, *Ovis canadensis cremnobates*, occupies the Peninsular Ranges from the San Jacinto Mountains southward (fig. 5.31). Like the California Bighorn Sheep, it is listed as threatened and may not be hunted legally. Legal hunting of all types of Bighorn Sheep was halted in 1883. Since then the sheep have not responded to protection as quickly as some would hope. One of the reasons for the establishment of Anza-Borrego Desert State Park was protection of the Peninsular Bighorn Sheep. (*Borrego* is the Spanish word for the sheep.) Another refuge occurs on the slopes of the Santa Rosa Mountains in the headwaters of Deep Canyon.

The Desert Bighorn Sheep, *Ovis canadensis nelsoni*, has responded to management better than the other two subspecies. These sheep occur in ranges throughout the Mojave Desert, and they also are found in the San Gabriel and San Bernardino Mountains. In 1987 the first legal hunt in 103 years was allowed. It was determined by the Fish and Game Department that the number of Desert Bighorns had reached about 3700, and some of the older sheep should be removed. The state legislature therefore passed a bill to allow hunters to take 15% of the adult rams from two herds in the eastern Mojave Desert. Thinning of a herd can have beneficial effects on the remaining sheep. It allows better utilization of resources and helps to retard epidemic diseases. The biggest threat to the existence of Desert Bighorn Sheep is the presence of feral Burros in many parts of the desert, a problem that will be discussed in chapter 9.

Of the mammals that avoid the high-country winter through hibernation, none has been studied more thoroughly than Belding's Ground Squirrel, *Spermophilus*

FIGURE 5.31 Peninsular Bighorn Sheep, *Ovis canadensis cremnobates*. Deep Canyon, Santa Rosa Mountains, Riverside County.

beldingi (fig. 5.32). These little squirrels, about 10 inches (25 cm) long, are gray on the back and buff on the sides and belly. They sit up straight on their hind legs and watch for danger, a posture that has earned them the common name of "Picket Pins" in reference to the stakes packers use to tether their livestock. These ground squirrels occur in colonies in Sierran meadows from about 6500 to 11,800 feet (2000-3700 m) in elevation, between Kings Canyon and Lake Tahoe. They are restricted to meadows where soil is abundant enough to construct burrows but does not remain waterlogged. In particular, they may be observed easily in any of the large meadows along the Tioga Pass Road in Yosemite National Park. In one of these, Dana Meadows, just east of Tioga Pass, researchers constructed small platforms atop tripods about 15 feet (4 m) above the ground. Here they sat, hour after hour, with binoculars, observing the behavior of Belding's Ground Squirrels.

These squirrels spend about eight months in hibernation. During summer months they fatten up by eating seeds and insects. The scientific name *Spermophilus* means "seed-loving." They double their body weight by increasing their fat reserves up to 15-fold. Males emerge first, in late April, when snow is still abundant. Females do

FIGURE 5.32   Belding's Ground Squirrel, *Spermophilus beldingi.*

not emerge until the snow has melted from the tops of their burrows. A few days after emerging, females become sexually receptive and remain so for only three to six hours on one day. Receptive females are followed by males, who attempt to mate with them and who chase and fight each other in order to be chosen. In actuality, a few large, old males do most of the mating. One study found that 71% of copulations were accomplished by 3 to 12 males. Females generally mate four to five times, with about three different males, and give birth to as many as eight offspring.

Gestation lasts 23 to 25 days. Females either dig their own burrows or inhabit abandoned gopher burrows. Each burrow has at least two entrances. Burrows often must be changed, as they may become flooded or dug up by predators such as Badgers, weasels, or Martens. The young spend their early days in the burrow, in a nest made of dry grass. After nearly a month of nursing, they appear aboveground, in late July and August. By that time some adults already have entered hibernation. Juvenile males disperse, but juvenile females remain near the nest.

Studies show strong kin recognition in ground squirrel families. Males and females raised together are nonaggressive toward each other. Female siblings separated experimentally at birth are able to recognize each other, but sibling males reared apart are aggressive. Females remain for many generations in the same area where they were born.

Juveniles enter hibernation last and these yearlings are the last to emerge the following spring. Yearling males are highly carnivorous. They must have a good protein source in order to overwinter and to be ready to reproduce in their second year of life. Protein is provided by insects, carrion, small mice, and young nursling ground squirrels. Infanticide is practiced by yearling males presumably as a protein source. It is also practiced by adult females, who prey upon the nurslings of other females. These nurslings are not eaten, but merely dragged from the nest and killed. This practice is assumed to increase the contribution of genetic material from the female that does the killing, by reducing competition from offspring other than her own. Neither yearling males nor females kill the offspring of relatives.

Females vigorously defend their nests. After juveniles emerge, young females co-operate to enlarge the defended territory. Juvenile females will hibernate together, and the following year, they will construct their own nest near their original home. This means that females living near each other are related. Nonrelated males and females are kept from entering the territory.

When predators approach, some ground squirrels give alarm calls that cause others in the family to seek shelter. This same behavior was described for California Ground Squirrels in the foothills. In the case of Belding's Ground Squirrel, the callers usually are large, old females. Because calling may attract the predator, callers are more frequently killed, but these old females are the most expendable of the group. This form of behavior, where one animal sacrifices itself to protect its descendants, is known as altruism. By her activity, which may lead to death, the female enhances her contribution of genetic material to future generations.

Of the forms of behavior that have been observed in Belding's Ground Squirrel, some have clear survival value or increase the probability of genes surviving in off-spring. It might also be argued that many behavioral features are associated with density-dependent regulation of population size. This means that mechanisms in the population function to keep the population from becoming so large that it outstrips the available resources. Consider infanticide. If food is abundant, females are able to forage near their nests and defend it from invasions by other squirrels. Abundant food therefore helps to ensure survival of nurslings. Likewise, if insects are abundant, yearling males may not need to prey on nurslings in order to receive adequate protein. The reciprocal of this is that if yearling males do not receive adequate protein, they may perish during hibernation, or they may survive in a weakened condition and not be part of the breeding pool the following year. They may not become reproductive due to poor nourishment, or they simply will be too weak to win the battles necessary to mate with a female.

Differential lifespan can also be linked to density-dependent regulation of popu-lation size. Females typically live four to six years, males only three to four. Some individuals live considerably longer, however. Females up to eleven and males up to six years of age have been reported. Differential mortality means that the sex ratio becomes skewed in favor of females. Because so few males actually succeed in mating, they are more expendable. When food is scarce, more females survive. The few males that survive are the strongest, and they become the parents the following year. It actually takes very few males to make all the females pregnant. The extra males are a luxury; they provide variation for the gene pool so that all the offspring are not sired by only a few males. This luxury, however, can be postponed until food is abundant. The fact that a female mates with several males is another mechanism to ensure that all babies are not fathered by the same male.

Of the major causes of death, two may be related to density-dependent regulation. In one four-year period, infanticide accounted for 8% of the deaths. The regulatory nature of infanticide was discussed earlier. Another study determined that 4% to 11% of the study animals were killed by predators such as Badgers, Coyotes, weasels, and hawks. These predators are opportunistic, feeding on whatever is abundant. When squirrels are common they feed on them more heavily, which also serves to reduce the size of the squirrel population when it is densest.

Apparently, the primary cause of death for these squirrels is the weather. Depending on the severity of the winter 54% to 93% of juveniles and 23% to 68% of adults perish during hibernation. This pattern selects for large, well-fed adults that are able to endure a long, harsh winter. If the winter is mild, those squirrels that emerge early have an advantage: their offspring have a longer time to feed and develop and they become large and fat. A critical balance between opposing forces is evident. If squirrels emerge too early, they may be caught by a late snowstorm, so this favors those squirrels that emerge late. Conversely, if squirrels emerge late, their offspring will not have as long a time to grow. The critical balance between early and late emergence dictates which squirrels will survive to pass on their genes. Variation is also important. If all squirrels emerged at the same time, a population could be obliterated by the weather. Weather-related mortality is a classic example of density-independent regulation: the initial size of the population has very little influence on the number of offspring that are killed.

The most conspicuous mammal of the high country is the Yellow-bellied Marmot, *Marmota flaviventris* (fig. 5.33). This large rodent occurs in meadows and rock piles from about 6200 feet (1900 m) to the tops of peaks. Although it lacks cheek pouches, it is correctly considered to be a large squirrel. Related to the Hoary Marmot (*M. caligata*) of the Rockies and the Woodchuck (*M. monax*) of the eastern United States, the Marmot is the largest of the Sierran squirrels. It reaches a body length of 20 inches (45 cm) and a weight of about 10 pounds (4.5 kg). By late summer about half of its body weight is fat, because, like the other high-country squirrels, it is a hibernator. During hibernation its body temperature drops from 97°F (36°C) to about 40°F (4.5°C). Its heart rate drops from about 100 beats per minute to about 4 beats per minute. It inhales about once every six minutes.

Marmots are common where there are rocks, and burrows are common under large boulders at the edges of meadows. They sometimes construct burrows among the roots of trees, and where little soil is present, they construct dens in talus slopes. A

FIGURE 5.33   Yellow-bellied Marmot, *Marmota flaviventris*.

den or burrow system usually has several entrances, and there is one sleeping chamber lined with grasses.

Mating occurs upon the marmots' emergence from hibernation. Females dig new burrows, and males wander from burrow to burrow seeking a mate. Unlike Belding's Ground Squirrel, mating takes place underground, so little is known about mating or territorial behavior. Presumably, a nonreceptive female drives males from her burrow until she is ready to mate, at which time the male joins her in the burrow. Gestation takes about 30 days, after which the male is evicted and offspring are cared for by the female for about six weeks.

Marmots spend a great deal of time basking in the sun. Apparently this is an energy-conserving device that enables them to maintain their body temperature. They will need all the energy they can store to get through the winter. It may seem that they are unduly exposed to predators while they bask, but, like other communal squirrels, they have an acoustic warning system. A single loud whistle from one member of the group causes others to dive for cover. To many back-country visitors this is the most familiar animal sound. Looking in the direction of the sound, a person often sees just the head of a marmot peering from the top of a boulder. There may be a dominance hierarchy established among marmots. Each seems to have its own high perch, and the largest animal is usually on the highest perch. Concentrations of feces and urine are often found on the tops of rocks and may be a territorial marking system.

The onset of hibernation in mammals has long been a mystery. Recent studies show that lowering of blood temperature causes the release of natural opiumlike chemicals (opiates) from a region of the brain known as the hypothalamus. This region is known to be associated with many other important physiological urges, such as thirst, hunger, and sleep. Extracts of hibernating Woodchuck blood can drive nonhibernators such as monkeys into a torpid condition. Furthermore, hibernating ground squirrels seem to show low sensitivity to morphine, another opiate. Apparently, natural opiates produce the suite of characteristics we call hibernation by activating certain receptor sites in the brain. Opiates such as morphine have little effect at this time because the receptor sites are already occupied by natural opiates.

Another common mammal of the alpine zone is the Pika or Cony, *Ochotona princeps* (fig. 5.34). These animals employ a third strategy available to alpine animals: They remain active throughout the winter. They do not migrate, and they do not hibernate. They live on stored piles of sedges and grasses stashed among rocks in talus slopes. They seldom venture from the rock piles except to gather food. Although they are rodent-like in appearance, Pikas are more closely related to rabbits and hares; they are lagomorphs. Similar to other lagomorphs, their distribution is seriously limited by the potential for overheating. They have a relatively high body temperature for a mammal, 104°F (40°C), and they can tolerate only a few degrees of warming before they die. The large ears of lagomorphs are renowned for their ability to dissipate body heat by radiation, and the ears of Pikas are proportionately larger than those of any other mammals of the alpine zone. However, as predicted by the rules proposed by Bergmann and Allen, relating to body size and limb length, Pikas have the smallest ears of the hares and their allies.

Studies in rock piles at various elevations show that the ability of Pikas to colonize new habitat depends on their ability to run without overheating from one pile to the next. At high elevation, where it is cooler, this is less of a problem, and Pikas seem to inhabit nearly every rock pile and talus slope. At the lower extremes of

FIGURE 5.34   Pika, *Ochotona princeps*.

their range, however, the rock piles are like cool ecological islands separated from each other on the basis of heat. Rock piles too far from a source of colonizers have no Pikas, whereas rock piles that may be reached during periods of cool weather maintain steady population size, with the number of colonizers balanced by the number that die. As might be expected in this situation, the apparent downhill dispersal of Pikas is limited by temperature, not by the abundance of rock piles or food.

Vocalizations of Pikas are also familiar to back-country hikers. They utter loud, short squeaks as a territorial signal. The sound is distinctly not whistle-like and is not likely to be confused with the sound of the marmot. As in the case of the marmot, a person searching the talus in the direction of the sound may locate the Pika peering from the top of a rock. Studies of Pikas in the Rocky Mountains have revealed a great deal of diversity in their vocalizations. They have long songs vocalized by males and females. There are also calls emitted during courtship, and there are wailing calls that signal the end of courtship. There are distress calls, aggressive calls, and territorial calls. Apparently, these territorial calls differ enough among individuals in a population that Pikas are able to recognize each other by sound alone.

Another aspect of the territorial call is that it is uttered only when the animal has a retreat in the talus. If a Pika is out on a meadow gathering food when a predator approaches, it utters no sound. It waits motionless, hoping for the danger to pass. When in the talus it utters its call, and if the predator approaches too closely, the Pika drops out of sight into the labyrinth of tunnels and cavities among the rocks. No call is uttered if the predator is a Marten or a Long-tailed Weasel, *Mustela frenata* (fig. 5.35); the Pika simply drops out of sight without warning the others. Apparently, the sound would attract the attention of the only predators able to follow the Pika into its retreat.

In the spring, Pikas establish territories in the talus in an alternating male-female pattern. Males court the females in areas where the territories overlap. If mating occurs, two broods of young are produced. After the first mating, about three young are produced within about 30 days. Mating occurs again, and the second brood is produced about 30 days after that. After the second mating, the male is driven from the territory, and the young are cared for by the female only.

During late summer, males and females venture into meadows to gather sedges and grasses, which are stored in the talus as "haystacks." After the first snows of the winter, Pikas continue to feed by burrowing in the snow or venturing out upon it to feed on nearby shrubs. They also eat crustose lichens, which they scrape off rocks. It is not until the snow becomes so deep that it would be too energetically expensive to dig that the Pikas remain in the rock piles feeding upon their stored hay.

Pikas are so efficient at gathering vegetation that they produce a gradient of grazing pressure in the vicinity of their talus piles. Preferred vegetation becomes depleted near the talus. If there are too many Pikas in the talus pile, they are forced to venture farther in search of food. If this happens, they are more likely to overheat or be caught by a predator. This is another example of density-dependent regulation of population size.

FIGURE 5.35   Long-tailed Weasel, *Mustela frenata*.

A variation of the two preceding strategies is illustrated by the Deer Mouse, *Peromyscus maniculatus* (fig. 8.44). This small mouse is notable for enjoying a wide range of distribution from below sea level in Death Valley to the alpine zone above 11,000 feet (3300 m). It has been collected as high as the summit of the White Mountains, at 14,250 feet (4240 m). On one hand, this mouse stores food in its nest to feed upon during winter months. On the other hand, its body temperature drops every day when it goes to sleep. It's as if the animal hibernates every day, which can be a very important energy-conserving technique, particularly for such a small mammal with a high surface-volume ratio.

A number of studies have been conducted on these mice in an attempt to determine how animals can live at high elevation. By raising mice at different elevations and then moving them up and down the mountain, a number of generalizations have been established. At high elevations, animals tend to develop larger hearts, increased lung volume, and a greater number of red blood cells. In accordance with Bergmann's rule, body weight increased with elevation, but only to about 10,000 feet (3000 m). Above that, body weight decreased, presumably because lack of oxygen restricted growth. Animals also exhibit very high metabolic rates at high elevation. Other sampling at various localities in the Sierra illustrated that up to about 10,000 feet (3000 m), limb length, ear length, and tail length showed a decrease, in accordance with Allen's rule.

Breeding experiments at various elevations and subsequent transport of animals to different elevations illustrated that these changes were a function of development and

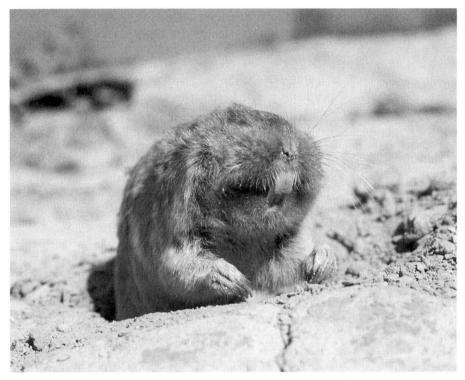

FIGURE 5.36   Pocket Gopher, *Thomomys* sp.

acclimatization rather than hereditary differences. An interesting hereditary component did become clear, however. Hemoglobin of mice born at high elevation has a
greater attraction for oxygen than it does in mice at low elevation. Further studies
showed that Deer Mice have polymorphic hemoglobins, which means that they are
genetically capable of producing several kinds of hemoglobins. The one they produce
as an adult is determined during development in the uterus. They produce the type
of hemoglobin that functions best at the elevation of early development.

Experiments at different temperatures showed that mice exposed to cold developed a greater amount of brown fat—the high-calorie, heat-generating tissue. Their
metabolic rate also went up, but this trend also was limited by reduced oxygen at
high elevation. More brown fat was produced, but the limit in oxygen caused the
metabolic rate to decline, so that heat production was actually reduced in spite of
the greater mass of brown fat. These animals were probably living at the very fringe
of existence.

Various species of gophers (*Thomomys* spp.) (fig. 5.36) range from the Great
Central Valley to the alpine zone of the Sierra. Unlike the Deer Mouse, different
species occur at different localities, but their habits are similar. In meadows they
construct lateral burrows extending to the surface, through which excavated earth

is dumped to the outside. Gophers usually feed on roots and underground parts of plants, such as bulbs and stems (rhizomes). At night, however, they venture from their burrows to feed on grasses and leaves. During winter they leave the ground and maintain burrows under the snow at the surface of the ground. There they are able to move about, feeding on plants under the snow. In spring, when the ground thaws, they excavate underground burrows once again, filling the snow burrows with excavated earth. After the snow melts, ridges of earth indicate the outlines of their snow burrows on the surface of meadows. Like other burrowing forms, gophers make a nest beneath the ground and line it with shredded plant parts. Six to eight babies are produced in the spring in these nests. Gophers are victimized by the usual predators of alpine animals, including the Great Gray Owl, as described previously.

Jack rabbits are technically classified as hares. The White-tailed Jack Rabbit, *Lepus townsendii* (fig. 5.37), is an interesting mammal of the alpine zone that has been poorly studied. This high-elevation form of the common White-tailed Jack Rabbit is widely distributed throughout the Great Basin. It is distributed in the southern Sierra, mostly in the subalpine zone, but it ranges widely into the alpine zone. It has been observed as high as 13,000 feet (4100 m) on Mount Langley. Compared to the desert members of this species, this jack rabbit clearly shows a trend toward enlarged body size and reduced size of ears and legs, as predicted by Bergmann's and Allen's rules. Furthermore, as predicted by Gloger's rule, during winter it grows white fur to protect it from predation and to increase its thermal efficiency. In cold weather it is an advantage for an endothermic animal to be white, because it loses less heat by radiation than a dark animal. Furthermore, because white hair has microscopic air spaces, it is a better insulator than pigmented hair. The switch to a dark color in the summer is likewise more efficient for heat loss. It was mentioned above that the distribution of hares and rabbits is largely controlled by temperature. In the winter this jack rabbit grows hair on its feet so that it may travel in snowshoe fashion across the snow. Food for the White-tailed Jack Rabbit during winter has not been

FIGURE 5.37 White-tailed Jack Rabbit, *Lepus townsendii*, on Mount Langley, Sequoia National Park.

identified. Presumably, it feeds on leaves, twigs, and bark, digging down to bush tops through deep snow.

The Snowshoe Hare, *Lepus americanus*, occurs widely through northern forests up to 8000 feet (2500 m), but it is not commonly seen due to its tendency to remain concealed. Although it is most common in the northern Sierra Nevada, the Snowshoe Hare reaches it southernmost distribution in Tulare County. It relies on protective coloration for concealment. Its preferred habitat seems to be dense creekside thickets, particularly where alders and willows abound. The Snowshoe Hare also occupies dense stands of manzanita that grow after a fire. Unlike the White-tailed Jack Rabbit, it seldom ventures into the alpine zone. Where it coexists with the White-tailed Jack Rabbit, the Snowshoe Hare can be distinguished by its short ears, scarcely longer than its head, and its large "snowshoe" feet and long hind legs. Like the White-tailed Jack Rabbit, the Snowshoe Hare changes color with the seasons.

6

Pacific Northwest Mountains

The northwestern corner of California is a mountainous region of diversified geology. Along the coast, the Klamath Province is a topographic upland characterized by moist forests and large rivers that have cut deep, steep-sided canyons. Elevation of the uplands ranges generally between 5000 and 7000 feet (1500 and 2150 m). Thompson Peak, in the Trinity Alps, is the highest, reaching 8936 feet (2725 m).

Most of this mountainous region is not accessible to the general public. This is particularly true in the Klamath Province, where there are large tracts of wilderness. Of the roads that have been built, most are logging roads that are closed off. The few paved roads that traverse the area follow the coast or major rivers. The average person traveling by automobile in the area would see no difference between the Klamath Province and the northern Coast Ranges.

A mode of entry that may become popular in the future is along abandoned railroads. Many of these are now being developed in northern California, usually on the bed of an abandoned logging or mining railroad. The advantage to these conversions is that they are seldom steep. They may be covered with planks to allow access by mountain bicycles. For example, a 25-mile trail in Lassen National Forest occupies the bed of the old Fernley and Lassen Railroad.

Along the coast (fig. 6.1), plant communities on the terraces are quite similar to those that will be discussed in association with the northern Coast Ranges. A belt of Coast Redwoods is extensive, particularly along Highway 101. Redwood National Park and Prairie Creek Redwood State Park are in this area. Most of the forested area in the Klamath Mountains is quite different, however. To see them, a person has to hike, ride a horse, or gain access to a logging road.

Above about 2000 feet (600 m) elevation, the montane forest of the Klamath Mountains takes on a different character. These forests have attracted attention among botanists because there are many endemics and relicts. Vegetation patterns are highly complex, and there is a great deal of species diversity. For example, there are over 20 species of conifers in the area, more than in any other part of California. Studies of fossils throughout the western United States suggest that the forests of the Klamath Province most closely resemble those that covered western North America until a million years ago. In this respect, Klamath Province vegetation represents living fossil-forests.

Associated with the Klamath Province are three of California's wild and scenic rivers. The region is drained by the Klamath River, the Trinity River, and the Smith River. The Smith River has been proposed as a wild-river national park. The fact that the Eel River joins the coast just south of the Klamath Province means that four of California's wild and scenic rivers are in the region. "Wild and scenic" means that the rivers must remain undammed, allowed to follow their natural course. In California,

FIGURE 6.1   The Pacific Northwest, where the forest meets the sea.

these are the only rivers in the state that still have reasonable runs of salmon and steelhead trout. The Klamath River is dammed in Oregon before it enters California, but in the California section it travels 150 miles (240 km) as a wild river.

The Klamath Province does not represent a single range. The Klamath and Trinity rivers have cut deeply into the upland so that several definable mountain ranges are evident (fig. 6.2). The northernmost range is the Siskiyou Mountains. This region overlaps into southern Oregon and is drained principally by the Smith River, which enters the Pacific Ocean south of the Oregon border. Other ranges include the Salmon, Marble, Scott, South Fork, and Trinity mountains. The Trinity Alps, as this range is known, is the southernmost and highest subunit of the region. This region is drained by the Trinity River, which joins the Klamath River before it dumps into the Pacific.

To the east of the Klamath Province is the southernmost extension of the Cascade Range. This is a volcanic province consisting mostly of rolling, forested terrain about 4000 feet (1200 m) in elevation. The southernmost of the Cascade volcanoes is actually represented by the Sutter Buttes, which project 2132 feet (656 m) from the sediments of the Sacramento Valley. In California, two well-known volcanic peaks, Lassen and Shasta, project boldly above the surrounding terrain. From a biological perspective, the southernmost extent of the province is marked by Lassen Peak, which reaches 10,457 feet (3187 m) in elevation. It and the surrounding region are included in Lassen Volcanic National Park. This is a region of open forests, hot springs, and fumaroles.

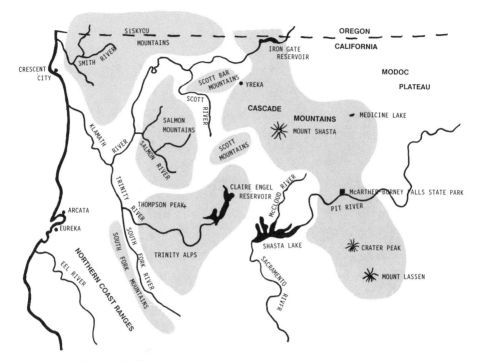

FIGURE 6.2   The Pacific Northwest. (Illustration by Phil Lingle.)

FIGURE 6.3   View of Mount Shasta from Mount Lassen.

To the north, Mount Shasta (fig. 6.3, pl. 8C) towers above the surrounding land-scape. Reaching 14,162 feet (4317 m), it is visible for many miles in any direction. Lassen and Shasta in California are but 2 of the 12 major peaks of the Cascades, which extend in a north-south line northward to Washington. The northernmost peak, Mount Baker, is about 500 miles (800 km) from Lassen.

In general, the Cascade Range lies west of the volcanic tableland known as the Columbia Plateau. It extends from southern British Columbia to California. The California portion of the tableland, known as the Modoc Plateau, lies in the rain shadow of the Klamath and Cascade Mountains. It is discussed in chapter 9, in the section on the Great Basin Desert.

CLIMATE

Precipitation in the Klamath Province is the highest in the state. Average annual precipitation in the redwood belt along the coast exceeds 80 inches (200 cm). In the wettest part of the Siskiyous, in Douglas Fir forest, annual precipitation is reported to reach 140 inches (350 cm). Most of this precipitation occurs in the winter, but temperatures are not particularly cold. Soil never freezes, even in the subalpine zone, where snowfall may reach 10 feet (3 m) and remain on the ground until July. This means that, unlike most regions characterized by conifers, most photosynthesis occurs during the winter months. This soil property also selects against winter-deciduous hardwoods. The driest month is July, but summer precipitation is common. The tail ends of Alaskan storms produce more summer rain in the Klamath Province than is found anywhere else in the state. It is the predictability of this precipitation that favors the growth and maintenance of relict forest species that occur nowhere else in the state. Many plant species of the Pacific Northwest cannot exist without summer rain. Precipitation remains high on slopes that face the coast, but to the interior, in the rain shadow, precipitation drops to about 20 inches (50 cm) per year. On the western slopes of Lassen and Shasta, precipitation averages about 60 inches (150 cm) per year.

The cool, moist climate of the Pacific Northwest not only encourages vigorous forest growth, but it also promotes conditions that discourage large forest fires. During drought years, however, particularly when long periods of fire suppression have allowed an accumulation of downed wood or other fuel, conditions favorable to large fires can occur. Such a situation occurred in 1987, a drought year. Summer thunderstorms started an unprecedented number of fires throughout the northern part of the state. An estimated 1.1 million acres (0.5 million ha) of forest burned in northern California and southern Oregon. The pall of smoke in the Klamath River Canyon was so thick that during September of that year, high temperatures averaged 27°F (15°C) below normal. In a scenario supportive of the hypothesis of a "nuclear winter," high temperatures in the area hovered in the mid-50°F (13°C) range, while similar areas not covered with smoke averaged temperatures in the low 80°F (28°C) range.

GEOLOGY OF THE KLAMATH PROVINCE

The structural framework of the Klamath Mountains is the same as that of the northern Sierra Nevada (fig. 6.4). The batholithic rock (granitic) of the Klamath region was formed by subduction at the same time as the Sierra batholith. This batholithic material intruded into a series of prebatholithic metamorphic rocks that occur in long belts to the west of the plutonic rocks.

The metamorphic rocks were added to the western border of North America by accretion. The youngest rocks, the last to be added, are those farthest to the west. There is a near-perfect matchup of these belts on the western side of the Klamaths and the Sierra Nevada. Fossils of animals that lived along the shoreline during Cretaceous time, about 130 million years ago, are found in some places along the western slope of the Klamaths and the Sierra Nevada. In many areas, former trench rocks have been uplifted and become accreted to the edge of the continent. Soils derived from these rocks, including serpentines, are known collectively as ophiolitic soils.

Apparently, about 130 million years ago, the two ranges became dismembered. The Klamath Mountains began to slide westward in a manner that geologists call extension. They are now about 60 miles (100 km) west of their point of origin, in line with the northern Coast Ranges.

The intrusion of granitics into these ranges occurred at about the same time as material was accumulating by accretion in the Coast Ranges. The presence of granite in the Klamaths and the Sierra, and the degree of metamorphism caused by the intrusion are the basic differences between these mountains and the northern Coast Ranges.

During the end of the Mesozoic, about 65 million years ago, the Klamath Mountains stood as an island. The northern Coast Ranges were still accumulating displaced terranes, but seawater covered what is now the Cascades and the Modoc Plateau.

About 65 million years ago, at the beginning of the Cenozoic, a long period of erosion and tectonic quiescence began. Materials eroded off the Klamaths and the Sierra Nevada and became deposited westward. The climate was relatively warm and humid. Lateritic soils (oxisols) formed along the western borders of the Sierra and Klamath provinces. These red clay soils are still present in many areas.

About 25 million years ago, at the beginning of Miocene, tectonic activity began again. The San Andreas Transform system began its march northward, and the southern Coast Ranges began their uplift. At this time, volcanic activity began in northeastern California, and black basaltic lava began to pour out over the Modoc Plateau, eventually filling the gap between the Klamath Mountains and the newly rising Sierra Nevada. As these volcanic rocks accumulated, the sea was displaced. Extension and faulting, associated with the Basin-Range Province, began. This activity culminated with uplift of the Sierra Nevada and the mountains of the Great Basin. Erosion of materials off the top of the Sierra batholith exposed masses of granitics to weathering. These sediments were carried westward to fill the Great Central Valley, pushing back the ocean even farther. The reason the Klamaths look different from the Sierra today, in spite of their common origin and structural similarity, is that the

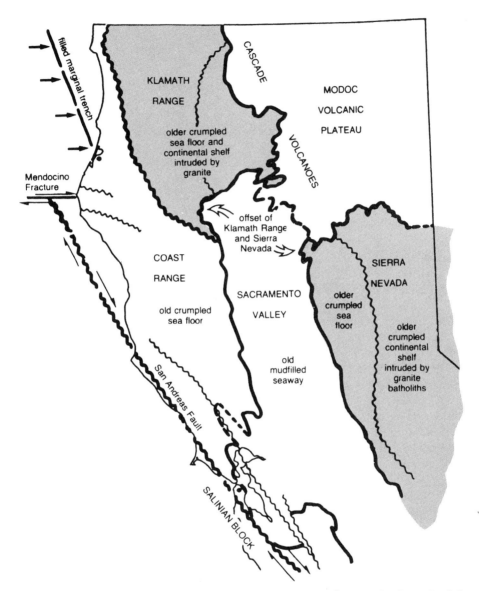

FIGURE 6.4   Geology of the Pacific Northwest. (From D. D. Alt and D. W. Hyndman. *Roadside Geology of Northern California*. Missoula, MT: Mountain Press, 1975. Reprinted with permission.)

Klamaths did not experience this secondary uplift and erosion. The Klamath Province is the product of millions of years of erosion under a dense forest cover.

Soon after the discovery of gold in the Sierra Nevada, prospectors found rich placer and lode gold deposits in the Klamath River area. The swiftness of the river made navigation nearly impossible, and the Indians in the area were hostile. Nevertheless, miners diverted the waters of the major rivers and mined the river gravels. After that, several hydraulic mining operations were undertaken, with incredible environmental degradation. On the South Fork of the Scott River from Etna Mills to Callahan, there are several miles of gravel piles left over from that period.

The threat of environmental degradation from mining operations is not over. A gold-mining process known as cyanide heap leaching has been developed. In this process, low-grade ore is piled up, and a cyanide solution is sprayed on top. The leachate contains the gold, which can be recoverd by passing the solution through carbon-filled columns. Obviously, there is concern that the highly toxic cyanide solution may escape into groundwater or streams, but miners assure all those concerned that the process is safe and efficient. Environmentalists are concerned because over 500 mammals and nearly 7000 birds were reported killed at cyanide extraction gold mines in Arizona, California, and Nevada between 1980 and 1989. Of the mammals that died, one-third were bats, many of which were classified as endangered, threatened, rare, or protected by government agencies. It remains to be seen how this procedure in the quest for gold fares with the environment.

In addition, several mining companies would like to establish viable strip mines in the Gasquet Mountain area of the Siskiyou Mountains. These companies propose to mine the laterite soils and extract cobalt, nickel, and chromium. The largest of these proposed mines would remove about 3.3 million tons (3 million t) of dirt annually in order to yield about 50 pounds of metals per ton (22 kg/t). Strip-mining laws require that spoils would have to be mulched, fertilized, and revegetated.

Obviously, this is an expensive operation. At world market prices it would not be economically feasible to operate these mines. The mine owners are hoping that the federal government will subsidize the operation because these are "strategic minerals," components of hardened alloys used in the aerospace industry.

Environmentalists are opposed to the plan because the mining operations are in the Smith River drainage, a wild and scenic river. Furthermore, the area has been proposed for inclusion in a new national park. Leach water from the mine could contaminate the water. Dams to supply water for the mining operation would become the only dams in the drainage. Severe air pollution from sulfur dioxide and nitrogen oxides, the major pollutants associated with acid rain, could occur. The mining operation could thus contribute to the formation of acid rain, which would fall on nearby wilderness areas.

GEOLOGY OF THE CASCADE PROVINCE

Overall, Cascade volcanics are relatively young. The process that formed the range began several million years ago and was responsible for uplifting volcanic peaks in excess of 14,000 feet (4300 m). Older volcanics, of the Tuscan Formation to the west, have been dated at about 5 million years of age. Apparently, the interval between eruptions is much greater than it was centuries ago, and there are few earthquakes in the area today. This reduction of activity indicates that the forces responsible are subsiding. Recent eruptions are from magma that formed a million years ago.

FIGURE 6.5   Bumpass Hell, Lassen Volcanic National Park. This region of geothermal activity is typical of areas associated with recent volcanism.

The California coast south of Cape Mendocino is an example of a rifted borderland (fig. 3.3). This is the area associated with the San Andreas fault. North of Cape Mendocino, California's most westerly projection, the coastline changes to the Andean type. Subduction is recent and may still be going on. Offshore there is a deep marine trench where the ocean floor slides beneath the continent. To the interior is an arc of volcanoes, above the region of magma formation. This volcanic arc is the Cascade Range. The higher Cascades, to the east, are younger than 5 million years, indicating that the leading edge of the subducted plate moved eastward under the North American continent. It is believed that the leading edge is now under Montana and is responsible for the volcanic and geothermal activity in the Yellowstone area. The eruption of Mount Saint Helens in 1980 was a reminder that this activity is still going on. Mount Shasta last erupted in 1786, and Mount Lassen (pl. 4A) erupted sporadically from 1914 to 1917. Geothermal activity in the area today proves that the region is still hot (fig. 6.5).

The primary type of volcanic rock in the Cascades is andesite. This type of rock is consistent with a subduction–volcanic arc borderland and is similar to what occurred to form the Andes of South America, which is why the rock is called andesite. Mount Lassen is composed of andesite and a related rock called dacite. Mount Shasta has two cones. The larger, older cone is composed of dacite. The smaller cone, known as Shastina, is composed of rhyolite, a light-colored volcanic rock that erupts in a more viscous state. Shasta, the higher peak, shows evidence of multiple glaciation, which indicates that it is quite young. An active glacier is still present on the top of Shasta.

BIOTIC ZONATION OF THE KLAMATH PROVINCE

Biotic zonation of the Klamath Province is shown in figure 6.6. Vegetation on the coastal terraces is similar to that of the northern Coast Ranges and will be discussed in detail in the next chapter. Shore Pines, *Pinus contorta contorta*, grow on stabilized sand dunes. On the first terrace is a well-established Coastal Prairie, which has been altered for agriculture, pastures, and urbanization. Moist pockets contain a forest of Alaskan affinities, including such species as Grand Fir, *Abies grandis*; Sitka Spruce, *Picea sitchensis*; and Western Hemlock, *Tsuga heterophylla*. On dry sites in this area, there is a closed-cone pine, the Knobcone Pine, *Pinus attenuata* (fig. 8.55). It often grows on poor soil that is either well drained or serpentine, and it usually gets its water from fog drip.

Riparian Woodland

The contrast between Riparian Woodland and surrounding communities is less dramatic in the Klamath Province than in parts of the state where there is a pronounced period of summer drought. At lower elevations along the coast, the forest understory contains many riparian species, including broad-leaved evergreens such as Pacific Madrone, *Arbutus menziesii* (fig. 6.7); Tanoak, *Lithocarpus densiflora* (fig. 6.8); and California Laurel, *Umbellularia californica* (fig. 7.9). Among the component deciduous

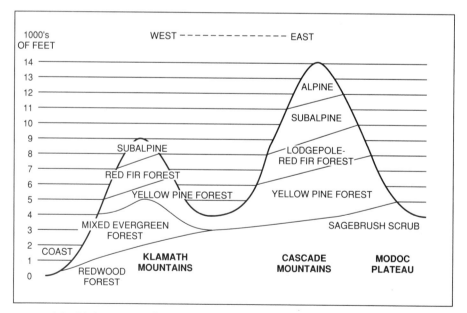

FIGURE 6.6   Biotic zonation of the Pacific Northwest Mountains.

FIGURE 6.7   Pacific Madrone, *Arbutus menziesii*. A. Leaves.

FIGURE 6.7 (*continued*)   Pacific Madrone, *Arbutus menziesii*. B. Flowers.

FIGURE 6.8   Tanoak, *Lithocarpus densiflora.*

species of the surrounding forest are Pacific Dogwood, *Cornus nuttallii* (fig. 4.55); Big-leaf Maple, *Acer macrophyllum* (fig. 6.9); and Oregon Ash, *Fraxinus latifolia.* In northern forests, Oregon Ash is one of the hardwood species with some commercial value. The yellowish wood is used for furniture, drawer sides, and cabinets.

Also typical of these coastal drainages are willows that are common in similar habitat throughout much of California, such as Pacific Willow, *Salix lasiandra*; (fig. 10.8) Sandbar Willow, *Salix hindsiana*; and Arroyo Willow, *Salix lasiolepis.* Below 500 feet (150 m) in these coastal drainages are several species of willow that are northwestern in distribution. Tracy Willow, *Salix tracyi*, occurs on gravel bars from Humboldt County to Del Norte County. In similar habitat, up to 1000 feet (300 m) in elevation, is the Smith River Willow, *Salix parksiana*; and restricted to the Smith River itself, between the elevations of 300 and 600 feet (100 and 190 m) is the Del Norte Willow, *Salix delnortensis.* Also near the coast, from San Luis Obispo County north, Velvet Willow, *Salix coulteri*, occurs, so named because of its silky lower leaf surface.

Right at the coast from Mendocino County north, two species of willow occur as large shrubs or small trees. Coast Willow, *Salix hookeriana*, occurs at the mouths of rivers and along lagoons as far north as Vancouver Island, British Columbia. Dune Willow or Piper Willow, *Salix piperi*, is rare in California. It occurs with Coast Willow, but in localized habitats as far north as Washington.

FIGURE 6.9   Big-leaf Maple, *Acer macrophyllum*, with winged fruit (samaras).

Upstream there is White Alder, *Alnus rhombifolia* (fig. 4.55), also common through-out the state. In the Pacific Northwest three other species of alder occur. Sitka Alder, *Alnus sinuata*, grows in marshes and stream bottoms in the wet coastal forest of the Klamath Province. It is a nitrogen-fixing, pioneer species in that area. Red Alder, *Alnus rubra*, grows in slightly drier areas of coastal forest, usually associated with Douglas Fir. Red Alder is a large species, reaching 80 feet (25 m) in height. It grows along the streams at lower elevations than White Alder. Its range overlaps both Sitka Alder and White Alder, but the three species rarely grow together. Red Alder can be a forest species, too.

Along with willows, Mountain Alder (*Alnus tenuifolia*) forms a typical montane type of riparian community resembling that of the Sierra Nevada. Mountain Alder is widely distributed along mountain lakes and streams of the eastern Klamath Province and the Cascades. The importance of alders as nitrogen fixers may be illustrated by a study conducted at Castle Lake, a nutrient-poor (oligotrophic) lake in the eastern Trinity Mountains. One-third of the lake's nitrogen is supplied by Mountain Alders that grow along the east side. Sampling of soil, spring water, and lake sediment from both sides of the lake revealed that the east side had far higher concentrations of water-soluble nitrogen compounds.

At higher elevations and on the interior slopes of the Klamath Province, the Riparian Woodland is more Sierran in appearance. This type of riparian habitat is discussed in chapter 4. Of special interest, however, is the presence of Water Birch, *Betula occidentalis*. Its distribution is patchy. In California, this Great Basin species occurs throughout the Klamath Province, in the interior of the northern Coast Ranges, and on Mount Shasta. Southward it reappears on the eastern slope of the Sierra Nevada from about 5000 to 9000 feet (1500–2700 m). This sort of disjunct distribution is similar to subalpine plants such as the Foxtail Pine, discussed in chapter 5.

At higher elevations, among the shrubby willows, usually above 5000 feet (1500 m) elevation, is a northern species known as Jepson Willow, *Salix jepsonii*. Jepson Willow also occurs at suitable localities in the Sierra Nevada. It inhabits a niche similar to that of Lemon Willow, *Salix lemmonii*, which occurs statewide. Mountain Willow, *Salix commutata*, occurs between 5000 and 7400 feet (1500 and 2300 m) in elevation in the Klamath Province and the Warner Mountains. Its range extends all the way north to Alaska. This species resembles Eastwood Willow, *Salix eastwoodiae*, of the Sierra Nevada.

Mixed Evergreen Forest

Above about 1000 feet (300 m) elevation, the Mixed Evergreen Forest dominates (pl. 5A). This forest is a mixture of broad-leaved evergreen species and conifers. Unlike the Coast Ranges, in the Klamath Province this forest is often dominated by Douglas Fir, *Pseudotsuga menziesii* (pl. 4B).

Various authors have divided Mixed Evergreen Forest into subcategories based on different dominant species. These subdivisions are, for the most part, an expression of moisture gradient or soil type. One author recognized 12 forest types on sedimentary, metasedimentary, volcanic, granitic, and ultrabasic (ophiolitic) parent materials.

A simpler way is to divide the forest into four categories, roughly associated with soil type, exposure, and moisture. On gentle slopes, north-facing slopes, ridges with deep soil, or river terraces with deep sediment, there is a luxuriant forest dominated by Douglas Fir. Commonly, these are soils weathered from sedimentary rocks. This forest is recognized by many authors as Douglas Fir Forest. Nearly 70% of forest cover is occupied by Douglas Fir, huge trees that may rival Coast Redwoods in size and growth rate. Of secondary importance in this forest are components of moist Yellow Pine Forest, including Sugar Pine, *Pinus lambertiana*; (fig. 4.33); Ponderosa Pine, *Pinus ponderosa*; and White Fir, *Abies concolor* (fig. 4.32). In this forest, broad-leaved evergreens play a minor role.

Of great importance in coniferous forests are the masses of underground filaments known as mycorrhizae. These are produced by a variety of fungi and form an interconnecting network of fine tubes that tap into the root systems of the trees. This arrangement increases the surface area available for absorption of water and nutrients, and it also provides a means for chemical communication between adjacent trees. One of the most important of these fungi is the Oregon White Truffle, *Tuber gibbosum*. Its range extends from British Columbia to northern California. Although it is most often associated with roots of Douglas Fir, it also is found in soil under various species of oaks. This is a convoluted mushroom that grows entirely beneath the ground. It is a favored food for rodents, particularly the Golden-mantled Ground Squirrel (pl. 12D), which digs up truffles and disperses the spores through its digestive tract. Also a favored food for humans, the flavor of this species of truffle has been likened to the European truffles considered gourmet delicacies. In fact, it has been the human quest for these underground mushrooms that has also revealed their presence in the Oak Woodlands of the northern Coast Ranges.

On granitic soils, typically at lower elevation than the Douglas Fir Forest, dominant trees are similar, but broad-leaved evergreens are more common. In particular, Tanoak, *Lithocarpus densiflora* (fig. 6.8), and Canyon Live Oak, *Quercus chrysolepis* (pl. 7A), form forests of broad-leaved trees in these areas. An interesting species in this community is Giant Chinquapin, *Chrysolepis chrysophylla*. This member of the beech-oak family (Fagaceae) occurs in tree form at widely scattered localities in Redwood and Mixed Evergreen forests. On dry sites, associated with chaparral species, it occurs in shrub form. In western Siskiyou County, distribution of the shrub form overlaps that of Bush Chinquapin, *Chrysolepis sempervirens* (fig. 4.49); hybridization of the two is believed to occur. Bush Chinquapin was discussed as an understory shrub in chapter 4, in the section on Lodgepole–Red Fir Forest.

On steep slopes where soil is coarse and well drained, dominance shifts to Canyon Live Oak, also known as Golden-Cup Oak. Douglas Fir is of minor importance in this community, representing a dry extreme of Mixed Evergreen Forest. In this form, the forest is quite similar to Canyon Live Oak woodlands that occur in canyons throughout the state. Canyon Live Oak is the most widely distributed oak in the state.

The fourth type of forest is associated with the ophiolitic soils, such as those derived from serpentine. Here we find strikingly different patterns of vegetation depending on exposure and mineral composition of the soil. In ravines are moist forests dominated by Port Orford Cedar, *Chamaecyparis lawsoniana*; Western White Pine, *Pinus monticola* (fig. 4.47); and, to a lesser degree, Douglas Fir. Port Orford Cedar, a member of the cypress family (Cupressaceae), occurs at patchy localities for about 200 miles (320 km) along the coast from Coos Bay, Oregon, to Humboldt County, California. It is often described as a serpentine endemic, but it also occurs on other soil types, in moist areas within Douglas Fir Forest. The fine wood of this forest tree is treasured for beautiful interior finish work, particularly in shipbuilding. It also has been planted extensively in the Pacific Northwest as a horticultural species known as Lawson Cypress. Western White Pine in this forest is the same species that occurs on dry exposed sites at middle elevations in the Sierra Nevada, most often in association with Lodgepole Pine.

In more exposed localities on ophiolitic soils, or on steep slopes, a forest more similar to dry Yellow Pine Forest occurs. Trees here include many that have been discussed previously, such as Incense Cedar, *Calocedrus decurrens* (fig. 4.28); Jeffrey Pine, *Pinus jeffreyi* (fig. 4.29); and Knobcone Pine, *Pinus attenuata* (fig. 8.55). Also possibly found here are Douglas Fir, Western White Pine, and Sugar Pine. This forest has a completely different appearance than other parts of Mixed Evergreen Forest. Trees are farther apart, occurring in rather open stands, sometimes single-species stands.

On ophiolitic soils in warm, dry localities, particularly on south-facing slopes, the Mixed Evergreen Forest gives way to Oak Woodland and Chaparral communities. Among the oaks found here is a form of white oak known as Garry Oak or Oregon White Oak, *Quercus garryana*. Some authorities refer to a community dominated by Garry Oak as Northern Oak Woodland. They consider this to be a form of Foothill Woodland in which there is a change in the dominant white oak from Blue Oak to Garry Oak. This tree resembles Blue Oak, often growing in savannas, and its associated species are similar to those found with Blue Oak. An example of ecological separation between Garry Oak and Blue Oak can be seen near Browns Creek, in Trinity County. Here Garry Oaks occur in open, rocky locations on ophiolitic soils within Mixed Evergreen Forest, whereas the Blue Oaks occur on disjunct patches of clay loam derived from shale.

Garry Oak is a northern oak species, occurring all the way to British Columbia, that reaches its southern limits in California. This is the only California oak that has widespread distribution beyond the state. Farther south, in the Coast Ranges, Garry Oak becomes a species of north-facing slopes, or those slopes that receive more precipitation than the surrounding areas, which may be dominated by Blue Oak. Also in the northern Coast Ranges, Garry Oak dominates on ridgetops up to 5000 feet (1600 cm) in elevation. These ridgetop communities, known locally as balds or bald hills, are dominated by grasses or by Garry Oaks, depending on the type of soil.

As soils become increasingly exposed and dry, tree species drop out. A rather continuous layer of shrubs may dominate, forming a chaparral-like community. Several species of shrubby oaks may coexist, including a shrub variety of Garry Oak. A scrub oak known as Huckleberry Oak, *Quercus vaccinifolia,* occurs here along with Deer Oak, *Quercus sadleriana.* These species of scrub oak do not have spiny margins on the leaves. Huckleberry Oak leaves are oblong, resembling those of a Huckleberry plant. The distribution of Huckleberry Oak is typically northwestern Californian, although its total range is from southern Oregon, through the Cascades, down the western Sierra foothills to the region of Yosemite National Park. It is the dominant scrub oak at Glacier Point, one of the most popular view points in Yosemite. The shrub form of Garry Oak also occurs along the foothills of the Sierra, but it extends as far south as Kern County.

Deer Oak is also known as Sadler Oak. Its distribution resembles that of Huckleberry Oak, but it does not occur eastward into the Sierra foothills. Leaves of Deer Oak resemble those of an alder or an elm. They are 2 to 4 inches (5–10 cm) long, and they are serrated but not spiny. Leaves are pale gray underneath and shiny on top.

Also in these shrub-dominated communities are shrub varieties of other common tree species of the northwest, such as Canyon Live Oak, Tanoak, and California Laurel. True chaparral species such as California Coffeeberry (*Rhamnus californica*), Buckbrush (*Ceanothus cuneatus*), and Hoary Manzanita (*Arctostaphylos canescens*) also occur here.

Overall, the patterns of community distribution just described have become complicated by a diversified history of fires and logging. Succession following a disturbance may vary depending on the intensity of disturbance. For example, Douglas Fir does not sprout; if an intense fire were to kill all the Douglas Fir in an area, or if clear-cutting were extensive, there would be no source of seeds. In this case, sprouting species such as Tanoak or Pacific Madrone would dominate for many years. Coast Redwoods also regenerate after a severe fire because they too are sprouters. If a fire is mild, or if many acres have not been logged, there could be a nearby source of Douglas Fir seeds. In this case Tanoak or, in very open areas, Pacific Madrone would dominate for a few years because they are sprouters. Seedlings of Douglas Fir could start in the partial shade of sprouting species, but eventually it would overtake the other forms. Douglas Fir is a long-lived species, reaching an age of 400 to 600 years. In old-growth situations, Douglas Fir is certain to dominate.

Moist Yellow Pine Forest

Some authorities use the term *Montane Forest* to include two communities that have been discussed previously: Yellow Pine Forest and Lodgepole–Red Fir Forest. On western slopes of the Klamath Mountains, these communities are present in their moist form.

From about 2000 to 4500 feet (600–1400 m) the moist Yellow Pine Forest is dominated by White Fir, *Abies concolor* (fig. 4.32). Douglas Fir may be common here as well. Subdominant species include Sugar Pine and Canyon Live Oak.

An interesting understory tree in this moist forest is Pacific Yew, *Taxus brevifolia,* a slow-growing, long-lived conifer. Pacific Yew is widespread in the west, ranging from Alaska to California and into the Rockies of Idaho and Montana. It is not common anywhere, usually occurring in isolation or in small stands in old-growth forest. In California, it occurs in the northern Coast Ranges, Klamath Mountains, the Cascades, and the northern Sierra as far south as Calavaras Big Tree State Park.

Pacific Yew is a small tree, seldom over 25 feet (8 m) in height. On drier soil it becomes shrublike. Because it grows in deep shade, its trunk is usually twisted and it has sprawling branches. Its needles resemble those of a fir, but each is prickly tipped. The bark has purple, papery scales under which there is a clear reddish hue. These trees differ from other conifers in that male and female reproductive structures are borne on separate trees. The female part, the cone, is red and fleshy, resembling a large berry with a hole in it. This sweetish, fleshy fruit is an important food for some birds. Pacific Yew has heavy, tough wood that is surprisingly resistant to decay. For that reason it has been used for gateposts. The wood also has a good deal of resilience and has been used for canoe paddles and bows for archery.

In 1962 a program conducted by the National Cancer Institute identified chemicals from the bark and roots of Pacific Yew known as taxanes, including taxol, as having the ability to inhibit tumors in mice. The National Cancer Institute initially contracted for 60,000 pounds (27,000 kg) of yew bark, which would require cutting down about 12,000 trees. By 1991 it was estimated that 38,000 trees would have to be harvested to satisfy demand for the drug during that year. Because the Pacific Yew is so sparsely distributed and grows so slowly, it may be unrealistic to expect such a quantity of bark ever to become available even with the use of cultivars. A synthetic substitute extracted from yew needles may solve the problem.

Pacific Yew is California's only true yew. It should not be confused with another member of this family (Taxaceae), which is known as California Nutmeg, *Torreya californica*. California Nutmeg occurs in the shade of canyons in the northern Coast Ranges and foothills of the Sierra Nevada, and it does not occur in the Klamath Mountains, where Pacific Yew is most common. The trees resemble each other, but *Torreya* has even stiffer prickly needles, and its fruit is blue-green with no hole. When its foliage is broken, it gives off a foul odor. In the Sierra Nevada it occurs at lower elevations and farther south than the Pacific Yew.

Red Fir Forest

Elevational gradients in the western Klamath Province are similar to those in the Sierra Nevada. Above Yellow Pine Forest there is a zone dominated by Red Fir, *Abies magnifica* (fig. 4.45). Occurring from about 4500 to 6000 feet (1400–1950 m) in elevation, this forest often borders meadows (fig. 6.10). Associated species include Lodgepole Pine, *Pinus contorta murrayana* (fig. 4.46); Western White Pine, *Pinus monticola* (fig. 4.47); and Mountain Hemlock, *Tsuga mertensiana* (fig. 5.3). At higher elevations Mountain Hemlock becomes the dominant species. Above 6000 feet (1950 m) Mountain Hemlock is joined by Whitebark Pine, *Pinus albicaulis* (fig. 5.5), in a typical subalpine community. On ophiolitic soils and on south-facing slopes Foxtail Pine, *Pinus balfouriana* (fig. 5.8), becomes the dominant subalpine species. The subalpine zone on the Klamath and Cascade mountains is discussed in chapter 5.

Forests of the Klamath Province are noted for the presence of relict conifers. Typically, there are species of northern affinities that reach their southernmost distribution in northern California. One exception is Foxtail Pine, which also is found in the southern Sierra Nevada. Its enigmatic distribution is discussed in chapter 5. The usual summer precipitation from the tails of Alaskan storms is deemed particularly important for these relicts.

Of special interest in the Siskiyou and Marble Mountains are two large fir species that resemble Red Fir. The Cascade or Lovely Fir, *Abies amabilis,* is common in the Olympic and Cascade mountains. It is scarce south of Crater Lake, Oregon. The tops of this species, also known as Pacific Silver Fir, may be sold as an expensive Christmas tree under the name "Silver Tip," although, as explained earlier, any of the true firs might be sold under that name. Noble Fir, *Abies procera,* occurs in association with Cascade Fir in the Cascades of Oregon and Washington. In California it occurs along with Red Fir on the western side of the Siskiyous. It is so similar to Red Fir that only an expert can tell the two species apart, and then only by closely examining a mature cone.

FIGURE 6.10   Stanshaw Meadow, Marble Mountain Wilderness, Salmon Mountains.

Another fir with restricted distribution occurs in the Red Fir Forest of the Salmon Mountains. This is the Subalpine Fir, *Abies lasiocarpa*. It grows on the edges of meadows on wet slopes, and its distribution is apparently expanding into the meadows. This is the most widely distributed fir in North America, occurring from Alaska to Arizona. Throughout most of its range it is a subalpine species, but on the coast of California it occurs lower. It is believed to have survived above the glaciers during the Pleistocene and to have extended its range down the mountain during the last 10,000 years or so.

Port Orford Cedar was mentioned previously as a relict occurring in moist Yellow Pine Forest. A close relative of this species occurs at higher elevations, in wet meadows and seeps: Alaska Cedar, *Chamaecyparis nootkatensis*. Where it grows in moist forests to the north, this is a large, stately species. At the few localities where it is found in the Klamath Mountains, it is low-growing and shrubby. Apparently, it reproduces vegetatively.

Spruces are not common in California. There are three species, all in the northwest. They resemble firs, but their needles are stiff, encircling the branches, and their cones hang down. Fir cones fall apart when mature, and they point upward on the stem. Spruces most nearly resemble Douglas Fir. Sitka Spruce, *Picea sitchensis*, mentioned earlier, is a component of the wet coastal forest in association with sand dunes. Engelmann Spruce, *Picea engelmannii*. is widespread in mountains of western North America. In California it occurs primarily on the east side of Russian Peak in the

FIGURE 6.11   Weeping Spruce, *Picea breweriana*.

Salmon Mountains. This spruce is concentrated in valley bottoms in the Red Fir and Yellow Pine forests, and its upper limit is about 6500 feet (2150 m). The third spruce is Weeping Spruce, *Picea breweriana* (fig. 6.11). This spruce is endemic to the Klamath Province of California and southern Oregon, and it gets its name from its long, down-drooping branches. It is a very beautiful tree, often standing by itself on a rocky outcrop. It does not grow in large stands but is associated with a wide variety of species at a wide range of elevations. It is probably fire-sensitive and cannot tolerate saturated soil. It is remarkably drought-tolerant, withstanding moisture stresses below −20 bars.

Dry Yellow Pine Forest

East of the main crest of the Klamath Mountains, vegetation zones follow a pattern similar to that of the western slopes, but the elevation of each zone is deflected upward about 600 feet (200 m). There is less precipitation on the east side of the mountains, so the forest takes on a more open appearance, and the moisture-loving species either drop out or become common only locally. Below about 4000 feet (1300 m) Ponderosa Pine, Sugar Pine, and California Black Oak, *Quercus kelloggii* (fig. 4.27), become important components of the forest, which more closely resembles the Yellow Pine Forest of the Sierra Nevada.

On ophiolitic soils in the western Klamath Province, the forest is also typical of dry Yellow Pine Forest, but the dominant pine is usually Jeffrey Pine. On the eastern slopes of the Klamath Mountains the dry Yellow Pine Forest becomes interspersed with chaparral species. Of particular interest is the occurrence of Leather Oak, *Quercus durata*, a serpentine endemic. The distributions of these serpentine-associated species are discussed in chapters 4 and 7.

BIOTIC ZONATION OF THE CASCADES

East of the Klamath Province, the volcanic soils of the Cascades make their appearance. In lowland areas the forest is typically moist Yellow Pine Forest dominated by Ponderosa Pine, Sugar Pine, White Fir, and Incense Cedar. Elevational relationships in the Cascades are similar to those in the northern Sierra Nevada. Forests on the west side are moist, and those on the east are drier. On the western side of the Cascades, Yellow Pine Forest occurs in a belt that covers about 1500 feet (500 m) in elevation. In some areas on the west side of the Cascades, the moist Yellow Pine Forest is particularly luxuriant. One such area lies in McArthur-Burney Falls State Park. One of the main attractions in this park is Burney Falls itself, a two-tiered waterfall (fig. 6.12). The upper part of the fall occurs where the water flows over the top of a cliff, and the lower part occurs at an interface between volcanic rock and old sedimentary rock. Water percolates downward through the volcanic rock and then flows horizontally along the sedimentary rock until it emerges halfway up the cliff to complete the waterfall.

On the east side of the Cascades, understory plants in the Yellow Pine Forest are typically those of Great Basin affinities. Trees in the forests of Ponderosa and Jeffrey pines are widely spaced, with abundant shrubs in between. Ponderosa Pine is more common to the north. Western Juniper, *Juniperus occidentalis occidentalis* (fig. 6.13), is an important tree species occurring with Jeffrey Pine to the south and east. Shrubs such as Great Basin Sagebrush, *Artemisia tridentata* (fig. 9.21A), and Antelope Brush, *Purshia tridentata* (fig. 9.21B), form the understory. This forest grades off to the east to the Modoc Plateau.

An interesting conifer known as Baker Cypress, *Cupressus bakeri,* grows on the volcanic soils of the east side of the Cascades in California. There are 10 species of cypress in California, and all of them have restricted ranges, usually in association with specialized soils such as serpentine. Baker Cypress grows primarily on volcanic soils, but a few groves also grow in the Siskiyou Mountains on ophiolitic soils. Distribution of the species is patchy, with groves separated by many miles. It grows at only eight locations in California and one in Oregon, 25 miles (40 km) south of Crater Lake.

FIGURE 6.12   Moist Yellow Pine Forest in McArthur-Burney Falls State Park.

FIGURE 6.13   Western Juniper, *Juniperus occidentalis occidentalis*, mixed with Great Basin Sagebrush, *Artemisia tridentata*. A community typical of the east side of the Cascade Range.

Baker Cypress grows straight and tall. It is an attractive tree, often having cherry red bark, particularly on young specimens. This is a unique species of cypress by virtue of its tolerance for snow and cold. Throughout most of its range it is associated with Ponderosa Pine, Knobcone Pine, Incense Cedar, Western Juniper, Garry Oak, and California Black Oak. In Plumas County, however, in the Red Fir Forest of the northern Sierra Nevada, Baker Cypress grows at an elevation of 7200 feet (2300 m). This is the highest elevation at which cypresses are known to grow in California.

At higher elevations, zonation of the Cascade Province is typically Sierran. Volcanic soils are coarse, so trees are well spaced. A variety of Red Fir, known as Shasta Fir, *Abies magnifica shastensis,* occurs here, primarily on the west side. The subalpine and alpine communities on the peaks are discussed in chapter 5, on mountaintops.

ANIMALS OF THE NORTHWEST FORESTS

Animals of Oak Woodland, Chaparral, and Yellow Pine Forest are similar throughout the state, but in the moist forests along the coast are a number of animals unique to California. Mostly, these are animals that reach the southernmost portions of their range here, and many of them enjoy widespread distribution along the coast farther north. However, conspicuous species are not numerous.

In an environment as productive as these moist forests, a considerable biomass of animal life can be sustained. One of the reasons that the forest seems to lack animal life is that there is a large community of detritus feeders and decomposers. There are fungi, slime molds, termites, and many kinds of insects. Banana slugs, *Ariolimax* spp. (fig. 7.22), are conspicuous detritus feeders. These large, shell-less molluscs, up to 6 inches (16 cm) in length, creep about on the forest floor consuming litter and debris. Banana slugs will be discussed in more detail in the next chapter.

Salamanders

The Pacific Northwest is the land of the salamander. Here in the northern forests there are at least 15 species, most of which reach the southerly limits of their distribution in the area.

Some of the salamanders are discussed in other chapters. The rassenkreis, or circle of races, of *Ensatina* (fig. 8.31) will be discussed in the chapter on cismontane southern California. In the northern part of the state, the spotted Sierra form, *Ensatina eschscholtzii platensis* (fig. 4.38), merges with a mostly solid-colored coastal form, *Ensatina eschscholtizii oregonensis.* Furthermore, a dwarfed form known as the Painted Salamander, *Ensatina eschscholtizii picta* (fig. 4.38), from the northern Coast Ranges, reaches its northernmost distribution here. Intergradation between the different subspecies occurs in the regions where the ranges overlap. In the Redwood Forest, along the coast, two species of newt (*Taricha* spp.) overlap their ranges (fig. 7.24).

Among the lungless salamanders (Plethodontidae), three species of climbing salamanders (*Aneides* spp.) overlap their ranges in these northern forests. The Arboreal

Salamander, *Aneides lugubris,* reaches its northern distribution in Humboldt County and is associated primarily with oaks. The Black Salamander, *Aneides flavipunctutatus,* ranges from Santa Cruz County to the Klamath Mountains, occurring mostly in rock talus along streams. The Clouded Salamander, *Aneides ferreus* (fig. 6.14A), the most arboreal of the three, is associated with Coast Redwoods, Douglas Fir, and Port Orford Cedar from Mendocino County to the Columbia River.

Other lungless salamanders are the Woodland Salamanders (*Plethodon* spp.). These salamanders occur only in the extreme northwestern corner of the state. The Del Norte Salamander, *Plethodon elongatus* (fig. 6.14C), occurs in wet, mossy rock slides and talus from Humboldt County to just north of the Oregon border. A close relative of the Del Norte Salamander is the Siskiyou Mountains Salamander, *Plethodon stormi.* An endangered species, it occurs only in the Rogue River area of the Siskiyou Mountains. Its range barely extends into California just south of the Oregon border, Dunn's Salamander, *Plethodon dunni,* occurs together with the Del Norte Salamander in talus along the Rogue River. It has not been collected in California, but its range occurs so near to the border that it probably will be collected here sooner or later.

The Shasta Salamander, *Hydromantes shastae,* is a cave-dwelling species that is endemic to limestone. This species is also endangered. Its range is restricted to the McCloud River area of Brock Mountain, north of Shasta Reservoir. Closely related to the Mount Lyell Salamander, its distribution is discussed in chapter 5 (fig. 5.30).

The mole salamanders (Ambystomatidae) differ from the lungless salamanders in that adults are terrestrial and larvae are aquatic. In this respect, they are similar to newts. Unlike newts, the adults are seldom seen, spending most of their lives underground. Also unlike newts, they seldom venture far from water.

Of special interest among the mole salamanders is the Pacific Giant Salamander, *Dicamptodon ensatus* (fig. 6.14B). Adults of this species are known to grow up to 12 inches (30 cm) in length. Adults are rarely seen, but they are distinctive, with a light brownish color and a marbling of brown to black blotches on their backs. They range from Santa Cruz County to British Columbia. In California they are associated with streams in the Redwood country, and they occur inland in the Siskiyous and Cascades. They are known to burrow in stream gravels, particularly at the heads of streams. When molested, they make a noise that has been described variously as a scream or a bark. This is the reason they are sometimes called barking salamanders.

Two other mole salamanders are closely related. The Northwestern Salamander, *Ambystoma gracile,* occurs in wet forests from southeast Alaska to Sonoma County. Adults are a uniform brownish to black, but they are seldom seen. They breed in quiet water. The Long-toed Salamander, *Ambystoma macrodactylum,* occurs in the Cascades, the eastern Klamath Mountains, and the northwestern parts of the Sierra Nevada. It ranges up to about 9000 feet (2900 m) in elevation, almost always near lakes. Sometimes adults are found under rocks and logs at the edges of lakes. It differs in appearance from the Northwestern Salamander by having an undulating light stripe down its back.

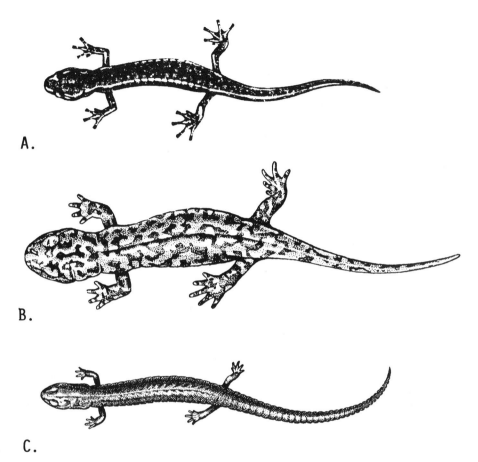

FIGURE 6.14   Some salamanders of the Pacific Northwest. *A.* Clouded Salamander, *Aneides ferreus.*
B. Pacific Giant Salamander, *Dicamptodon ensatus. C.* Del Norte Salamander, *Plethodon elongatus* (From
R. C. Stebbins. *Amphibians of Western North America.* Berkeley: University of California Press, 1951.)

The fourth mole salamander is the Olympic Salamander, *Rhyacotriton olympicus.*
This small salamander is associated with rapidly flowing mountain streams in the
coastal forest from Washington to Humboldt County. It may be found in the water
or under rocks on the water's edge. It is chocolate brown with black flecks on its back.

Birds

One would expect birds to be abundant in a forest. Most of the birds that are present
in the northwest are similar to those that occur throughout the forests of California,
but they are not particularly abundant. Most authorities recognize only seven kinds of

birds nesting in the coastal coniferous forests of northern California. Two of them are hummingbirds—the Rufous, *Selasphorus rufus*, and Allen's, *Selasphorus sasin*—both of which are also found in the Sierra Nevada.

Two grouses occur in the area, but only the Blue Grouse, *Dendragapus obscurus* (fig. 4.51), nests here. This species is discussed in the chapter on the Sierra Nevada. The other grouse is the Oregon Ruffed Grouse, *Bonasa umbellus*. It is a brownish bird and is more pheasantlike than the Blue Grouse. It reaches its southernmost distribution in the Klamath Mountains.

Among gleaners there are creepers, nuthatches, and warblers. The only nesting species is the Chestnut-backed Chickadee, *Parus rufescens*. This chickadee lacks the lyric call of its relative, the Mountain Chickadee, and differs in appearance by having a brownish-colored back.

A conspicuous bird of the forest is the Varied Thrush, *Ixoreus naevius*. This bird is similar in size and appearance to the American Robin, also in the thrush family (Muscicapidae). The Varied Thrush has a black band across its rusty-colored chest. It nests in the forests of the Pacific Northwest and winters southwards in the Coast Ranges or out in the Great Basin. Similar to the Robin, its clear whistle is a sound commonly associated with the forest.

Swallows and swifts are acrobatic birds that catch insects on the wing. Vaux's Swift, *Chaetura vauxi*, is a small dingy-looking swift. It looks like a swallow with no tail. The Black Swift, *Cypseloides niger*, is the largest of this group, about 8 inches (12 cm) in length. It is not a common bird in California, but one of the few places where it may be seen is over the cliffs in McArthur-Burney Falls State Park. Black Swifts make nests on cliffs by packing algae and moss into moist cracks. They often are solitary and may fly along with other species of swifts and swallows. One biologist described the flight of the Black Swift as looking like a great winged spider gone mad.

Large birds that are considered rare may occur here. During salmon or steelhead runs, Bald Eagles, *Haliaetus leucocephalus* (fig. 6.15), may be observed fishing in the larger rivers. The largest winter concentration of Bald Eagles in the lower 48 states occurs in the Klamath Basin. Approximately 500 may occur at one time in the Tule Lake National Wildlife Refuge, just south of the Oregon border. The Bald Eagle formerly occurred over much of the state, but because of hunting and widespread use of DDT, the number of nesting pairs by the late 1960s was reduced to 20. Protective measures were initiated in association with the Endangered Species Act of 1972, and the use of DDT was discontinued. Since that time, the number of Bald Eagles has increased markedly. As of 1989 there were 83 known pairs of nesting birds in the state, and the number of winter visitors had risen to over 600. Most of the overwintering birds were in the Klamath Basin of northern California, but about 30 made it as far south as Big Bear Lake in the San Bernardino Mountains, Lake Mathews in Riverside County, and Lake Henshaw in San Diego County. A pair of Bald Eagles was introduced to Santa Catalina Island in 1980 with the hope that they would thrive and reproduce. Apparently, enough DDT remains in the environment

FIGURE 6.15   Bald Eagle, *Haliaetus leucocephalus*.

at this southern California locality that the female continued to lay thin-shelled eggs. In 1989 a three-week-old chick from a nest in northern California was placed in the nest on Santa Catalina Island, and the adults apparently adopted it.

Pileated Woodpeckers, *Dryocopus pileatus,* also reach their southern, coastal distribution limits in the Klamath Province. The secretive Spotted Owl, *Strix occidentalis* (fig. 6.16), might also be observed in its daytime haunt, resting on a branch close to the trunk, where it is well camouflaged. Spotted Owls have been particular victims of habitat destruction. As inhabitants of old-growth forests, they are threatened by clear-cut logging. Furthermore, in the summer of 1990 the Northern Spotted Owl (*Strix occidentalis caurina*) was officially listed by the federal government as threatened, a move that is certain to provoke a prolonged conflict between logging interests and environmentalists.

One of the strangest birds that a person can expect to find in moist coastal forests is a seagoing bird known as the Marbled Murrelet, *Brachyrampus marmoratus*. This species, which spends most of its life out on the Pacific Ocean, nests in the tops of tall trees up to several miles from the sea. This is a robin-sized, stout-bodied bird with short wings. It is quite agile in flight, but it apparently experiences some difficulty getting airborne from a perch. When it takes off, it is said to require the height of a tall tree to build enough momentum for flight. The first Marbled Murrelet nest

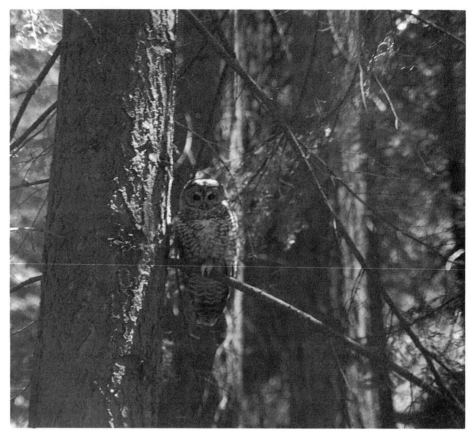

FIGURE 6.16   Spotted Owl, *Strix occidentalis*. (Photo by William B. Cella.)

discovered in California was found in 1973 in the Santa Cruz Mountains. It was 135 feet (42 m) up in a large Douglas Fir. This bird also has been proposed for threatened status by the U.S. Fish and Wildlife Service.

Mammals

Among the mammals of the coastal forest, squirrels are the most conspicuous. Three species overlap their ranges here. The Northern Flying Squirrel, *Glaucomys sabrinus*, is the nocturnal member of the group. The Western Gray Squirrel, *Sciurus griseus* (pl. 12B), occurs where there are acorns, and the Chickaree, *Tamiasciurus douglasii* (pl. 12C), feeds mostly on cones of various conifers. There are two species of chipmunk. The Sonoma Chipmunk, *Tamias sonomae,* occurs in open places in the forest and in chaparral. The chipmunk of the forest floor is Townsend's Chipmunk, *Tamias townsendii.* This is a wide-ranging species of northern forests that occurs as far south as Marin County and the central Sierra Nevada. This is the darkest species of chipmunk and is often used to illustrate Gloger's rule, that dark coloration is associated with moist habitats. One authority proposed to split this form into four separate species based on anatomy of the penis bone (baculum).

Another ecological principle illustrated by rodents of the coastal forest is parallel evolution. Mice of the subfamily Microtinae are known as microtine mice. They look very much alike, and it often requires inspection of teeth and skeleton to tell them apart. Included here are mice from three genera. They all have relatively small ears that may be nearly covered by long hair and they also tend to have short tails. They are separated by habitat and behavior, however. Meadow mice (*Microtus* spp.) (fig. 6.17) often occur in meadows and along streams. There are at least four species that may occur in these forests. Good swimmers, they often have been observed to swim underwater with their front legs folded back, propelling themselves with their hind feet. Many of them make tunnels through the grass, which they use to conceal themselves from predators.

There are two species of tree voles. The White-footed Vole, *Arborimus albipes,* lives on the ground. It is distinguished from other microtine mice by being the only species with white feet and a nearly hairless tail. It is a rare mouse, and very little is known about its life history. The Red Tree Vole, *Arborimus longicaudus,* can be distinguished from the others by its reddish color and long tail, which is usually about 65% of its total length. These are truly mice of the moist forests. They live high in the trees, seldom coming to the ground. Their diet consists of needles of fir, spruce, and hemlock. They make large nests of the inedible parts of the needles. Of particular interest to physiologists is the rather long gestation periods and small litters of these mice. There are usually only one to three offspring per litter, and the mother carries them up to 48 days. This is a low reproductive capacity for a mouse. It may be related to the low-calorie diet of fir needles, or it may mean that these rodents are so well adapted to their environment that they need not produce many young. An investigation has discovered that Red Tree Voles south of the Smith River have a different chromosome number than those north of the river. The two forms probably will be assigned separate species names.

The Western Red-backed Vole, *Clethrionomys californicus,* is another mouse of the deep forest. It usually lives on the forest floor, making a nest out of lichens under logs, but sometimes it occurs in wet meadows. These mice can be distinguished from Red Tree Voles by having a shorter, bicolored tail and grayish underparts. The back is not as rusty in appearance as that of the Red Tree Vole; it is more of a chestnut brown. These mice feed mostly on leaves and other green vegetation.

A unique rodent of moist northwestern forest is the Mountain Beaver, *Aplodontia rufa* (fig. 6.18). This large rodent is not really a mountain dweller, nor is it a beaver. It is a primitive squirrel-like creature that looks like a large gopher. Mountain Beavers grow up to 14 inches (35 cm) in length and have large claws, small ears, and a stubby tail. They spend most of the time underground. When they emerge from their burrow, it usually is at night. They make their burrows in thickets of wild blackberries, Salmonberries, and Thimbleberries, on which they feed. They also feed

FIGURE 6.17   California Meadow Vole, *Microtus californicus*. (From E. W. Jameson, Jr. and H. J. Peeters. *California Mammals*. Berkeley: University of California Press, 1988.)

FIGURE 6.18   Mountain Beaver, *Aplodontia rufa*. (From E. W. Jameson, Jr. and H. J. Peeters *California Mammals*. Berkeley: University of California Press, 1988.)

on a wide variety of green vegetation. During winter, at higher elevations, they burrow under the snow in a manner similar to a gopher. They often strip the bark from young White Firs during winter. There is only one species in the Mountain Beaver family (Aplodontidae). Its distribution is limited entirely to the forests of the Pacific Northwest and the northern Sierra Nevada.

Of the larger mammals, the most conspicuous is the Porcupine, *Erethizon dorsatum* (fig. 6.19). Porcupines are seldom reported in humid coastal forests, but east of

FIGURE 6.19   Porcupine, *Erethizon dorsatum*. (Photo by Steven D. Cain.)

the crest of the Klamath Mountains and throughout the Cascades, they are commonly observed as road kills. Porcupines are mostly nocturnal, but they are occasionally encountered during daylight hours sauntering along the trail, humming to themselves. During the daytime they usually conceal themselves in the foliage of a tree. In the summer they eat leaves and herbs, or they may climb into treetops and eat buds, an activity that may cause forking of treetops. During winter they primarily gnaw on the bark of young trees, and it is this habit that makes them the enemy of loggers. Actually, they may provide a beneficial thinning effect, because most of the trees they damage are saplings that do not grow well under the forest canopy. Their habit of erecting their spines and slapping with their spiny tail when molested protects them from most predators, although Martens have been reported to burrow under snow and attack Porcupines from beneath.

Another nocturnal mammal that is sometimes conspicuous is the Raccoon, *Procyon lotor*. This animal is widespread throughout northern forests, usually occurring along watercourses and lakes, where it feeds on nearly everything edible. The reason they are conspicuous is that they are apparently very curious. They also are clever and brazen. They have learned that campers are careless with food and that for a simple glimpse of a "wild" animal, humans will leave tempting morsels of food in easy-to-reach places. Many campers in public campgrounds are delighted by the visits of Raccoons to the campfire, and dismayed when they raid the larder.

Of the predatory mammals in the northwest forests, most important are members of the weasel family (Mustelidae). Every Pacific representative of this family can be found somewhere in the northwestern mountains, each in a different habitat. This list includes the Long-tailed Weasel (*Mustela frenata*) (fig. 5.35), Marten (*Martes americana*), Fisher (*Martes pennanti*), Ermine (*Mustela erminea*), Mink (*Mustela vision*), Wolverine (*Gulo gulo*), Badger (*Taxidea taxus*), Spotted Skunk (*Spilogale gracilis*), Striped Skunk (*Mephitis mephitis*), and River Otter (*Lutra canadensis*).

These mammals have a number of features in common, including highly developed scent glands, long bodies with short legs, and fine-quality fur. The rarest of these mammals are the Fisher and the Wolverine. The Fisher is now rare because its prime pelt has commanded high prices, and it has been hunted to the brink of extinction. Logging has also seriously reduced its available habitat. Fishers still live in the Trinity Mountains, Siskiyou Mountains, and inaccessible parts of the Sierra Nevada. They are probably misnamed, for they principally eat small mammals and birds.

The Wolverine was never common, and now it is listed as an endangered species. The Wolverine is largely a subalpine mammal. It is the largest of the terrestrial mustelids, weighting up to 35 pounds (16 kg). Their body form resembles a large, dark Badger. Instead of having white lines on the face, as a Badger does, it has a broad gray forehead. Its food consists of a variety of small mammals, including Porcupines, and sometimes it feasts on the remains of large animals. No one knows why the species is disappearing. Because it was always scarce, it was not the object of serious hunting. Its fur, however, is reputed to be of high quality. Apparently, Wolverine fur has been used to line hoods of parkas because frosty breath will not adhere to it. Wolverines today are reported occasionally at timberline in the Klamath Mountains and the central Sierra Nevada.

The River Otter is another protected mammal. Its short, thick fur was highly prized by trappers and was used for ceremonial purposes by Indians in northwest California. They still occur in small numbers in larger mountain streams and lakes in the Klamath Mountains and northern Sierra Nevada. They do not spend a considerable time on land, but they live in burrows of other mammals some distance from water. One of their interesting habits is to build a slide, which may be 25 feet (8 m) long, on the bank of a stream or lake. They repeatedly climb to the top and slide into the water, as if playing. Their food is primarily aquatic, consisting of fish, frogs, turtles, crayfish, and aquatic insects.

The largest mammal of this region is the Roosevelt Elk or Wapiti, *Cervus elaphus roosevelti* (fig. 6.20). Not to be confused with the somewhat smaller Rocky Mountain Elk, *Cervus elaphus nelsoni,* which occurs near Shasta Lake in a small part of its

FIGURE 6.20   Roosevelt Elk, *Cervus elaphus roosevelti*. Prairie Creek Redwood State Park.

former range in northeastern California, this is the subspecies that occurs in moist forests along the coast, as far north as Vancouver Island, British Columbia. In Europe members of this species are called Red Deer. Usually they occur in herds in the vicinity of meadows. A herd is generally composed of a single dominant bull and up to 12 cows. Sometimes young bulls may remain with the herd.

Mature bulls, usually at least five years of age, engage in fierce fights to establish dominance. These fights occur in autumn, the rutting season. Bulls sound a challenge by bugling. If the challenge is accepted, two bulls will charge each other head on. They may lock antlers, or they may charge several times. The winner is the stronger, the one that is able to push an intruder away from his territory.

One of the marvels of these fights is that bulls rarely hurt each other. Innate signals of aggression and appeasement ensure that these fights remain rituals and stop short of death or serious harm. It is not necessary to kill the loser in a fight to keep him from mating. Usually, the dominant bull succeeds in keeping his herd of females together and chasing away subdominant males. However, subdominant males occasionally sneak into a herd and successfully copulate.

Food of these elks includes grasses and leaves of trees. They feed a great deal, for an elk may weigh 1000 pounds (450 kg). They are not easily confused with deer, which are much smaller. Antlers of a bull elk also have a different branching pattern than those of a deer. The only native deer in California, the Mule Deer, *Odocoileus hemionus,* has antlers that fork in pairs. Elk antlers have one main beam with all of the branches aiming forward. Furthermore, the subspecies of deer, *Odocoileus hemionus columbiana,* that occurs in the northern Coast Ranges and Klamath Province is smaller than other deer in California. This subspecies, known as the Black-tailed Deer, ranges along the coast from California to Canada.

Roosevelt Elk are no longer common in California. Habitat destruction has taken care of that. They can be viewed by nearly everyone, however, in a large meadow next to Highway 101 in Prairie Creek Redwood State Park. This herd is so tame that thousands of people every year watch and photograph these stately animals.

7

Coast Ranges

California's Coast Ranges extend along the coast for about two-thirds of the length of the state. They run about 550 miles (880 km) from the South Fork Mountains of the Klamath Province on the north, to the Santa Ynez Mountains of the Transverse Ranges on the south. San Francisco Bay divides them into two ranges, the northern and southern Coast Ranges.

Steep slopes with exaggerated relief are common in the southern Coast Ranges, where the mountains rise abruptly from the sea. Overall, however, these ranges are not particularly high. Most peaks are less than 6000 feet (1800 m) in elevation. In the south Coast Ranges, the highest peaks are at the southern end, where the general orientation of the mountains is east–west, similar to the Transverse Ranges. North of Santa Barbara, Big Pine Mountain, at 6828 feet (2083 m), is the highest in the San Rafael Range. In the southeastern corner of the Coast Ranges, in a terrane that may be more appropriately a part of the Transverse Ranges, Mount Pinos reaches 8826 feet (2758 m). Mount Pinos lies just west of the juncture of the San Andreas and Garlock faults, about 40 miles (64 km) inland.

The beauty of the southern coast has been celebrated by poets, photographers, and naturalists. Robinson Jeffers, who lived at Big Sur, called the area "the greatest meeting of land and water in the world." Another Big Sur resident, novelist Henry Miller, declared, "This is the face of the earth as the Creator intended it to look." Highway 1, constructed with convict labor between 1924 and 1937, runs 92 miles (147 km) from Cambria to Carmel. It is considered by many to be one of the most scenic highways in the world.

The crown jewel of the southern Coast Ranges is the Santa Lucia Range, which rises abruptly from the Big Sur coast to a height of 5868 feet (1893 m) at Junipero Serra Peak. In this area there are at least 57 endemic plant species and over 220 total species, including Coast Redwood, which reaches its southernmost distribution here. Average precipitation at Big Sur is nearly 60 inches (150 cm) a year, but at higher elevations the annual total can exceed 100 inches (250 cm). The area's most impressive figure, however, is the highest official annual precipitation ever recorded in California, 161 inches (403 cm), which fell during the 1940–41 rainy season.

The northern Coast Ranges (fig. 7.1) are generally higher than the southern Coast Ranges. Just south of the Klamath Province, in the southwest corner of Trinity County, Solomon Peak reaches 7581 feet (2312 m). The longest primitive stretch of coastline in the state is found along the northern Coast Range about 70 miles (110 km) south of Eureka. This 23-mile (37-km) stretch of beach is south of the Mattole River along the King Mountain Range. In this area the crest rises over 4000 feet (1200 m) in view of the ocean. Highway 1 cuts inland to avoid the range, which has left this "lost coast" largely unvisited and unexploited. A single road penetrates this

FIGURE 7.1   Aerial view of northern Coast Ranges near Elk, Mendocino County, 15 miles (24 km) north of Point Arena. Note coastal terraces, north-south trending ridges and valleys, and vegetation mosaic with bald hilltops. (From E. H. Bailey, W. P. Irwin, and D. L. Jones. *Franciscan and Related Rocks. and Their Significance in the Geology of Western California*. California Division of Mines and Geology, Bulletin 183, 1964.)

remote area, which is administered largely by the Bureau of Land Management. A controversy has arisen over whether access should be improved or whether the area should be granted wilderness status and preserved in its pristine state.

The Coast Ranges consist of a series of north–south trending valleys and ridges that lie along a series of parallel faults and folds (fig. 7.2). This alignment causes many rivers to run northward, emptying into the ocean many miles from their source. In the northern Coast Ranges, the Eel River runs northward about 140 miles (230 km) to exit south of Humboldt Bay. In the southern Coast Ranges, the Salinas River runs about 100 miles (160 km) northward and exits at Monterey Bay. This is the long valley made famous by the writings of John Steinbeck. A major river of the northern Coast Ranges is the Russian River. It flows for about 40 miles (64 km) southward along the structural grain of the Coast Ranges. Near Healdsburg, however, it turns

SOUTHERN COAST RANGES

NORTHERN COAST RANGES

FIGURE 7.2 The Coast Ranges.

abruptly westward to cut through the range in a gorge nearly 1000 feet (300 m) deep, exiting on the coast near Jenner. This east–west orientation permits marine air to flow a considerable distance inland along the Russian River.

CLIMATE

To the interior of the Coast Ranges, drying occurs because of the rain-shadow effect. At its southern end, the rain shadow is so effective that the vicinity of the Great Central Valley near Taft is truly a desert. Much of the Coast Ranges vegetation is Oak Woodland or Foothill Woodland, similar to that of the western Sierra Nevada. In the southern Coast Ranges, however, Coastal Sage Scrub and lower Chaparral are important, particularly on south-facing slopes. Slope effect on the south coast is as distinct as will be seen anywhere in the world. Accentuated by Mediterranean climate, south-facing slopes suffer the extremes of drought. These slopes are covered with Chaparral that appears dry and brown by midsummer. In contrast, north-facing slopes are cloaked with evergreen oaks whose roots reach deeply to permanent water. The patterns in color form a visual contrast that bear witness to the profound influence of slope exposure.

On the coastal side of the Coast Ranges maritime climate predominates. The temperature of the ocean along the California coast is generally cold because the water flows southward from Alaska and heats slowly. The cold temperature causes condensation of water vapor in the air near the ocean surface. The result is frequent fog along the coast, which is held there by the Coast Ranges. This fog is very significant to the vegetation because it reduces water lost by transpiration, and it contributes significantly to soil moisture through fog drip. It has been determined that fog drip in the Berkeley Hills accounts for an equivalent of 10 inches (25 cm) of precipitation. In the northern Coast Ranges the fog drip is responsible for the belt of Coast Redwoods, which to many people typifies northern California.

GEOLOGY OF THE COAST RANGES

The Coast Ranges are folded and faulted on an axis that parallels the coastline. Formation of these ranges is generally attributed to events associated with subduction of the Pacific plate beneath the western border of North America. Island arc volcanics and materials deposited in a deep submarine trench apparently became accreted to the western edge of California as the ocean floor slid beneath the continental margin. Most of these rocks are late Mesozoic in age (150 to 65 million years old). Eastward-directed pressure folded and cracked the leading edge of the continent to form the parallel series of ridges and valleys that make up the present ranges.

Long-distance northward transport of rocks in Alaska indicates that a transform fault system must have existed along the western margin of North America until about 100 million years ago. Many of the rock units of the Coast Ranges had their origin much farther south than where they lie today. In the southern Coast Ranges batholithic rocks (granitics) form a major component of what is known as the Salinian block. These plutonic rocks were probably formed by subduction south of the present Sierra Nevada and carried to their present position west of the San Andreas fault during the last 25 million years by right-lateral slip. Uplift and emplacement of the southern Coast Ranges in its present position took place very recently compared with the formation of the northern Coast Ranges.

North of Red Bluff the boundary between the northern Coast Ranges and the Klamath Province generally lies along the South Fork Mountain fault. This is a thrust fault in which rocks of the Klamath Province, resembling those of the northern Sierra Nevada, have been thrust over the sedimentary rocks of the Franciscan Formation. Most of the northern Coast Ranges is an assemblage of Franciscan rocks that are late Mesozoic in age (fig. 7.3). These rocks are associated with the offshore trench that was formed during subduction of the ocean floor and were named for deposits near the city of San Francisco. Franciscan rocks are dominated by shales and sandstones that were formed by rapid erosion of a volcanic highland and deposited in deep marine basins. They are gray-green in color and known as graywackes. About 90% of Franciscan rocks are of this type. It has been estimated that these deposits are about 25,000 feet (7600 m) thick. Graywackes are interbedded with lesser amounts of dark-colored shale, occasional limestone, and reddish silica-rich cherts (fig 7.4). East of the Franciscan rocks is a belt of sedimentary rocks that formed along the continental shelf of the Mesozoic ocean. These rocks are known as the Great Valley sequence.

Franciscan sedimentary rocks have become intruded by igneous rocks that have been metamorphosed, probably by heated seawater, to become the waxy green rock known as serpentine or serpentinite. This attractive, hydrothermally altered rock has been designated the state rock. Mixed in with this assemblage are other igneous rocks, believed to be associated with ocean floor deposition, collectively known as ophiolites. The Greek work *ophidion* means "serpent," and ophiolites and serpentine are named for a mottled pattern that seems to resemble a snake's skin. These rocks are composed of a great variety of different minerals, and it is their weathering that has caused the enormous variety of soil types scattered like islands throughout the Coast Ranges. These soils, which may be called ophiolitic, serpentine, ultramafic, or ultrabasic, have in common an odd assortment of minerals. They are unusually rich in magnesium and iron, but they are deficient in calcium, sodium, and potassium. They also may contain large amounts of nickel, cobalt, and chromium. Many unique plants grow on the special soils, forming the edaphic ecologic islands that are numerous in the Coast Ranges and the Klamath Province. They also occur in the western foothills of the Sierra Nevada and sparsely in southern California.

North of San Francisco is a geothermal field that bears testimony to the fact that tectonic pressures still exist in the area. In an area along the Sonoma-Lake county line numerous hot springs, or fumaroles, occur. The area is generally known as "the Geysers." The steam produced here naturally by the earth's heat is used to generate electricity, which should be an efficient technique, because no fossil fuel or nuclear fuel need be used to create the heat. However, one glitch is that an oil company owns

FRANCISCAN ROCKS

GREAT VALLEY SEQUENCE

G R E A T

V A L L E Y

PACIFIC

SAN ANDREAS FAULT

SALINIAN BLOCK

NACIMIENTO FAULT

O C E A N

PALOS
VERDES
HILLS

0   50   100 MILES

SANTA
CATALINA ISLAND

FIGURE 7.3   Generalized map showing distribution of Franciscan rocks, the Great Valley
sequence, and the Salinian block. (After E. H. Bailey, W. P. Irwin, and D. L. Jones. *Franciscan
and Related Rocks, and Their Significance in the Geology of Western California.* California Division
of Mines and Geology, Bulletin 183, 1964.)

FIGURE 7.4   Franciscan rock, thinly bedded chert in the
Coast Range northwest of the Golden Gate Bridge.

the mineral rights to the steam. It seems that if the price of steam is kept artificially
high, geothermally generated electricity will not undermine the demand for fossil
fuel. Other political problems developed also, so that by 1988 the full potential of
the resource had yet to be realized. Nevertheless, some electricity for the area around
San Francisco is generated by the Geysers geothermal field.

In the southern Coast Ranges, Franciscan rocks lie east of the San Andreas fault.
West of the San Andreas is a zone of granitics and metamorphics, known as the
Salinian block (figs. 7.3, 7.5). Mount Pinos lies at the southern tip of this block.
The Salinian block represents a rock assortment similar to the Sierra Nevada and Transverse Ranges. It was formed south of the Sierra Nevada and carried northwest about
190 miles (300 km) by motion on the San Andreas fault. West of the Salinian block
is the Nacimiento fault, which separates the granitics from more Franciscan rocks to
the west. In cross section, the southern Coast Ranges have a central core of granitic
rocks separated from Franciscan rocks by major faults on either side. If the Salinian
block is aligned with the southern Sierra, the Nacimiento fault lines up south of the

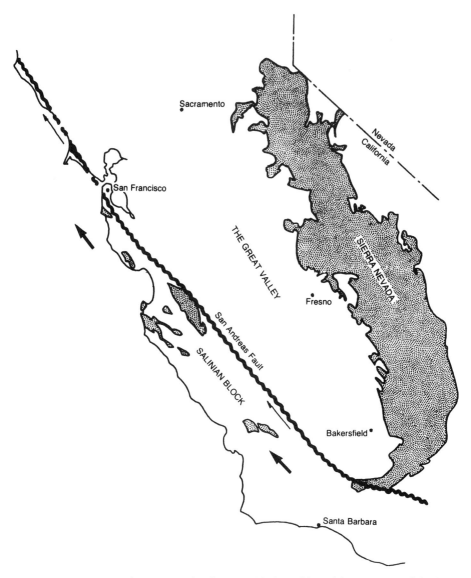

FIGURE 7.5   Granitics of the Salinian block, originally formed by subduction south of the Sierra Nevada. They were carried to their present position by northwest displacement along the San Andreas fault. (From D. D. Alt and D. W. Hyndman. *Roadside Geology of Northern California*. Missoula, MT: Mountain Press, 1975. Reprinted by permission.)

Motherlode fault. This is the fault on the western side of the Sierra that separates the granitic rocks from the western metamorphic complex, which also includes Franciscan rocks. To the south, the Nacimiento fault more or less coincides with the Newport-Inglewood fault, which parallels the Los Angeles Basin along the coastline. The granitics of the Peninsular Ranges formerly were in line with the Salinian block at its southern end.

The southern Coast Ranges are mainly composed of sedimentary rocks much younger than the Franciscan or granitic rocks. In early Miocene, over 20 million years ago, the sea covered much of the southern Coast Ranges, forming numerous bays, straits, islands, and inlets. In a setting similar to the modern Gulf of California, deep-water sediments such as the 700-foot-thick diatomaceous shales near Lompoc were deposited in deep, elongate basins. These and other sediments began to be uplifted only in the last 10 million years or so, making the southern Coast Ranges quite young. By the end of the Pliocene, 1 to 2 million years ago, the southern Coast Ranges were above sea level. These sedimentary rocks are reasonably soft and unstable, and they are easily eroded by surf, particularly during heavy winter storms. A series of wet winters since 1978 has greatly exacerbated the problem. All along the coast, people have built homes too close to the edge. In the Santa Cruz area, retreat of the cliffs away from the sea averages about a foot (30 cm) per year, and loss of 75 feet (24 m) has been recorded in a single year.

Furthermore, these sedimentary beds are not always horizontal; tectonic activity has tilted many of them. When these layers become wet, they slip on each other, causing landslides. The heavy rains of 1978 and 1983 have contributed to this wetting, but the condition is made even worse by homeowners on the cliffs who insist on planting landscapes that demand lots of water. Erosion by surf or landslides associated with overwatering have claimed many multimillion dollar homes on coastal cliffs.

Coastal terraces are formed by the action of surf on a rocky headland. Surf, with its load of sand, can be highly abrasive. The action of the surf is to cut at right angles into the rock along the shore. The outcome is a relatively flat, wave-cut bench or reef with a steep cliff on the shoreward side. Because the west coast is continually rising by tectonic activity, old wave-cut terraces have become elevated above present sea level. Superimposed on this uplift are intervals of changing sea level, which coincide with episodes of glaciation associated with the Ice Age (Pleistocene). During periods of glaciation, sea level was lowered as a great deal of the earth's water was bound up in polar ice caps. During interglacial intervals, sea level rose as the ice caps melted. Furthermore, expansion and contraction of the water itself is a temperature-related phenomenon. Warm water, like warm air, expands and takes up more space. Sea level today apparently is as high as it has been in the last 125 million years.

These series of flat terraces or platforms, rising like staircases on hills that border the ocean, are particularly conspicuous where they have been formed on rocky headlands. In the Palos Verdes area of Los Angeles County, 13 terraces are visible. In the Point Loma area near San Diego, there are 11 terraces. Perhaps the most terraces, 17, are visible on the southern coast near Ventura. Up and down the Coast Ranges, the number of visible terraces varies, although 5 to 7 are typical (fig 7.1).

BIOTIC ZONATION

Foothill Woodland

As illustrated in figure 7.6, throughout most of the Coast Ranges the predominant community is Foothill Woodland (fig. 7.7). Many authorities refer to the community as Oak Woodland. This apparent discrepancy has arisen because the Coast Ranges are not true foothills. In practice, it has become conventional to refer to the Foothill Woodland of the Coast Ranges as Oak Woodland and to reserve the term *Foothill Woodland* for the Sierran counterpart of the same community. For the purposes of this book, the two terms will be considered equivalent. This is a mixed community of trees and grasses. Many authorities refer to it as a savannah. Dominant tree species include Blue Oak, *Quercus douglasii*, (fig. 4.20), and Digger Pine, *Pinus sabiniana* (pl. 5B). At slightly higher elevations and on north-facing slopes, particularly in the northern Coast Ranges, California Buckeye, *Aesculus californica* (fig. 4.21), is locally common. Redbud, *Cercis occidentalis*, may be locally common in the northern Coast Ranges as well.

A community known by some authors as Northern Oak Woodland dominates ridgetops up to 5000 feet (1600 m) in the northern Coast Ranges. This community, dominated by Garry Oak or Oregon White Oak (*Quercus garryana*) rather than Blue Oak, is also discussed in chapter 6. In Humboldt and Mendocino counties, grassy "balds" and open woodlands of Garry Oak occur in patches on ridges in the Mixed Evergreen Forest. These bald hills occur in patterns caused by different soil types. This grass-tree mosaic reflects the soil mosiac associated with the diverse geologic nature of the region.

Other oaks include Coast Live Oak, *Quercus agrifolia* (pl. 7B), Interior Live Oak, *Quercus wislizenii*, and Valley Oak, *Quercus lobata* (fig. 10.13). To the south of the Coast Ranges, Blue Oak is ultimately replaced by Coast Live Oak. Where the two species occur together, in the southern Coast Ranges, Blue Oak tends to grow on south-facing slopes, and Coast Live Oak grows on north-facing slopes. Interior Live Oak and Valley Oak are more common toward the interior of the Coast Ranges where Oak Woodland grades into Valley Grassland. Valley Oak dominates in valleys and on gentle upper slopes with deep soils. These deep soils are the result of reduced erosion rates. One author describes these open woodlands of Valley Oak as montane savannahs that are ecologically equivalent to the open woodlands of Garry Oak. Valley Oak grows as far south as the Tehachapi Mountains, where it occurs on gentle, sloping ridges up to 6000 feet (1800 m) in elevation.

Old gnarled oaks can be very picturesque. Large specimens are spectacular. The largest Blue Oak, located in Alameda County, is over 6 feet (2 m) in diameter and stands 94 feet (29.4 m) high. Its crown spread is 48 feet (15 m). The largest Coast Live Oak, found near Gilroy, is even more impressive. With a diameter of over 9 feet (3 m), it stands 85 feet (26.6 m) high and has a crown spread of a whopping 127 feet (40 m). The largest Valley Oak is found in Butte County in the Great Central Valley. It is also an impressive specimen, standing 120 feet (37.5 m) high with a crown spread of 103 feet (32 m). Its trunk is also nearly 9 feet (3 m) in diameter.

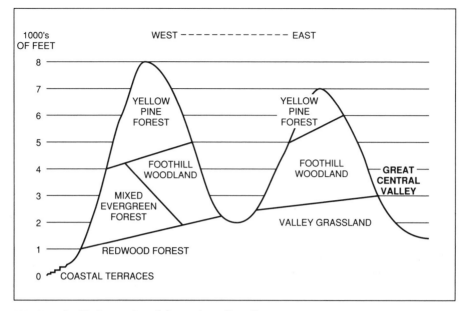

FIGURE 7.6   Biotic zonation of the northern Coast Ranges.

In canyons, particularly on north-facing slopes, there is Canyon Live Oak, *Quercus chrysolepis* (pl. 7 A). Canyon Live Oak resembles Coast Live Oak in size and shape but has small whitish hairs on the undersides of the leaves. In addition, the leaf margins of Canyon Live Oak are highly variable, ranging from smooth to spiny. Canyon Live Oak therefore may be identified at a glance by noting the undersides of the leaves and the variety of leaf shapes on a single tree. The largest Canyon Live Oak is a massive tree found in the Santa Ana Mountains of southern California. Its trunk diameter is nearly 11 feet (3.5 m), but it stands only 72 feet (22.5 m) in height. Its crown width is 80 feet (25 m). Another 70-foot (22-m) Canyon Live Oak, located at the foot of Duckwall Mountain in Tuolumne County, was lost in 1965 when it split apart and toppled during a snowstorm.

North of San Francisco the ranges of Coast Live Oak and Interior Live Oak overlap. Where this occurs, microclimatic preferences between the two species become apparent. Coast Live Oak tends to occur more commonly on the coast-facing slopes, where there is more soil moisture. Interior Live Oak prefers slopes that face away from the coast and becomes more common toward the interior of the Coast Ranges. Where the two species occur together, they may hybridize, which indicates that they have not been separate species for long. Identification of each species where their ranges overlap is complicated by hybridization, but in their pure forms, they can be identified by the color of their leaves. Interior Live Oak is bright green and shiny on both leaf surfaces. The leaf of the Coast Live Oak is a darker green and shiny only on the top surface. Coast Live Oak also has small tufts of hairs where leaf veins intersect on the lower surface.

FIGURE 7.7   Foothill Woodland of the northern Coast Ranges. Note Lace Lichen hanging from the tree in the left foreground.

Where fog is common, the vegetation is coated with a reticulated, filamentous lichen known as Lace Lichen, *Ramalina menziesii* (fig. 7.7). This yellow-green growth cloaks and dangles pendulously from everything that is bathed by the fog. The apparent function of the netlike branching is to increase the surface area available for condensation of water. Condensation not only supplies additional water to the lichen and promotes fog drip, but it also provides a warming effect that could enhance photosynthesis. The warming of a surface by condensation is the opposite of evaporative cooling, which is so important to organisms in hot climates.

Foothill Woodland may be a threatened community. For a variety of reasons, it seems that the number of hawks, owls, Coyotes, and Bobcats is decreasing. This change, if nothing else, has allowed an increase of rabbits, ground squirrels, gophers, mice, and deer. In addition, introduced annual weeds that produce a large number of seeds have led to an increase in seed-eating mammals. All these different herbivores have interfered with regeneration of Blue Oaks. In many areas there are no Blue Oaks younger than 50 years of age. Mule Deer, rabbits, and mice browse on young oaks from above while gophers attack the roots. Species composition in the Oak Woodland seems to be undergoing an important change. Coast Live Oaks seem not to suffer as much damage, so they are on the increase while Blue Oaks are disappearing.

Furthermore, wild pigs, *Sus scrofa* (fig. 12.36), are also becoming more common. The impact of wild pigs has yet to be addressed fully. These pigs are either escaped domestic pigs or descendents of European wild pigs (also *Sus scrofa*), which were introduced to Monterey County in 1923. Feral pigs uproot acorns and seedlings, and the abundance of acorns is an important limiting factor for many animals, including Mule Deer. At equal densities, wild pigs eat three times as many acorns as deer, which, if nothing else, could severely curtail the size of native deer herds. In addition, at the Pepperwood Ranch Natural Preserve in Sonoma County, pigs gnaw the bark off Knobcone Pines, ultimately killing them. Pigs also consume a wide variety of underground plant parts, including bulbs, corms, tubers, and fungi. It has been suggested that attempts to hunt wild pigs be intensified. The California Department of Fish and Game has authorized bag limits for pigs at one per hunter per day, and special depredation permits may be issued for private land owners if pig damage is extensive. It has been recommended that no more than six pigs per 40 acres (16/ha) be allowed to persist.

In most valleys, native marshes and grassland have been replaced by pastures or agriculture. In the south, these valleys produce a wide variety of crops, including cotton, corn, tomatoes, beans, and sugar beets. Castroville, near the mouth of the Salinas Valley, is known as the artichoke capitol of the world. Valleys of the northern Coast Ranges are renowned for grapes, producing some of the finest wines in the world. Many famous-name vineyards are in Napa Valley, northeast of San Francisco.

Maritime Chaparral

As figure 7.8 shows, Chaparral-covered slopes are common in the southern Coast Ranges (pl. 5C). Chaparral predominates on south-facing slopes and becomes more common toward the south. This community will be discussed in more detail in the chapter on cismontane southern California.

Maritime Chaparral is a unique kind of Chaparral that occurs in patches on the coastal side of the southern Coast Ranges. In general, the shrubs form low, conspicuous mounds in open areas among the woodlands of oaks or closed-cone pines. In the Monterey area, the community occurs on sandy soil, the remnant of Pleistocene sand dunes that occurred along the coast. The community seldom grows on shale.

The significant feature that differentiates this form of Chaparral from that in the southern part of the state is the presence of abundant summer fog. Data gathered from the Monterey Bay area indicated an average of 135 foggy days per year. The average distribution of fog during summer months was as follows: June, 14 days (9 hours/day); July, 20 days (13 hours/day); August, 22 days (14 hours/day), September, 17 days (12 hours/day). It is this foggy weather that also dictates where other ecologic-island species such as Coast Redwood and various closed-cone pines will grow.

Maritime Chaparral is dominated by a number of endemic manzanitas (*Arctostaphylos* spp.) and California lilacs (*Ceanothus* spp.). The community also includes Chamise, *Adenostoma fasciculatum* (fig. 8.17), the most common species in many chaparral communities. The amount of endemism in the Monterey area is remarkable and will be noted frequently in this chapter. The endemic shrubs that occur in Maritime Chaparral in the Monterey area include Hooker Manzanita, *Arctostaphylos hookeri*; Monterey Man-

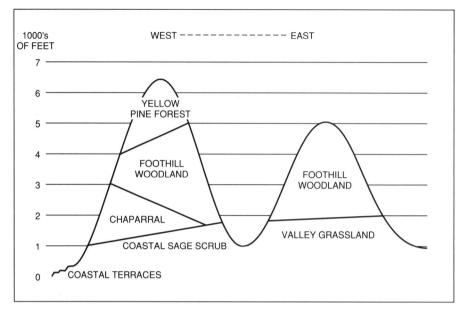

FIGURE 7.8   Biotic zonation of the southern Coast Ranges.

zanita, *Arctostaphylos montereyensis*; Pajaro Manzanita, *Arctostaphylos pajaroensis*; Sandmat Manzanita, *Arctostaphylos pumila*; Cropleaf Ceanothus, *Ceanothus dentatus*; Monterey Ceanothus, *Ceanothus rigidis*; and Monterey Goldenbush, *Ericameria fasciculata*. However, habitat destruction has nearly wiped out this community. Nearly every one of the endemic species mentioned is classified as threatened or endangered.

Mixed Evergreen Forest

In the northern part of the Coast Ranges, in Mendocino and Humboldt counties, precipitation increases markedly. On cooler, moister sites, particularly canyon bottoms, Oak Woodland merges with Mixed Evergreen Forest composed of conifers and broad-leaved evergreen trees (pl. 5A). Douglas Fir is an important component of this forest to the north. In the Klamath Province, as discussed in the preceding chapter, this community occurs in an even moister form.

Tanoak or Tanbark Oak, *Lithocarpus densiflorus* (fig. 6.8), is an evergreen species of the beech-oak family (Fagaceae) that is more closely allied to the oaks of southeast Asia. The tree is called Tanoak because it was once a major source of tannin, the substance used to preserve or tan leather. Except for the acorns, a person would not guess that this is an oak. The leaves are large, oblong, and leathery, up to 5 inches (13 cm) in length. They have a wavy, toothed margin, and the undersides are hairy. This is a relict, distributed in moist locations from southern Oregon to southern California. Along with Pacific Madrone, California Laurel, and Coast Redwood, it is a remnant of a forest that once enjoyed a much larger distribution. Indians found the fairly large acorns to be particularly palatable after the tannins were leached.

Pacific Madrone, *Arbutus menziesii* (fig. 6.7), looks like a large manzanita. It is an evergreen tree with large, oblong leaves similar in shape to those of the Tanoak. The leaves differ from those of the Tanoak by lacking the hairy underside and, usually, the toothed margin. Pacific Madrone grows as for north as Canada; as such it is the most northerly occurring evergreen hardwood tree. In California its distribution is similar to that of Tanoak, and the two species usually occur together. There should be no mistaking the two species, however. Tanoak has brown, deeply furrowed bark. Madrone has smooth, red bark that peels off in papery sheets on the branches. Flowers on Pacific Madrone are similar to manzanita flowers. They are white and urn-shaped, and they occur in clusters. The flowers are typical of the heath family (Ericaceae), to which manzanitas and Pacific Madrone belong. Also similar to manzanita, it produces bright orange to red berries in autumn. Pacific Madrone is a handsome tree that does well in residential landscapes when it gets adequate water. It is particularly attractive where it occurs among Coast Redwoods. The towering redwoods create so much shade that the Pacific Madrone, in its quest for light, commonly possesses a tortuously twisted trunk and is cloaked with bright green lichens.

California Laurel, *Umbellularia californica* (fig. 7.9), is an evergreen with dark green, lance-shaped leaves, up to 5 inches (13 cm) in length. The most distinctive feature of the leaves is a peppery, aromatic odor. They are shaped like bay leaves, and they may be used in cooking; therefore this tree sometimes is referred to as California Bay. The odor is quite pungent when the leaves are broken, and it is not wise to sniff it for too long because it is known to cause headaches. In small doses, however, it is very pleasant.

California Laurel is more common in southern California than the other evergreen species mentioned here. It is a frequent component of riparian communities there. This tropical relict belongs to the laurel family (Lauracaceae), which includes several trees of economic importance, such as avocado, cinnamon, and camphor. California Laurel is the only native member of this tropical family in California. The wood is very beautiful and is commonly used for carved figurines, gun stocks, trays, and bowls. Along the southern coast of Oregon the wood is known as myrtlewood, and the tree is called Oregon Myrtle. Carvings made of myrtlewood are a popular tourist attraction in Oregon, and they often carry a sticker erroneously stating that this tree is unique to the Oregon coast. How strange that they would make such a claim when the scientific name refers to the state of California.

In the northern Coast Ranges, California Laurel is commonly called Pepperwood. In the northern Coast Ranges alone, there are at least 10 localities called Pepperwood. In areas associated with serpentine-derived soils, particularly where springs keep the soil wet, California Laurel may form shrubby thickets. In contrast to the shrubby forms found on serpentine, an extremely interesting locality in Marin County, west of Novato, is occupied by a California Laurel savannah with trees up to 80 feet (24 m) in height.

FIGURE 7.9   California Laurel, *Umbellularia californica*.

In the southern Coast Ranges, Mixed Evergreen Forest is restricted to north-facing slopes at higher elevation. These sites, characterized by Tanoak and Pacific Madrone, may be highly localized. On disturbed sites, or where the soil is derived from granitics or schist, Coulter Pine, *Pinus coulteri* (fig. 8.27), is an important species. Coulter Pine is the southern California equivalent of Digger Pine. It is the most drought-adapted member of the yellow pine group, which includes Ponderosa and Jeffrey pines. It can be distinguished by its very long needles, often over 10 inches (25 cm) in length. Its volleyball-sized cone is the largest of all pine species. At the few high-elevation localities of the southern Coast Ranges where true Yellow Pine Forest occurs, Coulter Pine may coexist with Jeffrey Pine, with which it may hybridize. The two species can be distinguished by the size and shape of the cone. Coulter Pine will be discussed in more detail in chapter 8, in the section on southern California Chaparral communities.

Riparian Woodland

In the northern Coast Ranges, where annual precipitation is high, the Riparian Woodland is similar to that of the Klamath Province. Differences are not dramatic between the Riparian Woodland and the adjacent forest areas. Conifers such as Coast Redwood, Douglas Fir, and California Nutmeg, *Torreya californica*, are forest species that may be included in the Riparian Woodland. Broad-leaved evergreen species such as Pacific Madrone, Tanoak, and California Laurel may occur along the streams as well as in the adjacent forest.

Among the winter-deciduous trees that occur in the Riparian Woodland as well as the bordering forest are Big-leaf Maple, *Acer macrophyllum* (fig. 6.9); Pacific Dogwood, *Cornus nuttallii* (fig. 4.55); and Red Alder, *Alnus rubra*. Upstream, White Alder, *Alnus rhombifolia* (fig. 4.54), replaces Red Alder. In Oak Woodland areas, riparian species frequently are joined by Canyon Live Oak, *Quercus chrysolepis*. The most common willows of the Coast Ranges are Red Willow, *Salix laevigata*, and Pacific Willow, *Salix lasiandra* (fig. 10.8).

Shrubs associated with Riparian Woodland in the northern Coast Ranges are similar to those that occur in the Klamath Province. The common willow species are discussed in chapter 6. Among the shrubby dogwoods, that occur in moist localities in the Coast Ranges is Brown Dogwood or Smooth Dogwood, *Cornus glabrata*. This species resembles Creek Dogwood, *Cornus stolonifera*, with which it may occur, but the leaves are smaller, seldom over 2 inches (5 cm) in length, and the bark is brownish rather than bright red. This is truly a California species. Its range barely extends into southern Oregon, in the Siskiyou Mountains. It also has been reported at patchy localities in moist areas in the foothills of the western Sierra Nevada and in southern California.

A very attractive spreading shrub in the dogwood family (Cornaceae) is known as Bunchberry, *Cornus canadensis*. This little shrub grows only 3 to 9 inches (7–22 cm) high and has a whorl of four to six dogwood-like leaves. It is most spectacular when it is in fruit. A cluster of large, bright red berries is framed by the whorl of leaves. These plants grow as ground cover in swamps and moist places along the coast from Mendocino County northward.

In the moist northern forests from Monterey County to British Columbia grows a beautiful flowering shrub known as Western Rose-bay, *Rhododendron macrophyllum*. Related to Western Azalea, *Rhododendron occidentale*, with which it may occur, Western Rose-bay is an evergreen species with dark green, leathery leaves, up to 8 inches (20 cm) in length. Its leaves resemble those of a madrone, but this species is darker green, and it is always a shrub. Its large, funnel-shaped, rose-colored flowers, however, could not be confused with anything else. Sometimes these shrubs are cultivated in yards of the Pacific Northwest. They may be sold under the name rhododendron.

Farther south, where summer drought becomes an important climatic factor, species that are shared with the adjacent forest in the north become strictly riparian. Pacific Madrone, California Laurel, Big-leaf Maple, Pacific Dogwood, White Alder, and Canyon Live Oak range southward all the way to the Peninsular Ranges, where they occur along streams or strictly on north-facing slopes.

In the southern Coast Ranges, the Riparian Woodland becomes more southern Californian in appearance. Species such as Coast Redwood, Douglas Fir, Red Alder, and Western Azalea drop out. Western Sycamore, *Platanus racemosa*, and Fremont Cottonwood, *Populus fremontii* (fig. 8.54), become dominant species along with White Alder, Red Willow, and Pacific Willow.

Yellow Pine Forest

True Yellow Pine Forest occurs in the northern Coast Ranges at high elevations and on dry sites associated with serpentine or other ophiolitic soils. In the southern Coast Ranges this community occurs only on a few high peaks. Where it occurs, such as on Figueroa Mountain in Santa Barbara County, the forest is dominated by Jeffrey Pine. Also in the area may be found Coulter Pine, Digger Pine, Big-cone Douglas Fir, Canyon Live Oak, Blue Oak, Coast Live Oak, and Interior Live Oak. Such an interesting mix of species should provide ecologists many hours of study on microclimate preferences.

Edaphic Communities

Edaphic communities are those controlled by specialized soils. The significance of these soils to the distribution of plants has been emphasized already in the chapters on the Sierra Nevada and the Pacific Northwest. In particular, mention was made of the degree of specialization associated with serpentine soils. As mentioned before, serpentine is the state rock. Technically, the rock name *serpentinite* should be used for the rock composed of *serpentine* minerals. Common usage, however, of the word serpentine for both rock and minerals is acceptable. These soils occur in patches in the northwestern foothills of the Sierra Nevada, the Klamath Province, and the Coast Ranges (fig. 7.10). In the northern Coast Ranges, serpentine outcrops can usually be recognized by the presence of chaparral species such as Chamise, although on the coastal side, where moisture is more abundant, closed-cone pines or open stands of Jeffrey Pine and Incense Cedar may occur there. The bald hills of the northern Coast Ranges are also associated with special clay soils derived from shales.

There are also special soils derived from sandstone. For example, in western Fresno County near the town of Coalinga, there is an interesting area known as Anticline Ridge. Soft sandstone in this area weathers to sandy mounds that harbor a number of desert species, such as Narrowleaf Goldenbush, *Ericameria* (= *Haplopappus*) *linearifolius*, and Mojave Sand Verbena, *Abronia pogonantha*. Also found in this area is California Juniper, *Juniperus californica*, and some of its associates. Of particular interest is an abundance of Mormon Tea or California Joint Fir, *Ephedra californica*, a leafless shrub sometimes harvested for the purpose of brewing a rich tea. This plant contains tannins and small amount of a stimulant known as ephedrin, a component of some commercial decongestants. Commercial ephedrine, however, is either derived synthetically or obtained from an Asian member of this genus. The desertlike nature of this area is not only a product of its soils. Lying in the rain shadow of the southern Coast Ranges, this region experiences a pattern of precipitation characteristic of a desert. Desert plants of various types occur along the inner side of the southern Coast Ranges.

Biologists seem to emphasize the edaphic communities associated with serpentine. In the Coast Ranges, indicator species for serpentine outcrops include Leather Oak, *Quercus durata*; Muskbrush, *Ceanothus jepsonii*, and Interior Silktassel, *Garrya*

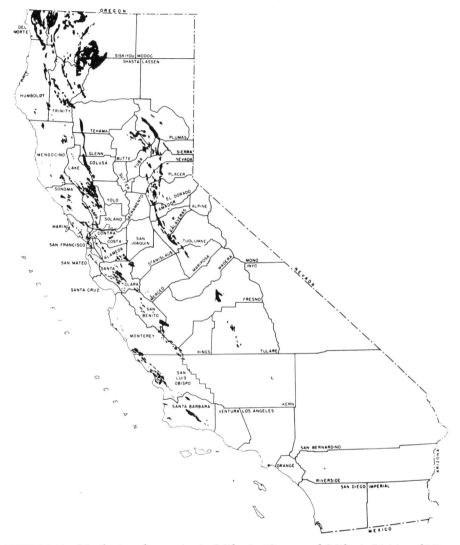

FIGURE 7.10   Distribution of serpentine in California. (Courtesy of California Division of Mines and Geology.)

congdonii. Serpentine soils of the inner Coast Ranges from Napa County northward are characterized by Macnab Cypress, *Cupressus macnabiana*. Sargent Cypress, *Cupressus sargentii*, occurs on serpentine soils of the outer Coast Ranges from Mendocino County southward. Among herbaceous species there are also many serpentine endemics. One group that has been studied extensively is *Streptanthus*, a highly diversified group in the mustard family (Brassicaceae).

FIGURE 7.11   New Idria Barrens, San Benito County. This is an area characterized by serpentine soils.

One interesting area characterized by serpentine soils is known as the New Idria Barrens (fig. 7.11). This region occurs in the Clear Creek Recreation Area of the inner Coast Ranges in San Benito County. This is a visually striking area characterized by yellowish soil nearly devoid of vegetation. Because of its apparent barren nature, the Bureau of Land Management has authorized this area for open use by off-road vehicles. Areas characterized by endemic plants have been fenced. Included here is a depauperate chaparral community dominated by Bigberry Manzanita, *Arctostaphylos glauca*. The area is also unique because of the occurrence together of Digger Pines, Jeffrey Pines, and Coulter Pines. Coulter Pines occur here at higher elevation and on south-facing slopes. The Jeffrey Pines are scarce and seem to be disappearing. The slow growth of plants associated with serpentine soils was dramatically illustrated by paired photos taken in 1932 and again in 1960. There was no apparent change in the size or abundance of vegetation during the 28-year interval.

Strategies of plants for tolerating serpentine soils include drought tolerance and the ability to deal with the peculiar minerals. Some species have acquired ways to exclude the undesirable elements, such as nickel and chromium. At the extreme are species called hyperaccumulators. For example, the serpentine endemic known as Milkwort

Strepthanus, *Streptanthus polygaloides*, can take up amounts of nickel in excess of 1000 parts per million.

As might be expected, where there are endemic plants, there are also endemic animals, particularly insects that feed or breed on specialized plants. One study documented nine species and subspecies of butterflies associated with the inner northern Coast Ranges alone. For example, the Muir's Hairstreak, *Mitoura nelsoni muiri*, occurs only on Sargent Cypress, and the Lacustra Skipper, *Erynnis brizo lacustra*, occurs only on Leather Oak. Similarly, certain butterflies are associated with the mustard genus *Streptanthus*. The California White, *Pieris sisymbrii*, is very nearly endemic on serpentine because it lays eggs mostly on the endemic members of the *Streptanthus* group. An unusual checkerspot, *Euphydryas editha luestherae*, is restricted to serpentine even though its two host plants, a paintbrush (*Castilleja* sp.) and a lousewort (*Pedicularis* sp.), also occur off of serpentine. In this case, there may be something special about the temperature and moisture regimes of serpentine that keep the butterfly there, or there may be something about the timing of growth periods and flowering that is unique to the plants growing on serpentine.

The Ecological Staircase of Mendocino County

Perhaps the most interesting example of biotic zonation occurs on the coastal side of the mountains in Mendocino County. On the coastal terraces near Fort Bragg, there is an ecological staircase where each terrace possesses a distinctive vegetation type (fig. 7.12). The cause of the zonation is a combination of factors including climatic differences associated with elevation, as well as soil differences associated with age. These terraces illustrate the succession of changes over time. The oldest terrace is at the top, about 650 feet (200 m) above sea level. There is a guided nature trail to the staircase in Van Damme State Park. A walk up the ecological staircase is, in fact, a walk back in time. It is also possible to think of it as a walk into the future, because it demonstrates what eventually will become of the lower terraces.

The Lowest Terrace: Coastal Prairie.   The lowest terrace is the youngest. It was formerly the beach and had its association of tide pools and beach dunes. The native community of this terrace today is a grassland known as North Coast Grassland or Coastal Prairie. It is characterized by grasses and spring wildflowers such as California Poppy, *Eschscholzia californica*; Owl Clover, *Orthocarpus erianthus*; and Beach Strawberry, *Frageria chiloensis*. There are no large tree or shrub species because heavy winds and salt spray produce a drying effect that perpetuates the coastal prairie. Hundreds of thousands of years of accumulation of organic material from the grasses and wildflowers have produced a rich, dark prairie soil (mollisol) highly prized for vegetable farming. Natural percolation of water from the next terrace above keeps the soil on this terrace wet enough that the vegetables do not have to be irrigated during the summer dry season. Furthermore, grasses remain green all summer, so the Coastal Prairie is also prize terrain for dairy cattle. A consequence of the economic importance of the Coastal Prairie is that most of it has been converted to agricultural or pasture land. As the population of California continues to grow, we shall probably see the phenomenon of urban sprawl creep over the north coast just as it has in the south.

FIGURE 7.12   The ecological staircase of Mendocino County. (Illustration by Geoff Smith, after W. W. Fox. "Pygmy Forest: An Ecological Staircase." *California Geology*, 29 (1): 4–7, 1976.)

Where percolation from upper terraces does not occur, the Coastal Prairie is subject to typical seasonal growth spurts. Primary productivity in such cases is low. For example, studies at Bodega Head revealed that during a 289-day growing season, photosynthesis accounted for about 4600 pounds of vegetation per acre (527 g/m²). Although this is more productive than a typical desert, it is only half as productive as most chaparral communities. This means that on a steady basis, Coastal Prairie is not capable of supporting much animal life.

Where there is some protection from salt spray, Coastal Prairie grades into a community of herbs and evergreen shrubs known as Northern Coastal Scrub. This community includes a number of species associated with Coastal Sage Scrub in southern California, such as Sticky or Orange Bush Monkey Flower, *Mimulus* (= *Diplacus*) *aurantiacus* (fig. 8.12), and Coyote Brush or Chaparral Broom, *Baccharis pilularis*. Northern Coastal Scrub differs from Coastal Sage Scrub by lacking a large number of drought-deciduous species and by possesing a large component of herbaceous species, many of which are components of the Coastal Prairie. In some areas the dominant plants are perennial lupines, such as Varicolored Lupine, *Lupinus variicolor*, and Yellow Bush Lupine, *Lupinus arboreus* (fig. 7.13). The former is a low-growing shrub about 1½ feet (30 cm) high. Its flowers may be yellow, pink, white, purple, or blue — hence the name "varicolored." Bush Lupine grows up to 9 feet (2.5 m) in height and has yellow flowers. Other conspicuous species include the invasive climber, California Blackberry, *Rubus vitifolius*, and Salal, *Gaultheria shallon*, a glossy-leaved evergreen often used for Christmas decorations. Its berrylike fruit is an important food for birds and other wildlife.

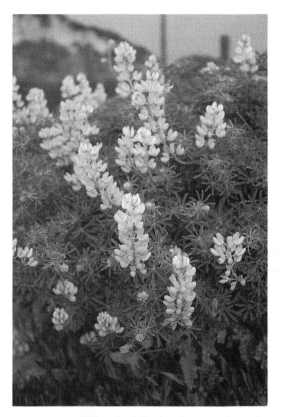

FIGURE 7.13 Yellow Bush Lupine, *Lupinus arboreus*, in Northern Coastal Scrub.

The Second Terrace: Redwood Forest. As time passes, these perpetually wet soils accumulate decay products and become increasingly acidic. This process, known as podzolization, leads ultimately to a fine-grained, ash gray soil with an acidic pH. These soils are known as podzols or spodosols. The upper terraces on the Mendocino coast are characterized by soils of this type and have been measured as the most acidic in the world. The soil here has been measured at pH 2.8.

The second terrace is about 200 feet (65 m) above sea level and is believed to be about 100,000 years of age. It is nearly a mile (1.6 km) back from the sea cliffs. Salt spray is much less of a factor here, and the increase in elevation is enough to cause an increase in precipitation, which measures 40 to 60 inches (100 to 180 cm) per year. It is here that the "towering rain forest" occurs, characterized by Coast Redwoods, *Sequoia sempervirens*, and Douglas Fir, *Pseudotsuga menziesii*. Western Hemlock, Tanoak, and Pacific Madrone are also important in this community.

This forest is best established on the forward portion of the terrace upon old sand dunes. Soil has become weathered to a light brown, and pH is about 5.0. This is a rich soil with abundant organic material and ample nitrogen. A constant shower of needles and leaves from the forest adds to the decay products.

The redwood forest of the north coast is one of California's treasures. Coast Redwoods are endemic to the state, occurring only near the coast from near the Oregon border to San Luis Obispo County in the south. On the Mendocino Coast the forest has been logged, but the second growth itself is impressive. In order to see pristine redwood forest, one must travel to Redwood National Park or one of the series of state parks scattered along the coast from near the Oregon border to as far south as Big Sur.

Because of its dependence on high humidity, provided by a combination of precipitation and fog drip, redwood forest does not occur far inland. Where it does occur inland, the forest is associated with river bottoms. Some of the most beautiful groves occur along the "Avenue of the Giants" in Humboldt County (fig. 7.14). Old Highway 101 in this area follows the course of the Eel River, winding its way among some of the most impressive trees in the world. In this area, redwoods extend inland about 10 miles (16 km) from the coast.

The ecology of redwood forests has been thoroughly studied. This is such an important lumber crop that logging companies have been willing to spend large amounts of money on research, particularly to determine why they grow where they do and what complex of factors makes them grow well. Coast Redwood and Douglas Fir are the two most important timber crops in the state. Redwood is valued for its rich color and resistance to termites and decay. At 365 feet (112 m), these are the tallest trees in the world, and they are among the fastest-growing. Redwoods accumulate more mass of wood per year than any other forest type. It has been estimated that a hectare (2.5 acres) of forest accumulates about 42 cubic meters of wood per year, or about 4000 pounds per acre (4525 kg/ha). Furthermore, in a redwood forest, the aboveground biomass, at about 1500 tons per acre (346 kg/m^2), is greater than in any other community in California. Douglas Fir (pl. 4B) is the most important source of construction lumber used to build the ever-increasing number of buildings required to accommodate the human population.

Distribution of redwood groves is patchy. This is an ecological-island situation associated with a complex set of factors including temperature, moisture, soil, and exposure. For example, it has been reported that Coast Redwoods prefer temperatures around 65°F (18°C). Moisture, however, seems to be the most important factor. The redwood forest is the southern extreme of the temperate rain forest that occurs along the coast from Alaska to California. In the wettest parts of its range, as in the Klamath Province, the forest is composed of Sitka Spruce, Grand Fir, Western Hemlock, and Douglas Fir. Some authorities propose that Coast Redwoods are actually a successional species, and that if precipitation in California were heavier, they would be replaced by the more moisture-loving species except in disturbed areas.

Coast Redwoods grow inland beyond the reach of salt spray, but not beyond the influence of maritime climate. A combination of precipitation and fog drip keeps them watered year-round. The importance of fog drip should not be underestimated.

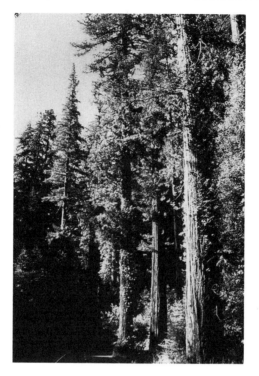

FIGURE 7.14   Coast Redwood, *Sequoia semper-virens*, along the Avenue of the Giants, Humboldt County.

In addition to about 60 inches (180 cm) of moisture contributed by rainfall, it has been determined that up to 12 inches (30 cm) is provided by fog drip. Coast Redwoods occur inland along river bottoms only where the canyon mouths face westward, so that interior heating can draw moist maritime air some distance inland. Along the Russian River near Cloverdale, Coast Redwoods occur as far as 23 miles (37 km) inland. Because most river valleys in the Coast Ranges run north to south, parallel to the coast line, Coast Redwoods seldom occur far from the coast. The reason they occur so far inland on the Russian River is that this is one of the few rivers that has an extensive westward run to the sea. It is also important to note that, in the interior groves, Coast Redwoods occur only on north-facing slopes. In these regions, the south-facing slopes are occupied by Douglas Fir (fig. 7.15).

The influence of wind patterns on the distribution of Coast Redwoods is illustrated by the Mattole River basin, where average precipitation is the highest in the area, and there is a large gap in redwood distribution. During summer, as the prevailing wind sweeps past the King Range, an eddy occurs, causing the wind to blow offshore instead of onshore. Dry downdrafts blow out to sea, and there is very little fog in the Mattole Valley. The area is characterized by Valley Grassland and Oak Woodland.

FIGURE 7.15 Slope effect in a grove of Coast Redwoods and diagrammatic representation of a Coast Redwood root system on a flood plain. (From E. Bakker. *An Island Called California.* Berkeley: University of California Press, 1971.)

Labels within figure:

DOUGLAS-FIR
COAST LIVE OAK
MADRONE
BAY
FERNS
SOUTH-FACING SLOPE
OCEAN FOG
NORTH-FACING SLOPE
RESPROUTING REDWOOD STUMP
SEEDLING IN HUMUS-FREE SOIL
NEW ROOTS AFTER BURIAL BY FLOOD
REDWOOD BURL
SOIL MOISTURE 18% IN AUGUST

The influence of soil on Coast Redwood distribution is also profound. Redwoods grow on sandy soils such as old sand dunes, alluvial deposits along river banks, or soils derived from weathering of sandstones. Abrupt boundaries in redwood distribution occur where soil is derived from rocks such as serpentine or other ophiolites. On these soils, with their strange mineral composition, there are no Coast Redwoods. Instead, these areas are occupied by Yellow Pine Forest species such as Jeffrey Pine, Ponderosa Pine, Sugar Pine, and Incense Cedar. At drier localities these ophiolitic soils are occupied by various closed-cone pines, which will be discussed later.

The boundary of a redwood forest is often abrupt. Where this boundary is associated with a change in soil, there may be a complete change of species within a few hundred yards (meters). One such area is at Red Mountain, in northern Mendocino County. A highly visible example is in Jedediah Smith Redwoods State Park.

Fire and flooding also play important roles in the dynamics of a redwood forest. Redwoods will stump-sprout. The well-known redwood burls sold throughout the northwest are examples of these buds, which will begin to grow if provided with ample water and light. After logging, or after a fire, the redwood trees will rejuvenate rapidly from burls at the base of the trunk. The importance of fire to the redwood forest was discussed in reference to Sierra Redwoods. Fire removes competing species, clears downed wood, recycles minerals, opens the forest canopy, and stimulates seedfall. It is ironic that the California State Park system still believes in fire suppression.

Along the rivers of the northwest, periodic flooding is a natural phenomenon. Each time a flood occurs, a new layer of soil is deposited on the alluvial flat. This deposition tends to clear out undergrowth and provides new fertile soil for the forest. Redwood trees grow a new set of surface roots that penetrate the new soil. The result is that the root systems of old redwoods penetrate deeply into the ground. They have multiple layers of roots, each corresponding to a former flood (fig. 7.15). At Bull Creek Flat, one researcher's crew dug down about 28 feet (9 m) into the alluvium. He found evidence of 15 different floods, at intervals of 30 to 60 years, dating back about 1000 years.

Each new deposit of sediment also creates ideal conditions for seed germination and seedling survival. In open areas, where light is abundant, the seedlings grow rapidly. At Stephens Grove, in Humboldt Redwood State Park, there was a flood in 1861. Seedlings that germinated that year, now over 100 years old, can be tracked exactly. In areas at the margin of the grove, where there has been abundant light, those trees are now over 180 feet (60 m) tall. In the interior of the grove, where light is not abundant, tree seedlings dating to the same flood are only about 30 feet (10 m) tall. It should be obvious that disturbance is important to the health of a redwood forest. A combination of fog, fires to open the canopy, and floods to stimulate proper germination represent the best of all possible worlds for a redwood forest.

Sphagnum Bogs.   On the second coastal terrace of northern California, the red-wood forest occurs primarily on the outer edge, in the vicinity occupied by former sand dunes. To the interior of the forest, in the center of the terrace, the soil is derived differently. The area is low-lying and boggy, fed by seeps and springs. In some areas these bogs dry out every summer. In other areas they remain moist and are invaded by thick layers of a moss called sphagnum. Water in sphagnum bogs is very acidic, from the accumulation of decay products. At this acidic pH, water-soluble nitrate (NO_3) cannot exist, which leads to a deficiency of nitrogen for bog plants. It is for this reason that carnivorous plants are associated with bogs. Carnivorous plants get their nitrogen from the protein in the insects they consume.

The largest of these carnivorous plants is the California Pitcher Plant or Cobra Lily, *Darlingtonia californica* (fig. 7.16). Its distribution is confined mostly to areas where a source of cold water flows through a serpentine substratum. Apparently, they seldom produce flowers, reproducing by underground runners. Most populations are clones.

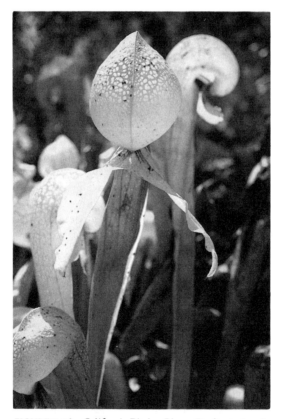

FIGURE 7.16   California Pitcher Plant, *Darlingtonia cal-ifornica*. Carnivorous plants grow on nitrogen-poor soil. They obtain nitrogen from the proteins of trapped insects.

Pitcher Plants are yellow-green with conspicuous veins. Their hollow stem is a modified leaf that is gradually enlarged upward into a rounded, dotted hood with an opening underneath. A two-lobed appendage under the hood gives the plant its cobralike appearance. Plants may be 1 1/2 feet (60 cm) tall. In the hollow part, or pitcher, is a liquid that contains digestive enzymes. Insects are attracted under the hood by light shining through transparent "windows," after which they fall into the digestive fluid. A series of small, downward-pointing hairs prevents the insects from climbing out once they fall in.

A less conspicuous carnivorous plant is the Sundew, *Drosera rotundifolia*. This small plant may be 4 inches (10 cm) across. It grows flat on the ground in a basal rosette. Its leaf blades are covered with tentacle-like reddish hairs that secrete a sticky fluid that traps insects. Entrapment is semiactive on the part of the plant; after an insect is trapped, the leaves are able to bend, which brings the prey in contact with more glands and sticky fluid. Sundews have a wider distribution than the Pitcher Plant. They may also occur in the Sierra Nevada as high as 8000 feet (2600 m) in elevation.

Upper Terraces: Closed-Cone Pine Forests.   On the ecological staircase of Mendocino County, closed-cone pines begin to appear on the interior of the second terrace, and they are the dominant form of vegetation on the outer margins of the third, fourth, and fifth terraces. Soil here has become more podzolized. It is shallow, nutrient-poor, and acidic. The closed-cone pine in this area is Bishop Pine, *Pinus muricata* (fig. 7.17). In its best-developed stands it forms a nice forest of trees up to 40 feet (13 m) in height. In more impoverished conditions the trees are short and scrubby, occurring in a Chaparral-like community, particularly in association with manzanitas. Whorls of firmly attached cones grow on the main trunks each year. These cones may remain closed for many years. If a fire occurs, the heat opens the cones, and seeds are dispersed. Because of this association with fire, most stands of Bishop Pines are even-aged.

Distribution of Bishop Pines is patchy, in the typical ecological-island pattern. The trees occur in groves from Humboldt to Santa Barbara counties. They also occur on Santa Cruz and Santa Rosa islands, where some authorities recognize another, closely related species—the Santa Cruz Island Pine, *Pinus remorata*. Bishop Pines usually grow on fine-grained, nutrient-poor, shallow, poorly drained soil with an acid pH. In the Lompoc area they occur on fine-grained diatomite, or diatomaceous shale. In areas where soil is dry, they water themselves with fog drip. They never grow far from the influence of the ocean.

The species is not limited to California, but it is nearly so. It also occurs in Baja California in one area near San Vicente. The closed-cone pine on Cedros Island is also assigned to this species by many authorities. This peculiar distribution is usually explained as remnants from a formerly widespread coastal distribution in the late Tertiary, several million years ago. Changing climatic conditions during the Pleistocene (the Ice Age) caused them to become isolated as relicts in their present localities.

FIGURE 7.17   Bishop Pine, *Pinus muricata*.

The pattern is similar for the other closed-cone pines. Knobcone Pine, *Pinus attenuata* (fig. 8.55), enjoys the largest distribution of the closed-cone species, and it also has rather specific requirements for fog, fire, and fine-grained soils. In Big Basin Redwood State Park in the Santa Cruz Mountains, the location of Knobcone Pines on the outer margins of upper terraces is analogous to locations of Bishop Pines on the Mendocino coast. Knobcones replace redwoods to the interior and on the ridges. Isolated Knobcone Pine populations also occur in southern California and Baja California. Those populations will be discussed in the chapter on cismontane southern California.

Another closed-cone pine with similar requirements is Monterey Pine, *Pinus radiata*. There is a widespread fossil record for Monterey Pine in coastal California, but now its natural distribution is limited to three widely spaced regions extending over 100 miles (160 km) on the central California coast. Far to the south, however, on Guadalupe Island, about 460 miles (730 km) from the southernmost population near Cambria, there is a population of closed-cones pines that have been designated as either Bishop Pines or Monterey Pines (fig. 7.18). Different authorities have different

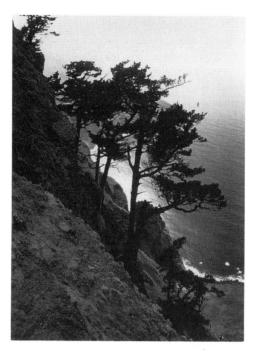

FIGURE 7.18   Monterey Pines, *Pinus radiata*, on a fog-shrouded cliff above the sea on Guadalupe Island.

opinions. As of this writing, the closed-cone pines of Cedros and Guadalupe islands are called Monterey Pines. They appear to be intermediate between the two species. Whatever the case, the distribution of the closed-cone pines is a fascinating case of biogeography and isolation.

Monterey Pine is a large, spreading tree under ideal conditions, but in its native range it often takes on a scrubby form, or it is flagged by salt spray. Monterey Pine has become one of the most commercially valuable timber crops in the world. It has been planted widely in the southern hemisphere, where, under optimal conditions, the trees grow straight and tall and reach harvestable size in 25 to 30 years.

The three species of closed-cone pines seldom grow together, although their ecological requirements are similar. The northern locality of Monterey Pine in the Año Nuevo area, about 30 miles (48 km) north of Monterey, is a region where Monterey Pine and Knobcone Pine occur in close proximity and hybridize. On the other hand, on the Monterey Peninsula on Huckleberry Hill, there is a small stand of Bishop Pines surrounded by Monterey Pines, and there is little or no hybridization.

If the three species were to occur together commonly, they would not be difficult to tell apart. Bishop Pine has needles in clusters of two, and the others have needles in clusters of three. The cones, which are persistent on the trees, are easy to tell apart, if by no other means than their size. Bishop Pines have the smallest cones; they are about 2 inches (5 cm) long, and they have prickly spines. Monterey Pine cones are about 3 inches (7.5 cm) long, they are distinctly rounder, and they have no spines. Knobcone Pines have cones that are 4 to 5 inches (10–12 cm) in length, and they are distinctly asymmetrical, with large, pointed cusps on each scale.

The possible reasons for different cone size are often debated. Why do some pine trees have such large cones? The answer is not certain, but it appears that pines in hot, dry climates have larger cones. If we look at the localities where the three closed-cone pines occur, this seems to be the case. Bishop Pine has the smallest cones, and Knobcone Pine, the most interior in distribution, has the largest cones. Large size may protect the seeds, or larger seeds may have more stored energy to help them germinate and endure the harsher climate.

Another group of conifers with localized distribution along the coast are the cypresses. There are 10 species of cypress (*Cupressus* spp.) in the state. They are characterized by gray, fleshy cones and scale-like leaves. Each is rather localized in distribution, usually associated with a specialized soil. Eight of the species are endemic, and the other two have limited distribution outside the state. Cedars, junipers, and cypresses are all in the cypress family (Cupressaceae). These common names cause a great deal of confusion.

Two species of cypress occur in the southern California area. Three others are localized foothill species found in the Sierra Nevada and the Cascades. The remaining

FIGURE 7.19   Monterey Cypress, *Cupressus macrocarpa*. This specimen, along the Seventeen Mile Drive on the Monterey Peninsula, has been shaped by wind and salt spray.

five species are coastal forms with requirements similar to the closed-cone pines. Perhaps the best known species is Monterey Cypress, *Cupressus macrocarpa*. Its natural distribution is on granitic headlands with thin marine deposits in the vicinity of Monterey. One population occurs in Point Lobos State Reserve; the other occurs along the famous Seventeen Mile Drive near Carmel. It is a picturesque species, occurring in gnarled form where it is exposed to wind and salt spray (fig. 7.19). Monterey Cypress in more favorable localities develops into a large, well-shaped tree. Near the Pebble Beach golf course is an old stand of large Monterey Cypress growing on a rich organic soil. Scattered among these trees, which are estimated at about 300 years of age, are old Indian middens. About 90% of the native population of Monterey Cypress grows in the Carmel area, but the species has been widely planted in landscapes, particularly along the coast. The phenomena of ecologic islands, specialization, endemism, and relicts are well illustrated by the pines and cypresses of the coast of California.

The Pygmy Forest.   The pygmy forest occurs on the most impoverished soils of the Medocino County ecological staircase. On the upper terraces to the interior of the Bishop Pine forest is a region of extreme podzolization. These soils were formerly bogs. Hundreds of thousands of years of leaching by the acidic water carried minerals into deeper soil, where they precipitated, forming a hardpan. Once a hardpan formed, percolation of water into deeper layers was prevented, and the acidification process was accentuated. The soil is white, it has a peculiar mineral consistency, it is very acidic, it is oxygen-poor, and it has poor drainage. Only specialized plants can survive here. Most characteristic of the species on the Mendocino coast that survive these conditions are dwarfed conifers that occur nowhere else in the world.

Of the two conifer species that inhabit the pygmy forest, one is a cypress, and the other is a pine. The cypress is known as Pygmy Cypress or Mendocino Cypress, *Cupressus goveniana pygmaea*, and it grows as a canelike dwarf. It may be centuries old, but it seldom stands more than 10 feet (3 m) tall. Its dwarf status is caused not by a lack of water, for the ground is frequently saturated, but by a lack of essential nutrients. Perhaps it is lack of oxygen, which could severely restrict metabolism in the root system. Ironically, when this species is planted in a favorable locality, it attains great size. In fact, a Pygmy Cypress nearly 100 feet (30 m) in height is one of the tallest specimens of cypress ever recorded.

The pine that grows in the pygmy forest is a variety of Lodgepole or Shore Pine. Known as Bolander Pine, *Pinus contorta bolanderi* (fig. 7.20), it is sometimes considered a distinct species, but it is probably best to consider it a subspecies of Lodgepole Pine. Whether it grows on impoverished soils or in more favorable conditions, the cones remain closed. In the pygmy forest, growth is very slow. Bolander Pines 4 to 5 feet (1.3–1.6 m) high were found to be about 60 years of age. Thickets of stunted trees often are found to be the same age, a reflection of their closed-cone habit and their fire-stimulated origin.

Other Upper-Terrace Communities

Huckleberry Hill on the Monterey Peninsula also has a pygmy forest. The upper terrace where this occurs is only 400 feet (130 m) in elevation. It is a terrace occupied

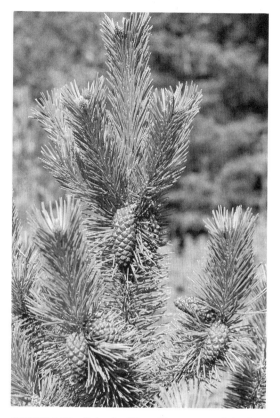

FIGURE 7.20   Bolander Pine, *Pinus contorta bolanderi*.
This dwarfed type of Lodgepole Pine grows on impoverished, acidic soil of the upper coastal terraces in Men-
codino County.

by an acidified, clay-pan soil similar to that in Mendocino County. The dwarfed
species here are Bishop Pine and Gowen Cypress, *Cupressus goveniana goveniana* (fig.
7.21). In this area, on better soil, the pygmy forest is surrounded by a forest of Monterey
Pine. This is the only place where these two closed-cone pines have survived together.

Of special interest on the upper terraces of the Santa Lucia range in Monterey
County is an endemic fir, the Santa Lucia Fir, *Abies bracteata*. It is also known as
Bristlecone Fir because its small, upright cones have spinelike tips on the scales.
These firs are found only in a strip about 13 miles (20 km) wide and 55 miles (90
km) long. Its distribution is limited to steep, rocky slopes and ridges, where it occurs
with Canyon Live Oak. More than any other factor, however, its distribution is limited
by fire. Unlike the closed-cone pines and cypresses, this fir cannot tolerate fire. Its
distribution is limited to the steep slopes and ridges with little fuel to carry a fire.
When it becomes established in adjacent Oak Woodland, it is soon eliminated by
fire.

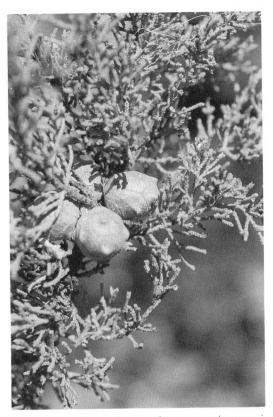

FIGURE 7.21   Gowen Cypress, *Cupressus goveniana goveniana*, on Huckelberry Hill, Monterey County.

ANIMALS OF THE COAST RANGES

Most animals of the Coast Ranges are not particularly distinctive, although the unique insects associated with serpentine were mentioned earlier. In the southern Coast Ranges, most animals are typical species of Foothill Woodland and Chaparral. They are discussed in the sections devoted to those communities. In the northern Coast Ranges, Foothill Woodland and forest species are similar to those discussed in chapter 4. The animals of the moist forests were discussed in chapter 6.

In the moist parts of the Coast Ranges there are many moisture-loving animals, such as insects, molluscs, and amphibians. Banana slugs (*Ariolimax* spp.) are bright yellow detritus feeders that are conspicuous on the forest floor. They are very important as processors of organic material. It has been proposed that one species, *Ariolimax columbianus* (fig. 7.22), be elevated to the status of state mollusc. Slugs do not have shells, but they are in the same group of molluscs (Gastropoda) as the snails. Of particular note is that slugs are hermaphroditic and have internal fertilization, mediated

FIGURE 7.22   Banana Slug, *Ariolimax columbianus*.

by a penis. When they mate, they impregnate each other. *Ariolimax dolicophallus* has a penis longer than its body.

Butterflies

Among insects of the Coast Ranges, perhaps none has captured people's hearts more than the Monarch Butterfly, *Danaus plexippus* (fig. 7.23). This is the only insect known to make a long-distance migratory round trip. On the eastern side of the Rocky Mountains, Monarchs migrate between Canada and the Sierra Madre of central Mexico. West of the Rockies, some 5 million Monarchs spend the winter months along the foggy California coast from Mendocino County to south of San Diego. The greatest concentration occurs along the central coast. They are particularly visible in Pacific Grove, where thousands roost in "butterfly trees," which are usually Monterey Pines or eucalyptus. Each October, to celebrate the return of the Monarchs, Pacific Grove has a Butterfly Festival and parade sponsored by the chamber of commerce.

The same butterflies do not make the entire round trip, but flocks do return to the same trees every year. During migration, they glide on the wind to save energy. They may travel 3000 miles (4800 km) and reach altitudes of 10,000 feet (3000 m). The adults feed on nectar during migration. At their winter sites they search for nectar during the day and bunch up at night in communal roosts. In the spring they leave the coast and fly northward and inland, lay their eggs on milkweeds (*Asclepias* spp.), and then die. Caterpillars (larvae), which feed on the milkweed, hatch from the eggs

FIGURE 7.23   Monarch Butterfly, *Danaus plexippus*.

in 2 to 12 days, depending on the temperature. They are greenish with black and yellow bands, and they have a pair of long filaments. The caterpillar continues to grow, shedding its skin (exoskeleton) about five times before weaving a bright green cocoon (pupa). In about two weeks, the metamorphosis to an adult butterfly takes place. The adults migrate farther north or farther east and repeat the process.

Researchers have marked thousands of adult Monarchs in attempts to track their migratory routes. East of the Rockies, a tagged Monarch flew from Toronto, Canada, to southern Mexico, a distance of over 2000 miles (3200 km). To date, the longest distance a California Monarch has been known to travel is 660 miles (1056 km). Between November 7, 1987, and April 9, 1988, this specimen traveled from Ellwood, in Santa Barbara County, to southeastern Arizona. Apparently, a California Monarch reproduces several times before returning to its winter roost. It is believed to take about four generations to make the round trip.

The mechanism by which Monarchs are able to navigate has also been the subject of some research. Because the same butterflies do not make the full round trip, learning has very little to do with it. The entire procedure must be instinctive. Furthermore, it has been demonstrated that Monarchs are able to find their direction by using sun orientation, an ability exhibited by nearly all migratory animals, including birds, whales, and salmon.

The fact that Monarch caterpillars feed on poisonous milkweeds has been known for a long time. The toxins, known as cardiac glycosides, are capable of killing most animals that would forage on the plant; that is the plant's way of defending itself. The butterfly, however, has become immune to the poison and uses it as a mechanism to defend itself from predation. This is known as coevolution. Similar patterns have been observed for other plants and insects. The case of willows and their associated beetles was mentioned in the section on Riparian Woodland in the Sierra Nevada.

Because potential predators, particularly birds, have learned that Monarchs are distasteful, if nothing else, they avoid them. This mechanism also has inadvertently protected other species of butterfly that resemble Monarchs. In time, the nonpoisonous butterflies become more and more similar to Monarchs in appearance, an evolutionary phenomenon known as mimicry.

Mimics need not be identical to be protected. In fact, it would be a disadvantage to be identical, because it would cause confusion between the species during mating. Birds seem to avoid nearly all orange butterflies as if they were poisonous. In California, this means that common butterflies such as silverspots or fritillaries, *Speyeria* spp., also receive a certain amount of protection from predation. The best-known mimic of the Monarch is the Viceroy, *Basilarchia archippus*, a common butterfly throughout the range of the Monarch in the eastern United States. In California, however, the Viceroy enters the range of the Monarch only along the southeastern border of the state.

In southern California, a butterfly known as the Queen, *Danaus gilippus*, is another poisonous milkweed feeder. It is closely related to the Monarch, which it resembles. This is also a form of mimicry, because the two species of poisonous butterfly, by resembling each other, derive cooperative protection. The resemblance reinforces the protective nature of the coloration. Again, it would not be advantageous for the two species to be identical, because confusion between mates could lead to considerable waste of reproductive effort.

Amphibians

Of special interest in the Coast Ranges are sedentary animals such as certain amphibians and reptiles. There are several cases of breaks in distribution that correspond to geologic breaks. A case in point is represented by slender salamanders (*Batrachoseps* spp.), in the family of lungless salamanders (Plethodontidae). It was indicated previously that distribution and diversity within this sedentary group of salamanders could be correlated with specific geologic terranes that experienced long-distance transport before becoming attached to the western border of North America (fig. 7.24). Breaks in distribution between species or subspecies occur along major fault lines or in association with major rock units with distinctive geologic histories. The separation of animals into species or subspecies populations usually requires spatial isolation over long periods of time. The implication is that fragments of land, like massive ferries, moved from positions to the south, carrying with them cargos of organisms. Once these ferries became docked to the North American continent, the animals were free to move onto the mainland. Many of these salamanders, however, are so sedentary that they apparently chose not to move and have remained in place on the displaced terranes. As evidence of their sedentary nature, one researcher found that over an entire lifespan the farthest one of these salamanders moved was about 4 feet (1.5 m).

To review the basic distribution of these salamanders, they are found in the western foothills of the Sierra Nevada, the Kern Plateau, and along the coast from southern Oregon to Baja California. They are associated primarily with various Oak Woodland communities. On the Kern Plateau they may be associated with conifers, and in southern California they occur in various moist habitats, including suburban gardens. They are found under logs, rocks, and debris. During summer they estivate in cracks and burrows. In the foothills of the southern Sierra Nevada—in particular, along the Kern River drainage—there are seven different forms occurring in isolated populations in association with specific displaced terranes or soil types. Most of these have yet to be assigned scientific names. In southern California there are two species, the Pacific Salamander, *Batrachoseps pacificus*, and the Black-bellied Salamander, *Batrachoseps nigriventris*. The former is a lowland form associated with suburban gardens, and the latter is primarily associated with Southern Oak Woodland occurring in the foothills at higher elevations than the Pacific Salamander.

In the southern Coast Ranges the Black-bellied Salamander is also associated with Oak Woodland, but primarily in the area of sedimentary rocks that have been high and dry only since the Pliocene, some 2 to 3 million years ago. The Black-bellied Salamander also occurs in the foothills of the southern Sierra Nevada on the east side of the Great Central Valley.

North of the sedimentary rock units occupied by the Black-bellied Salamander are two interesting units of rock associated with the Salinian block. The Santa Lucia Mountains occur along the coast south of Monterey and are occupied by an endemic subspecies of the Pacific Salamander. Directly east of the Santa Lucia Range, on the other side of the Salinas Valley, is a large block of granitic rocks known as the Gabilan Range, where there is another endemic subspecies of Pacific Salamander. The Gabilan and Santa Lucia ranges are comparatively high, remaining above sea level and forming islands during times of maximum inundation by seawater. These rocks are at least 100 million years of age. That, plus their separate origins from positions hundreds of miles to the south, are responsible for the isolation and subsequent derivation of two varieties of slender salamander. The two ranges stand today as examples of ecologic islands separated by a region of low relief that is now occupied by Valley Grassland and agriculture.

A third species of slender salamander, the California Slender Salamander, *Batrachoseps attenuatus* (fig. 7.25), occurs in the northern Coast Ranges and northern foothills of the Sierra Nevada. Its distribution is associated closely with Franciscan rocks. These are also old rocks, 70 to 150 million years of age. The coastal and northern Sierra populations are separated by the volcanics of the Cascades and the granitic-metamorphic complex of the Klamath Province. This is essentially a forest species, although it also occurs in association with oaks in the northern Coast Ranges and Sierra Nevada foothills.

A fourth species of slender salamander occurs in the Oregon Cascades, but it is not common. Known as the Oregon Slender Salamander, *Batrachoseps wrighti*, this is

FIGURE 7.24 Comparison of California's displaced terranes with distribution of slender salamanders and newts. Arrows indicate discontinuous distributions. (Displaced terrane map after D. A. Hendrickson. "Congruence of Bolitoglossine Biogeography and Phylogeny with Geologic History: Paleotransport on Displaced Suspect Terranes?" *Cladistics* 2(2): 113–129, 1986.)

Labels within the figure:

CALIFORNIA'S DISPLACED TERRANES

CALIFORNIA SLENDER SALAMANDER
BLACK-BELLIED SLENDER SALAMANDER
PACIFIC SLENDER SALAMANDER

ROUGH-SKINNED NEWT
SIERRA NEWT
RED-BELLIED NEWT
ZONE OF SYMPATRY
COAST RANGE NEWT

FIGURE 7.25   Some salamanders of the Coast Ranges. From top to bottom: California Slender Salamander, *Batrachoseps attenuatus*; Arboreal Salamander, *Aneides lugubris*; Coast Range Newt, *Taricha torosa* (terrestrial and aquatic stages). (From R. C. Stebbins. *Amphibians of Western North America*. Berkeley: University of California Press, 1951.)

a salamander of a moist forest of Douglas Fir, Western Hemlock, and Big-leaf Maple. It is separated from the other populations of slender salamander by about 200 miles (320 km).

Distribution of slender salamanders in California is further complicated by two isolated species that occur on the border of the desert. One, the Inyo Mountains Slender Salamander, *Batrachoseps campi*, occurs in a spring on the eastern side of the Inyo Mountains, on the edge of Saline Valley. The other, the Desert Slender Salamander, *Batrachoseps aridus*, occurs in a palm oasis on the desert side of the Santa Rosa Mountains.

Another salamander that shows differentiation in association with fault lines is the Arboreal Salamander, *Aneides lugubris* (fig 7.25). Another lungless salamander, it is commonly associated with Oak Woodland, where, in spite of its name, it is commonly found on the ground under rocks and logs. Its distribution parallels that of the slender salamanders, although it is seldom found away from oak trees. Although separate subspecies have not been named, different patterns of spotting are correlated with different geologic units. In the Gabilan Range there are forms with spots larger in diameter than 1 mm. In the Santa Lucia Ranges and elsewhere, spots are smaller than 1 mm. These salamanders occur generally above 300 feet (100 m) in elevation, and they do not occur below in the Salinas Valley. This appears to be an ecologic-island situation comparable to that described for slender salamanders. It is also noteworthy that the only other population of Arboreal Salamander with large spots is on South Farallon Island, a granitic outcrop that is also part of the Salinian block (fig. 7.5), but 90 miles (150 km) to the northwest of the Gabilan Range. This island is about 30 miles (50 km) west of San Francisco.

Breaks in the distribution of subspecies of the salamander genus *Ensatina* also correspond to similar geologic units (fig. 8.31). Distribution of *Ensatina* has been discussed already, and it will be analyzed thoroughly in the following chapter. These are the lungless salamanders that occur as spotted forms in the Sierra Nevada (fig. 4.38) and as solid-colored forms in the Coast Ranges. The total range of the species encircles the Great Central Valley, and at the southern end (fig. 8.32), where the ranges overlap, they do not hybridize. The pattern of distribution of the solid-colored forms parallels in a remarkable way that of the arboreal and slender salamanders of the Coast Ranges and Sierra foothills. The breaks in subspecies distribution parallel closely those of the slender salamanders.

Another family of salamanders is known as newts (Salamandridae). The most conspicuous salamanders in California, they are brownish on the back, and the underside is bright yellow, orange, or red, depending on the species. Apparently not fearful of predators, they are commonly active during daylight hours. Their skin secretions are toxic to most animals. When molested, they arch their backs and expose the bright color of the belly. Bright colors are often warnings, as has been discussed in other chapters.

These are not sedentary salamanders. They spend summer months estivating under rocks and logs or in cracks. With the first rains of autumn they migrate to water in large numbers. They reproduce in the water and remain aquatic throughout the breeding season. During this time their skin becomes smooth, and the tail develops into an oarlike fin. During their migrations, which often occur in daylight hours, they may be observed in great numbers. In the Berkeley area there are signs along roadways that say "Watch for Newts Crossing."

This migratory habit enables these salamanders, more than any other, to colonize new habitats. For this reason the breaks between populations are not as obvious as those for the lungless salamanders. Nevertheless, inspection of the ranges of the three California newt species will show that ancestral geographic barriers are the same as they were for the others (fig. 7.24).

Overall, distribution of the three species resembles that of the *Ensatina* group. They occur along the coast and around the north end of the Great Central Valley. In the Sierra Nevada they occur as far south as Kern County. Unlike *Ensatina*, the two arms of distribution do not overlap at the southern end.

The northernmost species is the Rough-skinned Newt, *Taricha granulosa*. It occurs in moist forests from southeast Alaska to Santa Cruz County, California. The southern boundary of its distribution coincides generally with the boundary between Franciscan rocks and the younger sedimentary rocks of the southern Coast Ranges. The Coast Range Newt, *Taricha torosa torosa* (fig. 7.25), occurs in canyons and along streams from the southern Coast Ranges to southern California. A closely related subspecies, the Sierra Newt, *Taricha torosa sierrae*, occurs across the Great Central Valley in canyons and streams of the Foothill Woodland. To the north, the ranges of these two subspecies overlap that of the Rough-skinned Newt, but hybridization is evidently not common. The third species, the Red-bellied Newt, *Taricha rivularis*, occurs in association with flowing water in the Coast Redwood Forest. Its range overlaps that of the Rough-skinned Newt and, at its southern end, that of the Coast Range Newt. The three species could occur together, but they seldom do. Presently the three species are separated ecologically, but they were likely separated geographically in former times. Their migratory habit apparently has brought them together. In particular, it seems that the Coast Range Newt has moved northward for some considerable distance, so that its range now overlaps those of the other two.

Genetic analysis of the newts, using gel electrophoresis, has been undertaken. Because of the great difference between the Rough-skinned Newt and the Coast Range Newt, it is estimated that they were geographically separated about 9 million years ago. This time corresponds well with the period of inundation of the southern Coast Ranges. A comparison of northern and southern populations of the Coast Ranges newts indicated that their time of divergence occurred about a million years ago. This coincides with uplift of the southern Coast Ranges, indicating that they probably migrated northward during that time.

Salamanders are not the only animals that show this pattern of diversification in association with geologic units. The Foothill Yellow-legged Frog, *Rana boylei*, and the Mountain Yellow-legged Frog, *Rana muscosa* (fig. 11.26), have the same two-armed distribution around the Great Central Valley. These two species occur together in southern California in the San Gabriel Mountains. In particular, they have been collected at the same localities in the North Fork of the San Gabriel River and in Bear Creek. Distribution of these frogs is discussed in chapter 11.

Reptiles

The Western Pond Turtle, *Clemmys marmorata* (fig. 7.26), occurs along the coast and in the Lake Tahoe area of the Sierra Nevada. There are two subspecies in the Coast

FIGURE 7.26   Western Pond Turtle, *Clemmys marmorata*. (From R. C. Stebbins. *California Amphibians and Reptiles*. Berkeley: University of California Press, 1972.)

Ranges, a northern and a southern form. Their ranges overlap in the central area north of Monterey.

Among lizards, the alligator lizards and the skinks are noted for their sedentary habits. Like salamanders, they spend a great deal of time under rocks, logs, and other debris. Both of these lizards are noted for their cigar-shaped (fusiform) bodies and small legs. They move in a snakelike fashion. Alligator lizards have conspicuous squarish scales on their backs. Skinks are very sleek and shiny and are noted for their bright blue or red tails.

Ranges of the Northern Alligator Lizard, *Elgaria coerulea* (= *Gerrhonotus coeruleus*), and the Southern Alligator Lizard, *Elgaria multicarinata* (= *Gerrhonotus multicarinatus*) (fig. 7.27), overlap in a manner similar to that of the newts, and subdivisions into subspecies occur in approximately the same places as in *Ensatina*. Similarly, ranges of the Western Skink, *Eumeces skiltonianus*, and Gilbert's Skink, *Eumeces gilberti* (pl. 15A), follow a similar pattern. Subspecies of Gilbert's Skink are also fragmented along similar boundaries. Alligator lizards and skinks are also found on the Kern Plateau and in southern California in association with Southern Oak Woodland.

The Ringneck Snake, *Diadophis punctatus* (fig. 8.52), is a sedentary species found under a variety of objects throughout its range. It occurs mostly in moist habitats such as forests and Oak Woodland, and it commonly feeds on slender salamanders. It is a small snake, seldom over 12 inches (30 cm) in length. It has a dark-colored head with a yellow to red ring around its neck. The belly is also bright yellow to red. When a Ringneck Snake is disturbed, it coils its tail like a corkscrew, which reveals the bright color. The snake waves the tail, presumably as a distraction. A Ringneck Snake is not able to shed its tail like a skink, but if a predator attacks the tail, more vulnerable parts of the body are likely to escape damage. The distribution of Ringneck Snakes is notable because it is very much like that of *Ensatina*. Its circle

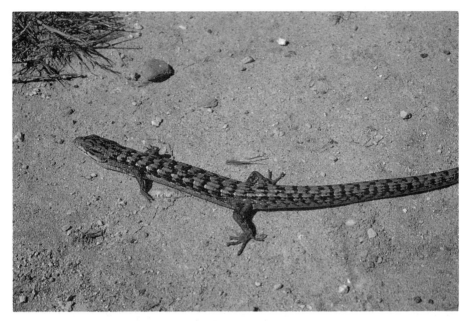

FIGURE 7.27   Southern Alligator Lizard, *Elgaria multicarinata*.

of subspecies is divided in much the same way, and the two arms of distribution overlap in southern California.

Distribution of all these species of amphibians and reptiles, taken as a group, illustrates a remarkable pattern of biologic differentiation caused by the interaction of climatic and geologic history. These are but more examples of how California's diversity is the product of an evolutionary laboratory.

Birds

Most birds and mammals of the Coast Ranges are discussed elsewhere in this book. Those of the northern forests are discussed in chapter 6. Those of Yellow Pine Forest are discussed in chapter 4. Oak Woodland species are discussed in association with Foothill Woodland, Southern Oak Woodland, or Chaparral.

Among the birds, those associated with oaks are the most conspicuous. This includes the Western Scrub Jay, *Aphelocoma californica* (pl. 13F), and the Acorn Woodpecker, *Melanerpes formicivorus* (fig. 7.28). The Scrub Jay is very important to Oak Woodland because it buries hundreds of acorns for future consumption, but it does not retrieve them all. This is a major mechanism for planting and uphill dispersal of oak trees.

The habit of Acorn Woodpeckers of drilling holes and storing acorns has been mentioned. Perhaps the most interesting thing about them, however, is their social behavior. Because they are typically associated with oaks, and because much of their behavior has been studied in the southern Coast Ranges, they will be discussed here.

FIGURE 7.28   Acorn Woodpecker, *Melanerpes formicivorus*.

Acorn Woodpeckers are conspicuous, gregarious birds that are easy to watch. They are dark birds with a white chin and a small red cap. When they fly, their white rump and white wing patches are conspicuous. They also attract attention because they make considerable noise. Their call is an easily recognized "wack-a, wack-a."

Apparently, the urge to fill a hole with an acorn is instinctive. If the hole happens to be in a cabin wall, Acorn Woodpeckers will continue to push acorns through it until one sticks or until the space in the wall becomes filled up to the hole. When the woodpecker sees an acorn in the hole, it loses the urge to stuff another one in there. According to one story, when a cabin in the Santa Ana Mountains was torn down, enough acorns were taken from the walls to fill two large trash barrels.

Acorn Woodpeckers are unique among birds in north temperate regions because they feed and breed in cooperative groups that may include 12 to 15 members. These social groups defend a territory, which consists of a tree full of holes into which acorns have been stuffed. These trees are known as granaries. In regions such as southern Arizona, where acorns are not abundant, these woodpeckers do not defend granaries, and they mate in single pairs. In California, where acorns are commonly abundant enough to provide food for the entire winter, these social groups have evolved.

Males in the social group are commonly siblings. Females are also commonly siblings but may be unrelated to the males. A social group may include one to three breeders of each sex; the remainder of the birds are nonbreeding helpers. Mate sharing is common among the breeders. The helpers gather food, defend the granary, and feed the young. When the granary is full, helpers drill more holes. If the granary is not full, they spend most of their time searching for food. Young birds are fed insects, not acorns. The acorns are food for the birds that gather insects to feed the young.

If mating birds die or disappear, new breeders are not recruited from the helpers. Rather, if all mating birds of one sex are gone, a mate vacancy appears. Groups of woodpeckers from nearby colonies will then appear at the granary, and a great deal of commotion ensues as mature birds compete, chase, and display for the privilege of filling the vacancy. When the vacancy is filled, it is by new sibling breeders, which immediately begin to destroy eggs and offspring belonging to the former breeders. This behavior ensures that new breeders will contribute genes to the next generation.

Competition between females takes place over which of the sisters will lay the first egg. Most females lay about five eggs. If one breeding female begins to lay eggs before another, the second breeder will remove the egg and carry it to another tree, where it is broken and eaten by the group. This procedure is continued until the second female begins to lay eggs. When two females are laying eggs in the same nest, the eggs cannot be told apart, and none of them is destroyed. This process ensures that more than one female contributes genetic material to the offspring, and the bird that removed the eggs will contribute more genetic material than the first to lay.

Sometimes, whole new colonies are formed by a merging of sibling coalitions — females from one group and males from another. Formation of a new colony requires an abundance of acorns and, more important, a granary. Each bird is capable of drilling only a few holes per year, and a granary has anywhere from a few hundred to a thousand storage holes. Marginal habitats are scarce, and it takes the work of many birds to create a new granary. New granaries are produced only when all existing holes are filled and acorns are still abundant.

The California Condor, *Gymnogyps californianus*, is primarily a species of the southern Coast Ranges, although its official range also includes the Tehachapi Mountains and southern Sierra foothills. As of 1988, however, there were no animals remaining in the wild. The last natural home of the California Condor was the Los Padres National Forest, east of Ventura. A captive breeding program was begun, and in 1992, when sufficient numbers of these birds were living again, captive condors began to be returned to their former range.

The California Condor is the largest flying bird in North America. It weighs about 20 pounds (8 kg) and has a wingspread of around 10 feet (3 m). A large vulture, it is black and has a naked head. It soars on rising currents of air, called thermals. It covers hundreds of miles in a day searching for carrion, which, similar to the Turkey Vulture, *Cathartes aura*, it probably locates by sight and odor.

The California Condor roosts and nests in tall trees and on cliffs, usually in remote areas. It flies during the day over pastureland and other open habitat, searching for food. A California Condor would typically soar over 120 linear miles (190 km) in a day. Because of its large size, it is not able to become airborne merely by flapping its wings. It must wait for the thermals and then launch itself from a high place into the rising air. When it does land on the ground it experiences great difficulty becoming airborne again, particularly if its stomach is filled with food. In this circumstance, birds have been observed to walk up a hill and then run back down, flapping their wings until they reach sufficient speed to take off.

Activities of humans drove the California Condor to the brink of extinction. In the old days, a large number simply were shot. Since the 1800s, loss of habitat has been very important. Conversion of Valley Grassland to farmland took away the feeding grounds. The prey as well as the predators were driven out. Carcasses of Tule Elk and Pronghorn were no longer available for food. In recent years the birds fed primarily on dead livestock and on Mule Deer that were shot and not located by hunters. Although deer carcasses, the remains of mountain lion kills, were still available, these were in Oak Woodland and Chaparral areas. After the turn of the century, following the introduction of a policy of fire suppression, brushlands became overgrown, resulting in a lack of open space for landing and feeding of California Condors. Deer moved into woodlands, where more food was available. The California Condor gradually disappeared.

Extirpation of the California Condor is not restricted to California. Fossil remains indicate that during the Pleistocene, about a million years ago, they occurred widely over North America. There is evidence of their existence from Canada to Florida. Their decline is associated with a general reduction in the number of bird and mammal species over the last few thousand years. This may be the result of climatic change, but a strong body of evidence relates the extinctions to a rise in human populations in North America. The La Brea Tar Pits include the remains of California Condors that lived up to 40,000 years ago. As recently as 2000 years ago they still occurred across Arizona, New Mexico, and Texas. California Condor remains are found in caves all over the southwest, often in association with Indian artifacts. Indians most certainly had an interest in these huge birds. Rituals involving sacrificial deaths of California Condors are known among San Diego Indians, and costumes and other artifacts made of California Condor skins or feathers are found in natural history museums. In fact, collecting of California Condors for display in zoos and museums has also taken its toll. By actual count, 177 California Condor specimens are known to exist in the world's natural history museums.

In the early 1800s the California Condor still occurred along the Pacific coast. In 1806, the Lewis and Clark expedition recorded instances of California Condors feeding on dead salmon washed up on the banks of the Columbia River. In the early 1900s they were eliminated from southern California. One of the early natural history studies of the California Condor took place in 1906 in Eaton Canyon, in the San Gabriel Mountains. Photographs taken with $5'' \times 7''$ glass plates are still among the best of nesting California Condors.

In the 1930s it was estimated that there were 60 to 70 birds left in the wild. In the 1940s an estimate of 60 birds was made. Some authorities claim that these estimates are not accurate, and that there must have been at least 150 birds as recently as the 1950s. The Sespe Condor Sanctuary, encompassing 35,000 acres (14,200 ha), was created in 1947. Then 18,000 acres (7300 ha) were added in 1951, and a 1,200-acre (485-ha) parcel around Sisquoc Falls was declared a sanctuary in 1973. In 1986, the 11,000-acre (4450-ha) Hudson Ranch was purchased by the U.S. Fish and Wildlife Service. Acquisition of this property, in the southeast corner of Kern County, put into public hands most of the natural range of the California Condor. The wild population continued to decline, however, and in 1965 there were an estimated 40 birds left. In 1983 there were 20, in 1986 there were 6, and the last wild bird was trapped and taken to a zoo in 1987.

Much of the decline in recent years can be attributed to factors other than habitat loss. From the 1960s on, thinning of eggshells due to DDT was a factor. Some birds were poisoned as victims of coyote and rodent extermination programs, and many others were poisoned from consuming lead, presumably in the remains of deer or other animals that were wounded by a hunter and died later. Many authorities today consider lead poisoning to be the major cause of the California Condor's decline.

The California Condor is now the rarest bird in North America. Federal and state agencies, under the auspices of the 1973 Endangered Species Act, have begun a recovery program including the establishment of critical habitat, research on habits of the species, and a captive breeding program. Regarding critical habitat, since 1969 over 4300 acres (1740 ha) have been acquired for management as reserves. As for research, observation posts were established where wild birds could be studied and photographed, and birds were fitted with tiny radio collars so their daily activities could be monitored. The most controversial part of the program has been the captive breeding program.

In a captive breeding program, birds in captivity produce and raise offspring that are destined to be released into the wild. Normally a California Condor lays a single egg every other year. This is a low reproductive rate, typical of long-lived, large animals that occur high on a food chain. If an egg is destroyed or removed, the California Condor responds by laying another egg, a phenomenon known as double-clutching. There is one known case of triple-clutching. In a captive breeding program, eggs are removed from nests of wild birds and hatched in captivity. The wild birds then lay another egg, which doubles the reproduction rate. Similarly, mated captive birds are stimulated to double-clutch. In 1983 there were 20 birds in the wild and 8 in captivity. By 1986 there were 6 birds in the wild and 21 in captivity. In 1992 when there were a total of 52 live birds in captivity, the first captive-reared California Condors were released into the wild. Captive birds are housed in Los Angeles and San Diego zoos and wildlife parks.

Part of the controversy involved whether or not there should by any birds left to reproduce in the wild. Various studies have indicated the importance of genetic diversity to survival of the species. Diversity is maintained by reproduction among as many breeding pairs as possible. The proponents of captive breeding contended that to achieve as much diversity a possible, all birds ought to be kept in captivity until there were enough to establish a viable population in nature. Furthermore, hatching success is much higher in captivity, where adverse conditions such as predation by Common Ravens, *Corvus corax* (fig. 9.51), can be eliminated.

Critics of the program said that if all birds were in captivity, their habitat would be doomed to destruction in their absence. Theoretically, there can be no critical habitat if there are no animals in the area to protect. Critics were also quick to point out that one California Condor death occurred from stress suffered during handling by a U.S. Fish and Wildlife biologist. Critics also fear that birds raised in captivity will be too tame to make it in the wild.

Because of the precipitous decline in the numbers of these wild birds, an agreement was reached in 1986 to remove them all from the wild. Meanwhile, in order to get a better idea of ranges and feeding behavior, female Andean Condors, *Vultur gryphus*, with radio collars were released into the California Condor refuge. If lead poisoning is indeed the major threat to further existence of this bird, precautions will have to be made to ensure that newly released birds do not contact carrion containing lead pellets. The problem of lead poisoning will have to be addressed sooner or later anyway. Whatever may be the result of this outpouring of effort and money, it cannot be stated that California Condors were ignored. With luck, future generations will once again see these magnificent birds in the wild.

The Golden Eagle, *Aquila chrysaetos* (fig. 10.19), is one of the few birds that might be confused with a California Condor in flight. With a wingspan exceeding 7 feet (2.1 m), and soaring with slightly upturned wing tips, the Golden Eagle may be seen over open country throughout the state. Golden Eagles build huge stick nests in tall trees or on cliffs where they are afforded a good view of open country. With their extremely keen vision, Golden Eagles search for a variety of diurnal rodents and carrion. Despite their protected status, they are often shot by ranchers, who accuse them of preying on sheep or other livestock. Although Golden Eagles are not rare in California, they are not common either, and it is possible that these large birds could face a fate similar to that of the California Condor. A recent study confirmed that 30% of the Golden Eagles sampled in the southern Coast Ranges contained high concentrations of lead in their blood.

Another victim of eggshell thinning is the Peregrine Falcon, *Falco peregrinus*. Its numbers declined markedly in association with the widespread use of DDT. This is not specifically a Coast Ranges bird, nor is it uniquely Californian. It is a species whose native range is in temperate regions throughout the world. This was the sovereign's bird of the Middle Ages, trained to the sport of falconry by noblemen and commoners. With a claim to fame as the "fastest bird in the world," it has been clocked at 217 miles per hour (347 kph) in a dive.

It is appropriate to discuss the Peregrine Falcon here because Morro Bay is one of the places in California where these birds have persisted in nature. In 1970 the pair at Morro Bay was one of only two nesting pairs known in the state. The other was in the Coast Ranges in Sonoma County.

These raptors feed on other birds, which they catch in midair in a spectacular display of aerial acrobatics. They are particularly fond of swifts, acrobats in their own right. Their primary natural enemies are Great Horned Owls and Golden Eagles, which prey on chicks in nests. An "unnatural" enemy is the ruthless falconer, who steals the eggs. Apparently there is a profitable black market for raptors in the Middle East, and wealthy falconers particularly covet Peregrine Falcons.

In California, the species was hardhit by pesticides. All of the southern California populations and most of those in the Sierra Nevada were extirpated. The remainder of the state retained less than 10% of its historic population. Before World War II there were from 200 to 300 pairs in California.

The Peregrine Falcon represents a success story for management practices. Since DDT was banned in the United States in 1972, the species has been making a comeback. Likewise, the threat of mass species extinction on a worldwide scale caused the abandoning, or at least curtailment, of DDT use all over the world, enabling Peregrine Falcons to make a global comeback.

In California, there is still a problem with thin eggshells. This problem is attributed to DDT, DDE, and various other chlorinated hydrocarbons still present in nature. The source of these chemicals is not certain, but there are four possibilities. Three involve local conditions. Pre-1972 residues may still be in the food chain, the chemical may be being used illegally, or it could be present as "impurities" in related pesticides. The fourth possibility is that various prey species for the falcons, particularly the swifts, are picking up the DDT when they migrate to Mexico, where the pesticide is still legally used.

In particular, management of the Peregrine Falcon represents a success story for captive breeding. Peregrines mate for life and annually breed in the same territory. Nests are built on cliffs such as Morro Rock and El Capitan in Yosemite. Breeding pairs in nature will double-clutch if eggs are removed from their nests. Many of these eggs are thin-shelled and will not hatch in nature. Pressure or weight of the nesting bird during incubation could cause them to break. The eggs that are removed from nests are hatched in an incubator, and the chicks are returned to the nest for the parents to raise. If the parents have successfully hatched their second clutch of eggs in the meantime, the total number of birds raised by the parents will be doubled. This is known as augmentation.

Another technique involves what is known as hacking. Young birds are fledged in an area where there are no adult birds. The juvenile is placed in a box on a cliff, and it is fed indirectly while it practices flying and catching its own prey. After five weeks of training, it is left to the process of natural selection. The success rate has been quite high using this technique. About 80% of these birds become established on their own—a number that is particularly striking since the natural survival rate for birds in their first year of life is only 25%.

One of the most interesting success stories of Peregrine Falcons is the fact that they have adapted to urban life. Throughout the United States and Canada, these birds are nesting in cities, on the ledges of skyscrapers. As of 1988, there were seven birds living in Los Angeles and six in San Francisco. To the delight of the people who work and live in these cities, these magnificent birds may be watched as they hunt, feeding particularly on the pigeons (Rock Doves), *Columbia livia*, so common in these areas. What an irony: the high-rise topography of cities that has displaced so many wild animals has become the home for one of the most endangered!

Each year the effect of these management techniques becomes more apparent. In 1977 two young from the captive breeding program were released; one survived. By 1983, however, over 200 had been released, either by hacking or fostering of young that were hatched in captivity. From the two breeding pairs known to exist in 1970, the number had risen to 103 by 1989. The Peregrine Falcon is returning to California, largely because of the captive breeding program. We cannot become complacent, however, because many birds, particularly older adults, are still laying thin-shelled eggs. DDT or its relatives are still in the environment, and the source is unexplained. Furthermore, there is still a profitable black market for raptors.

8

Cismontane
Southern California

The term *southern California,* as it is used by many people, refers to the southwestern portion of the state, where rapidly proliferating urban sprawl is covering the coastal lowlands. The word *cismontane* means "this side of the mountain." Thus the region covered by this chapter consists primarily of the coastal sides of the Transverse and Peninsular ranges, an area that includes the Los Angeles Basin. Technically, the Los Angeles Basin is part of the Peninsular Ranges, but the term specifically refers to an alluvial outwash that includes most of the Los Angeles and Orange counties, as well as western San Bernardino and Riverside counties. In terms of area, this region encompasses less than one-sixth of the state, but it contains over half of the human population, most of which is concentrated on the coastal plain. Above 1000 feet (300 m) elevation, cismontane southern California is mostly uninhabited brushland.

Southern California is the part of the state characterized by scrub vegetation, commonly known as Chaparral. The word *chaparral* is derived from Spanish and originally referred to a thicket of shrubby evergreen oaks. Now it is used to denote habitats characterized by dense stands of brush. Chaparral is not restricted to cismontane southern California, but in this region it is the dominant form of vegetation. Statewide, chaparral types of vegetation also occur in the drier parts of the Sierra Nevada foothills and the Coast Ranges, particularly on south-facing slopes or in association with serpentine or other depauperate soils. In total, variations of Chaparral represent one of California's most common communities, covering about 12 million acres (29 million ha) of terrain. In this chapter, four brushy communities will be discussed, all of which have been referred to at one time or another as Chaparral.

Scrub vegetation occurs throughout the world in regions with a Mediterranean climate. This type of climate, characterized by long, hot summers and moderate winter precipitation including snow at upper elevations (fig. 8.1), promotes native vegetation such as evergreen shrubs with relatively small leaves. Because the leaves of such shrubs are often covered with a waterproof coating of resinous or waxy material, some authorities prefer to call this sclerophyllous (hard-leaf) vegetation. Associated with the long summer drought, vegetation becomes very dry by autumn. At this time it is susceptible to fire. Chaparral therefore has evolved in conjunction with fire for millions of years. In many respects the chaparral communities require periodic burning for proper growth and vigor. The conflict between human habitation and periodic fires is never-ending.

The mountain ranges of cismontane southern California are shown in figure 8.2. North of the Los Angeles Basin lie the Transverse Ranges. These ranges are aligned on an east–west axis, an orientation quite different from all other mountain ranges of

FIGURE 8.1   Winter storm in the San Bernardino Mountains. View eastward from Rim of the World Highway.

the state. This alignment is caused by northward motion of the Pacific plate along the San Andreas fault. At the contact point between the Pacific plate and the westward-moving North American plate, there has been a good deal of rotation in subplates, which act as ball bearings between the two major plates. This rotation is reflected in the east–west orientation of the Transverse Ranges. From east to west, the three main ranges of this province are the San Bernardino Mountains, the San Gabriel Mountains, and the Santa Monica Mountains. The Channel Islands appear to be a westward extension of the Santa Monica Mountains where all but the mountaintops are covered by seawater. Cajon Pass, through which Interstate 15 passes, separates the San Gabriel and San Bernardino mountains. San Fernando Pass, through which Interstate 5 runs, separates the San Gabriel and Santa Susana mountains.

The Peninsular Ranges are located east and south of the Los Angeles Basin, although technically the basin is included in the Peninsular Ranges Province. They are called the Peninsular Ranges because they are the northernmost ranges of the series of mountains that make up the Baja California peninsula. From north to south, the main ranges of this province are the San Jacinto Mountains, the Santa Rosa Mountains, and the Laguna Mountains. The Santa Ana Mountains are also part of this chain, but they lie to the west of the San Jacinto and Santa Rosa mountains, separated from them

FIGURE 8.2   Cismontane southern California.

by a broad valley that includes the Hemet and Lake Elsinore areas. San Gorgonio Pass lies between the San Jacinto Mountains of the Peninsular Ranges and the San Bernardino Mountains of the Transverse Ranges. Interstate 10 lies in this gap.

Peaks of the Transverse and Peninsular ranges are remarkably high. Surrounding the Los Angeles Basin, which is slightly above sea level, peaks rise more than 2 vertical miles (3.0 km). San Antonio Peak (Mount Baldy), in the San Gabriel Mountains, rises to 10,064 feet (3068 m). Mount San Jacinto, at 10,805 feet (3293 m), is the highest in the Peninsular Ranges. Mount San Gorgonio (Greyback), in the San Bernardino Mountains, at 11,502 feet (3506 m), is the highest in southern California.

The Los Angeles Basin is a flood plain surrounded by mountains. Deep beneath the flood plain there is a series of north–south-trending faults, similar to the geologic picture in the Peninsular Ranges. This is the basis for including the basin as part of the Peninsular Ranges province. For millions of years floodwaters carried by the Los Angeles, San Gabriel, and Santa Ana rivers deposited alluvial outwash from the mountains. This alluvium is up to 14,000 feet (4200 m) thick and extends some 75 miles (120 km) from the coastline to the base of the San Bernardino Mountains. The series of faults buried beneath the alluvium have been responsible for major earthquakes in the recent past. Trapped in pockets associated with these faults are several large petroleum deposits. For this reason, the Los Angeles Basin has been one of the major oil-producing regions of the United States.

CLIMATE

The climate of the southern California area is the product of cold ocean water and latitude, a combination of maritime and Mediterranean climates. The maritime influence usually prevails in the Los Angeles Basin, causing a persistent marine layer or temperature inversion layer. Consequently, the area is often hazy, foggy, or smoggy. Many winter storms reach their southernmost latitude in southern California. During summer, the region lies under a high-pressure zone associated with descending dry air from the upper atmosphere. This persistent high pressure generally prevents precipitation in summer, although tropical storms sporadically work their way into southern California, particularly in the Peninsular Ranges (fig. 2.8). For example, in August 1981, a tropical storm dumped 11.5 inches (290 mm) on Campo, in San Diego County, in only 80 minutes.

Four distinct seasons occur in southern California (fig. 2.10), but the primary growing season is winter. Winter rain is followed by spring fogs, which give way to summer haze and smog. Summer temperatures are often in the 80s and 90s. Autumn brings Santa Ana winds, which blow from the Mojave Desert toward the ocean. They push the marine layer out to sea and become heated by compression as they drop into the basin. This is the season when scrub vegetation is driest. Fires can be fanned into holocausts by this hot wind. Winter is characterized by alternating rainstorms and clear, sunny days. This is a time of renewal, when burned vegetation resprouts and ephemeral plants provide hillsides and valleys with a brilliant green hue.

Precipitation at the Los Angeles civic center averages about 15 inches (38 cm) per year. Closer to the coast, however, it is half that. On Mount Wilson, in the San Gabriel Mountains, it is twice that. This range of precipitation, from 8 inches (20 cm) at the coast to 30 inches (75 cm) in the mountains, is a clear example of the effect of elevation on precipitation. Adiabatic cooling causes lower average temperatures at higher elevations. This cooling increases precipitation in the mountains and also increases the proportion of precipitation that falls as snow. Also, along the coast, the extremes of temperature are reduced through the influence of maritime climate (table 8.1). Close proximity of the ocean increases the amount of moisture in the air and tends to moderate temperature fluctuations.

The influence of rain-shadow effect may be illustrated by comparing records from two weather stations in the San Gabriel Mountains. Mount Wilson is directly above Los Angeles. This is the mountain with the television transmitters. Table Mountain, in the vicinity of Big Pines, is on the desert side of the San Gabriel Mountains. Both weather stations record the same average annual temperature, 56°F (13°C), but the average annual precipitation on Table Mountain is only 21 inches (52 cm), about 10 inches (25 cm) less than that on Mount Wilson.

Slope effect is superimposed upon the effects of temperature and precipitation. Mediterranean climate, with its long, hot summer, accentuates slope effect. South-facing slopes, with their greater degree of drought stress, are cloaked with drought-tolerant vegetation. This phenomenon is particularly evident in the Transverse Ranges because of their east–west orientation. The entire side of the ranges above the Los

TABLE 8.1   A Comparison of Average Temperatures at Three Points in the Los Angeles Area, Indicating Influence of Maritime Climate and Elevation

	Long Beach (coastal)	San Bernardino (interior basin)	Mount Wilson (San Gabriel Mts.)
Coldest month	53°F (12°C)	48°F (9°C)	32°F (0°C)
Warmest month	68°F (20°C)	80°F (27°C)	62°F (17°C)
Annual range	15°F (8°C)	32°F (18°C)	30°F (17°C)
Elevation	Sea level	400 ft (120 m)	5000 ft (1600 m)

Angeles Basin is south-facing. On that side, chaparral vegetation extends all the way up to about 5000 feet (1600 m). At that elevation on the north side (the desert side) of the mountains, Yellow Pine Forest occurs even though actual precipitation there is lower (pl. 6A). Water is more available because north-facing slopes experience less evaporation than south-facing slopes, and snow lasts longer before melting. In contrast, in the north–south-oriented Peninsular Ranges, vegetational zonation is more like that of the Sierra Nevada. As one would expect, Yellow Pine Forest occurs at a lower elevation on the coastal side of the mountain, where there is more precipitation.

SOUTHERN CALIFORNIA GEOLOGY

Southern California can be said to have many faults (fig. 8.3). Most of this region lies west of the San Andreas fault. About 25 million years ago (Miocene), right-lateral movement on this fault began carrying southern California to its present latitude from its former position adjacent to mainland Mexico. However, the area contains several other faults running in a parallel direction. From east to west, these are the San Jacinto fault, the Whittier-Elsinore fault, and the Newport-Inglewood fault. The Newport-Inglewood fault runs roughly parallel to the coast on the western edge of the Los Angeles Basin. It extends out to sea and remains offshore south of Corona Del Mar. At least two other major faults lie offshore. One lies between Santa Catalina Island and the mainland, and the other lies between Santa Catalina and San Clemente islands.

Motion along these faults has been up-and-down (dip-slip) and/or sideways (strike-slip). Dip-slip motion has resulted in uplift of fault-block mountains. Authorities generally place most of the uplift during the last 2 million years. Strike-slip motion has been right-lateral, similar to that of the San Andreas fault. The overall picture is that west of the San Andreas fault, a series of slices of continental crust are sliding against each other as everything westward is carried toward the north.

The Transverse and Peninsular ranges are all fault-block ranges. The San Jacinto and Santa Rosa mountains have been uplifted along the east side of the San Jacinto fault. The Santa Ana and Laguna mountains have been uplifted along the west side of the Whittier-Elsinore fault. The Palos Verdes Peninsula is an uplifted mountain lying in the western edge of the Los Angeles Basin just west of the Newport-Inglewood fault.

FIGURE 8.3   Some important southern California faults. (Reprinted with permission from P. Abbott. "The Rose Canyon Fault," *Environment Southwest*, 524: 12–16, Winter/Spring 1989.)

At many points along these faults there are hot springs. Borrego, Gilman, Eden, and Soboba hot springs are located along the San Jacinto fault. Agua Caliente, Warner, Murrieta, Elsinore, and Glen Ivy hot springs are on the Whittier-Elsinore fault. The therapeutic value of hot mineral baths is subject to debate; nevertheless, many of these springs are still operated in association with resorts. Some of these, such as San Jacinto and Elsinore, have had towns developed around them. In the Imperial Valley, to take advantage of this source of heat, geothermal electrical power plants have been constructed south of the Salton Sea.

There is a record of major earthquakes rocking the Los Angeles Basin as the earth slipped along these faults. The magnitude 6.3 earthquake near Long Beach in 1933 was on the Newport-Inglewood fault. This earthquake was the incentive to build homes that are more earthquake-proof. The well-known wooden-frame house with stucco exterior, considered in many parts of the United States to be a California-style house, was a response to a demand for a design that would flex and bend as the earth moved. The magnitude 6.6 earthquake in 1971 was on the San Fernando fault at the base of the San Gabriel Mountains. The 1987 magnitude 5.9 earthquake near Whittier was on the Whittier-Elsinore fault. Between 1968 and 1988, there were no fewer than five earthquakes of magnitude 6.0 or higher on these faults where they extend into the Colorado Desert east of the Peninsular Ranges.

The Transverse Ranges lie on the "big bend" of the San Andreas fault. Here, since the Miocene, the mountains have been rotated about 90° clockwise, so that they now lie on an east–west axis. The faults associated with them also run east–west. The San Fernando fault lies across the southern base of the San Gabriel Mountains, and the Santa Monica fault lies along the southern edge of the Santa Monica Mountains and the Channel Islands.

The position of the San Bernardino Mountains and two smaller ranges eastward represents a bit of an enigma. These members of the Transverse Ranges lie east of the San Andreas fault. The San Andreas passes between the San Bernardino and San Gabriel mountains and continues along the northern base of the San Gabriel Mountains on a mostly east–west line before turning northward once again. This is the "big bend." Paleomagnetic data in volcanic rocks of Miocene age provide evidence that the San Gabriel Mountains, the Santa Monica Mountains, and the Channel Islands have rotated about 90° clockwise. The absence of such volcanic rocks in the San Bernardino Mountains leaves us without proof that this range also has been rotated, although from outward appearances it seems to lie on a similar east–west line. The issue is further complicated by the fact that, because they lie east of the San Andreas fault, the San Bernardino Mountains must not have experienced the northward translocation exhibited by the other Transverse Ranges. Apparently, as the San Andreas continues its relentless motion, the San Bernardino Mountains will be left behind as the western portion of the Transverse Ranges is carried northward.

Rocks of the Transverse Ranges are among the oldest in California (fig. 8.4). The comparatively low precipitation in southern California has caused less erosion than in the Sierra Nevada. Consequently, many old rocks remain on top of the granitics of the Southern California batholith. A number of igneous and metamorphic rocks from the northwestern part of the San Gabriel Mountains apparently are older than a billion years. The oldest is a darkly banded gneiss dated at 1.7 billion years. This rock is visible on the Angeles Forest Highway near Mill Creek, where the highway passes through Singing Spring Tunnel (fig. 8.5). Included among the old rocks of the San Gabriel Mountains is another gneiss dated at 1.05 billion years of age. An igneous rock known as anorthosite, dated at 1.02 billion years, is visible west of the road at Baughman Spring. Anorthosite is rare on this planet, limited to a few pre-Cambrian localities, but interest was generated in this formation when the Apollo astronauts discovered that this rock constitutes the bright lunar highlands of the moon.

Correlation of old rocks with those in the Orocopia Mountains, 100 miles (160 km) southward, on the other side of the San Andreas fault, has been an important part of the evidence substantiating the magnitude of drift that has occurred. A green schist known as the Pelona Schist, which forms much of the eastern part of the San Gabriel Mountains, is found on the other side of the San Andreas fault in the San Bernardino Mountains, as well as in the Orocopia and Chocolate Mountains farther south. It is difficult to explain this distribution, but one hypothesis is that about 70 million years ago, as shallow subduction occurred, the schist, which has its origin to the west, was thrust on top of the eastern terrain. Later, about 25 million years ago,

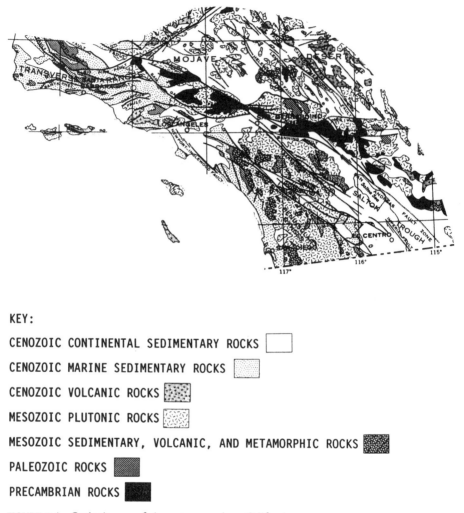

KEY:

CENOZOIC CONTINENTAL SEDIMENTARY ROCKS

CENOZOIC MARINE SEDIMENTARY ROCKS

CENOZOIC VOLCANIC ROCKS

MESOZOIC PLUTONIC ROCKS

MESOZOIC SEDIMENTARY, VOLCANIC, AND METAMORPHIC ROCKS

PALEOZOIC ROCKS

PRECAMBRIAN ROCKS

FIGURE 8.4   Geologic map of cismontane southern California.

when the San Andreas fault began its activity, the schist west of the fault was dragged northward. The schist formerly of the San Bernardino Mountains was deposited north of the San Gabriel Mountains by the same events that deposited it in the Orocopia and Chocolate mountains, but it now lies slightly to the south of the San Gabriels due to 100 miles (160 km) of displacement.

FIGURE 8.5   The oldest rock in the San Gabriel Mountains, 1.7 billion-year-old gneiss at Singing Spring Tunnel, Angeles Forest Highway.

In addition to the very old rocks just mentioned, there are rocks of Paleozoic age (700 million to 245 million years old), including schists, shales, sandstones, and limestones. These old rocks are exhibited in road cuts that traverse the Transverse and Peninsular ranges, especially in the San Gabriel and San Bernardino mountains. There are several cement plants where Paleozoic limestones are mined on the north side of the San Bernardino Mountains. For some reason, Paleozoic rocks are not common in the Peninsular Ranges. Those that are present are found mostly on the desert side of the San Jacinto and Santa Rosa mountains. Some Paleozoic limestone is mined for cement near Riverside.

Mesozoic rocks are best represented by the Southern California batholith. These are granitics and gabbros that became intruded into older rocks during the time of major subduction. Similar to the Sierra Nevada, all southern California ranges have a granitic component. In southern California, however, granite is often covered by older rocks. Where the older rocks have been stripped away by erosive processes, the granite is exposed and shows a weathering pattern similar to that of desert ranges. Lily Rock (Tahquitz) near Idyllwild is a good example of a granite dome. Where the Ortega Highway crosses the Santa Ana Mountains, near the summit is a well-exposed outcrop of the batholith. Similarly, where Interstate 8 crosses the Laguna Mountains between San Diego and El Centro, the granite is exposed.

Edaphic ecologic islands are found in the southern California area, too. In the Laguna Mountains are several gabbro outcrops that weather into reddish, iron-rich soil with peculiar chemical components. These gabbro soils resemble serpentine soils in that they have a high magnesium content. Gabbro soils support a large number of endemic plants found nowhere else in the world.

Processes associated with intrusion of the batholith have resulted in many mineral deposits of economic value. Eighteen different gold-mining districts have been described from the Transverse Ranges alone. Some of the earliest gold-mining operations in the United States were in the northwest part of the San Gabriel Mountains. As early as 1834, placer operations in gravels near Castaic were under way; Placerita Canyon gets its name from these operations. In the Peninsular Ranges, many small gold-mining operations were in operation in the early 1900s, particularly in the Santa Ana Mountains. Important gold mines were located in the Laguna Mountains, in the area around Julian. Of special interest in the Julian area was one of the few nickel mines. Nickel was mined from important sulfide minerals associated with gabbro deposits. Other metals mined in southern California include lead, zinc, and some copper.

Of special interest are gem mines along the San Luis Rey River on the southwestern side of the Agua Tibia Mountains. In this area, near the present town of Pala, transparent crystals of pink, green, and blue tourmaline are still being mined. Giant crystals from 5 to 20 inches (12–50 cm) in diameter and up to 3 feet (1 m) long have been collected. Some gem-quality topaz and garnet also were collected from these areas. During World War II, pink lithium-bearing mica, called lepidolite, was also mined here. On a worldwide scale, such high concentrations of rare minerals are uncommon. The reason for their occurrence here is unknown.

Mesozoic rocks in southern California also include island-arc volcanics that became accreted to the continent during subduction. Remnants of these volcanics are found in the Peninsular Ranges near San Diego and in the Santa Ana Mountains, where they exist as roof pendants. The Santiago Peak (Saddleback) volcanic rocks have been estimated to be 2300 feet (700 m) thick in some places.

Other Mesozoic rocks include some interesting fossil-bearing marine sediments. In the Santa Ana Mountains near Silverado Canyon, and through the southern Peninsular Ranges in San Diego County, there is an interesting section of upper Cretaceous marine sediments, approximately 80 million years old, that have yielded large fossil ammonites. These ammonites, up to a meter in diameter, represent a group of organisms that were once very common but now are nearly extinct. Although these organisms had octopuslike soft parts, they bore a large coiled shell that is preserved in fossils. The modern-day chambered nautilus is the only remnant of that formerly abundant group.

In many areas of the southern California mountains, the Cenozoic story (the past 65 million years) begins as it does in the desert, with extensive layers of rock missing, indicative of some 40 million years of erosion. In association with such an unconformity, Miocene rocks are often found on top of much older Mesozoic rocks. Where early Cenozoic rocks are present, they are mostly marine sediments. The thickest section of these sediments is in the Ventura Basin, where they have accumulated to a depth of nearly 5,000 feet (15,000 m). Included in this record are about 2500 feet (760 m) of sediments of terrestrial origin. These are red siltstones dated at about 35 million years. These beds, known as the Sespe Formation, are also found farther south, in the Vasquez Rocks of the northern San Gabriel Mountains. Sespe rocks are also found on both sides of the El Toro Valley, in Black Star Canyon and Laguna Canyon. The Los Angeles Basin includes about 14,000 feet (4200 m) of mostly marine sediments corresponding to the same time interval as those of the Ventura Basin.

Other old sedimentary beds scattered around southern California indicate that the area was under seawater for most of its history. There was an Andean type of shoreline until about 65 million years ago, when uplift of the coastline in conjunction with a tropical climate caused a great deal of erosion. Much of the eroded material was deposited offshore in a shallow marine environment. Shallow marshes and swamps occurred along the shoreline, and sediments from these terrestrial environments are found as siltstones and claystones, many red in color. These can be found near the entrance to Silverado and Santiago canyons on the western border of the Santa Ana Mountains (fig. 8.6).

In the Cajon Pass area, on the eastern end of the San Gabriel Mountains, there is a region where the San Andreas and San Jacinto faults are only about 2 miles (3.2 km) apart. The San Jacinto fault passes through Lytle Creek Canyon, and the San Andreas passes through Lone Pine Canyon, a couple of miles to the north. In this area some interesting sedimentary beds are exposed by road cuts and along the railroad. Among these are marine beds just northeast of the San Andreas fault. These are the youngest marine beds north of the San Gabriel Mountains. They are unique because of their age (40 million to 65 million years old) and because they lie on the north side of the San Andreas fault. The distinctive tilted sandstone beds known locally as Mormon Rocks (fig. 8.7) also lie north of the San Andreas in this area, but they are sandstones of terrestrial origin. They represent a river deposit that is perhaps only 5 million years of age.

About 25 million years ago (Miocene) the modern picture of coastal California, with its faulting and rifting, began to emerge. About this time, a large, mountainous island similar to, but much larger than, present-day Santa Catalina was uplifted on the western side of the Newport-Inglewood fault. This island was composed of metamorphic trench rocks (Franciscan Formation) formed from the former subduction zone. To the interior of this island, where the present coastal plain is located, there was a region of deep marine water covering what is now the Los Angeles Basin.

The Upper Miocene shoreline is represented by Topanga sandstone, a yellowish rock that contains many windblown hollows and caverns. It is found around the edge of the Los Angeles Basin in places such as Topanga Canyon, the mouth of Silverado Canyon, and in the San Joaquin Hills along Laguna Canyon.

In Middle Miocene, 12 to 15 million years ago, landslides and alluvial wash carried rock debris eastward from the large island. This debris, originally deposited underwater, is now located along the present shoreline, where it has become exposed by more recent uplift. This cemented landslide material is known as the San Onofre Breccia (fig. 8.8). It forms the headlands and reefs of the Orange County area, which

FIGURE 8.6 Sedimentary rocks of terrestrial origin near the junction of Silverado and Santiago canyons, Orange County.

FIGURE 8.7 Mormon Rocks near Cajon Junction, San Bernardino County.

FIGURE 8.8   Reconstructed paleogeography of the southern California border-land during deposition of the San Onofre Breccia (Lower and Middle Miocene). Locations of islands are shown for reference; they were not all islands at the time. (After Howell and others, 1974. From S. M. Rowland. "Geology of Santa Catalina Island," *California Geology* 37(1): 239–251, 1984.)

look somewhat like crude, wave-washed concrete. It is particularly well exposed as the cliffed headland at Dana Point.

Sediments from this deep-water episode include many small fossils of invertebrates such as sand dollars and pectens. These sediments are found up and down the coast from Monterey to San Diego, indicating an extensive, deep, but narrow marine basin, or several such basins. The nature of these sediments indicates that these basins were up to 15,000 feet (4300 m) deep. These sediments are now represented by thinly bedded shales, rich in diatoms. Where exposed, they often form whitish to buff deposits. The light-colored cliffs on both sides of upper Newport Bay are composed of this material, which is known as the Monterey Formation. As mentioned in the previous chapter, near Lompoc, north of Santa Barbara, there is a deposit about 700 feet (230 m) thick, which is mined and marketed as diatomaceous earth. This sediment was also rich in organic material and has yielded a significant amount of petroleum.

Miocene was also a time of volcanism along the coast. The Orange Hill area, east of the town of Orange, is made up of rocks known as El Modena volcanic rocks. They are exposed in a road cut on Chapman Avenue at the edge of Orange Hill. Miocene volcanic rocks are also found at the foot of the San Gabriel Mountains in the Glendora area.

The last 15 million years was marked by shallowing of basins, uplift of fault-block mountains, and a generally emerging coastline. Most evidence, however, indicates that the bulk of the uplift of the Transverse and Peninsular ranges has occurred in the last 2 million years, since the Pliocene, although some authorities would have most of the uplift occurring during that last million years. Because these mountains are young and because precipitation in the southern part of the state has not been as great as it has farther north, these mountains are steep and jagged. In the absence of severe erosion, many very old rocks are still in place.

Sediments exposed in the Capistrano, Puente, and Laguna areas have yielded fossils of shark's teeth and marine mammals in addition to many microfossils. This fossil evidence tells us what the marine environment was like at the time.

During the Pleistocene, when the Sierra Nevada and more northern mountain ranges were experiencing waves of glaciation, the Transverse and Peninsular ranges were mostly free of the glaciers. Glaciers are one of the most powerful forces of erosion; hence, as mentioned earlier, many very old rocks are still exposed in these southern ranges. Mount San Gorgonio is the southernmost peak to show evidence of glaciation. Popular landmarks such as Dollar Lake, Dry Lake, and Poopout Hill are actually glacial landforms.

Also during the Pleistocene there were changes in sea level associated with alternating periods of glaciation and global warming. When the polar ice caps melted, sea level rose and the Los Angeles Basin became flooded. At this time, high points such as Palos Verdes Hills, Baldwin Hills, and the Coyote Hills near Whittier became islands. During periods of maximal glaciation sea level was so low that the northern Channel Islands near Ventura were fused and became one large island. It is now assumed that even at its lowest point, the depth of the water between the mainland and the Channel Islands was never less than 300 feet (100 m). The distance between the Channel Islands and the mainland was probably never less than about 4.5 miles (7 km).

Elevation of the shoreline has exposed a series of marine terraces that reflect ancient shorelines. These wave-cut benches are represented by flattened terraces all along the coast. Most coastal cities and the Pacific Coast Highway are laid out along the first terrace. In profile, hills along the coast show a series of flat regions representing the older terraces. Studies of fossil marine organisms on these terraces reveal that the water was alternately warm and cold, and different marine organisms existed along the coast at different temperatures. The periods of cold water are correlated with the periods of glaciation in the Sierra and the periods of maximal flooding in the deserts.

SCRUB COMMUNITIES

Elevational zonation of vegetation in southern California mountains (fig. 8.9) is similar to that of the Sierra Nevada. Southern California differs, however, in its abundance

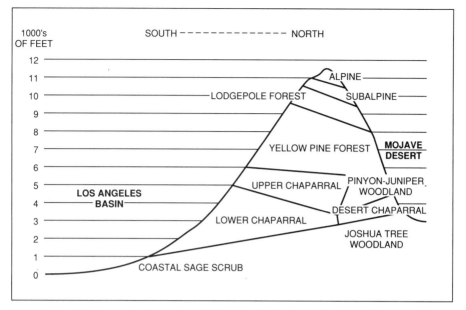

FIGURE 8.9   Biotic zonation in southern California. *A.* Biotic zonation in the Transverse Ranges.

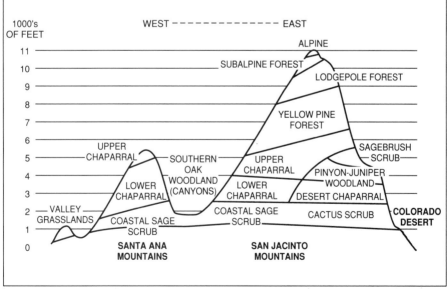

FIGURE 8.9 (*continued*)   Biotic zonation in southern California. *B.* Biotic zonation in the Peninsular Ranges.

of drought-adapted scrub vegetation. Plant communities of cismontane southern California consist primarily of different kinds of Chaparral. Chaparral communities dominate on the coastal side of the Peninsular Ranges (pl. 6C), Transverse Ranges (pl. 6B), and southernmost Coast Ranges (pl. 5C). The community also predominates southward to the Ensenada area, in northern Baja California. Forest and mountaintop communities have been discussed in previous chapters. It is important, however, to point out that the southern California forest communities are composed mostly of elements that predominate in the drier Sierra Nevada forests. For example, the dominant conifer of the Yellow Pine Forest is Jeffrey Pine, *Pinus jeffreyi*, not Ponderosa Pine, *Pinus ponderosa*, as is often reported. Sierra Redwoods are not native to southern California today, although they occurred here in the past, as indicated by cones found in the La Brea Tar Pits.

Pronounced slope effect complicates an otherwise simple picture of chaparral communities. Various attempts have been made to classify scrub vegetation into subgroups or communities. From 2 to over 10 subdivisions have been proposed. In this chapter, 4 communities will be recognized, based primarily on climatic considerations and easily recognizable generalizations in vegetative characteristics (table 8.2). Within these 4 communities, there are pronounced differences based on slope exposure. The effect is that within each community, most groupings of related species appear on north-facing slopes at lower elevations and on south-facing slopes at the upper reaches of their distributions.

Coastal Sage Scrub

The Coastal Sage Scrub community has been referred to by some authorities as Soft Chaparral because many of the dominant plants bend easily and/or have soft, flexible leaves. Many of the shrubs are odoriferous and drought-deciduous. Such vegetation usually grows about knee-high (pl. 6C), but even when taller shrubs are present, it is not difficult to walk through the community. This community occupies mostly alluvial soils at low elevation. It is not restricted to coastal regions but is found inland in suitable low-elevation valleys.

Coastal Sage Scrub does best under the influence of a maritime climate. Fog is important. Frost is also a critical factor; many of the component species do not do well where frost is common. The community is also remarkably drought-adapted. Throughout much of its coastal distribution, precipitation averages 10 inches (25 cm) per year or less. This precipitation regime qualifies Coastal Sage Scrub as a desert community. In some respects it is not inaccurate to think of it as such, but the high humidity and moderate temperatures typical of maritime climate keep evaporation rates low, so that this community seldom experiences the drought stress typical of true desert vegetation. However, some of the community's plants and animals are also found in the desert, and several of the indicator species have close relatives in the desert. Above-ground productivity is low but is intermediate between average desert and average chaparral communities in other areas. The nearest desert analog to Coastal Sage Scrub is the Cactus Scrub community of the Colorado Desert. Both communities

TABLE 8.2   A Comparison of Southern California Scrub Communities

Community	Slope Aspect	Growth Habit	Examples
Coastal Sage Scrub	South-facing	Drought-deciduous; small leaves; phytotoxins	California Sagebrush, Coast Brittle-bush, monkeyflowers, true sages
		Succulent	Prickly-pears, Chollas, Live-forevers
	North-facing	Evergreen; large leaves	Toyon, Laurel Sumac, Lemonadeberry, Fuchsia-flowered Gooseberry
Lower Chaparral	South-facing	Evergreen; small, sclerophyllous leaves	Chamise, California lilacs
	North-facing	Evergreen; oval, spiny, scelrophyllous leaves	Scrub oaks, Holly-leaved Redberry, Holly-leaved Cherry
		Vines	Wild peas, honeysuckles, wild cucumbers
Upper Chaparral	South-facing	Evergreen; vertically oriented sclerophyllous leaves; sun tracking	Manzanitas, silk-tassel bushes, Western Mountain Mahogany
	North-facing	Evergreen conifers	Big-cone Douglas Fir, Coulter Pine
Desert Chaparral	South-facing	Drought-deciduous	Desert Apricot, Desert Almond, true sages
		Succulent	Prickly-pears, chollas, Mormon teas
	North-facing	Evergreen; large leaves	Sugar Bush, Desert Scrub Oak, Bigberry Manzanita, Jojoba

have many drought-deciduous and succulent components. This is particularly true farther south, toward Ensenada.

Also similar to desert vegetation, many species produce large, showy flowers. When in full bloom, the Coastal Sage Scrub community is very beautiful. It is surprising that more species from this community have not been adopted for suburban landscapes. They are hardy and attractive, and they often have pleasant odors.

There is a pronounced difference between the shrubs on south-facing slopes and those on north-facing slopes. On south-facing slopes and exposed flats, the vegetation typically has small leaves and is drought-deciduous. California Sagebrush, *Artemisia*

californica, is one of the indicator species here. It has finely divided, almost filamentous herbage, which is shed during drought. When winter rains arrive, this is
commonly the first species to grow new leaves and shoots. In some areas this shrub is
so abundant that whole hillsides take on a blue-gray appearance. California Sagebrush
has a distinctive odor, similar to that of Great Basin Sagebrush, its close relative.
Unlike the sages of this community, California Sagebrush is in the sunflower family
(Asteraceae). Its flowers are not conspicuous, however, nor do they resemble typical
sunflowers.

A more typical sunflower of Coastal Sage Scrub is California Encelia or Coast
Brittle-bush, *Encelia californica* (fig. 8.10). This shrub resembles its relative in the
Cactus Scrub community, Desert Brittle-bush, *Encelia farinosa.* Desert Brittle-bush has
white leaves, whereas Coast Brittle-bush has light green foliage. Both are drought-
deciduous and display a spectacular canopy of bright yellow sunflowers that track the
sun. In low passes such as San Gorgonio Pass, these two species hybridize. Hybrids
are particularly common on disturbed sites such as road cuts.

True sages can be identified by several common characteristics. They are members
of the mint family (Lamiaceae); as such, they usually have a pungent odor. They have
two-lipped flowers with long anthers and stigma. They usually have square stems,
which, if not visible, can be detected by rolling the stem between the thumb and
forefinger. Finally the leaves usually occur in pairs, opposite on the stem. Most shrub
species have their leaves arranged singly on the stem, alternating on each side.

Several species of true sages also are drought-deciduous components of this community. Black Sage, *Salvia mellifera,* is perhaps most common. It gets its name from
its black stems, which become particularly conspicuous when the leaves drop. Leaves
of Black Sage are the darkest green of the sages, and hillsides predominantly of Black
Sage can take on a blackish appearance. Leaves are narrow and lance-shaped, and their
surface is rough and mealy to the touch. White to pale lavender flowers appear in
spring. Typical of sage flowers, they are tubular and two-lipped, resembling snapdragons (Scrophulariaceae). They differ from snapdragons by having long reproductive
parts (anthers and stigma) that project for some distance beyond the petals.

In contrast to Black Sage there is Purple Sage, *Salvia leucophylla* (fig. 8.11), named
for its purple flowers. Leaves of Purple Sage resemble those of Black Sage, except
that they are whitish, and flowers are rose-lavender. This species is common from
Orange County northward. Southward there is another species, *Salvia clevelandii,* that
is sometimes called Purple Sage, but it is probably more correct to call it Fragrant
Sage. It has flowers of a darker purple hue, but otherwise it resembles the northern
Purple Sage.

White Sage, *Salvia apiana,* has white leaves. This sage is very common and also
occurs on the desert side of the Peninsular Ranges. It differs from the others by having
much larger, velvety leaves. Also, its flowers are borne on long, whiplike stalks with
the leaves crowded at the base. It resembles, and may coexist with, its near relative
of the Cactus Scrub community, Wand Sage, *Salvia vaseyi,* whose name refers to its
long, wandlike flower stalks.

FIGURE 8.10   Coast Brittle-bush, *Encelia californica*.

The value of odor to plants has been the subject of some debate. The odor of flowers helps to attract pollinators, and the odor of herbage apparently is one of the mechanisms plants use to discourage herbivory. Presumably, these odors have evolved in conjunction with resinous coatings that help inhibit evaporation. Some plants produce toxic chemicals but do not produce odors; animals learn to avoid these plants by previous experience or through heredity. Odors, however, advertise that the plant may not be palatable.

Humans have come to appreciate the odors and flavors of many plants, some of which require getting used to. A good example is the flavor of juniper berries, which are what gives gin its distinctive flavor. There are also many examples of plants used as spices to flavor food, including the traditional parsley, sage, rosemary, and thyme. It is further interesting to note that the native habitats of many of these plants are associated with Mediterranean climates. The sage usually used in cookery is known as Garden Sage, *Salvia officinalis*. It is grown widely in the east, but originally it was imported from the Mediterranean region of Europe. Locally, *Salvia clevelandii* is an appropriate substitute for cooking. The leaves of the California Laurel, *Umbellularia californica* (fig. 7.9), a riparian tree in southern California, are a good substitute for commercial bay leaves, which come from a European shrub of Mediterranean origin known as Sweet Bay, *Laurus nobilis*.

Some of the most beautiful flowering shrubs in this community are the bush monkeyflowers. They are inconspicuous most of the year because they are small in size

FIGURE 8.11   Purple Sage, *Salvia leucophylla*.

and drought-deciduous. In the spring, however, when they come into bloom, entire hillsides are colored by their blossoms. These are in the same family as snapdragons (Scrophulariaceae), and their flowers are similar, with petals fused into a two-lipped tube. The tip of the pistil, the stigma, is divided into two conspicuous lobes. When a pollinator, such as a bee, visits the flower, it touches the stigma lobes, causing them to fold together (fig. 8.12). This change in appearance is a signal to the pollinator that the flower already has been visited, thus optimizing the efficiency of the pollinator and the plant.

There is a good deal of confusion about speciation in the bush monkeyflowers. As of this writing, Southern Bush Monkeyflower (*Mimulus longiflorus*), Red Bush Monkeyflower (*Mimulus puniceus*), and Island Monkeyflower (*Mimulus flemingii*) (fig. 12.33D) have been lumped into one species, known as the Sticky or Orange Bush Monkeyflower, *Mimulus aurantiacus* (fig. 8.12). Formerly, the northern, interior forms with deep orange to white blossoms were known as the Southern Bush Monkeyflower. The Orange Bush Monkeyflower occurred closer to the coast, and from the Santa Ana

FIGURE 8.12   Orange Bush Monkeyflower, *Mimulus aurantiacus*. Note that the stigma lobes are closed in the flower on the right.

Mountains southward. The Red Bush Monkeyflower, perhaps the most beautiful of all, with flowers ranging from brick red to orange, was found along the coast from Laguna Beach southward and on Santa Catalina Island. The Island Monkeyflower, an island endemic, occurred only on San Clemente, Santa Rosa, Santa Cruz, and Anacapa islands.

An interesting feature of these drought-deciduous shrubs is that during the dry season they may not become entirely leafless. Rather, they exhibit what is known as seasonal leaf dimorphism. During summer they may exhibit only small terminal leaves, which, although representing only a fraction of the total seasonal leaf area, are capable of maintaining low levels of photosynthesis during drought stress.

Another common plant associated with this community is California Buckwheat, *Eriogonum fasciculatum*. This low evergreen herbaceous shrub is one of the most common representatives of a very large genus with over 75 different species in California. The buckwheat family (Polygonaceae) includes a large number of plants found in nearly every habitat in the state. The common California Buckwheat has small waxy leaves borne in clusters or fascicles. Elongated flower stalks persist as dried structures long after the flowers have set seed. Indians would gather the small black seeds by the millions and grind them into a flour—hence the name "buckwheat flour." This species grows naturally in sunny disturbed areas, such as road cuts, from the coast to the desert. Sometimes it is deliberately planted to help stabilize soil along roads.

FIGURE 8.13 Coastal Sage Scrub showing differences between north-facing and south-facing slopes. San Joaquin Hills, Orange County.

On north-facing slopes, or where water is locally more abundant, the Coastal Sage Scrub vegetation is quite different (fig. 8.13). In these areas the vegetation is more Chaparral-like in that the shrubs are large and evergreen, and they possess large root systems that penetrate deeply. Furthermore, the leaves are large compared to other scrub species, and this distinguishes the plants from true chaparral species, which, even on north-facing slopes, usually have smaller leaves. Perhaps the most conspicuous of these large-leaved shrubs is Toyon, also known as Christmas Berry or California Holly, *Heteromeles arbutifolia*. The long, lance-shaped leaves do not truly resemble holly; the resemblance is based on the presence of toothed margins. Near Christmas, the plant may be quite showy, with large clusters of bright red berries. The famous city in the low hills north of Los Angeles was named Hollywood in honor of this shrub. Toyon is available in many nurseries, and it has been planted in many landscapes. Given abundant water, it grows quite large, resembling a many-stemmed tree.

Associated with Toyon at many localities is Laurel Sumac, *Malosma* (= *Rhus*) *laurina,* a member of a large tropical family (Anacardiaceae) that includes economically important products such as cashews and pistachio nuts. This large shrub has elongated leaves that tend to fold up like a taco shell when it gets dry. Unlike many members of the Coastal Sage Scrub community, it apparently seldom goes dormant, continuing to grow throughout the year. One of its distinctive features is that it is quite frost-

FIGURE 8.14   Lemonadeberry, *Rhus integrifolia*.

sensitive; frost causes it to turn brown and die back to the ground. However, when the weather warms in spring, new shoots rapidly grow back from the roots—as much as a full 3 feet (1 m) in a single year. After two years a person can barely tell that the shrub was damaged. In years past, locating this shrub was important for farmers searching for appropriate sites to plant citrus. Orange County was originally settled and inhabited in this way. Of course, most of the orchards are now being replaced by housing tracts and shopping malls. Here we see an interesting pattern of succession. Coastal Sage Scrub becomes replaced by citrus, which in turn becomes replaced by buildings.

Also in the cashew family is another associate on north-facing slopes, Lemonade-berry, *Rhus integrifolia* (fig. 8.14). This shrub has oval, leathery leaves that are usually toothed. The plant's large, flattened red berries are covered with a sticky, acidic secretion that can be soaked in water to make a drink that tastes very much like lemonade. This plant flowers early, as soon as winter rains begin. The flowers are borne in clusters and are white to rose in color. This is another shrub that does well in coastal landscapes. Its flowers provide winter color, and the fruits are attractive, too. One feature that makes this a particularly useful shrub in coastal communities is that it is mildly tolerant to salt spray. It occurs naturally on cliffs next to the ocean.

In interior valleys, where it is warmer, Lemonadeberry is replaced by a close relative known as Sugar Bush, *Rhus ovata*. Leaves of Sugar Bush are intermediate in appearance between Laurel Sumac and Lemonadeberry. They are leathery, similar to Lemonadeberry, but they are taco-shaped, similar to Laurel Sumac. The leaves are shorter and broader than those of Laurel Sumac, and the petioles (leaf stems) are usually red. Identification is sometimes difficult because where ranges overlap, the species sometimes hybridize.

Many plants in this family produce chemicals to discourage herbivores. Probably the most famous is Poison Oak, *Toxicodendron diversilobum* (fig. 8.15), which is most common in Southern Oak Woodland. The chemicals that cause the rash are phenolic compounds known as resorcinols and catechols. Many persons are sensitive to Poison Oak, and those that are especially sensitive will also get dermatitis from other members of the family.

Coyote Brush or Chaparral Broom, *Baccharis pilularis,* is another evergreen shrub that occurs in Coastal Sage Scrub. It is most common at low elevations, particularly where drainage increases soil moisture. This shrub has resinous oval leaves about $1/4$ to $3/4$ inch (1.5–2.0 cm) in length, and there are usually five to nine teeth along the margins. The flowering period of this species is late summer through autumn, during which time the plants are covered with clusters of white flowers. Close inspection of the flower will reveal that Coyote Brush is in the sunflower family, but it lacks the ring of petal-bearing flowers characteristic of other sunflowers such as Coast Brittle-bush. This attractive shrub is another component of Coastal Sage Scrub that is being used as a landscape plant. A dwarf or prostrate form, native to the coast from the Russian River south to Point Sur, is often used as a ground cover in domestic landscapes.

From Point Sur, Monterey County, north to southern Oregon there is a version of Coastal Sage Scrub that many authors refer to as Northern Coastal Scrub—an appropriate name because most of the sages go no farther north than the southern Coast Ranges. Furthermore, this community differs from Coastal Sage Scrub in that most of the shrubs are evergreen, and there is an important herbaceous element. Dominant shrubs include Coyote Brush; California Yerba Santa, *Eriodictyon californicum;* Salal, *Gaultheria shallon*; and Yellow Bush Lupine, *Lupinus arboreus* (fig. 7.13). This community occurs in a narrow coastal strip that is often mixed with coastal prairie, a community discussed in the preceding chapter.

At the southern end of its distribution, where it is drier, Coastal Sage Scrub is characterized by numerous succulent species. This has led some authors to identify a separate community known as Maritime Desert Scrub, which in some respects resembles Cactus Scrub, a desert community. A number of elements of Coastal Sage Scrub as well as numerous succulents, such as cacti, stonecrops, and live-forevers, occur here. Among the cacti are several species of prickly-pear and cholla, all of which are in the genus *Opuntia.*

There are at least three coastal species of prickly-pear. Where they coexist, they all hybridize, and in some areas there are three-way hybrid swarms. One such area is east of Orange in the El Modena area. A large hill that occurs here, known locally

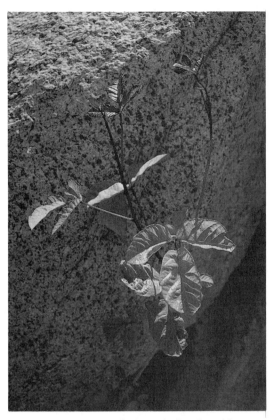

FIGURE 8.15   Poison Oak, *Toxicodendron diversilobum.*

as Orange Hill, is composed of Miocene volcanics. Here, amid two restaurants and numerous houses, is a hybrid cactus swarm.

The introduction of cattle in the 1800s greatly altered the composition of native vegetation in some areas. Among the plants that cattle seldom choose to eat are prickly-pear cacti. Therefore, in overgrazed areas, even where cattle are no longer present, prickly-pear cacti may spread out to form thickets.

Chollas are also among the dominant species. Coastal Cholla, *Opuntia prolifera,* is widespread along the coast. This thick-stemmed species occurs in dense stands on overgrazed sites, particularly on islands such as Santa Rosa, Anacapa, Santa Catalina, and San Clemente. In the interior valleys, the cholla of Coastal Sage Scrub is Cane Cholla, *Opuntia parryi,* a thin-stemmed, sparsely branched plant that grows up to 7 feet (2.4 m) tall.

Among the most handsome succulents of this community are various members of the stonecrop family (Crassulaceae), which are most common on rocky outcrops. Most are in the genus *Dudleya* and are known by that name, although they may be referred to as stonecrops or live-forevers. They are significant because they often are endemic, localized in distribution, and may be classified as rare or endangered. For example, in the San Joaquin Hills, near Laguna Beach, are two endangered species, Laguna Beach Dudleya, *Dudleya stolonifera,* and Many-stemmed Dudleya, *Dudleya multicaulis.* Their presence can be a frustration to developers because many sites where they occur are protected by law. Of wider occurrence, more common to the south, are other species such as Lance-leaved Dudleya, *Dudleya lanceolata,* and a large, attractive form known as Chalk Lettuce, *Dudleya pulverulenta* (fig. 8.16). These two species also occur on the desert side of the Peninsular Ranges.

To the interior, particularly on outwashed flood plains, there is another leaf succulent known as Our Lord's Candle, *Yucca whipplei.* This species is a common component of another variation of Coastal Sage Scrub known as Alluvial Scrub. Historically, this community was subjected to periodic flooding and consists mostly of the large, evergreen components of Coastal Sage Scrub in various stages of regeneration. Our Lord's Candle, similar to other yuccas, is pollinated by Yucca Moths (*Tegeticula* spp.). Unlike other yuccas, but similar to desert succulents known as agaves, it blooms once and then dies. This plant is recognized by its low-growing cluster of stiff, narrow, sharply pointed leaves, which give the appearance of a large pincushion. When it is time to blossom, plants send up a long stalk, up to 10 feet (3 m) in height, topped with a large cluster of white flowers. Hundreds of these plants may blossom at one time, providing a spectacular sight on flat flood plains.

In the interior valleys, changes in the composition of Coastal Sage Scrub reflect generally warmer conditions. Components of the community here are more desertlike. Coastal Cholla is replaced by Cane Cholla. Lemonadeberry is replaced by Sugar Bush. Coast Brittle-bush is replaced by Desert Brittle-bush. White Sage is joined by, and in some areas replaced by, Wand Sage. In the area around Santa Rosa Mountain, Black Sage becomes replaced by Santa Rosa Sage, *Salvia eremostachya.* Our Lord's Candle becomes locally common on sandy soils. Jojoba, *Simmondsia chinensis* (fig. 9.32), is a desert shrub with erect, semisucculent leaves that is also locally common on rocky soils.

In disturbed areas such as road cuts and abandoned fields, hybridization between coastal and interior species is common. This is particularly true among Sugar Bush, Laurel Sumac, and Lemonadeberry, as well as between the two brittle-bushes, various sages, and various cacti. In these disturbed habitats, natural barriers to germination and cross-fertilization apparently are lost. Seedlings of related species may become established in close proximity, which facilitates pollen transfer.

Aerial photographs taken between the 1930s and 1980s have been used to compare changes in vegetation in the Los Angeles Basin. These photographs show that the amount of area covered by grasslands has increased while that covered by Coastal Sage Scrub has decreased. Coastal Sage Scrub is a threatened community. Indicative of its threatened status, one authority has cited 13 plant species from this community as rare, endangered, or threatened. Furthermore, two birds—the California Gnatcatcher,

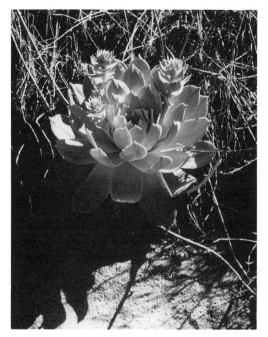

FIGURE 8.16   Chalk Lettuce, *Dudleya pulverulenta*.

Polioptila californica, and the Cactus Wren, *Campylorhynchus brunneicapillus*—have been proposed by the U.S. Fish and Wildlife Service for threatened status in this community. Formerly distributed widely from coastal bluffs to the foothills, Coastal Sage Scrub in most areas has been replaced by grazing, agriculture, and urbanization. Non-native grassland has invaded as a consequence of overgrazing and frequent fires. Fire frequency in grassland is high enough to prevent regeneration of Coastal Sage Scrub species.

Coastal Sage Scrub still exists in isolated pockets such as the Santa Monica Mountains parklands, the Camp Pendleton Marine Corps base, and in the San Joaquin Hills near Laguna Beach, much of which may be destined to be covered with houses and shopping malls. As of the 1980s, the Los Angeles Basin was second only to New York City in population density per acre. If Coastal Sage Scrub is eliminated, California will lose one of its most attractive shrub communities. With it will go many native species of plants and animals, not to mention natural open space. Open space, free of the visual and acoustic trappings of civilization, has been determined to be very important for the psychological well-being of humans.

Lower Chaparral

Lower Chaparral is also referred to as Warm Chaparral. This community occurs on the lower slopes of mountains, below the region where snow is the major form of precipitation. Thus Lower Chaparral is frost-tolerant but not snow-tolerant. A factor that separates this community from Coastal Sage Scrub is the significance of frost. Lower Chaparral, southern California's most common natural community of plants and animals, occurs at elevations from about 1000 feet (300 m) to 5000 feet (1600 m), between the frostline and the snowline.

As in other scrub communities, there is also a pronounced slope effect in Lower Chaparral. As is the case with Coastal Sage Scrub, south-facing slopes are characterized by shrubs with small leaves, and north-facing slopes have shrubs with larger leaves. Unlike Coastal Sage Scrub, however, plants of Lower Chaparral are seldom drought-deciduous. Most are evergreen, with resinous or waxy coatings on their leaves. These coatings, plus an increase of nondigestible fibers, make the leaves stiff to the touch. This consistency has led to use of the term *sclerophyll* ("hard-leaf") to describe chaparral vegetation. Chaparral plants also have woody stems and large root systems, and they grow to be much larger than most plants of Coastal Sage Scrub. A mature stand of Lower Chaparral may form an inpenetrable thicket of tangled branches up to 10 feet (3 m) in height.

Chaparral plants are physiologically different from those of Coastal Sage Scrub. Drought-deciduous and succulent plants of Coastal Sage Scrub are adapted for longer periods of drought. Their relatively shallow root systems absorb water as soon as it rains, and they quickly grow new shoots and leaves. In contrast, evergreen shrubs of Chaparral have two-layered root systems that, over a long period of time, continue to absorb water from both shallow and deep regions of the soil. New growth of evergreen shrubs takes place about four months later than that of most Coastal Sage Scrub plants, and it continues later into the summer.

A difference between the two physiological strategies of these communities is also reflected in their photosynthetic rates. During winter, the photosynthetic rate of drought-deciduous species is twice that of the evergreens. Drought-deciduous species, however, are only about half as resistant to water loss. At the height of summer drought, Coastal Sage Scrub species have lost most of their leaves, and they experience severe water stress at this time. One sage species was measured with the low water potential of -64 bars. This is equivalent to 64 times the atmospheric pressure, or nearly 1000 pounds per square inch (160 kg/cm^2). Effectively, they are dormant. In contrast, evergreen species at this time continue to photosynthesize, although at lower rates than during winter, and some species continue to photosynthesize at -85 bars. Evergreen species also apparently can carry on with photosynthesis over a wider range of temperatures, although there seems to be little difference in photosynthetic rate between the two communities in the range from $45°$ to $87°$F ($7-30°$C). This implies that the primary limiting factor on growth of evergreen chaparral shrubs is the short winter day length.

In Lower Chaparral, above-ground growth of evergreen shrubs takes place during about four to six months during the winter and spring. The rest of the year, growth goes into the roots. Overall, above-ground growth never seems great because, in order to discourage herbivores, much of the energy budget of evergreen plants goes into cellular maintenance and production of chemicals such as lignins and tannins. The gain provided by this effort is that leaves tend to stay on the plants for at least two years, whereas drought-deciduous species have to make a complete set of new leaves every year.

Lower Chaparral species have a number of other leaf adaptations that help them to deal with the stresses of their environment. Sclerophyllous leaves have reduced rates of water loss, and the hardened tissues and coatings make them difficult to digest—a discouragement to herbivores. In addition, it is notable that many species have serrated or spiny leaf margins. It is believed that the function of these spines is to increase surface area to help dissipate heat. A number of species roll their leaves, which traps air on the inside and reduces evaporation. Leaves of several species have fine hairs, which form a boundary layer that traps air. The hairs also provide a small amount of shade and help to dissipate heat. Other species have leaves that track the sun in order to optimize or minimize light intensity, and leaves of some plants are oriented vertically so that sun does not strike them directly.

Nutrient and water absorption in chaparral evergreens seems to be enhanced by mycorrhizal fungi. Chamise, scrub oaks, and manzanitas have been shown to possess these fine underground filaments. The absorption of phosphorus by mycorrhizae is believed to be one of the primary nutritional benefits. It also has been demonstrated that association of these fungi with the roots of seedlings helps prevent wilting during the first months after germination.

Lower Chaparral is the southern California community most likely to burn. The community has evolved over millions of years in association with fires, and in fact requires fire for proper health and vigor. Thus it is not surprising that most chaparral plants exhibit adaptations enabling them to recover after a burn. Many species are sprouters; the aboveground parts may be killed, but new growth arises from roots or buds at the base of the stem in a region known as a root-crown burl. Other species have seeds that require fire in order to break dormancy; they will not germinate unless they have been heated. The cones of some chaparral conifers open only after they have been heated. Some herbaceous species will not germinate unless there is ash on the ground when it rains. Large oak trees have a thick, fireproof bark.

Not only do chaparral plants feature adaptations that help them recover after a fire, but some characteristics of these plants, such as fibrous or ribbonlike shreds on the bark, seem to encourage fire. Other species contain volatile oils. In the absence of fire, a mature chaparral stand may become senile, in which case growth and reproduction are reduced. Without new growth and with fewer berries and seeds, there is less food for animals. The new growth of some shrubs contains about 14% protein. Browsers such as deer cannot survive without this kind of nutrition.

In the old days, prior to fire suppression, fires were seldom holocausts because the slopes were a mosaic of burned and unburned terrain. Usually new fires were limited by recently burned regions with very little fuel. Dead wood and other fuels could not accumulate for long. When a fire started, it was usually due to lightning, and the fire would burn during conditions of high humidity. Old records show that a fire might start in early summer and burn for months, moving slowly along the ground, sometimes smoldering for a while before blazing again.

Of course, in the "old days," there was very little habitation to worry about. Now there are homes and villages all over the Chaparral. When a fire breaks out, a tremendous amount of money and effort are expended to protect habitation areas. Unfortunately, most fires in southern California are caused by humans, either through arson or accidents. Arson fires are set during periods of Santa Ana conditions, when wind, low humidity, and heat are complicating factors. The accumulation of fuel and the great extent of unburned brush provides conditions ensuring that the fire will be severe.

These extremely hot, large fires have serious consequences. Burrowing animals that normally survive small fires are suffocated in their burrows. Animals that escape are forced to compete with those already established in the unburned areas. Thousands of acres may be burned all at once, drastically reducing total habitat. When the rains come, erosion is severe.

Dry creep or slow sliding is a characteristic of chaparral soils. Loose soil material is carried away with heavy rain. Furthermore, many chaparral plants produce waxy, nonwettable (hydrophobic) chemicals. These chemicals cause the soil to repel water, and this may inhibit germination of seeds under a healthy canopy. Water that supplies roots of mature plants gets there by trickling down branches and running into the soil at the base of the trunk. When a fire burns the litter, the chemicals are driven into the soil to form a nonwettable layer beneath the surface. After a fire, soil becomes saturated above the layer and washes away. Before the policy of fire suppression, when fires were small and cooler, this problem was not severe. Now large areas are denuded of vegetation, and runoff is increased. Tons of valuable soil are carried away, and homes below the burn area are flooded or damaged by mud slides.

Attempts to reduce the erosion-flood sequence usually are futile. Agencies concerned with management of chaparral habitats often reseed burn sites with nonnative grasses, particularly Perennial Ryegrass, *Lolium perenne*. Evidence has accumulated to indicate that this is not a good procedure. Unless the first rains are gentle, the grass will not germinate in time to do any good. If the first rains are gentle, the grass will take valuable water away from native species and retard their regrowth. Furthermore, grasses increase fire frequency.

A policy of outright fire suppression is disastrous for both plant and animal life. Government agencies are now undertaking programs to light fires deliberately in order to maintain natural habitats, a procedure known as prescribed burning. This requires careful analysis of fuel and climatic conditions. When conditions of humidity allow the fire to burn slowly, it can be controlled. The answer to the problem is to allow Lower Chaparral to return to more natural conditions, where there is a mosaic of burned and unburned terrain. Where human habitation encroaches on Chaparral, homes should be built of nonflammable materials, such as masonry walls and tile roofs.

The most abundant plant in Lower Chaparral is Chamise, *Adenostoma fasciculatum* (fig. 8.17). It is in the rose family (Rosaceae), but its white flowers are quite small, requiring close inspection to recognize the family characteristics. Chamise probably has the greatest biomass of any plant in cismontane southern California. It is charac-

FIGURE 8.17 Chamise, *Adenostoma fasciculatum*. A. Mature plants on the west slope of the San Jacinto Mountains.

FIGURE 8.17 (*continued*) Chamise, *Adenostoma fascicula-tum*. B. New shoots after a fire.

teristic of south-facing slopes, where it may occur in nearly pure stands. A textbook example of a chaparral shrub, it has small, drought-adapted leaves and a large root system, and it is fire-adapted.

Drought tolerance of this species is moderately high, although not as high as plants from Coastal Sage Scrub. Water potentials of −50 bars have been recorded, which places Chamise between Coastal Sage Scrub plants on south-facing slopes and those of north-facing slopes in terms of drought tolerance. This plant has tiny, resin-covered leaves that grow in clumps. The leaves are similar to those of the buckwheat mentioned previously but are often no longer than 1/4 inch (7 mm). Following a fire, Chamise reestablishes itself primarily through new shoots that resprout from its root crown or burl (fig. 8.17B). These shoots may grow a foot (30 cm) or more during the year following a fire.

Chamise also can regenerate by means of seeds, which are produced in enormous numbers. There are two kinds of seeds: those that require heat in order to germinate and those that do not. This variation, plus its ability to sprout, gives Chamise ample opportunity to become reestablished. Some experiments show that regeneration by seeds is more common following a high-intensity fire.

The relationship between fire and Chamise is illustrated by the plant's tendency to "encourage" burning. A thermometer was placed within a Chamise shrub as a fire approached, and the following changes were documented. At about 200°F (93°C) the plant began to wilt as its temperature approached the boiling point of water. At about 400°F (204°C) the plant began to emit combustible gases such as hydrogen, alcohol, and methane. At about 600°F (316°C) the shrub smoldered and began to turn black. At about 800°F (427°C) the plant burst into flames! This species must have evolved in association with frequent fires to have reached the point where it seems to encourage burning.

Another bit of evidence shows the evolution of these shrubs in association with fire. This is an example of coevolution. The color on the back of the Western Fence Lizard, *Sceloporus occidentalis* (fig. 8.18), closely matches the color of a burned Chamise stem. Data using a machine that measures reflected light (a reflectometer) showed that a Western Fence Lizard is nearly invisible when it rests on a burned Chamise stem. The surface that matches the lizard next best is granite.

Chamise may become the dominant plant on south-facing slopes in mature Chaparral by outliving the other species. If an area has gone unburned for 35 years or more, Chamise may seem to be the only species left, although it is not always completely healthy in these old stands. Although Chamise resprouts immediately after a fire, other shrubs dominate from 4 to 10 years after a burn. Common among these early successional plants are several species in the buckthorn family (Rhamnaceae) known generally as California lilacs (*Ceanothus* spp.). These include Hoaryleaf Ceanothus, *C. crassifolius*; Hairy Ceanothus, *C. oliganthus*; and Chaparral Whitethorn, *C. leucodermis* (fig. 8.19). These species of *Ceanothus* do not sprout; they must return from seeds after a fire. They mature quickly and produce a great number of seeds early in their lives. The seeds may remain dormant for hundreds of years, but heating

FIGURE 8.18   Western Fence Lizard, *Sceloporus occidentalis*.

stimulates them to germinate. The heat either melts or cracks the hard seed coat, allowing the uptake of water when it finally rains. Another characteristic of *Ceanothus* plants is that they throw their seeds. Seeds that bounce off a rock may be cracked by the impact, and cracked seeds can germinate without fire if they land in an appropriate open space. Of particular importance to the chaparral community is that *Ceanothus* plants have nitrogen-fixing bacteria associated with their roots. Hence new shoots and leaves are rich in protein, providing an important browse for deer and other herbivores. Guess why *Ceanothus cuneatus* is known as Buck Brush.

On some hillsides *Ceanothus* dominates in nearly pure stands, and some authors distinguish this special community as *Ceanothus* Chaparral. However, in southern California this is usually a successional community that exists until the *Ceanothus* plants die of old age or become overtopped by Chamise. Depending on circumstances, complete replacement by Chamise generally takes place within 10 to 30 years after a fire.

In the mid-1980s patches of *Ceanothus* with yellow leaves, a condition sometimes known as chlorotic decline, began to appear, particularly in the Transverse Ranges. At first, informed biologists assumed it was a consequence of fire suppression and that the shrubs were dying of old age. As researchers began to study the problem and the number of dying plants increased, however, other factors came to be suspected. The period from 1978 to 1983 was one of the wettest in history. It was followed by one of the worst droughts in history. Perhaps the additional precipitation stimulated so

FIGURE 8.19   Chaparral Whitethorn, *Ceanothus leucodermis*.

much growth that the plants were put under severe stress in attempting to maintain excessive foliage during the drought. Another complicating culprit may be dry fallout of nitrogen compounds from the polluted air. The excess nitrogen, particularly during periods of heavy rainfall, may also stimulate growth that cannot be maintained during drought.

Some herbaceous species or subshrubs have characteristics similar to *Ceanothus*. These species require heat for seed germination, and they have nitrogen-fixing bacteria in their roots. Among these are members of the pea family (Fabaceae), including a variety of lupines (*Lupinus* spp.) and a small shrub known as Deerweed, *Lotus scoparius*. Guess why it is known as Deerweed.

Apparently, chaparral fires cause a tremendous loss of nitrogen from the ecosystem by the burning of nitrogenous compounds such as proteins in plant tissues and detritus. It has been determined that a direct loss of 133 to 178 pounds of nitrogen per acre (150–200 kg/ha) could result from a moderate fire. During the first years after a fire, species equipped with nitrogen-fixing bacteria dominate because they grow quickly on the disturbed terrain, and they restore nitrogen to the system. Chaparral succession therefore is characterized in its early stages by herbs and suffrutescent (herbaceous) shrubs such as Deerweed.

For the first few years after a fire, Lower Chaparral is dominated by short-lived herbaceous plants, including many brightly colored wildflowers. Among these are the lupines and several members of the waterleaf family (Hydrophyllaceae), such as the shrub Yerba Santa (*Eriodictyon* spp.) and heliotropes or Canterbury-bells (*Phacelia* spp.).

Among the well-known wildflowers associated with chaparral are the paintbrushes (*Castilleja* spp.) (pl. 16A). There are about 34 species of paintbrushes in California, all associated with shrubs. They occur in a variety of communities from the desert to the mountains, and their often-brilliant red blossoms add a striking accent to the landscape. Paintbrushes are hemiparasites; that is, they are partially parasitic. They are photosynthetic and produce their own food like any free-living plant. In addition, paintbrushes tap into the root systems of shrubs to enhance their absorption of water and minerals. Therefore they are able to grow vigorously, even when surface layers of the soil become too dry for most small plants.

As might be expected, paintbrushes are not host-specific. They appear to parasitize a number of common shrubs, such as Chamise and California Buckwheat. Although this type of parasitism does not severely affect the host plant, during times of drought it has been shown that the host's growth and vigor are reduced. Another interesting study has shown that paintbrushes are also able to absorb phytotoxins such as alkaloids from host plants, thus parasitizing the chemicals that defend against herbivores.

Studies in the 1980s showed that compounds found in burned wood (charate or leachate) are capable of stimulating germination of a number of species. Among the wildflowers stimulated to germinate by charate are the phacelias. Also included in this group are common "fire followers," such as Whispering Bells, *Emmenanthe penduliflora;* Golden Yarrow, *Eriophyllum confertiflorum;* and Fire Poppy, *Papaver californicum.* At the same time these herbs germinate, *Ceanothus* and Chamise are also making a comeback. *Ceanothus* seems to dominate for about ten years. After that, Chamise dominates. The successional phases described before are apparently a function of growth rates and lifespan.

Other common associates of Lower Chaparral on south-facing slopes, particularly during early successional phases, are various members of the Coastal Sage Scrub community, such as Our Lord's Candle, California Buckwheat, White Sage, and Toyon. South-facing exposure provides the heat necessary for their proper growth.

On north-facing slopes in Lower Chaparral there is a community dominated by shrubs with comparatively large leaves, many of which have serrated or spiny leaf margins. The most important of these is California Scrub Oak, *Quercus berberidifolia* (fig. 8.20). The name *Quercus dumosa,* formerly used to denote California Scrub Oak, now refers to a separate species of scrub oak that grows in patches in canyon bottoms and on north-facing slopes within Coastal Sage Scrub. Acorns from scrub oaks are among the most important food items for chaparral animals. California Scrub Oaks can form a dense canopy up to 12 feet (4 m) in height, and their abundant leaf litter, up to 8 inches (20 cm) deep, often precludes growth of understory plants. This is an important habitat for woodrats (*Neotoma* spp.), who build their nests of branches and litter on the ground and in the branches of the oaks. California Scrub Oaks have dark green, thick, leathery leaves with soft, short hairs on the underside. The leaves have small lobes on the edge, but the margins are sometimes spiny. In some areas there is another scrub oak with spiny leaf margins. This is the scrub version of the

FIGURE 8.20   California Scrub Oak, *Quercus berberidifolia*.

Interior Live Oak, *Quercus wislizenii frutescens,* which is more common in the foothills of the Sierra Nevada. It can be distinguished from California Scrub Oak by its leaves; the undersides are not hairy, and both sides are shiny green.

More species are associated with California Scrub Oak than with any other chaparral plant, and nearly all of them have comparatively large, oval leaves. Among those that have leaves with serrated or spine-tipped margins are Holly-leaved Cherry, *Prunus ilicifolia,* and Holly-leaved Redberry, *Rhamnus ilicifolia.* Many of the species also have berries, such as California Coffeeberry, *Rhamnus californica,* and a number of wild currants (*Ribes* spp.). The importance of berries as a food for animals and as a means for dispersal of seeds is obvious. In particular, Coyotes, woodrats, and birds are known to feed on these fruits. It has been demonstrated that the seeds of Holly-leaved Cherry require the acid treatment of the Coyote's digestive tract or they will not germinate. This is an interesting irony, because the seeds, if cracked, release cyanide—another example of a defensive mechanism to discourage animals from eating the seeds. Apparently, the Coyote must eat the fruit without cracking the seeds. Does the Coyote learn this trick, or is it innate? This appears to be another example of coevolution.

Also common in Lower Chaparral are species of woody vines, such as honeysuckles (*Lonicera* spp.), wild peas (*Lathyrus* spp.), and wild cucumbers, or man-roots (*Marah* spp.). Being vinelike enables these plants to grow over the top of the shrub canopy so that they are not shaded or crowded out. Honeysuckles and wild peas bear attractive, tubular, hummingbird-pollinated flowers. Many consider the flowers of the various

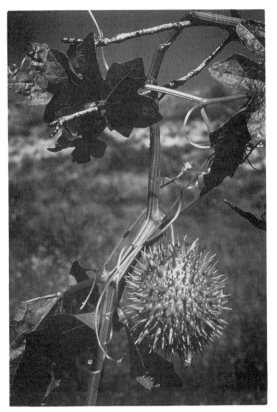

FIGURE 8.21   Chilicothe, *Marah macrocarpus*.

species of wild pea to be the most beautiful of the entire community. The most common of the wild cucumbers is known as Chilicothe, *Marah macrocarpus* (fig. 8.21). This vine produces many white, star-shaped flowers about $^{1}/_{4}$ to $^{1}/_{2}$ inch (8–13 mm) in diameter. Some people call the spiny, egg-shaped fruits "porcupine eggs." The plant returns each year from a large underground tuber and spreads widely over the vegetation. The name *man-root* refers to the huge tuber, which may reach the size of a man's body.

Many authorities consider California Scrub Oak and its associates to be a distinct community known as Scrub Oak Chaparral, pointing out that it occurs on north-facing slopes over a wide range of elevations from within Coastal Sage Scrub to Upper Chaparral. Scrub Oak Chaparral requires more moisture than communities on adjacent south-facing slopes, and it is more snow-tolerant than Chamise Chaparral. At upper parts of its range it occurs on south-facing slopes, and in the Transverse Ranges it occurs on both north-facing and south-facing slopes above about 3000 feet (900 m) elevation. This community also tends to respond differently to fire than Chamise-dominated chaparral. Most species associated with California Scrub Oak are sprouters that regrow rapidly after a fire. Even though herbaceous species are common for a year or two after a fire, it takes only a few years of vigorous growth to shift the dominance back to the common shrub and vine species.

Upper Chaparral

Upper Chaparral is also known as Cold Chaparral because much of the precipitation is provided by snow and fog drip. This community occurs on mountain slopes below the Yellow Pine Forest. Compared to Lower Chaparral, soil here is moderately organic, relatively deep, and usually acidic (pH 5.2–5.5). As in other chaparral communities, slope effect is pronounced. On south-facing slopes there are evergreen shrubs with thick, oval leaves. On north-facing slopes there are drought-tolerant conifers. This community is well established on the coastal side of the Transverse and Peninsular ranges from about 4000 to 5000 feet (1300–1500 m) elevation.

On south-facing slopes Upper Chaparral is dominated by various species of manzanita (pl. 7A). Some authors call this community Manzanita Chaparral. Particularly common are Eastwood Manzanita, *Arctostaphylos glandulosa,* and Bigberry Manzanita, *Arctostaphylos glauca* (fig. 8.22). In some areas manzanitas occur at lower elevations on north-facing slopes. At higher elevations, they are nearly always on south-facing slopes. Greenleaf Manzanita, *Arctostaphylos patula* (fig. 4.36), occurs this way, particularly on dry slopes in the Yellow Pine Forest. A manzanita is recognizable from a distance by its light green herbage. Up close, the manzanita is distinctive because of its smooth, bright red bark. Leaves on manzanita have a mealy, waxy surface and are often oriented vertically, which serves to reduce the amount of light that directly strikes leaf surface. Manzanita is a member of the heath family (Ericaceae). Many members of this family are notable for their distribution in snow zones. Manzanitas represent the drought-tolerant, fire-adapted heaths, but their tolerance for snow is typical of the family.

Manzanita is often associated with other cold-tolerant shrub species, such as Silk-tassel Bushes (*Garrya* spp.), which resemble manzanitas but whose bark is not red. Silk-tassel leaves are turned upward and arranged in pairs, opposite each other on the stem. The flowers are distinctive, hanging down in long chains like church bells (fig. 8.23).

Another common associate in Upper Chaparral is Western or Birch-leaf Mountain Mahogany, *Cercocarpus betuloides* (fig. 8.24). With its whitish gray bark, this shrub is distinctive. Its leaves are serrated, resembling a small birch leaf. Its fruits are dry, curled, featherlike structures. This shrub is in the rose family (Rosaceae), but it has nitrogen-fixing bacteria associated with its roots. It is therefore an important browse species, particularly in exposed, rocky locations, where it is important as food for Bighorn Sheep and Mule Deer.

An interesting characteristic of all three of these shrubs is that their leaves are oriented vertically, and to some degree they engage in sun tracking. This feature enables them to optimize light and heat for photosynthesis.

FIGURE 8.22   Bigberry Manzanita, *Arctostaphylos glauca*.

FIGURE 8.23   Silk-tassel Bush, *Garrya fremontii*.

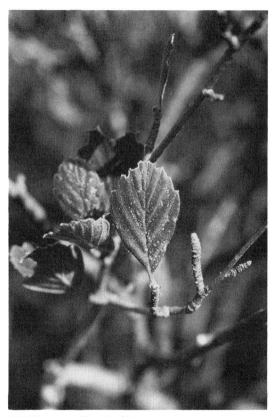

FIGURE 8.24 Birch-leaf Mountain Mahogany, *Cercocarpus betuloides*. Note the sun-tracking leaves oriented vertically.

Ribbonwood, *Adenostoma sparsifolium* (fig. 8.25), also known as Red Shanks or Ribbon Bush, occurs in the Peninsular Ranges. This member of the rose family is a relative of Chamise that favors north-facing slopes at elevations above Lower Chaparral. It is an associate of manzanitas and California Scrub Oak. On favored localities, particularly above 4000 feet (1300 m), it grows in nearly pure stands, and some authorities categorize this as a separate community known as Red Shanks or Ribbonwood Chaparral. In the San Jacinto Mountains, east of Garner Valley and south to Anza, there is an area along the Pines to Palms Highway (Highway 74) where a stand of Ribbonwood dominates a north-facing slope for many miles. At the lower reaches of its distribution, Ribbonwood is associated with California Scrub Oak and Hoary Ceanothus. At upper elevations it mixes with manzanitas. It appears to represent a transitional community between Lower and Upper Chaparral. Ribbonwood has small, filamentous leaves and red shaggy bark. It is a sprouter, growing new shoots vigorously after a fire.

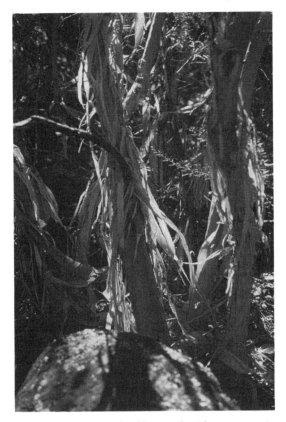

FIGURE 8.25   Bark of Ribbonwood, *Adenostoma sparsi-folium*.

Upper Chaparral has abundant leaf litter, which promotes a soil reasonably rich in organic matter. When there is a fire, the abundance of litter contributes to a deep ash layer with alkaline pH (ca. 7.4) that tends to inhibit germination of seeds. Therefore, after a fire, the abundance of annuals associated with other types of Chaparral is not as evident. About half of the manzanita species are sprouters that return readily after a fire. The other half become reestablished by seeds. Seeds of manzanitas, along with those of California lilacs and various herbs, must germinate in appropriate localities and compete for space. The abundance of seedlings of manzanitas and California lilacs after a fire maintains their dominance in the community at these times. California lilacs, however, are short-lived. Seedling California lilacs have a high mortality within the first two years after a fire, and once seedlings become established, California lilacs die before manzanitas. For this reason mature stands of Upper Chaparral may be composed entirely of manzanita.

A severe fire may burn the organic material in the soil and also burn dormant seeds. Recovery from such hot fires is very slow. In the Transverse Ranges there have been several large fires since the early 1960s. In these areas, there seems to be no reestablishment of Bigberry Manzanita, one of the species that does not sprout but returns from seeds. In the San Gabriel Mountains in 1980, there was a large, hot fire in San Antonio Canyon and Ice House Canyon on the south side of Mount Baldy. As of 1988, no manzanita seedlings were apparent. In the San Bernardino Mountains along Highway 18 between Arrowhead and Running Springs, there is a site that burned in 1959 that still has not returned to a manzanita shrubland. The area is showing early successional stages of dry Yellow Pine Forest, including Bracken Fern, Incense Cedar, and California Black Oak. Some Coulter Pines are also becoming established. Seedlings of these species normally would be precluded by deep ash and competition with the manzanitas.

The mechanisms associated with seedling germination after a fire are not well understood for species of manzanita. For example, in some areas sprouters occur with nonsprouters. Perhaps the most common crown-sprouting manzanita is Eastwood Manzanita. In an area east of San Diego it occurs equally with Bigberry Manzanita, a nonsprouting species. Bigberry Manzanita produces about eight times as many seedlings after a fire, but examination of soil in nearby unburned areas revealed about 25 times more Eastwood Manzanita seeds. As its name implies, Bigberry Manzanita has larger fruit, which would seem to increase the competitive ability of seedlings because there would be more stored food. It might also be assumed that larger fruit and seeds would provide better protection from fire. In light of these generalizations, it is difficult to explain why over 99% of Bigberry Manzanita seeds do not germinate after a fire.

Perhaps the size of the seeds is associated with some other adaptation, such as dispersal by animals. Here again, it would seem that larger fruit would attract more herbivores and therefore result in removal of a greater number of seeds from an area. This hypothesis was verified by predation studies. Presumably, Coyotes and ground-feeding birds removed the larger fruit from the area, which could explain why there are many more Eastwood Manzanita fruits remaining in the soil. But this does not explain why more Bigberry Manzanitas than Eastwood Manzanitas germinate. Perhaps the value of large fruits is to encourage dispersal of seeds. Further study may also show that passing of seeds through the digestive tract of an animal enhances its ability to germinate, as is the case with Holly-leaved Cherry.

On north-facing slopes in Upper Chaparral, shrub species are less common, and coniferous trees dominate. Although they seldom occur together, most common among these conifers are Big-cone Douglas Fir, *Pseudotsuga macrocarpa* (fig. 8.26), and Coulter Pine, *Pinus coulteri* (fig. 8.27). Big-cone Douglas Fir or Big-cone Spruce is related to the Douglas Fir of northern forests, but the cone of this species is twice as large. Distribution of Big-cone Douglas Fir is entirely southern Californian, extending from Santa Barbara to San Diego counties. Seeds germinate and grow well after a fire. It is notable that this conifer sprouts after a fire, but not from buds near the ground. These trees sprout from latent buds located at the bases of branches along the trunk. When a fire is too intense, the trees apparently fail to sprout, and regrowth must occur from seedlings.

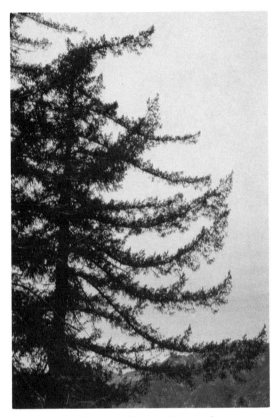

FIGURE 8.26 Big-cone Douglas Fir, *Pseudotsuga macro-carpa.*

Big-cone Douglas Fir is a moisture-dependent species commonly restricted to north-facing slopes and canyon bottoms above 3000 feet (980 m). It is notable that the only southern California occurrences of Pacific Madrone, *Arbutus menziesii* (fig. 6.7), are with Big-cone Douglas Fir on north-facing slopes. These sites are in deep canyons such as the West Fork of the San Gabriel River, Trabuco Canyon in the Santa Ana Mountains, and near Mount Palomar in the Agua Tibia Mountains. To the north, Pacific Madrone is normally associated with Coast Redwoods or other moisture-loving plants.

Coulter Pine resembles a short, stout Ponderosa Pine. Its thick foliage consists of long needles, often greater than 10 inches (25 cm) in length, which occur in clusters of three. One of these trees might be mistaken for a Ponderosa or Jeffrey pine were it not for its enormous cones, which may be larger than a volleyball. Similar to Digger Pine, the cones have large curled hooks on each scale. In the southern Coast Ranges, where the distribution of Digger Pine and Coulter Pine overlaps, the latter may be distinguished by its darker green needles and larger, light-colored cones. In some

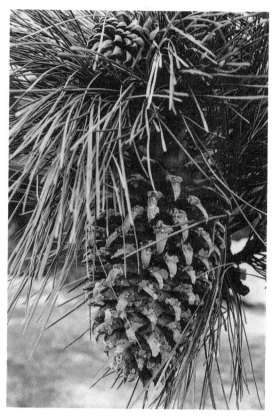

FIGURE 8.27   Coulter Pine, *Pinus coulteri.*

respects Coulter Pine may be considered the ecologic equivalent of Digger Pine in southern California.

It is notable that large cones seem to be associated with hot, dry habitats. Perhaps larger cones are needed to protect the seeds in these climates. However, the seeds of these conifers are also quite large. Perhaps large seeds are necessary to store enough food to support extensive root growth after germination, and large cones are merely coincident with large seeds.

Coulter Pines often occur in pure stands, although in the San Bernardino Mountains they are often associated with Canyon Live Oaks. This association is similar to what a person might find on upper north-facing slopes in the southern Coast Ranges. Flowering Ash, *Fraxinus dipetala,* is another northern associate on these north-facing slopes. These are large, winter-deciduous shrubs or small trees with pinnately compound leaves composed of three to seven leaflets. In the spring the shrubs become covered with white flowers, making them conspicuous on these slopes. Other associates include shrubs of Upper Chaparral, such as manzanitas.

Coulter Pines seem to be less fire-adapted than other chaparral species, although they survive low-intensity ground fires quite well. Unlike Big-cone Douglas Fir,

Knobcone Pine, and Jeffrey Pine, which may grow nearby, they show fewer special-izations that may be called fire adaptations. It is important, however, that the cones of Coulter Pines open slowly. This causes seedfall to be delayed until December, after the fire season is generally over.

Coulter Pine may be less drought-tolerant than other conifers in southern Califor-nia. Similar to the situation described previously for *Ceanothus*, large stands of Coulter Pines are dying. Weakened by drought and smog, the trees succumb to bark beetle infestations.

Distribution of Coulter Pine is a bit of an enigma. In the southern Coast Ranges it is an associate of Digger Pine, but it is absent from the Sierra Nevada in similar habitat. In southern California its distribution is spotty in the Transverse and Penin-sular ranges to northern Baja California. It and Big-cone Douglas Fir are the most common conifers in the Santa Ana Mountains. There is some evidence to support the contention that in southern California its distribution is associated with granite. It seems to be absent, for example, along the front range of the San Gabriel Mountains, where soils are derived mostly from metamorphic rock. Where Coulter Pines are com-mon, they form an open woodland on shaded flats and north-facing slopes. A region of great abundance occurs in the Chilao-Charlton Flats area near Mount Waterman in the San Gabriel Mountains. At higher elevations Coulter Pines are replaced by typical Yellow Pine Forest, although on rocky ridges they may extend up to 6000 feet (1800 m) elevation. In the San Bernardino and San Jacinto mountains, they may be found even higher.

Desert Chaparral

Desert Chaparral is found on the desert slopes of the Transverse and Peninsular ranges (fig. 8.28). It is also found on the inner slopes of the southern Coast Ranges bor-dering the dry southern end of the San Joaquin Valley. Technically, this community is not in cismontane southern California, because it is located in the rain shadow of the mountain ranges. Its obvious relationship to other chaparral communities, however, dictates that it be discussed here. In southern California this community usually occupies a zone below the Pinyon-Juniper Woodland but above the desert communities.

Desert Chaparral is an open type of community. Vegetation usually covers less than 50% of the terrain, but individual shrubs may be quite large, 10 feet (3 m) in height or more. Included here is a mixture of drought-adapted, snow-tolerant species found in other communities.

This community is less extensive on the desert slope of the Transverse Ranges than it is in the Peninsular Ranges. In the Transverse Ranges it may include Chamise as a dominant species. It also may include Bush Poppy, *Dendromecon rigida,* which is often considered a fire follower. This shrub is also called Tree Poppy, which is what the name *Dendromecon* means. The name "Bush Poppy" seems to be more appropriate, however, because the species seldom grows in a treelike form. Bush Poppy is characterized by large, bright yellow flowers with four papery petals.

FIGURE 8.28 Desert Chaparral, Santa Rosa Mountains, Riverside County.

In the Desert Chaparral of the Transverse Ranges, Bigberry Manzanita and Desert Ceanothus, *Ceanothus greggii,* may also be included. Desert Ceanothus resembles Hoaryleaf Ceanothus of Lower Chaparral; it has coarsely toothed margins, but the underside of the leaf is not white. Desert Chaparral is also characterized by localized patches of the shrub form of Interior Live Oak. At higher elevations Curl-leaf Mountain Mahogany, *Cercocarpus ledifolius,* may occur, a species more commonly associated with Pinyon-Juniper Woodland. This shrub is also a nitrogen fixer and therefore serves as an important browse species for Mule Deer and Bighorn Sheep.

An interesting species that occurs in Desert Chaparral and is also found in Chaparral of the western foothills of the Sierra Nevada is California Flannel Bush, *Fremontodendron californicum* (fig. 4.22), of the tropical Cacao family (Sterculiaceae). This large shrub has lobed leaves with a fine coating of hair. When it flowers in the spring, it becomes covered with large yellow blossoms. The blossoms are formed by bracts and sepals; there are no petals. During the dry season, leaves are shed a few at a time, but the plant seldom becomes leafless. This beautiful shrub is being cultivated for locations where no supplemental watering is available. When it is in bloom, very few shrubs can rival it for beauty. The blossom of this shrub is used on the logo for the California Native Plant Society journal, *Fremontia.*

On desert slopes of the Peninsular Ranges there is a more extensive belt of Desert Chaparral. The diversity here is extraordinary. In one study in upper Deep Canyon on the northeastern slope of Santa Rosa Mountain, over 50 species of perennial plants were identified, most of them shrubs. This diversity is a consequence of edge effect, a merging of communities. There is a mixture of species from Joshua Tree Woodland, Pinyon-Juniper Woodland, Cactus Scrub, Sagebrush Scrub, and Coastal Sage Scrub. Included are Sugar Bush, Desert Ceanothus, Western Mountain Mahogany, Bigberry

Manzanita, Holly-leaved Cherry, Bitterbrush (*Purshia tridentata glandulosa*), and Desert Scrub Oak or Muller's Oak (*Quercus cornelius-mulleri*). The Desert Scrub Oak differs from the California Scrub Oak, *Quercus berberidifolia*, by having small hairs on both surfaces. There are now three species of Desert Scrub Oak which were formerly known as *Quercus turbinella*. *Quercus turbinella* now refers to those populations that occur in the New York Mountains of the Eastern Mojave Desert and eastward into Colorado and Texas. Muller's Oak, *Q. cornelius-mulleri*, occurs on the desert side of the Peninsular Ranges from Baja California north to the San Bernardino Mountains. Tucker's Oak, *Q. john-tuckeri*, occurs from the north side of the San Gabriel Mountains to the interior side of the southern Coast Ranges. Bitterbrush is in the rose family (Rosaceae). It is spectacular in bloom, when it becomes covered with small cream-colored flowers. A similar shrub, Antelope Brush, *Purshia tridentata* (fig. 9.21B), is an important component of the Sagebrush Scrub community of the Great Basin.

There is some disagreement among authorities as to whether Desert Chaparral deserves recognition as a distinct entity. Because it contains plant species found in adjacent communities, some choose to consider it merely a transitional community, or ecotone. Others point out that the community contains many species from nonadjacent areas, and plants such as Sugar Bush, Desert Scrub Oak, and Desert *Ceanothus* are more common here than anywhere else. Furthermore, because most of the plants are shrubs, the term *Chaparral* is appropriate. Finally, because most of the birds and large mammals are the same as those found in other chaparral communities, it seems best to refer to the community as a form of Chaparral.

A number of species in this community produce showy flowers. They do not always blossom at the same time, however, so a person can expect to find things blooming from early spring onward. Among the most spectacular species is a shrubby sunflower (Asteraceae) known as Narrowleaf Goldenbush, *Ericameria* (= *Haplopappus*) *linearifolius,* which is locally abundant on rocky or sandy slopes. It has fine, linear, resinous leaves. When it flowers, whole hillsides appear covered by bright yellow sunflowers.

Because this community merges with Pinyon-Juniper Woodland at its upper reaches, it is understandable that there are many important foods here for animals. Cahuilla Indians gathered acorns, pine nuts (piñones), juniper berries, cactus apples (prickly-pears), and roots of yuccas while they took refuge from desert heat. In this community there is a group of drought-deciduous shrubs that were also useful to Indians. Among these is another member of the cashew family (Anacardiaceae), so important in chaparral communities. This is Squaw Bush, *Rhus trilobata*. Superficially, Squaw Bush appears to be a shrublike version of Poison Oak, but it seldom causes dermatitis. Whereas Poison Oak has leaflets in groups of three, Squaw Bush leaves are each divided into three lobes of about the same size and shape. Poison Oak occurs in moister habitats, and should not be feared in Desert Chaparral. The two species do occur together, however, on the coastal side of the Transverse and Peninsular Ranges, where Scrub Oak Chaparral mixes with Southern Oak Woodland. Squaw Bush was important to Indians because the stems are very flexible and were used in making baskets. Squaw Bush is one of the plants that shows measle-like splotching in the presence of ozone. Therefore it is being watched closely in some areas as an indicator of air pollution.

FIGURE 8.29   Desert Apricot, *Prunus fremontii*.

Other drought-deciduous species are two fruit-bearing members of the rose family: Desert Apricot, *Prunus fremontii* (fig. 8.29), and Desert Almond, *Prunus fasciculata* (fig. 8.30). In the spring Desert Apricot is covered with clusters of white flowers resembling those of many cultivated fruit trees. The fruit has thin meat and a large seed but was eaten by Cahuilla Indians nevertheless. Desert Almond produces many hairy fruits that probably were eaten as well. This is the shrub that is commonly infested with tent caterpillars (*Malacosoma* spp.) (fig. 9.24).

Succulent members of this community include two yuccas, Our Lord's Candle and Mojave Yucca (*Yucca schidigera*), as well as several species of cacti. The Desert Century Plant, *Agave deserti,* may also occur here, although it is more appropriately a member of the Cactus Scrub community. The prickly-pear found here is the Desert Prickly-pear, *Opuntia phaeacantha,* which is associated with pinyon pines throughout the deserts. Its fruit is another important food for animals. At least two species of cholla can be included as components of this community. *Opuntia echinocarpa* may be known as either Silver or Golden Cholla, depending on the color of its spines. Buckhorn Cholla, *Opuntia acanthocarpa,* is a similar but less spinescent species that gets its name from the fact that its branching may resemble the antlers of a deer.

FIGURE 8.30   Desert Almond, *Prunus fasciculata*.

Productivity in Scrub Communities

Water is a limiting factor in scrub communities. Primary productivity is therefore low. Figures reflecting food production in Chaparral vary, but Mediterranean climates produce an average biomass of about 5300 pounds per acre (600 g/m²) per year. This is about six times greater than a typical desert, but compared to other terrestrial communities it is low. A biomass of 5300 pounds will support about 530 pounds of herbivores and about 53 pounds of carnivores per acre. That is why there are so many small, ectothermic animals in scrub communities.

Variation in primary production within scrub communities is also high. Communities dominated by species of California lilac (*Ceanothus* spp.) are nearly twice as productive as the others. This type of Chaparral produces a biomass of nearly 9000 pounds per acre (1056 g/m²) per year. Furthermore, because nitrogen-fixing bacteria are associated with the roots of California lilacs, the food produced is rich in protein. About 80% of the production results in litterfall, contributing to a diverse community of insects that live in detritus. Many species of birds are ground dwellers that feed on these insects. It should be emphasized that California lilacs are usually short-lived successional species, and that high productivity lasts from about 4 to 10 years after a fire.

Productivity in Coastal Sage Scrub is low, reflecting the desertlike amounts of precipitation. Typical Coastal Sage Scrub produces only about 3000 pounds of food per acre (335 g/m²) per year. About 60% of that results in litterfall. Total aboveground biomass is small compared to chaparral communities. Aboveground biomass for Coastal Sage Scrub is about 10,430 pounds per acre (1172 g/m^2), and for *Ceanothus* Chaparral it is about 67,850 pounds per acre (7624 g/m^2). The total biomass for animals in Coastal Sage Scrub is correspondingly low.

ANIMALS OF SCRUB COMMUNITIES

Animals that live in scrub must deal with problems similar to those of animals that live in the desert. Overall, this is a hot, dry, food-poor ecosystem. As in the desert, there is an abundance of small, ectothermic animals, such as arthropods and reptiles, that have low metabolic demands and escape the harshest seasons by becoming dormant. Of the diurnal animals in Chaparral, birds are the most conspicuous. Many chaparral birds also occur in the desert, but others, such as the Western Scrub Jay, are primarily chaparral species. Most mammals are small and nocturnal. These include a number of species of rodents. The largest mammals are Mule Deer and Bighorn Sheep, and the largest predator is the Mountain Lion.

Insects are very common in chaparral habitats. Conspicuous are ants, grasshoppers, and butterflies, most of which are discussed in the following chapter. Predatory arthropods such as spiders and scorpions are also common but are far less conspicuous. Of special interest among arthropods are the ticks and mites. Although they are more closely allied to spiders than to other arthropods, they are not predators in the typical sense of the word. Altogether, they occur in practically all habitats and rival insects in diversity. Ticks are bloodsuckers, and as such they are considered to be ectoparasites. Experienced hikers have long known the importance of checking themselves for ticks after a day in the chaparral. Recently, the spread of a tick-borne malady known as Lyme disease has made this practice even more important. Lyme disease is spread by the bite of the small Deer Tick, *Ixodes pacificus.* Symptoms of Lyme disease include a rash at the site of the bite, which if left untreated is followed by an arthritis-like inflammation of joints and associated nausea and fever. The disease is caused by a bacterium, *Borrelia burdorferi,* and once the symptoms are recognized, it may be treated with antibiotics. The problem is that the symptoms may not show up for a month after the bite, by which time the victim may fail to associate the symptoms with the hike in the brush.

Mites are very small versions of ticks. Many of them are scavengers, and a large number of them are ectoparasites on plants and animals. Close inspection of lizards in chaparral areas, for example, commonly reveals groups of small red mites clustered near the ears or in the armpits. Of recent interest is the discovery that the larvae of harvest mites or chiggers (Trombiculidae) occur in Coastal Sage Scrub and adjacent grasslands. Even though some 150 species have been reported from California, they are not often encountered. In fact, it is a common belief that they do not occur here. Adult chiggers do not feed on humans, but the larvae may crawl up a person's legs and feed for a short time on skin cells. They do not burrow into the skin, as commonly believed, but when they become firmly attached to the host's skin they inject a digestive fluid that causes disintegration of skin cells. It is the digestive fluid that causes the itching and dermatitis associated by a chigger infestation. There are a few reports of the chigger *Eutrombicula belkini* in southern California, from Laguna Beach, Palos Verdes, and a couple of localities in Ventura County. In one interesting instance, forensic experts were able to link a murder suspect to the scene of the crime by virtue of the chigger bites on his legs.

Amphibians

Amphibians are not common in Chaparral because they typically remain near water. One interesting exception is the Monterey Salamander, *Ensatina eschscholtzii eschscholtzii*, which inhabits deep canyons and north-facing slopes, where it lives under rocks and logs. In summer, in order to estivate, these salamanders often move into burrows or under woodrat nests. They have smooth skin and are brownish on the back. Lungless salamanders (Plethodontidae), they breathe through their skin and the capillaries in their throat.

Distribution of the genus *Ensatina* in California was mentioned in the chapters on the Sierra Nevada, the Pacific Northwest mountains, and the Coast Ranges. The range of these salamanders illustrates a rare pattern known as a *rassenkreis* (fig. 8.31), a German word that means "circle of races." In California a single species of variable coloration inhabits a range that encircles the Great Central Valley; different color variants have been described as subspecies. *Ensatina* ranges from southwestern British Columbia to extreme southern California in the Peninsular Ranges. The ring of distribution represents a circular chain of subspecies that intergrade where ranges overlap. Coastal forms have a solid color pattern that grows lighter from north to south; these are known as Monterey Salamanders. The Sierra Nevada groups have yellow spots that become larger from north to south. These blotched forms occur at higher elevation, in association with Yellow Pine Forest. Similar to a pair of calipers, the two arms of distribution come together and form populations that overlap at the southern end, but they do not interbreed. In the vicinity of Mount Palomar and Julian in the Peninsular Ranges, the Monterey Salamander of lower elevation overlaps its range with the Large-blotched Salamander, *Ensatina eschscholtzii klauberi* (fig. 8.32), of Yellow Pine Forest. The two varieties may occur under the same bit of cover, but they do not hybridize. Farther north, in the San Bernardino Mountains, a similar situation occurs with a different blotched subspecies. At the upper end of Sawmill Canyon on Mount San Gorgonio, the Monterey Salamander hybridizes to a small degree with the Yellow-blotched Salamander, *Ensatina eschscholtzii croceator* (fig. 8.31). If an extinction were to occur in northern California where the solid form grades into the spotted form, the circle of races would be broken, and we would be obligated to identify two species: a solid form and a variable blotched form. A distribution pattern of this type is important to understand because it shows that the process of speciation is dynamic and still occurring.

Also of interest in the distribution of these salamanders is a peculiar disjunction in the range of the Yellow-blotched Salamander. In southern California these salamanders occur in the Tehachapi Mountains and on Mount Pinos to the west. They also occur in the San Bernardino Mountains to the east, but they have never been collected in

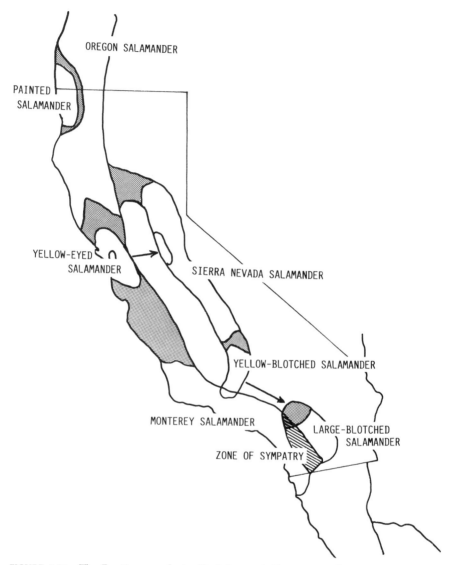

FIGURE 8.31 The *Ensatina* rassenkreis. Shaded areas indicate zones of intergradation between subspecies.

the San Gabriel Mountains in between. The cause of this disjunction has not been identified.

Reptiles

Reptiles are common and conspicuous in scrub communities. Many snakes and lizards are also found in the desert. Lizards are far more common than snakes, and, as in

FIGURE 8.32   Monterey Salamander, *Ensatina eschscholtzii eschscholtzii*, and Large-blotched Salamander, *Ensatina eschscholtzii klauberi*, from near Julian, San Diego County.

the desert, the most common lizards are in the iguana family (Iguanidae). The most common of these is the Side-blotched Lizard, *Uta stansburiana* (fig. 8.33), but the Western Fence Lizard, *Sceloporus occidentalis* (fig. 8.18), is nearly as common. These are primarily insect eaters. Side-blotched Lizards are also common in desert areas and get their name from a large black blotch located just behind the armpits. These small iguanid lizards are active all year and are particularly common in rocky areas. Females are usually brownish. Males may exhibit bright blue speckles on the top surface, and the lower surface of the throat may be blue and orange.

Side-blotched Lizards and Western Fence Lizards are conspicuous because of their basking behavior. They appear to do push-ups as a person approaches. The underside of the chin and belly of these lizards, particularly males, is brightly colored, and push-ups are a way for the lizards to expose the color. It is a form of behavior used to defend territories and for courtship. Western Fence Lizards are also known locally as "blue-bellied lizards" because the underside is an intense iridescent blue. The color on the top surface of these lizards closely resembles that of burned Chamise stems or granite. Hence predators would experience some difficulty seeing these lizards basking on these surfaces.

At upper elevations in southern California, the Western Fence Lizard is replaced by the Sagebrush Lizard, *Sceloporus graciosus*. This lizard ranges throughout the Great Basin, but in southern California its range is deflected upward in the mountains along with Great Basin Sagebrush. In the Transverse and Peninsular ranges the Sagebrush

FIGURE 8.33   Side-blotched Lizard, *Uta stansburiana*, in its defense posture, "doing push-ups."

Lizard is found in Upper Chaparral, Sagebrush Scrub, and Yellow Pine Forest. It is smaller than the Western Fence Lizard, and where the two species occur together, the Sagebrush Lizard can be distinguished by its rusty-colored armpits. At lower elevation, in the interior parts of the Peninsular Ranges, the Western Fence Lizard is replaced by the Granite Spiny Lizard, *Sceloporus orcutti.* This large, dark lizard is particularly common in rocky areas. In the coastal parts of the Peninsular Ranges the Western Fence Lizard is the usual species.

Another common chaparral lizard that is also found in the desert is the Western Whiptail, *Cnemidophorus tigris* (fig. 8.34). This lizard is distinguished by its black-and-white checkered pattern and long, dark tail. It is commonly seen foraging for insects in the litter under bushes. Those who like to capture lizards by noosing them find whiptails a frustrating challenge. They move incessantly, and even if they are snared, they usually wiggle free because their necks are thicker than their heads. On the coastal side of the Peninsular Ranges the Western Whiptail is replaced by an uncommon striped form known as the Orange-throated Whiptail, *Cnemidophorus hyperythrus* (fig. 8.35). Its distribution in southern California is the northern limit for its range, which extends southward to the tip of Baja California. Because it is an inhabitant of Coastal Sage Scrub, a community that is rapidly being replaced by pastures, agriculture, and development, the lizard is a candidate for being listed as rare or endangered.

Whiptail lizards range widely across the arid parts of the southwestern United States, but they actually represent only the northernmost forms of the whiptail family (Teidae), which extends across the tropics from temperate South America to the southern United States. In the southwest they are notable for a bizzare form of speciation in which all-female populations reproduce by parthenogenesis, that is, in the absence of males and without mating. It has been determined that these populations evolved in marginal habitats by hybridization between species with overlapping ranges. Genetic

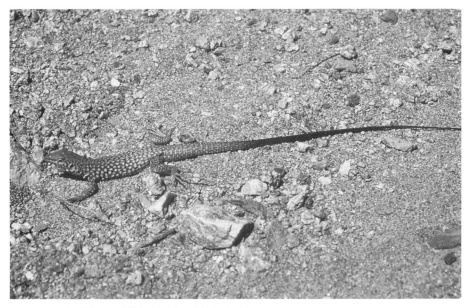

FIGURE 8.34   Western Whiptail, *Cnemidophorus tigris*.

FIGURE 8.35   Orange-throated Whiptail, *Cnemidophorus hyperythrus*.

integrity of the hybrids is maintained because the lizards do not reproduce sexually. Furthermore, some of the populations are characterized by a rare phenomenon in animals: they have triploid ($3N$) chromosome numbers. Typical sexually reproducing organisms have a diploid ($2N$) chromosome number that is maintained indefinitely by fusion of sperm and ova that contain only the haploid (N) number of chromosomes. Nine all-female parthenogenetic populations have been identified so far.

The Coast Horned Lizard, *Phrynosoma coronatum* (fig. 8.36), is another iguanid lizard. It ranges throughout the state except in the humid northwest and the deserts. In the deserts it is replaced by two other species: the Desert Horned Lizard, *P. platyrhinos,* and the Flat-tailed Horned Lizard, *P. mcallii.* These lizards are so similar in appearance that it takes experience to tell them apart. The Coast Horned Lizard usually has two rows of conspicuous spiny scales along the edge of its belly; the Desert Horned Lizard has only one, and the scales are smaller. The Flat-tailed Horned Lizard has a dark middorsal line. Habits of all horned lizards are similar. They frequent open spaces and sandy areas, where they eat primarily ants. They rely on protective coloration and a flattened body shape for concealment, and they usually remain motionless when approached.

In southern California, numbers of Coast Horned Lizards are declining rapidly. In California, the San Diego subspecies, *P. coronatum blainvillii,* occupies essentially the same range as the Orange-throated Whiptail and, along with some other species of Coastal Sage Scrub, is up for consideration as rare or endangered. The problem is related to habitat destruction associated with development, pastures, and agriculture. The situation has been complicated by the practice of fire suppression, which has allowed existing brushland to overgrow, reducing the amount of open space. The open spaces that remain, such as dirt roads, flood plains, and stream banks, are trampled by humans and off-road vehicles. In an effort to control flooding, stream courses have been channelized and lined with concrete. Also, children love to collect and play with horned lizards. It remains to be seen whether horned lizards and humans can coexist.

Snakes are far less common than lizards. They are larger, and they are all carnivores. Many snakes of scrub communities are the same species that occur in the desert. Among those distinctly associated with scrub is the Common Kingsnake, *Lampropeltis getulus* (fig. 8.37). This snake is common throughout the southwest in many habitats, but in California it is typically a lowland, coastal species. The Common Kingsnake is characterized by alternating dark and light bands or rings about the body (fig 8.37A). This pattern is found in other snakes, but the Common Kingsnake is the largest of the California banded species. Color variants are found throughout its range. In southern California, for example, there is a striped phase; in this snake a continuous stripe runs lengthwise along the top side of the body (fig. 8.37B). These snakes eat small rodents, lizards, and other snakes. They are called kingsnakes because they also will eat rattlesnakes, and they are not affected by rattlesnake venom. The Common Kingsnake is replaced by the California Mountain Kingsnake, *Lampropeltis zonata* (pl. 15C), in Upper Chaparral and Yellow Pine Forest.

The adaptive value of a banding pattern has been questioned frequently. Several other species, such as the Long-nosed Snake (*Rhinocheilus lecontei*), the Western Shovel-nosed Snake (*Chionactis occipitalis*) (pl. 15D) and the Banded Sand Snake (*Chilomeniscus cinctus*), show similar banding. These, however, are all nocturnal burrowers, whereas the kingsnakes are usually diurnal. If a snake with a banded pattern remains motionless under brush where filtered light makes a dark and light pattern, its pattern of alternating light and dark bands will help conceal it.

FIGURE 8.36   Coast Horned Lizard, *Phrynosoma coronatum*. (Drawing by Pat Brame from A. A. Schoenherr. *The Herpetofauna of the San Gabriel Mountains.* Special Publication of the Southwestern Herpetologist's Society, 1976.)

Conspicuous patterns can also serve as a warning to other organisms, a mechanism known as aposematic coloration. The Banded Krait, *Bungaris fasciatus,* of Southeast Asia, a venomous snake, has a black and white pattern that is very similar to that of the Common Kingsnake. Furthermore, studies of brightly colored snakes in Mexico and Central America confirm that mimicry occurs. There is remarkable convergence in color patterns where the ranges of nonvenomous species overlap those of venomous species such as coral snakes.

Venomous coral snakes of the southeastern United States and Mexico have banding, including red and yellow colors, that resembles the pattern of the California Mountain Kingsnake, but their ranges do not overlap. This disparity raises the question of whether mimicry could have been responsible for the bright colors of the California Mountain Kingsnake. Evidence for mimicry exists where the present range of the Arizona Coral Snake, *Micruroides euryxanthus,* overlaps the ranges of species resembling the California Mountain Kingsnake. These similarly colored species include the Long-nosed Snake and two species not found in California: the Sonora Mountain Kingsnake, *Lampropeltis pyromelana,* and the Milk Snake, *Lampropeltis triangulum.* It is possible that the coloration of the California Mountain Kingsnake can be traced to a time when its range overlapped that of a coral snake. It is also possible that a common ancestor of these three species of *Lampropeltis* (the California Mountain Kingsnake, the Sonora Mountain Kingsnake, and the Milk Snake) co-occurred with a coral snake, and the events responsible for speciation of the three took place after the mimicking pattern evolved.

Another bit of evidence to support the warning function of the California Kingsnake banding pattern is that rattlesnakes instinctively avoid kingsnakes. If a kingsnake and rattlesnake are placed together, the rattlesnake immediately retreats without rattling, which is *its* threat. Rattlesnakes have responded to the presence of kingsnake skin alone. In addition, there is evidence that rattlesnakes respond to

FIGURE 8.37   Common Kingsnake, *Lampropeltis getulus. A*. Banded color pattern.

FIGURE 8.37 (*continued*)   Common Kingsnake, *Lampropeltis getulus. B*. Striped color pattern.

kingsnake odor, leading to the question of whether there is odor mimicry that has escaped observation.

A color pattern that is more effective for moving through brush or grass without being seen is that of longitudinal stripes. These stripes break up solid color patterns, and they appear to remain stationary as the animal moves, particularly if it is only partly exposed. It is interesting that behavioral studies of kingsnakes show that those with the banded pattern tend to be ambush hunters, waiting motionless for prey to come near, whereas the striped forms are active foragers, frequently moving in search of prey.

The most common snake with longitudinal stripes is the Striped Racer, *Masticophus lateralis*. This snake is coachwhip-shaped and gets its name from its apparently rapid movement, although it probably moves no faster than about 4 miles (7 km) per hour. It is an active forager. It moves with its head raised, and its sinewy shape and longitudinally striped elongate body give it the appearance of great speed. Distribution of this snake is closely associated with Chaparral. It is conspicuous because it is diurnal. It feeds on a variety of foods, including lizards, birds, small mammals, and insects.

Other snakes with longitudinal striping include garter snakes (*Thamnophis* spp.) and the Western Patch-nosed Snake, *Salvadora hexalepis,* also relatively rapid-moving snakes. Garter snakes are found chiefly near water, but the Western Patch-nosed Snake occurs throughout desert and chaparral areas. This racerlike snake is not frequently encountered, however. It gets its name from the large, curved scale on the tip of its snout. This type of nose scale is also found on several other species of snake and is probably an adaptation for burrowing.

Several snakes of southern California are divided into coastal and desert subspecies, including the Gopher Snake, the Glossy Snake, the Western Patch-nosed Snake, and the Rosy Boa. In each case, the coastal form occurs throughout the scrub communities.

The Gopher Snake, *Pituophis melanoleucus* (fig. 8.38) is probably the most common snake in southern California. It certainly is the largest, measuring up to 8 feet (250 cm) in length. This large yellowish snake may have a diamond pattern on its back. This pattern, as well as its habit of hissing and vibrating its tail when alarmed, leads some people to mistake it for a rattlesnake. This snake is a good burrower, and it also enters the burrows of rodents such as gophers or ground squirrels. Depending on the size of the burrow, the snake may kill its prey by maneuvering past it and crushing it against the side of the burrow. Gopher Snakes also eat birds and some lizards, which they kill by constriction. It also has been reported that they eat bird's eggs, including chicken eggs.

It is not uncommon to find Gopher Snakes sunning on mountain roads, sometimes in a group of three or more. Such grouping usually occurs during spring and includes several males vying for the favors of a single female. This habit of lying on roads, plus the mistaken notion that they are rattlesnakes, has led to a decline in population numbers. These are beneficial animals that need not to be molested.

The Glossy Snake, *Arizona elegans,* resembles the Gopher Snake, but it is smaller and has smooth scales. It is more common in Coastal Sage Scrub than in Chaparral, and it tends to be nocturnal. Lizards and small mammals are its favored food.

FIGURE 8.38 Gopher Snake, *Pituophis melanoleucus*.

The Rosy Boa, *Lichanura trivirgata,* is a slow-moving pinkish snake with a blunt nose and tail. Boas in general possess two very small hind limbs, one on each side of the vent. These vestiges indicate that snakes come from ancestors that once possessed limbs. The limbless condition is most likely an adaptation for burrowing. The Rosy Boa is becoming scarce. It usually occurs in Coastal Sage Scrub or along lower stream courses, both habitats that are disturbed by the activities of humans. This extremely docile snake is favored by those who like to keep snakes as pets. Unfortunately, they do not always do well in captivity. They are usually nocturnal, feeding on small mammals, and they sometimes crawl about in the rain. They differ from most snakes by giving birth to their young alive. The Rosy Boa should not be confused with the Rubber Boa, *Charina bottae.* In southern California, the Rubber Boa is known only from three localities in the Yellow Pine Forest: Mount Pinos, Idyllwild, and near Lake Arrowhead.

The similarity between Coastal Sage Scrub and desert communities is apparent from the vegetation, but similarities between the animals also are apparent. For example, some typically desert reptiles may occur in Coastal Sage Scrub. Included here is the Desert Night Lizard, *Xantusia vigilis,* which is associated with Our Lord's Candle on coastal slopes of the San Gabriel Mountains. Similar to its role in the desert, this lizard eats mostly termites from the dead parts of various species of *Yucca.*

Also noteworthy is the presence on the coastal side of the San Gabriel Mountains of a desert dweller, the Western Collared Lizard, *Crotaphytus bicinctores*

(= *Crotaphytus collaris*) (pl. 15B). This lizard inhabits boulder-strewn washes in Lytle Creek and the East Fork of the San Gabriel River. These localities are adjacent to Lower Chaparral but are desertlike in their exposure. The lizards in Lytle Creek have not been seen in many years. Perhaps this disappearance is associated with the fact that this location is one of the open shooting areas designated by the U.S. Forest Service. On any weekend thousands of persons converge on the area in hundreds of vehicles to test their marksmanship on targets of various sorts.

Other desert forms that have been recorded in Coastal Sage Scrub include the Western Banded Gecko, *Coleonyx variegatus* (fig. 9.49), the Zebra-tailed Lizard, *Callisaurus draconoides* (fig. 9.42B), and the Coachwhip or Red Racer, *Masticophis flagellum* (pl. 15F). For unknown reasons the Coachwhip seemed to disappear in the 1960s, coincident with the loss of Coastal Sage Scrub along the front of the Transverse Ranges. In the 1980s, however, there have been many sightings of them in the Alluvial Scrub community of Big Tujunga Wash, near the western end of the San Gabriel Mountains.

Rattlesnakes also occur from the coast to the desert. These venomous snakes possess temperature-sensitive pits on each side of their nostrils, which they use to locate endothermic prey such as small rodents or birds. Similar to the bright color of other venomous snakes, the rattle is a warning device. A rattlesnake does not want to waste its venom defending itself.

In general, rattlesnakes are not highly mobile; they are stout-bodied and incapable of rapid locomotion, relying on quick reflexes and venom to immobilize their prey. Their typical hunting behavior is to locate by odor an area with suitable prey. They detect this odor with the forked tongue. Then they remain motionless, in ambush position, near a rock or log, often with their chin resting on top of the log. Mice run along the top or side of the log and unwittingly come too near. The rattlesnake senses the mouse's body heat with its labial pits, and it strikes. Another favorite rattlesnake trick is to crawl up into a bush and remain motionless among the branches until a bird or small mammal comes near.

Rattlesnakes may group in dens for the winter, where they are able to hibernate and share each other's body heat. In the spring they emerge from the den and migrate to hunting areas, where they will remain solitary except to mate. Rattlesnakes will migrate until they encounter an area that has an abundant supply of mice for food. They locate this site by its odor. As indicated before, odor molecules are picked up by the snake's forked tongue, but the odor is actually interpreted by two small pits, known as vomeronasal organs, in the roof of its mouth. When sufficient mouse odor is detected, the rattlesnake usually takes up residence in the area for the entire summer.

The typical rattlesnake of the Chaparral is the Western Rattlesnake, *Crotalus viridis* (fig. 8.39). This snake is widely distributed in California, occurring in nearly all cismontane habitats. Usually it is brown, with a diamond pattern on its back, but in the Yellow Pine Forest it may be completely black (pl. 15E).

In the Peninsular Ranges, and at lower elevations in general, the Red Diamond Rattlesnake, *Crotalus ruber*, is present. This is the largest but perhaps most docile of

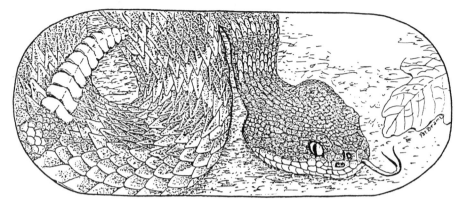

FIGURE 8.39   Western Rattlesnake, *Crotalus viridis*. (Drawing by Pat Brame from A. A. Schoenherr. *The Herpetofauna of the San Gabriel Mountains*. Special Publication of the Southwestern Herpetologist's Society, 1976.)

California's chaparral rattlesnakes. This large pinkish snake is a near relative of the Western Diamondback, *Crotalus atrox,* another desert snake. The venom of the Red Diamond Rattlesnake is less dangerous, however.

Another pinkish rattlesnake, but without the diamond pattern, is the Speckled Rattlesnake, *Crotalus mitchelli*. This is another species distributed in lowland desert and coastal communities in southern California. It inhabits mostly rocky areas from the southern Sierra Nevada to Baja California.

Birds

A large number of bird species are associated with scrub habitats, but most of them also occur in other communities. Many species are shared with Oak Woodland, riparian, grassland, and desert habitats. Species that are typically chaparral in distribution have certain features in common. They tend to have short wings and a long tail, which gives them maneuverability in flight. They are usually omnivorous because they must be opportunistic feeders. They eat berries and acorns when they are in season, and they eat insects, also relying on these foods for water during periods of drought.

The Western Scrub Jay, *Aphelocoma californica* (pl. 13F), typifies chaparral birds in all respects but one. The Scrub Jay is bright blue and conspicuous, whereas most chaparral birds are brown. The raucous call of the Scrub Jay also attracts attention. The jay is the alarmist that calls possible danger to the attention of the entire chaparral community. Factors separating the Scrub Jay from Steller's Jay of the Yellow Pine Forest include water and heat. Scrub Jays are able to derive all the water they need from the food they eat, and they are extremely efficient at dissipating heat from the unfeathered portion of their feet. During the hottest part of a summer day, they remain quiet in the shade of a shrub and dissipate heat without losing water.

The brown color of most chaparral birds makes them inconspicuous as they forage in the bushes, often on the ground. However, the lack of striking color poses some problems in attracting a mate. Many chaparral birds compensate for this with melodic songs, enabling them to communicate without being seen. The California Thrasher, *Toxostoma redivivum* (fig. 8.40), typifies chaparral birds in this respect. It is a large brown bird that is seldom seen, but its long lyric song is a familiar sound of the Chaparral. It is easily recognized by its long, hooked beak, which it uses to thrash about in leaf litter and uncover insects.

The bird that is known as the voice of the Chaparral is the Wrentit, *Chamaea fasciata*. A person rarely spends much time in the Chaparral without hearing its distinctive call, which resembles a bouncing pingpong ball. This smaller, long-tailed bird is seldom seen as it moves through the vegetation, gleaning insects.

Another bird with a long lyric song is the Rufous-sided Towhee, *Pipilo erythrophthalmus*. Although its color may seem conspicuous — it has a white breast, buff sides, a black head, and black wings with white spots — the bird is actually ideally colored for an environment with filtered light. It does not form a clear silhouette because of its broken color pattern. This is an example of disruptive coloration, an adaptation associated with birds that spend a good deal of time on the ground beneath bushes. The Rufous-sided Towhee and its relative the California Towhee, *Pipilo crissalis* (fig. 8.41), are two of the most common chaparral birds. They are ground-feeding birds with thick seed-eater beaks, but they are omnivorous. The Brown Towhee is a typical chaparral bird in appearance, similar in color and size to the California Thrasher. It has little to distinguish it visually other than its pale orange rump. Unlike many chaparral birds, it does not often produce pretty song. Most of the time, it utters a single tone, "peenk," which it may repeat after a pause.

Other birds frequently heard include the California Quail, *Callipepla californica* (pl. 13A), which makes a strange laughing sound ("a-ha-ha"); the Acorn Woodpecker, *Melanerpes formicivorus* (fig. 7.28), which utters a "wacka-wacka"; the Mourning Dove, *Zenaida macroura*, with its distinctive "coo"; and the Northern Flicker, *Colaptes auratus* (fig. 4.24), which utters a shrill "kee-oo." The Cactus Wren, *Camphlorhynchus brunneicapillus*, is one of the most familiar sounds of the desert, but it occurs in Coastal Sage Scrub and Lower Chaparral as well. Its call is a series of rapid "chuga-chuga" sounds. During spring, the call of the Great Horned Owl, *Bubo virginianus* (fig. 8.42), is a familiar sound after dark. This is the familiar deep-throated "Whoo" that is associated with owls in general.

Predatory birds of Chaparral include a variety of owls and hawks. The Great Horned Owl is an important nocturnal predator. This large owl commonly hunts from a perch, locating its prey, small nocturnal mammals, primarily by hearing them. Like other owls, they have good nighttime vision, but their hearing is even better. The ring of feathers that surrounds each eye collects sound in the same way as the external ear of a mammal. Owls can hunt in total darkness, and their wing feathers are specially adapted for silent flight. Their wing bones are hollow, containing extensions of their lungs, which makes them lighter. Owls usually return to a perch to feed.

FIGURE 8.40 California Thrasher, *Toxostoma redivivum*.

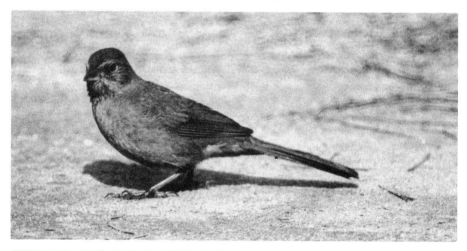

FIGURE 8.41 California Towhee, *Pipilo crissalis*.

After digesting their meal, they burp up a pellet containing hair and bones. When seen about the base of a tree, these owl pellets indicate that the tree is a favored owl perch. A good naturalist can identify the species of owl by the size and shape of the pellets. Pellets of a Great Horned Owl are almost as large as a chicken egg. It is not uncommon for owls to swallow their prey whole. Their pellets, therefore, commonly contain many intact bones, particularly skulls, which makes identification of prey species relatively simple. Some hawks produce pellets too, but because hawks tend to feed by tearing up the prey, their pellets contain fewer intact bones.

FIGURE 8.42   Great Horned Owl, *Bubo virginianus*. (Photograph by Lloyd P. Parratt.)

The most common hawks are the Red-tailed Hawks, *Buteo jamaicensis,* which may be seen soaring above cliffs and hilltops. They ride on rising columns of warm air known as thermals, and they feed on a variety of prey species, including small mammals, birds, reptiles, amphibians, and insects. A mature Red-tailed Hawk has a rust-colored tail. Immature Red-tailed Hawks have brownish tails with indistinct banding. If the red tail is not visible, the hawk's best distinguishing characteristic is a dark V-shaped band across the belly. In contrast to the Red-tailed Hawk is the

FIGURE 8.43   Red-shouldered Hawk, *Buteo lineatus*.

Red-shouldered Hawk, *Buteo lineatus* (fig. 8.43), which usually hunts from a perch. The Red-shouldered Hawk is slightly smaller than the Red-tailed Hawk, and it has black and white bands on its tail.

Mammals

The small-mammal fauna of scrub communities consists mostly of nocturnal rodents. However, California Ground Squirrels, *Spermophilus beecheyi* (pl. 12A), are diurnal. They occur from Desert Chaparral to the coast and are an important food item for predatory birds such as Red-tailed and Red-shouldered hawks.

In general, the small mammals of Coastal Sage Scrub closely resemble those of the desert. Both habitats support the Deer Mouse, *Peromyscus maniculatus* (fig. 8.44), the Desert Woodrat, *Neotoma lepida,* and the Desert Shrew, *Notiosorex crawfordi.* There is probably a greater variety of small rodents in Coastal Sage Scrub than in the other scrub communities.

Deer Mice are distributed in nearly all communities from the desert floor to the high mountains. By allowing their body temperature to drop every day while in their burrows, they require less food, an important strategy for animals living in a food-poor habitat. This lowered metabolic rate also serves to extend their lifespan. Deer Mice live about five years, longer than other species of small rodent. Most mice live only a year or so.

Several other species of *Peromyscus* can be found in Coastal Sage Scrub. They all have hairy tails and large ears, and they differ in color, size, and tail length. Collectively, they are found in nearly every habitat in the state, and they are particularly common in scrub communities. They feed on a variety of foods, including seeds, insects, and insect larvae. They differ from meadow mice or voles (*Microtus* spp.) in that they seldom eat grass, bark, or leaves. These differences in food habits, representing examples of niche partitioning, enable these mice to coexist in a food-poor ecosystem.

FIGURE 8.44   Deer Mouse, *Peromyscus maniculatus*.

A common inhabitant of Upper and Lower Chaparral communities is the California Mouse, *Peromyscus californicus*. This mouse is more common in mature Chaparral than the Deer Mouse. The California Mouse is one of the larger species of the genus, intermediate in size between a Deer Mouse and a woodrat. Otherwise it resembles them both by having large ears and a hairy tail.

Woodrats (*Neotoma* spp.) are also known as packrats or traderats. They get these names from their habit of picking up small shiny objects. If they are carrying one object and see another they like better, they will drop the first, pick up the second, and carry it back to their nest. If you happen to be living in a cabin, you may find this habit amusing or disturbing, depending on what is snatched. If a woodrat has exchanged the lid of a bean can for your fifty-dollar gold piece, you will probably be vexed. Your next step will likely be to locate the thief's nest and tear it up to see if it contains your treasure. You might find a wide assortment of things there, including other animals such as scorpions or rattlesnakes, which use woodrat nests for shelter.

Woodrats make their nests from available materials. In scrub areas, nests usually consist of a large pile of sticks. Odoriferous bits of sage may be used to conceal the odor of the woodrat. In desert areas, nests may be constructed entirely of pieces of cholla. Building materials may also include knives, forks, and perhaps some miner's treasure. Usually there are several false entrances, apparently to confuse predators. In the center of the mound is a hollow area lined with grass, string, or pieces of rags.

At higher elevations in Lower and Upper Chaparral, the Desert Woodrat is replaced by the Dusky-footed Woodrat, *Neotoma fuscipes* (fig. 8.45). Wood piles made by this species may be 6 feet (2 m) high. It has been reported that smaller piles or houses

FIGURE 8.45   Dusky-footed Woodrat, *Neotoma fuscipes*. (From E. W. Jameson, Jr. and H. J. Peeters. *California Mammals*. Berkeley: University of California Press, 1988.)

constructed in the branches of shrubs, usually California Scrub Oak, are the homes of males, whereas those on the ground are occupied by females. These woodrats subsist largely on acorns and oak leaves. They also eat a variety of berries in season. These are larger woodrats, similar in size to the introduced Old World rats, *Rattus rattus*, which are sometimes called Roof Rats or Black Rats. Woodrats are distinguishable by their large ears and hairy tails.

In rocky areas, woodrats make their nests in small caves or hollows in rocks. The entrances to these hollows are marked by small piles of debris, including pieces of wood, urine, and feces. These piles are known as middens. If they are out of the weather, protected from rainfall, the concentrated urine apparently acts to preserve the wood and plant material. This debris may be carbon-14 dated to determine its age. It turns out that these fragments of wood may be thousands of years old, from species that no longer grow in the area. As discussed in chapter 5, this accidental bit of preservation has enabled scientists to reconstruct patterns of vegetation and climatic change dating back to the Ice Age (Pleistocene).

Woodrats are able to endure the period of summer drought by deriving water from various species of prickly-pear cactus. This is true in the desert, and also in Coastal Sage Scrub. Whereas other rodents seem to experience a drop in density during the summer, woodrats maintain about the same population density all year long, probably because they are able to make use of prickly-pear cactus as their sole water source. During summer months they will actively defend patches of prickly-pear.

In addition to the rodent species that are shared between the desert and Coastal Sage Scrub, there are examples of paired species, or near relatives, that occur in both places. Examples may be found among the kangaroo rats (*Dipodomys* spp.) (fig. 9.48A), pocket mice (*Perognathus* spp.) (fig. 9.48B), and various white-footed mice (*Peromyscus* spp.). Habits of these species are similar no matter where they occur.

Kangaroo rats tend to forage for seeds in open areas between shrubs. Pocket mice forage for seeds under the canopy of the shrubs. These forms of niche partitioning will be discussed in the following chapter.

After a fire in Coastal Sage Scrub, animals associated with open areas become more common. At this time, the common small rodents include the Agile Kangaroo Rat, *Dipodomys agilis*, the Cactus Mouse, *Peromyscus eremicus*, and the Desert Woodrat. As the Coastal Sage Scrub recovers from the fire, kangaroo rats become less common, and the pocket mice and deer mice become the most common small mammals. After a fire in the chaparral communities, the Dusky-footed Woodrat and the California Mouse disappear. At this time Chaparral becomes occupied by an assemblage of species similar to those of Coastal Sage Scrub.

In certain parts of Riverside County, between the Santa Ana and San Jacinto mountains, the Agile Kangaroo Rat is replaced by Stephen's Kangaroo Rat, an endangered species that, by virtue of its status, has prohibited some forms of development.

In certain scrub communities, bare areas occur on the periphery. This is particularly true in some Coastal Sage Scrub areas or those dominated by *Ceanothus*. It has been determined that this is the result of grazing by small mammals, who pick up seeds and eat seedlings most vigorously near the existing stands of vegetation. This type of selective herbivory can also hasten the succession from *Ceanothus* to Chamise.

In Desert Chaparral, most small mammals are desert species. These include woodrats, kangaroo rats, and white-footed mice. One different species is the Pinyon Mouse, *Peromyscus truei* (fig. 8.46). This large mouse closely resembles the California Mouse, replacing that species on the desert sides of the ranges and farther north. The Pinyon Mouse occurs in Desert Chaparral, Pinyon-Juniper Woodland, and Foothill Woodland. The large mammals of Desert Chaparral are typically those also found in other chaparral communities, such as Mule Deer, Bighorn Sheep, Mountain Lions, Bobcats, and Coyotes.

In general, big fierce animals are scarce in scrub communities, just as they are in the desert. There is simply not enough biomass of animal life to support a population of large carnivores, which explains why one of the most important predatory mammals in Coastal Sage Scrub is the diminutive Desert Shrew. How do we justify a large carnivore such as a Mountain Lion, *Felis concolor*, in a food-poor ecosystem? First, Mountain Lions eat large prey, such as Mule Deer or Bighorn Sheep, and they have large home ranges. Second, they are very good at conserving energy. They typically hunt from an ambush position, and they spend a great deal of time lying in wait. This behavior uses a minimal amount of energy, and lying in the shade helps to keep the animal cool.

In southern California about 100 square miles (256 km^2) is the estimated typical range for a male Mountain Lion. Female Mountain Lions may have smaller ranges, and their ranges may overlap. Studies in the Santa Ana Mountains indicated that in the vicinity of Caspers Regional Park, four females had overlapping ranges averaging 77 square miles (197 km^2). The general density of Mountain Lions may be related to that of their favored prey, Mule Deer. An approximate ratio of one Mountain Lion per 200 deer is typical. At this ratio, there might be a total of 10 male Mountain Lions

FIGURE 8.46   Pinyon Mouse, *Peromyscus truei.*

and/or 40 females in an area the size of the Santa Ana Mountains. Similar densities probably occur in the other principal ranges in the Transverse and Peninsular ranges. One authority calculated that there might be 25 Mountain Lions in Orange County; however, to make an estimate of the total number of Mountain Lions in southern California is meaningless, because densities must be calculated for areas where a sufficiently large population is able to move about freely so that they can interact during breeding season and raise offspring. To locate a patch of land that is 10 miles by 10 miles (16 km × 16 km) surrounded by urbanization and expect a lion to choose to live there is absurd. Similarly, to dedicate narrow corridors for wildlife within vast acres of housing tracts is simply not to understand what wildlife really means.

Perhaps the most common large mammal in scrub communities is the Coyote, *Canis latrans* (fig. 8.47). Coyotes are opportunistic feeders, eating whatever is abundant. That is one of the reasons they are so successful. They eat insects, rodents, and a wide variety of fruits. Fecal piles, called scats, may be examined to determine what animals eat. Coyote scats are among the most abundant found in scrub communities, and they nearly always contain mostly vegetable material. One authority estimated that the diet of a Coyote is 80% vegetable.

In areas where housing developments have pushed into brush-covered hillsides, interactions between humans and wild animals have become troublesome. In southern Orange County, Mountain Lions have been sighted in suburban areas, but most interactions are with Coyotes. Excited by the prospect of seeing wild Coyotes, humans have taken to feeding them table scraps and dog food. Once Coyotes get accustomed to the easy calories, they begin to demand them. When the Coyotes become too brazen or aggressive, humans stop feeding them. That is when the Coyotes get truly aggressive, particularly if they are not accustomed to feeding on their own.

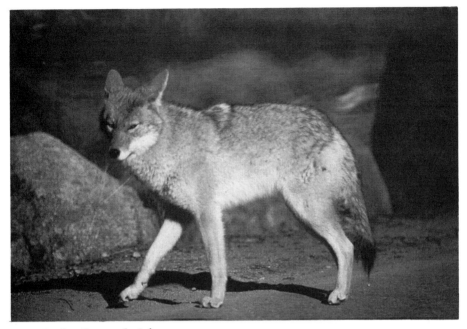

FIGURE 8.47   Coyote, *Canis latrans*.

Several incidents have occurred where dependent Coyotes attacked children once the parents stopped providing handouts. In one incident, a lame Coyote was the attacker. In an undisturbed situation the crippled Coyote would have been weeded out by natural selection, and the interaction with a human never would have occurred. These interactions between humans and wild animals, whether it involves Coyotes in San Clemente or Black Bears in Yosemite, could be prevented if humans would abstain from providing the animals with easy food.

Some serious interactions have occurred between Mountain Lions and humans. In southern California, the most highly publicized attack took place in Ronald W. Caspers Wilderness Park. This park, along the Ortega Highway in the Santa Ana Mountains, is surrounded on three sides by urban development, most of which originated in the mid-1980s. In 1986 a five-year-old girl was seriously mauled by a Mountain Lion. Mountain Lion attacks on humans are not common, but since 1750 there have been more than 65 incidents recorded in the Western Hemisphere. Very few interactions have been recorded for southern California, but most of the ones that have were recent and in the vicinity of Caspers Park. Apparently, civilization has encroached upon the former range of the Mountain Lions. They are unable to move farther into the national forest, because that area is already occupied by other Mountain Lions. This sort of competition, perhaps exacerbated by drought, forces the weaker Mountain Lions to take refuge in marginal habitats—in this case, a "wilderness" park. A small girl frolicking on a trail easily could be mistaken for a natural prey item, and if a Mountain Lion were hungry, it might assume that the girl is something normal to

FIGURE 8.48 Gray Fox, *Urocyon cinereoargenteus.*
(From T. I. Storer and R. L. Usinger. *Sierra Nevada Natural History.* Berkeley: University of California Press, 1963.)

eat. If Mountain Lion habitat continues to be replaced at the present rapid rate, more such interactions are certain to occur.

Other chaparral carnivores include the Gray Fox, *Urocyon cinereoargenteus* (fig. 8.48); the Bobcat, *Lynx rufus* (= *Felis rufus*) (fig. 8.49); and the Ringtail, *Bassariscus astutus* (fig. 8.50). These are all predators that feed on small rodents and birds. Scats and stomach contents of trapped animals have been examined to find out what these animals eat. Foxes are omnivorous, like Coyotes. However, their scats are smaller and often contain grass.

The Bobcat is also known as the Wildcat or Lynx, not to be confused with the Lynx, *Lynx canadensis* (= *Felis lynx*), of forests in northern North America. Bobcat scats rarely contain vegetable matter, and they contain many bones. Bobcats seem to be strictly carnivorous. Contrary to popular belief, they rarely eat game birds such as quail or doves, although they do consume a variety of birds. Studies indicate that they prey primarily on small rodents and birds, although there are accounts of bobcats killing small Mule Deer. Bobcats, with their relatively short noses, do not have as good a sense of smell as some other predators, so they hunt primarily by vision.

Bobcats are probably more common than observations indicate. Estimates indicate that there is about one animal for every 1 to 2 square miles (2.6–5.2 km²) of Chaparral. In spite of this density, they are rarely seen, as they characteristically lie quietly in wait, using their remarkable protective coloration to keep them concealed. Like Coyotes, Bobcats are widespread, ranging from Yellow Pine Forest to the desert. Also like the Coyote, the Bobcat may be seen abroad in daylight.

In recent years Bobcats have been subjected to a significant amount of trapping. The federal government has banned the importation of spotted fur to help stop the worldwide slaughter of spotted cats. Unfortunately for Bobcats, the demand for this fur has made it lucrative to trap them.

The Ringtail is in the Raccoon family (Procyonidae). It is not much larger than a Gray Squirrel, although its long bushy tail may give it a larger appearance. Some people call it a Ringtail Cat. Its distinctive features include enormous eyes and a bushy tail with black and white rings. Scats of Ringtails are seldom seen because

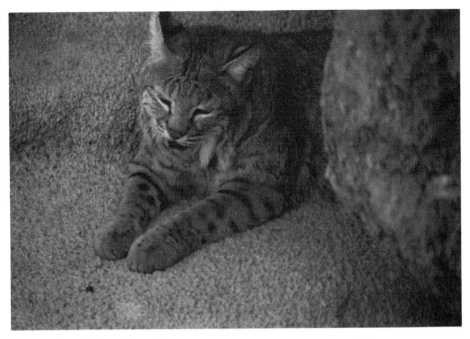

FIGURE 8.49 Bobcat, *Lynx rufus*.

FIGURE 8.50 Ringtail, *Bassariscus astutus*. (From E. W. Jameson, Jr. and H. J. Peeters. *California Mammals*. Berkeley: University of California Press, 1988.)

they are usually deposited in shelters rather than along trails or roads. Ringtails and foxes eat birds by climbing into the bushes to feed, whereas Bobcats are more likely to lie in wait and then pounce. Ringtails and foxes also may take birds that are asleep or that are on the nest. Many juvenile birds meet their end this way.

Observations of hunting behavior suggest that the Ringtail holds its tail over its back when it moves through open areas. This behavior may confuse a potential predator such as a Great Horned Owl, which presumably tries to grasp the tail and gets nothing but fur. Competition between Ringtails and other predators is avoided by the Ringtail's habit of feeding very late at night. This late-night activity means that it is seldom seen by humans. Ringtails are probably more common than is believed.

Physiological studies of Ringtails indicate that they may be the most drought-adapted of all mammals in North America. They can persist on water derived from food, and they conserve water by producing the most concentrated urine known among mammals.

The history of the Grizzly Bear, *Ursus arctos*, in California is the story of a disaster. California is the only state in the union that has an extinct animal as its symbol. In southern California, the last grizzly was killed in Trabuco Canyon in 1908. The last Grizzly Bear in the state was killed in 1922, in Horse Corral Meadows, in the Sequoia area of the western Sierra Nevada.

The Grizzly Bear should not be confused with the Black Bear, *Ursus americanus*, which is a forest bear and probably did not occur in the mountains of southern California until it was introduced in 1933. Apparently some 27 Black Bears were brought down from Yosemite National Park and released into the San Gabriel and San Bernardino mountains. Those bears prospered, and now there are thriving populations in the area. The population in the San Bernardino Mountains has expanded from 16 bears in 1933 to over 300 in 1989. Now they are breaking into cabins and raiding trash cans here just as they do in the Sierra Nevada.

The Grizzly Bear was a chaparral and grassland bear. Similar to Black Bears, however, Grizzly Bears were omnivorous, eating mostly small mammals, insects, grasses, berries, and various roots. The long claws and large muscle mass of the shoulders were adaptations enabling them to dig up roots, bulbs, and tubers, as well as tear up logs to get ants and termites. The ferocity of the Grizzly Bear is legendary. Bull and bear fights with the two animals roped together were usually won by the bears. Nevertheless, their extinction, encouraged by a $10 bounty, was unfounded.

The California Grizzly Bear was a subspecies of the Grizzly Bear that still inhabits portions of the northern Rockies. Of course, statements about the size of the animals often are exaggerated, but they probably averaged about 900 pounds—considerably larger than Black Bears and somewhat larger than other Grizzly Bears in the lower 48 states. Unlike Black Bears, they probably did not hibernate, because they commonly overwintered at lower elevations than the snow-covered forest communities. Grizzly Bears primarily roamed lowland areas of the state, from foothills to the coast, feeding on what was abundant. It was the encounters in the valleys that got them into trouble with humans. Here ranchers had encroached upon traditional Grizzly Bear hunting grounds, and cornered Grizzly Bears would attack domestic dogs and humans. To the humans of the time, it seemed it was "them or us," and the program of extermination was begun.

CONIFEROUS FORESTS

Composition of coniferous forests in southern California has been outlined in chapters 4 and 5. The dominant species of Yellow Pine Forest include Jeffrey Pine, Incense Cedar, and California Black Oak; these are joined by Sugar Pine and White Fir on moist sites. Ponderosa Pine, which is not common, reaches its southernmost distribution in the Laguna Mountains of San Diego County. Yellow Pine Forest is absent from the Santa Monica and Santa Ana mountains. Lodgepole Pines and Limber Pines are found on high peaks in the San Gabriel, San Bernardino, and San Jacinto mountains. The southernmost Limber Pines are found on Toro Peak, the highest peak in the Santa Rosa Mountains. The rest of the species mentioned here reach their southernmost distributions in Baja California.

SOUTHERN OAK WOODLAND

Southern Oak Woodland is the southern California equivalent of Foothill Woodland. Usually it is dominated by one of the large oak species. Three species of large oak trees occur in southern California; Coast Live Oak, *Quercus agrifolia* (pl. 7B); Canyon Live Oak, *Quercus chrysolepis* (pl. 7A); and Engelmann Oak, *Quercus engelmannii*. These three species are not always easy to tell apart, particularly where they grow near each other, because they frequently hybridize. These oaks have enormous root systems that enable them to tap into water supplies deep in the soil. Thus they are not forced into long periods of dormancy by summer drought. Their thick bark protects them from fire.

Coast Live Oak is most common along the southern Coast Ranges and at low elevations in southern California. It occurs at moist sites with deep soil, particularly canyon bottoms and north-facing slopes. Live oak woodlands exist as islands within Coastal Sage Scrub. In the southern Coast Ranges, Coast Live Oak occurs on the coastal side, usually on north-facing slopes. It resembles Interior Live Oak, *Quercus wislizenii*, by having spine-tipped leaf margins, but it differs by having curled leaf margins. The leaves are more oval, and the underside has hairs at the junctions of the veins. Interior Live Oaks have no hair on the underside of the leaves.

Coast Live Oaks are also known as California Live Oaks, and in many ways they symbolize southern California country living. In areas such as the San Fernando Valley, communities have incorporated the native oaks into their plans for urbanization. Place names such as Sherman Oaks and Thousand Oaks bear witness to this trend. Unfortunately, many people don't know how to treat these trees and wind up killing them. One obvious mistake for a tree such as this is to cover its enormous root system with concrete. The other major mistake is to plant a lawn or put water-loving ornamental shrubs around the base of the tree. These forms of vegetation require summer watering, and water during the summer causes a fungus to attack the roots of the oak, which in time will certainly kill it. The best advice for a person who has one of these oaks is to leave it alone. It probably has lived at that spot for hundreds of years, surviving on natural precipitation. If further landscaping is desired, the best bet is a mixture of shrubs from north-facing slopes of Coastal Sage Scrub. Attractive shrubs that are common associates of Coast Live Oak include Toyon, Lemonadeberry, and Fuchsia-flowered Gooseberry, *Ribes speciosum.*

Perhaps the most common associate of Coast Live Oak is Poison Oak, *Toxicodendron* (= *Rhus) diversiloba* (fig. 8.15). In spite of its name, Poison Oak is not in the same family as the oaks. It is a member of the cashew family (Anacardiaceae), which includes several other important southern California shrubs, such as Laurel Sumac, Lemonadeberry, Sugar Bush, and Squaw Bush. Poison Oak is winter-deciduous and is very beautiful in autumn, when its leaves turn bright red before they are shed. Poison Oak does not affect everyone equally. Apparently, American Indians were immune to its toxin. Those who are sensitive may be affected by contact with leaves, stems, or even smoke from a brushfire. It is a serious mistake to use it for a campfire. When hiking in canyons, sensitive individuals should proceed with caution, particularly during winter, when there are no leaves. If a sensitive person must hike with a dog, it is advisable not to pet it or hug it, because the dog is certain to have brushed against the Poison Oak.

Another southern California tree that is commonly associated with Coast Live Oak is California Black Walnut, *Juglans californica*, (fig. 8.51). This is the state's native walnut. Although the nuts are not as large as the commercial walnut, they are considered by many to be every bit as tasty. Squirrels commonly eat the nuts and are believed to play an important role in the dispersal of this species. This tree is winter-deciduous. Leaves are pinnately compound, meaning that what appears to be many leaves arranged opposite each other on the stem is actually a large single leaf with many leaflets. Distribution of California Black Walnut is patchy, from lower canyon mouths of the Santa Monica Mountains southward to about the Santa Ana River, where it becomes associated with Riparian Woodland. Many of these trees, particularly along the southern face of the Transverse Ranges, have been replaced by development. In the San Jose Hills, between Diamond Bar and Fullerton, is the state's last remaining extensive stand of California Black Walnut. Unfortunately, this site is trapped in the midst of urban sprawl, and it is hoped that plans to preserve this area as open space will not become sidetracked.

Canyon Live Oak occurs at higher elevations than Coast Live Oak. The name of this species refers to the large yellow cups on each acorn. The most widely distributed oak tree in the state, it occurs in similar habitat throughout the Foothill Woodland of the Sierra Nevada, Klamath Mountains, and Coast Ranges. It also occurs in the Providence and New York mountains of the Mojave Desert, where it associates with pinyon pines. In southern California, it is often called Canyon Live Oak because it seems to be most common in canyons. Canyon Live Oak is associated with north-facing chaparral species such as California Scrub Oak and Coulter Pine. Leaves of Canyon Live Oak differ from Coast Live Oak and Interior Live Oak by possessing white hairs on the underside. A bit of confusion may arise in relation to the leaves

FIGURE 8.51   California Black Walnut, *Juglans californica*.

because, on any tree, some have smooth margins and some spiny margins. If acorns are present, there should be no confusion, for no other oak has such large acorns with a sulfur yellow cup.

Engelmann Oak is also known as Mesa Oak. Its typical habitat is flat tablelands of the Peninsular Ranges, where the trees are widely spaced and the understory is a mixture of grasses and herbs. This type of habitat is often called an oak savannah. Engelmann Oaks formerly grew along the base of the San Gabriel Mountains between Pasadena and Claremont, but no woodland of this type persists in the area today. The community was a victim of urbanization and grazing.

Engelmann Oak is in the white oak group. This is the southern California equivalent of the Blue Oak, *Quercus douglasii*, which is characteristic of the Foothill Woodland surrounding the Great Central Valley. Engelmann Oak differs from Blue Oak by not having lobed leaves; its leaves are elongated and have smooth margins. Also, whereas Blue Oaks are winter-deciduous, Engelmann Oaks are semideciduous: they may lose many leaves, but they usually do not lose them all.

An interesting pattern of reproduction is emerging for these oak trees. Seedlings require shade, but this is a fairly open habitat. Seedlings and saplings therefore occur in groups near the dripline of the canopy of large old trees. These are known as nurse trees. Apparently, fog drip and shade are necessary for germination.

The woodland characterized by Engelmann Oaks is associated with deep, clay-rich soils. These soils are found on flatlands amidst California Scrub Oak and Upper Chaparral. A significant characteristic of these soils is poor drainage. Also found within these areas are temporary ponds known as vernal pools, which will be discussed later as ecologic islands. Engelmann Oaks as well as several vernal pools are now protected in a large Nature Conservancy reserve on the Santa Rosa Plateau in the Santa Ana Mountains southwest of Elsinore.

Animals of Southern Oak Woodland

For the most part, animals of Southern Oak Woodland are the same as those described for Foothill Woodland. Mammals and birds that eat acorns are associates, as are those that require cavities for nesting purposes. Conspicuous among these are California Ground Squirrels, Acorn Woodpeckers, and Western Bluebirds. Less conspicuous are Great Horned Owls and Band-tailed Pigeons, *Columba fasciata*. Many chaparral birds, during the heat of the day, take refuge in the cool canopy of the oaks.

Of particular interest in the southern California area are some of the lungless salamanders (Plethodontidae). Monterey Salamanders, as described earlier, are common inhabitants, living under bark and logs. They become active after the first rains of winter and remain among the moist leaf litter, feeding at night on small insects until things become too dry. They then migrate to rodent burrows or cracks in rocks, or they burrow deeply into rotten logs. Many take residence under woodrat nests.

Another lungless salamander is the Arboreal Salamander, *Aneides lugubris* (fig. 7.25). These salamanders are nearly always associated with oaks, from southern California through the Coast Ranges. In southern California, they are most often associated with Coast Live Oak, although near Crystal Lake, at 5000 feet (1500 m) in the San Gabriel Mountains, they are associated with Golden-cup Oak. They are called arboreal because they are known to climb trees and make nests in tree hollows. However, they are probably most common on the ground, where they are frequently found under the same rocks or logs as Monterey Salamanders. They are brown with small yellow spots. They are unique among salamanders by having a prehensile tail, which they curl and use to hold themselves in a tree or bush. They have very large jaw muscles, which give them an alligatorlike appearance. The teeth are probably used to help enlarge cavities in wood. They are capable of inflicting a bite and drawing blood, but that rarely occurs. Another distinctive feature of these salamanders is that they have expanded toe tips, which were once thought to function as an aid in climbing. This may be true, but it is now known that the toes are loaded with capillaries and aid the animal in its absorption of water and oxygen. It might be stated that these salamanders breathe through their toes. They also absorb oxygen through their skin in general, and particularly through capillaries in the mouth, which they ventilate by flapping the floor of the mouth up and down.

There are two more lungless salamanders associated with oaks in southern California. These are the slender salamanders, and they have been discussed in the chapters on the Sierra Nevada and Coast Ranges (fig. 7.24). Locally, there are two species: the Pacific Slender Salamander, *Batrachoseps pacificus*, and the Black-bellied Slender Salamander, *Batrachoseps nigriventris*. These salamanders are very well adapted for burrowing. They have long, wormlike bodies and very small limbs. They take refuge in any sort of crack, hollow, or burrow, and they probably do no actual digging. These are very sedentary, seldom moving far from their shelter.

The Pacific Slender Salamander is a lowland form, seldom occurring above 1000 feet (300 m) in elevation. It is the species that is frequently encountered under rocks, boards, or trash cans in suburban southern California. It is the larger of the two forms, sometimes reaching 4 inches (10 cm) in total length. It can be distinguished by its gray belly with small black flecks. The Pacific Slender Salamander is replaced by the Black-bellied Slender Salamander at higher elevations. In southern California, this salamander is not particularly associated with sedimentary rocks, as it is in the Coast Ranges. When the black-bellied form is found, it is in the same sort of habitat as the other lungless salamanders. This small salamander seldom exceeds 3 inches (7.5 cm) in total length. Its belly is black, speckled with minute white flecks.

There are two known relict species of slender salamander in southern California. One occurs at about 5000 feet (1500 m) in the North Fork of San Gabriel Canyon. It has yet to be named. Populations of the Black-bellied Slender Salamander occur nearby. Another relict species, known as the Desert Slender Salamander, *Batrachoseps aridus*, occurs in a most unlikely location. It is known only from one locality, a palm oasis in upper Deep Canyon, on the east side of the Santa Rosa Mountains. Presumably, during periods of heavier precipitation it was more widespread. It endures today in cracks wet by a permanent spring on a north-facing slope.

The association of these relict populations with terranes that have been translocated over long distances was discussed in relation to the Coast Ranges. A number of these associations occur in southern California as well. One such region is along the San Gabriel River. Faulting in the area has brought into close proximity at least three terranes of different origin. At various points along the river are populations of distinctive native animals. For example, this is the only southern California locality for the Foothill Yellow-legged Frog, *Rana boylii* (fig 11.26A), which here occurs in the same water with the Mountain Yellow-legged Frog, *Rana muscosa* (fig. 11.26B). The relict slender salamander (unnamed species) occurs here, and this is also the only place in the San Gabriel Mountains where the Yellow-blotched Salamander has been sighted. Unfortunately, this unofficial record has not been confirmed. Furthermore, along the East Fork of the San Gabriel River there is a population of the Collared Lizard, normally a desert form. The San Gabriel River is also one of the few localities in southern California that contains remnants of the native fish fauna.

A few reptiles seem to be associated particularly with Southern Oak Woodland in southern California. Unfortunately, with the encroachment of humans upon these habitats, the reptiles are far less common than they used to be, and some may have been extirpated. One such reptile is the Racer, *Coluber constrictor*. This snake is associated with oaks in the Coast Ranges, and it still occurs on the Santa Rosa Plateau in the Santa Ana Mountains. It still may be present in the Mount Pinos–Gorman area and has been sighted recently on the western end of the San Gabriel Mountains near Placerita Canyon.

The Racer is bluish gray above and yellow on the belly. The name for the local subspecies, *Coluber constrictor mormon*, is the Western Yellow-bellied Racer. It feeds

FIGURE 8.52   Ringneck Snake, *Diadophis punctatus*. (Drawing by Pat Brame from A. A. Schoen-herr. *The Herpetofauna of the San Gabriel Mountains*. Special Publication of the Southwestern Herpetologist's Society, 1976.)

on salamanders and skinks. Gilbert's Skink, *Eumeces gilberti* (pl. 15A), occurs as far south as the Mount Pinos–Gorman area also, but it is no longer found in southern California. These southern races of Gilbert's Skink differ from the northern races by having pink or reddish tails rather than blue tails during the juvenile phase. Sometimes they coexist with the Western Skink, *Eumeces skiltonianus*, which has a blue tail. In northern populations of Gilbert's Skink, the juveniles look very much like the Western Skink, but the two species seldom occur together. The Western Skink is apparently the only skink left in southern California. It occurs in Southern Oak Woodland and Yellow Pine Forest, where it is fed upon by the Mountain Kingsnake.

Several species of amphibians and reptiles characteristic of Southern Oak Woodland seem to have adapted to California gardens. Among these are secretive or burrowing species such as the Arboreal Salamander or slender salamanders. Of particular note is the appearance in gardens of the Ringneck Snake, *Diadophis punctatus* (fig. 8.52), and the California Legless Lizard, *Anniella pulchra* (fig. 8.53). These species prefer moist, sandy soil or leaf litter in which to burrow. Well-vegetated, watered gardens with mature shrubs and abundant litter, particularly where undisturbed native habitats occur nearby, seem to attract these species.

The Ringneck Snake is often small, about 12 to 15 inches (30–38 cm) long, but it may reach 30 inches (75 cm). This slender snake is bluish to nearly black, with a bright yellow to orange neck ring. Its underside is orange to red. When the snake is disturbed, it coils and turns over its tail, revealing the brightly colored underside. This is an apparent warning device, although the snake is not venomous. Ringneck snakes feed on salamanders, small lizards, and insects, all of which may also appear in gardens.

The California Legless Lizard looks like a small silvery snake, seldom exceeding 6 inches (15 cm) in length. Even though it has no legs, close inspection will reveal that it has eyelids, a characteristic of lizards. California Legless Lizards forage in the leaf

FIGURE 8.53 California Legless Lizard, *Anniella pulchra*. (Drawing by Pat Brame from A. A. Schoenherr. *The Herpetofauna of the San Gabriel Mountains*. Special Publication of the Southwestern Herpetologist's Society, 1976.)

litter at night for small insects and spiders. With the loss of habitat within Coastal Sage Scrub and Southern Oak Woodland communities, it was feared that these strange little lizards would become extirpated. Perhaps by default, these and other delicate animals may find refuge alongside humans.

RIPARIAN WOODLAND

Riparian Woodland of cismontane southern California resembles that of the southern Sierra Nevada and the southern Coast Ranges. Most of the riparian species are winter-deciduous; descriptions of these species are found in chapter 4. These are the trees that provide the autumn color in southern California canyons (pl. 7C). People from the east who yearn for autumn color can drive less than an hour from southern California's urban sprawl to any number of canyons in the Transverse and Peninsular ranges. If they want a more spectacular display, they will have to drive up to Bishop to see Quaking Aspens, or else go home.

At lower elevations, the dominant trees are Western Sycamore, *Platanus racemosa*, and Black Willow, *Salix gooddingii*. Red Willow, *Salix laevigata*, occurs up to about 5000 feet (1500 m), and Pacific Willow, *Salix lasiandra* (fig. 10.8), occurs up to 8000 feet (2500 m) in elevation. Shrubby willows such as Sandbar Willow, *Salix hindsiana*, occur to about 3000 feet (900 m), and Arroyo Willow, *Salix lasiolepis*, occurs up to 7000 feet (2100 m) in elevation. Fremont Cottonwood, *Populus fremontii* (fig. 8.54), is also a common species, but it is more often found at low elevations inland than it is along the coast. Black Cottonwood, *Populus trichocarpa* (fig. 4.54), occurs from the foothills to about 7500 feet (2300 m) in elevation. In the San Gabriel and San Bernardino mountains, there is a variety of Black Cottonwood with narrow leaves, less than 1 inch (25 mm) wide.

White Alder, *Alnus rhombifolia* (fig. 4.55), occurs from about 1000 feet to 6500 feet (300–2000 m) in elevation. At middle elevations, where streams cut through

FIGURE 8.54   Fremont Cottonwood, *Populus fremontii*.

Yellow Pine Forest, White Alder is commonly associated with Big-leaf Maple, *Acer macrophyllum* (fig. 6.9), and Pacific Dogwood, *Cornus nutallii* (fig. 4.56).

At upper elevations there is a variety of shrubby willows, including Lemmon Willow, *Salix lemmonii*; Scouler Willow, *Salix scouleriana*; and Yellow Willow, *Salix lutea*. Of limited distribution in the San Gabriel and San Bernardino mountains is Dusky Willow, *Salix melanopsis*.

Quaking Aspen, *Populus tremuloides* (pl. 8A), reaches its southernmost California distribution in the San Bernardino Mountains in an isolated colony just south of Heart Bar State Park, at an elevation of 7500 feet (2300 m) on Fish Creek. The only other known colony of aspens in southern California is also in the San Bernardino Mountains, southeast of Big Bear Lake. The presence of this species in these mountains is notable because it is approximately 150 miles (240 km) south of the nearest groves, in Tulare County of the southern Sierra Nevada. Perhaps even more remarkable is that a similar distance south of the San Bernardino Mountains, even larger groves occur in the Sierra San Pedro Martir of Baja California. It is unfortunate that these San Bernardino Mountain populations of Quaking Aspen are now threatened by introduced beavers (*Castor canadensis*).

Of the evergreen species associated with Riparian Woodland, only California Laurel, *Umbellularia californica* (fig. 7.9), and Pacific Madrone, *Arbutus menziesii* (fig. 6.7), occur in southern California. The odoriferous California Laurel is common in canyons as far south as the Laguna Mountains in San Diego County. Pacific Madrone has patchy distribution in canyons of southern California as far south as Mount Palomar.

Animals of Riparian Woodland include a wide variety of insects, amphibians, and birds. Most of these are discussed in other parts of the book. Of particular significance to southern California is that Riparian Woodland communities have become threatened; hence so have a number of the characteristic animal species. Channelization and flood control projects have destroyed many miles of Riparian Woodland. In addition, invasion of riparian habitats by the Brown-headed Cowbird, *Molothrus ater*, a nest parasite, has threatened a number of songbirds that require Riparian Woodland as a nesting habitat.

A specific example of a songbird that is threatened by Brown-headed Cowbirds is a small gray bird known as the Least Bell's Vireo, *Vireo belli pusillus*, once considered a common summer visitor in southern California. Many vireos are yellowish and have a distinctive white ring around the eye. The Least Bell's Vireo has no eye ring, and its color is light gray. It is considered to be the least distinct of all the vireos. Typical of drab-colored birds that remain hidden, these vireos have a beautiful lyric song, which was formerly one of the familiar sounds of the Riparian Woodland. Typically, these birds would arrive from Mexico in the spring. They would nest in willows or wild rose bushes, remarkably close to the ground, and raise two broods of young per year. The combination of cowbirds and habitat destruction has practically eliminated this bird. Down to fewer than 300 pairs, this subspecies is now listed as endangered by the federal government. The Brown-headed Cowbird is also a documented parasite on nests of the California Gnatcatcher, a Coastal Sage Scrub species mentioned before that has been proposed for threatened status by the U.S. Fish and Wildlife Service.

There are few pristine Riparian Woodlands left in the southern part of the state. One is found along Mono Creek near Santa Barbara, and another is along Santa Margarita Creek near Oceanside. In these areas during the summer, in order to protect the Least Bell's Vireo, federal workers trap and remove the unwanted Brown-headed Cowbirds.

ECOLOGIC ISLANDS

The concept of an ecologic island has been discussed frequently and refers to a region with rather specific ecological parameters surrounded by a habitat of a more generalized nature. Southern California's ecologic islands, some of which have been discussed elsewhere, include areas characterized by cypresses, Knobcone Pines, and vernal pools. Included among these regions is the pavement plain with its Great Basin relicts near Baldwin Lake in the San Bernardino Mountains.

The temporary ponds that occur in areas with poor drainage are known as vernal pools or hogwallows. These pools are found also in the Great Central Valley and Sierra Nevada foothills in grassland areas, where they may be associated with Blue Oak. In southern California they are located on Kearny and Otay mesas in San Diego County, and on the Santa Rosa Plateau in the Santa Ana Mountains, in association with Engelmann Oak.

These pools are formed by runoff during winter rains, but the water does not percolate into the clay soil. Rather, it remains standing to form pools of various sizes, which gradually disappear by evaporation in the spring. The word *vernal* means "spring." A distinguishing feature of these pools is that circles of annual wildflowers grow around the borders and follow the water's edge inward as the pools dry up. Because of the high rates of evaporation, soils are usually alkaline.

The wildflowers of these pools are often unique. A list of 101 species considered typical of vernal pools was compiled. Of these, more than 70% were native ephemerals, and over half were endemic to California. Two genera of rare grasses, *Orcuttia* and *Neostapfia*, are found only in association with vernal pools, and five species of *Orcuttia* are endemic to California. A meadow-foam, *Limnanthes gracilis*, is a small, delicate ephemeral that occurs in these moist areas of the Laguna Mountains. It also occurs about 800 miles (1280 km) to the north, in the Klamath Mountains. Such an incredible disjunct distribution is testimony to the relict nature of this species. The presence of summer rain in both areas may be related to such a pattern of distribution.

Many of the vernal pool species are rare or endangered. Habitat destruction due to development and grazing have caused the disappearance of many areas of vernal pools. It is to the credit of the Endangered Species Act that the remaining southern California vernal pools are protected from destruction.

A closed-cone pine associated with Upper Chaparral in southern California is the Knobcone Pine, *Pinus attenuata* (fig. 8.55). Its distribution here is extremely localized; it occurs naturally in only two areas. The larger area ranges over about 1000 acres (400 ha) at about 3500 feet (1000 m) elevation in the area around City Creek, on the south side of the San Bernardino Mountains. The other is at about the same elevation in the region of Pleasants Peak, in the Santa Ana Mountains. A third, southern stand is found near Ensenada, in Baja California. At the other localities where it occurs, it has been introduced by the U.S. Forest Service or county road crews.

Knobcone Pine is found at isolated localities throughout the state, particularly in association with serpentine soils in the Coast Ranges, Klamath Mountains, and northwestern Sierra Nevada. In the Santa Ana Mountains it is found on a very peculiar soil associated with hydrothermally altered volcanic material, which is likely serpentine. These are depauperate soils. They are fine-grained, of acidic pH (4.5–5.3), and of peculiar chemical composition. Water is not readily available to roots in these soils because the fine particles tend to retain moisture by adsorption. These trees maintain their dominance on these sites by surviving on fog drip, which has been measured at up to 4 inches (102 mm) per month during spring.

These are small three-needle pines, but they are not closely related to the yellow pine group. They are more closely allied with Lodgepole Pines. The cones are crescent-shaped, and they adhere to the main branches of the tree. They remain on the tree in a closed condition for many years. When the cones are heated, as by a fire, they open and shed their seeds. With precipitation and abundant light, the seeds become established, and new trees grow on the burned site. Where the trees have been introduced, there is no apparent germination of seeds after a fire. It appears that competition from rapidly growing species on sites with better soil precludes the establishment of Knobcone Pines where they are not native. They remain localized by

FIGURE 8.55   Knobcone Pine, *Pinus attenuata*. *A*. Cones before a fire.

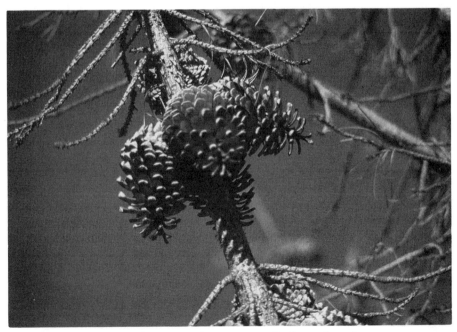

FIGURE 8.55 (*continued*)   Knobcone Pine, *Pinus attenuata*. *B*. Cones after a fire.

virtue of their association with specialized ecological conditions, namely, poor soil, fog, and fire.

One of the most interesting ecologic islands occurs on coastal sandstone bluffs near Del Mar in San Diego County. Here is where Torrey Pines, *Pinus torreyana* (fig. 8.56), grow. It has been estimated that the total population here consists of less than 7000 trees. At Santa Rosa Island about 175 miles (250 km) to the northwest, also on sandstone, is a second population of Torrey Pines, numbering about 2000 trees. This total, less than 9000 trees, makes this the rarest species of pine in the world. These trees are relicts from a former time when conditions were more moist. They survive today in a region where fog drip provides the moisture and where sandstone soils restrict competition from other species.

Torrey Pine is related to Digger Pine and Coulter Pine. These are the pines with large cones, although Torrey Pines have the smallest cones of the three. These are fire-adapted pines in the sense that the cones open only partially, releasing the seeds over a period of several years. Torrey Pines resemble Digger Pines with their candelabralike appearance, having many heavy branches in the crown. They resemble Coulter Pines by having very long, thick needles. Unlike the other two species, which have needles in clusters of three, Torrey Pines have needles in clusters of five. The needles are grayish in color, similar to those of Digger Pine. The pines on Santa Rosa Island are quite blue-gray in color.

The mechanism by which a species could become distributed in such an odd manner has been the subject of much debate. It is possible that the former distribution was fairly continuous, and that the remaining trees are relicts of that time. The distance between the Channel Islands and the mainland during the Pleistocene, when sea level was at its lowest, was about 4.5 miles (7 km). That distance would not be a significant barrier to dispersal, because cones can float that far, and birds such as Western Scrub Jays are noted for their ability to carry seeds or acorns in their throats. On the other hand, right-lateral movement of fault systems has carried land segments hundreds of miles northward, including the land on which both populations of Torrey Pines now grow. There are at least two faults lying between the populations as they occur today, and it is entirely possible that ancestors of the present Santa Rosa Island population originated south of the present population near Del Mar. If large cone size is an adaptation associated with drought conditions, it follows that the Torrey Pine would have smaller cones than its relatives, because of its more southerly and coastal origin. The fact that the island population has larger cones than those on the mainland also fits this hypothesis.

Two other conifers occur as ecologic-island populations within Lower Chaparral. These are the local cypresses. The relict nature of cypresses and their restricted distribution is discussed in chapter 7. A cypress resembles a juniper by its arrangement of scale-like leaves on the stem, and also by its fleshy cones. Cypress cones, which resemble small soccer balls, are larger than those of junipers, in some cases almost as large as a golf ball. They remain on a tree in closed conditions for up to 20 years, and heat from a fire causes them to open. After a fire, in a manner similar to Knobcone

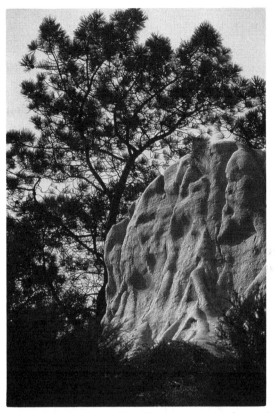

FIGURE 8.56   Torrey Pine, *Pinus torreyana*, and coastal sandstone.

Pines, they drop there seeds on bare mineral soil. The seeds germinate after the first rains.

The Tecate Cypress, *Cupressus forbesii,* is a variety of a Baja California species. In California the largest stands are near the Mexican border in the Peninsular Ranges. They occur there on the Otay, Tecate, and Guatay mountains on north-facing slopes, on alkaline clay soils derived from gabbro, a dark-colored plutonic rock rich in iron and magnesium. About 90 miles (144 km) to the north, on the northern end of the Santa Ana Mountains, a fourth stand of Tecate Cypress occurs. Just south of where Highway 91 passes through Santa Ana Canyon, on the northern slopes of Sierra Peak, Tecate Cypress grows in Coal, Gypsum, and Fremont canyons. It is here that the Paleocene (60 million-year-old) Silverado Formation occurs. This formation consists of sandstone soils formed in a shallow lagoon. The trees here are the oldest and largest of the Tecate Cypresses. Specimens over 200 years of age have been recorded. The largest, on the floor of Coal Canyon, has a trunk circumference of 8 feet (2.8 m) and a height of 35 feet (11 m).

Cones of Tecate Cypress from the La Brea Tar Pits, as well as fossils from the local deserts, attest to a former widespread distribution. They exist today by default on clay or sandy soils where they lack competition. Associated species in the northern groves are mostly disturbed-area plants, although a depauperate mix of species from Lower and Upper Chaparral occurs in the area as well. In the northern groves there are two associated species considered to be endangered. These are herbaceous species known as Heart-leaved Pitcher Sage, *Lepechinia cardiophylla*, and Braunton's Milkvetch, *Astragalus brauntonii*. In the southern groves, the largest Tecate Cypress stand is on Otay Mountain. Here are six rare or endangered species, including three specialized shrubs; Mexican Flannel Bush, *Fremontodendron mexicanum*; Otay Manzanita, *Arctostaphylos otayensis*; and Otay Ceanothus, *Ceanothus otayensis*.

Groves of Tecate Cypress are becoming smaller. They require fire to reproduce, but they take about 35 to 40 years to become mature. If fire occurs more frequently than that, or if the fire is too hot, the trees are burned before they can produce cones. Another problem can occur if a fire is followed by drought. Without the follow-up of precipitation, the seeds may die or be eaten before they can germinate. Historically, a summer storm accompanied by lightning was probably the combination of fire and precipitation that enhanced the propagation of Tecate Cypress.

Fire records and aerial photographs have revealed that the fire frequency on Tecate Peak in northern Baja California has increased to a 15–20-year interval. Similar data have been obtained for Otay Mountain in San Diego County. Apparently, these fires are associated with activities of humans. Continued expansion of settlements into back-country areas will no doubt threaten the continued existence of the Tecate Cypress.

The Cuyamaca Cypress, *Cupressus arizonica arizonica* (= *C. stephensonii*) (fig. 8.57), occurs on gabbro soils on the Southwestern side of Cuyamaca Peak in the Laguna Mountains. This localized form of the Arizona Cypress is the rarest cypress in California. It is known only from six stands covering a total area of only 43.5 acres (17.6 ha). Illustrating how reducing the interval between fires can take a toll, fires in 1950 and 1970 extirpated one stand and reduced another by 75%. At present, the existing trees appear healthy and vigorous. It is hoped that with proper fire management on the part of federal and state agencies, the Cuyamaca Cypress will continue to thrive in this restricted area.

The Peninsular Ranges in San Diego County also contain other gabbro endemics. Certain rare plants, such as Dehesa Beargrass, *Nolina interrata*, are restricted to these soils. The state's largest stand of this yucca-like succulent is found on McGinty Mountain, near Jamul, 20 miles (32 km) east of San Diego. This region, owned by the Nature Conservancy, contains a total of seven rare and endangered plant species endemic to gabbro-derived soils.

Perhaps the most spectacular ecologic island in southern California occurs at 6720 feet (2050 m) in the San Bernardino Mountains, east of Big Bear Lake. The area is known as the Baldwin Lake pebble plains. In the area, the California Native Plant Society has identified 14 rare or endangered species, 11 of which are endemic. This is the largest concentration of endemics in the state. Clay soils of the pebble plains

FIGURE 8.57   Cuyamaca Cypress. *Cupressus arizonica arizonica*, California's rarest cypress.

were left behind by a Pleistocene lake. Freezing conditions in winter cause round quartzite pebbles to become pushed to the surface; hence there is a layer of orange pebbles on the clay. This is an area where many relicts of the ice ages, most of them associated with the Great Basin, still exist. It is a habitat that superficially resembles an Alpine Fellfield. Most of the plants are low-growing, and some of them are similar to cushion plants. Apparently the area escaped glaciation, and somehow the relicts were preserved under these extremely harsh conditions.

Plants that are endemic to limestone also occur in the San Bernardino Mountains, associated with several east–west-trending ridges north of Big Bear. Four of these plants are listed in the California Native Plant Society's *Inventory of Rare and Endangered Vascular Plants of California*. The most limited in distribution is San Bernardino Bladderpod, *Lesquerella kingii bernardina*. It occurs only in Big Bear Valley and Van Dusen Canyon, near Holcomb Valley. Silvery-white Milk-vetch, *Astragalus albens*, and Parish's Daisy, *Erigeron parishii*, are confined to lower slopes and canyons near Cushenbury Springs, just above the desert floor. Perhaps the most beautiful is Cushenbury Buckwheat, *Eriogonum ovalifolium*. This plant occurs as white-leaved mats up to several feet in diameter, growing on stark white rocks. Limestone mining in the area may threaten these species in the future.

AIR POLLUTION

Air pollution in southern California is having an influence on local plants and animals as well as human health. Haze probably has always been a feature of the Los Angeles

FIGURE 8.58   Inversion layer over the Los Angeles Basin as seen from the San Bernardino Mountains.

Basin, because it is associated with the persistent temperature inversion layer. Cool marine air flows into the basin from the west, and cool air flows down from the mountains at night. This cool air is trapped by the surrounding mountains. Although the depth of this cool "puddle" of air varies from day to day, it is always there except during periods of Santa Ana winds or rain. Condensation of water vapor in the air produces a ground-hugging haze or, when the condition is more extreme, fog. Heated exhaust from vehicles and factories rises in the cool air but is unable to rise beyond the warmer air above, because that is where the density of the air and exhaust gases become similar. On most days, a view over the Los Angeles Basin from an airplane or the local mountains reveals a flat-topped mass of semi-opaque air trapped under the inversion layer (fig. 8.58). As sunlight shines on this air mass, chemicals in the exhaust are transformed into harmful pollutants.

Back in 1951, a Cal Tech scientist named A. J. Haagen-Smit described this phenomenon as photochemical smog. He explained that hydrocarbons (HC) and oxides of nitrogen (NO_x) react in the presence of sunlight to form ozone (O_3). He also explained that the reaction is circular, feeding upon its own by-products to produce more and more ozone, as long as the sun continues to shine (fig. 8.59). Oxides of nitrogen make the air yellow, ozone irritates the lungs, and one of the other by-products, peroxyacetyl nitrate (PAN), irritates the eyes. Furthermore, one of the oxides of nitrogen (NO_2) reacts with water (H_2O) in the air to form nitric acid (H_2NO_3), which falls back on the local mountains as acid rain or remains in the basin as acid fog. All of

PHOTOCHEMICAL SMOG — A VICIOUS CIRCLE

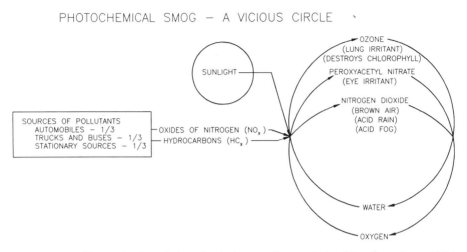

FIGURE 8.59   The production of photochemical smog. Factors depicted in this cycle are highly simplified, but pollutants increase in concentration in the presence of sunlight.

this is trapped under the inversion layer, making Los Angeles one of the smoggiest places in the world.

On December 6, 1982, a Cal Tech scientist monitoring acid fog in the Los Angeles Basin recorded a pH of 1.7 in Corona Del Mar, one of the most acidic fogs ever measured in the world. Apparently, in the Los Angeles Basin, measurements of 2.0 to 3.0 are routine. The well-known acid rains of the northeastern United States typically measure around 4.0. The threat of a possible killer fog similar to that which took about 4000 lives in London in 1952 is not out of the question for Los Angeles. It would take a stagnation of the inversion layer for several days, allowing the pollutants to accumulate without dissipating.

The ingredients in smog are produced by combustion in mobile sources, such as automobiles and trucks, as well as stationary sources, such as power plants and refineries. The automobile was deemed the most important source, so autos were fitted with positive crankcase ventilation (PCV) devices to recycle hydrocarbons, and catalytic converters were installed to intercept oxides of nitrogen. To reduce other sources of hydrocarbons, gasoline pumps were fitted with vapor recovery nozzles, and automobile gas tanks were fitted with tight caps.

Meanwhile, for economic reasons, refineries, power plants, and trucks remained virtually exempt. Environmentalists pointed out these discrepancies with dismay. Why, simply for economic reasons, should any source be exempt? Air pollution is a matter of health, not economics. A particular exemption that seemed to defy logic was diesel trucks, which produce proportionately more NO_x than gasoline engines. In fact, all trucks — gasoline or diesel — remained exempt. The South Coast Air Quality Management District reported that large trucks make up only 4% of all registered vehicles in the Los Angeles Basin, but they produce 17% of the air pollution. As of 1991, Los Angeles was still ranked the smoggiest city in the United States. Of

40 metropolitan areas, Los Angeles ranked last. The city had a total of 242 days of unhealthy air in 1984.

Air pollution is not healthy for humans. A link between ozone and respiratory problems such as asthma and emphysema is well documented. Evidence is also accumulating that links air pollution to lung cancer, although the primary cause of lung cancer is cigarette smoking.

The influence of air pollution on agricultural crops has also been documented. During spring and summer, the airflow in the basin is from west to east. Deserts are warmer than the basin, so smoggy air is carried up the canyons into the mountains every afternoon, bathing the Yellow Pine Forest and Chaparral in pollutants. Air flowing through San Gorgonio Pass carries smog on a daily basis to the "low desert," where vegetation in the vicinity of Palm Springs is subjected to the pollutants. This has led to concern over the potential for smog to kill native vegetation, including desert plants.

The effect is not limited to the "low desert." It has been noted in Joshua Tree National Monument that Squaw Bush, *Rhus trilobata*, develops measle-like splotches in the presence of ozone. This plant is now being used as an indicator of air pollution in desert areas.

The effect of smog on native vegetation seems to be of little significance to most public officials, although its influence is profound. In the 1950s people began to notice that Ponderosa and Jeffrey pines in the San Bernardino Mountains were dying. Needles were turning yellow and prematurely falling off trees. Whereas needles previously remained on trees up to five years, they were lasting only two to three years. The condition appeared to worsen during periods of drought. These weakened trees became susceptible to bark beetles, and they finally died. Foresters began to refer to the condition as "Crestline crud," because it was in Crestline, on the ridge above San Bernardino, that the condition seemed worse. Because the condition was characterized by a loss of chlorophyll, it became known technically as chlorotic decline. It was discovered that ozone was the culprit, and that Ponderosa Pine, Jeffrey Pine, and White Fir were the most seriously affected. It also has been noted that chlorotic decline and depressed acorn production in California Black Oak are consequences of ozone in the air. Some species, such as Incense Cedar, seemed not to be affected. The die-off of Coulter Pine mentioned earlier also may be a part of this pattern.

The long-term effects of smog on native vegetation are unknown, but some clues are emerging. Investigations of Coastal Sage Scrub indicate that ozone causes a reduction in total cover and species richness. Furthermore, old records indicate that the Lace Lichen, *Ramalina menziesii* (fig. 7.7), which is so common in the Coast Ranges, formerly was common in the Santa Monica Mountains, where it no longer occurs. When samples of this lichen were transplanted to the Santa Monica Mountains, they turned yellow and died within three months. The cause turned out to be air pollution.

Recent studies in chaparral and desert areas have uncovered other problems. In addition to the influence of ozone, increased amounts of nitrate chemicals seem to accumulate during summer on the leaves of native plants. The source is dry fallout from smoggy air. When the rains come, the nitrates are washed into streams and rivers, raising the nitrate levels above water quality standards. Furthermore, as described earlier there seems to be some correlation of pollution with local die-off of *Ceanothus* plants in chaparral areas. Foresters fear that the accumulation of dead wood poses a fire hazard. On the other hand, some biologists view the die-off as a natural consequence of fire suppression, because various species of *Ceanothus* are considered short-lived, successional forms. The biologists contend that if natural fires were allowed to create a vegetational mosaic, there would not be large stands with single-species composition, and the die-off would not be noticeable.

9

California's Deserts

California has three main desert regions, all of which lie to the interior of major mountain ranges. Thus California's deserts are all the product of rain-shadow effect. From north to south, the three regions are: the Great Basin, east of the Cascades and the Sierra Nevada (pl. 8D); the Mojave, to the interior of the Transverse Ranges; and the Colorado Desert (fig. 9.1), lying east of the Peninsular Ranges. A fourth arid region, the southern San Joaquin Valley, lies in the rain shadow of the southern Coast Ranges. The San Joaquin Valley will be discussed in more detail in the next chapter, on the Great Central Valley, although in many respects it qualifies as one of California's deserts.

CLIMATE

Traditionally, a region that receives less than 10 inches (25 cm) of precipitation per year is classified as a desert. In California, many desert regions receive far less than that. Bagdad, formerly a small community in the Mojave Desert on old Highway 66, was reported to be the driest place in the United States. Its annual precipitation averaged 2.2 inches (5 cm). Its truly remarkable record, however, was that from October 3, 1912, until November 8, 1914—a total of 767 days—Bagdad received absolutely no precipitation. Based on average yearly precipitation, Death Valley, at 1.5 inches (4 cm) per year, officially is the driest place in the state.

Without question, California's deserts are dry, but they vary considerably in temperature extremes and the timing of precipitation (table 9.1). For comparison, Bishop, in the Great Basin, averages 5.6 inches (14 cm) of annual precipitation, much of which is snow; Barstow, in the Mojave, averages 4.0 inches (10 cm), mostly winter rain; Imperial, in the Colorado Desert, averages 3.6 inches (9 cm), including winter and summer rain; and Bakersfield, in the Great Central Valley, averages 6.0 inches (15 cm) of winter rain per year.

The characteristics of a desert environment are:

1. Low, unevenly distributed precipitation, less than 10 inches (25 cm) per year
2. Temperature extremes
3. Windy (increased evaporation rates)
4. High light intensity
5. Nutrient-poor, alkaline soil
6. Low rates of primary production

Dryness influences the other characteristics associated with deserts. Dry air changes temperature rapidly, because there is little water vapor to moderate the change. A range of 50°F (28°C) between nighttime lows and daytime highs is commonplace.

FIGURE 9.1   Colorado Desert, Anza-Borrego Desert State Park. Cactus scrub community in foreground.

At the community of Imperial, in the Colorado Desert, the range of temperature from the record low to the record high is a full 130°F (54°C).

Air rises when it is warmed, and it sinks when it is cooled. Uneven heating coupled with rapid temperature change causes desert air to move rapidly from place to place. Hence deserts are windy. Wind accelerates evaporation, which adds another burden to the drought stress experienced by plants and animals.

Dry air is very clear. About 90% of available sunlight reaches the ground on a typical desert day, as compared with about 40% in a typical humid climate. This intense sunlight includes ultraviolet radiation that is capable of causing severe tissue damage to plants and animals. It also means that temperatures are very high during the long summer days, when the sun is high in the sky. The hottest temperature ever recorded in the Western Hemisphere was in the California desert. On July 10, 1913, at Furnace Creek, in Death Valley, the official temperature reached 134.6°F (57°C). This temperature is exceeded only by a world record at El Azizia, Libya, in 1922. There the temperature reached 136.4°F (58°C). Some authorities question the Libyan record because no other stations in the area reported such high temperatures on that date. In contrast, many stations in the Death Valley area on that memorable day recorded high temperatures. In addition, for nine consecutive days that same July, the high temperature was at least 125°F (52°C). The night before the record, the low temperature was 93°F (34°C).

Desert soil is also a product of the dry climate. Low precipitation coupled with a high evaporation rate causes the soil to be alkaline. Alkaline soils (aridosols) pose

TABLE 9.1 A Comparison of California Deserts

Desert	Features	Communities
Great Basin ("Cold Desert")	Winter precipitation, often snow Spring growing season	Blackbrush Scrub Sagebrush Scrub Shadscale Scrub Alkali Sink
Mojave ("High Desert")	Winter precipitation, some snow Winter, spring growing season	Joshua Tree Woodland Creosote Bush Scrub Shadscale Scrub Alkali Sink
Colorado ("Low Desert")	Winter, summer precipitation Winter, summer growing season	Cactus Scrub Creosote Bush Scrub Saltbush Scrub Alkali Sink Desert Wash Palm Oasis

an osmotic stress for desert plants, which are already drought-stressed. This problem is compounded by the fact that most desert soil is coarse. The soils tend to remain immature and are low in organic material. Coarse soil allows water to percolate rapidly. Therefore, after it rains, the soil remains wet for a comparatively short period of time.

Lack of water limits primary productivity. Photosynthesis, which requires water, is limited in desert areas; therefore food is scarce. The entire desert ecosystem must adjust to this limitation. The total amount of biomass that can be supported in a desert ecosystem is smaller than for any other terrestrial ecosystem.

THE GREAT BASIN DESERT

The Great Basin of California includes two geomorphic provinces, the Modoc Plateau and the Basin-Range Province. The Modoc Plateau (fig. 9.2, pl. 8C) is a volcanic tableland that lies in the lee of the Cascades in northeastern California. It is the southernmost extension of a large volcanic plateau known as the Columbia Plateau, which covers eastern Oregon, eastern Washington, southern Idaho, northwestern Nevada, and northeastern California. The Modoc Plateau has been converted extensively to agriculture and pasture. Large lakes in the area, such as Goose Lake and Eagle Lake, provide abundant water, which is distributed through irrigation systems. Except for its stark, flat appearance, it probably bears little resemblance to its condition before the advent of large-scale agriculture.

Most of the Great Basin is characterized by interior drainage. This is not so for the Modoc Plateau. If Goose Lake had no outlet, it would be a region of interior drainage. However, Goose Lake and the surrounding environs drain into the Pit River, which

FIGURE 9.2   Great Basin Desert, Modoc Plateau and Cascade Range.

flows southwestward toward the Great Central Valley. Formerly, water from the Pit River joined the Sacramento near Redding. Now it is impounded by Shasta Dam, forming one of many reservoirs that are part of the huge state water project, which ultimately carries water nearly 600 miles (960 km) to southern California.

Not all of the Great Basin is desert. There are numerous ranges — ecologic islands — that rise above the Great Basin Desert. East of the Modoc Plateau, in the very northeastern corner of the state, is an uplifted fault block known as the Warner Mountains (pl. 8C). This is the westernmost of a long series of alternating mountains and valleys making up the Basin-Range Province. The Warner Mountains are composed mostly of volcanic rocks that have been uplifted to 9722 feet (3015 m) at Eagle Peak. Among these volcanic rocks is an abundance of obsidian. The obsidian here includes the usual black variety, but much of it is a unique brown form known as mahogany obsidian. In this form, the iron is in its oxidized state. This high-quality obsidian was apparently very important to Indians as a material for making tools. Presumably from the Warner Mountains, it is found in chipping sites all over the southwest, including localities in southern California. The interesting forest of this area is discussed in chapter 5.

Directly east of the Sierra Nevada, the Basin-Range Province is represented in California by a series of north–south-trending mountains and valleys. South of Lake Tahoe, the eastern face of the Sierra is bordered by three basins. The northernmost of these is the valley drained by the Walker River in the vicinity of Bridgeport. The east and west forks of the Walker River drain northward into Nevada to flow into Walker Lake, another of the large lakes or closed basins of interior drainage, From Conway Summit south to Sherwin Summit is the Mono Basin–Long Valley Caldera, which is discussed in chapter 4 in the section on volcanic rocks of the Mammoth area. South of Sherwin Summit near Tom's Place, drainage is toward the Owens River, which flows southward toward Owens Lake and the Mojave Desert.

During the Pleistocene, the Ice Age, there were periods of heavy rainfall in the deserts. The Owens River flowed southward beyond Owens Lake to terminate in China Lake, near the present town of Ridgecrest. During periods of heavy flow, water continued to flow eastward into Searles Lake, near the present town of Trona. The large tufa towers south of Trona were formed underwater (pl. 11D). Testimony to the amount of water that formerly flowed in the Owens River is the deep gorge cut into the basaltic lava flows near the present town of Little Lake. A short distance to the east of Highway 395 is an old Indian chipping site on the edge of what must have been a spectacular waterfall. The area is known as Fossil Falls and is presently administered by the Bureau of Land Management.

The climate of the Great Basin Desert is cooler than that of the more southerly deserts. Almost all of the precipitation occurs during winter, much of it in the form of snow. The dominant vegetation reflects the cooler climate. Most growth is delayed until spring, whereas in the more southerly deserts the major period of growth is during the winter.

With the exception of the Modoc Plateau, drainage is internal, usually terminating at a salt lake. If precipitation and/or runoff is too slight, the lake may be dry most of the year. The dry lake bed may be composed of clay, or if many years of evaporation have taken place, it may be covered with salt (evaporites). Vegetation in these basins reflects the alkalinity and particle size of the soil. Moving from the edge to the center of a basin, soil becomes progressively finer in texture and more alkaline. The effect of this soil change is that different types of vegetation grow in concentric bands around a lake bed.

The distribution of vegetation in the northern parts of the Owens Valley is typical of the Great Basin Desert in California (pl. 8D). At the upper fringe of the desert in rocky soil, where the desert environment grades into the mountain environment, the dominant plant may be the Single-needle Pinyon Pine or the Western Juniper. At the eastern face of the Sierra Nevada, the pinyon pine belt is visible as the first band of dark-colored vegetation (fig. 4.5). Below this on gravelly slopes is a community called Blackbrush Scrub, so named because on the dominant plant, Blackbrush, *Coleogyne ramosissima,* the outermost blackish stems seldom bear leaves. Along Highway 395 from Bishop to Tom's Place, there is an extensive belt of Blackbrush. Below this, and south of Bishop, is where Great Basin Sagebrush, *Artemisia tridentata,* dominates (pl. 8D). The most common plant of the Great Basin Desert, Great Basin Sagebrush is typical of well-drained sandy soil. Many acres of the Great Basin are characterized by this blue-gray shrub. In fact, one biologist calculated that the standing biomass of Great Basin Sagebrush actually exceeds that of Coast Redwoods. Where soil becomes more alkaline, in low places and south of Lone Pine, this shrub is replaced by Shadscale, *Atriplex confertifolia,* a member of the saltbush family (Chenopodiaceae). Saltbush is also grayish, but a darker gray. The transition from Great Basin Sagebrush to Shadscale is usually marked by a distinct color change in the vegetation. Below the Shadscale zone, soil becomes very alkaline. If the soil remains wet, a community of shrubs with succulent leaves provides the last band of vegetation before water or bare clay dominates. This band is obvious along the shores of Owens Lake.

MOJAVE DESERT

The Mojave Desert is south of the Great Basin. In the Owens Valley the transition becomes apparent south of Olancha, where the Joshua Tree, *Yucca brevifolia,* and dark green Creosote Bush, *Larrea tridentata,* (pl. 9B) become the dominant vegetation, although these species also occur farther north, in the valleys of the Basin-Range Province. From a geological perspective, the Mojave is a large wedge-shaped basin lying between the Garlock fault on the north and the San Andreas fault on the south (fig. 9.3). To the southwest the Mojave Desert is bounded by the Transverse Ranges. To the northwest it is bounded by the Tehachapi Mountains and the southern Sierra Nevada. To the east it barely crosses the Colorado River to enter northwestern Arizona and southern Nevada near Las Vegas.

The Mojave Desert is the "High Desert" of the weather report, even though it includes Death Valley, with the lowest point in the United States (pl. 9C). Also included within the Mojave are Antelope Valley, Apple Valley, and Yucca Valley, all of which lie at about 3500 feet (1100 m) elevation. These other valleys all interconnect to form one large drainage basin. The Mojave is a large alluvial-filled basin into which many isolated mountain ranges of diverse geologic nature are projected.

The Mojave is a hot desert. Precipitation occurs mostly in the winter, but there are occasional summer thunderstorms. At higher elevations snow is common. Where snow falls in the winter, and where soil is coarse and nonalkaline, vegetation is unlike that of the other desert regions. Here the dominant life-forms are the leaf-succulent yuccas, the most conspicuous of which is the Joshua Tree. The outline of Joshua Tree distribution is effectively an outline of the Mojave Desert. Above the Joshua Trees is the belt of pinyon pines on rocky soils and ridges. Below the Joshua Trees, similar to the Great Basin, there may be a region dominated by Blackbrush. Below that is the vast expanse of sandy soil occupied by Creosote Bush, the dominant shrub of America's hot deserts and the most abundant shrub in California. Creosote Bush is the dark green resinous shrub with wandlike stems that grows with orchardlike regularity on flat slopes of the desert (pl. 9B). Creosote Bush fades out at the clay soils of dry lakes. Where soil becomes too alkaline, Creosote Bush is replaced by Shadscale. Cacti are more abundant in the Mojave than they are in the Great Basin, but they are mostly

FIGURE 9.3 Southern Great Basin, Mojave, and Colorado deserts. The northern boundary of the Mojave Desert is represented by the distribution of Joshua Trees and Creosote Bush. Note that it is north of the Garlock fault, the accepted boundary of the geologic Mojave Desert Province.

found on rocky slopes. Along washes there may be thickets of trees, primarily Desert Willows, *Chilopsis linearis,* or Honey Mesquite, *Prosopis glandulosa,* both of which drop their leaves in the winter.

COLORADO DESERT

California's "Low Desert" is the Colorado Desert. It is the California portion of a much larger region known as the Sonoran Desert. This southwestern desert region encircles the Gulf of California and includes northwestern Mexico, southwestern Arizona, southeastern California, and Baja California. Much of the Californian portion lies in the Salton Trough, an elongate valley separated from the Gulf of California by the delta of the Colorado River. This is a large, closed basin with the Salton Sea at its lowest point. East of the Salton Trough are ranges of mountains uplifted along the San Andreas fault, the Orocopia and Chocolate mountains. From these mountains eastward the terrain drops off gradually, interrupted by a few mountain ranges, such as the Chuckwalla Mountains south of Desert Center. The Colorado Desert ends at the Colorado River on the east. Much of the boundary between the Mojave and Colorado deserts is the ridge formed by the Little San Bernardino Mountains, the Pinto Mountains, and the Eagle Mountains. Joshua Tree National Monument lies astride this boundary and includes a mixture of vegetation from both deserts. East of the Eagle Mountains the boundary curves northeastward toward Needles so as to include the Turtle Mountains, the Whipple Mountains, and the Chemehuevi Mountains in the Colorado Desert.

The Colorado Desert experiences more summer precipitation than the northern deserts. Although yearly precipitation remains low, a significant portion of it falls in August and September, usually as thunderstorms. Data collected at the headquarters for Anza-Borrego Desert State Park indicate a yearly average of 6.9 inches (16.9 cm). Most precipitation falls from December to March, with January the only month averaging more than 1 inch (25 mm). On the average, thunderstorms in August and September add another inch (25 mm) to the yearly total. These thunderstorms may be severe. A total of 3 to 5 inches (8–14 cm) of rain may fall in a few hours, washing out roads, scouring washes, and uprooting trees. These storms are often local in distribution; a few miles away there may be little or no precipitation.

Sandy flats and slopes in the Colorado Desert are very similar to those of the Mojave Desert. Creosote Bush dominates over most of the area with saltbushes occurring where the soil becomes more alkaline. On upper rocky slopes, particularly on the eastern side of the Peninsular Ranges, there is a community of succulent and drought-deciduous plants known as Cactus Scrub (pl. 9A, fig. 9.1). There are many cacti in the Sonoran Desert, but the Colorado Desert differs from other subdivisions of the Sonoran by having mostly small cacti. Also in this region is a leaf-succulent plant known as Desert Agave or century plant, *Agave deserti.* These agaves are noted for their tall stalks topped with large yellow flowers. Among the drought-deciduous plants, the most distinctive is Ocotillo, *Fouquieria splendens.* Ocotillo plants are composed of many tall whiplike stems covered with long spines. In the spring each stem terminates

FIGURE 9.4   Some members of the legume family (Fabaceae) characteristic of Desert Wash. A. Blue Palo Verde, *Cercidium floridum,* a drought-deciduous tree. B. Ironwood, *Olneya tesota,* an evergreen tree. C. Honey Mesquite, *Prosopis glandulosa,* a winter-deciduous tree. D. Catclaw Acacia, *Acacia greggii,* a winter-deciduous shrub. (Drawings by Karlin Grunau Marsh from C. B. Clarke. *Edible and Useful Plants of California.* Berkeley: University of California Press, 1977.)

in a cluster of bright red, tubular flowers. The distribution of Ocotillo, effectively outlining the Sonoran Desert, extends northward nearly to Needles.

Another distinctive feature of the Sonoran Desert is the presence of many species of trees, most of them in the pea family (Fabaceae) (fig. 9.4). Throughout most of the Sonoran Desert, these trees are distributed widely among Ocotillos and large cacti. In the Colorado Desert, where it is drier, these trees are confined to washes. Blue Palo Verde (*Cercidium floridum*), Ironwood (*Olneya tesota*), mesquites (*Prosopis* sp.), and Smoke Trees (*Psorothamnus spinosa*) occur along dry water courses. Smoke Trees are nearly always leafless, and to some they resemble puffs of smoke. Their twisted, blue-gray image has become a symbol of the Colorado Desert, which is roughly outlined by the distribution of this species.

The California Fan Palm, *Washingtonia filifera* (pl. 8B), is another distinctive species of the Colorado Desert, occurring in seeps and oases. From the air, groves of California Fan Palms can be seen to outline the trace of the San Andreas fault. It is along faults such as this that water seeps to the surface to form springs. Glancing eastward from Interstate 10, motorists can see lines of palm trees along the San Andreas fault near the community of Thousand Palms.

The Peninsular Ranges, along the western edge of the Colorado Desert, show distinct banding of desert communities. Above the Cactus Scrub community there is a zone of shrubs known as Desert Chaparral, a diverse community discussed in chapter 8. Above the scrub community is the zone of pinyon pines, marking the transition to the mountain communities.

DESERT GEOLOGY

The lack of water in the desert has preserved ancient landscapes. Old rock materials that have washed away in other parts of California are still present in desert mountain ranges. In fact, geologists have deciphered the ancient history of western North America by examining rocks that are now exposed in desert areas (fig. 3.3).

Metamorphic rocks older than a billion years are found at scattered localities in the Mojave Desert. Such rock formations, including gneiss and marble, are found in the Ord and Old Woman mountains. The Pinto Gneiss is found in Joshua Tree National Monument, and at the southern end of the Marble Mountains there are old granites and schists.

From about a billion years ago to 600 million years ago, during the Proterozoic, a period of erosion stripped away many thousands of feet of rock throughout most of the southwest. This interval of erosion produced an unconformity in which 570 to 700 million-year-old (Cambrian and Ediacarian) rocks are now found lying on billion-year-old metamorphic rocks: nearly a half-billion years of rock is missing! One of the few remaining records for that period of time is approximately 10,000 feet (3000 m) of sedimentary rock exposed in the Nopah Mountains of eastern California. Here there are sandstones, shales, and limestones that fill the gap.

The Paleozoic Era, from about 600 million to 245 million years ago, is represented by shales, sandstones, and limestones that are exposed throughout the deserts, but particularly in the Basin-Range Province, where uplift of mountains along dip-slip faults has exposed them (fig. 9.5). These sedimentary rocks represent the interval of time when the western border of North America was a continental shelf covered by seawater. It was the trailing edge as the continent moved eastward toward its collision with Europe. Among the oldest rocks in this sequence are shales that contain trilobites (fig. 9.6), extinct marine crustacea that crept about like sowbugs on the ocean floor beyond the surf zone. Trilobites are found in the Marble Mountains, the Nopah Mountains, and in Saline Valley. Also in the Marble Mountains are limestones with circular structures, known as oolites, representing the remains of blue-green algae that lived in a warm, shallow lagoon-type environment.

The Mesozoic Era, from about 245 million to 65 million years ago, was a time of subduction, when the continent was moving westward over the ocean crust. The magma formed during this interval is represented by plutonic rocks throughout the west. These are the granitics of the western mountain chain. They are also the granitics of the Little San Bernardino Mountains in Joshua Tree National Monument. The granitics of the Chuckwalla Mountains in the Colorado Desert (fig. 9.7) are also of this age, as are those in the Granite Mountains and New York Mountains of the eastern Mojave. In the Basin-Range Province these granitics are found in the Alabama Hills near Lone Pine. In the desert climate, they form large spherical boulders that have been weathered by oxidation to a brownish color. They are among the most popular landforms for rock climbers.

During the Cenozoic Era, from about 65 million years ago to the present, the desert area accumulated freshwater sediments and volcanic rocks indicating that the terrain was above sea level. The oldest part of this record represents another unconformity throughout most of the west. An erosional period stripped away most of the rocks from about 65 million to about 30 million years ago. One exception to this is found on the north side of the El Paso Mountains near Red Rock Canyon. This area, uplifted along the El Paso fault, a portion of the Garlock fault system, includes a series of stream and lake deposits dated at about 58 million years of age. This area includes fossils of early crocodiles and a primitive mammal. Fossils of this age are found nowhere else in California. The next oldest fossils, of primitive monkeys, rodents, and a rhinoceros, are found near San Diego in rocks about 40 million years of age. In rocks dated from about 30 million years ago to the present are found scattered fossil localities that tell us much about prehistoric California and the evolution of mammals. In northern Death Valley, in Titus Canyon, there are fossils over 30 million years old that give us a picture of the area as a wet, wooded countryside. Included here are fossils of dwarf horses and deer, as well as tapirs, rodents, rhinos, and dogs.

About 25 million years ago (Miocene) the picture of California as we see it today began to emerge. About this time the west coast changed to become a faulted, rifted borderland. Land west of the San Andreas fault began its inexorable slide toward the north. This caused a stretching of the desert areas, a type of motion known as extension, which is accompanied by faulting and down-dropping. Faulting in the Basin-Range Province began. The Garlock fault cut diagonally along the southern edge of the Basin-Range Province. Mountains uplifted, and valleys sank. In the Death

FIGURE 9.5   Old limestones of the Ibex Hills, Death Valley National Monument.

FIGURE 9.6   Trilobite fossil in Paleozoic shale, Saline Valley, Inyo County.

FIGURE 9.7   Mesozoic granite, Chuckawalla Mountains, Riverside County.

Valley area, for example, it has been determined that the Panamint Range moved northwestward about 50 miles (80 km) from a position adjacent to the present Nopah Range. This allowed the intervening terrain to sink, forming Death Valley, at 282 feet (87 m) below sea level.

Right-lateral faulting along the San Andreas fault pulled Baja California away from what is now mainland Mexico. This rifting opened up the Gulf of California, of which the Salton Trough of the Colorado Desert is merely the northern end. It too has subsided, lying at 274 feet (88 m) below sea level. The delta of the present Colorado River holds back seawater from the Gulf of California.

Northward (right-lateral) movement along the San Andreas fault may be the driving force causing left-lateral movement along the Garlock fault. The wedge-shaped basin between the San Andreas and Garlock faults, forming the main portion of the Mojave, appears to be rotating clockwise due to motion along these two faults. Studies of paleomagnetic data in Miocene volcanic rocks indicate that about 25° of rotation has occurred in the last 15 to 20 million years. The Garlock fault runs northeastward from near the town of Gorman to the southern end of Death Valley, a distance of some 150 miles (240 km). Its trace is marked by an uplifted scarp that is clearly

FIGURE 9.8   Badlands at Zabriskie Point, Death Valley National Monument.

visible along the Tehachapi Mountains, southern Sierra Nevada, Red Rock Canyon, and the El Paso Mountains. The south side of the fault has been displaced eastward about 30 miles (48 km).

The Miocene record in California's deserts is represented not only by uplift and subsidence, but also by intermittent flooding and volcanism. Tuff, ash, and other volcanics interbedded with lake bed sediments are widespread. Red Rock Canyon has the oldest beds, at about 58 million years (pl. 11C). As indicated previously, however, there is very little record for periods before about 30 million years ago. Shales, siltstones, sandstones, and conglomerates mixed with volcanics are scattered about the southwestern deserts. Along the west side of Death Valley there is a scenic motor route known as Artist's Drive. Here a person can see playa deposits and conglomerates hundreds of feet thick. The colorful display known as Artist's Pallette is a mixture of lake beds and volcanics. In the badlands area near Zabriskie Point (fig. 9.8) are thousands of feet of lake sediments spanning millions of years of deposition. These beds have been tilted vertically by uplift along the fault on the east side of Death Valley.

Eroded lake bed deposits are called badlands because they will support very little plant life. Water sinks slowly, and the soil clings tenaciously to the water, so that it is difficult for plants to grow there. In the badlands east of Death Valley there is a plant in the buckwheat family (Polygonaceae) that grows nowhere else. This rare wildflower, *Gilmania luteola,* has a low, matlike growth habit. Its tiny yellow flowers are only 2 to 3 millimeters in diameter. It has hard-shelled seeds that are able to withstand long periods of dormancy. In those rare years when several consecutive rains succeed in wetting the clay soil, *Gilmania* puts on its display of germination, growth, and flowering. Such years occurred in 1939, 1976, and 1980. Only then, in recent times, have these plants been abundant.

Over the last 11 million years or so, the Salton Trough has been flooded on numerous occasions by either seawater or freshwater. In the Fish Creek and Coyote Mountains areas of the Colorado Desert there is a series of marine deposits known as the Imperial Formation. Near the town of Ocotillo in Imperial County these deposits have been uplifted along the Elsinore fault. These rocks, deposited about 7 million years ago, contain fossils of about 200 marine invertebrate species, as well as rare remains of marine vertebrates such as bat rays, sharks, giant barracudas, sea cows, and whales. Of the molluscs represented, 16% of the species have modern counterparts in the Caribbean, indicating that the former Gulf of California had a direct connection to the Carribbean. That is, at the time, the two continents were not connected by land. The Central American terrain that now connects North America to South America was not present.

Anza-Borrego Desert State Park contains a badlands formation known as the Palm Spring Formation. This sequence of beds, 2 miles (3 km) thick, was deposited from 1.5 to 4 million years ago in a flood plain and coastal lagoon setting. One of the most complete records of Pliocene terrestrial vertebrates in the southwestern United States is found here. The vertebrate fossils from this formation include llamas, camels, horses, donkeys, zebras, mammoths, mastodons, and sloths, as well as their predators, including lions, sabertooth cats, and bears.

The Pleistocene (1–2 million years ago) was a period of inundation in the deserts. Whereas heavy snowfall formed glaciers in the mountains, the deserts experienced heavy rainfall. Similar to glacial intervals, there were intervals when desert basins were large lakes. For example, in Death Valley there was Lake Manly, the waterline for which indicates it was about 600 feet (190m) deep. East of Death Valley, near the small towns of Shoshone and Tecopa, is a region of clays and silts representing old Lake Tecopa. These beds are about 400 feet (120 m) thick. They are still horizontal in orientation and have not been deeply eroded, indicating their recent deposition. Of interest here is a layer of pumice 12 feet (4 m) thick. This material, derived from volcanic ash that settled in the lake, indicates that many volcanoes must have been active in the area during the Pleistocene.

Other than the Salton Sea, at 235 feet (76 m) below sea level, which is fed today by irrigation runoff and effluent from the Mexicali area, the last major freshwater invasion of the Salton Trough ended about 500 years ago with the drying of Lake Cahuilla, which apparently was fed by the Colorado River. A waterline from that lake, 200 feet (60 m) above the water level of the present Salton Sea, is conspicuous along the base of the Santa Rosa Mountains on the west side of the Coachella Valley (fig. 9.9). Fifteen rows of fish traps used by the Cahuilla Indians lie along former western shorelines. The distances between these rows suggest that they were probably constructed once a year as the lake was drying. During that time, the lake level dropped about 4 feet (1.5 m) a year. Presumably about 1500 A.D., the Colorado River turned southward to dump into

FIGURE 9.9   Lake Cahuilla waterline along the base of the Santa Rosa Mountains west of the Salton Sea.

the Gulf of California, and Lake Cahuilla lost its input of freshwater. The lake is presumed to have taken 55 to 60 years to dry completely.

Volcanism in desert areas is mostly of Miocene age or younger. In the Great Basin, this includes the Modoc Plateau. Miocene volcanics are also scattered throughout the Mojave and Colorado deserts. The brilliantly colored Calico Mountains near Barstow are a mixture of volcanics and sediments of Miocene age. Perhaps some of the most interesting volcanic scenery is in the eastern Mojave between the Providence Mountains and New York Mountains. Here there are buff-colored rhyolitic flows alternating with ash deposits, forming spectacular steep-sided, flat-topped mesas that look like layer cakes. The hard rhyolite forms a protective cap over the softer ash deposits. A popular campsite in the Mid Hills area is known as Hole-in-the-Wall (fig. 9.10), in reference to many large cavities formed as gas pockets during the time the lava flowed. These buff-colored flows are also distinctive because they have picked up many small angular particles, forming volcanic breccias.

Younger volcanics are mostly dark-colored basalts. These rocks are abundant in Owens Valley. They began to form during the Pleistocene and have continued since then. Near Little Lake there are about 45 different volcanic formations, including cinder cones and basaltic flows. Rainbow Canyon is a spectacular area that lies east of Owens Valley. The highway from Owens Valley to Death Valley descends into Panamint Valley across spectacular red and yellow volcanics that border Rainbow Canyon. At one point the road traverses the inside of several cinder cones.

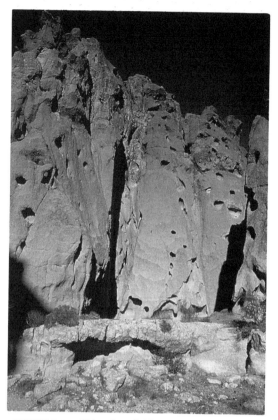

FIGURE 9.10   Volcanic rock (rhyolite) in the Mid Hills, near Hole-in-the-Wall Campground, San Bernardino County.

There are several conspicuous volcanic cones in the Mojave extending in a line from Barstow eastward. These craters, including Amboy and Pisgah craters, probably were formed by eruptions about 2000 years ago. The basalt fields around the craters are interesting because of numerous tunnels, vents, fissures, and collapsed blisters, indicating the plastic nature of the lava as it flowed.

At the northern end of Death Valley is a peculiar volcanic formation known as Ubehebe Crater (pl. 11A). *Ubehebe* is an Indian word that means "big basket." This distinctive feature probably was formed by steam and volcanic ash that erupted and fell back upon itself, forming layers of bedded sediments. The material is basaltic in composition, but there are no associated lava flows.

In the Colorado Desert, recent volcanics are represented by a line of pumice and obsidian domes near the southern end of the Salton Sea. This region is still mildly active. There were mud pots and steam vents in the area until about 1954, when the rise of the Salton Sea covered them. Some mud pots are still visible near the town of Niland.

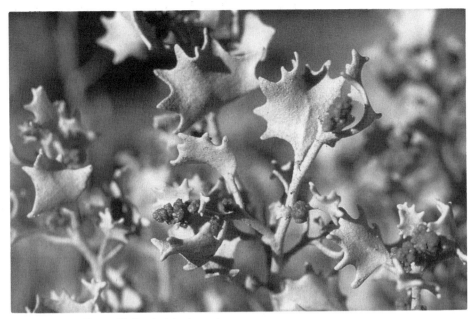

FIGURE 9.11   Desert Holly, *Atriplex hymenelytra*.

Areas of recent volcanism provide the opportunity to use the earth's heat to generate electricity. The geothermal facility at Geysers was mentioned in chapter 7. Quite a number of geothermal facilities for desert areas are in the planning stages. As of 1991, there were several operating south of the Salton Sea, and a new facility was generating electricity near the southern end of the Coso Range near Ridgecrest. Several localities near Mammoth Lakes were also in the planning stages. One such proposal, near Hot Creek (fig. 4.9), is controversial because the Owens River in the area is a fishery for native trout. In Mexico, just south of the border, at Agua Prieta, there is one of the oldest functioning geothermal power plants.

One interesting feature of volcanic landscapes is that they are often associated with specific vegetation. One plant that is conspicuous in volcanic areas is a saltbush known as Desert Holly, *Atriplex hymenelytra* (fig. 9.11). This small shrub gets its common name from its small, toothed, hollylike leaves, found on no other saltbush. Its white herbage stands out starkly against dark volcanic soils.

Mining has been an important economic activity in California's deserts since the mid-1800s. Significant amounts of silver, lead, and zinc have been mined in the Inyo Mountains, Panamint Mountains, and Argus Mountains of the Basin-Range Province. The most important silver mines in the Mojave Desert were in the Rand Mountains, south of the Garlock fault. Gold was obtained from mines in the Panamint Mountains, Rand Mountains, and Cargo Muchacho Mountains in the southeast corner of the Colorado Desert. Silver and gold also were obtained from the mine at Bodie, near Mono Lake. Small amounts of tungsten were extracted by placer mining from gravels on the southeastern side of the Rand Mountains.

The effort to extract gold from the desert is not over. The process known as cyanide heap leaching, described in chapter 6, may be a means of mining low-grade desert ore profitably. The oldest mine utilizing this technology in the state is the Picacho Mine, located near the Colorado River in Imperial County. Since 1980 about 9500 tons (8600 t) of ore have been mined per day, yielding about 25,000 ounces (710 kg) of gold per year. When the mine is no longer profitable. the enormous leach pads will be purged of cyanide, the land reshaped, and native vegetation replanted.

The use of cyanide heap leaching for extracting gold is also being used at the Colosseum Mine on Clark Mountain near Mountain Pass and has been proposed for a site in the scenic Castle Mountains of eastern San Bernardino County. There is also talk of a similar operation at Bodie, a state historic park. Apparently, the plan is to remove the 400-foot (125-m) Bodie Ridge situated behind the townsite, and move the material to another location for processing. Environmentalists are opposed to this form of mining because of possible groundwater contamination and/or danger to wildlife, particularly birds and bats. Between 1980 and 1989 a total of 7609 animal deaths were reported for 97 mines in Arizona, Nevada, and California.

Among the most famous old mines was the Cerro Gordo Mine, near the crest of the Inyo Mountains. Beginning in 1860, significant amounts of silver and lead were mined, but in the early 1900s zinc became the most important product. The ore was deposited by hydrothermal solutions into Paleozoic carbonate rocks. So rich was this mine that a sizable community of miners, many of them Chinese, once occupied the area. By means of a bucket-tram system, metal was brought down the mountain to the town of Keeler, on the edge of Owens Lake. Here the ingots were loaded aboard a steamer and transported across the lake to be loaded on wagons. In later years the ore was loaded from the steamer to a railroad. There is a story that a steamer loaded with silver once sank in Owens Lake and was never recovered. Presumably, the load was so heavy that the entire steamer and its contents sank beneath the muddy lake bottom and is still buried there, totally concealed by the sediments! Part of the mining operation at Cerro Gordo included smelting the ore. Charcoal for this process was produced in the charcoal kilns located along Cottonwood Creek on the west side of Owens Lake. Wood for the kilns was obtained from the forest on upper Cottonwood Creek.

Another famous silver mine was at Panamint city in the Panamint Mountains. The town grew to a population of 1500 in the 1870s, when the mine was most productive. A cloudburst and flash flood wiped out the town and the smelter in 1876, but by that time most of the ore had been mined. The mine was reopened for a short time in the mid-1980s when the price of silver was very high. Other famous silver mines were the Minietta and Modoc mines of the Argus Mountains. Charcoal for smelters of these silver mines was produced at beehive-shaped charcoal kilns in the Pinyon-Juniper Woodland at the northern end of the Panamint Mountains. These charcoal kilns have been restored, and the site is now a part of Death Valley National Monument.

Significant amounts of iron were also mined from desert localities. The largest iron mine was in the Eagle Mountains on the northern border of the Colorado Desert. Kaiser Steel Company operated this mine until the middle 1900s. The railroad down

Salt Creek Wash carried ore from this mine to the Southern Pacific Railroad on the eastern border of the Salton Sea. It is interesting that a new use for the old railroad has been proposed: to haul trash from Los Angeles to be dumped into the huge pits at the old Eagle Mountain mine. Some estimates indicate that the site could absorb Los Angeles trash for 125 years. Remains of another iron mine, the Vulcan Mine of the southern Providence Mountains, can still be seen as a "glory hole" several hundred feet deep, where it penetrates Cambrian limestones. The Vulcan Mine operated in the middle 1940s. Its close proximity to the old Union Pacific railroad station at Kelso also makes it a potential landfill.

Most of the mining today is for sand and gravel, but minerals in salts (evaporites) are also valuable in deserts. Such mining operations occur in the salt deposits of Owens Lake, Bristol Lake near Amboy, and Searles Lake near Trona. The mine at Trona is a large operation that produces potash, a potassium mineral used in fertilizers. The town of Trona is named after a rare mineral that can be obtained from the salts of Searles (dry) Lake.

Borates are other important minerals found in Searles Lake. Boron is used as an additive in jet fuel, and some borates are used in detergents and in fiberglass insulation. Boron was infused into lake water by volcanic gas emissions that occurred millions of years ago, when huge lakes filled many basins in the desert. As a result of evaporation, crystalline borate minerals may also be found among the salts of some lake beds. Other lake deposits with borate minerals are found in the Mojave Desert. Death Valley contains borate minerals known as colemanite and ulexite. Near the town of Boron is a large mine where borate minerals such as ulexite, colemanite, and kernite are profitably mined.

Plaster of Paris is gypsum, an evaporite composed of calcium sulfate. It also is an important component of various kinds of plasterboard used in construction. In the Colorado Desert, just east of Split Mountain Canyon, near Anza Borrego Desert State Park, is a 100-foot-thick (30-m) deposit of gypsum that has been mined for many years. A narrow-gauge railroad carries the gypsum south to Plaster City, where it is processed. During the Renaissance, a solid form of gypsum known as alabaster was a common material used in the carving of statuary.

Other than the saline minerals, most mining today is for talc. Talc is a magnesium mineral used in making paper, soap, and toilet powders. It is concentrated at the contact points between certain limestones and intrusive bodies such as granite. Profitable talc mines have operated from time to time in the Cottonwood Mountains, Ibex Mountains, Argus Mountains, and around the southern end of Death Valley in the Panamint and Black mountains.

One group of interesting elements mined in the California desert is known as rare earths. These represent a group of elements used in the glassmaking, petroleum, and metallurgy industries, particularly those involved in research and production of superconducting materials. Virtually all rare-earth production in the United States involves a mineral known as bastnaesite, taken from an open pit mine near Mountain Pass, where Interstate 15 crosses the Clark Mountains between Baker and Las Vegas. Approximately 97% of U.S. and 33% of world rare-earth production comes from this one mine in the Mojave Desert.

Structure of a Desert Basin

In order to understand why desert plants grow where they do, it is necessary to become familiar with the structure of a typical desert basin. To some degree, all desert terrain is basinlike. In the Basin-Range Province, basins are narrow and elongated. Different aspects of a slope are easily distinguishable as bands or zones of vegetation.

In most hilly terrain, water is the most important erosive force. This is true for deserts as well. The difference, however, is that most of the erosion took place thousands of years ago, during periods of heavy rainfall associated with ice ages. Desert landscapes were shaped many years ago, and they have been preserved by a lack of rainfall since that time. In this sense, deserts have fossil landscapes. Heavy rainfall occurs sporadically today, usually associated with a localized thunderstorm. On such occasions, erosion occurs rapidly, and land is rearranged, after which it may lie for another thousand years relatively undisturbed.

During long periods of time with no significant rainfall, the surfaces of desert rocks become darkened. This darkening, known as desert varnish or rock varnish, is due to oxidation of minerals such as iron and manganese. According to present theory, the actual varnish, less than $1/2$ millimeter thick, involves a fine patina of clay that is deposited by wind over the rocks, and the minerals are in the clay. In exposed areas where the pH is neutral, oxidizing bacteria concentrate black-colored oxides of manganese that help to cement the clay in place. In protected areas, such as dust-filled depressions or the undersides of rocks, an alkaline pH inhibits the growth of the bacteria, and a bright orange iron oxide is formed instead. The long period of time required for the varnish to form is illustrated by locations where Indians have overturned or removed varnish-covered rocks to form giant intaglios on the desert floor. One such locality near Blythe, in the Colorado Desert, is believed to be at least 400 years old. Using a technique known as cation-ratio dating, petroglyphs in the Mojave Desert are now known to be thousands of years old.

The uppermost part of a desert slope is an erosion surface known as the pediment. *Ped* means "foot," and the term *pediment* refers to the foot of the mountain. There is very little soil on the pediment, as it has been carried away by wind and water. Rocks in the area are heavily varnished. Canyons in desert ranges cut across the pediment, and at canyon mouths are fan-shaped piles of rocks and gravel that have been carried by runoff from the mountains. These are known as alluvial fans. Because these fans have remained undisturbed for thousands of years, upper surfaces on the fans have become varnished. It is not until a major storm occurs that enough water flows out of a canyon to turn over old rocks and deposit new ones. New or overturned alluvium is easy to spot because of the absence of varnish. Carbon-14 and cation-ratio dating in Death Valley have revealed that the varnish at the top or head of one alluvial fan is 50,000 years old. Varnish gradually becomes younger toward the bottom or toe of the fan. The varnish there is 14,000 years old, indicating that these were the last rocks to be deposited.

The alluvial fans spread out at their lower borders, and the edges of adjacent alluvial fans overlap (fig. 9.12). This part of a slope, where alluvial fans coalesce below the pediment, is known as the *bajada,* which is a Spanish word that means

FIGURE 9.12   Desert landforms. Alluvial fans emerging from the north side of the Avawatz Mountains merge to form an outwashed bajada. Note the parallel lines of Creosote Bush in the foreground.

FIGURE 9.13   Skid boulders on Racetrack Playa, Death Valley National Monument.

"lower." It refers to the lower aspect of the long slope that begins high up on the mountain bordering each valley. The bajada is composed of gravels and sand, and particle size becomes smaller toward the center of the valley. If the center of the basin is clay, it remains relatively free of vegetation and is known as a *playa,* which means "beach" in Spanish. A salt flat in the center of the basin is known as a *salina.*

The nature of a clay playa is best appreciated by a visit to Racetrack Playa, in Death Valley National Monument (fig. 9.13). Apparently, when the clay is wet, it is so slippery that wind is able to blow rocks around on the surface. The tracks left in the clay indicate changes in wind direction. Sometimes the tracks actually loop back upon themselves. Another theory about the tracks is that the rocks become imbedded in ice and are then blown about. During a period of heavy rainfall the lake may fill to a depth of 1 or 2 feet. If freezing occurs, the top 12 inches or so may turn to ice. As the lake begins to thaw, the heavy boulders are buoyed up by the ice, and wind transports these ice-boulder rafts floating on the remaining water. The fascinating part of this story is that apparently no one has ever seen the wind blow one of these rocks. All evidence is circumstantial.

STRATEGIES OF DESERT PLANTS

In general, strategies of desert plants (table 9.2) are based on ways to cope with drought, alkaline soil, temperature extremes, intense light, and a short growing season. In general, however, the distribution of desert vegetation (fig. 9.14) reflects the water-holding capacity and alkalinity of the soil, both of which increase toward the center of a basin.

Succulents and Drought-deciduous Plants

On the pediment and upper alluvial fans, water runs off or percolates rapidly. Therefore it is available for a short period of time. In this region most plants are either succulent or drought-deciduous. Succulent plants grow on the coarsest of soils. They store water, which they draw upon slowly between rainstorms. Plants such as cacti are called stem succulents because they store water in their stems. Plants such as yuccas and agaves store water in succulent leaves and are called leaf succulents. Succulents have deciduous root hairs that are shed when the soil becomes dry. When this happens, water will neither enter nor leave the roots. When it rains, the plant grows new root hairs. Growth and photosynthetic rates of succulents are slow.

Drought-deciduous plants range from the pediment to the upper bajada. They drop their leaves during drought. After it rains, they rapidly grow new leaves, which are often comparatively large for desert plants. Most drought-deciduous plants drop their leaves only once a year, but Ocotillo is reported to lose and grow new leaves up to seven times a year. Drought-deciduous plants grow and photosynthesize rapidly.

Evergreen Shrubs

On the middle and lower bajada most of the plants are evergreen; that is, they retain leaves year-round. In the Great Basin, the dominant evergreen shrub is Great Basin Sagebrush. In warm southern deserts, the dominant evergreen shrub is Creosote Bush. These shrubs are characterized by large root systems. They are capable of absorbing water from all levels of the soil, relying on their deepest roots during the dry season. Photosynthetic and growth rates are slow. Leaves are small and often possess a waxy

TABLE 9.2   Strategies of Desert Plants

Succulent
   Leaf succulent: yuccas, agaves, live-forevers
   Stem succulent: cactus:
      Associated with coarse, rocky soil
      Store water; deciduous root hairs
      Store carbon at night; CAM photosynthesis
      Shallow, widespread roots
Drought-dormant
   Drought-deciduous: Ocotillo, Desert Brittle-bush
      Associated with coarse soils
      Lose leaves during drought; dormancy maintained by roots and stems
   Geophytes: Desert Lily, Coyote Melon
      Regions with predictable precipitation
      Lose aboveground parts during drought; dormancy maintained by below-ground parts (i.e.,
        bulbs, corms, tubers)
   Ephemerals (Annuals)
      Regions with unpredictable precipitation
      Entire life cycle during one season; dormancy maintained as seeds
         Winter annuals: Evening Primrose, Sand Verbena
           C_3 photosynthesis; require early winter precipitation.
         Summer annuals: Unicorn Plant
           C_3, C_4 photosynthesis; require midsummer precipitation
      Rapid growth
      Large leaves
Drought-enduring
   Xerophytes
      Evergreen perennials: Creosote Bush, Great Basin Sagebrush
        Associated with medium-grade soils, lower bajadas
        Large root systems
        Small, drought-adapted leaves; lose leaves a few at a time
        Slow growth of aboveground parts; most of growth in roots
Drought-avoiding
   Associated with permanent water
   Phreatophytes
      Winter-deciduous: Fremont Cottonwood
      Evergreen: California Fan Palm
        Large leaves
        Large root systems
   Desert wash plants
      Winter-deciduous: Honey Mesquite, Desert Willow
      Drought-deciduous: Smoke Tree, palo verdes
      Evergreen: Ironwood
        Small leaves
        Large root systems
Salt-tolerant
   Xerophytic halophytes: saltbushes
      Associated with fine-grained, alkaline soil
      Small leaves
      Excrete salt on leaves
      C_4 photosynthesis
   Succulent halophytes: pickleweeds, Iodine Bush
      Store water to dilute salt

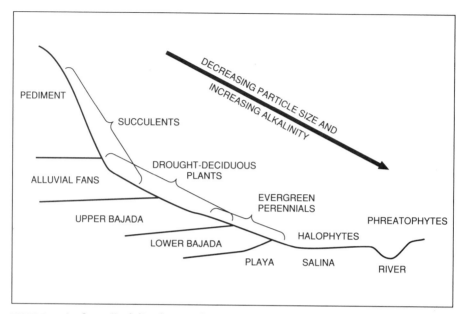

FIGURE 9.14   Generalized distribution of vegetation on a desert slope. See text for explanation.

or resinous coating to inhibit water loss. One of the most important characteristics of these plants is tolerance for drought. They are able to conduct photosynthesis under the highest levels of water stress known among plants.

Halophytes

The lowermost portions of the bajada are more alkaline. Plants of these soils are called halophytes and include members of the saltbush family (Chenopodiaceae). Saltbushes are also evergreen shrubs, but they tolerate alkaline soils by absorbing both salt and water. The salt is then excreted upon the surface of the leaves, which is one of the reasons that most saltbushes have a silvery sheen on the leaves. As soil becomes more alkaline, the leaves on these saltbushes become more succulent. Apparently, water storage helps to dilute the salts that become concentrated in tissues. Iodine Bushes, *Allenrolfea occidentalis,* and Pickleweeds, *Salicornia subterminalis,* are the most succulent and the most salt-tolerant, growing on the edges of salty bodies of water such as the Salton Sea.

In the center of a basin, very little vegetation occurs. Either the soil is too alkaline, or there is too much clay. Clay absorbs and releases water slowly. Plants do not grow well in clay because water adheres strongly to the fine particles of soil and is unavailable to the plants. Furthermore, oxygen is unable to reach the roots, which limits cellular respiration there. Many areas of old lake beds composed of clay soils are devoid of plants. These regions, when uplifted, erode in a characteristic way, forming deeply furrowed topography. Such topography, particularly if it lacks vegetation, is known as badlands. Well-known badlands occur at Zabriskie Point (fig. 9.8) in Death Valley and at various localities around the Salton Sea.

Phreatophytes

Deeply rooted plants that tap permanent water are known as phreatophytes. This word means "well-plants," implying that these plants grow near a well. Where soil is unstable, or where precipitation is unpredictable, plants must be extremely deep rooted, or they are ephemeral. Sand dunes and desert washes typify unstable soils. Mesquites and Desert Willows are typical of deep-rooted plants that grow either in washes or sand dunes. Roots of mesquites may be more extensive than those of any other desert plants. They are commonly 30 feet (10 m) deep, and they have been recorded in mines as deep as 250 feet (80 m). Similar to other phreatophytes, mesquites and Desert Willows are winter-deciduous.

Phreatophytes are unable to conserve water. Many phreatophytes, such as Fremont Cottonwood, *Populus fremontii* (fig. 8.54) are not true desert plants. Cottonwoods actually avoid the true desert by growing only where there is abundant water. Typical of riparian plants in many parts of California, these trees are winter-deciduous, dropping their leaves in the cold season. It has been calculated that a three-year-old Fremont Cottonwood loses through transpiration about 10.3 gallons (38.9 l) per day. In comparison, 100 square meters of drought-tolerant vegetation transpire only 2 to 3 gallons of water (8–12 l) per day.

Ephemerals

Ephemeral or annual plants endure drought in dormant, seed form, which makes them particularly suited for survival in areas where precipitation is unpredictable, such as deserts. Ephemerals in deserts make up about 40% of the species, whereas in other habitats they seldom make up more than 15% of the species.

Old stands of Creosote Bush often are associated with an abundance of annuals. Little else grows with Creosote Bush in these areas. After it rains, the bare spaces between Creosote Bushes may become carpets of flowers.

Annual plants also grow in unstable soils. When wind or water move the soil, the seeds move with it. When adequate water is available, water-soluble inhibitory chemicals are washed out of the seeds, and germination occurs. Following germination, growth is rapid; an ephemeral plant must complete its entire life cycle in one season. In California, almost all annual plants are adapted to germinate and grow during winter. Similar to alpine plants, they show a suite of characteristics designed to accelerate growth and optimize heat. Leaves grow flat on the ground in a basal rosette. Flowers and leaves track the sun. Photosynthetic rates are high. Brown-eyed Evening Primrose, *Camissonia claviformis,* a common annual plant of the Mojave and Colorado deserts, has the highest photosynthetic rate ever measured.

In order to optimize the growing season, germination of ephemeral plants should occur early in the winter. If an inch (25 mm) or more of precipitation falls in late September or early October, inhibitors will be leached from the seeds, resulting in mass germination and a carpet of wildflowers for a spectacular spring show. If rainfall doesn't arrive until mid-December, then germination will require an inch (25 mm) of rain coupled with soil temperature greater than 50°F (10°C). Late rainfall must be coupled with warm temperature to ensure that growth occurs rapidly, because the entire life cycle must be accomplished in a shorter time. Apparently, the seeds are also sensitive to temperature. One other opportunity for germination of winter annuals occurs if 2 inches (50 mm) of precipitation occur by early April. In the midst of a five-year drought, heavy rains during March 1991 stimulated a spectacular bloom of some winter annuals. With abundant water, these winter annuals are able to complete an entire life cycle in an abbreviated growing season.

Precipitation during summer does not cause germination of winter annuals. Apparently, if the weather is too warm, germination will not occur; winter annuals cannot be "fooled" into germinating during the wrong season. Conversely, annuals that depend on summer precipitation cannot be "fooled" into germinating during winter. Most summer annuals grow very rapidly and complete their life cycles in only a few weeks. Summer annuals are not common in California, but they occur more frequently in the eastern parts of the Sonoran Desert, where summer rainfall is more predictable. One well-known weed, Russian Thistle or Tumbleweed, *Salsola tragus* (= *S. australis*), is a summer annual that has become well established in California, primarily because agricultural fields are irrigated during the summer.

During a year with adequate precipitation, the number of ephemeral plants that bloom simultaneously is amazing. These annual species must compete for pollinators with each other, as well as with the perennial species that are also in bloom. Some species produce very large flowers; others produce a great number of flowers. Some species avoid competition by becoming associated particularly with certain pollinators. For example, tubular flowers that are red or yellow are frequently pollinated by hummingbirds. White flowers that bloom at night are often pollinated by moths.

The native Jimson Weed, *Datura discolor,* is a white-flowered ephemeral of the southeastern part of the Colorado Desert. It is one of some 25 species of *Datura* found throughout the world. Three other species, also known as Jimson Weeds, have been introduced to California. They are widely distributed in disturbed areas of the arid southwest, including cismontane southern California and the Great Central Valley. The nonnative species are perennials that die back each summer and return from rootstock after spring rains. Jimson Weeds are in the nightshade family (Solanaceae). Characteristic of this family, they contain poisonous compounds—in this case, alkaloids such as atropine and scopalamine, which are sometimes called "belladonna" after a related plant, *Atropa belladonna*. The name *belladonna* means "beautiful lady." Apparently, European women used the sap to dilate the pupils of their eyes, a characteristic that was supposed to make them more beautiful. These chemicals are also found in some popular decongestants. These alkaloids were also used in the puberty ceremonies of several North American Indian tribes, in which consumption of a Jimson Weed drink caused hallucinations and finally unconsciousness. The name *Jimson Weed* is a corruption of "Jamestown Weed," a refence to an episode that occurred in 1676 when British soldiers in Jamestown, Virginia, become intoxicated by eating a salad that contained *Datura* leaves.

Jimson Weeds have large, white, fragrant, trumpet-shaped flowers that open in the evening. They are pollinated by hawk moths or sphinx moths (*Manduca* spp.) that have remarkable proboscides (tongues) over 4 inches (10 cm) in length. Apparently, the moths become addicted to the alkaloids in the nectar, which keeps them returning to the flowers for another "fix," thereby accomplishing pollination. This is another example of the interdependence of plant species and their pollinators. Furthermore, the larvae of the moths, known as tomato or tobacco hornworms, feed on a variety of other poisonous species in the nightshade family, such as tobacco. In this way the larvae are rendered poisonous or distasteful to predators.

An interesting example of competition between ephemeral species occurs where the range of the Ghost Flower, *Mohavea confertifolia* (Scrophulariaceae) overlaps that of the Sand Blazing Star, *Mentzelia involucrata* (Loasaceae) (fig. 9.15). The Ghost Flower may be considered a mimic. Its cream-colored blossom with purple dots in the center is similar in coloration to the Sand Blazing Star, but the Ghost Flower produces no nectar to reward the pollinator, a bee of the genus *Xeralictus*. The bees innately recognize the Sand Blazing Star as a rich source of nectar. Most of the time they visit the Sand Blazing Star rather than the Ghost Flower, but when the bees are abundant and competition occurs for nectar, extra male bees visit the Ghost Flower. The Ghost Flower is thus pollinated without investing energy in the production of nectar. In this way, the Ghost Flower might be considered a pollinator parasite.

Geophytes

The word *geophyte* means "earth-plant." Geophytes are plants that shed their above-ground parts during the dry season. This is a strategy that is intermediate between drought-deciduous and ephemeral plants, but it accomplishes a similar end: the plants are dormant during the dry season. Dormancy is maintained by underground organs, modified roots or stems known variously as bulbs, tubers, corms, or rhizomes. Geophytes tend to occur in sandy, relatively stable soils where precipitation is predictable. If an inch (25 mm) of precipitation occurs early in the winter, these plants will have adequate moisture and time to produce aboveground leaves, stems, and flowers. Included among the desert geophytes are a variety of lilies, wild cucumbers, and the nonnative Jimson Weeds mentioned earlier.

C₄ Photosynthesis

Three variations in the process of photosynthesis convey certain advantages to desert plants. In the type of photosynthesis that occurs in most plants, CO_2 is absorbed in such a way that the first chemical compound produced has three carbon atoms. This is known as C_3 photosynthesis. A disadvantage to this type of photosynthesis is that above 77°F (25°C) the rate of photosynthesis actually declines. One of the problems is that the enzyme controlling the process becomes inhibited by oxygen. As more photosynthesis occurs, more oxygen is produced, and the excess oxygen feeds back negatively to inhibit the reaction.

FIGURE 9.15   An example of mimicry and pollinator parasitism. *A.* The Sand Blazing Star, *Mentzelia involucrata,* is a rich source of nectar.

FIGURE 9.15 (*continued*)   An example of mimicry and pollinator parasitism. *B.* The Ghost Flower, *Mohavea confertifolia,* produces no nectar. Instead it relies on its resemblance to the Sand Blazing Star, near which it grows, to attract pollinators.

One variation of the process is known as C_4 photosynthesis. This type of photosynthesis is characteristic of many grasses, saltbushes, and summer annuals. In this variant, the first chemical compound produced has four carbon atoms instead of three, and the process is not inhibited by oxygen. It functions in low concentrations of CO_2, and it takes place at a higher temperature than the C_3 process. The ability to function at low concentrations of CO_2 means that the plant can continue to photosynthesize with its stomates nearly closed. Stomates are small pores in the leaf surface surrounded by specialized cells that allow CO_2 to enter. Water also leaves the plant through these pores. During hot weather, plants close their stomates to minimize water loss; however, this decreases the amount of CO_2 that can enter, and it traps oxygen inside the leaf. The C_4 process takes place in the outer cells of the leaves. The C_4 chemical is then passed to the cells that surround the veins of the leaves, where the standard C_3 process takes place as the carbon is donated from the C_4 chemical rather than directly from CO_2. In this way, photosynthesis operates more efficiently and at a higher temperature, to the advantage of a desert plant.

The third variation in the photosynthetic process is actually a variant of C_4 photosynthesis. It is known as crassulacean acid metabolism, or CAM photosynthesis. This process takes place in succulent plants and is named for a family of plants, Crassulaceae, that includes many leaf succulents, such as live-forevers. In CAM photosynthesis, CO_2 is fixed into a C_4 compound at night and the light-dependent C_3 process takes place by day. This photosynthetic mechanism requires more energy than either the C_3 or the C_4 process, but it enables the plant to absorb CO_2 at night and store it for use in the daytime. The advantage to this is that the plant can close its stomates during the day in order to reduce water loss. In effect, succulent plants carry on photosynthesis using stored water and stored carbon dioxide. The energy demand, however, dictates that CAM plants have very slow growth rates.

DESERT COMMUNITIES

Desert zonation (figs. 9.16–9.18) is less a function of elevation than of soils and latitude. The influence of soils is most important locally, causing distinctive bands of vegetation. Latitude influences zonation due to its effect on temperature and day length. Northern latitudes are colder and receive more precipitation as snow; therefore northern communities may appear at higher elevations toward the south. Growing season is postponed until spring and early summer. Very little precipitation occurs during summer, and summer photoperiods are very long during the time of greatest drought stress.

Creosote Bush Scrub

Creosote Bush, *Larrea tridentata* (= *L. divaricata*) (fig. 9.19A), is the dominant shrub of the Mojave and Colorado deserts (pl. 9B). In total, Creosote Bush Scrub covers more land than any other community in California—over 21 million acres (12,000,000 ha). Creosote Bush is most common on well-drained soils of bajadas and flats. Usually it occurs in association with Bur-sage or Burro Bush, *Ambrosia dumosa* (fig. 9.19B).

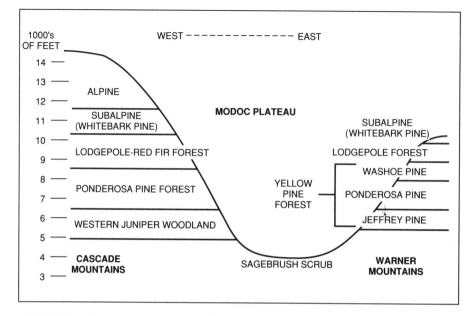

FIGURE 9.16 Biotic zonation of the Great Basin in California: Modoc Plateau.

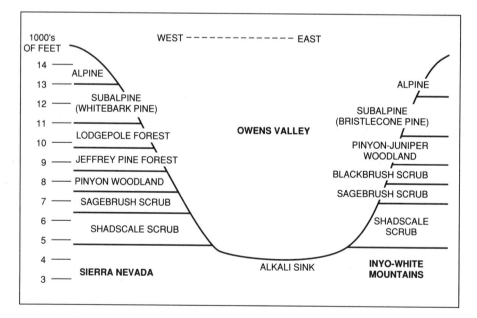

FIGURE 9.16 (*continued*) Biotic zonation of the Great Basin in California: Northern Owens Valley.

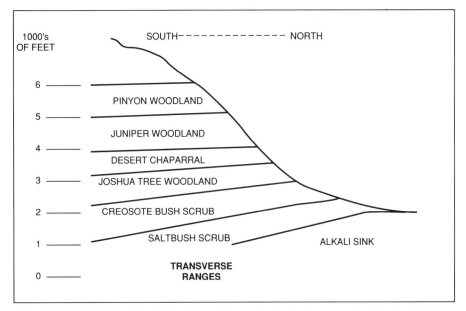

FIGURE 9.17   Biotic zonation of the Mojave Desert.

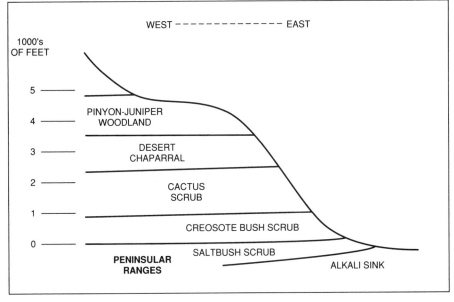

FIGURE 9.18   Biotic zonation of the Colorado Desert.

Creosote Bush has dark green, resinous leaves borne on wandlike stems. Bur-sage is a short, gray, densely branched shrub with small, lobed leaves. The association of these two shrubs occurs in varying proportions, the reasons for which are not clear. It may be a function of age: Creosote Bush outlives Bur-sage. Or it may be a function of precipitation: Creosote Bush can tolerate drier soil. Another factor involves chemicals produced by the roots of Creosote Bush that inhibit growth of Bur-sage roots, a phenomenon that has been suspected but was proved only in 1991.

Creosote Bush also occurs in the Chihuahua Desert of southern Texas and northern Mexico, and there are similar species in the deserts of South America. It appears that the dispersal of Creosote Bush has been from the south, and some evolution has occurred as it dispersed. Studies of chromosome numbers show that the Chihuahua Desert forms have a diploid (2N) number of 26. Specimens from the Sonoran Desert have 52 chromosomes (4N), and those in the Mojave have 78 (6N). This multiplication of chromosome numbers, known as polyploidy, is a common mechanism of speciation among plants. In the case of Creosote Bush, it has caused different races, but apparently they are not yet separate species.

Creosote Bush is the "champion" desert plant. It can tolerate drought stress in the form of negative water potential (pressure) more than any other shrub. Water potential is used as a measurement of water stress. It is measured in bars, with 1 bar

FIGURE 9.19 Dominant plants of Creosote Bush Scrub. A. Creosote Bush, *Larrea tridentata*.

equivalent to the pressure of the atmosphere, about 15 pounds per square inch (1.08 kg/cm^2). Typical agricultural or garden plants begin to wilt if the negative water potential of their tissues exceeds 10 to 15 bars. Creosote Bush functions very well at -50 bars and has been found to function at -120 bars. This is roughly equivalent to a negative pressure of 1800 pounds per square inch (288 kg/cm^2). The critical water potential is about -70 bars. Below that, cellular respiration exceeds photosynthesis, and the plant cannot long endure.

Cell division, the addition of new cells to growing shoots, can continue to take place while Creosote Bush is under water stress. Directly after it rains, the new cells absorb water and elongate, giving the appearance of rapid growth. Lengthening of stems up to 1 $^1/_4$ inches (3 cm) has been observed after it rains. It has been reported that the water potential must be above -24 to -28 bars for this stem elongation, as well as flowering, to take place.

The regular spacing of Creosote Bush on broad, flat terrain is remarkable (fig. 9.12); plants seem to be spaced with orchardlike regularity. It was once assumed that the spacing was due to a water-soluble chemical inhibitor produced by the leaves or

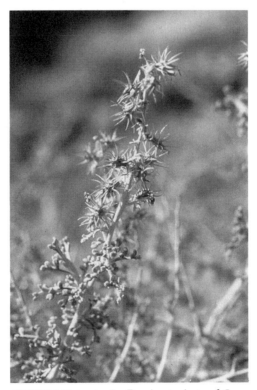

FIGURE 9.19 *(continued)* Dominant plants of Creosote Bush Scrub. *B*. Burro Bush, *Ambrosia dumosa*.

roots that prevented germination of Creosote Bush seeds in the vicinity of a mature plant. In well-watered areas, plants are taller and grow closer together. In spite of evidence that Creosote Bush roots inhibit those of Bur-sage, no evidence has been developed to support the presence of an inhibitor that works between individual Creosote Bushes. At the present time it is supposed that Creosote Bush is so efficient at absorbing water that germination of seeds is prohibited within the scope of a mature root system. The regular interval of spacing represents the reach of root systems of adjacent plants. Because water is distributed equally over these desert flats, the shrubs presumably all grow at the same rate. Thus they are equally spaced. Because Creosote Bush is long-lived, these areas of regular spacing seem to represent even-aged stands.

Germination of Creosote Bush seeds, however, is not as difficult as the paucity of Creosote Bush seedlings may make it seem. Apparently, seeds germinate abundantly following winter rains, but they die very early of water stress. This stress is accentuated if the seeds germinate within the scope of the root system of a mature plant. Perhaps more critical than that, however, is the effect of heat close to the ground. Heat accelerates water stress, and the temperature at ground level in the summer is near 160°F (71°C). Before its root system becomes established, Creosote Bush is unable to endure that kind of stress. Apparently, in nature young Creosote Bushes can only become established if there is a period of three to five years of cool, moist weather. Because this condition does not often occur, we do not find many young Creosote Bushes.

The age of Creosote Bushes has generated a bit of controversy. Aerial photographs show that in old stands of Creosote Bush, circles of shrubs are apparent (fig. 9.20). Subsequent study shows that the bushes involved in a circle contain the same genetic material; that is, they are clones. There may be two to nine shrubs in these rings, all "identical twins." The circles can be explained by the habit of Creosote Bush to generate new stems from an underground crown. New stems are produced from the outside of the crown, and the oldest stems are in the center. Eventually the central stems die, but the shrub continues to expand until the living stems form a ring. As this ring enlarges, it breaks up into bunches of stems, each representing a different plant. Actually, the different components of the circle originated from a single root system. The original plant had a taproot, but the different members of the clone do not have taproots.

In order to determine how rapidly these circles enlarge, carbon-14 dates were established for bits of wood found within the circle and cross-referenced with annual growth rings on the stems. It was found that the circles of shrubs in a clone enlarge at very slow rates. Many Creosote Bush clones about 20 feet (6 m) across were found. These were estimated to be about 3000 years of age. The oldest clone in the Mojave is located in Johnson Valley near the town of Lucerne Valley. It is 67 feet (22 m) across and has been named King Clone. It has been dated at approximately 11,700 years of age. Another clone in the Sonoran Desert near Yuma has been dated at 18,000 years of age. If we consider that the different shrubs in the clone actually represent one living plant, then these shrubs are by far the oldest living things. They germinated during the wet years following the last ice age and have been living ever

FIGURE 9.20   A circle (clone) of Creosote Bushes.

since. In other words, they are as old as the desert itself! To protect King Clone and its associates, the Nature Conservancy has purchased the land around it, and the area shall be maintained as a preserve.

The question of whether or not succession takes place in deserts is another controversy that can be answered in part by studying Creosote Bush Scrub at different localities. In sites that have disturbances of known age, such as areas disturbed by mining activities, there is an assemblage of plants different from mature stands. Roads at the Skidoo townsite in Death Valley have not returned fully after five decades, and tank tracks where George Patton's army practiced are still clearly visible in the eastern Colorado Desert after four decades. In areas of historic disturbance there is a greater abundance of plants such as Desert Trumpet, *Eriogonum inflatum;* Desert Senna, *Cassia armata;* and Bur-sage. In the Colorado Desert, Teddy Bear Cholla, *Opuntia bigelovii,* seems to be an early successional species. Young Creosote Bushes are discernible because they have a single central stem. As a stand ages, the number of associated species declines, and Bur-sage and Creosote Bush remain as the dominants. In very old stands, the abundance of Bur-sage declines. Annual plants seem to be more common in old stands of nearly pure Creosote Bush, particularly where precipitation is unpredictable. Apparently, succession does occur in deserts, but the rate is so slow that it is difficult to observe within a human lifespan. Studies encompassing a 72-year period in the Sonoran Desert near Tucson show little change other than those associated with variations in precipitation.

Early successional species usually are not long-lived. They have good dispersal ability, with many possessing plumed seeds that are carried by the wind. Creosote

Bush and Bur-sage are dispersed by animals. They have fruits that adhere to fur or feathers. Creosote Bush has white, hairy fruits, and Bur-sage has fruits with small spines (fig. 9.19B); its name refers to the burlike fruit. Bur-sage is in the sunflower family, but it produces inconspicuous flowers. Flowers of different sexes are borne on the plant separately, and they are wind-pollinated.

Creosote Bush produces an abundance of bright yellow flowers after the first heavy rains (fig. 9.19A). Approximately 1 inch (25 mm) of rain is required. Pollinators include various insects. Once the flowers are pollinated, the petals make a quarter turn so that the flowers are far less conspicuous. In this way, pollination efficiency is optimized.

Creosote Bush and Bur-sage have small leaves, typical of evergreen plants in desert areas. The high surface-volume ratio of small leaves is believed to enhance cooling by radiation without increasing water loss. Evaporative water loss is reduced by resinous or waxy coatings. Creosote Bush is renowned for the odor of its resinous coating, which is particularly pungent during and after rains, giving the entire desert a distinctive odor. As the dry season progresses, plants drop their leaves a few at a time. Bur-sage loses its leaves faster than Creosote Bush, leading some authorities to consider it drought-deciduous. Apparently, however, if all leaves are lost, the plant will not recover.

The amount of detritus from leaf fall that accumulates around the base of these shrubs is significant. A whole community of detritus feeders, including beetles and millipedes, live beneath these shrubs. In addition, when the wind blows, more organic and inorganic material is caught by the shrubs. A mound of sand may be found at the base of every shrub, and numerous seeds are brought in by the wind. Many desert rodents, such as pocket mice and kangaroo rats, make their burrows in the soil at the base of these plants and feed on the seeds that collect there. The canopy of the shrub helps to conceal foraging animals from predators. Efficient pocket mice may never have to leave the protective canopy of the Creosote Bush under which they have their burrows.

Sagebrush Scrub

Sagebrush Scrub is the dominant community of the Great Basin (pl. 8D). Some authors refer to it as Sagebrush Steppe. Great Basin Sagebrush, *Artemisia tridentata* (fig. 9.21A), is the dominant shrub, although it is often joined by Antelope Brush, *Purshia tridentata* (fig. 9.21B), on coarse soils. In its pristine condition, this community also includes perennial bunchgrasses such as wheat grasses (*Agropyron* spp.) and fescues (*Festuca* spp.). Other species of *Artemisia* may also occur as subdominants. In recent years, overgrazing has altered sagebrush communities significantly. Species composition has shifted toward a greater proportion of sagebrush and less Antelope Brush, and the replacement of perennial bunchgrasses with introduced annual grasses.

Great Basin Sagebrush is also known as Big Basin Sagebrush. This plant and Antelope Brush have elongated leaves with three rounded teeth at the tip. The portion *tridentata* of the scientific name refers to these three teeth. Great Basin Sagebrush is whitish gray, and Antelope Brush is dark green. Native browsers such as Pronghorn, Bison, and Bighorn Sheep preferred Antelope Brush, but their densities were never sufficient to deplete one of the species excessively. With the introduction of cattle and sheep, however, overgrazing has become a reality. In some areas Great Basin Sagebrush is the only species left, and it has been pruned severely.

Overgrazing also opens the way for encroachment by introduced weedy species, such as Russian Thistle, *Salsola iberica* (= *S. australis*), also called the Tumbleweed. This extremely hardy member of the saltbush family is a summer annual. Its life cycle in its native habitat in Asia is keyed to summer precipitation, but it survives very well in this country, particularly where irrigation of crops provides a source of summer water. Its incredible mechanism for distribution includes being tossed and tumbled by the wind; during its travel hundreds of seeds are tossed about the landscape. In the early 1870s, Russian Thistle was introduced accidentally to central Canada by seeds that were mixed in a shipment of winter wheat. Within 25 years it rolled and tumbled all the way to Mexico, where it thrives on summer precipitation!

In the past, fire may have been an important factor in altering species composition. Succession after fire caused a shift in species composition, favoring Antelope Brush and perennial grasses that were able to resprout from undamaged rootstock. Great Basin Sagebrush does not resprout after a fire, so it is effectively eliminated until seedlings can become reestablished, which takes about 20 years. One successional species that is common after fires or on other disturbed sites is Rabbitbrush, *Chrysothamnus nauseosus*. Rabbitbrush is also known as Mojave Rubberbrush, a name that refers to the high rubber content of its herbage. It has been determined that if the price of rubber were to rise high enough, it would be economically feasible to harvest this species or actually cultivate it. Rabbitbrush may be nearly leafless, but when leaves are present, they are fine and resin-covered. Its flowers bloom in autumn, taking advantage of pollinators during a time when very few other plants are in bloom. The bright yellow flowers of Rabbitbrush are a common sight along roads and other disturbed areas throughout the Great Basin. Rabbitbrush is another member of the sunflower family that produces wind-distributed, plumed seeds. It is a good pioneer species.

During May 1980, Mount Saint Helens erupted in the Washington Cascades. The ash fall blanketed large portions of the Great Basin to the east. Experiments in the area showed that the blanket of ash initially caused an increase of soil moisture by inhibiting evaporation; but later, increased reflection from the white surface increased temperature and transpiration rates in the vegetative canopy. Great Basin Sagebrush was able to tolerate this stress by dropping up to 75% of its leaves. Coincident water conservation allowed the development of flower buds during the dry, hot summer so that autumn flowering and seed set occurred as usual. The implication of this study is that volcanism in the Cascades favored the growth of Great Basin Sagebrush over other species, and it may have been the extensive ash fall associated with eruptions of Mount Mazama, about 6700 years ago, that favored dispersal of Great Basin Sagebrush into the rain shadow of the Cascades.

Great Basin Sagebrush is ideally suited for the climate in the Great Basin. It tolerates cold weather. When snow melts in late winter, Great Basin Sagebrush is

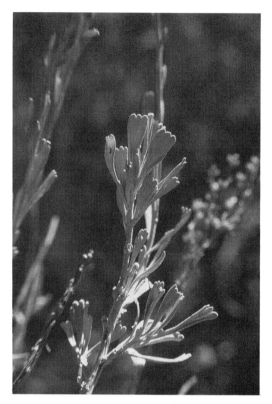

FIGURE 9.21   Dominant plants of Sagebrush Scrub.
A. Great Basin Sagebrush, *Artemisia tridentata*.

still unable to grow new shoots and roots. The cold temperature inhibits growth until late spring, and then all of the new growth must take place in a few weeks, before soil moisture is exhausted. It is not surprising that most of the growth goes into new roots rather than aboveground parts; the plants must optimize water absorption. It is this investment of productivity into underground biomass that makes this community particularly susceptible to overgrazing. Availability of moisture dictates whether or not the plants will flower. Another member of the sunflower family, Great Basin Sagebrush has flowers that are small and inconspicuous and are wind-pollinated.

One notable characteristic of sagebrush is its odor. Odoriferous chemicals often are produced by plants to discourage herbivory, and in the case of Great Basin Sagebrush it seems to have worked on native species of herbivores. There is one animal, however, that can defoliate vast acreage. It is the larva of the moth *Aroga websteri*. The ultimate significance of the moth is that by increasing the amount of fuel in the form of dead foliage, it makes the community more susceptible to fires. It is possible that the moth indirectly serves to rejuvenate old stands of sagebrush by precipitating fire, which recycles mineral nutrients.

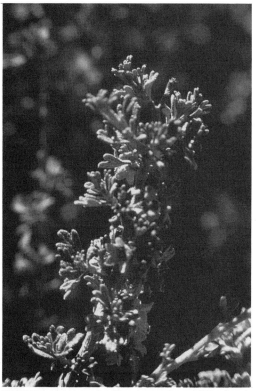

FIGURE 9.21 (*continued*)   Dominant plants of Sagebrush
Scrub. *B.* Antelope Brush, *Purshia tridentata*. Note that
both of these species have leaves with three teeth at the
apex.

Native ephemerals are not typical of this community. Delayed germination due
to snow cover and cold temperature does not favor annual species. The growing
season is simply too short and cool for native ephemerals to complete their life cycle.
Introduced annual grasses aided by C_4 photosynthesis and irrigation are able to hang
on in spite of the climate.

The Sagebrush Scrub community is not restricted in distribution to the Great
Basin. It is also found at high-elevation sites southward to Baja California. At these
sites, the community is restricted to coarse, well-drained soils, usually in flat areas locally referred to as meadows. Kennedy Meadows in the southern Sierra Nevada is one
such site, at about 7000 feet (2100 m) elevation. Another large area of Sagebrush Scrub
occurs in Garner Valley, at about 5000 feet (1500 m) in the San Jacinto Mountains of
southern California. In these southern California localities, Great Basin Sagebrush is
joined by Bitterbrush, *Purshia tridentata glandulosa*, which is the southern California
equivalent of Antelope Brush. Bitterbrush and Antelope Brush are in the rose family

(Rosaceae). In spring they become covered with yellow flowers with many anthers, typical of this family.

On a large flat area near Baldwin Lake in the San Bernardino Mountains is one of the largest regions of Sagebrush Scrub in southern California. Also in this region is an edaphic community known as a pavement plain, which was discussed as an ecologic island in chapter 8. Located here is an Alpine Fellfield type of habitat at about 6720 feet (2050 m) elevation where a pocket of Great Basin species reaches its southernmost distribution. The greatest concentration of endemics in the state occurs here. These low-growing species are alpinelike but of Great Basin affinities. Surrounding the pavement plain is the Sagebrush Scrub community. Also found in the area, reminiscent of eastern Oregon and the eastern Sierra Nevada, is Western Juniper, *Juniperus occidentalis*. Another common affiliate at these mountain localities is Jeffrey Pine.

Shadscale Scrub

The Shadscale Scrub community inhabits fine-grained alkaline soils of the Mojave and Great Basin deserts. In some areas of the Mojave it also occurs on rocky soil with rapid drainage. The community contains three dominant shrubs. Two of these are in the saltbush family (Chenopodiaceae): Shadscale, *Atriplex confertifolia,* and Winter Fat, *Krascheninnikovia* (= *Eurotia*) *lanata*. The third dominant is Bud Sagebrush, *Artemisia spinescens*. These shrubs resemble each other. They are usually well-rounded, compact, and seldom over 2 feet (60 cm) high. The leaves are almost white and mealy-surfaced. Shadscale has oval leaves, Winter Fat has linear leaves, and Bud Sagebrush has leaves with five to seven small teeth at the tip. After it loses its flowers, the sagebrush is left with naked spiny stems. It has been reported that in Utah, because of its giant salinas, there is more Shadscale than Great Basin Sagebrush. Shadscale Scrub is more tolerant of dry conditions than Sagebrush Scrub.

Similar to Sagebrush Scrub, in this community most of the growth goes into root systems. Although these plants have remarkably shallow roots, it has been reported that the ratio of root growth to shoot growth is 7:1 in Shadscale and 4:1 in Winter Fat. As much as one-fourth of the Shadscale root system is replaced annually; therefore more than 75% of Shadscale productivity goes into its roots. It is suspected that by dropping a portion of the root system every year, the plants conserve energy by reducing the amount of tissue that carries on cellular respiration.

Saltbushes have salt glands on their leaves. They absorb salt and water from the alkaline soil, and then they excrete the salt upon the leaves, which is one of the reasons they have a silvery appearance. Excreting salt is an energy-demanding process, and saltbushes are able to cope with this energy demand because of their high-efficiency C_4 photosynthesis, which operates at high temperatures with the stomates closed. Tearing the leaf of a saltbush and magnifying the cut edge with a hand lens reveals that the chlorophyll is concentrated in the cells around the veins.

Another saltbush found on these fine-grained soils is Desert Holly, *Atriplex hymenelytra* (fig. 9.11). Mentioned previously as one of the few shrubs on soils of volcanic origin, where they stand out as white, rounded shrubs against a background of black soil. Leaves of Desert Holly are oval and toothed, resembling miniature holly leaves.

This community provides important forage for browsing animals. During the dry season, kangaroo rats are also known to eat saltbush leaves because they contain a higher amount of water than many other plants. The fastidious kangaroo rats scrape the salt off the leaves with their teeth first, because ingesting salt would complicate absorption of water.

Alkali Sink

Alkai Sink is a moist, alkaline habitat. It occurs in the bottom of basins where water remains standing for long periods of time or where the subsurface terrain is moist. The largest Alkali Sink community is on the edge of the Salton Sea in the Colorado Desert, but the community is also common at places such as Death Valley (pl. 9C), Saline Valley, Mono Lake, and the San Joaquin Valley. These areas are covered with a layer of silt when they dry. Ephemerals are unable to become established in such a habitat, but saltbushes, with their mechanisms for coping with salt, are able to colonize the otherwise hostile habitat.

Some authors divide this community into two separate units. In areas where salinity ranges from 0.2% to 0.7% (2000–7000 ppm) it is called Saltbush Scrub. Where salinity is greater, ranging from 0.5% to 2.0% (5000–20,000 ppm), it is called Alkali Sink. Actually, one community grades into the other, with the soil becoming more alkaline toward the lowest portions of a basin. The community is typical of basins in all of our deserts, including salty areas of the Great Central Valley.

The least alkaline and driest areas in the community are characterized by saltbushes known as Cattle Spinach, *Atriplex polycarpa,* and Wingscale, *Atriplex canescens.* These are both important forage species, and they resemble each other. Where they occur together, they are difficult to tell apart. They both have narrow, elongate leaves. Wingscale, however, has distinctive fruits with flat, scale-like wings. Cattle Spinach occurs in all deserts, but Wingscale is more typical of coarser, drier soils of the Mojave and Colorado deserts. They commonly grow on sandy mounds at the edges of playas or salinas.

In the Mojave and Colorado deserts, these saltbushes are often associated with Honey Mesquite, *Prosopis glandulosa* (fig. 9.4C). This deep-rooted shrublike tree is a phreatophyte: it taps into permanent groundwater. As discussed previously, where it grows, water is said to be no deeper than about 30 feet (10 m).

These trees are often found on the edges of sand dunes growing out of a huge mound of sand, with a base of many buried trunks (fig. 9.22). There is often an abundance of dead wood beneath the mesquite canopy, and this wood is ideal for campfires, for it burns without smoke. It is also revered for its hot coals, which are ideal for broiling meat. A person wishing to gather mesquite for a campfire should keep in mind that the tree is winter-deciduous. What may appear dead may simply be leafless. The dead wood is found under the canopy, and a person gathering it is sure to become scratched and lacerated by thorns.

FIGURE 9.22 Honey Mesquite, *Prosopis glandulosa,* in mounds of sand near Stovepipe Wells, Death Valley National Monument.

In the spring, the apparently dead branches come to life. Leaves are compound; each has a two-parted, wishbone-shaped stem (petiole) with many small leaflets. Mesquite is a legume (Fabaceae), and its beans are an important staple for desert animals, including Coyotes. Indians depended heavily on Honey Mesquite beans for sustenance.

As soil becomes more alkaline, plants increasingly have succulent leaves. These are still members of the saltbush family, however, and it is interesting that they also grow along the edges of estuaries and tidal flats at the shore of the ocean. A transitional species between slightly salty and very salty soils is a conspicuous, low, blue-gray plant known as Inkweed or Desert Blite, *Suaeda torreyana.* A related plant, Sea Blite, *Suaeda californica,* is a component of the coastal Salt Marsh community. The name *Inkweed* comes from the black ink that can be extracted from the herbage. Cahuilla Indians in the vicinity of the Salton Sea used this ink in their artwork. This plant can tolerate salinity up to 1.0% (10,000 ppm). In many playa areas, this is the last species encountered before the lake bed becomes bare. Next to Highway 395, on the edge of Owens Lake, a distinct band of blue-gray vegetation marks the region occupied by Inkweed.

The "champion" desert halophyte is Iodine Bush, *Allenrolfea occidentalis.* It resembles the pickleweeds (*Salicornia* spp.) that also occur in coastal Salt Marshes. One species, *Salicornia subterminalis,* may co-occur with Iodine Bush in the Alkali Sink community. Iodine Bush and pickleweeds are nearly leafless, but their stems are composed of a series of succulent sections separated by joints. The stems appear to be composed of a series of elongate green beads. These plants have deep taproots and absorb salt and water. By storing water in their tissues, these plants dilute the concentration of salts; thus they become more and more succulent as they grow. Small sections at the tips of the stems eventually dry out, die, and fall off; in this way salts are shed by the plant. These plants grow on the edge of water that is over 2.0% salt (20,000 ppm), where no other plants can grow.

Blackbrush Scrub

At higher elevations in the Great Basin and Mojave deserts there is a community of drought-deciduous and succulent plants called Blackbrush Scrub. This community occurs on coarse, rocky soils of upper bajadas where a significant portion of the precipitation falls as snow. In the Great Basin, Blackbrush Scrub occurs on slopes above the Great Basin Sagebrush community. In the Mojave it lies above Creosote Bush Scrub. In many areas this community is composed of nearly pure stands of Blackbrush, *Coleogyne ramosissima* (fig. 9.23). The name *Blackbrush* refers to the appearance of the community from a distance; an entire slope may be gray-black in appearance. The color is on the leafless outer stems of the shrubs.

These are drought-deciduous shrubs, although some authors would categorize them as partially deciduous. Leaves are lost from the outside first, revealing many twiggy branches with blackish bark. In the center of the bush small green leaves are retained long into the dry season. The outer envelope of twigs forms a "lathhouse" that helps to shade leaves in the center of the plant. The twigs also form a boundary layer of trapped air that helps insulate the center of the shrub from temperature extremes.

Blackbrush is in the rose family (Rosaceae). When in full leaf it roughly resembles Antelope Brush, with which it may co-occur. Blackbrush flowers are yellow with many stamens, but the leaves are not toothed. It differs from other members of the rose family also in that its flowers have no petals. Instead, there are four yellow sepals that resemble petals. On most plants, sepals are green.

Many members of the rose family are drought-deciduous and fruit-bearing, and they may bear names that indicate how closely related they are to domestic fruit trees. They are in the same genus (*Prunus*) as the domestic fruit trees. In various desert areas, usually on rocky slopes, Blackbrush and Antelope Brush may be joined by shrubs such as Desert Apricot, *Prunus fremontii* (fig. 8.29); Desert Peach, *Prunus andersonii;* and Desert Almond, *Prunus fasciculata* (fig. 8.30). Desert Peach and Desert Apricot are noted for their showy flowers. Desert Peach occurs from the Mojave northward into the Great Basin. Desert Apricot and Desert Almond were discussed as components of the Desert Chaparral community of the Peninsular Ranges.

One way of identifying many of these plants in the rose family is that they are commonly infested with webs of tent caterpillars, *Malacosoma* spp. (fig. 9.24). These caterpillars share their body heat, which is generated by twitching. By remaining together they are able to conserve heat energy trapped within the webbed tent. Although these caterpillars seem to be associated most commonly with plants of the rose family, they may also be found on the Plateau Gooseberry, *Ribes velutinum*. Studies on the defoliation process associated with these caterpillars indicate that they seldom

FIGURE 9.23   Blackbrush, *Coleogyne ramosissima.*

inhabit the same bush for more than three years because there is a lowering of food quality with each successive year. Furthermore, the caterpillars apparently communicate from one bush to another, presumably about the food quality, with airborne chemicals. After metamorphosis, the adults live only a few hours. During that time they mate and select a new, healthy plant on which to lay their eggs. Thus as the food quality of one species is degraded, they move to another species. This allows recovery of the original species.

When the caterpillars are in their tents, they are conspicuous to predators. Apparently, however, they are seldom attacked. Studies of tent caterpillars in the eastern United States show that they consume cyanide compounds from the plants. When they are attacked, they regurgitate a fluid containing the toxin, and this repels the predator. This is another example of the coevolution of plants and animals that use plant toxins as a defense mechanism.

In the Mojave, Blackbrush is joined on upper coarse slopes by a drought-deciduous shrub known as Bladder Sage or Paper-bag Bush, *Salazaria mexicana* (fig. 9.25). This shrub is leafless much of the time, and it has sinewy green stems. Most notable are its rose-colored, papery inflated pods, which remain on the shrub for long periods of time. Wind or water can carry these seedpods for long distances. Antelope Ground Squirrels, *Ammospermophilus leucurus,* are known to climb in these shrubs and extract the seeds. Bladder Sage is a member of the mint family (Lamiaceae), although it lacks the square stems and odor of most mint species.

FIGURE 9.24   Tent caterpillars, *Malacosoma* sp., often found in species of the rose family.

Among the succulent plants in this community are various mormon teas (*Ephedra* spp.). A mormon tea has succulent stems and no leaves. There are separate male and female plants, each bearing conelike reproductive structures. The seeds produced are important forage for ground squirrels. The stems possess tannins and small amounts of ephedrine, a stimulant drug related to amphetamines and one of the components in certain decongestants. Commercial ephedrine, however, is extracted from an Asian member of the group. A tasty tea may be brewed by boiling these stems in water.

Another interesting succulent-stemmed shrub is Desert Rue, *Thamnosma montana*. This aromatic shrub is a member of the rue family (Rutaceae), the same family that includes citrus fruit trees. Usually leafless, its green stems bear small glands yielding an odorous oil that is a skin irritant. When fruits are produced in spring, the plants are conspicuous. The fruits are about the size of peas and resemble miniature oranges. They are yellow-green and bear many of the oil-producing glands. Indians claimed a number of medicinal uses for the oil.

In the Mojave Desert, the most conspicuous succulent plants of Blackbrush Scrub are two similar yuccas: the Banana Yucca or Spanish Bayonet, *Yucca baccata*, and the Mojave Yucca, *Yucca schidigera*. These are large leaf-succulent plants, with leaves often over 2 feet (60 cm) long. Mojave Yuccas are larger and can appear treelike, with a large trunk capped by many succulent leaves. Banana Yucca gets its name from a very large fruit that was roasted and eaten by Indians. The two yuccas resemble each other, but where they grow together it can be seen that they are different in color. Banana

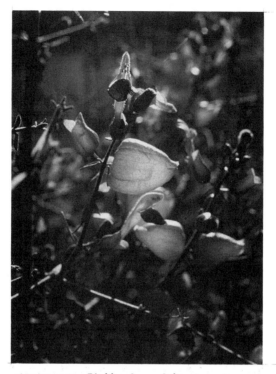

FIGURE 9.25 Bladder Sage, *Salazaria mexicana*, a drought-deciduous shrub of the Mojave Desert.

Yucca is blue-green, and Mojave Yucca is yellow-green. Banana Yucca occurs in the eastern Mojave, and Mojave Yucca occurs on upper bajadas and rocky slopes all over the Mojave. In the Peninsular Ranges, Mojave Yucca becomes associated with pinyon pines and junipers on the desert sides of the ranges. These two species of yucca were very important to desert Indians. Not only did they eat the fruits, but they made a soap from the roots and used fibers from the leaves for baskets and cloth.

When yuccas bloom, a high stalk of large white flowers projects above the leaves. White flowers are commonly pollinated at night, and the relationship between the night-flying yucca moths (*Tegeticula* spp.) and yuccas is often used as an example of mutualistic symbiosis. Yucca moths have to pack pollen onto the stigma of yucca flowers to accomplish pollination. After that the moth drills a small hole into the ovary of the flower, where it lays its eggs. Larvae develop inside the fruit. This is the only way that yuccas are pollinated, and this is the only place where yucca moths lay their eggs.

An apparent case of convergent evolution with yuccas occurs in the beargrasses (*Nolina* spp.), although their evolutionary relationships have been subject to controversy. These large plants, resembling bunchgrasses on a trunk, are included in

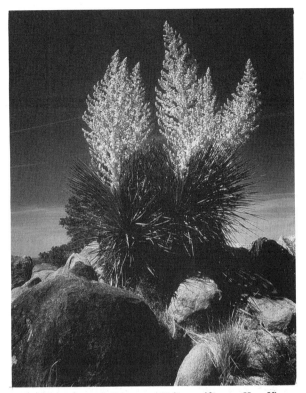

FIGURE 9.26   Wolf's Beargrass, *Nolina wolfii,* near Keys View, Joshua Tree National Monument.

the family Dracaenaceae, which allies them with palmlike plants such as the Dragon Tree, *Dracaena draco,* native to the Canary Islands. Formerly they were grouped with the yuccas and century plants (*Agave* spp.), in a different family, either Agavaceae or Lily-aceae. Some species of beargrass are very yuccalike in appearance. When they are in full bloom, beargrasses may be the most beautiful of all desert plants. The flower stalks, like giant plumes covered with white flowers, are often twice as high as the rest of the plant. Wolf's Beargrass, *Nolina wolfii* (fig. 9.26), of the eastern Mojave Desert, may grow in a cluster of long, narrow leaves with flower stalks up to a full 12 feet (4 m) in height. Spectacular specimens may be seen in the Kingston Mountains or Joshua Tree National Monument. Parry's Beargrass, *N. parryi,* occurs in the Domelands Wilderness of the southern Sierra Nevada and on the eastern slopes of the San Jacinto and Santa Rosa mountains. Bigelow's Beargrass, *N. bigelovii,* a smaller species, occurs in the southern part of the Colorado Desert at lower elevations than the other two. Classification of the beargrasses currently is under investigation. It may be that the desert beargrasses mentioned here, as well as those in cismontane southern California, may soon be realigned and renamed.

Joshua Tree Woodland

Joshua Tree Woodland is very similar to Blackbrush Scrub. It occurs at similar elevation, with similar climate, where snow is a common form of precipitation. There are many species in common between the two communities, and some authorities would lump them; however, Blackbrush is rarely found in Joshua Tree Woodland, and vice versa. Blackbrush is associated mainly with steeper, rocky slopes. Typical Joshua Tree habitat is well-drained loose gravel and sand, on the upper part of gentle slopes.

Joshua Trees, *Yucca brevifolia* (fig. 9.27), form a conspicuous overstory in this community. Although they appear to dominate, in terms of actual biomass they are probably less important than some of the understory species. Joshua Trees are the symbol of the Mojave Desert; their distribution more or less outlines the Mojave. They are ecologically similar to other yucca species; for example, they are pollinated by yucca moths. They do not flower every year, but when they do, great masses of white flowers are produced. Flowering is regulated by an unknown combination of temperature and precipitation.

Germination of Joshua Tree seeds occurs in association with abundant winter precipitation, but young Joshua Trees are usually gnawed off by rodents. It seems that the only Joshua Trees that escape predation are those that germinate under the protective cover of shrubs known as nurse plants, which include a variety of species. After three to four years the Joshua Tree emerges from the canopy of its host and eventually replaces it.

FIGURE 9.27   Joshua Tree, *Yucca brevifolia,* Joshua Tree National Monument.

FIGURE 9.28   The small world of a Joshua Tree. (From E. Bakker. *An Island Called California.* Berkeley: University of California Press, 1984.)

A number of animals are known associates of Joshua Trees (fig. 9.28). Yucca moths are obvious examples. Another associated insect is the Yucca Weevil, *Scyphophorus yuccae,* whose larvae kill the growing tip of a stem, causing it to branch. Flowering also causes branching. A young Joshua Tree will grow as a single trunk until either beetle larvae or flowering causes branching. After that, repeated branching is caused by the same stimuli, ultimately resulting in the largest species of flowering plant in the Mojave Desert. The largest of all Joshua Trees is located on the desert side of the San Bernardino Mountains. It is 32.3 feet (10.4 m) in height and has a crown diameter of 32.7 feet (10.5 m). Leaves of a Joshua Tree are smaller than those of other yuccas. After the growing tip is killed, the leaves turn brown and fold backward, forming what looks like a small straw umbrella. The next year, one or two branches form below that point.

At least 25 different species of birds have been reported to use Joshua Trees for nesting. Conspicuous among these are woodpeckers such as Northern Flickers, *Colaptes auratus* (fig. 4.24), and Ladder-backed Woodpeckers, *Picoides scalaris.* There are few trees in the California desert, and Joshua Trees have the softest wood for making a nest. Woodpeckers eat termites, and termites are constant associates of Joshua Trees. Branches fall off, or strong winds blow down entire Joshua Trees, and termites live in and feed on this downed wood. A lizard known as the Desert Night Lizard, *Xantusia vigilis,* also feeds on these termites. These lizards are found under and within the fallen Joshua Tree, and they are also associated with other species of yucca. Most of this foraging occurs during daylight hours, but because the lizards rarely leave the cover of fallen boughs, it was once thought they were strictly nocturnal—hence the misnomer *night lizard.* Small snakes such as Night Snakes, *Hypsiglena torquata,* also live under these boughs, where they feed on the lizards and a variety of insects.

The western part of the Mojave Desert is known as the Antelope Valley. This area contains the towns of Lancaster and Palmdale, which were the fastest-growing cities in the state in the 1980s. The rapid rate of development here led to fears that Joshua Trees would be uprooted at an inordinate rate. Ordinances were passed requiring botanical reports to be prepared before desert vegetation could be destroyed. Requirements to replace Joshua Trees and other sensitive species were initiated, and a tree bank has been proposed where plants can be put into storage until they can be transplanted.

Cactus Scrub

The coarse soils of the upper bajada and rocky slopes of the Colorado Desert are inhabited by a different mix of drought-deciduous and succulent species (pl. 9A, fig. 9.1). Just as Joshua Tree Woodland is truly a Mojave community, Cactus Scrub is truly a Colorado Desert community. Snow is rare in this warm desert community, and summer precipitation is significant.

The cactus family (Cactaceae) is American in origin. Succulent plants in Old World deserts resemble cacti, but these Old World plants are often in the euphorbia family (Euphorbiaceae), plants characterized by milky juice. The common Christmas ornamental, Poinsettia, is an example of a euphorbia with leaves. There are native euphorbias in the New World, but there are no native cacti in the Old World.

Cacti are remnants of a tropical family. In the American tropics today, large cacti are common on dry sites within the forest. Presumably, millions of years ago, tropical forests occurred where our present deserts lie. With increasing aridity and advances of cold climate during the Ice Age, tropical forest retreated, leaving behind those species that were drought-adapted. With the increasing aridity since the Pleistocene, cacti expanded their ranges from localized, warm dry refugia. The limit to northward distribution today is still cold climate. As one progresses northward, the number of species of cacti is reduced markedly.

Some authorities believe that the cactus family and the rose family are closely related. A group of primitive cacti from the Caribbean known variously as lemon vines or gooseberries (*Pereskia* spp.) show characteristics intermediate between the two families. These are long-stemmed drought-deciduous plants with leaves that arise from the stems along with spines. Superficially, they resemble Ocotillos. Rose flowers and cactus flowers are similar in that they possess many stamens. Rose flowers, however, usually have only five petals, whereas cactus flowers usually have many. The many-petaled rose flowers that adorn suburban gardens are products of horticultural tampering, and they rarely occur wild in nature.

Cactus flowers seem disproportionately large and colorful for the plant on which they grow. This illustrates an adaptation for dry climate, where precipitation is not predictable. When there is adequate rainfall, desert plants invest a major portion of their productivity on reproduction. They produce lots of flowers, and flowers are large. With all the flowers competing for pollinators, bright colors and large size are important. Very few desert flowers have odors, because odor requires moisture. The animal sense of smell requires a wet membrane for interpretation, and it apparently does not function well in dry air.

Cacti blossom in the winter, in keeping with their tropical heritage. Tropical plants are short-day plants; they flower only during a short photoperiod. Physiologically, they are unable to flower during summer, when day length exceeds 14 hours. When cacti become sufficiently hydrated and day length is short, they produce flowers. This coincides with winter precipitation in our deserts. The number of flowers produced by any one cactus plant is proportional to the amount of water it receives.

Cacti show other adaptations that make them ideal for rocky soils and hot climate. The advantages to water storage and crassulacean acid metabolism (CAM photosynthesis) have already been discussed. A reduced leaf surface reduces potential water loss, but the true function of leaves that have been modified into spines is not clear. Perhaps the most useful contribution of the spines is a boundary layer of trapped air that helps to insulate the cactus from rapid temperature change. The spines may also provide increased surface area to help dissipate heat, and they probably also produce a "lathhouse" effect, reducing the intensity of light that actually falls on the stem. It also has been stated that spines discourage browsing by herbivores, which is probably true to some degree, although the concentration of metabolic acids associated with crassulacean acid metabolism makes cactus flesh unpalatable, if not noxious. Nevertheless, certain animals, such as woodrats, consume cactus as a water source. In times of drought, large mammals such as Bighorn Sheep and cattle will also eat cactus.

Other features that reduce light intensity on cactus plants are vertical orientation of the stem and irregularities of surface, such as lumps, ridges, and grooves. These features ensure that light strikes photosynthetic surfaces at an angle and that no surface receives direct light all of the time.

There are many species of cacti in Cactus Scrub. Common forms include barrels, hedgehogs, pincushions, chollas, prickly-pears, and beavertails. The largest of the Colorado Desert cacti is the Barrel Cactus or Bisnaga, *Ferocactus acanthodes*. This form occurs in the rockiest of locations. Sometimes the only soil is found in cracks in rocks, and that is where the Barrel Cactus has its roots (fig. 9.29). The story of cutting the top off a Barrel Cactus and finding standing water within is an exaggeration. True, a considerable amount of water is stored in a Barrel Cactus, but it is contained within pulpy inner tissue. To obtain water from this tissue, a person would have to squeeze it vigorously, and the small amount produced would scarcely be palatable because of the metabolites from crassulacean acid metabolism.

Prickly-pear, beavertail, and cholla are common names for a variety of cacti in the genus *Opuntia*. Prickly-pear and beavertail are flattened stem succulents. Their spines emerge in clusters from localized patches of tissue arranged symmetrically on the stem. There are two kinds of spines: long ones and short, furry ones known as glochids. Glochids produce no pain when they stick to a person's skin, but there are so many of them and they are so small that they are difficult to remove. They can cause itching if they become caught in clothing.

Beavertail Cactus, *Opuntia basilaris,* is a dominant species in the Cactus Scrub community, although it also grows at appropriate localities within Creosote Bush Scrub as far north as the Mojave Desert. This cactus is blue-gray and often grows only one pad high. An obvious feature that distinguishes it from similar species of prickly-pear is that Beavertail Cactus has no long spines, only glochids. This is a favorite species for woodrats to gnaw on for a summer water source. The flowers on this species are a brilliant pinkish violet. In years with abundant rainfall these small cacti are spectacular, with rows of large, brightly colored flowers.

Various species of prickly-pear cactus may also occur in this community, although they are more common in the Mojave or at higher elevation. Prickly-pear cacti can tolerate more cold. These plants may be quite tall, with many stem joints. They are called prickly-pears because flower pollination is followed by production of a large red fruit that is full of sugar but covered with spines. Animals eat the fruit and then deposit the seeds at some other location in their feces. The sugar is the reward for the animal, and the bright color attracts the animal to eat the fruit. Birds and mice consume much of the fruit, but Coyotes eat the fruit whole. Coyotes are probably one of the most important dispersal agents for seeds of these cacti.

One species of this group is remarkably cold-tolerant. This is the Old Man Cactus or Mojave Prickly-pear, *Opuntia erinacea*. This species has very long spines that give it the appearance of having long gray hair. The abundant "hair" may provide the

FIGURE 9.29   Barrel Cactus, *Ferocactus acanthodes,* and Desert Agave, *Agave deserti,* growing from cracks in rocks.

insulation that enables this species to survive being buried in the snow. It occurs in snow-tolerant communities such as the Joshua Tree and Pinyon-Juniper woodlands.

Chollas have spines that are very close together, representing the ultimate in the boundary layer concept. Teddy Bear Cholla, *Opuntia bigelovii,* a dominant species in Cactus Scrub, appears downright furry. Its yellow thatch of spines dies at the base, giving the lower portion of the plant a blackish appearance. The joints of these cacti are fragile and easily broken. Consequently, on the ground in the area of Teddy Bear Cholla are many pieces of plants ready to "jump" on some passerby. These are the famous jumping cacti. Of course, they don't jump, but they do seem to find ways to become attached to animals, who carry them for some distance before they are able to knock them off. This is the way cholla gets dispersed. Each of the small sections is capable of growing a new set of roots, and thus the plant is able to colonize new areas. These chollas are sometimes considered pioneer species because they are particularly abundant in areas that have been disturbed.

Spines on these chollas are very sharp and barbed (fig. 9.30). They penetrate skin easily, but they are difficult to remove. It is a simple task for one of these fallen sections to become attached to a passing animal. The reason they seem to jump at humans is that a section of the plant is commonly picked up in the sole of one's shoe. When the person takes another step, the cactus becomes inadvertently planted in the back of the other leg. It certainly seems to have jumped there. Cholla spines also have a thin sheath around them. It is believed that this sheath is another example of a boundary layer, helping to keep the individual spines cooler.

FIGURE 9.30   Spines of Teddy Bear Cholla, *Opuntia bigelovii,* can be a trap to species unaccustomed to them. This Clark's Nutcracker, a mountain bird, caught its feet on the barbed spines and could not escape.

In spite of the nasty spines, some animals are able to use the cholla for their own interests. Desert Woodrats commonly gather cholla stems, which they heap into piles to form nests. The nest is in the center of the pile, and any animal attempting to dig out the woodrat is sure to experience a good deal of pain in the process. Several species of birds also make their nests in the cholla. The Cactus Wren, for example, builds its nest of grasses within the protective arms of the cholla plant. The Cactus Wren nest is distinguishable from those of most other birds by the entrance, which is on the side of the nest.

There are also leaf-succulent species in Cactus Scrub. The most conspicuous is the Desert Agave or Century Plant, *Agave deserti* (fig. 9.29). The base of this plant is a rosette of thick, fleshy leaves. When these plants blossom, they send up a tall stalk that may grow as much as a foot (30 cm) a day. The large yellow flowers are perfectly designed to be pollinated by nectar-feeding bats. In northern portions of the range of the Desert Agave, such bat species apparently no longer occur. Either they retreated southward with increasing aridity, or the plants have been carried out of their range by northward motion of the land west of the San Andreas fault. Other

FIGURE 9.31   Desert bees are able to steal nectar from the Desert Agave without accomplishing pollination. *A.* Carpenter bee, *Xylocopa* sp. *B.* Honey Bee, *Apis mellifera.* (From J. A. Powell and C. L. Hogue. *California Insects.* Berkeley: University of California Press, 1979.)

potential pollinators, such as moths, ants, hummingbirds, and Honey Bees (fig. 9.31B), are able to extract the nectar without touching the anthers, that is, without accomplishing pollination. Throughout most of the Colorado Desert, therefore, the Desert Agave is left to reproduce primarily by asexual means, which it accomplishes by producing smaller plants in a circle about the base of the parent plant.

Desert Agaves and nectar-feeding bats have evolved together. With the absence of nectar-feeding bats in this area, Desert Agaves are now forced either to reproduce by clones, which could be an evolutionary dead end, or to evolve in association with a different pollinator. Evidence of this evolution can be seen in a population of Desert Agaves near Los Alamos in northern Baja California. Here large-bodied California Carpenter Bees, *Xylocopa californica* (fig. 9.31A), contact the anthers when they gather nectar, so some pollination takes place. Pollinations occur more frequently if anthers and stigma are shortened, so shorter reproductive parts are favored. As might be expected, anthers and stigma are significantly shorter in the flowers near Los Alamos, and as time passes, they should become shorter as the efficiency of pollination improves.

Desert Agaves are called Century Plants because they grow for many years before producing flower stalks. Contrary to popular belief, they do not wait 100 years before producing blossoms. Rather, evidence shows the interval to be about 20 to 25 years. During this time, water and carbohydrates are stored in the leaves. The process of flower stalk growth exhausts the entire supply of water and stored food. After it flowers, the plant dies, leaving the clone of small plants at its base. Of course, if the plant has succeeded in producing seed, it has not died in vain; the expenditure of energy was worth it. In the northern part of this population, pollination rarely occurs, and the plant's death could be considered pointless. The plant has succeeded in reproducing vegetatively, however, and in time may evolve to accommodate a different pollinator, perhaps the California Carpenter Bee.

As in Joshua Trees, the rare seedlings of Desert Agave require a nurse plant. In this case, the seeds that germinate are usually under a desert bunchgrass known as Galleta

Grass, *Hilaria rigida*. It has been determined that Galleta Grass provides necessary shade and increased soil nitrogen for the Desert Agave seedlings.

A shrub of rocky slopes that has semisucculent leaves is Jojoba, *Simmondsia chinensis* (fig. 9.32). It enjoys patchy distribution from around Twentynine Palms southward to Arizona and Mexico, pretty well outlining the Sonoran Desert. It also occurs west of the crest of the Peninsular Ranges in dry Coastal Sage Scrub and Desert Chaparral. Leaves of this shrub are covered with a mealy, waxy surface and are oriented vertically, presumably to avoid the direct rays of the sun. Furthermore, the leaves track the sun. Depending on the temperature, they turn the flat surfaces away from or toward the sun's rays.

The fruits of these shrubs are borne on female plants. The fruits are about an inch (25 mm) long and contain about 50% high-quality oil, similar to Sperm Whale (*Physeter catodon*) oil. These fruits have been gathered for many years from wild plants for the purpose of extracting the oil. This enterprise was a major source of income for Indians in Arizona, and recently, Jojoba plantations have been started at various locations throughout the Sonoran Desert. It is hoped by entrepreneurs and environ-

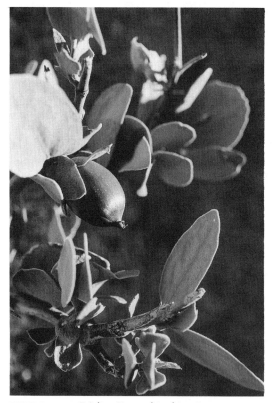

FIGURE 9.32 Jojoba, *Simmondsia chinensis*.

mentalists that large-scale use of Jojoba oil will replace Sperm Whale oil. The main problem is that, typical of most desert agriculture, in order to optimize growth, the plants have to be irrigated. Also, it takes a number of years before the plants produce fruit. It is therefore debatable whether the investment will produce a return sufficient to warrant the expense of leveling, road building, and irrigation. Originally, there were tax incentives, but these may not be continued. If too much Jojoba oil is produced, the price will drop, and it will be economically unfeasible to continue irrigating the shrubs.

Two common drought-deciduous species are components of the Cactus Scrub community. These are Desert Brittle-bush, *Encelia farinosa* (fig. 9.33A), and Ocotillo, *Fouquieria splendens* (fig. 9.33B). Desert Brittle-bush is in the sunflower family (Asteraceae). When it gets adequate water, it produces a large canopy of bright yellow sunflowers at the ends of long stems. These flowers track the sun to optimize the temperature of reproductive parts. A person viewing these plants with the sun to his or her back will see every flower straight on, in a blaze of color. At the height of flowering, a broad band of bright yellow on a hillside testifies to the abundance of this plant in its preferred habitat. The bright white leaves are over an inch (25 mm) long, reasonably large for a desert plant. As the growing season progresses, smaller, hairier leaves are produced, and the larger, more water-consuming leaves are dropped. Finally, when conditions get too dry, all the leaves are dropped, and the plant goes dormant. In its summer state the plant is leafless, and the long dead flower stalks stick out all over the canopy. These stalks break easily, giving the plant its name.

Another name for this plant is Incienso. Orange crystals of resin exude from the stems, and early padres would burn this resin as an incense. Indians chewed the resin and smeared it warm upon their bodies to reduce pain. It was also melted and used as a varnish. This plant is a close relative of Coast Brittle-bush, with which it hybridizes in low passes where their ranges overlap.

Ocotillo is the symbol of the Sonoran Desert. In the Colorado Desert it is distributed on rocky slopes or on gravels of the upper bajada. Bright red tubular flowers, perfect attractors of hummingbirds, occur in clusters at the end of tall, whiplike stems. When these flowers are in bloom, the plants form a band of red color on the hillsides, often just below the yellow band formed by the blooming Desert Brittlebushes.

Ocotillo is the "champion" drought-deciduous plant. It may grow and lose leaves up to seven times a year. Within two days after a good period of winter rain, leaf buds appear at the base of the thorns. One day later, the leaves are nearly 1/2 inch (1 cm) in length. By the end of the fifth day, the oval leaves are an inch (25 mm) long and fully mature. Then the stems elongate in proportion to the amount of rain. In a good year the stems may grow up to 3 feet (1 m). Examining the stems will indicate how much growth has been added each year, revealing a crude record of past years of precipitation.

On the new growth, leaves of a different shape are produced. Each leaf has a long, tapering stem (petiole) with the leaf blade folded backward at its tip. When the leaf

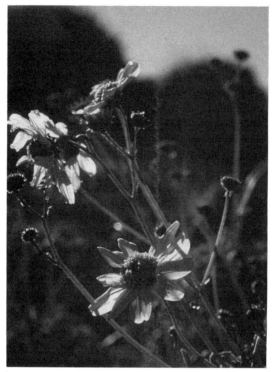

FIGURE 9.33   Drought-deciduous plants of the Cactus Scrub community. *A*. Desert Brittle-bush, *Encelia farinosa*.

FIGURE 9.33 (*continued*)   Drought-deciduous plants of the Cactus Scrub community. *B*. Ocotillo, *Fouquieria splendens*.

blade is shed, the petioles become new spines. The final picture is of a plant with 25 to 30 long, spiny stems up to 15 feet (5 m) in length. These are the tallest plants in the Colorado Desert. Similar to the Desert Agave, they attract pollinators by growing their flowers high, where there is less competition.

Desert Wash

The Desert Wash or Wash (Microphyll) Woodland consists mostly of deciduous, deep-rooted shrubs and trees. In the Mojave, these washes are outlined by thickets of Desert Willows, *Chilopsis linearis*. These are not true willows; they belong to a tropical family (Bignoniaceae) that includes many species of vines and trees with large, snapdragonlike flowers. Similar to cacti, these are relicts of a former time when precipitation in deserts was much greater. These trees are winter-deciduous. They are leafless during the rainy season, instead relying on water that remains deep within the sands of the wash during summer. Leaves are long and narrow when they are present. When in bloom the tree is covered with pinkish flowers that resemble snapdragons. The flowers are similar to those of the Jacaranda, a popular ornamental tree in the same family. After blooming, the tree produces long seedpods that resemble beans; however, these are not legumes. In some areas of the Mojave, Desert Willows are joined by Honey Mesquite, *Prosopis glandulosa,* another deep-rooted, winter-deciduous species. Like Honey Mesquite, Desert Willows grow on sand dunes. For example, the trees growing partway up Kelso Dunes are Desert Willows.

Desert Wash communities are most characteristic of the Colorado Desert. Desert Willow occurs here also, but it is joined by a number of trees in the pea family (Fabaceae) (fig. 9.4). Included here are Honey Mesquite; Ironwood, *Olneya tesota;* Blue Palo Verde, *Cercidium floridum;* and Smoke Tree, *Psorothamnus* (= *Dalea*) *spinosa*. Foliage on these trees is similar in appearance. Leaves are pinnately compound, with a single petiole bounded by small leaflets arranged opposite each other. Reflecting slightly different microhabitats, the trees differ in deciduousness. Mesquite is winter-deciduous. Ironwood is evergreen, but it loses its leaves a few at a time during the dry season. Blue Palo Verde is drought-deciduous, and after the leaves fall, it continues to photosynthesize with chlorophyll in the bark. Smoke Trees are similar to Blue Palo Verdes but rarely have leaves.

Little-leaf Palo Verde, *Cercidium microphyllum,* is a small tree with limited distribution in California, although it is widely distributed in the Arizona portion of the Sonoran Desert. It is found where the Colorado Desert extends northward in eastern San Bernardino County, in the Whipple Mountains, west of the Colorado River. It is noteworthy that this area is also one of the few places in California where the giant Saguaro Cactus, *Carnegiea gigantea,* occurs naturally. Little-leaf Palo Verde differs from Blue Palo Verde by having a greater number of leaflets and slightly different flower, fruit, and seeds. Flowers of the pea family are characterized by one petal, known as the banner petal, that stands upright and possesses special coloration that serves to attract insects. On Blue Palo Verde, this petal has small red dots. No such dots are found on Little-leaf Palo Verde. Furthermore, after a flower is pollinated, a change occurs that serves to signal potential pollinators that the flower has been visited.

FIGURE 9.34   Flower of the Blue Palo Verde, *Cercidium floridum*, with banner petal folded down, indicating to pollinators that it already has been visited.

On Blue Palo Verde, the banner petal folds down and covers the throat of the flower (fig. 9.34). On Little-leaf Palo Verde, the banner petal changes from yellow to white. Experiments have shown that this color change is triggered by a pH change in the flower that is activated by the act of pollination.

Seeds of the desert legumes are very important forage for animals. Indians also ate these seeds, which are tasty when green. Mature seeds are covered with an extremely hard coat and must be ground into a meal to be eaten. The value of this hard coat to the seed is that it prevents germination until it is cracked or broken, a process known as scarification. In nature, the mechanism that cracks the surface is rolling and tumbling of the seeds along with rocks and gravel when water rushes down washes. This ensures that seeds will not germinate unless there is enough water. Once the seeds germinate, a few leaves are produced. After that, most of the growth is in the roots, and at this time root growth is very rapid. Mesquite roots can grow more than 4 inches (10 cm) a day, about 10 times the rate of most plants. The green part of the plant remains small and close to the surface of the soil for several years, during which time the root system penetrates toward a potential water source. Once the roots are deep enough to provide adequate water, the upper part of the plant becomes enlarged. The deep roots of these trees serves two useful purposes: they provide for water absorption, and they serve to anchor the plant in what may be a disturbed habitat. Cloudbursts can excavate the gravels of a Desert Wash, uprooting all plants but those with the deepest root systems.

FIGURE 9.35   Phainopepla, *Phainopepla nitens.*

Catclaw Acacia, *Acacia greggii,* is a legume that grows on the edges of washes in the Mojave and Colorado deserts. It is a shrub, not a tree, but otherwise it resembles the other legumes in the washes. Similar to mesquites, it is winter-deciduous. The name *Catclaw* refers to its dark, recurved thorns, which snag anything that brushes up against it. Some old-timers call it the "Wait-a-minute Bush." The tops of these bushes are commonly infested with Desert Mistletoe, *Phoradendron californicum,* the seeds for which are deposited there in the droppings of the Phainopepla, *Phainopepla nitens* (fig. 9.35), a black, crested bird that perches commonly in the uppermost branches.

On the edges of Desert Washes is a community of drought-deciduous shrubs. These shrubs are able to become established on the shoulders of a wash that are disturbed by only the largest of storms. To a degree, these are successional species that are good at reseeding once a spot has been disturbed.

A common drought-deciduous shrub of the Mojave and Colorado deserts is Cheesebush, *Hymenoclea salsola.* A successional species, it is one of the first to colonize new soil after a desert storm has reworked the soil of a wash. The resinous herbage of this shrub smells cheesy when crushed. Leaves, when present, are filamentous, resembling the stems. This is a member of the sunflower family, but it has scale-like fruit resembling a saltbush.

One of the most spectacular drought-deciduous shrubs occurring on the shoulders of a desert wash is Chuparosa, *Justicia* (= *Beloperone*) *californica* (fig. 9.36). *Chuparosa*

FIGURE 9.36 Chuparosa, *Justicia californica,* a hummingbird-pollinated flower.

FIGURE 9.37 Black-throated Sparrow, *Amphispiza bilineata.*

is the Spanish name for the hummingbird; it means "suck-rose." This shrub becomes covered with long bright red tubular flowers typical of those that are hummingbird-pollinated. Birds such as Verdins (*Auriparus flaviceps*), House Finches (*Carpodacus mexicanus*), and Black-throated Sparrows (*Amphispiza bilineata*) (fig. 9.37) bite off the flowers to get the nectar. Indians formerly ate the flowers. This is the only California member of a large family of ornamental tropical shrubs, the acanthus family (Acanthaceae).

Sand Dunes

Sand dunes require a source of sand and a prevailing wind. The source of sand could be a river or a playa. If wind blows consistently in the same direction over a playa, sand becomes deposited at its leeward end. The side of a dune toward the wind is inclined at about a 5° to 10° angle. Wind constantly carries sand from this slope to the top of the dune, where it slides down the other side. The slope out of the wind, known as the slip-face, is a good deal steeper, lying at a consistent 33° to 34° angle.

Major dune fields are found in each desert. These areas are ecologic islands characterized by endemic plants and animals. In California, the most spectacular dunes are the Eureka Dunes, Dumont Dunes, Kelso Dunes, and Algodones Dunes.

The Eureka Dunes are the northernmost. Eureka Valley lies between northern Owens Valley and northern Death Valley. The dune field is 3 miles (4.8 km) long and 1 mile (1.6 km) wide. These are the highest dunes in North America, reaching 680 feet (207 m) in height. There are several dune endemics, including three plants and five species of beetles. Some authorities call dune plants *psammophytes,* which means "sand-plants." Notable among them is the Eureka Dunegrass, *Swallenia alexandrae.* Typical of dunegrasses, it keeps up with shifting substratum by spreading out with underground rhizomes. Perhaps the most spectacular endemic plant is the Eureka Valley Evening Primrose, *Oenothera californica eurekensis* (fig. 9.38), of the evening primrose family (Onagraceae), so named because the flowers open in the evening and remain open at night. Both of these plants are listed by the federal government as endangered, and in response the Bureau of Land Management has enforced a policy of no off-road vehicles in the area.

Geologists have determined that these dunes are older than 10,000 years, making them the oldest in North America. The presence here of a large number of plant species with Great Basin affinities implies that the desert species remained in the valley during the Pleistocene. Another interesting thing about the Eureka Dunes is that no source area for the sand can be located. Old waterlines indicate that the valley once was filled with water, and there is a playa there today, but the sand particles in the dune have not been derived from the adjacent playa. The best guess is that very high winds during the ancient past carried the sand from a source to the north that today is outside the valley.

Kelso Dunes (fig. 9.39) are located 35 miles (56 km) south of Soda Dry Lake, near Baker. This large dune field covers some 45 square miles (115 km^2). Sediments

FIGURE 9.38   Eureka Valley Evening Primrose, *Oenothera californica eurekensis.*

carried by the Mojave River flowing toward Soda Lake are its source of sand. These dunes rise 656 feet (200 m) above the surrounding desert floor, nearly as high as the Eureka Dunes. Kelso and Eureka dunes are the only two dune fields in California that "sing" when the sand is disturbed. Sometimes they are called booming dunes. This production of sound occurs when the etched surfaces of the sand grains rub on each other. The cause of the sound is not understood, but the moisture content of the sand must be less than 1% for the sound to occur.

Endemism in the Kelso Dunes is not as great as it is in the Eureka Dunes, but the field does harbor seven species of endemic insects, including the Kelso Dunes Giant Sand Treader, *Macrobaenetes kelsoensis* (a camel cricket); the Kelso Dunes Jerusalem Cricket, *Ammopelmatus kelsoensis;* and the Kelso Dunes Shieldback Katydid, *Eremopedes kelsoensis.* The Mojave Fringe-toed Lizard, *Uma scoparia,* is not endemic to the dunes, but it is rare everywhere else. A number of plants that are rare outside of dune fields are also found here.

The sensitive nature of the Eureka and Kelso dunes has prompted federal officials to close them to use by off-road vehicles. However, they still allow grazing and sand-mining on the Kelso Dunes—an apparent conflict of priorities. As an example of the effect of intensive use, the Dumont Dunes of the Amargosa Valley have little growing on them because they are open for dune buggy use. On any weekend, hundreds to thousands of dune buggies and off-highway vehicles buzz around on these sands.

The Colorado Desert contains the largest continuous dune field, the Algodones Dunes. The Spanish word *algodon* means "cotton." These dunes get their sand from ancient Lake Cahuilla and the present-day Whitewater River. Winds blow southward, pushing these dunes farther into Baja California. The field is 40 miles (64 km) long

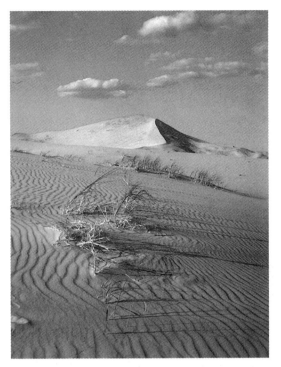

FIGURE 9.39   Kelso Dunes, San Bernardino County.

and up to 6 miles (10 km) wide, and the dunes are as high as 300 feet (95 m). Portions of the dune field near Glamis are closed to off-road vehicles in order to protect the specialized plants and animals. This dune field contains the largest number of dune endemics in North America. There are six kinds of plants that occur nowhere else. For example, the interesting Desert Buckwheat, *Eriogonum deserticola* (fig. 9.40), grows here. This plant may grow up to 5 feet (160 cm) high. In this shifting sand it continues to extend a single stemlike root in an attempt to keep the photosynthetic part of the plant above the sand. When the sand blows away, this sinuous, elongate root becomes exposed, arching up out of the sand 10 to 15 feet (3–5 m) away from the green part of the shrub. On some occasions, plants such as Creosote Bush or Mormon Tea also take this form.

One of the strangest plants in the Algodones Dunes is a root parasite often associated with Desert Buckwheat. This plant is called Sand-food, *Pholisma* (= *Ammobroma*) *sonorae*. Most of the plant lies beneath the sand, where it taps into roots up to 5 feet (1.5 m) down. The portion of the plant on the surface is a fleshy flower disc that resembles a partially buried bagel. Indians ate them raw or roasted. This nonphotosynthetic plant derives its entire sustenance from the plant it parasitizes. How seeds of this plant germinate is a mystery. The seeds are so small that they could not store enough energy for the stem of this plant to penetrate deeply enough to reach the

FIGURE 9.40 Desert Buckwheat, *Eriogonum deserticola,* with stemlike root exposed by shifting sand. Algodones Dunes, Imperial County.

root system of its host plant. The latest theory is that ants carry the seeds into their burrows, where they germinate in proximity to the roots they will parasitize. They may also germinate in this way in rodent burrows.

Because sand constantly shifts and dunes migrate, this is an unstable habitat, and certain ephemeral plants are typical. One of these is Sand Verbena, *Abronia villosa.* This member of the four-o'clock family (Nyctaginaceae) is common along roads and in sand dunes. It is a trailing, viny species with brilliant rose-purple flowers borne in small, rounded clusters. This is one of the few desert species with an odor. Its sweet fragrance is characteristic of spring nights in the desert. A good place to see acres of Sand Verbena is in the dunes near Palm Desert after a good period of winter rain. At least 1 inch (25 mm) of rain by late autumn is required for the best show of annual wildflowers.

The other common annual of sandy areas is Dune Primrose, *Oenothera deltoides,* which resembles the Eureka Valley Evening Primrose (fig. 9.38), mentioned earlier. This prostrate, spreading annual has large white flowers with four petals. As is often the case with white flowers, these are pollinated by a moth, the White-lined Sphinx Moth, *Hyles lineata.* This plant is another exception to the rule that desert flowers have no odor. Odors are more useful to plants in the desert at night, because this is the only time of day when the air is humid enough for the sense of smell to function well. Moths have a particularly good sense of smell, which helps them locate this flower at night.

Larvae of this moth are black, green, and yellow. They feed on leaves and flowers of the primrose, and when larvae are abundant, as occurred in 1991, most of the plants become defoliated. When this happened in the past, Indians would collect larvae in great numbers and eat them. When Dune Primrose plants become old, the stems have a peculiar way of rising upward and bending back to converge on themselves at the top. Plants that dry in this way form a sort of bird cage. At curio shops in the desert these dried plants, known as bird cage plants, are available complete with an artificial bird.

Geophytes, plants that regrow from an underground storage organ, are also found in sandy areas. Desert Lily, *Hesperocallis undulata* (fig. 9.41), is a large white lily common in the Mojave and Colorado deserts that grows from a bulb. The bulbs are surprisingly deep, up to 24 inches (60 cm) below the surface. Obviously, it takes a significant rainfall to reach one of these bulbs and stimulate growth. It is believed that these plants propagate primarily by seeds. A sphinx moth is one of the main pollinators. Indians ate the bulbs, which are reported to have an onion or garlic flavor. Sometimes this plant is alled *Ajo,* which is the Spanish word for "garlic."

A common member of the cucumber family (Cucurbitaceae) is a vine of sandy areas known as the Coyote Melon, *Cucurbita palmata.* This vine returns each year from a large bulbous root. Green to yellow gourds about the size of baseballs make these vines conspicuous. Indians ground and ate the seeds, which are quite nutritious. A similar vine, *Cucurbita foetidissima,* has a rank odor to its foliage. It is also known variously as Coyote Melon, Calabazilla, or Buffalo Gourd, and its noxious odor is the source of the Indian name Coyote Melon. According to the Indian story, Coyotes spoil anything that is good, and they urinated and defecated on the plant to give it a rank odor, hence leaving the nutritious fruit for themselves. There have been proposals to grow these plants commercially as a source of protein and cooking oil. The seeds average 31% protein and 30% oil.

Large dune fields are also water reservoirs. For this reason it is not uncommon to find deep-rooted trees, usually associated with desert washes, growing on the dunes. Honey Mesquite (fig. 9.22) and Desert Willow are found on dunes in the Mojave Desert. In the Colorado Desert other desert wash species, such as Blue Paloverde, grow on dunes, too.

Some dune areas are characterized by specialized lizards that "swim" under the sand. These are the fringe-toed lizards (*Uma* spp.) (fig. 9.42A), and they occur in the Algodones Dunes, the Coachella Valley Dunes near Palm Springs, and Kelso Dunes. There are two other species in Mexico. Restricted to fine, windblown sand, these lizards dive head-first into the sand and wriggle out of sight. Adaptations to this habitat include elongated fringe scales on the toes, to facilitate running on the sand, and a number of specializations to keep sand out of body openings, such as valved nasal and ear openings, sand-trap nasal passages, a countersunk lower jaw, and overlapping eyelids.

In order to protect the endangered Coachella Valley Fringe-toed Lizard, *Uma inornata,* three tracts of land in the Coachella Valley, representing about 10% of the lizard's known habitat, are administered as preserves by a coalition of agencies including

FIGURE 9.41   Desert Lily, *Hesperocallis undulata*, a geophyte.

the Bureau of Land Management, the U.S. Fish and Wildlife Service, the California Department of Fish and Game, and the Nature Conservancy. The Willow Hole–Edom Hill reserve contains 2500 acres (1000 ha), and the Whitewater Floodplain Preserve contains 1230 acres (492 ha). The Coachella Valley Preserve, near Thousand Palms, is a 13,000-acre (5,200-ha) tract of land that also includes one of the finest examples of a California Fan Palm oasis in the California desert (pl. 8B). This oasis is also being used as a refuge for the endangered Desert Pupfish, *Cyprinodon macularius*.

Similar in appearance to the fringe-toed lizard is the Zebra-tailed Lizard, *Callisaurus draconoides* (fig. 9.42B). Males have two dark bands on each side of the body just behind the armpits. During breeding season, the area around these bands becomes a bright blue-green. Interestingly, this is one of the few species in which females take on a breeding color. They develop an orange throat patch and become orange on the sides behind the armpits. This color change in a female appears to be a signal that she already has mated and is designed not to attract a courting male. This lizard is most common in sandy and gravelly areas, but it also occurs on desert flats with a scattering of small rocks. It favors the sand of desert washes and the margins of sand dunes. Its most distinctive feature is the underside of its tail, which bears black bars in a zebra or gridiron pattern. When the lizard is at rest but alerted, it curls its tail forward to reveal the black and white markings. It seems to wag the tail nervously, which may function to distract a potential predator to the conspicuous markings. If the predator goes for the tail first, it can be sacrificed and later regrown. This is one of California's fastest lizards. It has been clocked at 18 miles per hour (29 kph), and it can run 40 to 50 yards at a time, stopping and veering abruptly. When running

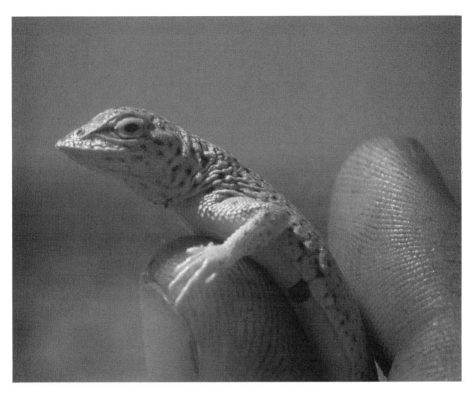

FIGURE 9.42 Two species of sand-dwelling lizards. *A*. Mojave Fringe-toed Lizard, *Uma scoparia*.

FIGURE 9.42 (*continued*) Two species of sand-dwelling lizards. *B*. Zebra-tailed Lizard, *Callisaurus draconoides*.

at high speed it uses only its hind legs. It holds its forelimbs to its side and curls its tail over its back, apparently for balance, as it sprints over the sand. This is truly a remarkable sight.

Desert Pavement

Desert pavement is produced when wind blows away all the sand from an area. The larger pebbles and stones that remain form an armored surface preventing any more sand from being blown away. Evaporation of water from this surface leaves calcium carbonate, which can become a cement that holds the stones together, similar to icing on a cake.

The dark surface of a desert pavement must be one of the hottest habitats in the world and is a difficult substratum for plants. Long-lived shrubs that grew there before the pavement was formed are able to continue using water that percolates between the rocks. However, very little new establishment is possible. One interesting exception is a small annual plant in the buckwheat family (Polygonaceae) known as Spiny-herb, *Chorizanthe rigida* (fig. 9.43). It is found in desert pavement of all California deserts,

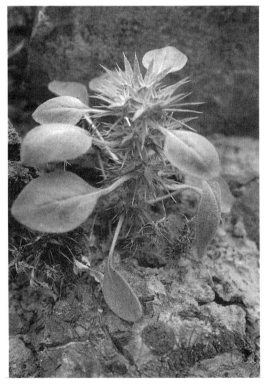

FIGURE 9.43 Spiny-herb, *Chorizanthe rigida*. A. As it appears with leaves, when it first grows.

and sometimes it is the only thing growing to tolerate temperatures higher than any other known plant can endure. When the plant comes up, it has a short, spiny stem with many oval leaves. After the plant dies, all that remains is a dry vertical mass of spines that may persist for years. Many people erroneously believe that this is a dead cactus.

Pavement plains are deceptively thin-skinned. A person walking upon the surface gets the illusion that it is as firm as blacktop. A vehicle such as a motorcycle, however, breaks through with little effort, and the tire track becomes an erosion channel. Wind and water carry away soil from the track. When it rains, water flows through the track and is carried away from the area, causing it to be drier than before. Plants may die as a result. It is difficult to understand what a fragile balance these desert ecosystems represent.

Riparian Woodland

Flowing streams enter the desert on the transmontane side of the Sierra Nevada, the Transverse Ranges, and the Peninsular Ranges. In addition, in various desert

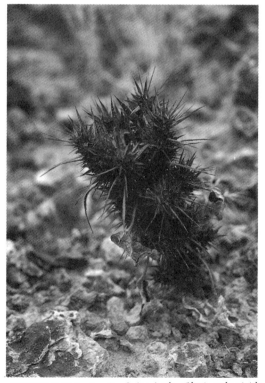

FIGURE 9.43 (*continued*)   Spiny-herb, *Chorizanthe rigida*.
B. As it appears in its dried state.

ranges there are springs with sufficient flow to produce permanent streams bordered by riparian vegetation. Furthermore, there are a few rivers in California deserts that maintain permanent flow over at least a portion of their courses. In the Great Basin are the East and West Walker rivers and the Owens River. The Mojave River and the Amargosa River maintain permanent flow over a portion of their courses in the Mojave Desert, and the Whitewater River has some permanent flow in the Colorado Desert. The largest river in the California desert is the Colorado River, which flows along the eastern edge of the Mojave and Colorado deserts, forming the border between California and Arizona.

Fremont Cottonwood, *Populus fremontii* (fig. 8.54), and Black Willow *Salix gooddingii,* are the dominant native trees in desert Riparian Woodland. Black Willow primarily occurs below 2000 feet (900 m) in elevation and is particularly common in the Colorado River drainage. On smaller streams, Fremont Cottonwood and Black Willow may form a gallery forest along the main flow. Along the Colorado River, however, these two species are most common in secondary channels. The establishment of seedlings depends on spring flooding, which deposits seeds in moist silt. Recruitment of seedlings is difficult along the main channel. Because the Colorado River flow is controlled by so many dams, the native Riparian Woodland along its banks is a seriously threatened community.

Narrowleaf Willow, *Salix exigua,* so named for its long, narrow leaves, is a shrub that grows up to 15 feet (5 m) in height. Leaves are 2 to 5 inches (5–12 cm) in length and about $^1/_3$ inch (8 mm) in width. It occurs below 8000 feet (2500 m) on desert streams from Imperial County north to Modoc County.

Mule fat, *Baccharis salicifolia* (fig. 10.9), is a willowlike shrub in the sunflower family (Asteraceae) that grows up to 12 feet (4 m) in height. It occurs along slow-moving streams from the Colorado Desert north to Owens Valley. Other species in this genus, such as Desert Broom or Broom Baccharis (*B. sarathroides*) and Squaw Waterweed (*B. sergiloides*), are nearly leafless, carrying on photosynthesis in their broomlike stems. Squaw Waterweed is a common water indicator of the Mojave and Colorado deserts. It is a shorter plant, seldom over 6 feet (2 m) in height. Under ideal conditions, Desert Broom may reach heights of 12 feet (4 m). It occurs in the Colorado Desert east to Arizona.

Arrowweed, *Pluchea sericea,* is another willowlike shrub in the sunflower family. Like Mulefat, the flowers occur in clusters of small heads, with no surrounding ray flowers. Arrowweed differs in appearance by having violet flowers and long, straight stems; these were frequently used by Indians to make arrows and baskets. The narrow, pointed leaves of Arrowweed are usually less than 2 inches (5 cm) in length, and the leaf blades are attached directly to the stems (i.e., without petioles). Arrowweed and Mulefat are probably the most common riparian shrubs in the Mojave and Colorado deserts.

Two small ash trees are associated with moist localities in mountains of the southwestern deserts. Arizona or Velvet Ash, *Fraxinus velutina,* grows along streams as far west as the desert slopes of the Sierra Nevada. Single-leaf Ash, *Fraxinus anomala,* barely ranges into California. It occurs where streams flow through Pinyon-Juniper

Woodland in the eastern Mojave Desert. The name *anomala* refers to the leaves of this species, which seldom occur in the typical pinnately compound arrangement. They are usually simple and oval—very un-ashlike in appearance. Oregon Ash, *Fraxinus latifolia*, has been reported to occur along the northern base of the San Bernardino Mountains, but this is most likely an erroneous reference to Arizona Ash.

Desert Oasis

There are springs and seeps in every desert region. In the Great Basin, these areas are characterized by winter-deciduous species associated with riparian habitats. Sedges, rushes, and cattails form thickets bordering the water. Riparian trees such as Fremont Cottonwood occur where their roots can reach permanent water.

In the Mojave, cottonwoods are joined by Screwbean Mesquite, *Prosopis pubescens*, named for its tightly coiled beanpod, an important forage for animals. Honey Mesquite also grows here, but it is more common away from the water.

In the Colorado Desert all of these species are joined by the California Fan Palm, *Washingtonia filifera* (pl. 8B), the only palm native to California. It is another tropical relict that has inhabited wet sites for millions of years. Its northern distribution today is probably due in part to movement northward about 200 miles (320 km) along with the Baja California peninsula, by motion along the San Andreas fault. These palm oases are located along both sides of the Salton Trough where water comes to the surface along fault systems.

Indicative of its tropical heritage, the California Fan Palm clearly has the largest leaves of California's desert plants, and this explains why it must always grow near water. One advantage to the large leaf surface is that it increases the amount of evaporative cooling that can take place. Evaporation of water cools the leaves, but it restricts the plant to areas with wet soil.

The distribution of heavy palm seeds from oasis to oasis has been the subject of considerable discussion. It cannot be explained merely from the point of view of relictism. Even during periods of heavy precipitation, palm distribution was probably spotty. The best guess today is that the seeds were carried in the digestive tracts of Coyotes. These animals are known to eat the sweet fruit, and Coyote scats filled with palm seeds are found all over the desert. However, some palm groves are found outside of the Colorado Desert. Although coyotes could have carried the seeds in a day's time from the San Andreas fault region, near Thousand Palms, to outlying localities such as Twentynine Palms, such a distribution mechanism could scarcely account for palms in the Kofa Mountains of Arizona. It would have to be a badly constipated Coyote to travel that far without a bowel movement. Perhaps birds dispersed the seeds; the American Robin has been observed to eat the palm fruit. Another explanation is that Indians carried the seeds and planted the palms. Indians not only ate the fruit, but they used fibers from the palms for cloth and mats and used the fronds for thatched roofing.

Fire is an important component of palm oases. Palms are fire-tolerant, but other oasis vegetation is not. Burning off understory vegetation increases the amount of water available for the palms by decreasing transpirational water loss through the other species. Fires also open up the habitat, allowing palm seedlings to become established. Suppressing fire in these oases works to the detriment of the palm community.

Because oases often have surface water and shade is commonly available, a greater variety of animals may be observed in an oasis than in any other desert habitat. Most of these animals, however, are not restricted to an oasis. One of California's most unusual insects is a palm oasis inhabitant. This is the Giant Palm-boring Beetle, *Dinapate wrightii*. The adult is nearly 2 inches (5 cm) in length, with a huge head and powerful jaws. The female lays its eggs by drilling a small hole in the wood. The large, pale yellow larvae (grubs) live inside palm trunks, boring extensive dime-sized tunnels in the wood. The actual duration of the larval stage is unknown, but one record documents emergence after seven years. The adult emerges from its tunnel after dark, and in reverse. Apparently, it must back out of the tunnel because the abdomen is its largest part, and it would be a disadvantage for the insect to exit head-first and become stuck by the abdomen with its legs flailing the air. Old or dead palms typically show the exit holes of the Giant Palm-boring Beetle, and there is some debate as to whether the beetle is responsible for killing the trees or whether the old trees, by virtue of their age, become probable hosts for the beetle. Nevertheless, about 45% of California Fan Palms over 35 feet (10 m) tall show the presence of beetle exit holes.

An insect that benefits from the activities of the Giant Palm-boring Beetle is the Southern California Carpenter Bee, *Xylocopa californica* (fig. 9.31A), the largest bee in California. They are robust, black or metallic-blue bees that often construct their own burrows. In California Fan Palms, however, the females lay their eggs in the empty exit tunnels of the beetle. On almost any spring day, the bees may be seen entering the tunnels to feed their developing young. Although great numbers of these bees may be observed at a time, they are actually solitary bees, with no social life. As explained earlier, these are the bees that pollinate some Desert Agaves.

Perhaps the greatest threat to oases and riparian habitats in general is encroachment by exotic species such as tamarisks (*Tamarix* spp.). Tamarisks were imported originally from the eastern Mediterranean and east Asian regions. In the United States they were first noted growing in the wild in 1916 following a flood on the upper Gila River in Arizona. By 1940 they dominated the riparian vegetation along that river. Now tamarisks have spread into all kinds of moist habitats throughout the southwest.

There are two widespread forms of tamarisk. A tree also known as Salt Cedar, *Tamarix aphylla,* is often used for windbreaks. Occasionally, it escapes into the wild. The most common form, and the one that causes the most problems, is a shrub, Chinese Tamarisk, *Tamarix ramosissima* (fig. 9.44). These are water-demanding species, and they are easily dispersed by the wind. Seeds are small and plumed. Once established, Chinese Tamarisks reproduce rapidly by underground shoots or rhizomes. A thicket of these plants is capable of taking over and replacing native species within a few years, after which all surface water may be dried up. It has been determined that a three-year-old Salt Cedar transpires about 13.5 gallons (49.5 l) of water per

FIGURE 9.44   Chinese Tamarisk, *Tamarix ramosissima*.

day. Oases and streamsides are the most productive desert habitats; loss of palatable vegetation and surface water can be catastrophic for animals.

In some areas, in order to restore wildlife habitat, tamarisk eradication projects involving pruning and herbicides have been undertaken. The National Park Service has expended long hours and a large amount of money removing tamarisk from riparian habitats in Death Valley. At Saratoga Spring, the home of the endemic Saratoga Spring Pupfish) *Cyprinodon nevadensis nevadensis,* all tamarisk plants have been removed. A showcase for the effect of tamarisk eradication is in Death Valley at Eagle Borax Spring, where tamarisk had dewatered the habitat. It took 10 years for the National Park Service to remove it all, but the effort restored the water and rendered the habitat once again usable by migratory water birds.

Tamarisks are not restricted to freshwater. The name *Salt Cedar* was coined because the trees can live in salty water, and they have cylindrical, jointed leaves resembling those of a conifer. On the surface of these leaves are salt glands, which enable the tree to excrete salt. The grayish color of the foliage is due to a coating of salt.

Limestone Endemics

Among the ecologic-islands of the deserts are outcrops of limestone that harbor specialized plants and animals. These deposits are remnants of the time when the sea covered vast areas of the western United States. The alkaline nature of soils derived from limestone poses special problems for plants. The cluster of limestone endemics that occurs along Convict Creek on the eastern side of the Sierra Nevada is discussed in chapter 4, and the limestone endemics in the San Bernardino Mountains are discussed in chapter 8. The occurrence of Bristlecone Pine and several of its associates on dolomite soil in the White Mountains is discussed in chapter 5. In the Basin-Range Province between the White Mountains and Death Valley, there are several regions of limestone endemism. Of particular interest are plants that occur on limestone cliffs in the Death Valley area. A list of the limestone endemics is impressive. Some species are widespread but only occur on limestone; others occur at only a single locality.

One of the most spectacular limestone endemics is July Gold, *Dedeckera eurekensis*. When in bloom, it becomes covered with bright yellow flowers. This shrub, in the buckwheat family (Polygonaceae), occurs in a few areas in the White Mountains and the Last Chance Mountains near Eureka Valley. It is listed as endangered by the federal government. The shrubs occur only on steep alluvial slopes below limestone outcrops, and they seem to form mounds. It turns out that all of the living shrubs are quite old, up to 400 years. There is no evidence of reproduction. It appears that the living plants date back to a time when far more precipitation occurred in the area, perhaps during the "little ice age." One interesting aspect of their growth habit is a consequence of their great age and the fact that the alluvial soil on which they grow is constantly sliding downhill: the root systems are buried in the soil several feet uphill from the aboveground parts of the plant.

The list of endemics from cliffs in the Death Valley area includes Lime Penstemon, *Penstemon calcareus;* Death Valley Monkeyflower, *Mimulus rupicola;* and Death Valley Maurandya, *Maurandya petrophila.* These attractive flowers are in the figwort family, Scrophulariceae. The word *petrophila* in the scientific name of the maurandya means "rock-loving." There are also other buckwheats, such as Napkin-ring Buckwheat, *Eriogonum intrafractum,* and Heermann's Buckwheat, *Eriogonum heermannii.* An interesting member of the euphorbia family is the Holly-leaved Tetracoccus, *Tetracoccus ilicifolius.* This is a hollylike shrub that grows in a mound up to 4 feet (1.3 m) high. It is found in the Grapevine Mountains of northern Death Valley. In the waterleaf family (Hydrophyllaceae) there are two attractive herbaceous shrubs associated with limestone: Panamint Phacelia, *Phacelia perityloides,* and Roundleaf Phacelia, *Phacelia mustelina.*

HISTORY OF DESERT VEGETATION

The history of California's deserts is tied closely to the uplift of mountain ranges and the subsequent development of a rain shadow. The forces leading to the uplift of the Basin-Range Province, including the Sierra Nevada, began about 25 million years ago and continue today. Evidence of drying as exhibited by changes in Great Basin vegetation indicate that a significant rain shadow formed by western mountain ranges had occurred by 11 million years ago. Uplift of the Sierra Nevada, Transverse Ranges, and Peninsular Ranges accelerated about 2–5 million years ago so that during the Pleistocene they were well-developed ranges. Evidence of montane glaciers occurs as far south as Mount San Gorgonio. During the 20 or so episodes of glaciation, heavy rainfall occurred across the deserts, and large basins such as Death Valley and Panamint Valley were filled with water. Lake Manly, in Death Valley, was 8500 feet (2575 m) deep.

By the close of the Pleistocene, about 11,000 years ago, a drying trend began. Studies of woodrat (packrat) middens in the southwest indicate that at that time a subalpine sort of forest, including Limber Pine and Bristlecone Pine, occurred extensively across what is now the Great Basin Desert and at higher elevations in the Mojave Desert. As mentioned previously, a woodrat midden on Clark Mountain revealed that Rocky Mountain White Fir has grown there continuously for 28,000 years. Most of the present-day Mojave and Sonoran deserts were occupied by a Pinyon-Juniper-Oak Woodland. The lower Colorado River Valley was occupied by a Mojave type of Creosote Bush Scrub that included Joshua Trees. This area may have been a desert refugium since the Pliocene, some 5 million years ago.

The presence of large grazing mammals such as horses, camels, Bison, and mammoth, as well as large browsers, including mastadons and ground sloths, implies that grasses and herbs were abundant in the Pleistocene woodlands. Perhaps there were extensive savannahs or open grasslands among the trees.

Coincident with uplift of the mountains, the ocean water off California became colder. In combination, these changes caused drying to the interior and all but eliminated summer rainfall throughout the Great Basin and Mojave areas. In the Sonoran region, where biseasonal rainfall still occurs, a woodland persisted until about 9000 years ago. The present vegetation did not appear until 4000 years ago. Some common plants, such as Ironwood and Ocotillo, seem not to have arrived until about 600 years ago.

During the last 10,000 years in the Mojave and Great Basin, desert communities such as Creosote Bush Scrub and Sagebrush Scrub pushed northward to their present latitudes. Over that time, through the mechanism of polypoidy, Creosote Bush evolved into different races in each of the major desert regions. Also, ash fall from volcanic eruptions in the Cascades may have favored the invasion of Great Basin Sagebrush. While Creosote Bush Scrub and Sagebrush Scrub dispersed northward, the Subalpine and Pinyon-Juniper woodlands retreated to mountaintops. The history of the latter communities is discussed in chapter 5.

STRATEGIES OF DESERT ANIMALS

Desert animals must adapt to three interrelated stresses: drought, temperature extremes, and sparse or unpredictable food supply—all functions of low or unpredictable precipitation.

In general, animals deal with temperature extremes by avoidance. Desert summer temperatures are the hottest of all the ecosystems. In cases of overheating, nearly all animals use some form of evaporative cooling. However, this process can be risky where water is in short supply, so keeping cool without relying on evaporative cooling is a major strategy of desert animals.

Dealing with drought is primarily a function of water conservation: keeping cool saves water. Animals accomplish this primarily through behavioral means. They avoid the heat of the day by remaining in the shade or in burrows. Activity periods are limited to dawn, dusk, or nighttime. When the climate is too severe—either too cold, too hot, or not enough food—animals go into a state of torpor; they hibernate or estivate.

One of the raw materials for photosynthesis is water. Where water is limited, photosynthesis is limited. A desert therefore is a food-poor ecosystem. Animals with low metabolic rates have an advantage; therefore there are many cold-blooded (ectothermic) animals in the desert. Deserts are inhabited by a large number of arthropods, such as insects, spiders, and scorpions. These are animals with exoskeletons of chitin and jointed appendages. Because the skeleton is external, the legs bend at conspicuous joints, as in a suit of armor. Among the vertebrate animals, reptiles are most common. There are 53 known reptile species in the California desert: 30 lizards, 21 snakes, and 2 turtles.

Dealing With Drought

Many animal adaptations for desert existence resemble those of desert plants. Common strategies include water storage, heat avoidance, dormancy, drought-tolerance, boundary layers, body orientation, and waterproof integument.

Storage of water is a cactuslike adaptation. Coupled with low metabolic rate during long periods of torpor, this is enough to get some animals through long periods of drought. For example, the Chuckwalla, *Sauromalus obesus,* stores water in lymph spaces under the skin along the sides of its body.

The Desert Tortoise, *Gopherus* (= *Xerobates*) *agassizii* (fig. 9.45), can store about a quart (liter) of water in its body, mostly in its urinary bladder. The scientific name *Gopherus* alludes to its digging ability. The tortoise emerges from its burrow in spring to feed on moisture-rich leaves and flowers, particularly those of ephemeral plants. During this time it accumulates reserves of water and fat that will carry it through a long period of dormancy including summer, fall, and winter.

The Desert Tortoise is on the state list of threatened species. The gentle nature of these animals has made them desirable as pets. Some people use them for target practice. An increase in the number of Common Ravens, probably in association with open dumps, has also threatened tortoises because ravens prey on hatchlings, which still have soft shells. One researcher counted the shells of 250 young tortoises around the nest of a single pair of Common Ravens. In addition, tortoises must compete with cattle, sheep, and donkeys for food. In the face of such competition, malnutrition has cut their reproductive rate, and they are becoming rare. Some studies indicated that Desert Tortoise populations have dropped about 90% in the last 50 years. In the western Mojave Desert their numbers declined 50% between 1980 and 1989.

Within its native range in the Mojave and Colorado deserts, certain areas have been set aside as refuges for the Desert Tortoise. It is a crime to collect one or to engage in any activity destructive of its native habitat. It is hoped that such protective measures

FIGURE 9.45   Desert Tortoise, *Gopherus* (= *Xerobates*) *agassizii*.

will enable the population to rebound. Captive breeding and release of juveniles may
not be a good idea for tortoises, depending on where the animals were raised. It is not
always a good idea to release animals into the desert once they have lived for some
time in a moister climate. It has been determined that contagious infections—in
particular, a lung fungus—may be introduced in this way into the wild population.

As unlikely as it may seem, several species of toad are associated with deserts. The
Great Plains Toad, *Bufo cognatus*, is able to store water in its urinary bladder equal to
about 30% of its body weight. The "champion" desert toads are known as spadefoot
toads. Couch's Spadefoot, *Scaphiopus couchi* (fig. 9.46), occurs in the southwest deserts
where there are periods of summer rain. In California they occur along the Colorado
River flood plain. They come up from deep burrows after the first heavy rains of
summer and congregate in temporary ponds to reproduce. Apparently, sound is the
stimulus to break dormancy. The sound of thunder, in particular, brings them up.
Unfortunately, they can be fooled by the loud sound of a dune buggy or motorcycle,
in which case they may emerge to find no water and subsequently die.

When conditions are right, Couch's Spadefoot Toads congregate at night in large
numbers at temporary ponds. Their mating calls sound remarkably like bleating
lambs. Eggs are laid and fertilized in these ponds. The development of these toads
is among the most rapid known for a vertebrate, for it must take place before the
ponds dry up. Development from egg to larva takes about 2 days. Larvae swim about
in the ponds, feeding on algae and detritus. In about 10 days the tadpoles lose their
tails and grow legs, and at this time they will be soon ready to leave the water.
They will dig a burrow and become dormant as soon as it becomes too dry to remain

FIGURE 9.46   Couch's Spadefoot, *Scaphiopus couchi*. (From R. C. Stebbins. *Amphibians of Western North America*. Berkeley: University of California Press, 1951.)

aboveground. The total period of development from egg to dormancy may last four to six weeks.

While they are in their burrows, spadefoot toads survive on water stored in their urinary bladders. As they use up water and fat stores, they gradually lose weight. If they were to urinate, they would lose valuable water, so nitrogenous waste (urea) becomes concentrated in their bodies. These toads can tolerate a 40% weight loss, and they can concentrate urea to the point that their body fluids equal half the concentration of seawater (16,000 mg/l). By concentrating body fluids, they are able to absorb water from the soil in a plantlike fashion. When the soil becomes too dry, they form a waterproof coating that prevents further water loss. In this cocoonlike structure, they wait until it rains again.

Reptiles, birds, and insects conserve water by converting their nitrogenous waste to uric acid, a substance that is not soluble in water. Therefore they are able to excrete the waste products of protein metabolism without losing water at all. This metabolic feature is another reason that these three groups of animals are so well represented in desert and scrub communities.

Water conservation is the primary means of desert survival, but making use of every possible water source is also important. Birds and large mammals are mobile enough to move to known water sources when they need to rehydrate. Temporary pools may hold water for long periods of time after a rain. Depressions in granite may be quite large. These storage ponds are known as *tinajas,* which is a Spanish word for "tank." Other animals concentrate their activities near permanent water. These animals are no more desert creatures than the deep-rooted, water-loving plants known as phreatophytes.

Making use of unique sources of water is important for desert survival. Doves are unique among birds because they can drink dew; they can swallow with their heads down. Small burrowing reptiles such as the California Legless Lizard, *Anniella pulchra* (fig. 8.53), or the Western Slender Blind Snake, *Leptotyphlops humilis,* are able to drink capillary water between sand particles. Many animals derive water from moist food. The Desert Woodrat, *Neotoma lepida,* eats prickly-pear cactus. Bighorn Sheep, *Ovis canadensis,* eat the rapidly growing flower stalks of agaves, a source of water and carbohydrate.

Any carnivore gains water by feeding. Because insects are very common in deserts, there are many insectivorous animals. Grasshopper mice (*Onychomys* spp.) are unique rodents because they feed on insects and small mammals. There are two species in California, one in the Great Basin and one in the Mojave and Colorado deserts. Because they are carnivores, they have large home ranges—up to 8 acres (3.2 ha).

Grasshoper mice can attack and kill mice that are twice their size. They immobilize these mice by biting through the spinal cord just behind the skull. The grasshopper mouse eats the brain first, and depending on how long it has been since the last feeding, it may or may not eat the rest of the body. Grasshopper mice even eat scorpions and stink beetles. They eat scorpions by first biting off the stinger. Stink beetles (*Eleodes* spp.) are common black beetles with a large, bulbous abdomen. They are avoided by most predators because of an obnoxious odorous liquid they emit when molested. When pestered, a stink beetle puts down its head and elevates its abdomen, which is enough warning to cause any other predator to leave it alone. The grasshopper mouse grabs the beetle with its forepaws, jams its abdomen in the sand, and eats off only the head end.

One very peculiar aspect of the hunting behavior of the grasshopper mouse is that it "howls." Soon after it emerges from its burrow for an evening's hunt, it climbs to a small rise and emits a long, shrill whistle that carries for about a hundred yards (meters). Apparently, they claim territories and establish dominance with these vocalizations, in a manner similar to Wolves, Coyotes, and many birds.

Bats are also common in desert areas. Most of them obtain water from the insects they eat. Their mechanism for locating flying insects with "sonar" is well known. Once a prey item is located, the bat scoops it into its mouth with the membranes between its fingers, which also serve as wings. Furthermore, unlike most mammals, bats conserve energy by allowing their body temperature to drop during the time they are in their shaded daytime roosts. In the evening, when they become active, they raise their body temperatures by shivering. Muscle contractions generate the heat necessary for them to become active, and they forage for insects at dusk, avoiding the heat of the day.

Many desert birds are also insectivorous. These include swallows, swifts, wrens, and a variety of flycatchers and gnatcatchers, which are discussed elsewhere. An interesting desert gleaner is the Verdin, *Auriparus flaviceps.* This small gray bird is noticeable by its bright yellow head and throat. It is an inhabitant of the Colorado Desert, where it often makes its nest in Smoke Trees. A Verdin nest is recognized by its spherical shape and side opening. Verdins typically glean insects in palo verde trees, although they are also known to eat nectar-laden flowers such as those that attract humming-birds. They are able to obtain all the water they need in this way. One researcher has calculated that they eat about two-thirds of their body weight in insects each day. During summer they spend about 50% of their active time foraging, and during winter almost 90% of their activity is spent on foraging. This high rate of activity also generates body heat, so it is important for keeping warm in the winter. It also has been shown that the enclosed nest is a very good insulator against the cold and wind.

An interesting water source is reclaimed water vapor. Long-nosed mammals are able to reabsorb water from exhaled air. This reabsorption is enhanced by certain mammals who plug the entrance to their burrows. As a result the humidity of the air in the burrow remains high, enabling the mammal to reclaim its water merely by breathing through its nose. Likewise, large mammals such as camels and antelopes reclaim a significant amount of water through their long, narrow nasal passages.

Another means of water reclamation occurs in Greater Roadrunners, *Geococcyx californianus* (fig. 9.47). Newly hatched nestlings produce urine-filled pouches that are excreted in the nest. Adult Roadrunners eat these sacs, reclaim the water, and excrete the nitrogenous waste a second time.

Roadrunners are important predators in desert and chaparral areas. The Spaniards called them *Paisanos,* meaning "country men." They are also known as Chaparral Cocks, in reference to their common occurrence in Chaparral. They eat insects, lizards, snakes, mice, and berries, and they are known to many as predators of whiptails, horned lizards, and rattlesnakes. The Roadrunner is the only member of the cuckoo family (Cuculidae) that occurs in the arid southwest. These crow-sized birds with long tails are best known for their habit of running rather than flying. They are able to fly, but they seem to prefer to run or glide and have been clocked at 15 miles (24km) per hour. An interesting habit of the Roadrunner is to bask in the sun in the morning. The bird positions itself in an opening or on a rock with its back to the sun. It fluffs its feathers and spreads its wings in order to maximize the surface for absorption. Roadrunners also have black skin on their backs under the feathers, which enhances absorption of heat. This is an energy conservation device that enables them to lower their body temperature at night and warm up again without burning food calories. It has been calculated that sunning Roadrunners conserve an average of 551 calories per hour. Furthermore, they conserve heat by placing their nests in dense trees or shrubs. This placement is also vital to survival of nestlings. Two density-dependent factors also keep Roadrunner populations in line with food supply. First, the number of eggs in a nest is correlated to the immediate food supply, and second, adults eat weak or lethargic nestlings. Nothing is wasted.

Another common bird that supplies itself with adequate water by being carnivorous is the Loggerhead Shrike, *Lanius ludovicianus.* This bird is conspicuous, hunting for insects, lizards, and mice from an open perch. In this position or when it flies, revealing white wing patches, it resembles a Northern Mockingbird, *Mimus polyglottos.* Close inspection, however, reveals that the shrike has a black eye mask, and, like a raptor, it has a small hook on the tip of its beak. This bird has gained the nickname Butcher Bird by its curious habit of hanging its prey, like sides of beef, on sharp thorns or the barbs of a barbed wire fence. The fact that this bird seems to kill more

FIGURE 9.47   Greater Roadrunner, *Geococcyx californianus.* Keeping cool conserves water. This bird is exhibiting four methods of cooling itself, three of which use no water: (1) panting, (2) drooping its wings, (3) elevating itself on a rock, and (4) standing in the shade.

animals than it could eat has puzzled biologists. It now seems clear, however, that a courting male provisions a larder and displays it conspicuously to "prove" to the females that it is a good hunter. The stored food will be used to feed the young. A highly successful male is able to mate with more than one female and supply enough food for more than one family.

The importance of metabolic water to desert animals cannot be overlooked. Waste products of cellular respiration are carbon dioxide and water. To most animals this metabolic water is insignificant, but to desert animals it contributes a significant proportion of their total water. There are several species of kangaroo rats (*Dipodomys* spp.) (fig. 9.48A) in California's deserts. Kangaroo rats are able to go their entire lives without drinking a drop of liquid water. They use various water conservation techniques and derive enough water solely from metabolism and food.

Kangaroo rats are more closely allied to squirrels than to rats. They are members of a family of rodents (Heteromyidae) that in desert areas have long, kangaroolike hind limbs and fur-lined cheek pouches. They subsist nearly entirely on seeds, which they gather at night and store in their burrows. During the day, when the burrow is plugged, humidity in the sleeping chamber rises. Water vapor is reclaimed through the animal's nasal membranes, and the humidity absorbed by the seeds is reclaimed when the seeds are eaten. Inside the sleeping chamber, the temperature remains at a relatively constant 80°F (27°C) even though the temperature of the soil surface

FIGURE 9.48   *A.* Merriam's Kangaroo Rat, *Dipodomys merriami.*

FIGURE 9.48 *(continued)*   *B.* Little Pocket Mouse, *Perognathus longimembris.* Note the similarity between these two species, which often coexist. The kangaroo rat hops on its hind legs and forages in the open, whereas the pocket mouse walks on all fours and forages under shrubs.

outside may rise to 180°F (82°C). The temperature in the burrow is ideal for heat and water conservation. A kangaroo rat is not required to raise its metabolic rate to heat itself, nor is it required to resort to evaporative cooling to dissipate heat. Kangaroo rats eat their own feces in order to reclaim water lost there. They can concentrate their urine to 30% salts and urea, reducing urinary water loss to an absolute minimum. Kangaroo rats are the "champion" desert rodents, marvels of efficiency.

Animals that store fat have another source of metabolic water. Fat helps them get through long periods of torpor by supplying calories. In addition, due to a peculiarity of fat metabolism, 1.1 grams of water are produced for every gram of fat that is metabolized. In contrast, a gram of carbohydrate produces only 0.6 grams of water. Camels have long been famous for storing fat in their humps.

In North America, several lizard species store fat in their tails, drawing upon it for energy and water during long months of torpor underground. For example, Gila Monsters, *Heloderma suspectum,* in the Sonoran Desert of Arizona and Mexico, store fat in their tails. They emerge in spring to eat insects, bird eggs, and baby birds. These are the only venomous lizards in the United States, and they are brightly colored as a warning.

In California, some persons confuse Gila Monsters with Chuckwallas, which are also large lizards with fat tails. The Chuckwalla's tail, however, is mostly muscle, and, as indicated earlier, they store water beneath the skin. Chuckwallas are primarily vegetarian. They live in rocky habitats, emerging from cracks in the morning to sun themselves. When they are sufficiently warm, they move into nearby vegetation to feed. If frightened, they dive into a crack in the rock and lodge themselves there with their muscular legs and tail, also inflating their lungs. Indians used to eat Chuckwallas. They would extract them from the cracks by tugging on a foot or the tail while poking a sharp stick into the animal's side to let out the air. Chuckwallas do not lose their tails as do other lizards.

The Western Banded Gecko, *Coleonyx variegatus* (fig. 9.49), looks too fragile to be a successful desert lizard. Its pinkish, fine-scaled integument is nearly transparent. It has large, conspicuous eyelids over bulging eyes. Geckos are nocturnal animals that are often found on the road, where they are endangered by cars. Another threat to the animals are snake fanciers, who collect them to feed to their pets.

Geckos emerge in spring to feed on small insects. Like Gila Monsters, they store a significant amount of fat in their tails. Unlike Gila Monsters and Chuckwallas, they shed their tails when molested. It is more important for this lizard to escape and reproduce than it is to maintain enough fat for the next dry season. One small burrowing snake, the Spotted Leaf-nosed Snake, *Phyllorhynchus decurtatus,* seems to prey heavily on gecko tails.

In addition to conserving water and utilizing unique sources of water, some desert animals have notable tolerances for desiccation. Humans can lose up to 10% of their body weight due to dehydration, and a loss of 25% is usually lethal. In contrast, the Desert Bighorn Sheep can endure 20% depletion of body weight, representing a 30% loss of total body water, without showing ill effects. Old World animals such as camels and donkeys can also lose up to 30% of their body weight through

FIGURE 9.49 Western Banded Gecko, *Coleonyx variegatus.*

FIGURE 9.50 Gambel's Quail, *Callipepla gambelii.*

dehydration. They are able to restore their body water with heavy drinking. A camel can drink 30 gallons (110 l) of water in 10 minutes. As indicated earlier, spadefoot toads can lose up to 40% of their body weight. Birds are the most notable in this respect because they have no urinary bladder. Doves can lose up to 40% of their body weight, and Gambel's Quail, *Callipepla gambelii* (fig. 9.50), can survive a 50% weight loss due to dehydration.

Coping with Heat

Coping with heat poses a series of related problems in desert animals. Evaporation of water from a surface with a good blood supply is the most efficient mechanism for cooling an overheated animal. However, because water is in limited supply, the animal's best strategy is never to get overheated. Animals alter their daily and seasonal activity periods to avoid the heat. In general, animals regulate their body temperatures by moving in and out of the sun. Desert animals burrow or rest in the shade. To avoid the hot ground, snakes and lizards climb into the branches of vegetation. It can be cooler by 100°F (38°C) in the shade 2 feet (60 cm) above the ground.

Ectothermic animals obtain a significant amount of their body heat from the environment. In contrast, endothermic animals gain most of their heat from metabolism. Because heat in the desert is not in short supply, and because food is scarce, ectothermic animals, with their low metabolic rates, have an advantage; they don't have to waste valuable calories keeping their bodies warm.

Heat is gained by metabolism, conduction, convection, and radiation. Metabolic heat gain is minimized in animals with low metabolic rates. Heat loss also can be enhanced by conduction, convection, and radiation. The advantage to an animal that loses heat by one of these mechanisms is that it can do so without losing valuable water.

It is often assumed that desert animals should be light-colored in order to reflect light. Although it is true that dark objects absorb more heat, it is also true that they emit more heat by radiation. A phenomenon known as Allen's rule was discussed in chapter 5, where it was pointed out that endothermic animals in cold climates tend to be white. Conversely, for ectothermic animals in hot climates, where the major source of heat is external, it is logical that diurnal animals should be light-colored. One searches, then, for an explanation for the black coloration of the Common Raven, *Corvus corax* (fig. 9.51). This member of the crow and jay family, Corvidae, is most common in deserts. Unlike most members of the family, Common Ravens soar hawklike while searching for food, primarily carrion. It would seem that its dark color would enhance heat absorption by radiation. However, the Common Raven avoids overheating in a number of ways. In the first place, it is cooler high above the ground. Second, the large surface area of the bird's wings allows conduction of heat to the environment without water loss. Movement of the air over the wings transports heat away by convection. Furthermore, soaring is an effortless activity, so the bird generates minimal metabolic heat. Finally, if all these factors are not enough to keep the Common Raven cool, it simply rests in the shade, at which time its black color enhances its heat loss by radiation.

It cannot be disputed that the lifestyle of the Common Raven is successful. Ravens have expanded their ranges considerably and are now common in many habitats. The Breeding Bird Census of the U.S. Fish and Wildlife Service indicated that the Common Raven population in the United States has been growing at about 3% per year, presumably in association with the birds' ability to thrive in open dumps. Their numbers have increased by more than 300% in the Mojave Desert. Some wildlife

FIGURE 9.51 Common Raven, *Corvus corax*.

officials are calling for a program of poisoning and shooting to reduce their numbers in the Mojave Desert, where predation on juvenile Desert Tortoises has caused a severe decline in that species.

Antelope Ground Squirrels or White-tailed Antelope Squirrels, *Ammospermophilus leucurus* (pl. 12E), are unique among ground squirrels because they remain active all year. They are diurnal and can be seen scurrying about in the dead of summer, gathering fruit and seeds. White-tailed Antelope Squirrels look like white-tailed chipmunks. When they overheat they can drop their body temperature up to 7°F (4°C) by pressing their bodies into cool sand in the shade of a bush. This is heat loss by conduction. If overheating is excessive, they will lose some valuable water and shift to evaporative cooling, which they accomplish by drooling, panting, and licking their forelimbs. Almost all animals resort to panting when they overheat. Evaporative cooling from capillaries in the lungs is a rapid, effective way to lose body heat.

Black-tailed Jack Rabbits, *Lepus californicus* (fig. 9.52), utilize radiation to cool themselves. Their long limbs and ears are ideal surfaces for dissipating heat away from their bodies. Typically, they remain in the shade on the north side of a bush facing the clear northern sky. They can continue to lose heat in this way, particularly through their ears. They enhance convective heat loss by wiggling their ears, which moves heated air away from the ear surface.

The White-tailed Jack Rabbit, *Lepus townsendii,* of the Great Basin was discussed in chapter 5, in the section on the alpine zone. Compared to the mountain form, the desert White-tailed Jack Rabbit has longer legs and ears and a thinner body. This surface area enhances radiative heat loss, illustrating Bergmann's and Allen's rules.

FIGURE 9.52   Black-tailed Jack Rabbit, *Lepus californicus.*

Jack rabbits, also known as hares, do not live in burrows; they simply hide in the shade of a shrub. Sometimes Coyotes use this habit to their advantage. A Coyote will flush a jack rabbit from hiding, and instead of running after it, the Coyote watches where it hides next. The Coyote then flushes it again. Running repeatedly from bush to bush causes the hare to overheat, and it drops from heat exhaustion. The Coyote, having conserved its energy, is able to catch the overheated jack rabbit even though it is no match for it on a dead run. Also, the Coyote is able to utilize more efficient evaporative cooling by drooling and panting. Like all dogs, Coyotes cool themselves by evaporating saliva from the surface of their tongue.

Cottontail rabbits are true rabbits, not hares. The Desert Cottontail, *Sylvilagus auduboni,* has much shorter legs and ears than the jack rabbit. The cottontail avoids overheating by becoming nocturnal in the summer, and it lives in a burrow, rather than taking cover in a bush. Cottontails also take care of their young for longer periods of time than do jack rabbits. Juvenile cottontails are born in the burrow in a nest lined with the mother's soft belly hair, and they are nursed for several weeks before they attempt to gather their own food.

Large African mammals such as camels and elands have another trick. These animals cool themselves by perspiration when they overheat. To avoid this, they allow their body temperatures to drop as much as 12° to 14°F ($7-9^\circ$C) during the night. During the daytime they heat up slowly by radiation to about 108°F (42°C) before they begin to sweat. When they exhale, they reclaim water by condensation in their long nasal passages. If they overheat, water evaporates from these surfaces when they inhale.

This evaporation helps to cool their blood, which is then shunted to the brain, the tissue most sensitive to overheating. This country no longer has many large native desert mammals. It is unknown whether the Pronghorn or Desert Bighorn Sheep allows its body temperature to fluctuate.

Invertebrates and ectothermic vertebrates undergo a greater range of daily fluctuation in body temperature than is tolerated in endothermic animals. Similarly, ectotherms have a greater tolerance for high temperatures. The upper temperature an animal can tolerate before dying is known as its critical thermal maximum (CTM). The CTM of 122°F (50°C) for desert invertebrates that have been tested, such as scorpions, sun spiders, and stink beetles, is the highest known among animals. Not only do these animals tolerate high body temperatures, but they are covered with a waxy integument that inhibits water loss. Among vertebrates, certain lizards of the iguana family (Iguanidae) can tolerate high body temperatures. In this respect, the Desert Iguana, *Dipsosaurus dorsalis* (fig. 9.53), is the "champion." It has been found to have a rectal temperature of 117°F (47°C).

Two factors lead to thermal death in animals. One is that enzymes have a narrow range of thermal tolerance. If enzymes function poorly, critical chemical reactions fail, and the animal soon dies. Lizards such as the Chuckwalla and the Desert Iguana have evolved enzymes that function over a wide range of temperatures. A second factor is that hemoglobin, the pigment in blood that carries oxygen, is also very temperature-sensitive. At high temperatures it loses its ability to transport oxygen. Such high body temperatures are also associated with increased metabolic rate. To cope with this problem, Chuckwallas and Desert Iguanas have an increased capacity to function in the absence of oxygen. They can function anaerobically, accumulating lactic acid in concentrations that would immobilize most animals. When it becomes cooler they process the lactic acid by heavy breathing. The amount of oxygen required to process stored lactic acid is known as the oxygen debt.

Among birds and mammals, high body temperatures are associated with very small animals. Coincidentally, these animals are common in deserts. At 105°F (41°C), hummingbirds have one of the highest body temperatures among birds. The high metabolic rate of these small animals is necessary to produce enough heat to keep them warm in the face of their high surface-volume ratio. Living in a hot environment lowers their metabolic demand. Hummingbirds are nectar feeders, and nectar is a nutritious, high-calorie food. Fortunately for desert plants, hummingbirds do well in hot environments. The coevolution of hummingbirds and long, tubular flowers is a desert phenomenon. There is abundant nectar in desert flowers, and plants such as Ocotillo and Chuparosa are distinctly adapted to accommodate hummingbirds as pollinators. Hummingbirds minimize their metabolic demand by allowing their body temperature to drop when they are at rest, particularly at night. For every 18°F (10°C) that an animal lets its body temperature fall, there is a 50% reduction in metabolism. A hummingbird in flight increases its metabolic rate fourfold over its resting rate. It has been calculated that a hummingbird eats about 50% of its body weight in sugar each day. If it were not for its ability to drop its temperature at night, it might have to eat four times that much.

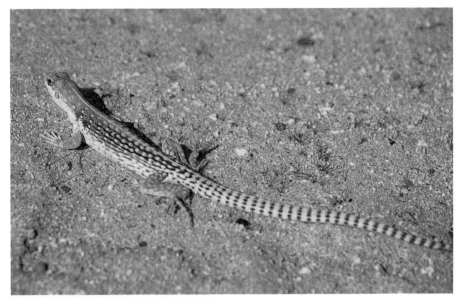

FIGURE 9.53   Desert Iguana, *Dipsosaurus dorsalis*.

The smallest mammal in the desert is the Desert Shrew, *Notiosorex crawfordi*. It is particularly common in the Cactus Scrub community of the Colorado Desert. These tiny carnivores must eat more than their own body weight each day. They eat mostly insects, but take mice as well. Problems and adaptations concerning metabolic rate in these animals are similar to those of hummingbirds. These ferocious little mammals are also unique in that they are venomous. This is an adaptation for eating large prey, as animals with venom are able to immobilize prey that are large enough to fight back. In the case of the shrew, practically all prey species are larger than it is.

Survival in a Food-poor Ecosystem

The total biomass of animals in the desert is small. This is because the desert is a food-poor ecosystem. Photosynthesis produces about 890 pounds per acre per year ($100 \text{ g/m}^2/\text{yr}$) of edible biomass. An acre of desert land will sustain about 89 pounds (36 kg) of herbivores and less than 9 pounds (3.6 kg) of carnivores. Productivity of deserts, however, may double in a wet year because of the tremendous increase in annual plants. But the animals able to respond to this "bonanza" of food must be short-lived. In long-lived animals such as Desert Tortoises, reproduction may be delayed until there is a bumper crop of annuals. In general, this kind of productivity favors small animals with short lifespans, high reproductive rates, and good dispersal. Arthropods (insects, spiders, and scorpions) and reptiles are favored in deserts.

The most common herbivorous animals are insects. Because desert plants invest so much energy in reproduction, seed eaters are very common. The most common seed-eating animals in the desert are ants. Other common arthropods are leaf-eaters

FIGURE 9.54 Soldier blister beetle, *Tegrodera* sp. This beetle has eaten all the petals off the ray flowers of this Brittle-bush (*Encelia farinosa*). Note the pollen on its head.

such as grasshoppers, beetles, and bugs. Large, orange soldier blister beetles (*Tegrodera* spp.) (fig. 9.54) eat mostly flower petals. Termites eat dead wood. Most termites in the desert are subterranean. When it rains, they build mud shells around dead sticks and other debris, encasing the wood of a dead shrub up to a foot (30 cm) or so above the ground. After they consume the wood, all that is left is the mud shell.

Some insects specialize. They are abundant only when their favored food is abundant. Among these are nectar feeders such as Honey Bees, butterflies, and moths. Juvenile forms of these insects partition resources by eating different food than the adult. The example of sphinx moth larvae was mentioned earlier.

Plants are specialized to attract certain pollinators. As has been mentioned before, the shape of flowers is associated with certain pollinators. For example, long tubular flowers are pollinated by moths or hummingbirds. Wide open flowers such as sunflowers are often pollinated by beetles. Colors of flowers are also associated with particular pollinators. White or pale yellow flowers attract nocturnal pollinators such as moths and nectar-feeding bats. Red or yellow flowers attract hummingbirds. Red flowers are seldom pollinated by insects because insects cannot see red. Color vision

FIGURE 9.55   Painted Lady, *Vanessa cardui*. (From
J. A. Powell and C. L. Hogue. *California Insects.*
Berkeley: University of California Press, 1979.)

in insects is shifted to the violet end of the spectrum; they are blind to red, but they see violet and ultraviolet quite well. Vertebrates are blind to ultraviolet. It should be no surprise, therefore, that in order to attract insects some flowers incorporate ultraviolet patterns into their blossoms that are invisible to humans.

Adult butterflies take only liquid food such as nectar. When flowers become abundant, so do butterflies. Outbreaks of the Painted Lady, *Vanessa cardui* (fig. 9.55), have been recorded in the Mojave and Colorado deserts, where motorists reported them flying northward by the thousands. Heavy rains in March 1991 stimulated such an outbreak. They fly a few feet off the ground, rising vertically to avoid obstacles. Adults continue northward toward Oregon until they die. There is no return flight. The Painted Lady is not restricted to deserts. It is said to be the most widely distributed butterfly in the world, adapting to habitation. It is sometimes called the Thistle Butterfly because larvae feed on a variety of thistles (*Cirsium* spp.). They also feed on other disturbance-area plants, such as fiddlenecks (*Amsinckia* spp.) and mallows (*Malva* spp., *Sphaeralcea* spp.), which they defoliate during outbreaks.

Butterflies such as the Mojave Sooty-wing, *Pholisora libya,* are more typically desert in distribution. Larvae of this species feed on a variety of saltbushes (*Atriplex* spp.) and seem particularly associated with Wingscale, *Atriplex canescens.* This gray to blackish butterfly presumably takes advantage of its coloration to absorb heat rapidly by basking in the sun, or to lose heat equally fast by resting in the shade.

Millipedes and ground-dwelling beetles eat detritus. The most common ground beetles are in the darkling beetle family (Tenebrionidae). Distribution of this family in the United States is concentrated in the southwest. Here there are more than 1200 species, over 400 of which occur in California. One of these, *Asbolus verrucosus,* is so common that at one locality in the northern Mojave, its biomass was calculated at nearly 2 pounds per acre (275 g/ha), more than the combined biomass of mammals, birds, and reptiles in the area. Another study found a related form, *Asbolus laevis,* in the Algodones Dunes to be so common that on one occasion 100 specimens were visible at the same time.

FIGURE 9.56 Stink beetle, *Eleodes* sp., in its threat position.

Darkling beetles have a number of adaptations that enable them to thrive in the desert. They are opportunistic feeders, eating all sorts of detritus. They retreat from heat by moving into cracks or under rocks, and some of them dig their own burrows. Most of them do not fly, but they use their first pair of wings, known as wing covers (elytra), as a bubble-shaped chamber to trap air. This acts as an insulation. On the ironclad beetles (*Phloeodes* spp.) the body is so hard that blows from a hammer may be needed to push an insect pin through it. Some beetles (*Asbolus* spp., *Cryptoglossus* spp.) have a distinctive way of increasing their insulative surface. They secrete a mass of microscopic waxy hairs on their backs that act as a boundary layer to trap air. This also causes them to change color. When it is hot and dry, they turn a bluish white with the waxy secretions. When it is cool or moist, they turn black, as the waxy hairs are lost. The color change also influences their abilities to absorb or radiate heat. Many darkling beetles can tolerate a wide range of humidity without significant water loss. The most important source of water loss for the stink beetle is its defensive secretions. The defensive posture of a stink beetle, known as head-standing, in which its abdomen is raised conspicuously, is a warning to potential predators (fig. 9.56). The stink beetle would rather not lose any water defending itself. This posture is so effective that it is mimicked by other beetles, even though they produce no nasty secretions.

The Desert Spider Beetle, *Cysteodemus armatus,* is a flightless beetle in the blister beetle family (Meloidae). They have a large, inflated abdomen and superficially resemble the darkling beetles. These beetles have an uncanny ability to gather a layer of pollen in pits on their elytra, which also acts as a boundary layer. These beetles often appear yellow or cream-colored because of the pollen.

PLATE 1   *A*. Yosemite Valley, Yellow Pine Forest in winter. *B*. Eastern Sierra Nevada, dry Yellow Pine Forest dominated by Jeffrey Pine. Wilson Butte, a volcanic outcrop, in background. *C*. Lodgepole Forest, McCabe Lake, Yosemite National Park. Mountain Hemlock against horizon at left center.

PLATE 2   *A*. Upper Kern Basin from Wright Lakes, a glaciated landscape in Sequoia National Park. *B*. Subalpine zone dominated by Foxtail Pines on the Kern Plateau. *C*. Subalpine zone dominated by Whitebark Pines. View southward from Pioneer Basin. Glaciated U-shaped valleys in background are Third and Fourth Recesses.

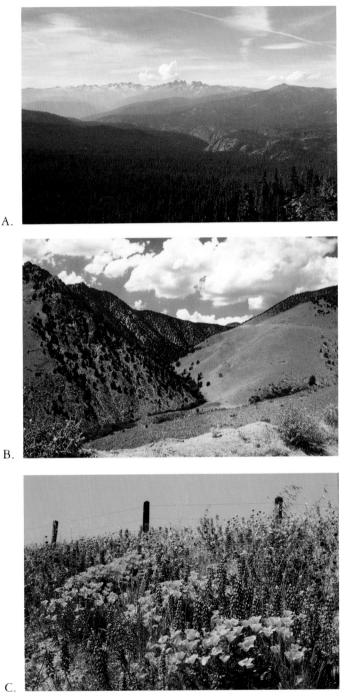

A.

B.

C.

PLATE 3   *A*. Western Sierra Nevada. View northward across Fish Creek and upper San Joaquin River. Minarets in background. Lodgepole–Red Fir Forest. *B*. Eastern Sierra Nevada. View westward up Ninemile Canyon showing slope effect. Pinyon pines on north-facing slope, desert vegetation on south-facing slope. *C*. Spring wildflowers, including lupines, *Lupinus* sp., and California Poppies, *Eschscholtzia californica*.

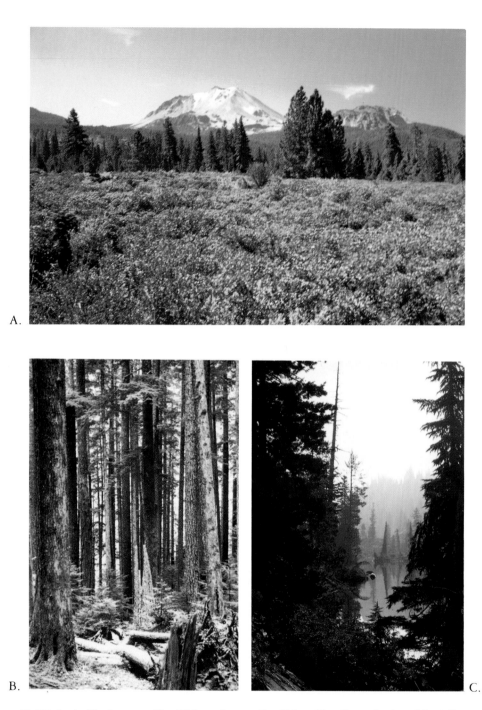

PLATE 4   *A.* Northeastern side of Mount Lassen. Dry Yellow Pine Forest dominated by Jeffrey Pine and manzanita. *B.* Old-growth Douglas Fir Forest, Siskiyou Mountains. *C.* Moist subalpine community of the Klamath Province. Cuddihy Lakes, Salmon Mountains.

PLATE 5   *A*. Mixed Evergreen Forest, northern Coast Ranges. *B*. Oak Woodland dominated by Blue Oak, southern Coast Ranges. *C*. Slope effect on coastal side of southern Coast Ranges. Oak Woodland on north-facing slope, Chaparral on south-facing slope. Coast Redwood in canyon bottom.

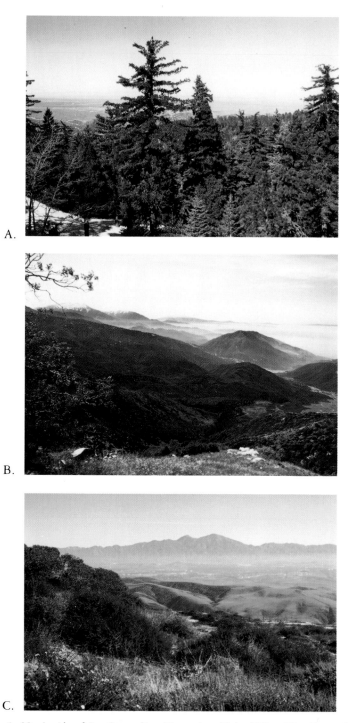

PLATE 6 *A*. North side of San Bernardino Mountains. Moist Yellow Pine Forest dominated by Sugar Pine and White Fir. Mojave Desert in distance. *B*. View eastward on south side of San Bernardino Mountains. Chaparral dominates. Typical spring day with fog in the Los Angeles Basin. *C*. View of Santa Ana Mountains eastward across El Toro Valley. Coastal Sage Scrub dominates in foreground. Notice the inversion layer in the valley.

PLATE 7   A. Santa Rosa Mountains. Upper Chaparral on south-facing slope dominated by manzanita. North-facing slope dominated by Golden-cup Oak. B. Southern Oak Woodland dominated
by Coast Live Oak on north-facing slope in San Joaquin Hills, Orange County. C. Western Sycamore
and Coast Live Oak in Black Star Canyon, Santa Ana Mountains.

PLATE 8 *A.* Quaking Aspen in autumn, near Glass Mountain, Mono County. *B.* Thousand Palms, a California Fan Palm oasis and sanctuary for the Desert Pupfish, *Cyprinodon macularius. C.* View westward across Modoc Plateau from Warner Mountains. Mount Shasta in background. Rabbitbrush, Great Basin Sagebrush, and Jeffrey Pine in foreground. *D.* Owens Valley and east side of Sierra Nevada. Great Basin Sagebrush dominates in foreground.

A.

B.

C.

PLATE 9   *A.* Cactus Scrub community, Colorado Desert. *B.* Creosote Bush Scrub community, typical of Mojave and Colorado deserts. *C.* Alkali sink community at Badwater, Death Valley, the lowest point in the United States. Panamint Mountains in background.

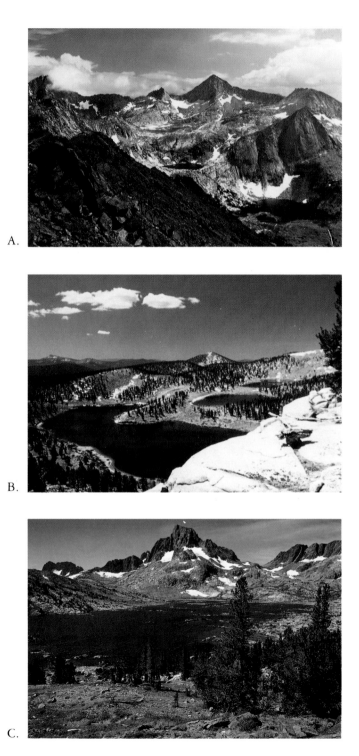

PLATE 10   *A*. A paternoster of cirque lakes. View southward toward Sawtooth Peak from Black Rock Pass, Sequoia National Park. *B*. Kettle lakes in Rocky Basin, Inyo National Forest. *C*. Thousand Island Lake, a large tarn in a glacial scour. Mount Banner and Mount Ritter in background.

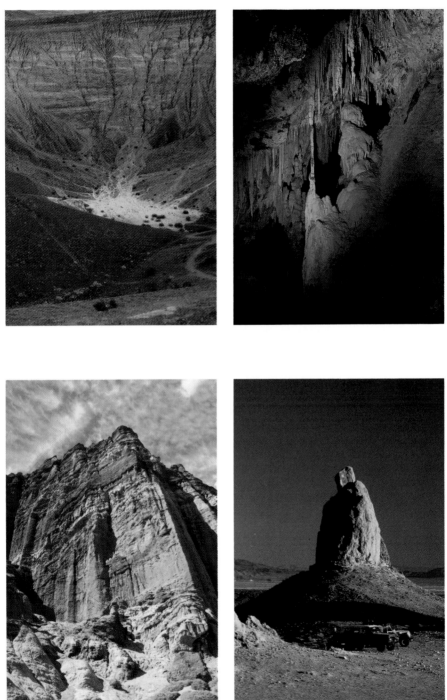

PLATE 11   A. Ubehebe Crater, Death Valley National Monument. Volcanic ash deposited on a lake bottom. B. Mitchell Caverns, Providence Mountains State Park. A limestone cavern. C. Red Rock Canyon. Volcanic tuff, ash, and old lake beds of the Ricardo Formation uplifted along a portion of the Garlock fault system. D. Trona Pinnacles, old tufa towers near Searles Lake.

PLATE 12 Some California rodents. A. California Ground Squirrel, *Spermophilus beecheyi*. B. Western Gray Squirrel, *Sciurus griseus*. C. Chickaree, *Tamiasciurus douglasii*. D. Golden-mantled Ground Squirrel, *Spermophilus lateralis*. E. White-tailed Antelope Squirrel, *Ammospermophilus leucurus*. F. Yellow-pine Chipmunk, *Tamias amoenus*. G. San Joaquin Antelope Squirrel, *Ammospermophilus nelsoni*. H. Desert Woodrat, *Neotoma lepida*. (Photograph by Greg Stewart)

PLATE 13 Some California birds. *A*. California Quail, *Callipepla californica*. *B*. Hooded Oriole, *Icterus cucullatus*. *C*. Wood Duck, *Aix sponsa*. *D*. Western Bluebird, *Sialia mexicana*. *E*. Red-winged Blackbird, *Agelaius phoeniceus*. *F*. Scrub Jay, *Aphelocoma coerulescens*. *G*. Belted Kingfisher, *Ceryle alcyon*. *H*. Black-billed Magpie, *Pica pica*.

PLATE 14 Some water birds. *A*. Forster's Tern, *Sterna forsteri*. *B*. Ruddy Duck, *Oxyura jamaicensis*. *C*. Brown Pelican, *Pelecanus occidentalis*. *D*. Long-billed Curlew, *Numenius americanus*. *E*. Great Blue Heron, *Ardea herodias*. *F*. Snowy Egret, *Egretta thula*. *G*. Sora, *Porzana carolina*. *H*. American Coot, *Fulica americana*.

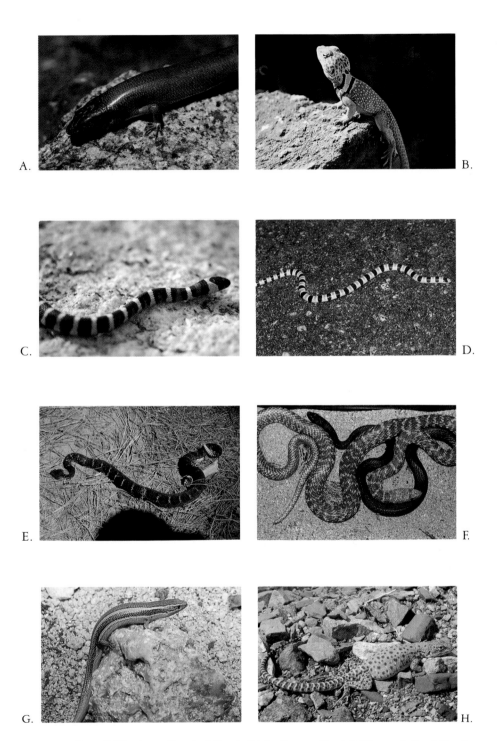

PLATE 15 Some California reptiles. *A.* Gilbert's Skink, *Eumeces gilberti*. *B.* Western Collared Lizard, *Crotaphytus bicinctores*. *C.* Mountain Kingsnake, *Lampropeltis zonata*. *D.* Western Shovel-nosed Snake, *Chionactis occipitalis*. (Photo by Charles Z. Leavell.) *E.* Melanistic Western Rattlesnake, *Crotalus viridis*. *F.* Two color forms of the Coachwhip, *Masticophis flagellum*. *G.* Western Skink, *Eumeces skiltonianus*. *H.* Long-nosed Leopard Lizard, *Gambelia wislizenii*.

PLATE 16   Some Mountain Wildflowers. *A*. Paintbrush, *Castilleja* sp. (Photo by Diana Cosand.) *B*. Scarlet Gilia, *Ipomopsis aggregata*. *C*. Harlequin Lupine, *Lupinus stiversii*. *D*. Leopard Lily, *Lilium parvum*. *E*. Red Columbine, *Aquilegia formosa*. *F*. Alpine Columbine, *Aquilegia pubescens*. *G*. Helleborine, *Epipactis gigantea*. *H*. Owl Clover, *Orthocarpus purpurascens*.

In their juvenile phase, periodical cicadas (Cicadidae) feed underground on fungus and juices obtained from roots. The Seventeen-year Locust of the eastern United States is actually a cicada. California species spend two to five years underground. When nymphs emerge they crawl up the nearest shrub or tree, where they molt, splitting the skin down the back. When the adult emerges, its wings fill with fluids and the new skin hardens. Concealed in vegetation, the adult "sings" loudly by vibrating membranes on its underside. This noise is a territorial and mating call. After mating, eggs are laid on twigs. Newly hatched nymphs drop to the ground, burrow in it, and the cycle repeats.

Internal juices of plants are nutritious, particularly during periods of vigorous growth. At this time insects such as aphids (Aphidae) become very common. They tap into the new growth with piercing mouthparts and suck the juices. Some discharge a sugary solution known as honeydew from the anus. Ants are attracted to the honeydew and may foster the spread of aphids by carrying wingless forms to new locations. Aphid life cycles are complex, involving winged and wingless forms. Some reproduce parthenogenetically: eggs develop without being fertilized. Parthenogenetic forms may appear at different times, or they may alternate seasonally.

Larvae of various gossamer-winged butterflies (Lycaenidae) also produce a type of honeydew that is attractive to ants. Included in this family are small butterflies known as hairstreaks (Theclinae), coppers (Lycaeninae), and blues (Polyommatinae). A number of these are associated with deserts. The Leda Hairstreak (*Ministrymon leda*) is associated with Honey Mesquite (*Prosopis glandulosa*), as are Edward's Blue (*Hemiargus gyas*) and Reakirt's Blue (*Hemiargus isola alce*). The Pygmy Blue (*Brephidium exile*) and the San Emigdio Blue (*Plebulina emigdionis*) are often associated with Shadscale Scrub.

The large Gray Snout-weevil, *Enpagodeves desertus* (fig. 9.57), also feeds on plant juices. This is a large beetle in the weevil family (Curculionidae), one of the most diverse families of organisms in the world. No other family in the animal kingdom has as many species. There are more than a thousand species in California alone.

Of the vertebrates that are herbivorous, most are birds and mammals, although not many can afford to be so specialized as to eat only plant material. Food is too scarce. Of the reptiles, there are a few herbivores, including the Desert Tortoise, the Desert Iguana, and the Chuckwalla. One problem with herbivory is that large amounts of potassium or other salts may be consumed in plant foods. Desert reptiles deal with this by expelling the excess salts through nasal salt glands and then snorting the fluid from their nostrils.

It is interesting to note that the herbivorous reptiles tend to be larger than the carnivores. Eating plant material generally produces fewer calories per bite, but much less effort is expended in gathering the food. Plant life is 10 times as abundant as animal life, and it doesn't attempt to escape. Herbivores therefore are able to move their large body masses with minimal energy expenditure, investing their calories in mass rather than locomotion. This principle also explains why grassland mammals tend to be larger than the predators. Based on these size relationships, a person might speculate that juvenile reptiles eat insects, and that their diet changes when

FIGURE 9.57   Gray Snout-weevil, *Enpagodeves desertus*.

they become larger. This is apparently not the case. It seems that whatever is the preferred diet of a reptile, it remains so throughout the life of the animal.

Of the mammals in deserts, herbivores such as rabbits and Bighorn Sheep eat leaves and twigs, but most of the herbivorous mammals are seed-eating rodents. Most herbivorous birds, such as quail and doves, are seed eaters but are not obligated to plant material, supplementing their diets with insects whenever possible.

Because seeds may be abundant in the desert, and because they are high-calorie items, they are objects of intense competition. Ants, rodents, and birds seem to compete for the same resource. How does niche partitioning avoid this problem?

Some insight into the problem of competition among seed-eating animals (granivores) can be gained by studying harvester ants. In Arizona where there is summer and winter precipitation, there are many kinds of seeds on a yearly basis. Ants are renowned for carrying loads that are disproportionately large for their body size. It has been proposed that ants, in order to be more efficient in carrying a load, might select seeds of a certain size and in this way partition the resources. In Arizona there are five to seven species of seed-harvesting ants, each of which is a different size. It appears that each species is adapted to carry seeds of a different size. In California deserts where there is only winter rain, the most common harvester ant, *Veromessor pergandei,* is polymorphic in body size. Depending on which type of seed is abundant, a different size of worker ant is apparent. This is only circumstantial evidence, but it is supported by the fact that in Arizona there are also five to seven size groups of granivorous rodents. Apparently, seed eaters in general avoid competition by gathering different sizes of seeds.

Further studies of rodents show that different species forage in different places. Kangaroo rats (*Dipodomys* spp.) (fig. 9.48A) forage in the open. Their bipedal form of locomotion (hopping) enables them to move rapidly and escape predators. Pocket mice (*Perognathus* spp.) (fig 9.48B) superficially resemble kangaroo rats. They are in the same family (Heteromyidae), but they are smaller. In spite of having enlarged hind legs, pocket mice move around on all fours: they are quadrupedal. Pocket mice forage beneath the shrubs. When seeds are abundant the pocket mouse need not move from under the protective canopy of the shrub, under which is the entrance to its burrow.

Seasonal variation in diet is another factor that reduces competition for seeds, particularly with birds. When seeds are abundant in spring and early summer, sparrows, doves, and quail eat primarily seeds. Later in the year they switch to insects. Black-throated Sparrows, *Amphispiza bilineata* (fig. 9.37), in particular are noted for their fly-catching behavior during the dry season, which frees them from seed competition and provides them with a food source that is rich in water. They are also noted for eating entire flowers to obtain the nectar within.

The Phainopepla, *Phainopepla nitens* (fig. 9.35), is a fly-catching species that switches to the fruit of mistletoe when it is abundant. Phainopeplas are in the family of silky flycatchers (Ptilogonatidae), which are closely related to the waxwings. Black birds with a large, slender crest, they are conspicuous as they perch in the tops of large shrubs or trees along washes. From this perch they search the sky for flying insects. When Desert Mistletoe comes into fruit, Phainopeplas feed heavily on the berries. The seeds pass through their digestive tracts, and while they perch they distribute the seeds to uninfested branches. It is primarily through the Phainopepla that the Desert Mistletoe, so common in Catclaw Acacia and Honey Mesquite, is disseminated.

In some parts of the Mojave Desert there are three species of ground squirrel that seem to feed on the same things: the Mojave Ground Squirrel (*Spermophilus mojavensis*), the Round-tailed Ground Squirrel (*Spermophilus tereticaudus*), and the White-tailed Antelope Squirrel (*Ammospermophilus leucurus*) (pl. 12E). They scurry about in the spring, feeding on seeds, flowers, and leaves. The Antelope Ground Squirrel is active year-round, but the other two species, doubling their weight in spring, are dormant from August to March, thereby conserving a great deal of energy. The three species avoid competition by feeding together only when food is abundant. The rarest of the three species, the Mojave Ground Squirrel is now on the state list of threatened species. The Antelope Ground Squirrel hibernates in the northern part of its range. There it overlaps with only one other species, Townsend's Ground Squirrel, *Spermophilus townsendi,* another hibernator. All of the ground squirrels avoid competition with other seed gatherers to some degree by climbing into the shrubs or trees and feeding on the seeds before they fall to the ground.

Most of the carnivores in the desert are insectivorous because insects are the most common animals. The most common carnivores are probably scorpions, but spiders and centipedes are also abundant. These are all venomous predators. Scorpions inject the venom with the tail stinger, and spiders and centipedes do so by means of fangs on their jaws called chelicerae.

In California there are no scorpions that are deadly to humans, although there are several in southern Arizona and Mexico. In most cases, a scorpion sting can be painful but is not much worse than a bee sting. Scorpions spend the day hiding under rocks or debris or in small burrows, emerging at night to forage. They do not see well, but they are effective hunters. Usually they stand and wait, sensing the approach of potential prey by feeling vibrations in the soil with their legs. The scorpion can orient to these vibrations in the same way other animals orient to sound. When the prey comes near, the scorpion grabs it with its pincers and stings it. The scorpion then crushes the immobilized prey with its pincers, tears it apart, and sucks up the fluid remains.

What wanders around the desert at night and falls prey to scorpions? Most studies indicate they eat other arthropods. A surprise that emerged from studies in the Coachella Valley is that a significant portion of food for scorpions is other scorpions. A large species, *Paruroctonus mesaensis,* makes up 95% of the scorpion population of the area, and in addition to its usual arthropod prey, it feeds heavily on three other species of scorpion. It seems to prey particularly on juvenile and male scorpions. Studies of behavior also indicate that the other species have evolved activity patterns that help them avoid predation.

Spiders usually trap their prey in a web. The prey, typically a flying insect, hits the web, causing vibrations that alert the spider. The spider then injects venom into the prey and wraps it with silk to prevent it from escaping. Regurgitated digestive enzymes liquefy the internal tissues of the insect, and the spider returns later to suck out the digested material. It does not eat the exoskeleton.

One prey item that is sometimes attacked by a spider is the millipede, a common detritus feeder. Millipedes, however, have a very interesting defense. They produce a tranquilizing chemical that puts the spider to sleep after it feeds. This does not protect the millipede that gets bitten, but the spider, if it survives its period of drug-induced sleep, will avoid millipedes as a prey species in the future. The millipede that gives up its life to a spider altruistically helps the survival of the remaining millipedes.

Few spiders in California are dangerous to humans. The only spider here that is likely to harm a human is the Black Widow, *Latrodectus mactans.* These spiders are most often associated with human habitation. Woodpiles and outhouses are their favorite haunts. They do not normally bite humans, and they are rarely deadly. Symptoms include pain, abdominal cramps, dizziness, nausea, and vomiting. The usual treatment is simply to relieve pain and includes tranquilizers. A typical adult human recovers fully in about four days.

In recent years a legend has been building about the dangers of being bitten by the Brown Recluse or Violin Spider, *Loxosceles reclusa.* These are rare, nonnative spiders that occur only around habitation. For some reason, there is more concern about this rare, introduced species than about the four native species of *Loxosceles* that are also known as brown spiders or violin spiders. The most widely distributed is the Desert Brown Spider, *Loxosceles deserta,* which occurs in the southern San Joaquin Valley as well as the Mojave and Colorado deserts. The other three species have localized distributions in Riverside County, Death Valley, and Palm Oases of the Colorado Desert.

There are only sporadic reports of bites from these spiders, but because the possibility exists, the symptoms of a Brown Recluse bite are worth noting. There may be a severe reaction, but it is rarely deadly. The bite may have a transient, local effect, or it may produce an ulcer that persists for several days. In some cases, severe tissue damage occurs, and skin grafting is required. Very few people get anything more than a local effect, which involves pain at the site from two to eight hours after the bite. Treatment ranges from topical cortisone to reduce inflammation, to surgical excision of the damaged tissue.

Few predatory insects are as interesting as the praying mantis. The name refers to the manner in which they hold their front legs, as if they were praying. There are several species of these tree-dwelling predators. They grasp their prey, usually another insect, and dismember it while they eat it alive. The mating behavior of some species of praying mantis is legendary. Once the male begins to copulate, the female bites off his head. This act stops the flow of a hormone produced in the brain that inhibits copulation. Because the copulatory organ is on the posterior end of the mantis, the female is now free to eat the remainder of the male while continuing copulation. The basis of this strategy is that once the female has been impregnated, the male would merely be a competitor for food. Killing the male reduces competition for food, which enhances survival of the female and the offspring. Although it is not common, a similar strategy may be employed by a female Black Widow, a behavior that is responsible for the species' common name.

Very common among carnivorous insects are red ants (*Formica* spp.). These ants are actually carrion eaters. In less than an hour, a swarm of red ants can dismember and carry away the remains of a large insect, such as a grasshopper or dragonfly. Red ants also eat the seed-gathering, black harvester ants.

Bees and wasps are related to ants. One group of wasps in which the females are flightless is known as velvet ants (*Dasymutilla* spp.). These wasps are covered with a boundary layer of long hairs. Their color ranges from bright red, to orange, to yellow, to white. They are distributed throughout the state. The most common desert forms are white and look like a bit of fluff blowing along the ground. They possess a stinger, with which they can immobilize prey, often ground-nesting bees and wasps. If molested by a human, they may produce a painful, stinging welt, but they are not dangerous.

Among the most interesting wasps are the large, orange-winged tarantula hawks (*Pepsis* spp.). A number of wasps have evolved to be associated with certain species of prey. Tarantula hawks attack tarantulas or trap-door spiders.

Tarantulas live in a silk-lined burrow. When a prey species disturbs the web near the entrance, usually at night, the tarantula rushes out and bites it, feeding in typical spider fashion. The adult tarantula hawk feeds on nectar, usually of milkweed flowers. It also walks about the desert, often at night, searching for tarantula burrows. When it finds one, it disturbs the web, causing the tarantula to rush out, and the fight begins. Once the spider is taunted into rearing back into its attack position, the wasp stings it at a precise location on the underside where it is able to pierce the spider's armor. Often the spider escapes, but if it gets stung, the wasp's venom paralyzes it without killing it. The wasp is unaffected by the spider venom. If, however, the spider bites the wasp at the same time that it is stung, its paralysis can cause the wasp to become impaled on the fangs. The wasp, unable to get free, will die.

After the spider is paralyzed, the wasp may enlarge the spider burrow by making a side chamber, it may make a new burrow, or it may use the burrow of another animal. Eventually, the wasp drags the paralyzed spider down the burrow and lays an egg upon it. The egg hatches into a white larva in a few days. Then, for about 30 days, the larva devours the paralyzed, still-living spider. When the spider is consumed, the larva pupates, and the adult wasp emerges the following year. A successful adult wasp can paralyze up to 20 spiders, ensuring that 20 new wasps will emerge the following year.

Sometimes while the wasp is underground, enlarging the chamber, another wasp will locate the paralyzed spider. It will attempt to claim it, dragging the spider away from the burrow. Usually the original wasp discovers the thief, and a fight ensues. The winner will kill the other wasp and claim the spider.

These large black wasps with orange wings are conspicuous. This color is probably important for defending territories and attracting a mate. During the day, males perch on top of large shrubs, particularly along a ridge line, where they will be easily observed by flying females. When a female appears, the male courts by displaying his wings. After mating, the female presumably spends the next night on the prowl, attempting to entice a tarantula from its burrow.

Although the wasp completes its life cycle in less than a year, female tarantulas are long-lived. One female in captivity lived for 30 years. They reach maturity in about 5 years, after which they produce 50 to 100 babies per year. Males do not mature for 8 to 10 years, but they die soon after mating. The female selects a mate that is about the same size as she is. Because females continue to grow for their entire lives, females of all different sizes require males of all different sizes. Males therefore mature at various sizes and ages to provide the variety of sizes to catch the female size groups. The tarantulas commonly seen in the spring during the day, sometimes in large numbers, are usually males out searching for females.

Most insects attack other arthropods, but a few bloodsucking insects attack mammals. Mosquitoes and horseflies are well known to humans, whom they pester. A lesser-known pest is the Western Conenose Bug, *Triatoma protracta,* a large, elongated bug in the assasin bug or kissing bug family (Reduviidae). These pests usually are found in woodrat nets, but sometimes they invade cabins. They typically prey upon woodrats, but on occasion they will bite a human, producing a painful, itching bite that may form a large welt up to 3 inches (7.5 cm) in diameter. Approximately 5% of those who are bitten develop an allergic reaction that requires antihistamine treatment. In Mexico and South America, related bugs introduce a blood parasite, a protozoan known as *Trypanosoma cruzi.* The subsequent affliction is a form of sleeping sickness known as Chagas' disease. At the present time, it is unknown in California.

Among vertebrate animals in deserts, lizards and snakes are the primary carnivores. The number of lizard and snake varieties in the desert is far too numerous for thorough discussion. Many of them also occur in cismontane southern California, and these were discussed along with southern California's scrub communities. Most lizards eat insects. A few carnivorous lizards, such as the Western Collared lizard, *Crotaphytus*

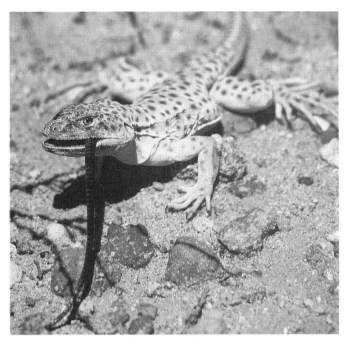

FIGURE 9.58   Long-nosed Leopard Lizard, *Gambelia wislizenii*. Note the tail of a recently swallowed Western Whiptail, *Cnemidophorus tigris,* hanging from the mouth of the lizard. (Photograph by Greg Stewart.)

bicinctores (pl. 15B) and the Long-nosed Leopard Lizard, *Gambelia wislizenii* (fig. 9.58) eat other lizards.

With so many insect-eating lizards, it is not surprising that an array of mechanisms to avoid competition exists. Niche partitioning among desert lizards is based on food preference, size, and favored habitat (fig. 9.59). Insectivorous sand dwellers include fringe-toed lizards (*Uma* spp.) (fig. 9.42A), the Zebra-tailed Lizard (*Callisaurus draconoides*) (fig. 9.42B), and horned lizards (*Phrynosoma* spp.) (fig. 8.36). Fringe-toed lizards live in sand dunes, Zebra-tailed Lizards lie along washes, and horned lizards feed in sandy areas almost exclusively on ants.

Of special note are the horned lizards. There are several species in the desert, but they all have the same basic lifestyle, eating 150 to 200 ants per day. This diet of ants adds a load of sodium that is excreted by the nasal salt gland. Horned lizards, in turn, are preyed on by Roadrunners, but their primary enemies are off-road vehicles.

The Desert Spiny Lizard, *Sceloporus magister* (fig. 9.60), and the Banded Rock Lizard, *Petrosaurus mearnsi,* are large lizards that feed on large insects. They also occur in different habitats. The Desert Spiny Lizard primarily lives in trees, including Joshua Trees. The Banded Rock Lizard, as its name implies, lives in rocks.

The Long-tailed Brush Lizard, *Urosaurus graciosus,* and the Side-blotched Lizard, *Uta stansburiana* (fig. 8.33), are small insectivores. The Long-tailed Brush Lizard lives

FIGURE 9.59 Ecological segregation of lizards of the family Iguanidae in the Sonoran Desert. (Illustration by Gene Christman from R. C. Stebbins. "Reptiles: Adaptations to Desert Ecosystems," *Environment Southwest*, 522:13–16. Reprinted with permission.)

in trees and brush. This lizard rests on branches in the shade and ambushes small insects. The Side-blotched Lizard also feeds on small insects, but it prefers to feed in the open.

Banded Geckos (fig. 9.49) are small, nocturnal insectivores. Leaf-toed Geckos, *Phyllodactylus xanti*, are also small, nocturnal insectivores, but they live and feed almost entirely under rock flakes. The Desert Night Lizard, *Xantusia vigilis* (fig. 9.61), is a small insectivore that feeds primarily on termites under the fallen boughs and trunks of yuccas.

All snakes are carnivores, eating all forms of insects and vertebrates. Because of this, snakes are scarce. They make up only a portion of the less than 9 pounds per acre (1 g/m^2) carnivore biomass. Because they are not common, and because they are easy to maintain, they have become desirable pets to some people. Snake collecting at night along desert roads has become a hobby and a vocation for quite a number of people. Unfortunately, this collecting has seriously threatened many species of snake, and it is now illegal to collect or sell wild amphibians and reptiles. A loophole in the law allows the sale of animals raised in captivity, those that are offspring of animals possessed prior to the law. The result is that a number of poachers continue to collect animals illegally, claiming that they were raised in captivity. Unless they are caught in the act, they cannot be prosecuted.

FIGURE 9.60 Desert Spiny Lizard, *Sceloporus magister*.

FIGURE 9.61 Desert Night Lizard, *Xantusia vigilis*.

Of great interest to many people are the venomous snakes. In California, all truly venomous snakes are in the rattlesnake family (Crotalidae). About six different species of rattlesnake are present in the deserts. A couple of others occur in marginal habitats and are found occasionally in what might be called a desert habitat.

Rattlesnakes are pit vipers. They have a temperature-sensitive pit beside each nostril, and this gives them "stereo" heat perception useful in locating endothermic (warm-blooded) prey and predators. Typical of venomous animals in general, they can immobilize prey species that are large enough to do them harm. In typical snake fashion, jaws disarticulate to allow the prey to be swallowed, even though it may be larger than the snake's head. Teeth curve backward, and each half of the lower jaw moves independently. The snake, when it swallows, moves one half of its lower jaw at a time. In this way it can "crawl" around its dinner. The rattle is a threat, nothing more. Its function is to warn some foolish animal that is too big to eat. The snake has no intention of wasting its venom to protect itself except as a last resort. Any human threatened by a rattlesnake simply should walk slowly away. Most bites occur by accident, when the snake is stepped on, or when it is being handled.

One of the most interesting rattlesnakes is the Sidewinder, *Crotalus cerastes* (fig. 9.62). Sidewinding is a form of locomotion that many kinds of snakes use to move over loose sand. Sidewinders use this type of locomotion on all surfaces. They are restricted to sandy areas, where, similar to other rattlesnakes, they lie and wait for small animals, usually rodents. Sidewinders have a small horn over each eye that acts like a gable on a roof. It keeps sand out of the eyes of the snake as it lies in wait, buried except for its nostrils and eyeballs. A parallel development has occurred in an African pit viper. This species looks and acts like an American Sidewinder, but it has no rattle.

The Mojave Rattlesnake, *Crotalus scutulatus,* is sometimes known as a Mojave Green even though it is rarely greenish. This rattlesnake is notable for its potent venom. In most rattlesnakes, the venom has a hemolytic action; it digests tissue. Mojave Rattlesnakes have a venom that has hemolytic and neurotoxic properties, making this snake a bit more dangerous than other species. It is important to realize, however, that rattlesnake bites are rarely deadly. Symptoms include pain and swelling, and sometimes weakness and nausea. The latter two symptoms are more likely the result of anxiety. No first aid should be administered unless the victim is more than three hours from a hospital—a rare circumstance in California. Once in the hospital, the victim can be watched. If a serious reaction begins to develop, an antivenom (antivenin) will be administered. If a victim is more than three hours from a hospital, the best treatment is to splint the limb and wrap it to inhibit lymph circulation beneath the skin. By no means should a tourniquet be used, or should the wound be cut and blood sucked out. Chilling or cryotherapy also has been proved to have little value.

A few rear-fanged snakes occur in California. Among these are Lyre Snakes (*Trimorphodon biscutatus*) and Night Snakes (*Hypsiglena torquata*) (fig. 9.63). Strictly speaking, these are venomous snakes, but they are not common and are not likely to bite a human. Even if a person is bitten, the location of the fangs at the rear of the mouth precludes the introduction of much venom. There are no California records of a human

FIGURE 9.62   Sidewinder, *Crotalus cerastes*.

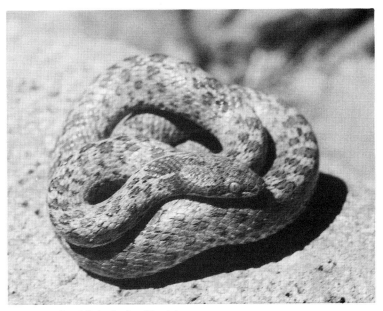

FIGURE 9.63   Night Snake, *Hypsiglena torquata*.

experiencing difficulty from the bite of a rear-fanged snake. They are found under debris such as fallen Joshua Tree boughs or under rock flakes on cliffs.

There are no large carnivores in the desert, simply because there is not enough food to support a population of large animals that eat nothing but other animals. With the desert capable of supporting less than 9 pounds per acre, the range of a 100-pound carnivore would have to be spread over 11 acres, and there would be no food left for any other carnivorous species, even an insect. There are carnivorous birds such as Golden Eagles, hawks, and owls. Their home ranges by necessity are quite large, which is not usually a problem for a bird. Poor-wills (*Phalaenoptilus nuttallii*) (fig. 9.64), nighthawks (*Chordeiles* spp.), swifts (Apodidae), and bats (Chiroptera) are insectivorous. They avoid competition by foraging at different elevations, and at different times of day.

It was mentioned earlier that Roadrunners allow their body temperatures to drop during the night, thus conserving metabolic energy. A more extreme example of this phenomenon is exhibited by the Poor-will, which hibernates during the winter, conserving a great deal of energy during the time that flying insects are least abundant. The Poor-will was the first bird discovered to be a hibernator. It is now known that swifts are also hibernators.

The larger mammals with reputations for being carnivores are actually omnivorous. These include foxes, Badgers, and Coyotes. The Kit Fox, *Vulpes macrotis,* is small, about the size of a house cat. Its size is an adaptation to a food-poor environment. It takes a smaller biomass of food to support a population of Kit Foxes than it does to support, for example, a population of Gray Foxes, *Urocyon cinereoargenteus*. Kit Foxes eat insects, scorpions, mice, and fruits. They are nocturnal and apparently very curious, because they are common visitors to campsites. Often they approach closely enough to be clearly visible from the light of a campfire. Their large ears indicate that hearing is important for their foraging, but they probably are just as important for radiating heat.

The Coyote, *Canis latrans* (fig. 8.47), has a worse reputation among ranchers than any other animal. They have been shot, trapped, and poisoned, but somehow they endure. The problem is clear. The Coyote has a reputation for preying on lambs and calves, not to mention house cats and small dogs. Vast acreage of desert is leased for grazing. Of 171 million acres administered by the Bureau of Land Management, 150 million are authorized for grazing. Coyotes are opportunistic, feeding on whatever is abundant. They will take meat when they can get it. If an opportunity arises, they will take a lamb or calf, particularly if there is a family of pups to be fed. Coyotes are normally solitary; the only time they hunt in packs is during winter when food is scarce. Grouping up is more common in the Great Basin than in other deserts.

As of 1982, the U.S. Fish and Wildlife Service had an annual budget of $8 million for animal control. The bulk of that money was spent on Coyote control, and most of that was spent in the western deserts to protect cattle and sheep. Several authors have calculated that, from an economic point of view, it would be cheaper to pay a rancher directly for lost livestock than to continue attempting to reduce Coyote populations. Coyotes are marvelously density-dependent. A female is capable of producing two

FIGURE 9.64 Poor-will, *Phalaenoptilus nuttallii*, basking in the sun after emerging from hibernation.

to eight pups, depending on the size of the Coyote population. When population density is reduced, Coyotes respond by having larger families.

Coyotes are a natural control on other pests, such as rats, mice, and rabbits. Jack rabbits are also remarkable examples of density-dependent animals. If predators are removed, the jack rabbit population explodes, and the rabbits invade fields and eat crops. Even where they don't eat crops, jack rabbits can have a significant effect on desert vegetation. Another calculation showed that killing five Coyotes increases the jack rabbit population to the degree that they eat the same amount of forage as a steer. In the state of Arizona, 1864 Coyotes were killed in 1969, the last year that these data were published. Competition from increased jack rabbits potentially cost ranchers grazing land that would support an additional 373 cattle. In other words, killing Coyotes actually reduced the cattle herd by increasing competition from jack rabbits. It actually cost the ranchers more money than if they had allowed the Coyotes to remain.

Until the early 1900s, Gray Wolves, *Canis lupus,* also roamed the Great Basin, feeding on Pronghorn and Bison. Conversion of the Great Basin to pasture nearly eliminated the large native herbivores, and the predator extermination program finished off the Gray Wolf. Gray Wolves today are on the list of endangered species, occurring only in a few protected habitats along the U.S.-Canadian border and in national parks such as Glacier and Yellowstone. The former Gray Wolf population of the Great Central Valley will be discussed in the next chapter.

Overgrazing by cattle and sheep is a reality. Only 20% of BLM land is not overgrazed. Livestock browse selectively, shifting the composition of natural vegetation toward unpalatable species; livestock enhance the distribution of weeds. Compaction of soil by livestock causes increased erosion. Old photographs taken at the turn of the century show that the southwest desert had a different appearance before the introduction of livestock. Steep-sided, dry arroyos are caused by increased runoff associated with overgrazing. There were few arroyos prior to the introduction of livestock.

The problem is that the desert's low productivity will sustain very few livestock. It takes about 10 acres (24.7 ha) to support a single steer or five sheep, and this disregards the existence of all other herbivorous animals, including native insects, lizards, rodents, birds, and mammals. In actual practice, for deserts to support cattle with minimum impact, there should be no more than one animal for every 70 to 100 acres (30–40 ha). Deserts simply are not appropriate for livestock grazing. The number of cattle grown on desert ranges is but a fraction of total beef production in this country. In California, a mere 0.3% of beef production occurs in the desert. If cattle grazing here were stopped entirely or greatly reduced, it would have minimal impact on beef production, but it would be a step toward recovery of our desert ecosystems. Abandoning desert grazing would also save the millions of dollars per year now spent trying to control Coyotes.

The damaging effect of overgrazing and other disturbances on desert soil has been well documented, but only recently has it been shown that the effect on cold deserts such as the Great Basin is even more dramatic than was previously thought. Disturbance of the soil surface can destroy a microbiotic crust that includes stabilizing filaments of cyanobacteria (blue-green algae) and nitrogen-fixing lichens. This filamentous mat in a spongelike way absorbs water and prevents erosion. It takes about 10 years for these mats to form, without which wind and water carry away the soil. Another problem with overgrazing is associated with feral animals, those that were domesticated but have gone wild. These include Feral Horses or Mustangs, *Equus caballus,* in the Basin-Range Province, and Burros or Donkeys, *Equus asinus,* in the Mojave. In 1985 the number of Feral Horses and Burros in the western states was estimated at more than 60,000. Compared to the 4.1 million domestic livestock animals, that number seems barely significant.

Until 1971 government agencies hunted feral animals to keep them under control. Sometimes meat was sold for pet food; other times it was exported to Europe, where it is consumed by humans as a delicacy. In 1971 Congress passed the Wild Horse and Burro Act, which made it a federal crime to kill or even molest these animals.

The number of Feral Horses is increasing slowly. In California, the problem evidently has not reached crisis proportions, and it may not. The total number of Feral Horses in California has been estimated at about 2100, and research shows that the total number of animals has remained stable for many years. There may be as many as 750 Feral Horses in the Coso and Argus ranges on land managed by the China Lake Naval Weapons Center. The largest single herd, containing about 150 animals, is located in the Montgomery Pass area, east of Mono lake.

The main problem is that ranchers view Feral Horses as direct competition for cattle. Ranchers want Feral Horses removed, but the herds roam across state lines and occur on property managed by different government agencies. The Bureau of Land Management established a program to round up Feral Horses and have them adopted, and from time to time the U.S. Navy contributes Feral Horses to this pool from their herds. Only about one-third of the animals are adopted. In the late 1980s the federal government was spending about $17 million a year just to feed those that nobody wanted. The BLM then got another idea. They would waive the $125 adoption fee if a rancher would graze the Feral Horses on his property. After a year, if the Feral Horses were not adopted, the rancher could keep them. What aggravated some people is that most of the Feral Horses were not adopted, and after the waiting period was over, some ranchers illegally sold them. Some of them became rodeo stock, but others were sold for meat. In 1988 the BLM suspended the fee-waiver arrangement.

The Burro problem is another matter. As of 1986 their numbers were continuing to increase dramatically. With no natural enemies, Burros have overgrazed and compacted vast stretches of Mojave terrain to the detriment of native plants and animals. Burros eat about 10 pounds (4 kg) of vegetation per day. One recent estimate for Saline Valley put the Burro population at one per acre (0.4 ha), which, similar to cattle, would put them over carrying capacity, even if there were no other herbivores in the area. In the Death Valley region, experimental exclosures were built to keep Burros out of certain areas. Three times as many plants were found inside the exclosures as on the outside, where the Burros grazed. Furthermore, the ratio of dead shrubs outside to dead shrubs inside was 27:1.

One of the animals most seriously affected by Burros has been the Desert Bighorn Sheep, *Ovis canadensis nelsoni*. Although this is the most common of the three types of Bighorn Sheep in California, there is cause for alarm when one considers the rate at which the Burro population is increasing. Competition for food is an obvious problem, but of greater concern is that aggressive packs of Burros take over water holes in the summer. They foul the water with waste products, and they will not let the sheep drink. Sheep populations in some areas have dwindled rapidly.

Since 1971 the Bureau of Land Management has sponsored an "adopt-a-Burro" program in order to dispose of Burros "humanely." They have unloaded about 50,000 Burros, but they still have thousands of unadopted animals that cost over $700 each year to maintain. In 1985 the BLM was funded $16 million to round up 17,000 more Burros for adoption. Not only has it been difficult to find people to adopt Burros, but the program has experienced some difficulty keeping up with the birthrate in captivity.

10

The Great Central Valley

The Great Central Valley, also referred to as the Central Valley or the Great Valley, is an elongate depression that lies between the Coast Ranges and the Sierra Nevada. It is about 430 miles (690 km) long and about 75 miles (120 km) wide. At its extreme northern and southern ends, the elevation is about 400 feet (120 m). At its center, east of San Francisco Bay, it is slightly below sea level.

The Great Central Valley is actually two large valleys lying end to end, each drained by a major river. North of San Francisco Bay, the Sacramento Valley is drained by the Sacramento River. To the south, the San Joaquin Valley is drained by the San Joaquin River. The confluence of these two rivers occurs east of San Francisco Bay. This area, the Sacramento–San Joaquin Delta, was formerly a massive wetland. It is now one of California's important agricultural areas.

It is difficult to establish precise boundaries for the Great Central Valley (fig. 10.1) because at its edges the biological communities, such as Valley Grassland, grade into Foothill Woodland or Oak Woodland in an irregular manner. (Foothill Woodland is discussed in chapters 4 and 7.) Elevation considerations are not precise either, because the floor of the valley grades into the foothills over a series of terraces (fig. 10.2), and a number of low-lying adjacent valleys of the Coast Ranges and Sierra Nevada foothills are dominated by biological communities that are typically associated with the Great Central Valley. In general, the borders of the Great Central Valley are formed by the zone where alluvial soils grade into bedrock features and the landscape is dominated by Foothill Woodland.

This geomorphic province more than any other has been altered by activities of humans. In its pristine state, it contained three primary communities of plants and animals: Valley Grassland, Freshwater Marsh, and Riparian Woodland (fig. 10.3). In 1987 a report entitled *Sliding toward Extinction* was prepared at the request of the California Senate Committee on Natural Resources and Wildlife and commissioned by the California Nature Conservancy. In this report, the state of natural communities in the Great Central Valley is clearly depicted. Valley Grassland, a community of perennial bunchgrasses, was once the most common community. This was California's prairie. There were more than 22 million acres (9,000,000 ha) present in the early 1800s, and it is now 99% gone. In low spots there were numerous Freshwater Marshes fed by winter precipitation and runoff from the mountains. About 94%, or 3,750,000 acres (1,540,000 ha), of this community have been lost. Cutting through the valley were large rivers fringed with a gallery forest of Riparian Woodland. About 89%, or 819,000 acres (334,000 ha), of it are lost.

The Great Central Valley is one of California's arid regions. As such, it shares many characteristics with the desert provinces. Desert communities such as Saltbush

FIGURE 10.1   The Great Central Valley. (From O. Hackel. "Summary of the Geology of the Great Valley." In E. H. Bailey, ed. *Geology of Northern California.* California Division of Mines and Geology, Bulletin 190, 1966.)

FIGURE 10.2   Biotic zonation of the San Joaquin Valley.

Scrub and Alkali Sink are distributed extensively in low-lying areas throughout the southern San Joaquin Valley.

CLIMATE

The climate of the Great Central Valley promotes widespread grasslands. Precipitation occurs during winter months, but it is reduced because of the rain shadow of the Coast Ranges. To the north, in the Sacramento River Valley, average annual precipitation is moderate. To the south it is reduced to desert proportions. At four weather stations, from north to south, average annual precipitation has been measured as follows: Redding, 38 inches (95 cm); Sacramento, 18 inches (46 cm); Fresno, 10 inches (24 cm); and Bakersfield, 6 inches (15 cm).

Cold-air drainage from the surrounding mountains becomes trapped, forming a persistent inversion layer in the Great Central Valley. During winter this is manifested in a dense, ground-hugging fog known as tule fog. In association with these dense fogs, massive, chain-reaction traffic accidents occur nearly every winter along Interstate 5 or Highway 99. Sometimes the sun fails to penetrate for weeks on end. During summer the inversion layer "burns off," but photochemical smog becomes a problem. Summer days are hot and hazy.

GEOLOGY

The Great Central Valley is a huge basin filled with sediments. Sands and gravels over 30,000 feet (9500 m) deep lie upon Sierran basement rocks that extend downward at

Fresh Water Marshes in California

Former Extent
(Prior to 1850)

N

Riparian Woodland in the Central Valley of California

Former Extent
(Prior to 1850)

N

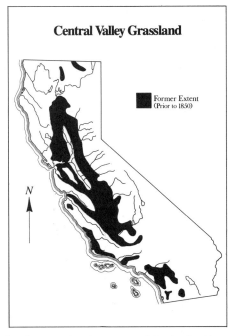

Central Valley Grassland

Former Extent
(Prior to 1850)

N

FIGURE 10.3 Former distribution of native communities in the Great Central Valley. (From P. Seligmann. "Changing California," *Nature Conservancy News*, 31: 18–23, 1981. Reprinted with permission.)

an angle from the western slope of the Sierra Nevada. The deepest region of sediments is off-center, near the eastern edge of the Coast Ranges; presumably, there is a deep fault system in that area. A thrust fault zone occurs along the western edge of the valley. The underlying basement rocks simply are a continuation of the landform that makes up the Sierra Nevada.

The deepest parts of the gravels and sands are marine sediments that have accumulated since late Jurassic time, about 145 million years ago. Apparently, the sea retreated from the valley at about the same time that the southern Coast Ranges were uplifted, and during the long history of accumulation of marine sediments, the basement rock continued to subside. During most of the Pleistocene the area was occupied by shallow brackish and freshwater lakes, particularly in the southern San Joaquin Valley.

During the last 5 million years, sediments accumulated as alluvial deposits washed out of the mountains. These deposits are only a few thousand feet (1000 m) deep over most of the valley floor. Depths up to 10,000 feet (3300 m) occur in some places, indicating that the valley floor was not always as monotonous as it is today.

The only topographic relief that occurs in the valley today is near Marysville, where Sutter Buttes project above the valley floor to an elevation of 2100 feet (640 m). These are plug domes of andesite that are about the right age to be the southernmost of the old Cascade volcanoes. Their origin, however, is controversial.

Trapped beneath the sediments of the San Joaquin Valley is one of California's richest oil fields. Oil has been the keystone of Kern County's economy since the 1920s. As of 1987, 9.5 billion barrels of crude oil had been removed. Some estimates indicate that there may be 6 billion barrels more to be recovered. Unfortunately, San Joaquin Valley crude oil is very thick, making it a high-cost, low-price product. Its production therefore is highly subject to the vagaries of world oil prices. When oil prices drop, it is not economically feasible to pump oil in the San Joaquin Valley. The resulting layoff of thousands of employees sends the Kern County economy into a slump, with unemployment rates sometimes rising to 20%. When world oil prices go up, the economy revives.

NATIVE VEGETATION

Valley Grassland

Valley Grassland once covered all well-drained areas in the Great Central Valley as well as larger valleys in the Coast Ranges and cismontane southern California. As indicated earlier, only about 1% of the grassland today could be considered pristine. Even in its disturbed form, Valley Grassland is still one of California's most common communities, covering over 22 million acres (8,980,000 ha) of land (fig. 10.4). Pristine grassland, however, was dominated by perennial bunchgrasses such as needlegrasses (*Stipa* spp.), triple-awned grasses (*Aristida* spp.), bluegrasses (*Poa* spp.), and rye grasses (*Elymus* spp.). By far, the dominant species was Purple Needlegrass, *Stipa pulchra*.

FIGURE 10.4 Rolling hills near Taft, western San Joaquin Valley. These introduced Mediterranean grasses have largely replaced native bunchgrasses.

Bunchgrasses grow upright in dense tufts of stems that arise from a perennial root crown. With the onset of winter rains, these grasses produce new growth. During winter, cool weather and persistent overcast inhibit growth and photosynthesis. Rapid growth, flowering, and maturity normally occur from April to June.

Pristine grasslands also contained annual grasses and herbs, although the annual grasses were not as abundant as the perennial forms. Some of the wildflowers produced displays of color that are legendary. Among these wildflowers were numerous annual species and geophytes, perennials that returned each year from bulbs.

Geophytes include members in the lily (Liliaceae) and amaryllis (Amaryllidaceae) families. Among the lilies, the mariposa lilies (*Calochortus* spp.) are the most beautiful. It is not certain how they got the name *mariposa*, which means "butterfly" in Spanish. The allusion could be a reference to the shape and color of the flower petals, or it could refer to some of the common pollinators. These plants usually grow about a foot (30 cm) tall, and they are usually capped by a single three-petaled blossom about 2 inches (5 cm) across. Depending on the species, petal color varies from white or violet to yellow or orange, and the base of each petal usually has a blotch of vivid color—purple, red, or orange.

Members of the amaryllis family have flowers in starburst clusters known as umbels. Sepals and petals are the same color, so it appears that each flower has six petals. There are numerous species in this group, varying in size from Blue Dicks, *Dichelostemma capitatum*, to White Brodiaea, *Triteleia hyacinthina*. Blue Dicks usually has a few bright blue flowers in a dense cluster less than an inch (2.5 cm) across. The plant is usually no more than a foot tall (30 cm). White Brodiaea, in contrast, may be 6 feet (2 m) in height. The surrounding vegetation dictates the height to which it will grow. In the foothills, this species may grow among shrubs, in which case it grows up through them in order to flower above. A cluster of 4 to 10 white flowers, each over an inch (2.5 cm) in diameter, caps the elongated stem.

Perhaps the most spectacular of the wildflowers are lupines (*Lupinus* spp.); California Poppies, *Eschscholtzia californica* (pl. 3C); and Purple Owl Clover, *Orthocarpus purpurascens* (pl. 16H). Descriptions of fields of wildflowers by early writers such as John Muir are common in the literature. Perhaps the best is that of John Steinbeck. In his book *East of Eden* he describes flowers in the Salinas Valley:

> On the wide level acres of the valley the topsoil lay deep and fertile. It required only a rich winter of rain to make it break forth in grass and flowers. The spring flowers in a wet year were unbelievable. The whole valley floor, and the foothills too, would be carpeted with lupins and poppies. Once a woman told me that colored flowers would seem more bright if you added a few white flowers to give the colors definition. Every petal of blue lupin is edged with white, so that a field of lupins is more blue than you can imagine. And mixed with these were splashes of California poppies. These too are of a burning color—not orange, not gold, but if pure gold were liquid and could raise a cream, that golden cream might be like the color of the poppies. When their season was over the yellow mustard came up and grew to a great height. When my grandfather came into the valley the mustard was so tall that a man on horseback showed only his head above the yellow flowers. On the uplands the grass would be strewn with buttercups, with hen-and-chickens, with black-centered yellow violets. And a little later in the season there would be red and yellow stands of Indian paintbrush. These were the flowers of the open places exposed to the sun.

Other carpets of wildflowers may include various members of the sunflower family (Asteraceae). Among these are small species such as Goldfields, *Lasthenia californica* (= *L. chrysostoma*), that occur in untold millions. Often mixed with Goldfields are larger members of the sunflower family, such as Tidy Tips, *Layia platyglossa* (fig. 10.5), whose name refers to the fact that each yellow petal is tipped with white.

Tarweeds and thistles bloom long after the grassland becomes dry. By blooming during summer, they capitalize on a lack of competition for pollinators. Common Tarweed, *Madia elegans*, stands about 2 feet (60 cm) high. It has yellow blossoms about 2 inches (5 cm) across, and each petal has three small lobes at the tip. These plants have glandular hairs that produce a tarlike substance. This resinous material helps to retard water loss during the long, hot summer. Also to help retard water loss, flower heads close up about midday. They open after dark and remain open during the next morning.

Thistles (*Cirsium* spp.) are prickly plants that usually have purple flowers. These are sunflowers without the usual circle of ray flowers around the edge. The disc flowers in the center provide the color. In some overgrazed areas, the only thing remaining is Artichoke Thistle or Cardoon, *Cynara cardunculus* (fig. 10.6). This plant was introduced in the 1920s from Europe, where it was used for food. It first appeared near Benecia in the inner Coast Ranges and has spread into overgrazed areas of the western Great Central Valley. It is also widespread in similar areas in southern California. If harvested in the bud stage, this plant provides an edible artichoke. When it goes into bloom, its purple flowers put on a spectacular display. Cattle

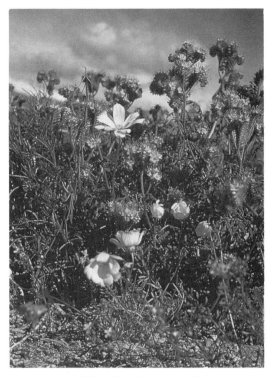

FIGURE 10.5 Tidy Tips, *Layia platyglossa*, and Fremontia Phacelia, *Phacelia fremontii*.

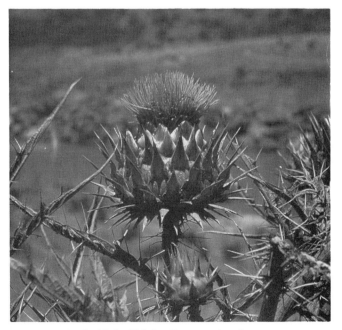

FIGURE 10.6 Artichoke Thistle, *Cynara cardunculus*.

and sheep avoid it, so once it becomes established, it spreads rapidly to infest entire pastures. Its beauty is the only redeeming feature of overgrazing.

The Carrizo Plain lies in a broad, flat valley west of Taft. The Temblor Range, a low range of hills uplifted along the San Andreas fault, lies between the Carrizo Plain and the Great Central Valley. Some people therefore would contend that the Carrizo Plain is merely one of the valleys of the southern Coast Ranges. It is truly a Valley Grassland ecosystem, however. It is home for some of the Great Central Valley's endangered species, such as the San Joaquin Valley Kit Fox, *Vulpes macrotis mutica*, and the Blunt-nosed Leopard Lizard, *Gambelia sila*. Moreover, although it has suffered the same sorts of disturbances as the Great Central Valley, it also has areas that contain native Valley Grassland in a relatively undisturbed condition. The California Nature Conservancy has purchased 82,000 acres (32,800 ha) of this valley with the ambitious intention of restoring it to the largest single tract of Valley Grassland in the state. If the project meets with success, large grazing animals such as the Pronghorn, *Antilocapra americana*, and Tule Elk, *Cervus elaphus nannodes*, will be reintroduced.

Corral Hollow is another valley of the inner Coast Ranges that contains vestiges of native plants and animals characteristic of the Great Central Valley. Situated about 8 miles (13 km) southwest of Tracy, in the southwestern portion of San Joaquin County and the eastern edge of Alameda County, the area has been used primarily for grazing sheep and cattle. Some of it has been converted to the Carnegie State Vehicular Recreation Area, a motorcycle playground. A portion of Corral Hollow was purchased by the federal government as part of a nuclear testing facility known as the Lawrence Livermore Laboratory. In 1974 part of the test facility was determined to be surplus property. Particularly because of its interesting population of amphibians and reptiles, The California Department of Fish and Game expressed interest in obtaining the parcel. The title was transferred to the department in 1976, and it is now operated as an ecological reserve.

The Corral Hollow Ecological Reserve is a 99-acre (24-ha) site composed of approximately 30% Riparian Woodland and 70% grassland. It is the home of a wide variety of amphibians and reptiles. The California Red-legged Frog (*Rana aurora draytoni*), the Foothill Yellow-legged Frog (*Rana boylei*) (fig. 11.26A), and the Western Pond Turtle (*Clemmys marmorata*) (fig. 7.26) have a refuge here in the riparian habitat. Seven species of reptile reach their northernmost distribution in this area. These species are the Side-blotched Lizard (*Uta stansburiana*) (fig. 8.33), Gilbert's Skink (*Eumeces gilberti*) (pl. 15A), the San Joaquin Whipsnake (*Masticophis flagellum ruddocki*), the Glossy Snake (*Arizona elegans*), the Long-nosed Snake (*Rhinocheilus lecontei*), the Western Black-headed Snake (*Tantilla planiceps*), and the Night Snake (*Hypsiglena torquata*) (fig. 9.63).

Furthermore, Corral Hollow is one of the places featuring serpentine soils and its unique vegetation. It is also a locale for some plant species, such as the Desert Olive (*Forestiera neomexicana*) and Iodine Bush (*Allenrolfea occidentalis*), that usually are associated with desert habitats. Honey Mesquite, *Prosopis glandulosa* (figs. 9.4C, 9.22), also has been recorded there, but much of it has been uprooted by ranchers. There may still be some of these plants located on private property.

Of particular interest in Corral Hollow is the presence of a species in the borage family (Boraginaceae) that is on the state and federal engangered lists: the Large Flowered Fiddleneck, *Amsinckia grandiflora*. Its entire known distribution consists of about 50 plants located on a half-acre (625-m^2) site within the confines of the Lawrence Livermore Laboratory. This is a robust ephemeral species associated with fine-grained soils. It stands about 2 feet (60 cm) tall and bears bright, showy, orange-red flowers about 3/4 inch (14–18 mm) in length. The name *fiddleneck* refers to a scroll-like arrangement of flowers that resembles the carving at the end of a violin neck. It is a characteristic of the borage family and the heliotrope or waterleaf family (Hydrophyllaceae), as exemplified by phacelias (fig. 10.5).

Vernal Pools

Vernal pools or "hogwallows" occur where the hardpan is close to the surface. There are three kinds of pools in the Great Central Valley: valley pools, pools of volcanic areas, and terrace pools. Valley pools, most common in low places of the San Joaquin Valley, occur in basins or valleys in saline or alkaline soils. Vegetation of these areas includes typical salt-tolerant plants such as Salt Grass, *Distichlis spicata*.

One of the most interesting plants that is widespread in vernal pools is a spore-bearing plant known as Quillwort or Merlin's Grass, *Isoetes howellii*. Inclusion of this aquatic plant in the family Isoetaceae aligns it with so-called "primitive" plants such as club mosses and horsetails. The name *Quillwort* refers to its rather yucca-like appearance, a mass of long quills. What makes it especially interesting is that it is an aquatic plant that uses crassulacean acid metabolism, a type of photosynthesis usually associated with drought-adapted succulent plants. Apparently, the mechanism is important in conserving CO_2. During a typical day, the dense vegetation of a vernal pool takes up all available dissolved CO_2. The Quillwort compensates for this depletion by storing CO_2 as a 4-carbon acid when it is available, continuing photosynthesis for the rest of the day by drawing upon its stored product.

Pools of volcanic areas are found throughout the state. They are typified by those on the Vina Plains, in Tehama County, and Mesa De Colorado, in Riverside County. Floristically, they are similar to the terrace pools.

Terrace pools occur on some of the oldest soils in the state: ancient flood terraces on higher ground. Water accumulates during the winter because it is unable to percolate into the ground. During spring, the rim of a pool becomes encircled by wildflowers. As the water evaporates, the ring of wildflowers moves inward. Toward the center of the area the soil becomes increasingly alkaline, favoring specialized species of plants. Endemism is high in these ecologic islands. All five species of Orcutt grasses (*Orcuttia* spp.) are restricted to vernal pools, and Crampton's Orcutt Grass, *Orcuttia cramptonii*, is known from only one pool in Solano County.

Associated with vernal pools on these terrace soils are peculiar mounds known as "mima mounds," up to 6 feet (2 m) in height. The terrain has a rolling, mounded appearance with vernal pools in the low spots. There are many theories about the origin of these mounds, including wind deflation of old stream channels and the piling of soil around old shrub fields. Soil scientists list several places in the world typified by mima topography, but there is no satisfactory explanation for the mounds because of the diversity of climates and geologic processes in the localities where they occur.

Vernal pool vegetation attains its highest development on terrace soils of the east side of the Great Central Valley. Many of these areas have been destroyed by activities of humans. The report *Sliding toward Extinction* indicated that 66%, or nearly 2.8 million acres (1,131,000 ha), of Central Valley vernal pools has been lost. The best pools today are on the higher terraces. Similar pools occur in other parts of the Great Central Valley, the Coast Ranges, and the mesas of the Peninsular Ranges. Vegetation of the vernal pools is discussed in more detail in chapter 8.

Freshwater Marsh

Many wetland habitats were part of the pristine conditions in the Great Central Valley. Enormous marshes occurred where runoff from the mountains accumulated. Tulare County gets its name from the tules that were abundant in the area. Tule fog gets its name from the fact that thick fog often hung over these marshes.

Wetland habitats characterized by a mixture of water and emergent vegetation are known variously as swamps, marshes, and bogs. These terms mean different things to different people. Swamps have the greatest proportion of open water and are characterized by various species of trees that tolerate flooding of their roots. True swamps do not occur in California, but spring flooding of riparian vegetation creates a similar habitat. Bogs are the wetlands characterized by the least amount of water. These are habitats composed of soggy or supersaturated substrates. They are said to be dystrophic, because the high acidity of the water prohibits water-soluble nitrates from forming. The vegetation therefore suffers from nutrient deficiencies. What water is present is often coffee brown in color due to accumulated decay products. In California, sphagnum bogs of moist northwest forests are a good example of this habitat. Vegetation of these bogs is discussed in chapter 7.

Freshwater marshes typically occur in flatlands where water accumulates in shallow depressions. True freshwater marshes are no longer common in California. Formerly, they were widely distributed in basins where input of stream water was roughly balanced by evaporation. Marsh habitat commonly bordered large, shallow lakes.

In California's virgin waterscape, there were three large lakes in the Great Central Valley. Tulare Lake, Buena Vista Lake, and Kern Lake, with their bordering marshes, sloughs, and connecting channels, formed the largest wetland habitat in the state (fig. 10.1). The water source for these lakes was runoff from the Sierra Nevada, particularly by means of the Kern, Tule, Kaweah, and Kings rivers. According to estimates, there were over 2100 miles (3360 km) of shoreline marsh habitat before draining and damming "dewatered" them.

Tulare Lake represented the largest freshwater lake west of the Mississippi River. It covered over 700 square miles (1800 km^2) and was fed by the four major rivers just mentioned. The lake was named for its extensive bed of tules. Early accounts indicated that tules formed a belt 100 yards (meters) wide around the edge of the lake and extended southward for 15 miles (24 km).

Other extensive freshwater marshes occurred in desert regions such as the Owens Valley, and along the Mojave and lower Colorado rivers. In southern California, marshland was extensive throughout the Los Angeles basin in association with the Los Angeles, San Gabriel, and Santa Ana rivers. The region of Los Angeles known as La Cienega was formerly a freshwater marsh. (*La Cienega* is Spanish for "the marsh.")

Regardless of the surrounding terrain, freshwater marshes throughout the state were remarkably similar. Where marshes still remain, studies of habitat and native plants give us an idea of what the extensive marsh systems were like. One such area is the Creighton Ranch Reserve, a 3200-acre (1280-ha) relict of Tulare Lake. Another is the San Joaquin Marsh Reserve in Orange County near the University of California, Irvine. This 202-acre (80-ha) region of wetlands is part of the University of California Natural Reserve System. In addition, various marshland reserves are operated by the Department of Fish and Game as waterfowl management areas. Gray Lodge is a beautiful marsh reserve north of Sutter Buttes. Its 8400 acres (3400 ha) form some of the most intensively used and developed wetlands in the Pacific Flyway. Ash Creek Wildlife Area covers more than 14,100 acres (5755 ha) on the Modoc Plateau in northeastern California. At its heart is Big Swamp, 8000 acres (3265 ha) of natural wetlands that are closed to entry so that wildlife will remain undisturbed.

Marsh vegetation is distributed in distinct bands. Ecological requirements for each of the plant types are precise enough that they occur in single-species clumps or zones that appear as bands on the edge of the water mass. Farthest out in the water are floating plants called macrophytes, a word that means "large plants." Floating macrophytes give way to rooted macrophytes in the shallow water, and some of these remain submerged. A distinct progression of rooted plants then occurs from the shallow water to drier land.

Freshwater marshes are dominated by reedlike plants that grow in water-saturated soil. Various species occur throughout differents parts of the state, but they essentially fall in four groups. Most common are rushes (*Juncus*) and bulrushes (*Scirpus*). Locally common are sedges (*Cyperus*) and cattails (*Typha*) (fig. 10.7). It is not always easy to tell these plants apart because they all have a similar, grasslike appearance. Cattails are the easiest to identify. They are the tallest, growing up to 10 feet (3 m) in height. They have long bladelike leaves and dense flower spikes that look like long brown sausages. They cannot tolerate deep water; therefore they occur at the outer fringes of the marsh. Sedges and rushes are shorter, about 3 feet tall (1 m). Leaves, if present, are usually located at the base of the plant. Above the leaves, a solid stem extends. Sedges have triangular stems, whereas most rushes have round stems. (Sedges have edges, and rushes are round!) Bulrushes are the forms commonly called tules, and they are related to sedges. As such, many of them have triangular stems, although the stems vary from round to triangular. They grow up to 6 feet (2 m) in height, and their flowers are borne atop leafless stems in umbels.

On higher ground in the marshes are various water-loving trees such as willows. Black Willow, *Salix gooddingii*, is the most common willow in marsh habitats of

FIGURE 10.7   Freshwater marsh dominated by cattails, *Typha* sp.

the San Joaquin Valley, although Red Willow, *Salix laevigata*, and Pacific Willow, *Salix lasiandra* (fig. 10.8) also occur on the edges of marshes. Some of these trees may branch close to the ground, resembling large shrubs. They have elongate, lance-shaped leaves. Pacific Willow has bright red branchlets. Yellow branchlets of Black Willows snap off easily and may float to a location where the water is shallow enough for them to root. Plumed seeds of willows are easily carried by the wind, which also aids dispersal.

On higher ground is a group of shrubs that superficially resemble willows and that typically occur where the water is more alkaline. One common form known as Mule fat, *Baccharis salicifolia* (fig. 10.9), is distributed throughout the Great Central Valley and southward along the coast. To the east it occurs in desert areas from the Owens Valley southward. These plants are willowlike in appearance, and sometimes they are called Seep-willows, but they are in the sunflower family (Asteraceae). Flowers are small and white. The plants do not possess brightly colored ray flowers, only disc flowers. As in willows, their plumed seeds are wind-disseminated.

In the Great Central Valley, a plant known as Buttonbush or Button-willow, *Cephalanthus occidentalis*, is a large shrub associated with these marshes. Its lance-shaped leaves have smooth margins and are opposite or whorled on the stem. The flowers occur in a spherical head up to an inch (25 mm) in diameter. This is another example of a plant left over from a more tropical period. It belongs to the madder family (Rubiaceae), which is widespread in the tropics today. The family includes many plants of economic importance, such as coffee and cinchona, the plant from which quinine is derived. It also includes ornamental plants such as gardenias.

FIGURE 10.8 Pacific Willow, *Salix lasiandra*.

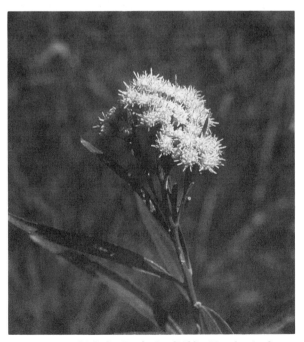

FIGURE 10.9 Mule fat, *Baccharis salicifolia*. Note by the flowers that this species is in the sunflower family (Asteraceae), even though the leaves resemble those of a willow.

The only California species in the lizard-tail family (Saururaceae) is found where water may be somewhat alkaline. This is Yerba Mansa, *Anemopsis californica* (fig. 10.10). This plant has straplike leaves and often grows about a foot (30 cm) high in pure stands on soggy ground. It is spectacular in blossom, producing a vertical cluster of white flowers. All of the plants seem to bloom at the same time, producing spectacular fields of white flowers. These plants occur in localized masses throughout the state from inland valleys to coastal estuaries, wherever appropriate brackish habitat occurs. In Spanish, *Yerba Mansa* means "gentle or mild herb," and the plant has been used for diseases of skin and blood.

In areas of open water, there are low-growing aquatic plants that emerge only a few inches above the water. Important among these is Watercress, *Rorippa nasturtium-aquaticum* (= *Rorippa officinale*), an edible member of the mustard family (Brassicaceae). This tasty herb, with small circular leaves, grows where water is cool and flowing. In some areas it is cultured for salads. Watercress decomposes rapidly. In autumn when there is a major die-off, 80% of the nitrogen is returned to the ecosystem within three weeks. Pacific Marsh Purslane, *Ludwigia palustris*, is an herb similar in appearance and may grow with Watercress. The purslane differs by having its leaves arranged in opposite pairs along the stem.

Also in open water may be dense mats of floating plants such as Water-fern, *Azolla filiculoides*, or duckweeds (*Lemna* spp.). Water-fern is a small, mosslike fern with many branched stems covered with minute, overlapping, bilobed leaves. Water-fern contains a symbiotic cyanobacterium (blue-green alga), *Anabaena azollae*, a nitrogen fixer that helps enrich the whole marsh ecosystem. For this reason, in some areas Water-fern is harvested and dried for cattle feed. It also may be used as a fertilizer for fields of rice, a cultivated marsh plant.

Duckweeds occur as minute, floating, leaflike structures that totally cover the water, giving it the appearance of a closely mowed dichondra lawn. The suspended roots of duckweeds dangle in the water and are often covered with nitrogen-fixing bacteria. Like Water-fern, duckweeds help to enrich the system. Decomposition of these mat-forming plants may add considerably to the organic matter that accumulates on the bottom as detritus. If the water is warm, the bottom muds may become anaerobic, forming a thick, black, gelatinous ooze that may bubble hydrogen sulfide (H_2S) gas.

Large numbers of nonnative floating plants such as Water-hyacinth, *Eichhornia crassipes,* sometimes accumulate in these open water areas (fig. 10.11). In tropical areas these plants become so abundant that they interfere with navigation. In California they are locally abundant in the Great Central Valley, the Los Angeles Basin, and a few localities in San Diego County. They have long oval leaves about 4 inches (10 cm) long. The stems (petioles) of the leaves are inflated, which keeps them afloat. During spring and summer, many blue flowers are borne in a spikelike cluster. When these plants are blooming, it is a beautiful sight, for they cover large areas of water. At such a time it is difficult to perceive the species as a noxious introduced pest that crowds out native plants. These plants are renowned for their rapid growth and rapid rate of absorption of dissolved nutrients. Some authorities have suggested that

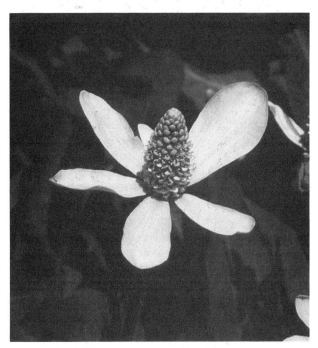

FIGURE 10.10   Yerba Mansa, *Anemopsis californica*.

FIGURE 10.11   Water-hyacinth, *Eichhornia crassipes*, an introduced floating plant that can become a pest.

Water-hyacinth represents a possible solution to the rapid accumulation of organic matter in sewer outfalls. After the plants absorb the nutrients, they could be dried and used as a source of organic biomass for bacterial decomposition and generation of natural gas (methane).

Another floating plant that may be introduced is the Yellow Pond-lily, *Nuphar polysepalum*. These plants occur naturally in ponds and slow-moving water in the northern two-thirds of the state, but because of their attractive large flowers and large floating leaves, they have been introduced into a great variety of quiet waters. Again, the problem is that they crowd out native vegetation and contribute greatly to the amount of organic matter that accumulates on the bottom of the marsh.

Marsh ecosystems are known to be among the most productive in the world. An abundance of photosynthesis results in a large biomass of vegetable material per year, most of which feeds back into the system as detritus. Activity of microorganisms recycles material back into water-soluble chemicals that reenter the water mass. Rooted aquatic plants absorb the nutrients from the sediment and directly from the water. The comparative roles of direct absorption and root absorption have not been thoroughly studied, but some evidence indicates that the roots may be more important for their anchoring quality than for absorption of nutrients.

Marsh Animals. High productivity means that a marsh ecosystem is capable of supporting a large biomass of consumers. Most animals, however, are unable to feed on the vegetative parts of marsh plants, so a large proportion of the edible biomass winds up as detritus that feeds back into the system through decomposition. The higher plants in the marsh, however, produce an abundant seed crop that is an important food for birds. In addition, shelter provided by the dense foliage is important for bird nests, as well as homes for small invertebrates. There is an abundance of aquatic invertebrates in marshes; these are discussed in detail in the following chapter.

The most conspicuous animals in marshes are the birds. Migratory species such as swans, geese, ducks, and shorebirds visit wetlands of the Great Central Valley in great numbers. However, they have suffered a decline because of the activities of humans; old reports indicate that water birds covered plains and waters in countless numbers from October to April. Many of the birds of Freshwater Marshes also occur in Salt Marshes. The discussion of marsh birds occurs in the section on estuaries in chapter 12.

Many mammals are attracted to water, particularly in hot, dry places such as the Great Central Valley. Most of these mammals, however, are not truly marsh species. One exception is the Muskrat, *Ondatra zibethicus* (fig. 10.12). Muskrats are ratlike rodents, about half the size of an average house cat. They have rich brown fur and a long, scaly, sideways-flattened tail, which they wiggle from side to side to help them swim. They eat tules, rushes, and cattails, and in some places they have been introduced to help keep the water clear of aquatic weeds. They make their homes of aquatic plants, often with the entrance underwater. These conical piles of vegetation may project 2 to 3 feet (1 m) above the water. They may live in holes with submerged entrances dug in the banks of ditches and ponds. This practice can cause considerable damage if the holes are dug in the levees of ponds or irrigation ditches.

FIGURE 10.12 Muskrat, *Ondatra zibethicus*. (From T. I. Storer and R. L. Usinger. *Sierra Nevada Natural History*. Berkeley: University of California Press, 1963.)

Muskrats are important fur-bearing animals. The fur is of average quality and has been marketed as "Hudson Seal." Muskrat hats have enjoyed some popularity. In California, the original range of the Muskrat was along the Colorado River and on the Modoc Plateau. It has been introduced in many parts of the state, primarily for its fur. Now it is abundant in the Great Central Valley. Muskrats are also edible, and in some southern states the meat is sold as "marsh hare."

The Beaver, *Castor canadensis* (fig. 11.9), occurs in streams and small lakes throughout the northern two-thirds of the state. They are not specifically marsh animals, but their occurrence in the Sacramento–San Joaquin Delta is of significance. In that area they typically live in burrows in the levees, and some of the levee breaks are due, at least in part, to the activity of Beavers. Their activities as dam builders are discussed in chapter 11.

Riparian Woodland

The most extensive Riparian Woodlands in the state formerly occurred in the Great Central Valley. Often known as gallery forests, they bordered the large rivers that cut across the valley—particularly the San Joaquin and Sacramento rivers and their tributaries. Riparian Woodlands reached their greatest development on the natural stream terraces or levees that rose from 3 to 20 feet (1–6 m) above the streambed. In some areas the woodlands were 10 miles (16 km) wide. Historical accounts suggest that in the middle 1800s there were about a million acres (400,000 ha) of Riparian Woodlands in the Great Central Valley. Today's estimate of 102,000 acres (41,600 ha) may be generous, and much of this Riparian Woodland has been seriously degraded. Only about 1%, or 10,000 acres (4000 ha), could be considered pristine.

Vegetation of the Riparian Woodlands consists of water-loving shrubs and trees. Because distribution of water may be patchy, these species are usually equipped with good mechanisms for dispersal, such as plumed seeds. Among the shrubs are Mule fat and several species of willows (*Salix*). Most spectacular in the pristine woodlands were the trees. These were mostly winter-deciduous species and included Western

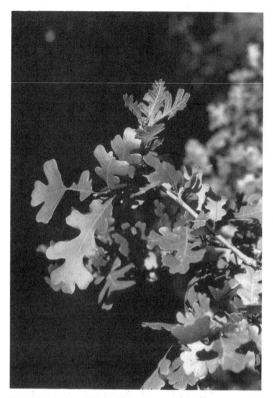

FIGURE 10.13   Valley Oak, *Quercus lobata*.

Sycamore, *Platanus racemosa* (pl. 7c); Box Elder, *Acer negundo*; Fremont Cottonwood, *Populus fremontii* (fig. 8.54); and the three species of willow mentioned in association with marshes. Perhaps the most impressive tree in the Riparian Woodland is Valley Oak, *Quercus lobata* (fig. 10.13). There are records of Valley Oaks 27 feet (9 m) in circumference. These trees, along with Western Sycamores, grow more commonly on the higher terraces. The largest remaining stand of Valley Oak is in the Nature Conservancy's Cosumnes River Preserve, between Stockton and Sacramento. This 1000-acre (405-ha) preserve includes not only Riparian Woodland but endangered marshland as well.

The fact that these trees drop their leaves in the winter is testimony that the environment along stream courses is similar to that of the eastern United States. There is abundant water, and winter temperatures are cold—a very "un-California-like" climate. These trees are relicts from a time when California's climate was very different. Winter temperatures along these streams are a product of cold-air drainage, short day length, and frequent fog. The average low temperature during winter ranges from 32° to 38°F (0°–4°C), and may dip as low as 15°F (−9°C).

Some of California's rarest, most endangered plant species are restricted to Riparian Woodlands of the Great Central Valley. One example is the California Hibiscus,

Hibiscus californicus. This is an ephemeral plant, which is a rare strategy for a riparian community. Flowers of this species are white with a crimson center. It is restricted to undisturbed slough banks from the Sacramento Delta north to Butte County.

Animals of Riparian Woodlands.   Riparian Woodlands are among the most productive habitats in the state, capable of supporting a large biomass of animals. Most of the animals are visitors from neighboring habitats seeking water, food, and shelter, but the total list of species is impressive. One researcher listed 39 species of mammals, 6 species of frogs, 7 species of lizards, 6 species of snakes, and a turtle for the Sacramento Valley Riparian Woodland. Sixty-nine species of breeding birds have been recorded for the Riparian Woodland of the Sacramento Valley. Of that number, 21 species have their primary affinity with Riparian Woodlands. The number of insect species must be enormous. Seventeen species of butterflies alone have been described as native to the Sacramento Valley Riparian Woodlands. Most of these species are described elsewhere in this book, but a few that are characteristic of lowland watercourses will be mentioned here.

Insects.   Of the enormous number of insects associated with Riparian Woodlands, two are worth mentioning because they are listed as threatened by the federal government. They are the Delta Green Ground Beetle, *Elaphrus viridis*, and the Valley Elderberry Longhorn Beetle, *Desmocerus californicus dimorphus*. The former is now known only from two regions of vernal pools in Solano County. These bright green $^1/_4$-inch (6-mm) ground dwellers (only one has ever been observed to fly) scurry along the edges of vernal pools in search of females or soft-bodied prey, including small gnats, beetle larvae, and springtails. The Valley Elderberry Longhorn Beetle is known only from the Riparian Woodlands of Sacramento, Yolo, and Merced Counties. It requires the Mexican Elderberry, *Sambucus mexicana* (= *S. caerulea*), as a host plant.

A number of butterflies are characteristic of these lowland Riparian Woodlands, and many of these are also conspicuous around cities. The largest and most common is the Western Tiger Swallowtail, *Papilio rutulus* (fig. 10.14A). The larvae are bright green with big "false eyes" behind the head that may serve to intimidate predators. Caterpillars feed on many riparian species, including willows, cottonwoods, alders, and sycamores.

Lorquin's Admiral, *Basilarchia lorquini* (fig. 10.14E), is an attractive, dark butterfly with broad white bands on its wings and orange wing tips. It resembles its relative, the California Sister, *Adelpha bredowii californica* (fig. 10.14D), which occurs along foothill and mountain streams in the vicinity of oaks. Larvae of Lorquin's Admiral feed on leaves and other riparian plants, and they overwinter in a case made from a leaf.

Another common butterfly is the Mourning Cloak, *Nymphalis antiopa* (fig. 10.14B). This butterfly is black to brownish purple with a cream-colored border to the wings. Adults hibernate under pieces of bark or other debris during winter. The black, hairy larvae feed on a variety of plants, including various species of imported elms (*Ulmus* spp.). Along streams, they feed on willows. The Satyr Anglewing, *Polygonia satyrus*, is one of the orange butterflies with brown spots. Similar to other anglewings, the edges of the wings appear torn and ragged. When the Satyr Anglewing is at rest on a tree trunk with its wings closed, it is nearly impossible to see because its color

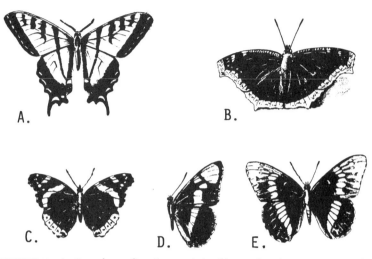

FIGURE 10.14   Some butterflies characteristic of lower-elevation Riparian Wood-lands. *A*. Western Tiger Swallowtail, *Papilio rutulus*. *B*. Mourning Cloak, *Nymphalis antiopa*. *C*. Red Admiral, *Vanessa atalanta*. *D*. California Sister, *Adelpha bredowii*. *E*. Lorquin's Admiral, *Basilarchia lorquini*. (From J. A. Powell and C. L. Hogue. *California Insects*. Berkeley: University of California Press, 1979.)

blends perfectly with the bark. The larvae of these butterflies feed on Creek Nettle, *Urtica holosericea*. The larvae also create a tent or shelter of the nettle leaves by partially cutting the midrib from beneath, allowing the leaf to droop downward. By using silk threads, a larva draws the margins of the leaves together from beneath. These tents superficially resemble those of the Red Admiral or Alderman, *Vanessa atalanta* (fig. 10.14C), whose larvae feed on the same plant. Larvae of the Red Admiral, however, draw the margins of the leaves upward so that the lower surface is exposed. The Red Admiral has red banding on its wings, and the tips of the wings are black with white spots.

Birds.   The Western Yellow-billed Cuckoo, *Coccyzus americanus*, has been described as a barometer for conditions in Riparian Woodlands. Its distribution is closely restricted to cottonwood-willow forest, and its decline has paralleled the decline of riparian vegetation in general. Some authorities relate the decline of the Yellow-billed Cuckoo to heavy use of DDT and other pesticides, which began in the late 1940s. This bird fed on insects and, in some areas, on caterpillars of the Nevada Buck Moth, *Hemileuca nevadensis* (fig. 4.30C). These caterpillars are black with yellowish stripes down the back and sides. They have yellowish or brownish branched spines that can produce a stinging rash. The black and white adults fly in the fall. These caterpillars were so abundant that they defoliated the Black Willows, *Salix gooddingii*, every year. In the late 1950s and 1960s Nevada Buck Moths became rare, and for some years the willows were not defoliated. The return of the Nevada Buck Moth in 1969 again caused defoliation, but the Yellow-billed Cuckoo apparently has not returned to most of its former range.

This bird is grayish brown above and white below. Its wing tips are reddish, and the underside of its tail is banded with black and white. In the early 1900s it nested in Riparian Woodlands of coastal streams from San Diego County north to Sonoma County and throughout the Great Central Valley. Its distribution in the Great Central Valley today is probably restricted to a few pairs along the Sacramento River between Colusa and Red Bluff. Nine to 10 pairs may occur in the Riparian Woodland along the South Fork of the Kern River above Lake Isabella, and there may be a few pairs nesting along the Colorado River. It is listed as threatened by the state government.

The Yellow-breasted Chat, *Icteria virens*, has also declined in numbers. The largest of California's wood warblers (Parulidae), the Yellow-breasted Chat is about 6 inches (15 cm) in length. It is olive green on the back and has a bright yellow breast. A black stripe bordered with white runs from the bill through its eye, and the eye is ringed with white. It resembles the smaller Common Yellowthroat, *Geothlypis trichas*, which has no eye ring and a smaller bill. The bill of the Yellow-breasted Chat seems rather large and its tail rather long for a warbler.

The Yellow-breasted Chat feeds on insects or, occasionally, fruits and seeds. This is a summer visitor to Riparian Woodlands, where it prefers tangles of willows and other thick streamside vegetation. Even when it was a more common visitor, it was an inconspicuous bird because it kept to the brush. It is probably best known for its variety of noises, which, like those of the Northern Mockingbird (*Mimus polyglottos*), are uttered at all times of the day and night. Also like the Northern Mockingbird, the Yellow-breasted Chat is a good mimic. To its benefit, this is one bird that is able to cope to some degree with the nest parasitism of the Brown-headed Cowbird, *Molothrus ater*. When the Brown-headed Cowbird lays an egg in the nest of the Yellow-breasted Chat, the mother chat has been observed to destroy the egg of the invader along with its own, but the chat is then free to lay more eggs.

Other birds that have declined in abundance along with Riparian Woodlands are tree-nesting ducks such as the Wood Duck, *Aix sponsa*; the Common Merganser, *Mergus merganser*; the Red-breasted Merganser, *Mergus serrator*; and the Hooded Merganser, *Lophodytes cucullatus*.

The male Wood Duck (pl. 13c) is probably the most beautiful bird in the state. In the words of W. L. Dawson, an early California ornithologist, the male Wood Duck is "of almost indescribable elegance." It is the only duck in the state that has a long, slicked-back crest on its head. Like "racing stripes," white lines from the bill and eye run backward along the crest. The eye is orange, and the bill is orange, white, and black. The head is iridescent, appearing green, purple, blue, or black, depending on the light.

Wood Ducks formerly ranged through the Riparian Woodlands of the northern part of the state. They are no longer common in the Great Central Valley, although they still range to some degree along streams into the foothills where appropriate habitat is present. On the verge of extinction in the early 1900s, they have recovered to their present rare state primarily through the efforts of captive breeders. They seem to prefer quiet, undisturbed woodlands.

Wood Ducks are agile fliers, dodging effortlessly through the trees. They perch on branches with ease. They feed heavily on acorns in season; otherwise they forage in water for aquatic plants and insects. They nest in the hollows of trees, particularly oaks, willows, and sycamores. Often they nest in deserted woodpecker holes, such as those of the Pileated Woodpecker, *Dryocopus pileatus*. Preferred nest sites overlook the water so that the ducklings, when they hatch, are able to tumble from the nest to the water. If the nesting tree is away from the water, the young birds tumble to the carpet of leaves beneath the tree. If the distance is too great, the mother carries the ducklings to the ground and leads them to the nearest water. Another threat to this species has been the spread of European Starlings, *Sturnus vulgaris*, which invade the nest cavities and replace the native birds.

Mergansers are fish-eating ducks. They have narrow, serrated bills with a hook on the end and were formerly common along lakes and rivers with wooded shorelines. The Hooded Merganser (fig. 12.22) was never abundant, but the Common and Red-breasted mergansers have declined in abundance along with Riparian Woodlands. The Red-breasted Merganser is more likely to be observed year-round in brackish water or sloughs along the coast.

Disappearance of Native Vegetation

The demise of native vegetation in the Great Central Valley goes back to the period of Spanish missions in the 1700s. Originally, there were some 23 million acres (9 million ha) of California prairie. Its disappearance is not a consequence of grazing per se, because Valley Grassland evolved for millions of years in association with large mammalian grazers. Rather, the problem is *over*grazing. Whereas native large mammals migrated seasonally, and numbers were kept in check by natural ecological constraints, domestic mammals may occur year-round or in numbers that far exceed carrying capacity. The Spanish introduced small, long-horned cattle and small, long-legged sheep known as Churro. As the missions spread northward, the numbers of livestock increased phenomenally. At the height of the mission period, there were about 400,000 head of cattle and 300,000 sheep. In addition, there were large numbers of horses and mules, many of which had gone wild.

Old records document a drought between 1828 and 1830, when no rain fell in coastal California for 24 months. Such a drought would be a hardship for the perennial bunchgrasses and would favor establishment of introduced annual grasses capable of remaining dormant in seed form (fig. 10.15). This kind of drought would also promote overgrazing. There would be no water for plant regeneration, and introduced livestock would eat every available blade of grass before starving. It has been estimated that 40,000 horses and cattle perished during that drought.

The late 1840s saw the decline of Mexican influence in California and the Gold Rush. Vast numbers of livestock were introduced to feed the forty-niners. By 1862 there were about 3 million cattle and 9 million sheep. During that year, unbelievably heavy precipitation flooded the Great Central Valley, forming a lake about the size of Lake Michigan. The prairie was underwater, and livestock drowned. Another two-year drought, and overgrazing reduced the Great Central Valley to a dust bowl. By the

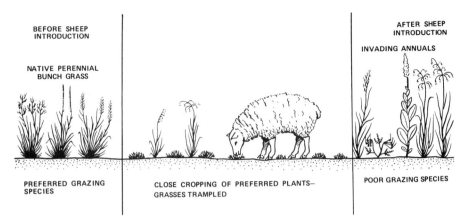

BEFORE SHEEP
INTRODUCTION

NATIVE PERENNIAL
BUNCH GRASS

AFTER SHEEP
INTRODUCTION

INVADING ANNUALS

PREFERRED GRAZING
SPECIES

CLOSE CROPPING OF PREFERRED PLANTS—
GRASSES TRAMPLED

POOR GRAZING SPECIES

FIGURE 10.15   History of alien grass invasion in native grassland. (From E. Bakker. *An Island Called California*. Berkeley: University of California Press, 1984.)

time normal precipitation returned to the valley, during the winter of 1864–1865, the numbers of livestock had declined markedly.

Cattlemen became discouraged by the vagaries of climate; not so the sheepherders. Whereas the number of cattle declined to a mere half-million by 1870, the sheep population was increasing markedly. Sheep required less water, and they could be herded easily, to take advantage of available forage. At this time it was common practice to herd sheep into meadows of the Sierra Nevada during summer. In fact, the great John Muir was originally such a shepherd. It has been estimated that by 1875 there were 5.5 million sheep. By that time, damage to rangeland was so complete that the Great Central Valley never recovered, and total livestock never again reached those numbers.

Where did the introduced grasses come from? They were of Mediterranean origin, introduced as seeds in the coats and digestive tracts of introduced livestock. They were also introduced as livestock food brought from the Mediterranean along with the animals. The history of the replacement of native grasses by introduced grasses is recorded in the adobe bricks that the Spanish and other early settlers used to build dwellings. Dry grass was used as a binding to help hold together the clay in the bricks. Botanists, by identifying species of grasses in bricks of known age, have been able to document the replacement of species.

Herbaceous species other than grasses were also introduced. Although the history of introductions is not always clear, many of these, such as sow thistles (*Sonchus* spp.), may have been introduced as food plants. These ephemerals have large, lyre-shaped leaves that were eaten raw or boiled. Other introduced food plants were various members of the geranium family (Geraniaceae), such as Red-stem Filaree or Storksbill, *Erodium cicutarium*. It appeared in California early enough that it became a favored food of the Indians, who ate it raw or boiled.

Other food plants were introduced by the missionaries. For example, some of the members of the mustard family (Brassicaceae) that are so common today owe their introductions to missionaries. The mustard genus *Brassica* includes a number of species with small, yellow, four-petaled flowers. These mustards cover many acres in the spring, and the leaves may be eaten raw or boiled. Actually, all members of the genus *Brassica* in California, including a number of important cultivated food plants, are introduced. For example, broccoli, cabbage, cauliflower, brussels sprouts, kale, and kohlrabi are all variants of the same species, *Brassica oleracea*. Turnips are cultivated varieties of the common Field Mustard, *Brassica rapa*.

Wild Radish, *Raphanus sativus*, is another introduced member of the mustard family. The flowers have four whitish petals with pink tips. Its greens are eaten in the same way as the others, or the young seeds may be eaten in salads. The root of the Wild Radish is too tough to be eaten like the domestic radish, although it has a similar flavor. The domestic radish is a cultivated variety of the same species.

Horehound, *Marrubium vulgare*, is an introduced member of the mint family (Lamiaceae) that has been used for medicinal purposes. It is boiled to produce a bitter fluid that is sweetened and formed into candy used to soothe sore throats and coughs.

The period of the late 1800s in the Great Central Valley was marked by a new form of land use. Large mechanized wheat farms extended from Fresno to Chico. For the most part, these wheat farms depended on natural precipitation, a technique known as dry farming. On the west side of the Great Central Valley, farmers continued to raise wheat by this method at least until the late 1920s. The beginnings of irrigated agriculture go back to the 1850s, but its widespread use came later. Around the turn of the century, wheat prices began to drop. Improved irrigation systems and refrigerated rail cars ushered in the era that continues today.

Most of California's multibillion dollar agricultural industry is concentrated in the Great Central Valley. Encouraged by cheap available land, inexpensive water, and government price supports, California farmers have prospered. In a single year, the income from California's agriculture is greater than the total value of all the gold mined since 1848. Of the total agricultural income in California, about 42% is generated by four farm products. As of the mid-1980s dairy products topped the list, with beef, grapes, rice, and cotton close behind. About half of the 42% is attributed to dairy and beef production. The cheapest way to feed grazing animals is to allow them to eat what grows naturally. Nevertheless, hay and alfalfa production, for feeding the animals, also ranks high in terms of state agricultural income.

Another aspect of California's agriculture is that a large part of it, approximately 30%, can be classified as "cash crops." These are crops that are not required by most people for everyday existence; they are part of the luxuries of life. They are things we do without when money becomes scarce, so demand for these crops fluctuates with the economy. Farmers who grow these crops depend on cheap water, inexpensive land, and various subsidies, or they cannot survive periods of low demand. When demand is high, they reap enormous profits. The 1980s were difficult times for these farmers.

Consequences of poor agricultural practices can be seen all over the valley. Overgrazing has compacted the soil, encouraging gully (arroyo) formation (fig. 10.16). Winds blow soil away from land that has been ground into dust by too many hooves. On lands that are irrigated for crop production, signs of overuse include soil erosion and salt buildup. A 1985 report from the American Farmland Trust stated that

FIGURE 10.16   Overgrazed pastureland near Panoche, San Benito County. Note the steep-sided arroyo indicative of soil compaction.

about one-third of California's 31 million acres (12.4 million ha) of crop and rangeland suffer from excessive soil erosion. Another report stated that by the year 2000, over one-third of the state's 35 million acres (12.5 million ha) of farmland will be destroyed by salt. Another 44,000 acres (17,600 ha) per year are gobbled up by urbanization.

The valley's difficulties are compounded by water problems. Most valley land including pastures is irrigated by groundwater pumping. The massive groundwater overdraft of 1.5 million acre-feet per year is causing water tables to drop, promoting draining of wetlands, drying of springs, and subsidence. Marshes and Riparian Woodlands have suffered from this dewatering. Subsidence of the land in some parts of the San Joaquin Valley is as much as 30 feet (10 m). Lowering of the water table means that wells must be dug deeper, which increases the energy cost to pump the water.

Riparian Woodlands also have suffered from dewatering due to dam building and channelization. Furthermore, trees have been removed for firewood and wood chips, and to increase available land for agriculture or pasture. Today the Sacramento–San Joaquin Delta is made up of diked "islands" covered with agriculture. These islands are frequently lower than the surrounding watercourses, which make up about a thousand miles (1600 km) of braided channels.

Mass transport of water through aqueducts adds to the problems. Irrigation of big tracts of land, using water subsidized by public funds, has encouraged large-scale agribusiness oriented toward immediate profit, rather than long-term land use. In 1981 two-thirds of the state-irrigated land in the southern San Joaquin Valley was managed by only eight companies, three of which were oil companies. This type of agriculture involves large-scale energy input for pumping and farm machinery. Heavy use of chemical fertilizers, herbicides, and pesticides brings high productivity for a short time. Human labor is minimized, and small family farms with owners who depend on long-term productivity are forced out of business.

Leach water containing a variety of chemicals pollutes groundwater. Banned pesticides such as DDT and dieldrin have accumulated at high levels in the sediments of the San Joaquin River and its tributaries. This problem is even more severe on the west side of the valley where marginal lands are used for agriculture. In this area a shallow hardpan causes accumulation of groundwater just beneath the surface. This accumulation concentrates chemicals and salts in the root zone of plants. To help solve the problem, the Bureau of Reclamation built a large drain to carry away water from some 180,000 acres (72,000 ha) of farmland where rising groundwater was a problem. The canal known as the San Luis Drain was originally proposed to carry water 188 miles (300 km) to San Francisco Bay. After the state spent $40 million and built only 82 miles (130 km) of canal, the project was halted. Money became scarce, and environmentalists objected to the prospect of the wastewater being discharged into San Francisco Bay. The canal ended at a marsh known as Kesterson Wildlife Refuge, and between 1978 and 1981, water quality in the refuge worsened. Birds that hatched there showed congenital defects. In 1983, 246 birds were found dead, and 106 were deformed. The culprit was determined to be high levels of selenium. The selenium was leached out of the soil in the agricultural area and had accumulated in the water of the refuge. In 1986 the drains were closed. It appeared that the farmland was doomed to accumulate salty groundwater. The government apparently chose to reopen the drains, renew the contract to deliver water to the district at a fraction of the true cost and transfer wastewater to the Tulare Lake Basin, but the problem of Kesterson was not resolved. The reservoir was dried up in 1986 and later covered with $6 million worth of fill dirt. The problem now is that pools of rainwater in the low areas draw up toxic selenium through the dirt. Furthermore, evaporation ponds in the Tulare Lake Basin have now become the cause of dead and deformed birds.

These problems are not restricted to the Great Central Valley. California's Imperial and Coachella valleys are part of an agricultural empire that includes adjacent Mexico and southwestern Arizona where about 90 percent of America's fall and winter produce is farmed. Problems with overuse of pesticides in the area led to highly publicized massive epidemics of immune pests. Runoff from these fields enters either the Salton Sea or the lower Colorado River. The selenium accumulation has caused health advisories to be posted regarding consumption of fish from the Salton Sea. In addition, there has been a documented crash in numbers of breeding birds such as egrets, herons, and cormorants. The number of documented nests dropped from over 1700 in 1987 to 19 in 1990. Similarly, the number of overwintering American White Pelicans, *Pelecanus erythrorhynchos,* dropped from 40,000 in 1987 to 650 in 1991. It is not certain what caused the decline, but increasing salinity, pesticide residues, heavy metals, selenium, and boron, all products of agricultural runoff, have been implicated.

When activities of humans cause lands to become desertlike, it is called desertification. Desertification in the Great Central Valley is continuing. All the symptoms are there: salty soil, erosion, gully formation, subsidence, and replacement of native vegetation by weeds. The causes are overgrazing, poor agricultural practices, groundwater overdraft, and poor water management in general. A comprehensive plan, involving environmentally sound principles, will have to be enacted soon, or agriculture in California will suffer the same fate as that of the Fertile Crescent in the Tigris and Euphrates valleys. In the sixth century B.C. that was the richest agricultural region in the world. Now it is a salty wasteland.

ANIMALS OF THE GREAT CENTRAL VALLEY

Animals of Freshwater Marsh and Riparian Woodland have already been discussed. The discussion here will be mostly on the animals of the native and altered grassland. Productivity in Valley Grassland is not high. This is a drought-adapted, and therefore food-poor, ecosystem. The animal biomass supportable by such a grassland is between that of the desert and that of the scrub communities. Consequently, insects such as ants and grasshoppers are the most common animals. Among vertebrates, reptiles are most common. Many species that occur in deserts and scrub communities also occur in grasslands: these have been discussed in the chapters on deserts and cismontane southern California.

Reptiles

Some of the reptiles in the valley are unique. Among these is the Blunt-nosed Leopard Lizard, *Gambelia sila* (fig. 10.17). A similar species, the Long-nosed Leopard Lizard

FIGURE 10.17   Blunt-nosed Leopard Lizard, *Gambelia sila*. (Drawing by Ellen Blonder from U.S.D.A. Forest Service, California Region. *List of Endangered, Threatened, Rare, or Unique Species to Be Considered in National Forest Planning and Management Activities*, 1976.)

544 THE GREAT CENTRAL VALLEY

(*G. wislizenii*) (fig. 9.58), occurs in southwestern deserts. The Blunt-nosed Leopard Lizard is an associate of Alkali Sink, dry wash, and bunchgrass habitats in the southern part of the Great Central Valley and adjacent foothills. It is now federally listed as endangered, another victim of habitat destruction. This is a large-headed, carnivorous lizard that feeds on insects, lizards, and small mammals. Its spotted pattern is well suited to its habit of waiting for prey in the shade of a bush.

Birds

Among birds of the Great Central Valley, those associated with wetlands were once most numerous. Ducks, geese, and shorebirds abounded. They will be discussed in chapter 12. These and other game birds, such as grouse and quail, were ruthlessly shot out. Introduced species, such as Chuckar, *Alectoris chukar*, and Ring-necked Pheasants, *Phasianus colchicus*, compounded the problem by creating competition for the little remaining habitat. Grouse and quail retreated to the mountains.

The story of the California Condor is outlined in chapter 7. Its relative the Turkey Vulture, *Cathartes aura* (fig. 10.18), is still a familiar sight in the Great Central Valley. This carrion eater is not as large as the California Condor, but it has a wingspread of 6 feet (2 m). No bird other than the Golden Eagle, *Aquila chrysaetos* (fig. 10.19), reaches this size in the Great Central Valley today. The Turkey Vulture can be easily distinguished from other soaring birds because it holds its wings in a V shape, noticeably above the horizontal. Most other birds soar with their wings flat.

The Turkey Vulture, like the California Condor, has a red, naked head. It is believed that the value of this featherless skin is to dissipate heat; a black bird is apt to absorb heat by radiation. Another possible role of a featherless head is related to the carrion-feeding habit. The back of the head is one of the places where a vulture has trouble cleaning its feathers. Perhaps by not having feathers on its head, it avoids accumulating bacteria and decayed meat from the carcasses upon which it feeds.

Adaptations for feeding on carrion are apparent in Turkey Vultures. Similar to hawks or owls, they have a hooked beak, which they use to tear meat from a carcass. Unlike hawks or owls, their feet are weak, not equipped for grasping prey. Their feet are more like those of a chicken. One interesting adaptation is that a Turkey Vulture has a sense of smell, whereas most birds do not. The Turkey Vulture is particularly sensitive to the odor of rotting flesh. What it detects are chemical compounds known as mercaptans. These are sulfur compounds with pungent odors. This ability of Turkey Vultures was discovered when it was noted that soaring Turkey Vultures could be used to locate leaks in gas lines. Natural gas in nature is odorless, but the gas company adds a mercaptan to natural gas so that leaks in homes will not go undetected.

Predatory birds (raptors) include the same species that were discussed in chapter 8. Red-tailed Hawks and Red-shouldered Hawks (fig. 8.43) are common. Particularly notable among the raptors are those that have adapted to and benefited by activities of humans. Of particular interest is the Black-shouldered (White-tailed) Kite, *Elanus leucurus* (fig. 10.20). Kites get their name from their habit of hovering with flapping wings, giving the impression of a kite on a string. This is an adaptation for hunting

FIGURE 10.18   Turkey Vulture, *Cathartes aura*.

FIGURE 10.19   Golden Eagle, *Aquila chrysaetos*.

FIGURE 10.20   Black-shouldered Kite, *Elanus leucurus*. (Photo by Charles Z. Leavell.)

in an open habitat. They search the ground for rodents and insects, swooping down from the hovering position. These beautiful birds had largely disappeared, but they have made a remarkable comeback. An estimated 50 pairs remained in the state in the early 1950s. Now they are a common sight, hunting for prey on the edges of fields and freeways. Because they have pointed white wings with black tips, they look like a seagull hovering next to the road.

Another conspicuous raptor that has benefited from human activities is the American Kestrel (Sparrow Hawk), *Falco sparverius* (fig. 10.21). This is a bird of agricultural lands and parks. California's smallest falcon, it also hunts while hovering, although an alternative habit is to hunt from a perch. These birds are quite commonly seen perched on telephone wires and fenceposts. These elevated positions give them a good view of the edges of fields and roadways, where mice and insects abound. Sometimes they will also take small birds. The American Kestrel can be told from other raptors by its small size and pointed wings. When it first lands on a perch, it pumps its tail up and down as if trying to catch its balance. These are pretty birds, with blue-gray wings and a reddish tail. Their face has two black bars on a white background, which is particularly conspicuous on males.

Few predators are more conspicuous in these disturbed areas than Black-shouldered Kites and American Kestrels. It is interesting to note, however, that Burrowing Owls, *Athene cunicularia* (fig. 4.26), also may be found along roads, particularly where they have been able to move into abandoned ground squirrel burrows. Common Barn Owls,

FIGURE 10.21   American Kestrel, *Falco sparverius*.

Tyto alba, are another example of this phenomenon. They are nocturnal, hunting more by sound than by vision. Their daytime roosts are usually in dark places in city and farm buildings. These pale-colored owls are seldom seen, but they are reasonably common. On occasion, they are found dead on the road after being hit by a car or truck at night while swooping along a roadway.

Throughout the book, many communities have been said to contain a member of the crow and jay family (Corvidae) that is noisy and conspicuous. In agricultural areas and urban woodlands, it is the American Crow, *Corvus brachyrhynchos* (fig. 10.22), that fills this role. These birds are smaller than a Common Raven but nevertheless are up to 18 inches (45 cm) in total length. In flight, it can be told from a Common Raven by its smaller size and squared, fan-shaped tail; a Common Raven has a more pointed or wedge-shaped tail. Common Ravens also usually are solitary, whereas American Crows usually occur in flocks. These are noisy, raucous birds that are famous for raiding farmers' crops. Their "cah, cah" is a familiar sound to many people. The American Crow's habit of carrying walnuts high into the sky and cracking them by dropping them on pavement has given them the reputation of being clever. Some biologists argue whether this behavior constitutes tool use. One researcher at the University of California at Davis suggested that American Crows purposely drop walnuts on the

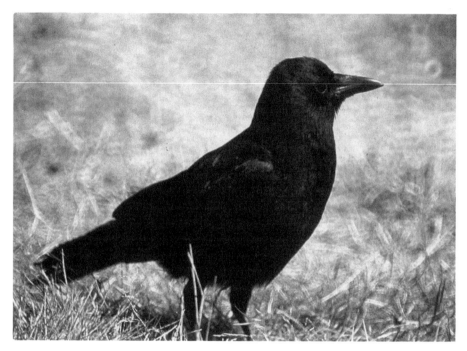

FIGURE 10.22   American Crow, *Corvus brachyrhynchos*.

road in front of cars and, in so doing, have invented the world's first gasoline-powered nutcracker.

Most farmers consider American Crows to be pests. They have been shot and poisoned, but still they abound. Like the Coyote, they have thrived in spite of humans, adapting well to urban and rural woodlands. According to the Federal Breeding Bird Survey, California's population of American Crows is growing at the healthy rate of 4% per year. At that rate, the population will double every 17 years.

Another member of this family that is conspicuous in grasslands is the Yellow-billed Magpie, *Pica nuttalli*. These are beautiful birds with very long tails. They are nearly as large as an American Crow. They have black and white markings, and the black of their wings and tail has iridescent green highlights. The bill is bright yellow. These birds are common in much of the Great Central Valley and in valleys in the Coast Ranges and foothills of the Sierra Nevada. They often feed in flocks, but not as conspicuously as American Crows. They frequently nest in groups, in groves of trees. At the northern end of the Great Central Valley, a similar bird, the Black-billed Magpie, *Pica pica* (pl. 13H) is an occasional winter visitor. This is a bird of northern prairies and the Great Basin. It occurs on the Modoc Plateau and south to the Owens Valley along the eastern side of the Sierra Nevada. Sometimes it wanders into the Great Central Valley in the winter. Except for its black bill, it is nearly identical in appearance to the Yellow-billed Magpie.

Mammals

In a wide-open habitat such as a grassland, there are basically two strategies for native herbivorous mammals. Either they are burrowers or they are large grazing species that take refuge in herds. Of the burrowers, the Great Central Valley includes its assemblage of rabbits, hares, ground squirrels, gophers, mice, and kangaroo rats. Characteristics and strategies of these mammals have been discussed in other parts of the book. The Great Central Valley also includes endemic species. However, because of the vast amount of habitat destruction, some of them, such as two of the kangaroo rats, have become endangered species. Others, such as the California Ground Squirrel, are probably more common because of their ability to colonize disturbed sites, such as abandoned fields and road cuts, and because of the increased abundance of seeds associated with introduced Mediterraneran weeds.

Of greater interest has been the fate of California's large herds of grazing animals. This story is not unique to California; the fate of animals in the Great Plains has been similar. Early accounts of Bison herds in the midwest are well known. Similar accounts for the Great Central Valley paint a picture of large herds of Mule Deer, Pronghorn, and Tule Elk darkening the landscape.

The accounts of deer are of interest. These animals have now vanished from the valley, and there is no way to know exactly which subspecies was involved. Presumably, it is the Mule Deer, *Odocoileus hemionus hemionus* (fig 4.43), which now migrates back and forth between foothill and forest. The influence of humans on early deer herds is discussed in chapter 4.

The Pronghorn, *Antilocapra americana*, formerly was considered to be the only living member of the family Antilocapridae. The Pronghorn is not a true antelope, such as those that live in Africa, but it is now classified in the family that includes African antelopes (Bovidae) as well as domestic cattle, sheep, and goats. Similar to African antelopes, Pronghorns are able to run very rapidly. They are among the fastest animals in the world. Speeds of 65 miles per hour (104 kph) have been recorded, but their ability to maintain high speed for a sustained time is phenomenal. They have been observed to travel 35 miles per hour (53 kph) for 4 miles, and 55 miles per hour (88 kph) for 1/2 mile.

Speed is an important adaptation for animals that live in wide-open habitats. All fast animals of the world live in such habitats. Their speed, plus their habit of remaining in herds, provides the protection they need to escape from predators.

Pronghorns stand about 3 feet (1 m) high at the shoulder. They are tawny with white patches on the face, chest, and rump. The bright color of the rump enables the herd to keep together when running. Both males and females have horns, which are shed in midwinter, leaving a bony core. New skin soon covers the bone, and new horns are replaced from the tip downward. The animal gets its name from a single branch, or prong, that grows forward on each horn.

The former range of the Pronghorn included all open terrain in California, including parts of the deserts. The western portion of the Mojave is still called Antelope Valley, in reference to former habitation by the Pronghorn. Pronghorns were rare in the Great Central Valley by 1875. People did not want herds of Pronghorns in their wheat fields. The only place in the state where they still occur naturally is in sagebrush country on the Modoc Plateau. Because much of the Modoc Plateau is under cultivation, they are not common there. Efforts have been made to reintroduce them to the Modoc Plateau and to a Nature Conservancy preserve on the Carrizo Plain in San Luis Obispo County.

The Tule Elk or Tule Wapiti, *Cervus elaphus nannodes* (fig. 10.23), disappeared with the Pronghorn. The biology of this species, endemic to the Central Valley, is similar to that of the Roosevelt Elk (Wapiti) of the northern coastal forests, but the Tule Elk is much smaller. Some authorities claim that the dwarf size is merely a function of poor food. Other authorities claim that the two will not hybridize, and therefore they are separate species.

Unlike the case with the Pronghorn, as humans destroyed the prairie, Tule Elk retreated to the vast Freshwater Marshes that covered hundreds of thousands of acres. In the tules, higher than a man's head, they made a labyrinth of trails. Then the wetlands began to be drained and the land cleared. The Tule Elk retreated even farther. By 1885 there was only one band of animals left, near Lake Buena Vista in the southern corner of the San Joaquin Valley. In 1904 it was estimated that only 145 animals remained, although at its smallest, the population may have numbered fewer than 10. A rancher in the area, Henry Miller, took pity on the small elk and established a refuge on his ranch. A number of transfers were attempted, but the only band that prospered was in Yosemite National Park. In 1933, the 26 Tule Elk remaining in Yosemite were transferred to the Owens Valley. The next year, 28 from the refuge were added to the herd. There they prospered, returning from the brink of extinction. This is one of the success stories for principles of wildlife management, although the prospect of a genetic bottleneck arising from too few progenitors is presently under study.

The number of Tule Elk in the Owens Valley had risen to 300 by 1960, at which time the California Department of Fish and Game decided that the range was overstocked. Part of the problem was that the animals had a propensity for knocking down fences and raiding fields of alfalfa. The Department of Fish and Game recommended a hunt, to kill 150 (half) of them. Screams of protest from animal lovers succeeded in aborting the hunt, but an overstocked range did not help the Tule Elk. In 1971 a state law was passed that forbade hunting of Tule Elk until their number reached 2000. To alleviate the problem of an overstocked range, animals were tranquilized and transported to other parts of the state and placed in other refuges. As of 1985 there were about 1800 Tule Elk located in refuges around the state. There are estimated to be about 600 in the Owens Valley. When the total population reaches 2000, the California Department of Fish and Game probably will propose a hunt in order to thin their numbers. Disadvantages of overpopulation include disease and starvation, and game management principles dictate that cropping of a herd that is too large is just as important as saving a herd that is too small.

What predators kept these herds from overpopulating before humans began to hunt them? Early accounts indicated that Mountain Lions, Grizzly Bears, and Gray Wolves,

FIGURE 10.23   Tule Elk, *Cervus elaphus nannodes*. (Photo by Michael G. Webb.)

Canis lupus, were also inhabitants of the Great Central Valley. Grizzly Bears probably were not too successful in capturing Tule Elk or Pronghorn. Moutain Lions certainly were important, but they probably were more common in the Riparian Woodlands and preyed on deer.

It is likely that Gray Wolves were an important component of the ecosystem. Wolves hunt in packs. Usually, they take lame or stray animals, and they commonly feed on squirrels and mice. Nevertheless, a pack of Gray Wolves could follow a herd of Tule Elk or Pronghorn and crop those that tire first. One of the interesting accounts of the early animal life of the Great Central Valley is that of the legendary James C. "Grizzly" Adams. He and other early settlers have left us with numerous accounts of the Gray Wolves in the Great Central Valley. Authentic Gray Wolves were trapped in the Providence Mountains in 1922 and in Lassen County in 1924. After that they were presumed to be extinct. In 1962, however, a wolf was killed near Woodlake on the edge of Sequoia National Park. Identification of this animal was verified by qualified mammalogists, but it is now believed that the animal was an escaped pet of Asiatic origin. The skin and skull are in the Museum of Vertebrate Zoology at the University of California in Berkeley.

Coyotes and foxes also occur in the Great Central Valley, and with the demise of the Gray Wolves their numbers, particularly Coyotes, likely have increased. Notable among these canids is the San Joaquin Valley Kit Fox, *Vulpes macrotis mutica* (fig. 10.24). Similar to the Desert Kit Fox, these small foxes live mostly on small rodents.

FIGURE 10.24   *A*. San Joaquin Valley Kit Fox, *Vulpes macrotis mutica*. *B*. Range of the San Joaquin Valley Kit Fox. (Drawing by Ellen Blonder from U.S.D.A. Forest Service, California Region. *List of Endangered, Threatened, Rare, or Unique Species to Be Considered in National-Forest Planning and Management Activities, 1976*)

In the Great Central Valley they are an important natural control on nonnative rodents such as Black Rats, *Rattus rattus*, that invade grain crops. Habitat destruction, trapping for fur, and deliberate poisoning have driven these beautiful animals to the brink of extinction. Of further concern is new evidence that Coyotes may be preying on them. If this proves to be the case, it will be a sticky problem for management policy. The San Joaquin Valley Kit Fox is now listed as endangered by the federal government.

Inland Waters

The study of the physical, chemical, and biological properties of inland waters is known as limnology. In general, inland waters include freshwater lakes and rivers, but some lakes are very saline, particularly in deserts. Because of its varied climate and topography, California has a great diversity of aquatic habitats distributed over 2674 square miles (6845 km^2) of inland waters.

Various classifications for inland waters have been established. Some are based on geologic processes; others are based on factors such as size, appearance, location, biota, or chemical constituents of the water. Various governmental agencies, such as the state Department of Fish and Game, have established classifications of aquatic systems based on mixtures of characteristics. One such classification lists 23 kinds of lakes or impoundments and 27 kinds of streams in California.

LAKES

Lakes owe their origin to geologic processes. A lake is a low spot in the terrain that captures and holds water. Lakes are often classified into different types based on the geologic nature of the basin. Limnologists have recognized at least 11 categories, each of which has been further subdivided. Nearly every type of lake that has been described can be found somewhere in California (fig. 11.1).

Glacial Lakes

The carving and scouring action of a glacier as it passes over bedrock leaves behind an irregular terrain. Low spots that become filled with water are glacial lakes called tarns. The Sierra Nevada abounds in such lakes (fig. 11.2). Basins formed in canyons, with a high, amphitheater-like back wall, are called cirques, and tarns in these basins are called cirque lakes (fig. 4.14). The southernmost cirque lake is Dollar Lake on Mount San Gorgonio. A series of these lakes, one above the other, is known as a paternoster, a word that refers to a rosary or string of beads. Paternosters of cirque lakes occur in nearly every canyon of the Sierra Nevada, particularly on the steep east side of the range. Perhaps the most spectacular of these is on the east side of the western divide near Sawtooth Pass. Southwest of Black Rock Pass, three lakes, carved into granite, lie below in a staircase (pl. 10A).

Most tarns are small mountain lakes that lie in depressions produced by glacial scouring. Large, glacially carved valleys commonly have tarns scattered about on their bottoms. One of the largest lakes in the Sierra Nevada, Thousand Island Lake, at the head of the San Joaquin River, is a huge but shallow tarn (pl. 10C). The view down on a Sierran basin from a pass usually includes several tarns (fig. 11.3).

Other lakes of glacial origin owe their existence to the moraine left behind when the glacier retreated. Where active glaciers still occur, a moraine lake filled with azure

FIGURE 11.1   Lakes and reservoirs of California. (From M. Hill. *California Landscape: Origin and Evolution.* Berkeley: University of California Press, 1984.)

water can be found at the lower end of the glacier. The lake at the toe of the Palisade Glacier is a good example. The color of the water is due to tiny particles of ground rock suspended in the water. The Big Pine Lakes below Palisade Glacier are examples of cirque lakes in a paternoster, filled with such water.

A moraine may occur at the outlet of a tarn, forming a dam that enables the lake to hold more water. Other moraines may form nearly the entire lake basin. These large moraine lakes are often found at the mouths of canyons on the east side of the Sierra. Convict Lake is one of the best examples of a moraine lake. Also, circular lakes known as kettles sometimes occupy a hollow in a large moraine field. Such lakes are common in Minnesota and Wisconsin, where huge continental glaciers formerly

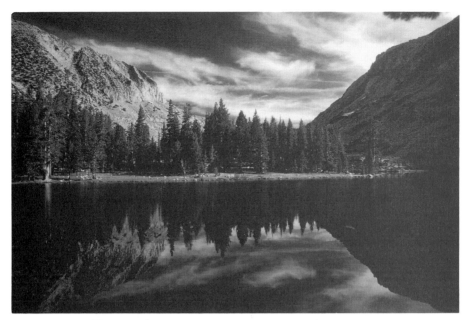

FIGURE 11.2   Sallie Keys Lake, Sierra National Forest. A typical Sierra Nevada tarn.

FIGURE 11.3   Tarns in glacially scoured depressions. View northeastward from Bishop Pass, Inyo National Forest.

occurred, but they are present in mountain regions as well. A kettle forms in a depression left behind by the melting of a small fragment of glacier. In the southern Sierra Nevada there are two well-known lake basins in which most of the lakes are kettles. These basins, in the Golden Trout Wilderness, are known as the Cottonwood and Rocky basins (pl. 10B). They lie at about 11,000 feet (3300 m), southwest of the town of Lone Pine. Tulainyo Lake, lying at 12,800 feet (3925 m) north of Mount Whitney, is also a kettle lake. This is the highest lake in the Sierra Nevada. To the east of it is a smaller, unnamed kettle lake at the base of Mount Russell.

Tectonic Lakes

Tectonic lakes lie in basins formed by warping, folding, fracturing, and faulting of the earth's crust. Fault-block mountains of the Basin-Range Province alternate with valleys that may contain impounded water. This is known as horst-graben topography, and a lake formed in such a basin is known as a graben lake. The name *graben* is German for "grave," implying that the lake lies in a low place. These grabens are formed by a combination of uplift and subsidence, usually along a dip-slip fault. One side of the fault rises, forming a mountain range, and the other side sinks. The consequence of this geologic activity is a valley that may contain a lake.

All of the large lakes that formerly lay in valleys of the Basin-Range Province were graben lakes. These particular graben lakes were also examples of pluvial lakes, because they existed primarily during the periods of heavy rainfall that occurred during the Pleistocene. The lake in Saline Valley today is such a graben lake, but it is quite small compared to the one that occurred there during the Pleistocene. On the Modoc Plateau today, Goose Lake is an example of a large graben lake.

One of the most spectacular graben lakes in the world is Lake Tahoe (fig. 11.4), which lies in a valley between the Sierra Nevada and the Carson Range. The valley floor lies on a block that sank between two fault systems, forming a steep-walled, flat-bottomed lake basin. Subsequent damming by a lava flow at one end deepened the lake considerably. At a depth of 1643 feet (501 m), Lake Tahoe is the largest, deepest lake in California, and, next to Crater Lake in Oregon, the second deepest in North America. The largest mountain lake in North America, Lake Tahoe covers 122,000 acres (49,780 ha) and has a 72-mile (115-km) shoreline.

When an earthquake occurs, movement of the land may create—literally overnight—a new lake basin. These earthquake lakes often lie directly over a fault. The source of water could be springs that upwell along the fault zone. These lakes are often called sag-ponds, because the depression was formed by subsidence. In Inyo County, on Highway 395 south of the town of Lone Pine, there is a sag-pond known as Diaz Lake. This lake appeared following the famous 1872 earthquake on the Lone Pine fault.

Another sag-pond, known as Lost Lake, lies on the San Andreas fault at the mouth of Lone Pine Canyon near the eastern end of the San Gabriel Mountains. Jackson Lake is another sag-pond on the same fault, about 17 miles (11 km) to the west. It is in a popular resort area on Highway 138 in the San Gabriel Mountains. Perhaps the

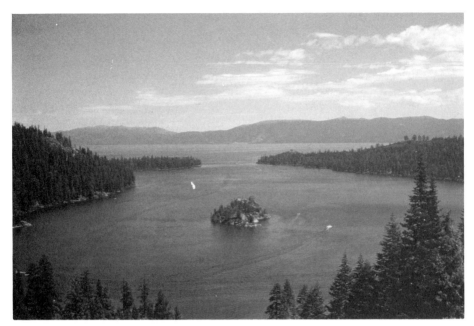

FIGURE 11.4 Emerald Bay, Lake Tahoe. Lake Tahoe is a large graben lake.

FIGURE 11.5 Lake Elsinore, Riverside County. This lake is a sag-pond on the Whittier-Elsinore fault that is kept filled with Colorado River water purchased from the Metropolitan Water District.

largest sag-pond in California is Lake Elsinore (fig. 11.5), occurring on the Whittier-Elsinore fault east of the Santa Ana Mountains. Today it is kept full with imported water from the Colorado River.

Sometimes crustal warping is enough to create a depression that will hold water. Thurston Lake on the Modoc Plateau is such a lake. Water in this lake is also impounded by a volcanic mud flow.

Landslide Lakes

Many lakes throughout the world owe their existence to impoundment of stream valleys by rock slides or mud flows. Sometimes the event triggering the rock slide is an earthquake. These lakes are often short-lived because the river, once it is impounded, overflows the dam, and subsequent erosion carries away material, restoring the area to a river. If the dam is substantial enough, a landslide lake may last for many years. On the Kern River at the southern end of the Sierra Nevada are two landslide lakes, known as Kern and Little Kern lakes. The event that precipitated the two landslides was probably an earthquake on the Kern fault, along which the river flows.

Perhaps the most famous landslide lake is Mirror Lake, in Yosemite National Park. This lake, beneath the north face of Half Dome, is an impoundment on Tenaya Creek and has been filling with sediment for many years. Formerly, the National Park Service maintained it as a lake by dredging out the sediment. Now, however, it is National Park Service policy not to tamper with nature. Mirror Lake soon will be a meadow, and photographs of Half Dome reflected in the lake will become antiques.

Volcanic Lakes

Volcanoes often occur along faults, so it is not surprising that a combination of volcanic and tectonic activity might cooperate to create a lake basin. A lava dam at the north end of Lake Tahoe is partly responsible for its great depth. The Truckee River flows over the dam at the outlet of the lake.

Clear Lake is a large lake that lies in a valley of the Coast Ranges north of San Francisco. This is the largest lake that lies entirely within state boundaries. Two arms of the lake lie in grabens, but water is impounded by a lava dam at its southern end. It is a relatively shallow lake for its size, only about 30 feet (9 m) deep. Clear Lake is famous in California for its fishing and tourism. It is also famous worldwide as one of the first localities where DDT worked its way up the food chain and reached sufficient concentration to kill aquatic birds. Much of the concept known as biological magnification was formulated from data gathered there.

In the Cascade and Modoc Plateau provinces, there are numerous lakes formed by volcanic processes. In Lassen National Park, Snag Lake was formed by a lava dam, Hat Lake was formed by a volcanic mud flow, and Manzanita Lake was formed by a landslide of volcanic rocks associated with the 1914–1920 eruptions.

Another kind of volcanic lake is a caldera, which results when the summit of a volcano collapses. This occurs when the reservoir of molten magma empties from beneath. The deepest lake in the United States, Crater Lake, Oregon, lies in a caldera.

FIGURE 11.6   Mono Lake, a closed-basin, hypersaline lake.

It is nearly 2000 feet (610 m) deep. Perhaps the best example of a caldera lake in California is Medicine Lake, on the Modoc Plateau, just south of Lava Beds National Monument. The original caldera was about 6 miles (10 km) long, 4 miles (6 km) wide, and 500 feet (150 m) deep. Later eruptions built a ring of eight small volcanoes, nearly obscuring the basin. Medicine Lake lies in the remainder of the basin. The Long Valley Caldera, which contains the city of Mammoth Lakes on its southwest edge, contained a large lake during pluvial times (Pleistocene). At the present time Lake Crowley, a reservoir on the Los Angeles Aqueduct system, lies in the bottom of the Long Valley Caldera.

A volcanic crater that has not collapsed may also hold water. Technically, this is not a caldera. Such a lake is found in Crater Butte, in Mount Lassen National Park.

Mono Lake (fig. 11.6), on the east side of the Sierra, is the remainder of pluvial Lake Russell, which during the Pleistocene was about 900 feet (300 m) deep. This is also known as a closed-basin lake, which means that it lies in a region of interior drainage. All the water from the surrounding mountains has been draining into it for years, and there is no outlet. Evaporation causes water to be lost, but the dissolved minerals accumulate. Mono Lake therefore is hypersaline. It is the oldest lake in California and has been accumulating salts for thousands of years. The tufa towers along its shoreline are the product of precipitation of limestone caused by fresh water bubbling up through the brine. The fact that the towers were formed underwater and now stand high and dry is testimony to a former lake level. Similar towers, now high and dry, can be found south of Trona near Searles Dry Lake (pl. 11D). Mono Lake today is about 14 miles (23 km) long and 10 miles (16 km) wide. In this century its greatest depth was 169 feet (51.5 m), and it has lowered considerably due to evaporation.

Since 1941, when diversions of water to the Los Angeles Aqueduct began, the water level has been dropping. Between 1941 and 1988, its level dropped 40 feet (13 m) because its primary source of fresh water was taken away.

Fluviatile Lakes

Fluviatile lakes lie in depressions caused by flowing water. When rivers flow over flat gradients, they meander back and forth across a flood plain. The meanders constantly change direction, and old meanders that have become separated from the present flow may still contain water. Because of their shape—rounded on one side—they are known as oxbow lakes. Such lakes are present in the Great Central Valley in association with large rivers. Three good examples are Peter Slough, near the San Joaquin River; Murphy Lake, near the Feather River; and Horseshoe Lake, near the Sacramento River.

Lakes can also be formed by flowing water when sediment produced by a tributary dams up the main river. These are known as fluviatile-dam lakes. The best example is Tulare Lake, which was formed when sediment deposited by the Kings River dammed a portion of the San Joaquin Valley. The Salton Sea basin was also formed in this way by damming from the Colorado River Delta. The huge Lake Cahuilla (fig. 9.9), which formerly occupied the basin, lay in a graben dammed by the Colorado River Delta.

Shoreline Lakes

Shoreline lakes are those impounded by barriers of sand. In California these occur within a mile or so of the ocean. The sand accumulates by the combined action of wind and water. If a sand-spit gets large enough, it can block the entrance to an estuary, allowing it to become a freshwater lake free of tidal flushing. Sometimes a large dune field forms a barrier that traps water. In the large Nipomo dune field near Guadalupe, south of Pismo Beach, there are several such bodies of fresh water. Oso Flaco Lake is a popular example (fig. 11.7).

Solution Basins

Some rocks are water-soluble. Pits and depressions may occur in granite where water-soluble minerals have become dissolved. In deserts, these depressions catch rainwater and provide an important water source for animals. These depressions are known as *tinajas*, which is a Spanish word for "tanks." Where limestone is the bedrock, water can create large cavities. In the Sierra Nevada, Boyden and Crystal caves are limestone caverns. Mitchell Caverns, in the Providence Mountains, is a limestone cavern in the Mojave Desert. If the roof of a cavern collapses, a subterranean lake may be exposed. Devils Hole, in Death Valley National Monument, is a small solution basin that was formed in this way.

Reservoirs

Reservoirs are man-made bodies of water formed by damming rivers. True reservoirs are primarily for storing water, which is released at a later time for irrigation, drink-

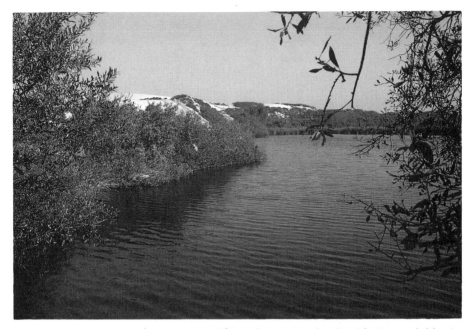

FIGURE 11.7   Oso Flaco Lake, in San Luis Obispo County, is a shoreline lake impounded by the Nipomo Dunes.

ing, or industrial use. Some reservoirs, however, are constructed primarily to generate hydroelectric power. This is one of the cheapest ways to generate electricity. For this purpose, electric companies own and operate several large lakes on the western side of the Sierra Nevada. These include Lake Thomas Edison, Huntington Lake, Florence Lake, Shaver Lake, and several others. After the water leaves Lake Thomas Edison on Mono Creek, it passes through eight different power plants before flowing out to Millerton Reservoir on the floor of the Great Central Valley. Waugh Lake, Gem Lake, and Agnew Lake are power reservoirs located on Rush Creek on the east side of the Sierra near Mono Lake.

Many reservoirs serve multiple purposes. They may be used simultaneously for drinking, irrigation, recreation, and to generate electricity. Sometimes, dams are built for flood control. These reservoirs, of necessity, must not be allowed to hold large amounts of water, or they would be worthless during a flood.

Nearly every river in California has been dammed. Many dams and impoundments in California are associated with major aqueducts (fig. 11.8). There are 18 reservoirs on the California Aqueduct alone. On the east side of the Sierra Nevada, reservoirs such as Grant Lake and Lake Crowley are part of the Los Angeles Aqueduct system. Another series, including the lakes Havasu, Parker, and Mathews, is part of the Colorado Aqueduct. In addition, many artificial impoundments in southern California were created merely to provide recreation or for their visual quality. Some of these are associated with exclusive residential communities.

FIGURE 11.8   A schematic map showing California's major aqueduct systems. (From M. W. Parratt and M. E. Parratt. *A Spaceship Called Earth: Our Living Environment*. Dubuque, Iowa: Kendall/Hunt, 1985. Reprinted with permission.)

Other animals create dams, too. Of greatest significance is the activity of the Beaver, *Castor canadensis* (fig. 11.9). Native distribution of this animal in California includes the rivers of the Great Central Valley and the Modoc Plateau. In large rivers they usually do not build dams, but in smaller rivers their activities can seriously alter natural stream flow. Where they have been introduced into the Sierra Nevada,

FIGURE 11.9   Beaver, *Castor canadensis*, California's native dam builder. (From E. W. Jameson, Jr. and H. J. Peeters. *California Mammals*. Berkeley: University of California Press, 1988.)

they fell aspens and willows, producing dams that may flood meadows or cause sedimentation that covers gravel used by spawning trout. In the late 1800s, Beaver pelts were very valuable, and the quest for Beavers was a major factor that helped to open up the west. Beavers were almost extirpated in California during that time. In recent times, natural reproduction and numerous introductions have enabled the Beaver to establish itself in many parts of the state, usually to the detriment of the native flora and fauna. California's southernmost groves of Quaking Aspen, *Populus tremuloides*, in the San Bernardino Mountains, may be in jeopardy because of the introduced Beavers.

Lake Succession

As lakes become older, they go through a process leading to their own demise. By their very nature, lake basins accumulate material and become filled with sediment. A lake ultimately becomes a meadow. Virtually all nutrients come from outside a lake, and as a lake becomes older, water becomes enriched with these minerals and nutrients. This process is known as eutrophication; the term *trophic* means "nourish."

The nutrient state of a lake can also be used as a basis for its classification (table 11.1). A eutrophic lake is one that is nutrient-rich. Usually, it is a fairly old lake. Young lakes are nutrient-poor and are called *oligotrophic* lakes, which means "few nutrients." As a lake ages, it goes through a series of stages, including oligotrophic, mesotrophic, eutrophic, and finally senescent.

Most mountain lakes are typical oligotrophic lakes. They contain clear, blue water and may have very little sediment on the bottom. While there is a great deal of variation in shape and size, typical oligotrophic lakes are deep, clear, cold, and nutrient-poor. The water contains low concentrations of dissolved minerals and a high concentration of dissolved oxygen. Fish such as trout, with small heads and small gill surfaces, would be content here.

TABLE 11.1   A Comparison of Oligotrophic and Eutrophic Lakes

Characteristic	Oligotrophic	Eutrophic
Age	Young	Old
Nutrient state	Poor	Rich
Clarity	Clear	Cloudy
Color	Blue	Green to brown
Depth	Deep	Shallow
Temperature	Cold	Warm
Dissolved oxygen	High, well distributed	Low, only near surface
Total dissolved solids	Low	High
Sediment	Sparse, coarse	Deep, muddy
Locality	Mountains	Valleys
Fish	Trout	Catfish

Eutrophic lakes usually occur in lowland areas. Having had long periods of time to accumulate materials, they contain water that is murky. They are green to brownish green in color. The sediment of such a lake is rich in organic material, forming a muddy ooze. The abundance of particles in the water helps to absorb and hold heat, so the water tends to be warm and oxygen-poor. Trout would not be happy here because they cannot tolerate concentrations of dissolved oxygen lower than 5 milligrams per liter. Eutrophic lakes contain large-headed fishes with abundant gill surface, including catfish, carp, bass, and panfish such as bluegill or crappie, none of which is native to California. The Sacramento Perch, which will be discussed later, is one of the few fishes of this type that is native.

In California, most eutrophic lakes become stratified during the summer (fig. 11.10). This means that there is a distinct layering of water of different temperature and density. The upper portion of the lake is warm, but the deeper parts are much cooler. If a person treads water in such a lake, it is not uncommon for his or her feet to be in cold water while the rest of the body is warm. The region where the water changes temperature over a relatively short range of depth is known as the thermocline. Above the thermocline, water is warm. Below the thermocline, it may be as much as $45°F$ ($25°C$) cooler. Often the temperature drops over $0.5°F$ per foot ($1°C/m$). This temperature change is analogous to the inversion layer that occurs in the air of a basin. In a lake, the cold water below the thermocline has greater density, and it is not disturbed easily. Above the thermocline, the water has less density and may be stirred by the wind. This stirring mixes oxygen with the water, but only above the thermocline.

A person would think that the deeper water, by virtue of its colder temperature, would hold more dissolved oxygen. What happens is that bacteria living in the rich sediment deplete the oxygen. Because the oxygen cannot be stirred downward below the thermocline, the deep water may actually become anaerobic. Fishes therefore are forced to occupy the warmer water near the surface.

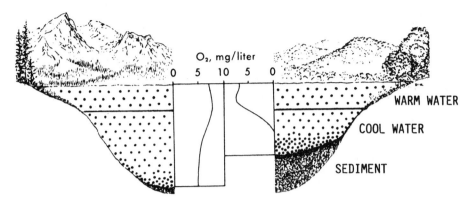

FIGURE 11.10 Diagrammatic comparison of an oligotrophic lake (left) and a eutrophic lake (right) during summer stratification. Horizontal lines indicate the regions of greatest temperature and density differences associated with a thermocline. Dots indicate distribution of an equal amount of plankton and particulate matter. Graphs indicate differences in dissolved oxygen. (After G. A. Cole. *Textbook of Limnology*, 3rd ed. Prospect Heights, Ill.: Waveland Press, 1983, reissued 1988. Reprinted with permission.)

In the warmer water, fishes are placed in double jeopardy. Warm water increases their metabolic rate, so they require more oxygen when less is available. Actually, the problem is more complex. Fishes must ventilate their gills by pumping water over the gill membranes. They do this with a bellows-like action of the bony operculum that covers the gills. Muscle activity to operate the operculum requires fully one-fourth of the fish's metabolism. In other words, because water is heavy, a fish uses one-fourth of its food and oxygen to pump water over its gills. When a fish lives in warm water, its metabolic rate is high, but there is less oxygen dissolved in the water; therefore the work required to ventilate its gills is disproportionately large, requiring an even greater amount of oxygen. This represents triple jeopardy.

Water Quality

Various characteristics of lake water may be measured as indicators of eutrophication. Aquatic biologists want to know the nutrient state of a lake so they may estimate what kinds of organisms live there and what sort of biomass and growth rates should be expected. Indicators of water quality are also used to determine whether or not the water is appropriate for introduction of certain fish species. In areas of habitation, these types of measurements are used to determine if the water is suitable for human consumption. Humans prefer to drink oligotrophic water.

A measure of the quantity of organic material in water is the biological oxygen demand. This is a measure of the oxygen consumed by microorganisms in a certain period of time. The organic material is food for microorganisms; therefore if lots of organic material is in the water, lots of oxygen is used. Such a test involves keeping a sample of the water in a sealed container in the dark. Dissolved oxygen in the water is measured before and after storage. This measure of water quality is usually expressed as the decrease in oxygen, in milligrams per liter (mg/l), over a five-day period.

Another indicator of eutrophication is the amount of photosynthesis that occurs in phytoplankton over some period of time. This is known as primary production. The measurement is accomplished by introducing a measured amount of radioactive CO_2 to a sample of water. The amount of radioactive carbon (carbon-14) absorbed by the plankton is measured with a Geiger counter, and it usually is expressed in milligrams of carbon per unit time in proportion to surface area (e.g., mg $C/m^2/day$). For comparison, in 1974, data for Clear Lake, a large eutrophic lake in the Coast Ranges, indicated that phytoplankton absorbed 433 mg $C/m^2/day$. In Lake Tahoe, a large oligotrophic lake, during the same season and year phytoplankton absorbed only 174 mg $C/m^2/day$. On a yearly basis, oligotrophic lakes fix from 0.7 to 25 g C/m^2, whereas eutrophic lakes fix from 75 to 250 g C/m^2. Heavily polluted or senescent lakes might fix from 350 to 700 g $C/m^2/year$.

Measuring biological oxygen demand and primary productivity requires specialized equipment and skilled technologists. The best results are obtained from analyzing water samples in a laboratory. Persons working in the field are always looking for simple techniques that lead to similar conclusions. by comparing data from various indicators of water quality, limnologists have decided that a good estimate of eutrophication may be obtained by measuring the amount of dissolved material in the water. This bit of information may by obtained in several ways. The most accurate measure is total dissolved solids (TDS), which is the same as salinity. Obtaining this information accurately involves weighing a sample of water, then evaporating the water, burning organic material out of the residue, and weighing the ash. The amount of ash per liter of water is then calculated and expressed in milligrams per liter (mg/l) or equivalently, in parts per million (ppm).

In a study of 112 lakes at various elevations in the Rocky Mountains, TDS values varied from an average of 14.9 mg/l for alpine lakes to 202.9 mg/l for lakes in the prairie. These are reasonably accurate indicators of eutrophication, and they indicate that elevation plays a role. Lakes at lower elevation have greater nutrient input and longer seasons of productivity.

In the Sierra Nevada, similar values were calculated for a series of lakes in the Convict Lake Basin. Bunny Lake, at an elevation of 11,000 feet (3354 m), had only 5 mg/l TDS. Lake Crowley, at 6800 feet (2073 m), had 200 mg/l. In Bunny Lake, the small quantity of nutrients dictates that growth rates are slow. The oldest Brook Trout on record, 24 years old, was captured there. It was 8 inches (20 cm) long, and it weighed only 1/4 pound (115 g). In contrast, fishes in Crowley Lake grow from 1 ounce (20.5 g) to 1 pound (456 g) in a single year. At this lake, 2-pound (1-kg) fishes 15 inches (38 cm) long may be no older than 1 1/2 years.

Because TDS is a measure of the amount of dissolved minerals in water, hydrologists have developed an even simpler way to measure it. They determine how well the water conducts a current of electricity. This measure of water quality is called conductance. The more minerals that are dissolved in the water, the better it conducts electricity.

The attractiveness of this method is that any person with a few minutes of training can carry a battery-powered instrument to a body of water and measure its conductance. The water need not be returned to a lab for analysis, so the investigator gets an instantaneous reading. For all practical purposes, conductance will reveal what an investigator needs to know about the eutrophic state of a body of water.

Seasons in a Lake

In high-mountain lakes there are only two seasons: winter and summer. During winter the duration of ice cover is the critical factor. Because wind is the source of oxygen for lake water, a lake that is covered by ice for too long cannot sustain a fish population. The larger the lake, the greater the oxygen reservoir; therefore large, deep lakes are able to maintain fish populations under ice for a longer period of time. A shallow lake will not sustain a fish population during an average winter.

In typical eutrophic lakes there are four seasons (fig. 11.11). During summer concentrations of phytoplankton are low because dissolved nutrients such as nitrates (NO_3) and phosphates (PO_4) have been exhausted. Plankton that were abundant in spring have died and settled to the bottom. This season may be referred to as summer exhaustion. At this time, bacteria in the sediment decompose the dead organisms, depleting the oxygen in the deeper part of the lake. If oxygen concentrations in the deep become too low, decomposition is carried on by anaerobic bacteria that may produce toxic by-products, such as hydrogen sulfide (H_2S). Decomposer organisms also return soluble nitrates and phosphates to the lake water at the bottom.

As autumn approaches, day length becomes shorter, and the sun moves to a lower position in the sky. As a result, surface water receives less warming each day. Air temperatures also begin to drop. Water at the surface of the lake cools first. When the temperature at the surface is cooler than that of the deep water, surface water begins to sink, producing a stirring effect known as the autumn turnover. When this happens, nutrient-rich water from the bottom rises to the top. If the deep water has been anaerobic, this turnover may be accompanied by a fish kill. The deep water rising to the surface may be so oxygen-poor and loaded with hydrogen sulfide that it is insufficiently diluted, a combination that may be lethal to fish.

The upwelling of nutrients often causes an autumn plankton bloom, but it is short-lived because day length is too short and water temperature too cool to maintain phytoplankton for very long. Then the period of winter stagnation begins. Eutrophic water is clearest during this time. This stage occurs even if there is no ice cover.

If there is a cover of ice during winter, a second turnover during spring may occur when the ice melts. Ice, at $32°F$ ($0°C$), is less dense than water that is slightly warmer, which is why ice floats. When the ice melts, the cold water produced sinks to the bottom, initiating a spring turnover. Water at the bottom of a lake is the densest and usually is about $39°F$ ($4°C$).

During spring, day length increases. The sun rises in the sky and shines more directly on the lake, and air temperature increases. As the surface water becomes warmer, phytoplankton become more numerous, absorbing abundant nitrates and

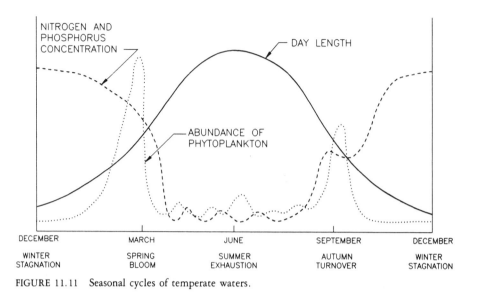

FIGURE 11.11   Seasonal cycles of temperate waters.

phosphates. This is the spring bloom. Lake water at this time may turn from clear to cloudy green in a few days. Algae that are capable of nitrogen fixation appear first. These are blue-green algae (cyanophyta or cyanobacteria). They are followed by green algae (chlorophyta) and small animals (zooplankton). Stimulated by abundant food and warm water, large aquatic animals such as frogs and fish begin to breed. Juveniles hatch and thrive on the abundant food. When the nitrates and phosphates become exhausted by the phytoplankton, there is a population crash, followed by clearing of the water. This is the beginning of a new phase of summer exhaustion, another critical time for frogs and fishes. When food becomes scarce, only the hardiest will survive; often these are the oldest and largest. All of the dead organisms, from plankton to vertebrates, will sink to the bottom, contributing to the organic ooze in which bacteria are busy decomposing and recycling.

Cultural Eutrophication

If nutrients such as nitrates and phosphates are added to a lake artificially, eutrophication may occur at an accelerated rate. This type of artificial eutrophication can be serious enough that an oligotrophic lake can become green and murky in a short period of time. If the process goes far enough, deep water becomes anaerobic, and a fish kill could result. This has occurred in the Great Lakes, where sewer discharge carries nitrogen from human urine and phosphorus from detergents.

Of serious concern is accelerated eutrophication in Lake Tahoe. A combination of gambling casinos, ski resorts, and great beauty have attracted large numbers of visitors to the area. The lake's remarkable clarity is one of the reasons for its striking beauty. In the 1950s objects on the bottom could be viewed to depths of 130 feet (40 m). In the 1960s, clarity began to be lost, and attached algae began to grow on rocks around the lake's margin. Between 1960 and 1980 primary production in phytoplankton more than doubled, from about 40 g C/m^2/year to over 80 g C/m^2/year. In an attempt to halt the eutrophication process, the Environmental Protection Agency sponsored construction of an advanced sewage processing plant. This involved tertiary treatment of the water to remove nitrates and phosphates as well as organic material. In addition, all processed sewer water was pumped out of the basin. Nevertheless, eutrophication continued. The source of nutrients was determined to be the forest ecosystem in the basin. So much construction was going on that soils were being disturbed at an unprecedented rate. Runoff from the forest carried nutrients that normally would cycle through the forest ecosystem. The outcome was eutrophication of the lake water in spite of the advanced sewer system. A moratorium on development in the 1980s stirred a storm of protest. A compromise somehow must be worked out among private-property owners, the U.S. Forest Service, and the states of California and Nevada.

Cultural eutrophication may also affect streams and lakes in regions of clear-cut logging. Again, it is runoff from disturbed land that creates the problem. This is particularly serious in regions of heavy precipitation, such as the Klamath Mountains.

STREAMS

Flowing water may be characterized in several different ways. Terms such as *river, creek*, or *brook* are based on relative size. However, it is foolish to quibble because the terms mean different things depending on the region of the country. A river in California might be called a creek in the eastern part of the United States.

Types of Flowing Water

Sometimes rivers are described according to permanence of flow. A permanent stream flows year-round. An intermittent stream dries up during a portion of the year. An interrupted stream is one that flows aboveground in portions of its run and underground in others. This vocabulary can reveal a great deal about a stream. A fisherman who knows that a certain stream is interrupted will not be dismayed to find a dry stream channel. A walk upstream will, sooner or later, lead to a region where there is permanent water. A wise hiker will read the symbols on a topographic map in order to know, before he or she arrives, whether a stream is permanent, intermittent, or interrupted. Most desert streams are intermittent. Most streams in southern California are interrupted.

Sometimes the appearance of the flow is used as a basis for comparing streams. Water that flows smoothly is said to be laminar, a situation that occurs in large rivers where the water flows slowly. Most rivers are characterized by various degrees of turbulence, reflecting a combination of speed and irregularities of the stream bottom.

Another means of comparison is based on the rate of fall, a combination of speed and turbulence based on stream gradient. Water moves fastest when it flows straight down without friction on the streambed. This is a waterfall. All cliffs over which a stream falls, however, are not vertical. Water falling over a surface that is not vertical is very turbulent as it moves over and around irregularities in the streambed. At some arbitrary point it is called a cataract rather than a waterfall. Turbulent flow over a nearly horizontal surface is known as a rapids.

The Sierra Nevada abounds in waterfalls, cataracts, and rapids. For example, some of the most spectacular waterfalls in the world are found in Yosemite National Park. Two of the 10 highest waterfalls in the world are in Yosemite Valley. At 2425 feet (739 m), Yosemite Falls is currently recognized as the fifth highest in the world, although some people quibble because it falls in two steps divided by a cataract. Angel Fall in Venezuela, at 3212 feet (979 m), is the highest. The eighth highest waterfall is Sentinel Falls in Yosemite Valley. It drops 2000 feet (609 m) in several steps. Ribbon Fall in Yosemite Valley drops 1612 feet (491 m) in a single drop. It ranks among the top 20 in total height, but among the top 10 in highest single fall.

Falling water directs a great deal of energy at the stream bottom. In a waterfall, nothing remains that is not attached. In a cataract, only large boulders remain. In a rapids, large and small boulders remain in the flow. As the stream gradient lessens, smaller particles remain in the bed, grading from gravel to sand to mud. In a mud-bottom pool, water barely flows.

The speed of falling water depends on the stream gradient. If it moves too fast, it not only carries along sediment, but organisms as well. The optimal flow for a typical stream is only about 1 to 3 feet (1 m) per second.

To a biologist, velocity of stream flow in itself is not a particularly useful item of information. It is more important to think in terms of volume of water flow per unit of time, a measure known as discharge. It is typically expressed in cubic feet per second (cfs). A rate of 1 cfs is equivalent to 28.3 liters per second. The amount of discharge varies with the width, depth, velocity, and sediment load of a stream. Niagara Falls, on the St. Lawrence River between New York and Canada, is an impressive sight. Its discharge has been estimated at about 220,000 cfs. The Mississippi River at New Orleans looks big but is not as impressive as Niagara Falls. However, discharge of the Mississippi at New Orleans has been estimated at 1,740,000 cfs. The difference is that it's deeper.

When large volumes of water are involved, discharge is often expressed in acre-feet per year. One acre-foot covers an acre (0.4 ha) to a depth of one foot (30 cm). The Mississippi River discharges 450 million acre-feet per year. In the west, the largest river is the Columbia. Its discharge has been measured at 141 million acre-feet per year. In California, typical discharges per year of the major rivers are as follows: Sacramento River, 17.1 million acre-feet; Klamath River, 12.5 million acre-feet; Colorado River, 10.5 million acre-feet; and the San Joaquin River, 3.3 million acre-feet. Although the Klamath River is dammed in its upper reaches, most of the flow in California is undammed. Is it any wonder why agricultural interests view the Klamath as a wasted river? On the other hand, salmon and salmon fishermen are delighted that the Klamath is a wild river.

A number of years ago limnologists attempted to devise a system of classification that would remove most of the subjective judgment from the vocabulary. This led to the concept of stream order, a classification of flowing water on the basis of number of tributaries, drainage area, total length, and age of water. First-order streams are the beginnings of a river system. These are the youngest segments, where the water begins to flow; they have no tributaries. Second-order streams are formed by the junction of two first-order streams. A third-order stream is fed by four first-order streams, fourth-order stream is fed by eight first-order streams, and so on. Tenth-order rivers are rare. The Mississippi is probably the only one in North America.

Obviously, correct classification of a stream requires careful examination of a detailed topographic map, which would be complicated by intermittent streams and would be only as reliable as its level of detail. Unfortunately, the system of stream orders is so complex that only limnologists can communicate with each other, and even they can not agree on whether the Mississippi is a tenth-, eleventh-, or twelfth-order river. Think of what would happen to literature if a romantic scene were described as taking place on the banks of a third-order stream.

California's rivers (fig. 11.12) are divided into seven major drainage systems. The Sacramento–San Joaquin system has the largest watershed and the greatest discharge, but the Klamath system carries a greater volume of water in proportion to its watershed. Conversely, in the southwest deserts there are numerous streams with large watersheds but low discharge. The system of stream orders would be meaningless for comparing these three areas of the state.

Formation of Stream Channels

At upper elevations, stream channels and valleys have a U-shaped bottom (fig. 4.17), the result of glacial sculpturing. In the Sierra Nevada, U-shaped valleys and stream channels occur all across the high country. As the waters flow toward lower elevations, they pass through V-shaped river valleys. A river, as it flows, cuts a notch into its bed. As the notch becomes deeper, weathering, gravity, and side streams work to eliminate the steep walls of the notch. The result is the typical V-shaped valley. Prehistorically, the U-shaped valleys of the high country began as V-shaped valleys but were reshaped later by passage of a glacier through the notch. The scenery of Yosemite Valley was formed in this way (pl. 1A). The large waterfalls that pour into the valley from all sides flow from the mouths of hanging valleys. The glaciers in the hanging valleys were smaller and did not cut as deeply into the bedrock as the glacier flowing down the main channel. Hence the water from the tributaries today plunges over a cliff before joining the main channel. Several miles below the entrance to Yosemite Valley, the Merced River flows through a V-shaped gorge. This gorge is below the point that was reached by the Pleistocene glaciers.

The physics of water as it cuts a stream channel have been studied thoroughly. A stream may be thought of as having the "goal" of flowing in a smooth arc from its headwater to its mouth. At its upper end, where less water is involved, the curve is steep. At its lower end, the curve flattens out. If an ideal curve is achieved, the

FIGURE 11.12 California rivers. (From M. Hill *California Landscape: Origin and Evolution*. Berkeley: University of California Press, 1984.)

stream uses all its energy to carry sediment over a smooth bed. If the gradient of the hill lessens, the energy in the water decreases, and the stream responds by dropping some of its load of sediment. This causes the stream channel to become filled, and the stream gradient is increased. If the stream flows over a high spot, such as a waterfall, it picks up energy and cuts away at the headwall. In this way, a waterfall moves up valley, leaving behind a steep gorge. This is exactly the way the gorge of the Merced River below Vernal and Nevada falls (fig. 11.13) was formed. These spectacular waterfalls are still cutting away upstream.

Limnologists construct stream profiles. A stream at base level flowing over its ideal curve is said to be at grade. Where a waterfall flows over a cliff, it is above grade and picks up energy. Where the water flows into a lake, it is below grade; it loses energy.

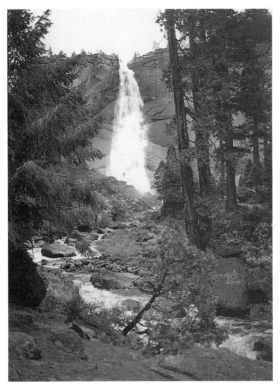

FIGURE 11.13   Nevada Fall on the Merced River, Yosemite
National Park.

By building a dam, engineers create a situation where the water is placed artificially
above grade. The energy gained is used to generate electricity as the water falls. Of
course, the reservoir above the dam is below grade, so it is doomed to become filled
with sediment.

At the stream's lower end, where the grade is flattened, coriolis effect begins to have
a profound influence on the flow of water. In the Northern Hemisphere, flowing
water turns to the right. This causes streams to flow to the right across a flood plain,
such as the Great Central Valley. Eventually, however, the flow will reach a point
where if it were to continue flowing to the right, it would be forced to flow uphill.
That is not possible, so the stream turns to the left, flowing downhill until coriolis
effect once again draws it to the right. The result is a stream channel that meanders
back and forth across a flood plain.

Fluctuations in flow associated with normal variations in precipitation cause a river
to flood and subside. The result of flooding is deposition of new topsoil, which is one
of the reasons that the Great Central Valley has been such a rich agricultural region.
Overflow and deposition form natural levees, creating the terraces upon which natural vegetation establishes itself. Overflowing also supplies water to flood plains, which

can help recharge the water table. As a river erodes its channel on the outside of a bend, it deposits sediment on the inside. The meander in this way moves down the valley, depositing new soil behind it.

Controlling rivers with dams and concrete channels disrupts the natural order of things. Without rejuvenation, soil is lost, not gained. Fertilizer must be applied artificially. All the symptoms of desertification discussed in the previous chapter may be related to poor agricultural practices based on short-term financial gain. Accumulation of salt, erosion, groundwater overdraft, and subsidence are problems involving agriculture and water management that must be faced in the near future.

AQUATIC ANIMALS

In lakes and rivers, there are three sources of nutrients: photosynthesis, material carried by downflow in streams, and material from the land (fig. 11.14). An analysis of the relative importance of these three sources has indicated that most nutrients enter the system from the outside. Leaf litter and other debris washed off the land or dropped from trees represent the greatest amount of input in streams and lakes. This is especially important where alders are part of the riparian community. About one-third of the biomass is tied up in this detrital form. Most of that material goes through a decay cycle before it becomes available for typical animal consumption.

Because most of the biomass in an aquatic system is involved in the decomposition process, the greatest amount of organic material in the system lies in the sediment or becomes dissolved in the water. The dissolved organic matter (DOM) is distributed nearly equally through the water and sediment and represents about half of the available food. If half the organic material in the system is dissolved and one-third is tied up in detritus, only one-sixth of the organic biomass is left to become incorporated into living organisms. Furthermore, the bulk of the living organisms are either microscopic algae or bacteria; therefore it should be no surprise that animals are not conspicuous in many aquatic ecosystems.

In stream ecosystems, the amount of organic material washed in is roughly equivalent to the amount washed out. The contribution of photosynthesis is small because only attached microorganisms and mosses are not carried away. As material is carried downstream in a river, however, the system becomes more productive. The contribution of photosynthesis increases because there are more nutrients, and the stream is wide enough for light to shine directly on the water. The amount of fine particulate organic matter and dissolved organic matter increases in downstream areas.

Aquatic insects that metamorphose into flying adults cause a net loss of organic matter for aquatic ecosystems. These organisms do most of their feeding in the water, and when they emerge, they carry their organic compounds into the terrestrial system. In one study of a desert stream, 97% of the emergent insect biomass was transferred to neighboring terrestrial ecosystems.

In lakes, attached and floating microorganisms play an important role. The contribution of photosynthesis increases in direct proportion to the nutritional state, or degree of eutrophication. In marshes, the photosynthetic contribution provided

FIGURE 11.14   Process and trophic relations in a stream. Predation occurs throughout but is omitted here. (P & N, phosphorus and nitrogen; 1°P, primary production; Prc, herbivore piercers; Scr, herbivore scrapers; Shr, shredders; Col, collectors; DOM, dissolved organic matter; FPOM, fine particulate organic matter; MF, microbial uptake and flocculation.) (From G. A. Cole. *Textbook of Limnology*, 3rd ed. Prospect Heights, Ill.: Waveland Press, 1983, reissued 1988. Reprinted with permission.)

by macrophytes is the greatest of any aquatic ecosystem. Nevertheless, the role of decomposition in the system also increases proportionately. In a senescent system there is so much bacterial activity that little or no oxygen is left for large animals. The consequence of this trend is that large animals such as fishes and frogs are more conspicuous in lakes at the lower stages of eutrophication. In marshes, nearly all the biomass is tied up in producers and decomposers (microconsumers).

Invertebrates

With so much organic matter represented by water-soluble molecules and microorganisms, a specialized group of small invertebrates has evolved that is able to harvest this resource. Of particular interest are the crustaceans and aquatic insects, many of which spend at least part of their life cycles in fresh water. These animals belong to the phylum Arthropoda. Two-thirds of all the animal species in the world are arthropods.

Based on feeding behavior, there are four ecological types of arthropods (fig. 11.14). Shredders feed on coarse particulate matter such as leaf litter. Grazers scrape algae off rocks. Collectors are organisms that gather plankton and floating organic matter. Predators feed on the other three types.

In upper reaches of streams, shredders and collectors are most common. Downstream, grazers become more common. In midsized streams, collectors and grazers form the bulk of the invertebrates. Downstream in large, slow-moving rivers, collectors make up about 90% of the invertebrates; the remainder are predators.

In lakes and ponds, phytoplankton such as diatoms and green algae are an important food resource. Grazers on this resource include small shrimplike creatures known collectively as crustaceans (fig. 11.15). Among the small crustaceans in the animal plankton (zooplankton) are three basic types. A fourth group of crustaceans is composed of large bottom dwellers such as crayfish.

Among the three groups of crustaceans in the zooplankton, one is composed of the branchiopods, a word that means "gill-foot." Included among branchiopods are fairy shrimp and brine shrimp. These are very important animals in saline lakes such as those in the desert. These small, shrimplike creatures swim on their backs, feeding on small suspended particles. In Mono Lake, an endemic brine shrimp, *Artemia monica*, is an important component of the food base that supports a large breeding colony of California Gulls, *Larus californicus*. Diversions of water to the Los Angeles Aqueduct have caused significant lowering of the water level in Mono Lake. It appears that the coincident increase in salinity associated with evaporation may negatively affect the brine shrimp population and thus reduce the food supply for the gulls. Furthermore, after the lake level dropped, Negit Island became connected to the mainland. It was on this island that the gulls laid their eggs. Between 1982 and 1985 the combination of increased salinity, reduced populations of brine shrimp, and exposure of the eggs and chicks to terrestrial predators contributed to a reproductive failure in the California Gulls. Heavy precipitation from 1983 through 1986 restored water to the lake, and the gulls reproduced again. Drought in the late 1980s and early 1990s lowered it again. The controversy over Mono Lake continues.

Brine shrimp are also quite common in temporary ponds. Their fertilized eggs are capable of withstanding drying and high temperatures. They lie in the dried muds until the next rainstorm forms a new pond. These are analogous to annual plants, and brine shrimp accurately could be thought of as "annual" animals.

The largest members of the branchiopods are tadpole shrimps (*Triops*). Like brine shrimp, they are annual animals, found in a number of playas in the southwestern deserts. They may be 2 inches (5 cm) or more in length. They have a large carapace that covers the front half of their body, so that they superficially resemble a tadpole swimming in the water. These animals have biting mouthparts, and they can chew on detritus or prey on other animals, including brine shrimp.

Other small branchiopods in the zooplankton are Cladocera. This order includes water fleas (*Daphnia*), which are often sold in tropical fish stores for live fish food. Water fleas also have a carapace, but it covers the back part of the body except for the head. Reproduction in water fleas is interesting. During the spring bloom they reproduce rapidly by parthenogenesis, that is, from unfertilized eggs. These offspring are all females. Later in the year some males are produced. Fertilized eggs

FIGURE 11.15 Some freshwater crustaceans. *A.* Opossum shrimp. *B.* Brine shrimp. *C.* Water flea. *D.* Tadpole shrimp. *E.* Amphipod. *F.* Copepod. *G.* Crayfish. (After G. A. Cole. *Textbook of Limnology*, 3rd ed. Prospect Heights, Ill.: Waveland Press, 1983, reissued 1988. Reprinted with permission.)

carried by females that overwinter are very resistant to cold and even drying. When optimal conditions return the following year, the population reappears seemingly from nowhere.

The second group of crustaceans in the zooplankton are the copepods, a name that means "oar-foot." There are over 10,000 known species. Most of them occur in the sea, but there are three common types in fresh water. Copepods are shrimplike in appearance, without a carapace. Their bodies are fatter at the head end, tapering to a thin tail composed of a pair of appendages. They are quite small, seldom over a few millimeters long. One group of copepods, known as anchor worms (Lernaeopods), is parasitic on fishes. They could be a problem if they appeared in a small population of fishes, such as some of the rare or endangered species. Cladocera and copepods are the most common members of the zooplankton community and represent an important link in the food chain between microscopic and visible life forms.

The third group of planktonic crustaceans is known as the ostracods, a word that means "shelled." These tiny creatures have unsegmented bodies enclosed in a pair of hinged valves that form a carapace. This gives them the appearance of tiny, transparent clams. Their antennae stick out of the carapace, and they use them for swimming. Actually, these are not abundant in the plankton community. Most commonly they live on the bottom, feeding on detritus. Nevertheless, they also form a link in the food chain that supports visible animals.

The largest and most diversified group of crustaceans is known as the malacostracans, which means "soft-shelled." There are four different groups of malacostracans in fresh water, three of which include small but visible shrimplike creatures. These groups are known as mysids, isopods, and amphipods. The mysids include a strong-swimming lake dweller, one of the opossum shrimps, *Mysis relicta*. This species occurs normally as a component of deep northeastern oligotrophic lakes such as the Great Lakes. It is a relict of marine origin that became isolated in fresh water during or soon after the Pleistocene. It feeds on zooplankton and is itself fed upon by fishes. Adults are about 1 inch (25 mm) long. Because it is an easily transported organism, it has been introduced far outside of its normal range as a forage species for game fish. The assumption was that introducing opossum shrimp would allow a greater biomass of predatory fishes such as lake trout to be supported. Obviously, introducing another link in the food chain means that fewer large fishes, not more, can be supported on the same food base. The increase in size and abundance of game fish is a temporary phenomenon and lasts only until the food base is exhausted.

The introduction of opossum shrimp into Lake Tahoe in 1969 had a profound effect on the natural zooplankton community. By the early 1970s opossum shrimp had increased dramatically, and cladocerans had practically disappeared. In the absence of cladocerans, copepods also increased in numbers.

Studies of zooplankton in Lake Tahoe indicated that they migrate on a daily basis. They migrate away from the shoreline, and also up and down. At night they move to the surface to feed on phytoplankton. When it is light they move to deeper water to avoid predation. Weak swimmers, such as some of the copepods, are unable to expend the energy that it takes to penetrate the dense water of the thermocline in the top 60 feet (20 m) of the lake.

The opossum shrimp migrate to the bottom, to a depth of nearly 1000 feet (300 m) every day, but during summer they remain below the thermocline, avoiding the upper, warmer waters. This behavior allows some of the copepods to escape predation above the thermocline. Other copepods, particularly in their larval stages, remain in very deep water, below the greatest concentration of opossum shrimp. The result of these behaviors is a layering of crustacean species promoted in particular by predation of the introduced form. This layering of animal life can deplete oxygen in regions of high density. It can also localize phytoplankton where there is less predation. Uptake of nitrogenous wastes produced by the zooplankton can also increase phytoplankton in certain layers.

Isopods are small, flattened, creeping crustaceans. Among the terrestrial members of this group are the familiar sowbugs or pill bugs. In aquatic systems, isopods such as *Asellus* are most commonly found in streams, where they feed on detritus. They are particularly abundant where leaves have accumulated, and they can be found by separating wet leaves or looking under small stones on the stream bottom.

Amphipods are important components of stream bottom and lakeshore habitats. They are thin, laterally flattened forms known as scuds, side-swimmers, or freshwater shrimp. They feed on fallen leaves and detritus caught in algal mats or clumps of aquatic moss. They are more characteristic of lowland habitats, but they are locally common in mountain or high-elevation lakes. The amphipod *Gammarus* was found to represent about half of the bottom fauna of Mildred Lake, a medium-sized but shallow lake at 9800 feet (3200 m) elevation in the Convict Lake basin. By comparison, in Bright Dot Lake, at 10,500 feet (3400 m) in the same basin, cladocerans were found to be the most common crustaceans at a depth of 50 to 60 feet (12–20 m).

Isopods and amphipods are important to the aquatic ecosystem because they are shredders. Shredding increases the surface area for action of micro-organisms, which greatly accelerates the recycling of organic material.

The fourth group of malacostracans is the group known as decapods. The name means "10-legged" and refers to the organisms' five pairs of walking legs. These are mostly predatory bottom dwellers. In California this group is represented by freshwater shrimp and crayfish.

Only a few species of freshwater shrimp have been recorded in North America, but three of these are endemic to California. The Pasadena Freshwater Shrimp, *Syncaris pasadenae*, has been extinct since the 1930s. It formerly occurred in low-gradient streams near Los Angeles. The California Freshwater Shrimp, *Syncaris pacifica*, now known from only five streams in Marin, Napa, and Sonoma counties, is on California's list of endangered species. These nearly transparent shrimp grow up to 2 inches (5 cm) in length. They live in shallow, low-gradient streams with good riparian cover and undercut banks. The Hilton Shrimp, *Palaemonetes hiltoni*, is a rare brackish water species of southern California. Unfortunately the habitats of these three species are seriously degraded.

Crayfish are lobsterlike animals up to 8 inches (20 cm) in length. Common in almost all warm-water habitats, they ingest crustaceans, worms, insect larvae, and small fishes. They also feed readily on carrion. In this respect, they are the scavengers of the system. Crayfish are preyed on by large fish, frogs, and humans. Crayfish may be caught with a fishing rod and a piece of bacon or liver for bait. No hook is required, because crayfish will cling so tenaciously to the bait that they can be dragged from the water. The tails and claws of crayfish provide a tasty treat. In some places crayfish are sold under the name *langostino,* which means "little lobster." Another name for them is crawdads.

The center of crayfish evolution in the United States is in the southeast, where there are more than 40 species. In California, there are only 4 native species, all in the genus *Pacifastacus.* Due to habitat destruction, an endemic species, the Shasta Crayfish (*Pacifastacus fortis*), is on California's list of threatened species. A very similar species, *P. nigrescens,* is endemic to streams of the San Francisco area. The most common crayfish in the state is an introduced species known as the Swamp Crayfish, *Procambarus clarki.* This is one of the species of crayfish commonly dissected in biology laboratories.

Insects are the most common arthropods. On a worldwide scale, about three-fourths of all animal species fall in this group. It is primarily a terrestrial group, however. They have not succeeded in invading the marine environment to a significant degree, and only 3% of them are aquatic at some point in their life cycles. Nevertheless, there are about 30,000 species of aquatic insects, distributed among 13 orders (table 11.2).

The evolutionary story of insects is interesting. Insects evolved first on land and then invaded water. It appears that they first invaded water in the cool headwaters of streams. From there they spread to warmer, lower reaches of streams and then to ponds and lakes. This last step required the evolution of tolerance for higher temperatures. Temperature is very important to the distribution of insects. Most evidence indicates that insects are sorted into niches within their habitats primarily on the basis of preferred temperature rather than competition for food or other resources.

Five groups (orders) of insects have at least one aquatic stage in nearly all their species (fig. 11.16). In these groups, the adults are terrestrial flying forms. They reproduce by laying their eggs in the water, where the immature forms, known as larvae or nymphs (naiads), develop. These five groups are caddisflies (Trichoptera),

TABLE 11.2   Aquatic and Semiaquatic Insects

Order	Common Name	Active Aquatic Stages
Collembola	Springtails	Immature, adult
Ephemeroptera	Mayflies	Nymph
Odonata	Dragonflies, damselflies	Nymph
Orthoptera	Grasshoppers, crickets, katydids	None (semiaquatic)
Plecoptera	Stoneflies	Nymph
Hemiptera	True bugs	Nymph, adult
Neuroptera	Spongillaflies, dobsonflies	Larva
Trichoptera	Caddisflies	Larva, pupa
Lepidoptera	Moths	Larva
Coleoptera	Beetles	Larva, adult
Hymenoptera	Bees, wasps	Larva (parasitic)
Diptera	True flies	Larva

SOURCE: After G. A. Cole. *Textbook of Limnology,* 3rd ed. Prospect Heights, Ill.: Waveland Press, 1983, reissued 1988.

FIGURE 11.16 Some aquatic insects. *A,B.* Caddisfly (adult and larva). *C,D.* Mayfly (adult and nymph). *E, F.* Stonefly (adult and nymph). *G, H.* Dobsonfly (adult and larva). *I, J.* Dragonfly (adult and nymph). (After G. A. Cole. *Textbook of Limnology*, 3rd ed. Prospect Heights, Ill.: Waveland Press, 1983, reissued 1988. Reprinted with permission.)

mayflies (Ephemeroptera), stoneflies (Plecoptera), dobsonflies (Neuroptera), and drag-onflies (Odonata).

Adult caddisflies, mayflies, and stoneflies are similar in appearance, with large, membranous wings. Usually the adult stage is of short duration. The larvae or nymphs spend their lives underwater, coming out of hiding to feed on detritus or algae at night. They commonly live in streams, so they are equipped with hooks and are often flattened or streamlined to withstand the current. The emergence of adults is known as "the hatch." At this time, trout fishermen attempt to catch fish by offering dry flies that mimic whatever is hatching.

Some larvae of caddisflies are known as case builders. They pick up bits of debris from the bottom and build protective shells around themselves. Different species in different habitats use different materials. Some caddisfly larvae cut up bits of leaves, others use pine needles, and some use small stones. One species in the southwest deserts builds a small coiled shell of stones so that it comes to resemble a small snail. In mountain lakes the forms that use pine needles are conspicuous. A person peering into the shallow water of a high Sierra lake may be surprised to see what appears to be a 1–2-inch (25–50-mm) bundle of pine needles lurching slowly along the bottom. Other caddisfly larvae are known as net spinners. These forms live in streams and build sticky nets to trap materials that drift with the current.

Dobsonflies are closely related to antlions and lacewings (Neuroptera). Adults are about 2 inches (5 cm) long, and they superficially resemble dragonflies and dam-selflies, but dobsonfly wings are much longer than their bodies. The larvae, known as hellgrammites, can be found under stones at the edges of streams and ponds. They look like underwater centipedes and have large, chewingmouth parts, which they use to chew detritus or insect larvae. Hellgrammites live three years in the water before emerging as adults.

Dragonflies and damselflies are related. They are included in the same order, Odonata, but they differ in appearance and habits. Adult dragonflies always keep their wings extended. These are large-bodied, brightly colored insects with very large eyes. They have two pairs of wings with conspicuous veins and cross-veins. They often fly over water, where they prey on flying insects such as mosquitoes. They mate in midair. Sometimes they may be seen dipping their tails into the water as they lay their eggs. Dragonfly nymphs or naiads are large, predatory, grublike creatures. They may spend up to five years in the water, gradually metamorphosing to an adult. When they emerge from the water, they molt for a final time into the winged stage.

Damselflies in flight look like slender-bodied dragonflies. Unlike dragonflies, when they land they rest with their wings folded back. Many are found in the same sorts of habitats as dragonflies, and they may be conspicuous, flitting over mountain lakes. They mate in midair, after which they lay their eggs in the stems of aquatic plants. They do this by crawling head first down the stem until they are underwater, and they pierce the stem and lay the eggs in the tissues of the plant. After the eggs hatch, the nymphs spend their immature period crawling about the lake bottom eating detritus.

True flies (Diptera), true bugs (Hemiptera), and beetles (Coleoptera) also have their aquatic members. These large orders of insects are very common in terrestrial habitats, but because they are such large groups, they are important components of aquatic communities as well. Aquatic larvae of true flies represent a very large portion of the aquatic insect biomass, and they occur in a wide variety of microhabitats. Flies with aquatic larvae include mosquitoes, midges, gnats, and blackflies (fig. 11.17). As adults, they are all small, delicate insects with a single pair of wings. The name *Diptera* means "two wings." Most insects have four wings (two pairs).

Mosquitoes (Culicidae) are among the best-known insects. Male and female adults feed on nectar and other plant juices. In most species, females have two stomachs. The second stomach is for blood that they obtain from a vertebrate animal. They require at least one blood meal to stimulate ovarian development and reproduction. Because they may fly from person to person, sucking blood, they carry several important diseases, the best-known of which is malaria.

Although malaria is not a major problem in California today, it was epidemic in the mining camps of the 1850s, when it was also known as "miner's fever." Until about 1880 there were frequent sharp, local epidemics. After that time the disease began a slow decline, interrupted by local outbreaks associated with the introduction of new irrigation systems or mining operations. For example, in the early 1900s, an area encompassing 13 counties in the Great Central Valley had a malarial death rate twice that of Mississippi, which was then considered one of most malarial states in the nation. In the year 1916, those counties, composing an area half the size of Mississippi, had a malarial death rate of 14.2 per 100,000 persons. Around 1920, the disease began a comparatively rapid decline, in spite of the continued abundance of one of the known vectors, Freeborn's Mosquito, *Anopheles freeborni*. Three other species of *Anopheles* are known to occur in California, but only one other, *A. punctipinnis*, was considered an important carrier of malaria. It may be that this species was formerly more common than Freeborn's Mosquito, and as it declined in abundance in association with alterations of wetland habitats, so did the incidence of malaria.

Different species of mosquitoes carry different diseases. The only mosquito-borne disease that is significant in California today is western equine encephalitis, sometimes incorrectly referred to as sleeping sickness. This disease is carried primarily by *Culex tarsalis*. Another species of mosquito, *Aedes triseriatus*, is known to carry a similar disease, called California encephalitis, which was first described from Kern County. Some mosquito abatement districts in California keep chickens in pens in strategic locations. They periodically sample the blood of these chickens to learn if mosquitoes in the area are carrying encephalitis. Mosquito abatement districts also engage in spraying programs or introduce small predatory fish species to permanent standing water to control the numbers of mosquito larvae. These districts also promote the concept of source reduction, which is essentially an attempt to reduce the amount and duration of standing water in an area. Some wetlands are drained and converted to fertile land for agriculture. In this way, the standing water for mosquitoes is removed, but so is the habitat for many other water-dependent organisms.

Because mosquitoes are widely considered to be such pests, much time and money has been spent to determine how to control them. On a worldwide scale, beginning in the 1940s, DDT was used principally for the purpose of controlling mosquitoes that

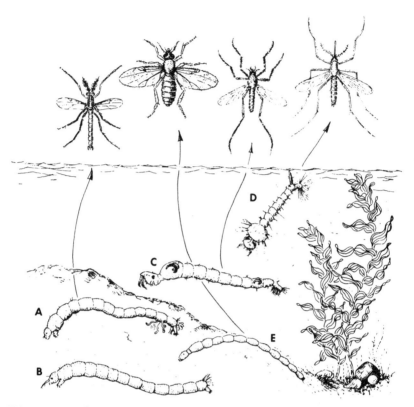

FIGURE 11.17   Some aquatic flies. *A, B*. Nonbiting midges. *C*. Phantom midge. *D*. Mosquito. *E*. Biting midge. (From G. A. Cole. *Textbook of Limnology*, 3rd ed. Prospect Heights, Ill.: Waveland Press, 1983, reissued 1988. Reprinted with permission.)

carried malaria. Widespread use of the chemical for that purpose was quite effective until the mosquitoes evolved immunity. The only mosquitoes reproducing were those not killed by DDT. The impact of the indiscriminate use of DDT is now a well-known story.

To keep mosquitoes from biting humans, a number of attempts have been made to develop a mosquito repellant. The most successful has been a chemical known as toluamide or DEET, which stands for one of the forms of toluamide. Mosquitoes locate potential blood sources by a combination of heat, odor, and carbon dioxide. Toluamide works by blocking the receptors for carbon dioxide on the proboscis of the mosquito. The mosquito may find you by the heat you produce, but it won't recognize you as a potential blood meal if it can't detect the odor of the CO_2 emitted by your skin!

Mosquito larvae are known as wigglers. These are small wormlike creatures that hang just below the surface of the water and breathe with an air tube that projects toward the surface. When the water is disturbed, the larvae wiggle and squirm.

Presumably this wiggling helps them move to a new location and distracts predators that would attack from beneath. Many aquatic predators feed on these larvae. Where mosquitoes occur naturally, there are usually predators specialized for eating mosquito larvae. In natural bodies of water, therefore, it should be unnecessary for mosquito abatement districts to introduce mosquito-eating animals, in particular the nonnative Mosquitofish, *Gambusia affinis*, which is known to eliminate native fishes by a variety of means.

A family closely related to mosquitoes includes species of nonbiting flies known as midges or gnats. One particular form, the phantom midges *(Chaoborus* spp.), are of interest because their transparent larvae are predatory members of the zooplankton communities of some large lakes, such as Clear Lake in the northern Coast Ranges. In fact, these larvae are the only insect members of the zooplankton. Because the larvae are nearly invisible and the adult seems to appear from nowhere, they are known as phantom midges.

At Clear Lake, tourists and summer residents have long complained about the enormous numbers of Clear Lake Gnats, *Chaoborus astictopus.* At the height of the emergence season, up to 3.5 billion flies may leave the lake on a single evening. In an attempt to control these nonbiting midges, deemed a nuisance because of their swarming around lights and stoves, in the early 1960s the people of Clear Lake authorized the application of DDT to the surface of the lake. The result was an ecological disaster. Concentrations of DDT increased as the chemical passed through the food chain. Fish-eating birds, such as grebes, began to die. It was determined that the cause was DDT poisoning, and this was one of the first documented cases of biological magnification. Such evidence ultimately led to the banning of DDT.

Another attempt to control the Clear Lake Gnat also was a biological disaster. This episode involved the introduction of nonnative species of fish. Bluegill *(Lepomis cyanellus)* were introduced in the 1940s, after which the native minnow, the Clear Lake Splittail *(Pogonichthys ciscoides)*, suffered a precipitous decline. Finally, in 1967, the Mississippi Silverside *(Menidia audens)* was introduced. The silverside replaced the Bluegill *and* the native splittail. The Clear Lake Splittail officially has been pronounced extinct.

Larvae of the other aquatic flies are most often found in the sediment of lakes and rivers. Of particular importance are the nonbiting midges (Chironomidae) that produce great swarms of adults that swirl about and follow humans as they walk along a lakeshore. The adults, which look like very small mosquitoes, are short-lived and have reduced mouthparts; they do not feed. The swarms are mating swarms, composed entirely of females. Solitary males select a female from the swarm, and mating takes place in a nearby shrub.

Larvae of these nonbiting midges, called bloodworms, form a highly significant portion of the biomass in the sediment of many lakes. Bloodworms get their name from their red color. This is one of the few insects to possess hemoglobin, the red respiratory pigment found in the blood cells of vertebrate animals. Bloodworms have no blood cells, but the pigment is suspended in their "blood." These larvae may be quite abundant in the sediment under nearly anaerobic conditions. The affinity of the pigment for oxygen gives them the ability to capture what oxygen molecules are available. Chironomid larvae (bloodworms) are extremely important as forage for fishes. In some situations, gut contents of fishes are composed of nothing but these larvae.

Closely related to the nonbiting midges are the biting midges (Ceratopogonidae), also known as punkies or "no-see-ums." These are the tiny bloodsuckers that sneak up on you during the heat of the day. One species is known in desert areas and along the north coast as the Bodega Gnat, *Leptoconops kerteszi*. Their orange-colored larvae seem to prefer sandy soil on the edge of a tidal marsh or saline lake. Another species is the Valley Black Gnat, *Leptoconops torrens*. Larvae of these midges prefer finely compacted clay soils in the western part of the San Joaquin and Santa Clara valleys.

Black flies (Simuliidae) are small, compact flies that vary in color, frequently black, gray, or yellowish tan. Females are bloodsuckers. In California they seem mostly to annoy wild or domestic birds and mammals, and when they emerge in spring or summer, they may bite humans. Black flies seem not to be affected by the usual repellents. A black fly bite is recognizable by a small red hole in the center of the swelling. The bites itch a great deal, and some sensitive individuals develop large welts. In some parts of the world these animals carry tiny parasitic worms that cause river blindness (onchocerciasis), but this is not a problem in California.

Black fly larvae occur in flowing water, attached to stones, vegetation, or other objects, often in the swiftest parts of streams. They are most conspicuous in clear mountain streams where water flows in a sheet over a smooth rock surface. Here they are visible as rows of small, black, wormlike objects, resembling moss in ridges. They attach by means of a sucker near the tail end, with their heads oriented downstream. Larvae possess a pair of large mouth brushes, which are spread out to strain food particles. A person who takes the time to sit near a mountain stream and watch these larvae will see that they are able to move about on the rock without being carried away. They do this with a looping motion involving the sucker on one end and a leg on the other. They also produce small silken threads that enable them to cling spiderlike to rocks in the current.

To the uninformed, bugs (Hemiptera) and beetles (Coleoptera) superficially resemble each other. They are easy enough to distinguish, however. An informed observer may retort, "That's not a bug, it's a beetle." *Coleoptera* means "sheath-wing," and on beetles the horny front wings, known as elytra, meet in a straight line down the back. In contrast, on bugs the front wings are thick and leathery at the base, and the tips are membranous and overlap. *Hemiptera* means "half-wing." In addition, true bugs possess a conspicuous triangular scale on the back, known as a scutellum, located at the attachment of the front wings.

Adults and immature stages of beetles and bugs are associated with fresh water (fig. 11.18). Most species are terrestrial, but these groups are so large that the aquatic species form a significant part of the animals in aquatic ecosystems. The adults are air breathers. Either they carry air down with them or they return to the surface frequently to breathe.

FIGURE 11.18 Predaceous aquatic insects and some comparisons. *A.* Mouthparts of predatory stonefly naiad, *Isoperla. B.* Mouthparts for shredder-scraper stonefly naiad, *Pteronarcys.
C.* Larva of predatory diving beetle, *Dytiscus,* and side view of a larva's head. *D.* Adult
diving beetle, *Dytiscus. E.* Spongillafly larva, *Sysyra,* a piercing predator, and its freshwater
sponge prey. *F.* Underside of piercing predatory backswimmer, *Buenoa,* and side view of its
head, showing the sharp rostrum. *G.* Adult giant water bug, *Belostoma. H, I.* Side view
of head of dragonfly naiads, *Macromia* and *Aeschna,* showing grasping mouthparts. (After
G. A. Cole. *Textbook of Limnology,* 3rd ed. Prospect Heights, Ill.: Waveland Press, 1983,
reissued 1988. Reprinted with permission.)

Adult beetles and bugs form a significant portion of the biomass in most shallow
water, where they play important roles at intermediate stages of food chains. Nymphs
(naiads) and larvae are important components of the bottom fauna.

Water bugs occupy a wide variety of habitats. They are found in saltwater pools, hot
springs, mountain lakes, and large rivers. In general, however, they are characteristic
of shallow, quiet waters. In particular, they inhabit ponds, backwaters, and shoreline
habitats of lakes. Most water bugs overwinter as adults. They lay eggs in the spring
and go through their developmental phases during summer. Their eggs are sticky
and when laid become glued to various objects in the water. They do not lay floating
eggs, as do many other aquatic insects.

Giant water bugs (Belastomatidae) are large, flattened predators. The largest aquatic insect a person is likely to encounter is a giant water bug known as *Lethocerus americanus*, sometimes called the Electric Light Bug, because it will fly to lights at night. In California, it may be over 2 inches (45–60 mm) in length. Giant waterbugs capture and suck dry a variety of prey, including insects, tadpoles, and small fishes. They are also known as fish killers and toe biters.

Giant water bugs may be encountered in any shallow warm-water pool or stream, from the desert to the coast. Usually they lie concealed in shallow water among mats of leaf litter or other debris. In two genera, *Abedus* and *Belostoma*, the eggs when laid are deposited on the back of the male. What better way of protecting them? There seems to be no predator that would dare approach one of these fierce insects. There must be something that eats giant water bugs, however, because they have defense mechanisms other than biting. When they are disturbed, they become rigid and feign death. If removed from the water, they also may squirt an obnoxious liquid from the anus.

In spite of their reputation, in some parts of the world giant water bugs are eaten by humans. In Asia, one species, *Lethocerus indicus*, is eaten roasted or boiled and is said to have a strong flavor like that of Gorgonzolo cheese. In Thailand, many sauces and curries are flavored with this insect. In Mexico, water bugs of the genus *Belostoma* are either roasted or used in stews, sometimes mixed with other insects.

Most numerous of the aquatic bugs are water boatmen (Corixidae). They get their name from their oarlike hind legs, which they use to propel themselves through the water. While underwater, they carry a bubble of air on their underside and use it as a source of oxygen. This bubble gives the underside of the body a silver appearance.

Water boatmen play an important role in aquatic communities because they are shredders of leaf litter and debris. Other food for these bugs consists of small midge and mosquito larvae. Furthermore, they are fed upon by many large fishes, and they are the preferred diet item of fishes in some habitats.

Water boatmen are distributed from below sea level in Death Valley to alpine lakes in the Sierra Nevada. Many species are restricted to certain habitats and therefore may be used as ecologic indicators. For example, one group (*Trichocorixa*) occurs in briny habitats, such as the salt pools owned by Leslie Salt Company on the south shore of San Francisco Bay. They also occur in the alkaline closed-basin lakes of the southwest deserts. They are the dominant insect in the Salton Sea, and they also are found at Badwater, in Death Valley. In the Salton Sea they are an important forage item for game fish. Another group (*Corisella*) is an indicator of septic conditions. These are found in Little Borax Lake of the northern Coast Ranges and in sewage-oxidizing ponds.

Occurring in many habitats with water boatmen are bugs known as backswimmers (Notonectidae), which get their name from the fact that they swim on their backs (upside down). They are longer and narrower than water boatmen, and their backs (undersides) are shaped like a boat bottom. These fast-swimming predators feed on anything they can overpower, including crustaceans, larvae of aquatic insects, and small fishes. A person choosing to handle a backswimmer should expect a very sharp bite.

Another widespread family is known as creeping water bugs (Naucoridae). They can be recognized by their flattened shape and their mottled, yellow to green color pattern. They are predatory and will bite humans. This group of bugs is not well known because they are often concealed among stones or vegetation. Typically they inhabit flowing water at low elevations. One species, *Ambrysus mormon*, has been collected along the shoreline of Clear Lake, Eagle Lake in Lassen County, and Lake Tahoe. This is the dominant insect species in the saline waters of Pyramid Lake, Nevada, and it is common in most large streams of the Great Central Valley and northern Coast Ranges. It is replaced to the south and in the desert by other, similar species.

Other water bugs are the sticklike water scorpions (Nepidae), which lie in wait for prey among tangled debris. On the surface long-legged water striders (Gerridae) or riffle bugs (Veliidae) may be found. Bugs in these two families move about on the water surface, feeding on small prey items. They are kept from sinking by the presence of many tiny water-repellent hairs on their feet. The effect of increased surface area of the feet of these bugs can be best appreciated by watching the shadow of a water strider on the bottom of a shallow pool. On the shadow, it appears that each foot terminates in a large circular disc that looks like a catcher's mitt.

Throughout the state, along the edges of streams and ponds or on lakeshores and beaches, inconspicuous bugs such as shore bugs (Saldidae) or toad bugs (Gelastocoridae) may occur. Shore bugs may be overlooked because they run or fly quickly at the slightest disturbance. Some are secretive, hiding in vegetation or shady spots. Shore bugs are scavengers and predators, eating a variety of living and dead organisms on the damp soil. Toad bugs are broad, flattened bugs with a warty appearance. Their mottled coloration enables them to blend in with the sand along the edges of streams and ponds. These bugs seem to hop like a toad when approached. Their short, grasping front legs are used to catch prey such as other insects.

There are about 10 families of water beetles. The most common are the diving beetles (Dytiscidae). Adults of this family spend most of their time underwater, obtaining air by surfacing rump first or backing into bubbles formed by aquatic plants. They carry the air under their elytra, and they swim with oarlike hind legs. Both larvae and adults are predacious. Eggs are laid on or in underwater plants. When the larvae, sometimes called water tigers, mature, they leave the water to form a pupa in damp soil nearby. Diving beetles are most common in ponds and slow-moving streams, where they inhabit weedy shallows. There are a few species in fast-moving streams, saline pools, and hot springs.

A group of beetles very similar to the diving beetles often occurs in the same water, particularly in marshes. These are the water scavenger beetles (Hydrophilidae). Water scavenger beetles differ slightly in appearance, being flat rather than rounded on the underside. Also, their antennae are clublike instead of threadlike. More importantly, they are herbivorous rather than predatory. They swim more slowly than diving beetles, using their legs alternately as if they were walking underwater. A person watching these two kinds of beetles in a pool would notice that diving beetles come to the surface for air rump first, but the scavenger beetles break the water with their antennae. Life histories of the two kinds of beetles are similar. Larvae of both groups are predatory.

A unique group of beetles is the water pennies (Psephenidae). In this group, only the larvae are aquatic. They are small, oval, flattened creatures that cling to rocks in well-aerated flowing water, often near waterfalls. They occur in waters of varying chemical composition, but seldom above 6000 feet (1800 m) in elevation. In headsprings where CO_2 concentration is quite high, they may seem to be the only living organisms. The adults are small black beetles, sometimes found on the rocks near a stream.

Among the invertebrates that inhabit fresh waters throughout the state, snails are perhaps the least studied. There are many species, and there is a high degree of endemism, which makes studies of snail distribution important to understanding the historic distribution of fresh water. There are too many species to discuss here, but essentially there are two types of aquatic snails: those with gills and those with a saclike lung.

Snails with a lung are called pulmonate snails. Most of them are terrestrial, but some are aquatic. All snails with gills are aquatic, and they can be distinguished from pulmonate snails by the presence of an operculum, which is like a trap door that may be pulled over the opening when they are out of water. In this way they are able to retreat inside their shell and tolerate temporary drying of habitat. Nearly all snails are herbivores or detritus eaters, harvesting their food with a rasplike tongue (radula) that is used to shred vegetation. This is such a ubiquitous group that it is too bad scientists don't spend as much time learning their natural histories as they do classifying them. The Trinity Bristle Snail, *Monadenia setosa*, is the only mollusc on the state list of threatened species.

Fishes

Freshwater fishes are the most common aquatic vertebrates (table 11.3). They range from coastal estuaries to alpine streams to desert springs. There are three kinds of fishes in fresh water. Primary freshwater fishes are those that cannot tolerate salt water. Secondary freshwater fishes are those that usually live in fresh water but can tolerate salt water. Marine fishes are those that live in seawater, although some may be found in coastal streams a considerable distance inland.

Primary Freshwater Fishes.   Of the native primary freshwater fishes, nearly all fall in three families (fig. 11.19). They are either minnows (Cyprinidae), suckers (Catostomidae), or trout (Salmonidae). Minnows and suckers make up the bulk of the native fishes. This may come as a surprise to a person accustomed to catching bass, Bluegill, crappie, or catfish, but these are all species introduced to California as game fish. Approximately 50 introduced species inhabit fresh water in California, often to the detriment of native species. Distribution of native primary freshwater fishes is of great interest to biogeographers because studies of modern-day distribution can lead to broad generalizations about ancient waterways and help to explain the relative positions of ancient land masses.

TABLE 11.3 Fishes in Major Drainage Systems of California

	Klamath	Sacramento–San Joaquin	Lahontan	Death Valley	Colorado River	Southern California	All California
Endemic species	6	17	5	8	6	2	25
Primary freshwater species	10	20	7	3	4	4	34
Secondary freshwater species	7	8	1	4	1	0	17
Anadromous species	10	11	0	0	0	1	15
Catadromous species	0	0	0	0	1	0	1
True marine species	1	3	0	0	0	2	3
Introduced species	17	36	14	25	25	30	49

Salmonidae
  Mountain Whitefish
  Bull Trout
  Cutthroat Trout
  Redband Trout
  Golden Trout
  Rainbow Trout

Cyprinidae
  Sacramento Blackfish
  Hardhead
  Hitch
  Sacramento Squawfish
  Colorado Squawfish
  Bonytail Chub
  Blue Chub
  Tui Chub
  Arroyo Chub
  Thicktail Chub
  Sacramento Splittail
  Clear Lake Splittail
  California Roach
  Speckled Dace
  Lahontan Redside

Catostomidae
  Lost River Sucker
  Shortnose Sucker
  Santa Ana Sucker
  Mountain Sucker
  Humpback (Razorback) Sucker
  Sacramento Sucker
  Klamath Smallscale Sucker
  Modoc Sucker
  Tahoe Sucker
  Owens Sucker
  Klamath Largescale Sucker

Centrarchidae
  Sacramento Perch

Embiotocidae
  Tule Perch

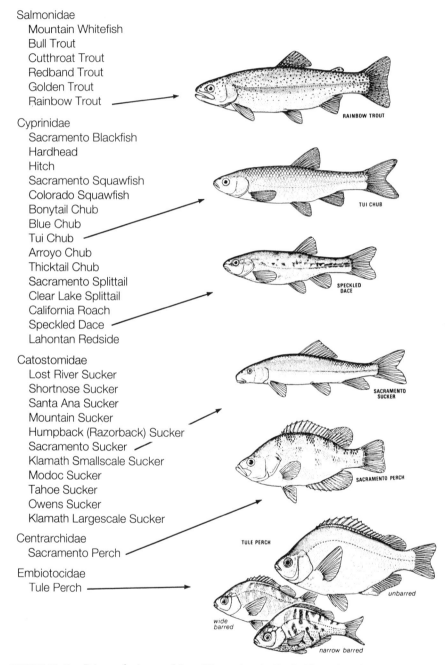

FIGURE 11.19 Primary freshwater fishes. (Illustrations by Doris Alcorn from S. M. McGinnis. *Freshwater Fishes of California*. Berkeley: University of California Press, 1984.)

The minnow family is the largest family of native freshwater fishes. They usually live in flowing water and, as such, are streamlined with elongated bodies and large fins. They are found all over the state, but there is a good deal of endemism. Of the 15 native species, only 2 are found outside of a single drainage.

The most widespread species is the Speckled Dace, *Rhinichthys osculus* (fig. 11.19). These are slender minnows with a speckled pattern on the back. They are small, seldom reaching over 4 inches (10 cm) in length. These minnows are usually riffle fish. That is, they occur in streams where the bottom is rocky and the water is turbulent. Their mouths are directed downward, which is an adaption for feeding on the bottom. They eat various kinds of small invertebrates such as snails and insect larvae. In spite of their obvious association with cool flowing water, they also occur in a variety of other situations, such as Lake Tahoe, where they live along the shoreline, and desert streams, such as the Owens River. In Death Valley, they occur in the outflows of desert springs.

The question arises: How does a freshwater fish become distributed throughout so many freshwater habitats? It is certainly true that during periods of heavy rainfall, various freshwater habitats, including those of the deserts, were interconnected. However, it is difficult to explain how a freshwater fish can cross a mountain range. The answer seems to be what is known as headwater stream capture. Streams that are above grade eat backward into their beds. At the summit, between two drainages, headwaters erode toward each other. If one stream cuts into the rock faster than the other, it is possible for the stream on one side to intercept the stream from the other side of the ridge. In so doing, it also may intercept its fishes. Distribution of Speckled Dace all over the west seems best explained by headwater stream capture. These fish are most common in the upper, fast-moving reaches of streams, and they occur on both sides of major drainage divides, such as the Rocky Mountains. In California, they are on both sides of major ranges such as the Sierra Nevada and the Transverse Ranges.

Another widespread minnow is the Tui Chub, *Gila bicolor* (fig. 11.19). Native distribution of this species includes all drainages except the Colorado River and coastal Southern California. This is a species of slow-moving water. It may occur in association with the Speckled Dace, but chubs prefer sandy or mud-bottom pools. They are most common in relatively lowland habitats—weedy shallows of lakes or sluggish rivers. They are also found in Lake Tahoe and some other large lakes, such as Eagle Lake in northeastern California. They are larger than dace, reaching 14 inches (40 cm) in length. Their heavier body is typical of the form associated with flowing but slow-moving water. These are opportunistic feeders, consuming everything from aquatic insects to detritus.

Tui Chubs have undergone considerable differentiation throughout their range, indicating a highly adaptable, plastic species. Many subgroups have been identified, and two coexist in Lake Tahoe, theoretically by feeding on different foods.

Of particular interest are the Blue Chub, *Gila coerulea*, of the Klamath drainage, and the Arroyo Chub, *Gila orcutti*, a southern California species. These are relatives of the Tui Chub that are different enough to be identified as distinct species, which implies that they have been geographically separated for thousands of years. Interesting theories involving plate tectonics have been advanced to account for these differences. Consider that the Klamath Mountains were once in line with the northern Sierra Nevada, much farther east of their present location. There is also evidence that the Klamath region has experienced about 70° of clockwise rotation, with over one-third of that occurring during the last 20 million years. It is highly probable that waters that now flow directly to the Pacific were once part of the ancient Sacramento River system. Both Tui Chubs and Blue Chubs occur in the Klamath system today. Could the Blue Chub represent early separation of fish populations associated with translocation and rotation of the Klamath Mountains? Perhaps the Tui Chub became introduced more recently through mechanisms of headwater stream capture.

The populations of the Arroyo Chub in coastal southern California are of interest because closely allied chubs occur today on the coastal side of Sonora, Mexico. The Arroyo Chub most likely rode the land mass to its present location from a position that was to the south, when the Baja California peninsula was attached to what is now mainland Mexico.

Dispersal of chubs to Mexico is part of a long and complicated history. It appears that during the Miocene, less than 25 million years ago, chubs began their odyssey at the upper reaches of the Colorado Plateau, in a region that is now the eastern part of the Great Basin in Utah. They crossed the Rockies and, through headwater capture, entered the upper reaches of the Rio Grande. They swam down the Rio Grande to Mexico and then southwestward up the Rio Conchos to the mountains of western Mexico. Headwater stream capture then carried them to the rivers of Mexico that drained westward toward the Pacific. Thereafter, northward displacement along the San Andreas fault brought them to their present location, on the coastal side of the Transverse and Peninsular ranges.

The final leg of this journey from Mexico may have involved about 90° of clockwise rotation of the San Bernardino Mountains. Arroyo Chubs also occur in the upper reaches of the Mojave River, on the desert side of the San Bernardino Mountains. If such rotation occurred, it could mean that the present-day Mojave River formerly flowed westward on the coastal side of the mountains, and was turned to its present drainage away from the coast by rotation of the mountain range. Evidence for rotation of the Transverse Ranges lies in magnetic lines of force trapped in volcanic rocks during the Miocene. The reason there is no evidence of rotation in the San Bernardino Mountains is that there are no suitable outcrops of Miocene volcanic rocks, but if rotation occurred in the other Transverse Ranges, it is likely to have taken place in the San Bernardino Mountains as well. Some authorities contend that the chubs probably were introduced. Other authorities speculate that they could have gotten there by headwater capture from the Santa Ana River.

Whatever is responsible for coastal species on the desert side of the San Bernardino Mountains, other aquatic species have similar distribution. A small fish, the Three-spine Stickleback, *Gasterosteus aculatus* is present in coastal streams and also on the desert side in the Holcomb Creek and Baldwin Lake areas. Likewise, the Western Pond

Turtle, *Clemmys marmorata* (fig. 7.26), has its only desert populations in the Mojave River.

Two subspecies of the Tui Chub are also found in desert rivers. The Owens Tui Chub, *Gila bicolor snyderi*, formerly occurred throughout the Owens River. Threatened with extinction by dewatering of its habitat, it is now listed by the federal government as endangered. The Mojave Tui Chub, *Gila bicolor mohavensis*, is also listed as endangered. It formerly occupied the lower reaches of the Mojave River. It was almost lost through hybridization with the Arroyo Chub, after which its total range was a spring system and pond next to Soda Lake that was operated as a "health resort" known as Zzyzx. The facility is now operated as a center for desert research in collaboration with the Bureau of Land Management and a consortium of California state universities.

Coexisting in Lake Tahoe with Tui Chubs and Speckled Dace is the most beautiful of the minnow species in California, the Lahontan Redside, *Richardsonius egregius*. Both sexes of this species bear bright golden and red lines on the sides of their bodies. In Lake Tahoe they occur in large schools, and in early summer they can be seen in shallow water, where they spawn. These are small minnows, rarely over 3 inches (8 cm) in total length. Presumably, the three minnow species avoid competition through niche partitioning, but they all spawn in the shallows at the same time of year, so occasional hybrids are produced.

Chubs of the Colorado River system illustrate another example of the plasticity of genetic systems (fig. 11.20). A series of closely related forms are adapted for varying degrees of turbulence and speed in stream water. These forms have been separated into species and subspecies on the basis of their anatomy. At this time, three species are recognized for the mainstream Colorado River.

Roundtail Chubs, *Gila robusta*, which occur in slow-flowing water of the Colorado River, look very much like Tui Chubs. They are streamlined (i.e., trout-shaped). In areas of rapidly flowing water, chubs develop a suite of characteristics that apparently enables them to cope with the swift flow. The Bonytail Chub, *Gila elegans*, shows these characteristics to a moderate degree. These fish have an elongated, narrow posterior body and greatly enlarged fins. In addition, an enlarged hump is present on the head. Water flowing over this hump may serve to thrust the fish against the bottom so that it is able to maintain position in the swift flow. These adaptations reach their greatest extreme in the Humpback Chub, *Gila cypha*, which inhabits the swift-flowing, turbulent waters of Grand Canyon. Unfortunately, the native distribution of these chubs has been influenced by severe alterations to the Colorado River. Damming and channelization have all but eliminated the turbulent flow and the spawning grounds for the native fishes. The Bonytail Chub is now probably extinct in California, although it still occurs in the upper Colorado River in Utah. It is on the federal list of endangered species.

Parallel development of a large hump behind the head has occurred in the Razorback Sucker, *Xyrauchen texanus* (fig. 11.20). These large suckers are also inhabitants of turbulent water in the mainstream Colorado River and are listed as endangered by the state of California and the federal government. In spite of the scientific name for

FIGURE 11.20   Fishes of fast-flowing waters of the Colorado River drainage.
A. Mountain Sucker, *Pantosteus clarki*. B. Razorback Sucker, *Xyrauchen texanus*. C.
Bonytail Chub, *Gila elegans*. D. Humpback Chub, *Gila cypha*. E. Colorado River
Roundtail Chub, *Gila robusta*. (From G. A. Cole. *Textbook of Limnology*, 3rd ed.
Prospect Heights, Ill.: Waveland Press, 1983, reissued 1988. Reprinted with
permission.)

this species, which implies they are from Texas, the species is restricted in distribution
to the Colorado River system.

The most spectacular of the fishes in the minnow family also formerly occurred in
the lower Colorado River. This is the Colorado Squawfish, *Ptychocheilus lucius*. Most
people would never believe that this is a minnow. Fish larger than 5 feet (160 cm) in
length formerly were caught by fishermen, and weights up to 100 pounds (45 kg) were
recorded. Like the Bonytail Chub and the Razorback Sucker, the Colorado Squawfish
was unable to adapt to the series of impoundments on the lower Colorado River. It
still occurs in the upper Colorado River, but the extraordinary large sizes have not
been recorded there. The Colorado Squawfish is also on the federal list of endangered
species. A similar fish, the Sacramento Squawfish, *Ptychocheilus grandis*, also occupies
the Sacramento–San Joaquin river system. The Sacramento Squawfish is also large,
but specimens over 3 feet (1 m) in length are not common. With the disappearance
of the Colorado Squawfish, this is now California's largest native minnow species.

Squawfish are big-river fish. They occupied the position of top carnivore in the
pristine river systems. In a manner similar to salmon, they would migrate upstream
to lay their eggs in gravels of smaller streams. Unlike salmon, they did not die after
spawning, nor did they swim all the way to the ocean to spend their adult lives.

The demise of California's native fishes has accompanied changes in big-river systems that result from the activities of humans. Damming of rivers blocked spawning

runs and changed characteristics of flow. Rivers formerly experienced seasonal fluctuations of temperature, turbulence, and silt load; now they are monotonously clear and cold. The water in flowing portions of the rivers comes from the bottoms of the reservoirs, and fluctuations in flow occur on a daily basis rather than seasonally. Finally, the large number of imported game fish has caused near elimination of the native species, many of which are classified as rare, threatened, or endangered. Reestablishment of Colorado Squawfish, Razorback Suckers, and other native fishes is a major responsibility of government agencies such as the California Department of Fish and Game and the U.S. Fish and Wildlife Service.

The greatest assemblage of minnows occurs today in and about the San Joaquin–Sacramento river system. Before it became a disturbed system, there were at least nine species of minnows nicely separated through niche partitioning. Introduction of many nonnative species, including five kinds of minnows, created serious problems for the native fishes. Introduced species, coupled with channelization, draining, damming, and pollution, led to the demise of the native assemblage.

In the system's pristine condition, Sacramento Squawfish were top carnivores, swimming up and down the large rivers. Hitch, *Lavinia exilicauda*, are plankton feeders that inhabit slow-moving, deep-water streams. Their ecologic niche has been largely taken over by the introduced Threadfin Shad, *Dorosoma petenense*, a member of the herring family (Clupeidae). The Hardhead, *Mylopharodon conocephalus*, is a large bottom dweller that feeds on invertebrates and aquatic plants. Its ecologic niche is threatened by introduced Inland Silversides, *Menidia beryllina*; Common Carp, *Cyprinus carpio*; and Goldfish, *Carrassius auratus*.

In smaller streams the Speckled Dace inhabited many habitats that have been taken over by introduced Red Shiners, *Notropis lutrensis*; Golden Shiners, *Notemigonus crysoleucas*; and Fathead Minnows, *Pimephales promelas*. The Tui Chub inhabited similar habitat in the Pit River portion of the drainage. The Speckled Dace still dominates in its favored habitat: riffles and rocky areas in smaller streams.

In backwaters, the Thicktail Chub, *Gila crassicauda*, wandered through tule beds, feeding on detritus and invertebrates such as mosquito larvae. The Splittail, *Pogonichthyes macrolepidotus*, lived in deeper water of sloughs and backwaters. The Sacramento Blackfish, *Orthodon microlepidotus*, was a filter feeder in fertile warm backwaters. Destruction of wetlands through draining and channelization has pretty much destroyed the habitat of these backwater species. The Thicktail Chub is extinct, and the Splittail is only locally common.

In the intermittent tributaries that may become reduced to interrupted pools, the California Roach, *Hesperoleucus symmetricus*, feeds on algae. Along with the Speckled Dace, this is one of the most widespread species in the state. It can tolerate water temperature up to 95°F (35°C) and dissolved oxygen down to 1.0 ppm.

Suckers (Catostomidae) are the second most common fishes in California. They are closely related to minnows and show similar patterns of distribution. These fishes are adapted to a variety of habitats, but their mouths are specialized for feeding on the bottom. Those that occur in streams have hard edges on their jaws for scraping algae, small invertebrates, and detritus off of rocks. The largest, as discussed previously, is the Razorback Sucker of the Colorado River. In the San Joaquin–Sacramento river system there are four subspecies of the Sacramento Sucker, *Catostomus occidentalis* (fig. 11.19). This is a slow-growing species that eventually reaches a size up to 18 inches (0.5 m). This species has adapted very well to reservoir life, and some anglers prefer fishing for them.

There are 11 native species of suckers in California, most with localized distributions. The Tahoe Sucker, *Catostomus tahoensis*, is the counterpart of the Sacramento Sucker in the lakes and streams of the Tahoe Basin. The Mountain Sucker, *Catostomus platyrhynchus*, occurs in the Lahontan drainage east of Lake Tahoe; the Owens Sucker, *Catostomus fumeiventris*, occurs in the Owens River; and the Santa Ana Sucker, *Catostomus santaanae*, occurs in streams of the Los Angeles Basin. The Modoc Sucker, *Catostomus microps* is an endangered species that occurs in Johnson Creek, Modoc County.

There are four species of sucker in the Klamath drainage. They are the Lost River Sucker, *Catostomus luxatus*; the Shortnose Sucker, *Chasmistes brevirostrus*; the Klamath Largescale Sucker, *Catostomus snyderi*; and the Klamath Smallscale Sucker, *Catostomus rimiculus*. The Klamath Smallscale Sucker is the smallest of the four species, and it is the only one that is still common. The other three are large, deep-water species, and their habitats have been threatened by draining of large lakes. The Lost River Sucker and the Shortnose Sucker are listed as endangered species.

Suckers are considered ugly by many people, and there is a mistaken idea that if suckers are present, something is wrong with the water. Nothing could be farther from the truth. In fact, they are fairly good to eat. It has been said that many Indian groups preferred suckers to trout as a food source. Because of habitat destruction, six native species are endangered. Others, such as the Santa Ana Sucker, are now so localized in distribution that they may be proposed for listing.

The most romantic of California's native freshwater fishes are in the trout family (Salmonidae). There are five native species of trout and one whitefish. These large, colorful fishes are the epitome of game fish in California. Many meals feature trout, many holidays are organized around trout fishing, and the largest fraction of the budget for the Department of Fish and Game is devoted to raising and planting trout in California waters.

Similar to minnows and suckers, trout are streamlined in shape, implying that they evolved in flowing water. Trout are basically stream fishes. Their habit of maintaining position in quiet water, downstream from a large boulder, is an adaptation for feeding. When a food item is carried downstream, the trout darts from the quiet water to catch it. The impression that high-country lakes have always been the home of trout is not true. Even though trout are widely distributed in streams and lakes today, the only high-country lake that originally contained members of the trout family is Lake Tahoe.

Lake Tahoe originally was the home for two members of the trout family, although there is some debate as to how common they actually were in the lake itself. Rivers and streams on the east side of the Sierra Nevada in the Lake Tahoe region are part of what is known as the Lahontan drainage. Lake Lahontan was an enormous body of water that occupied, during pluvial times, most of the northwestern part of Nevada and northeastern California. That drainage today includes Pyramid Lake in Nevada. In California, remnants of the drainage include Lake Tahoe, as well as Eagle Lake and Honey Lake, large saline lakes in northeastern California. Streams and rivers on the eastern side of the Sierra in that region are part of the Lahontan system. The major river in the system is the Truckee, which carries water from Lake Tahoe to Pyramid Lake.

The Mountain Whitefish, *Prosopium williamsoni*, is a small-mouthed, large-scaled member of the trout family. It has widespread distribution throughout the Great Basin, but in California it is limited to the Lahontan system. It occurs generally in lakes and deep pools from about 4500 to 7000 feet (1300–2100 m) in elevation. In Lake Tahoe, they are found mostly in deep water, except in the spring, when they move into shallow water to spawn. They feed on the organisms that inhabit the bottom. They are tasty fish, and they achieve reasonable size—about 18 inches (50 cm) in length. For some reason, they are not relished as a game fish by California fishermen. In other parts of the United States, whitefish are considered a prized game fish and a delicacy.

In similar water with the Mountain Whitefish, the Lahontan Cutthroat Trout, *Oncorhynchus* (= *Salmo*) *clarki henshawi,* formerly occurred. This trout was so common that it once supported a commercial fishery. For example, in 1900 over 9600 pounds (4360 kg) of this species were harvested commercially from the Truckee River. This is a typical trout, but it is renowned for its large size and the ease with which it is caught. Salmon-sized cutthroats over 3 feet (1 m) in length, weighing up to 30 pounds (13.6 kg), formerly were caught in Pyramid Lake. A Lahontan Cutthroat is recognizable by its olive to yellow color and many black spots. In particular, these trout can be distinguished from Rainbow Trout because the spotting occurs on the belly. Cutthroats get their name from a red slash that occurs on each side, just under the lower jaw. A highly colorful subspecies with very little spotting is known as the Paiute Cutthroat, *Oncorhynchus* (= *Salmo*) *clarki seleniris*. It occurs in Silver King Creek, in the Carson River drainage just south of Lake Tahoe. Both of these subspecies are listed as threatened by the federal government. A third subspecies of cutthroat, the Coastal Cutthroat, *Oncorhynchus* (= *Salmo*) *clarki clarki*, occurred in small coastal streams. Like steelhead, they migrated back and forth to the sea.

Other than Golden Trout, *Oncorhynchus* (= *Salmo*) *aguabonita*, of the Kern Plateau, Mountain Whitefish and two subspecies of cutthroat were the only high-country trout before humans started introducing them. With the exception of Lake Tahoe, as mentioned previously, lakes of the high Sierra were fishless. Most of the lake basins were the product of Pleistocene glaciation. After the glaciers retreated, trout were unable to make it to these lakes because the terrain was too steep. Waterfalls were barriers to the dispersal of trout.

The Coastal Rainbow Trout, *Oncorhynchus mykiss irideus* (= *Salmo gairdneri*) (fig. 11.19), originally was a fish of foothill and coastal streams from Los Angeles County northward. It was first discovered and described in 1855 from specimens obtained from the Redwood Creek drainage of eastern San Francisco Bay. Rainbows that move into seawater to spend their adult lives are called Steelhead Trout and are exactly the same subspecies as Rainbows that do not migrate to the sea. Like salmon, in order to reproduce, Steelhead return to the stream where they originally hatched.

Rainbows occur in a wide variety of colors and patterns. They have adapted well to rearing in hatcheries, and have been distributed far beyond their native range. Most of the hatchery trout raised in California are Rainbows, but they have been hybridized with other forms to the degree that pure Rainbow Trout may be difficult to find.

The Redband Trout, *Oncorhynchus* (= *Salmo*) *mykiss gairdneri*, is of Great Basin affinities. It is considered to be an inland version of the Rainbow Trout. These trout are found in isolated pockets throughout the western Great Basin. In California, true Redband Trout are found in Sheepheaven Creek, Siskiyou County. Apparently, former distribution included the Pit River that drains the Modoc Plateau. They were also found in Goose Lake at the head of the Pit River and in the upper Klamath drainage. This pattern of distribution is important, as it shows the relationship of Great Basin species to those of the Sacramento River. The implication is they evolved in the Great Basin and made their way to the Sacramento–San Joaquin system by traveling down the Pit River (or its predecessor), which drains the Modoc Plateau.

Redband Trout resemble Rainbows, but they tend to be pale yellow with a brick red stripe on the side. In contrast, Rainbows tend to have a pink stripe on a silvery background. Redband and Rainbow Trout are so closely related that they interbreed freely. It appears that, at some point, Rainbows that were able to disperse through seawater moved up the Sacramento–San Joaquin system and swamped, through hybridization, the genetic identity of most trout populations.

The Golden Trout is presumed to be a highly derived Redband Trout that evolved in isolation on the Kern Plateau of the southern Sierra Nevada. These fish are native to high-elevation streams such as Golden Trout Creek and the South Fork of the Kern River, which cut through the large meadows of the Kern Plateau. Because of its beauty, the Golden Trout has been named the state freshwater fish. Breeding males have a bright golden color on the lower sides, and the belly and cheeks are a bright red, as is the lateral band. The assumption is that Golden Trout reached the southern Sierra by means of the San Joaquin River. Ancestors in the San Joaquin were similar to Redband Trout. At times of high water on the floor of the Great Central Valley, the Kern, draining into Tule Lake, could overflow into the San Joaquin, and the trout could make their way eventually all the way up the Kern to the high country. If glaciation pushed them out of high-country basins, they remained in southern refugia such as Golden Trout Creek and the South Fork of the Kern. They were not able, however, to invade the high-country lakes. Distribution of trout to the thousands of high lakes in the Sierra Nevada is entirely the result of human efforts. The Rainbow Trout of the mainstream Kern River has also been described as a separate subspecies, the Kern River Rainbow Trout, *Oncorhynchus* (= *Salmo*) *mykiss gilberti*.

The story of Golden Trout and its introduction to high-country lakes is particularly interesting. In 1876 there was a sawmill on Cottonwood Creek, an east-side stream of the southern Sierra Nevada near Lone Pine. At the same time, across the Owens

Valley in the Inyo Mountains, the Cerro Gordo Mine was operating. This was a large, profitable enterprise that required charcoal to extract gold and silver from the ore. Logs cut in Cottonwood Creek were converted to charcoal in a set of kilns located on the shore of Owens Lake. Hundreds of people were employed in these operations. To provide fresh fish for his employees, the owner of the Cottonwood sawmill introduced Golden Trout to Cottonwood Creek. The initial stocking was 12 trout carried in a coffeepot over the pass from Mulkey Creek, a tributary of the South Fork of the Kern River. The trout prospered, supplying food for the employees.

In 1891, in order to increase the sawmill's capacity, Cottonwood Creek was diverted to a new channel. As the old channel dried up, Golden Trout trapped in the pools were harvested. Some were kept alive and introduced to the Cottonwood Lakes, a fishless basin. So began the practice of stocking high-country lakes with Golden Trout.

Since 1918, Golden Trout have been introduced by the Department of Fish and Game into lakes and streams all over the Sierra, usually at elevations above 9000 feet (2700 m). Golden Trout also have been introduced to other western states. Golden Trout require clear, cold water. Generally, they will not tolerate water temperatures above 70°F (22°C).

The Department of Fish and Game harvests eggs and sperm from the Golden Trout at Cottonwood lakes. These are fertilized artificially, and the hatchlings are raised in the Mount Whitney Fish Hatchery near Independence. These fish are then introduced to high-country lakes.

For many years the State Department of Fish and Game has been busily introducing new fish species. Brown Trout, *Salmo trutta*, were first introduced to North America in 1883. In 1894 a strain from Scotland known as the Loch Leven Trout was introduced to California. The more common German Brown Trout was introduced in 1895 and is now common in waters all over the state. Brown Trout grow to large size. They are bottom feeders, and, to a large degree, they eat other fishes, a habit that has led to the reduction of other fish species that occur in the same water. Introductions of Brown Trout have been implicated in the extinction of the native Bull Trout and reduction in numbers of the rare Modoc Sucker. Those events are discussed later.

In 1872 the first Brook Trout, *Salvelinus fontinalis*, were imported from New Hampshire and Wisconsin. Native to the eastern United States, Brook Trout belong to a group of trout known as chars. Brook Trout is one of the few species of trout that does well in the high-country lakes. Brown Trout are known to hybridize with Brook Trout, and the sterile hybrid is known as the Tiger Trout, in reference to the distinctive banding on their sides. Although the two species are not related closely enough to produce fertile offspring, the hybrids do possess what is known as hybrid vigor. Where Tiger Trout have been introduced, they are known for their voracious feeding.

Chars (*Salvelinus* spp.) can be distinguished from other trout by their large mouth and pointed nose. The state's native char is known as Bull Trout, *Salvelinus confluentis*. The Bull Trout is on the state list of endangered species, although it is probably extinct in California. It formerly occurred in the upper Sacramento drainage in the McCloud River. There are two dams on the drainage today, and nonnative Brown Trout occur there as well. In other parts of its range, the Bull Trout was eliminated through hybridization with introduced Brook Trout. Hybrids are sterile. Some authorities contend that a contributing factor to the demise of the Bull Trout was the loss of salmon in the Sacramento River. Apparently, salmon fry were an important food item. Its distribution today is in large bodies of water in the upper Great Basin, particularly in Idaho and Montana, where they grow to 3 feet (1 m) in length and may weigh 30 pounds (14 kg). The Bull Trout is another example of a Great Basin species with its California distribution in the Sacramento River drainage.

There are also tales that sea-run Dolly Varden Trout, *Salvelinus malma*, occasionally enter the Klamath River. The popular name of this species apparently refers to Dolly Varden, a character from a Charles Dickens tale, *Barnaby Rudge*, whose clothing was brightly colored and was a popular style in the 1870s. In reference to its bright color and spotting, the name *Dolly Varden* or *Calico Trout* was used for the fish in those days.

Neither Brook Trout nor Golden Trout grow very large in typical high-country lakes, but not all species of trout can survive and reproduce in the high country. Nevertheless, anglers yearning for large trout sometimes conduct unauthorized stockings of fishes such as Rainbows, Cutthroats, or Brown Trout, which are known to achieve large size.

Indiscriminate or unauthorized stockings can spell disaster for native fishes. Golden Trout in particular are threatened by the introduction of other fishes. Alien trout may become cannibalistic and eat the young of the native species. If Rainbows or Cutthroats are introduced, they hybridize with the Golden Trout, and the genetic integrity of the species is lost. Brook Trout normally do not hybridize, because they spawn in the fall whereas all of the native trout spawn in the spring. Brook Trout, however, are known to overproduce offspring, which causes serious competition for available resources, leading to stunted growth. Brook Trout are especially susceptible to stunting of their own populations, not to mention the effect that their overproduction has on the native species.

If introduced species of fishes were not enough of a problem for native Golden trout, Beavers have been introduced to many trout streams. Damming activity of the Beavers has destroyed spawning habitat by allowing the accumulation of sediment over the clean gravels where eggs are laid.

In response to these problems, the Department of Fish and Game began a program of remediation. Introduced species were removed by poisoning, and Golden Trout were reintroduced. Barriers to upstream dispersal were constructed to prevent natural encroachment by species from downstream warm-water habitats. Special angling regulations were adopted to prevent overharvesting. Beavers were trapped and removed and their dams destroyed. Thousands of dollars were spent to protect the Golden Trout. After all, it is the official freshwater fish of a state already stung by extinction of the California Grizzly Bear, adopted in 1953 as the state mammal. How would it look if the state were unable to protect its unique animals from extinction?

There are only two species of native primary freshwater fishes that are not in the minnow, sucker, or trout family. They are found in the Sacramento–San Joaquin drainage, where, through niche partitioning, they have coexisted with all the min-nows and suckers. This is the largest drainage in the state, and it has the largest assemblage of species. The Sacramento Perch, *Archoplites interruptus* (fig. 11.19), for-merly inhabited sloughs, sluggish water, and lakes of the Central Valley floor. This is a relict species, the only member of the sunfish family (Centrachidae) that occurs west of the Rocky Mountains. It is a deep-bodied, "slab-sided" fish with a large head and gills. It is adapted to moving through tules and aquatic vegetation in warm-water habitats. Large specimens may grow to 2 feet (60 cm) in length. Introduction of other sunfishes, such as Bluegill (*Lepomis macrochirus*) and crappies (*Pomoxis* spp.), have practically eliminated the Sacramento Perch from its native habitat. Evolving in a habitat with little competition, these perch are no match for other, aggressive fishes. Ironically, introduction of this species into the Great Basin, far outside of its native range, has preserved the species. Unlike most members of the sunfish family, Sacra-mento Perch can tolerate alkaline waters. This feature, plus their large size, makes them a desirable game fish in waters that are hostile to most sunfish. To preserve the species in California, the Department of Fish and Game has tried to encourage their propagation in California farm ponds.

The other native primary freshwater fish is the Tule Perch, *Hysterocarpus traski* (fig. 11.19), the only freshwater member of the surfperch family (Embiotocidae). They are small—up to 6 inches (15 cm) in total length—and they are slab-sided. They occur naturally in slow-moving waters in association with aquatic plants. Like the Sacra-mento Perch, they feed primarily on aquatic invertebrates. Formerly they inhabited the San Joaquin Valley marshes. They are still locally common in the Sacramento Val-ley and some large lakes such as Clear Lake, but their overall distribution is greatly reduced. They are victims of habitat degradation, particularly drying of marshes, increased turbidity, pollution, and reduced cover.

Secondary Freshwater Fishes. Secondary freshwater fishes are able to tolerate salt water, but they spend most of their lives in fresh water. Because of their ability to tolerate a wide range of salinity, they are said to be euryhaline. Two groups of native fishes make up the bulk of these species: the sculpin and killifish families (fig. 11.21).

The largest group of secondary freshwater fishes is the sculpins (Cottidae). This group has its origins in the north. It entered California by dispersal down the coast or from the northern Great Basin via the Pit River system. California has 10 species of sculpin associated primarily with fresh water. This is a small part of what is primarily a marine family. These are bottom fish that seldom exceed 4 inches (10 cm) in length. Their brown, mottled coloration conceals them as they lie motionless on the bottom. They have large, flattened heads and large, fanlike pectoral fins. These adaptations help them maintain position on the bottom, even in fast-flowing water.

The most abundant sculpin in California is the Prickly Sculpin, *Cottus asper* (fig. 11.21). It is a fish of northern affinities, ranging from Alaska to the Ventura River in southern California. They occupy a wide range of bottom habitats, from salt water to fresh water, and occur in all sorts of water quality and flow. Most typically, they inhabit low-elevation, moderate-sized streams with abundant sand-bottom to mud-

Cottidae
  Staghorn Sculpin
  Rough Sculpin
  Slender Sculpin
  Coastrange Sculpin
  Prickly Sculpin
  Pit Sculpin
  Marbled Sculpin
  Paiute Sculpin
  Riffle Sculpin
  Reticulate Sculpin

Cyprinodontidae
  California Killifish
  Desert Pupfish
  Owens Pupfish
  Amargosa Pupfish
  Salt Creek Pupfish
  Cottonball Marsh Pupfish

Gasterosteidae
  Threespine Stickleback

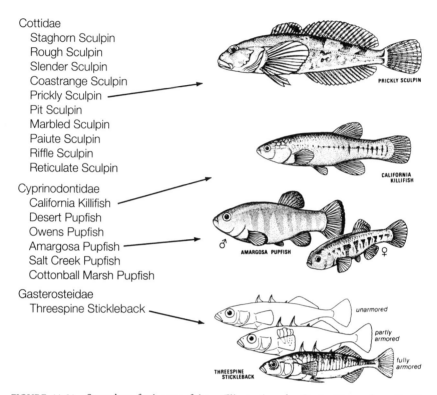

FIGURE 11.21   Secondary freshwater fishes. (Illustrations by Doris Alcorn from S. M. McGinnis. *Freshwater Fishes of California*. Berkeley: University of California Press, 1984.)

bottom pools. They feed on aquatic invertebrates that inhabit the bottom, particularly immature aquatic insects.

The reproductive behavior of Prickly Sculpins is interesting. They migrate downstream to breed, sometimes into salt water. Fishes that migrate to salt water to reproduce are said to be catadromous. Males construct a nest, usually under a large flat rock or other object on the bottom. These days, it may be in a beer can. Eggs are attached to the ceiling of the nest. The male defends the eggs and, with his pectoral fins, keeps a current of water flowing through the nest. After the fry hatch, for a few weeks they are members of the plankton community. They settle to the bottom and move slowly upstream to where their adult life will be spent.

Other species of sculpins have more restricted distribution, but it is not uncommon for similar species to occur together, making identification nearly impossible. Some species occur in a single drainage, and a few, such as the Paiute Sculpin (*Cottus beldingi*), have limited distribution in California. In the Pit River, three species may overlap.

The Paiute Sculpin occurs in Lake Tahoe and its tributaries and is locally common. In streams they occupy riffles, where they lie in wait until prey species come close enough to be grabbed. In Lake Tahoe they feed mostly at night. During daylight hours, they remain motionless in shallow water, relying on their coloration to conceal them.

These are the most abundant fish in the Lahontan system. In Sagehen Creek, densities of six adults per square meter have been recorded. Because this is also a trout stream, relationships between sculpins and trout have been studied. It has been determined that the diets of Paiute Sculpins and trout overlap by only 20%. Trout eat mostly drift organisms, and sculpins eat mostly what is on the bottom. In Lake Tahoe there is even less overlap (fig. 11.22). Moreover, a large part of the diet of trout is sculpins, so the ecological role of sculpins is as a forage fish. It is the link between the bottom-dwelling organisms and the top carnivores.

Killifish or tooth carps (Cyprinodontidae) reached California from the south. They are found worldwide in tropical freshwater and marine habitats. Because of their bright coloration and interesting behavior, many members of this family are popular aquarium fishes. The California Killifish, *Fundulus parvipinnis* (fig. 11.21), is a marine species that lives in brackish lagoons and estuaries as far north as the mouth of the Salinas River, near Monterey. In a few localities they have moved into fresh water. In San Juan Creek, in southern Orange County, an entirely freshwater population formerly existed near the town of San Juan Capistrano. This population has been extirpated by habitat destruction. San Juan Creek is now a concrete-lined ditch along its lower course. A freshwater species still survives near San Ignacio, Baja California.

Of greater interest, perhaps, are the pupfish (*Cyprinodon* spp.) (fig. 11.21) that inhabit warm, often saline bodies of water in the desert. In California there are five native species. Including the Death Valley system as a whole, there are seven species and six subspecies of pupfish and killifish in California and nearby Nevada. Each of these forms is characterized by a rather restricted distribution. The Devils Hole Pupfish, *Cyprinodon diabolis*, is a species 1 inch (25 mm) long that occupies a collapsed limestone cavern with about 180 square feet (20 m^2) of surface water. This is the smallest known range of any vertebrate animal in the world. While this area is technically in Nevada, it is in a detached portion of Death Valley National Monument that lies a few miles east of the California-Nevada border. Devils Hole is actually part of the largest oasis system in the Mojave Desert. This area is known as the Ash Meadows National Wildlife Refuge, and it contains 20 endemic species. This is the largest number of endemic plants, fish, and invertebrates for an area this size in the continental United States. It is the home of four endemic killifishes that are federally listed as endangered.

The species with the largest natural distribution in the southwest is the Desert Pupfish, *Cyprinodon macularius*. They were formerly common in sloughs and backwaters associated with the lower Colorado River and the Gila River in Arizona. This is the largest of the North American pupfish. Although they may reach 3 inches (75 mm) in length, they are seldom more than half that size. Typical of their preference for quiet water and aquatic vegetation, they are deep-bodied and slab-sided.

FIGURE 11.22 Feeding relationships of Lake Tahoe fishes, modified from R. G. Miller (1951). Numbers represent percentage of the diet by volume. Kokanee data are from Cordone et al. (1971). (From P. B. Moyle. *Inland Fishes of California.* Berkeley: University of California Press, 1976.)

Tolerance for environmental extremes is a notable feature of the Desert Pupfish. This is important because desert habitats experience wide variations in temperature, salinity, and dissolved oxygen. The critical thermal maximum of $112°F$ ($44.6°C$) for this species is the highest ever recorded for a species of fish. This ability to tolerate hot water also enables them to live in hot springs. In such a habitat the pupfish may feed on blue-green algae that live in water hotter than its critical thermal maximum. It does this by hovering in water as hot as it can tolerate and then darting into the hotter water for a quick bite of food. The thermal minimum of the Desert Pupfish is $40°F$ ($4.5°C$). The Owens Pupfish, *Cyprinodon radiosus*, lives under ice at Fish Slough, north of Bishop.

Also recorded for the Desert Pupfish is the lowest tolerated minimum for dissolved oxygen, at 0.13 mg/l. The species' range of tolerance for salinity is also high. Adult Desert Pupfish tolerate water from distilled to 70 g/l (twice the concentration of seawater). The Cottonball Marsh Pupfish, *Cyprinodon salinus milleri*, a resident of Death Valley, holds the record for the highest salinity tolerated by a fish. Living fish were observed in saline pools on the floor of Death Valley at five times the concentration of seawater.

Introduction of nonnative species and habitat destruction have threatened the fishes of the desert. Of the 18 kinds of California fishes listed as threatened or endangered, 10 are considered to be desert species. Four kinds of pupfish are on the list. The Cottonball Marsh Pupfish and the Tecopa Pupfish, *Cyprinodon nevadensis calidae*, are on the state list of threatened and endangered species. The Tecopa Pupfish is now extinct, however. The Owens Pupfish and the Desert Pupfish are listed by the federal and state governments as endangered.

The range of the Desert Pupfish has been diminished to two general localities in the United States. One population is in Quitobaquito Spring, in Organ Pipe Cactus National Monument in Arizona. The other population is in California and occurs in two streams that are tributaries of the Salton Sea. The species is found only in San Felipe Creek on the west side and Salt Creek on the east side of the Salton Sea (fig. 11.23). Formerly, they were the most common fishes in shoreline pools of the Salton Sea, but they have been all but eliminated from that habitat by interactions with introduced species of fishes.

Of course, the present Salton Sea is not a natural body of water, owing its continued existence to irrigation runoff. In prehistoric times the Salton Trough was occupied by Lake Cahuilla, (fig. 9.9), which dried about the year 1500, taking with it what was essentially an assemblage of fishes native to the Colorado River. The cause of its drying was a change in the direction of flow of the mouth of the Colorado River. It had been dumping into the Salton Trough, but as a result of southward meandering its flow was diverted into the Gulf of California. Estimates indicate that Lake Cahuilla took about 55 to 60 years to dry completely. Between 1840 and 1905, at least seven times the Salton Sea basin was reflooded by overflow from the Colorado River. The present body of water began with flooding of the Colorado River and rupturing of earthen irrigation ditches along the Mexican border. The Desert Pupfish was reintroduced to its former range at that time.

FIGURE 11.23   Desert Pupfish (*Cyprinodon macularius*) habitat in upper Salt Creek, Riverside County.

An interesting series of old waterlines lie on the west side of the Salton Sea. The highest waterline (fig. 9.9) is marked by a visible crust formed by precipitation of travertine ($CaCO_3$) in association with algae that lived along the shoreline. Lower waterlines are marked by rows of fish traps that were constructed by Cahuilla Indians. These traps consist of rows of rocks in a V shape. Fish that entered the structures were trapped by closing of the apex with a large rock. The rows of traps are nearly 5 feet (160 cm) apart in elevation, which corresponds to the known evaporation rate of water in the area today. Fifteen rows of traps mark the fall of water over a 15-year period. The absence of traps beyond that suggests that the lake became too saline for most of the large fish species preferred by the Indians. As the lake evaporated, it became unsuitable for the fishes that were more at home in fresh water of the lower Colorado River.

Runoff of irrigation water from fields in the Coachella and Imperial valleys continues to add water to the Salton Sea. The introduction of game fish from the Gulf of California has been successful, and a good sport fishery was established, although it is now threatened by increasing salinity and toxins such as selenium. Tests conducted by the U.S. Fish and Wildlife Service revealed concentrations of toxic substances comparable to the ill-fated Kesterson Wildlife Refuge, mentioned in chapter 10. The game fish, however, have not been the problem for the pupfish in the Salton Sea. Whereas predation probably eliminated them from the lower Colorado River, in the Salton Sea it was the introduction of small nonnative fishes that led to the decline. A total of 29 fish species have been recorded from drains and canals in the Salton Sea area. Only one of these was native—the Desert Pupfish.

Subtle behavioral interactions with two species seem to have caused the problem. Sailfin Mollies, *Poecilia latipinna*, were introduced about 1964. These are aquarium fish, and no one is certain how they were introduced. Male Sailfin Mollies seem to court any fish that is about the right size, regardless of species or sex. By 1979 these represented 98% of the fishes in shoreline pools. By sheer numbers they interfered with mating and courtship of the pupfish, which apparently escaped by moving into shallow water in the canals.

However, in 1973 the Coachella Valley Water District introduced a "weed-eating" fish to the canals in the hope that it would control the aquatic weeds. This fish, Zill's Cichlid, *Tilapia zilli*, is an aggressive African cichlid, but adults cannot live in water less than a few inches deep. Pupfish can live and breed in water about an inch (25 cm) deep, but juvenile cichlids in this shallow water can interfere with reproduction in the following way. A dominant male pupfish has a bright blue color and patrols a territory that it keeps clear of other males and other fishes. Females are lured into the area, where they lay eggs in the sand or in algal mats. The male responds by releasing sperm over the eggs and then vigorously guarding the spawn. However, when he is busy chasing intruders, subdominant males, which look like females, enter the spawning ground in an attempt to fertilize an egg or two. These are the "sneak" maters. In an attempt to maximize their contribution, they also eat some of the dominant male's spawn. Likewise, when the dominant male discovers another male's spawn, he eats it. The result is that if too much interference occurs, males eat each other's spawn, and reproduction is curtailed. Apparently, swarms of juvenile cichlids promote this kind of interference, and pupfish reproduction fails to keep up with the natural death rate.

The two habitats where Desert Pupfish are hanging on, San Felipe and Salt creeks, are small, interrupted streams. They are not ideal for pupfish, because there is not always quiet water and there are extreme variations in flow. As buffers against extinction, the species has several refugia in the Colorado Desert (pl. 8B).

How did all these pupfish of isolated drainages reach their habitats in the southwestern deserts? They all occur in tectonically active areas and may have experienced some degree of translocation along with migrating terranes. However, it is simpler to provide aquatic connections between the various localities. Similar to killifish, it seems that the pupfish's centers of origin are from the south. In some instances they are estuary dwellers, similar to the California Killifish. It appears that the Desert Pupfish or a very similar species inhabited the Bouse Embayment, a Mio-Pliocene estuary that covered what today is the lower Colorado River and the Salton Trough. Fossil pupfish of about that age are known from as far north as Nevada. Similarly, fossil killifish have been found as far north as Lake Lahontan, and fossil sticklebacks also occur throughout the southwest.

Retreat of the marine water from the Bouse Embayment could have left the pupfish isolated in streams and springs. During the Pleistocene, heavy precipitation in desert areas caused the formation of a series of interconnected lakes and streams with the

FIGURE 11.24   Mono–Death Valley drainage system during the Ice
Age (Pleistocene). (From M. Hill. *California Landscape: Origin and
Evolution.* Berkeley: University of California Press, 1984.)

general direction of flow toward Death Valley (fig. 11.24). Dispersal throughout the
system could have occurred at that time. The implication is that speciation among the
pupfishes occurred in the last 20,000 years, accompanied by reduction of precipitation
and stranding in isolated desert spring systems. It appears that all of the Death Valley
pupfishes evolved from the Desert Pupfish or a similar ancestor. Of particular interest
in this hypothesis is that the Owens Pupfish is the most closely related to the modern
Desert Pupfish, yet its range, in the upper Owens Valley, is the farthest away.

An alternative hypothesis is that, similar to the chubs, pupfish were carried from
latitudes of present-day Mexico in springs and streams west of the San Andreas fault.
During pluvial times they dispersed through the interconnecting system of desert
lakes. The absence of pupfish in Baja California and the Peninsular Ranges, however,
speaks against this hypothesis.

The stickleback family (Gasterosteidae) is the third group of secondary freshwater fishes in California. There is one species in California today, the Threespine Stickleback (*Gasterosteus aculeatus*) (fig. 11.21), although the fossil record indicates that in Miocene times, about 20 million years ago, there might have been several species. The family is abundant in Europe, northern Asia, and North America. It appears that in California its origin is from the south, in a pattern similar to that of the killifish family.

Sticklebacks are distributed in coastal streams and estuaries up and down the coast of California, and they are common throughout the Great Central Valley. Seldom over 3 inches (75 cm) in length, they have three sharp dorsal spines and a series of armored plates on each side. These features may help protect them from predation.

Sticklebacks have been divided into three subspecies on the basis of habitat. Anadromous populations spend most of their time in salt water and migrate into fresh water to spawn. They have been identified by some authorities as a subspecies. Those fish that spend their entire lives in freshwater have been named another subspecies. The anadromous form has plates of armor completely along each side, whereas the freshwater forms are armored only in the head regions. Finally, in the Los Angeles basin, there were populations that were unarmored. These have been identified as the third subspecies. They occurred as far south as San Juan Creek, where they were associates of the freshwater killifish. The Unarmored Threespine Stickleback, *Gasterosteus aculeatus williamsoni*, is now listed as endangered by the federal government. It occurs primarily in protected habitat in the Santa Clara and Cuyama rivers.

Recent studies have indicated that the degree of armoring is a function of predation pressure, and this has clouded the naming of subspecies. When the armored varieties are raised in habitats with no predators, they produce little or no armor. The mechanism for this variation has not been worked out, but it bears testimony to the genetic plasticity of this group.

Of special interest is the presence of sticklebacks in the upper reaches of the Mojave River drainage in Holcomb Valley, on the desert side of the San Bernardino Mountains. This is similar to the pattern of distribution of chubs and pond turtles. Some authorities contend that those on the desert side were introduced. However, those in Holcomb Valley are darkly pigmented, indicating that they represent a special variety that may have evolved in isolation. Recently, a population of the unarmored variety was discovered in a small creek near Big Bear Lake. The fact that this is an endangered subspecies disturbs plans for a major housing development in the area.

Breeding in sticklebacks has been studied heavily. Males develop a bright red belly in the breeding season. They defend territories among beds of aquatic plants. Fighting behavior in the males is stereotyped so that they do not kill each other. It has been determined that the signal to begin fighting is the sight of the red belly. The fight is stopped when the loser stands on his head to conceal the color, analogous to the submission posture assumed by deer and elk. Experimenters were able to elicit fighting behavior in male sticklebacks by placing in the water practically any object that was red on the bottom. Similarly, any object that resembles a female with a swollen belly will stimulate courtship.

Overall, breeding behavior is similar to that of sculpins. Males build nests, which they defend vigorously. After eggs are laid in the nest, the male causes water to circulate over them by fanning with his pectoral fins. After the eggs hatch, the male guards the school of fry. If one of the juveniles wanders from the school, the male picks it up in his mouth and spits it back into the school.

In spite of the armor, these are important forage fish. They are fed upon by trout and large chubs as well as predatory birds.

Marine Fishes. Salt water fishes that appear in fresh water are of three types. There are the anadromous species, which breed in fresh water; catadromous forms, which breed in salt water; and the true marine species, which may have a single member that has become adapted to fresh water (fig. 11.25).

The most economically important anadromous fishes are salmon, which are in the same family (Salmonidae) as the trout. There are five species in California waters, although two of them make up the bulk of the catch. Chinook and Coho Salmon are the most common. Sea-run Rainbow Trout, known as Steelhead, are another important anadromous fish.

Chinook Salmon, *Oncorhynchus tshawytscha* (fig. 11.25), are also known as King Salmon. These are the largest of the Pacific salmon, reaching 31 inches (80 cm) in length. The California record for weight of these salmon is 88 pounds (40 kg). These are the least abundant of the Pacific salmon, but in California they are the most common. In good years they make up 90% of the commercial salmon catch. In addition, up to 130,000 are caught each year by sport fishermen.

In years past, Chinook Salmon spawned as far south as the Ventura River. Today they are concentrated from the Sacramento River northward. Historically, the Sacramento–San Joaquin system supported a substantial run of Chinook Salmon, but about 96% of the historic salmon habitat in that river system is gone. Formerly, most spawning took place in the autumn when the first rains increased stream flow and lowered the water temperature to 77°F (25°C) or less. For maximum egg survival, water temperature must be less than 57°F (19°C). Eggs laid in the autumn hatch in spring and embryos remain in stream gravel for a few weeks. When hatchlings emerge from the gravel, they migrate downstream and enter the sea at about two months of age. This rapid exit from fresh water is an adaptation to California's Mediterranean climate. It is associated with the tendency for California streams to experience very low flow or drying in the summer. This phenomenon seems to explain why Chinook Salmon, the least abundant of the Pacific salmon, are the most common in California. Among salmon, they stay in fresh water for the shortest period of time. These autumn runs are a thing of the past in most rivers because dams now regulate the flow, in some cases blocking the salmon runs completely.

An interesting variant behavior has developed for salmon in the Sacramento River. Water is released from Shasta Dam in order to provide consistent supplies for irrigation. This water comes from the bottom of Shasta Reservoir and is therefore cold. This cold water creates havoc for many of the native species of freshwater fishes that require warm water to spawn, but it has stimulated increased spring spawning in

ANADROMOUS

Petromyzontidae
  Pacific Lamprey
  River Lamprey
  Pacific Brook Lamprey
  Pit-Klamath Lamprey
  Kern Brook Lamprey

PACIFIC LAMPREY

Acipenseridae
  White Sturgeon
  Green Sturgeon

lateral plates

WHITE STURGEON

Salmonidae
  Pink Salmon
  Chum Salmon
  Coho Salmon
  Chinook Salmon
  Sockeye Salmon
  Steelhead

round spots
both lobes

KING OR CHINOOK
SALMON

Osmeridae
  Eulachon

EULACHON

CATADROMOUS

Mugilidae
  Striped Mullet

STRIPED MULLET

TRUE MARINE FISHES

BAY PIPEFISH

Syngnathidae
  Bay Pipefish

Gobiidae
  Tidewater Goby

TIDEWATER GOBY

Pleuronectidae
  Starry Flounder

STARRY FLOUNDER

FIGURE 11.25   Marine fishes found in fresh water. (Illustrations by Doris Alcorn from S. M. McGinnis. *Freshwater Fishes of California.* Berkeley: University of California Press, 1984. Bay Pipefish from S. Hinton. *Seashore Life of Southern California.* Berkeley: University of California Press, 1987.)

Chinook Salmon. Although there always have been some fish that would spawn in the upper, perennially cool portions of the drainages, there are now more fish that run upstream in midwinter and spawn in spring. Eggs laid in the spring hatch in late summer. This has created two major seasons for salmon hatching, which has the potential to greatly increase productivity throughout the state.

Adult salmon spend five to seven years at sea, after which they return to their home stream to spawn. They die soon after. Elaborate experiments on migrating salmon have determined that they recognize their home stream by its odor. Furthermore, they migrate up and down the coast using visual cues such as polarized light and, possibly, familiar submarine landmarks.

Coho Salmon, *Oncorhynchus kisutch*, are known also as Silver Salmon. These may reach a length of 2 feet (60 cm), and the California record for weight is 22 pounds (10 kg). Unlike Chinook Salmon, Coho Salmon spend at least a year in fresh water before they move out to sea. They spawn in cooler, smaller streams than the Chinook Salmon, and they are absent from intermittent streams. At sea they spend most of their time near the coast within 100 miles (160 km) or so of their home stream.

There are two kinds of male spawners. Sneak-mating males, known as jacks, grow and mature rapidly. These males are smaller than the large, hook-jawed males that return from the sea after three to five years. These large males actually grow and mature more slowly than the jacks, but by defending territories they contribute more offspring to future generations. The sneaks, on the other hand, by reproducing early without going to sea, are more likely to live long enough to reproduce.

Coho are the easiest salmon to raise in hatcheries. Furthermore, they can spend their entire lives in fresh water. Larger and larger numbers of hatchery-raised salmon are being released in California rivers. The result of this program is that, in spite of habitat degradation, particularly because of logging, the total number of Coho Salmon seems to be increasing. Coho Salmon "Silvers" are also being planted in many large lakes and reservoirs, where they feed on introduced schooling fishes such as Threadfin Shad. These salmon now occur in catchable numbers in lakes such as Lake Berryessa and in reservoirs such as Lake Mead on the Colorado River.

The decline in numbers of salmon has been a significant factor in the economic collapse of the Pacific Northwest. The cause of the decline is controversial. Loggers and dam builders blame fishermen, and vice versa. Commercial fishermen blame Indians, and vice versa. All are to blame to some degree. The combination of overfishing and habitat destruction has reduced the salmon harvest to a fraction of its former numbers. Warm water associated with the El Niño condition of the early 1980s also had an effect, and warm water released from low reservoirs during the drought of the late 1980s practically wiped out the Sacramento River winter runs. Both winter-run Chinook and Coho Salmon are being considered for endangered status.

The Klamath River and its tributaries remain the most productive salmon fishery in California. Prior to 1900, migrating fish could travel all the way to its headwaters. Today the few dams on the Klamath system are near its headwaters. Iron Gate Dam regulates the main flow near the Oregon border. Nevertheless, from there to the coast the Klamath flows as a wild river, and the fall run of salmon is still significant.

Furthermore, the Smith River system, to the north of the Klamath, still is a wild river.

The American salmon fishermen and the federal government have worked out fishing quotas in an attempt to prevent overfishing. The quota system, however, is complicated by Russian and Asian fishing boats, which are less likely to respect our attempts to limit harvest. Furthermore, Canadian interests must be respected. Last but not least is the issue of native fishing rights. Indians are allowed to fish without regard to seasons, limits, or techniques, so long as their catch is for subsistence only. In effect, this tends to promote illegal sales of salmon by Indians, who view it as their inalienable right to catch salmon whenever, wherever, and however. Obviously, for the benefit of all concerned, there must be limits on the total harvest. Details of those limits must be worked out cooperatively and adhered to, or else all concerned parties, especially the fish, will lose.

Of special interest among anadromous species are the lampreys (Petromyzontidae), eel-like fishes with no paired fins. They are remnants of a very primitive group of jawless fishes, the Agnatha. There are six species in California, and their distribution is similar to that of salmon. Two of the species are predatory. These are the Pacific Lamprey, *Lampetra tridentata* (fig. 11.25), and the River Lamprey, *Lampetra ayresi*. The Pacific Lamprey is the largest, reaching two feet (60 cm) in length. The River Lamprey is half the size.

The life history of these lampreys is interesting because the larval stage is long and the adult stage is short. Larvae are sedentary filter feeders. They live for five to seven years in mud-bottom streams with their heads projected into flowing water. They metamorphose when they are but a few inches in length. The two predatory species migrate to the sea, where they prey on soft-bellied fishes such as salmon or herring. As adults, they have a suction cup for a mouth, which they use to attach to the belly of a fish. With their rasplike tongue they scrape a hole in the fish and suck out body fluids. Some authorities prefer to call these fish parasites because they do not eat their prey in its entirety, and sometimes the prey species is not killed. As adults, they live in the sea one or two years, after which they return to fresh water to spawn. Similar to salmon, they die after spawning.

The four species of brook lamprey remain in the fresh water their entire lives. Most have restricted distribution. The Pacific Brook Lamprey, *Lampetra pacifica*, enjoys the widest distribution, occurring in streams along the north coast and the Sacramento–San Joaquin delta. They also have been reported in the Los Angeles basin. These are not predatory, because adults do not feed, living only long enough to reproduce. Larvae live about four years as filter feeders. In order to reproduce, they metamorphose at about 8 inches (20 cm) in length. Similar to the strategy of many aquatic insects, the adult stage is for reproduction only.

The sturgeon family (Acipenseridae) includes two anadromous species in California. The Green Sturgeon, *Acipenser medirostris*, is not common in fresh water, although some specimens are found in the Klamath, Sacramento, and San Joaquin rivers. The White Sturgeon, *Acipenser transmontanus* (fig. 11.25), spawns in these large rivers. This is America's largest freshwater fish, reaching lengths in excess of 13 feet (4 m).

They grow slowly and live up to 100 years. They become sexually mature at about 13 years of age. They are cherished for their tasty roe, which is American caviar.

Because of their long life and late maturity, these fish do not respond well to environmental disturbance. They were common "nuisance" fish in the late 1800s, but an acquired taste for caviar and sturgeon flesh nearly extirpated them by 1909, when commercial fishing for them was halted. They have recovered slowly, and it is now legal to fish for them as a game fish.

Sturgeon are cigar-shaped with large diamond-shaped scales. Their mouths are underneath a broad, flat, sharklike nose. They have barbels with taste buds near the mouth, which they use to search in the mud for food. They have a mouth that resembles a flexible suction hose, which they use to slurp up invertebrates and carrion in the mud. Fishermen in the Sacramento–San Joaquin delta fish for them using small grass shrimp as bait. Sometimes, because of its value as a delicacy, all they keep is the egg mass, which they call "black gold." Also because of the value of the caviar, a program has been initiated to raise sturgeons in fish hatcheries.

The smelt family (Osmeridae) includes a number of small schooling species that are important forage fishes in bays and lagoons. The Eulachon, or Candlefish, *Thaleichthys pacificus* (fig. 11.25), is an anadromous form that in spring spawns in the Klamath River and a few small streams in Humboldt and Del Norte counties. In spite of their oily flesh, many people enjoy eating them. It is legal to fish for them with a dipnet. Indians not only ate them, but dried and burned them as if they were candles. They are important forage species for salmon and sturgeon. Other smelt species are also sometimes found in fresh water. For example, the Delta Smelt, *Hypomesus transpacificus*, a candidate endangered species, occurs in fresh water of the lower Sacramento and San Joaquin rivers. One species, the Wakasagi, *Hypomesus nipponensis*, was introduced to a few reservoirs as a forage fish and subsequently found its way into most northern coastal rivers.

The mullets (Mugilidae) are estuary fishes. In the lower Colorado River they are catadromous, returning to seawater to reproduce. California's only species, the Striped Mullet, *Mugil cephalus* (fig. 11.25), is conspicuous in estuaries and bays. For unknown reasons, they are often seen leaping from the water. They reach about 2 feet (60 cm) in length, and when a fish this size leaps clear of the water and lands on its side with a resounding smack, it is conspicuous. They feed on detritus, so they are seldom caught on a hook, but they are tasty eating. They invaded the Salton Sea soon after it began to fill, and by 1915 they were so numerous that a successful commercial fishery developed for them. They were netted in great numbers. Commercial fishing ceased in the early 1950s. They are now extinct in the Salton Sea, presumably because it is too saline for the eggs.

Of the true marine fishes that occur in fresh water, there are three families with a single member that may have incidental distribution in fresh water. Bay Pipefish, *Syngnathus leptorhynchus* (fig. 11.25), are small, green, elongated fish that live in eelgrass. They are in the seahorse family (Syngnathidae), and, similar to seahorses, eggs are incubated in brood pouches of males. They have been found living in beds of filamentous green algae in the Navarro River in Mendocino County.

The flounder family (Pleuronectidae) is a group of bottom-dwelling flatfish. They are notable for having both eyes on the same side of their head, so they may lie on their sides, flat on the bottom. The Starry Flounder, *Platichthys stellatus* (fig. 11.25), is relatively common in fresh water in the Sacramento–San Joaquin delta and various coastal streams. They have even made it into San Luis Reservoir by way of the California Aqueduct. When found in fresh water, they are not always in good condition.

The goby family (Gobiidae) is a group of bottom-dwelling fishes that superficially resemble the sculpins. Unlike the sculpins, these fishes have a peculiar suction cup formed by fusion of the pelvic fins on the front half of their underside. This suction cup helps to hold them on rocks in the intertidal zone, where there may be waves to contend with. In fresh water, the suction cup helps hold them on the bottom in flowing water. The Tidewater Goby, *Eucyclogobius newberryi* (fig. 11.25), is the only native species that enters fresh water. They have a wide range of distribution from San Diego to Arcata, but they are not common except in the Morro Bay area. The introduced Yellowfin Goby, *Acanthogobius flavemanus*, is becoming increasingly common in fresh water in California. It is native to the coast of Japan, Korea, and China. It was first discovered in 1963, in the Sacramento–San Joaquin delta. It probably arrived from the Orient, attached by its sucker to the bottom of a boat.

Amphibians

There are many unique, interesting species of amphibians in California, all limited to some degree by the distribution of water. Because salamanders are largely terrestrial, they have been discussed in association with the specific regions where they are common. Frogs, on the other hand, are largely aquatic. Their larvae (tadpoles) develop in water, and the adults leave water only temporarily.

There are only three native species in the "true" frog family (Ranidae) that enjoy widespread distribution in California. The state's largest native frog is the Red-legged Frog, *Rana aurora*. Its body length may reach 5 inches (13 cm). This is a pond frog. Formerly it was common in lowland, slow-moving waters and marshes throughout the state except for the Great Central Valley and deserts.

Breeding behavior of Red-legged Frogs is typical of the group. For protection from predators, they mate at night. In late winter, when day length begins to increase, males gather in ponds and begin to "sing." These breeding choruses are designed to attract females. If a female is ready to breed, she will call back. Frogs hear well, possessing large eardrums on the sides of their heads. A male is able to locate the position of the female by sound alone. Upon hearing her call, he will swim toward her. Upon reaching her, he climbs on her back and grasps her by the armpits. This is called amplexus. During the breeding season, males have an enlarged nuptial bump on the first finger of each hand. This bump is apparently important for tactile stimulation of the female's armpits, causing her to lay eggs. From a position on her back, the male is able to shed sperm over the eggs as they are laid. Floating masses of fertilized eggs develop into tadpoles.

Communication between male and female is largely acoustic. A male attempting to locate the female that responded to his call will grasp anything in the water that is the proper size. If he grasps a female that is not ready to shed eggs or if he grasps another male, the unwilling partner will utter a warning croak. If no warning croak is uttered, the male assumes he has grasped a willing female. Unfortunately, if he grasps a rock, log, or beer can of the right size and texture, he has no choice but to hang on and wait for something to happen. Fortunately, if nothing has happened by dawn, the clear light of day will reveal the mistake, sending the frustrated lover into hiding until the next night. In frog mating systems, the rule of thumb is, "If an object is silent, too large to eat, but not large enough to eat you, hang on for dear life."

California's largest frog is the introduced Bullfrog, *Rana catesbeiana*. This is the frog whose booming call is sometimes described as "jug-o-rum." This species is native east of the Rockies, but because frog legs are a delicacy, it has been introduced all over the west. These frogs may reach 8 inches (20 cm) in body length. They are highly predatory, feeding on crayfish, frogs, and fishes. Sometimes they even eat small snakes! Unfortunately for the native Red-legged Frog, the two species occur in the same habitat. What habitat destruction has not done, the Bullfrog has through resource utilization and predation. The Red-legged Frog is now becoming scarce.

At higher elevations the Red-legged Frog is replaced by the Foothill Yellow-legged Frog, *Rana boylei* (fig. 11.26A). The body length of these frogs is seldom over 3 inches (8 cm). The underside of the legs and the belly are yellow. This is a frog of rivers and streams, but it does not occur south of the San Gabriel Mountains. It occurs in riffles, where it rests with head and body out of the water, counting on its mottled yellow coloration to conceal it. If alarmed, it dives into the water and remains motionless at the bottom of the pool. For inexplicable reasons, this frog species is disappearing from its known habitat. It is now believed to be gone in the San Gabriel Mountains.

In the Sierra Nevada above 6000 feet (1800 m), the Foothill Yellow-legged Frog is replaced by the Mountain Yellow-legged Frog, *Rana muscosa* (fig. 11.26B). In southern California, from the San Gabriel Mountains to Mount Palomar, this species occurs in the habitat of the Foothill Yellow-legged Frog. At two localities in the San Gabriel Mountains, Bear Creek and the North Fork of the San Gabriel River, the two species formerly coexisted. Unfortunately for the Foothill Yellow-legged Frog, much of its habitat in the lower reaches of the San Gabriel drainage has been destroyed by dams and off-road vehicles. The Foothill Yellow-legged Frog has not been seen in the San Gabriel Mountains since the early 1960s.

The Mountain Yellow-legged Frog, the common frog of the high Sierra, has habits similar to those of the Foothill Yellow-legged Frog. It lives in a harsh habitat up to 12,000 feet (4000 m) in elevation, and it breeds when lakes and streams are ice-free. Tadpoles are then faced with a serious problem: They must grow and metamorphose in an abbreviated season. Because the growing season is so short in the high country, tadpoles may overwinter for two years. undergoing metamorphosis during their third season. Postponing metamorphosis provides another advantage for these frogs, because the larvae are better able than the adults to tolerate conditions of low oxygenation under the ice. In an attempt to optimize temperature conditions that will accelerate

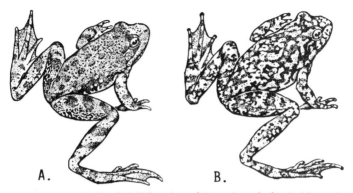

FIGURE 11.26   *A*. Foothill Yellow-legged Frog, *Rana boylei*. *B*. Mountain Yellow-legged Frog, *Rana muscosa*. (From R. C. Stebbins. *Amphibians of Western North America*. Berkeley: University of California Press, 1951.)

growth, larvae spend daylight hours basking in shallow water, usually on granite slabs, where the water temperature may warm considerably. They feed on algae that accumulate on these rocks as well. At night they move to deeper water, where heat is retained. While basking in shallow water, the tadpoles are protected from predation by fishes, but when they move to deeper water, they are fed on by trout. In shallow water, where they are relatively free from predation by trout, Yellow-legged Frogs may become very common. Trout fishermen are aware that a lake with a large frog population seldom is good for fishing, and it has been documented that frog populations decline after trout are introduced.

Adult Yellow-legged Frogs produce an odorous mucous that helps protect them from predation, but they still are fed upon by fishes, garter snakes, and birds. Brewer's Blackbird, *Euphagus cyanocephalus*, and Clark's Nutcracker, *Nucifraga columbiana* (fig. 5.12), have been observed to gather at the water's edge and feed upon the frogs as they emerge from the water during metamorphosis. Tadpoles may also be fed upon by California Gulls, *Larus californicus*, and Great Blue Herons, *Ardea herodias* (pl. 14E). Like the Foothill Yellow-legged Frog, the Mountain Yellow-legged Frog is disappearing. Although solid evidence is lacking, predation by introduced trout is believed to be a significant factor in its decline.

The Spotted Frog, *Rana pretiosa*, occurs on the Modoc Plateau in cold streams and pools. This is a frog of the northern Great Basin. Its range barely extends into California. A relative of the Spotted Frog is the Cascades Frog, *Rana cascadae*. This mountain frog occurs in habitats similar to those of Yellow-legged Frogs, ranging from Mount Lassen northward in the Cascade Mountains. When disturbed, unlike Yellow-legged Frogs they swim rather than remaining motionless on the bottom.

The most common frog in the United States is the Northern Leopard Frog, *Rana pipiens*. The natural range of this frog barely reaches California along its eastern border, where it may occur in isolated, sporadic localities in the desert. A small population in San Felipe Creek on the southwestern side of the Salton Sea represents an endangered subspecies. Because the Northern Leopard Frog is the familiar laboratory frog, it has been introduced all over the state. Feeling pity for them, students, faculty, and researchers release them in nature when they have outlived their usefulness in the lab. This is a very bad practice. It introduces not only an aggressive competitor, but many unwanted diseases as well.

Another introduced frog that has created havoc for native species is the African Clawed Frog, *Xenopus laevis*. This is a member of a family of tongueless frogs (Pipidae) that is not even native to North America. The species was originally imported for the purpose of conducting human pregnancy tests. When injected with urine from a pregnant woman, a female African Clawed Frog responds to hormones in the urine and ovulates. It is now known that a similar reaction occurs in many native species as well. Because it is completely aquatic, the African Clawed Frog also became popular as an aquarium species. It is easy to maintain, and the species in captivity is known to live 15 years.

The sources of African Clawed Frogs that have been released into the wild are not known, but once they become established they multiply rapidly and become major predators. As adults they seem to have no natural enemies. Their skin secretions are distasteful, if not poisonous, to all known potential predators. In reservoirs, large predatory fish keep them under control by eating the tadpoles, but in streams or small ponds the frogs take over. One of the most serious situations occurred in the Santa Clara River of Los Angeles County, critical habitat for the endangered Unarmored Threespine Stickleback. African Clawed Frogs appeared in 1978 in a tributary of the Santa Clara River. A decade later they had moved into the area occupied by sticklebacks and threatened to wipe out the population. The California Department of Fish and Game has begun a program of trapping to remove the frog. It is hoped that, at the very least, they can keep the population small enough to prevent obliteration of a fish that is listed as endangered by the state and federal governments.

Many people confuse frogs with toads. "True" toads are in the family Bufonidae. Frogs are mostly aquatic, but toads as adults are mostly terrestrial. Toads have rough skin that is nearly waterproof, and most can also be distinguished by a thin yellow stripe down their backs along the midline. Their hind legs are shorter than those of frogs, and when they are on land they commonly walk rather than hop. They hop mainly when they are excited. In addition, the web between their toes is not nearly as well developed as it is in frogs.

The Western Toad, *Bufo boreas*, occurs statewide in all habitats except the southern deserts. It is the common toad found in residential gardens. South of Kaiser Pass in Fresno County, it occurs all the way up into the alpine zone. Similar to frogs, they breed in water. During the dry season, in order to estivate, they may bury themselves in loose soil or enter rodent burrows.

In desert areas, there are several species of toads with localized distribution. These have behavioral habits very much like those of the spadefoot toads (*Scaphiopus* spp.) that were discussed in chapter 9. The largest "desert" species is a toad known as the Colorado River Toad, *Bufo alvarius* (fig. 11.27). It occurs on flood plains along the lower Colorado River and may be up to 6 inches (15 cm) in body length. It is

FIGURE 11.27   Colorado River Toad, *Bufo alvarius*.

renowned for its toxic secretions. Native animals know instinctively to avoid these creatures, but occasionally a domestic dog will bite one. The result is copious frothing of the mouth and temporary paralysis. It could seriously harm a small dog. The Colorado River Toad is becoming scarce. It is apparently a victim of the dams that no longer allow periodic flooding.

A truly remarkable toad of the high Sierra Nevada is the Yosemite Toad, *Bufo canorus* (fig. 11.28). These toads inhabit high-country meadows from about 6500 to 11,500 feet (2000–3500 m). They breed in temporary ponds fed by snowmelt and in the warm shallows of permanent lakes. One of the places where they have been studied is Dana Meadows, near Tioga Pass. This is the same area where populations of Belding's Ground Squirrels were studied.

Unlike other frogs and toads, Yosemite Toads are diurnal. This change in behavior is necessitated by the cold alpine nights. Yosemite Toads are the only toads with distinct sexual dimorphism. The males and females differ in size and color. Adult females are about 3 inches (75 mm) in body length, and they are gray or brown with distinct dark blotches on the back. Males are slightly smaller, and they are olive green with only faintly visible blotches. The different colors may be associated with protective coloration, or they may be related to reproduction.

Perhaps the different coloration of the two sexes is related to visual mating cues, a process associated with daytime mating. Females spend daylight hours in meadows or foraging at the meadow's edge under willows, where the blotched pattern may help conceal them. Males spend much of their time floating in shallow water or sitting at the water's edge attempting to entice females to mate. Similar to other true toads, males utter a musical trill. Females attracted by the call move to ponds, and mating

MALE   FEMALE

FIGURE 11.28   Yosemite Toad, *Bufo canorus*. Note the different size and appearance of the two sexes. (From R. C. Stebbins. *Amphibians of Western North America*. Berkeley: University of California Press, 1951.)

proceeds in a manner similar to that described for frogs. Unlike other frogs and toads, there are silent males, too. The silent males are "sneak" maters. They sit or float near the calling males, and when receptive females approach the calling males, the silent males attempt to intercept them.

Yosemite Toads hibernate in rodent burrows or in cracks under rocks and logs, emerging when the snow melts from their winter refuges. They are most vulnerable when they cross snowfields. At this time they are quite conspicuous to predators such as California Gulls and Clark's Nutcrackers. The noxious secretions that discourage most predators seem not to bother these birds. Nutcrackers have been observed to wipe the toads repeatedly on the ground before swallowing them. Presumably, this removes some of the secretion.

Walking on snow seems as if it would impose a hardship for an ectothermic creature such as a toad. Yosemite Toads cope with the problem in a way that might be expected: They walk on their toes with their bellies well elevated. Once off the snow, they bask in the sun to restore body heat.

After mating, eggs develop quickly in warm, shallow water and hatch in about 10 days. After they hatch, tadpoles move and feed in the ponds. Similar to the tadpoles of the Mountain Yellow-legged Frog, they gather in the shallows during daylight hours and move to deeper water at night. It takes seven to eight weeks for metamorphosis to occur. After that there may only be a few weeks of vigorous feeding before the adults must enter hibernation. Adults eat a variety of arthropods, including things such as millipedes, spiders, and bees that other predators find distasteful.

During their larval stages, toads are preyed upon by birds and fishes. In temporary ponds where fishes are absent, major predators are diving beetles and dragonfly larvae. The major cause of death, however, is dehydration. Often the pond dries out before they have had enough time to metamorphose.

In order for toads to avoid death by desiccation, early breeding is a necessity. On the other hand, if toads emerge and breed too early, an unexpected spring snowstorm can cause high mortality. Once the males break hibernation, they do not have the energy stores to reenter the dormant state. One feature of a toad population that serves as insurance against mass mortality is that all of them do not emerge from hibernation at the same time. During a year when spring arrives early and the weather remains favorable, toads that emerge early have an advantage. A late spring storm favors those that emerge later. Variation in the biological clock that regulates hibernation is a necessity in dealing with such vagaries of climate. Similar to the Yellow-legged Frogs, Yosemite Toad populations are on the decline. In fact, amphibian populations in general seem to have declined since the 1960s. Although these declines are not easy to explain, they will bear watching by the scientific community. Like canaries in a mine, loss of amphibians may be a signal that serious widespread environmental degradation is occurring.

Treefrogs (Hylidae) also are common in aquatic habitats. These are small frogs, about 2 inches (5 cm) in total length. They are easily recognized by their long legs and adhesive toe pads. These frogs are agile jumpers. A person driving along a canyon road on a rainy night might be surprised to see these little frogs crossing the road in giant leaps that may carry them over 3 feet (1 m) into the air.

Most common of the treefrogs is the Pacific Treefrog, *Hyla* (= *Pseudacris*) *regilla* (fig. 11.29A). They have a black eyestripe and occur in a variety of colors, but most often they are greenish. In a few minutes, they are able to change color to match their surroundings. These are the most commonly heard frogs in California. Their call may be described as a loud two-part sound, "kreck-ek." It is the call of this frog that has been joked about. Many people think the call sounds like "rib-bit."

Pacific Treefrogs occur in every freshwater habitat from the coast to over 11,000 feet (3350 m) in the mountains. In spite of its name, this is chiefly a ground dweller. Its usual habitat is in low vegetation along the borders of slow-moving water such as marshes, ponds, and roadside ditches. In alpine meadows, they may be found in habitats similar to the Yosemite Toad. In the Sierra Nevada they are even known to inhabit talus on the edges of alpine lakes. Treefrogs breed in the spring, although breeding choruses in southern California have been heard as early as December. Mating behavior is similar to that of other frogs. The Pacific Treefrog usually calls from a floating position near the shore, in shallow water.

The other treefrog in California is known as the California Treefrog, *Hyla* (= *Pseudacris*) *cadaverina* (fig. 11.29B). A southern California species, it occurs in canyons of the Transverse and Peninsular ranges from the foothills to about 3000 feet (900 m) elevation. It is less common on the desert sides of the mountains, but it does occur in palm oases in the Colorado Desert. Adults of this species are usually light gray

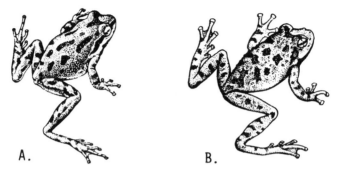

FIGURE 11.29 Treefrogs. A. Pacific Treefrog, *Hyla regilla*. B. California Treefrog, *Hyla cadaverina*. (From R. C. Stebbins. *Amphibians of Western North America*. Berkeley: University of California Press, 1951.)

and exhibit marvelous protective coloration. They tend to rest in depressions on large rocks, a situation that gives these boulders a warty appearance. Close inspection is required to discern that the lumps on the rocks are actually frogs.

At some localities in southern California, the two treefrogs occur together. Simultaneous breeding choruses have been observed in the western San Gabriel Mountains and the Santa Susana Mountains. At these localities, the Pacific Treefrog calls from a floating position in the water, and the California Treefrog calls from the water's edge. The California Treefrog utters a short, ducklike quack. It seldom produces a two-part sound similar to that of the Pacific Treefrog.

Formerly, the California Treefrog was considered to be the same species as the Canyon Treefrog of Arizona and New Mexico. An interesting investigation into speciation revealed that the California populations were, in fact, a different species. The two species are nearly identical in appearance, and even experts have difficulty telling them apart. The two populations, however, do not overlap. Most of the Colorado Desert lies between ranges of the two species. In nature, it would not be possible for a California Treefrog to meet a Canyon Treefrog; therefore there is no opportunity for them to breed with each other. If they could interbreed and produce fertile offspring, we would be obligated to call them one species even though their ranges do not overlap. On the other hand, if they are identical in appearance and their ranges do not overlap, what is there to make us believe that they are not the same species with a divided range? In listening to the calls of the two species, experts noted that the Canyon Treefrog makes a 1- to 3-second whirring noise on one note, rather than the short burst of sound uttered by the California species. As might be expected, recordings of the calls played for members of the other species fail to attract attention. If their mating calls are different, they can't attract a mate, and they won't reproduce. But suppose they did mate. Could they produce fertile offspring? Artificial insemination studies in the laboratory solved the question. Eggs fertilized by sperm from the opposite species failed to develop. The two frogs of identical appearance are therefore two separate species.

FIGURE 11.30 Tailed Frog, *Ascaphus truei*. (From R. C. Stebbins. *Amphibians of Western North America*. Berkeley: University of California Press, 1951.)

One other amphibian should be mentioned. This is the Tailed Frog, *Ascaphus truei*, (fig. 11.30), sometimes incorrectly known as the Bell Toad. Their range and habitat, in rapidly flowing coastal streams from Washington south to Humboldt County, are similar to those of the Olympic Salamander. They are very primitive frogs. What appears to be a tail is actually a copulatory organ that the male uses to transfer sperm to the cloaca of the female. These are unique frogs because fertilization is internal. After birth, larvae cling to rocks in fast-moving water with a suction cup sort of mouth. By this means they are even able to maintain position in waterfalls. This is a marvelous mechanism for larvae to develop in an environment free of predators.

Reptiles

Few reptiles are characteristically riparian in distribution. In California, there are two general kinds: garter snakes and turtles. Garter snakes (*Thamnophis* spp.) (= *Nerodea* spp.) get their name from their resemblance to a colorful garter. Most of them are of moderate size, although large ones reach about 4 feet (130 cm) in total length. They usually have a yellow stripe down the back and two lateral stripes. Their heads are slightly wider than the body, which leads some people to confuse them with rattlesnakes. Because they swim well, some uninformed persons call them water moccasins. Water moccasins do not occur west of Texas.

Garter snakes usually occur around or in water. They feed on all sorts of animals, including fishes, salamanders. frogs, toads, small mammals, and birds. Sometimes they remain motionless underwater, waiting for a fish or tadpole to come close enough to be nabbed. Very few animals prey on garter snakes. When they are molested, they curl around the molestor and defecate. Mixed with the excrement is material secreted from musk glands. The combination produces an odorous excretion designed to convince the predator that this item is too disgusting to eat. It is likely that the bright colors are part of a warning system to advertise that fact.

Classification of the different garter snakes in California has been a complex problem. There are three common species, all of which overlap their distribution in the Coast Ranges and northern California. In the Klamath Mountains, a fourth species enters the picture: the Northwestern Garter Snake, *Thamnophis ordinoides*, which reaches its southernmost distribution in California. Garter snakes are absent from the desert regions except for one species. The Checkered Garter Snake, *Thamnophis marcianus*, has moved into the Colorado Desert from the east by following irrigation ditches and canals.

It would be time-consuming to describe each of the three common species, but the only one that lacks the central stripe down its back is the Western Aquatic Garter Snake, *Thamnophis couchii*. This snake ranges throughout the state except in the deserts. It is the most common one in southern California. Above about 8000 feet (2400 m), particularly in the Sierra Nevada, the only garter snake is the Western Terrestrial Garter snake, *Thamnophis elegans*. In spite of its name, it occurs in and around water. The most colorful of the group is the Common Garter Snake, *Thamnophis sirtalis*. These snakes usually have red on the sides and may have blue-green bellies. They are most common in the Coast Ranges.

There is only one native species of turtle in California. The Western Pond Turtle, *Clemmys marmorata* (fig. 7.26), occurs in streams, marshes, and ponds of the Coast Ranges, Transverse Ranges, Peninsular Ranges, and the Great Central Valley. In the desert area, they only occur in the Mojave River. These are sedentary animals, spending lots of time basking. They feed on aquatic plants, insects, and carrion. Distribution of this turtle in southern California, in association with destruction of riparian habitats, is becoming seriously diminished.

Other aquatic turtles in California have been introduced. In some cases, the introductions have occurred because people have released unwanted pets. It is sometimes possible to find a Snapping Turtle, *Chelydra serpentina*, a large-headed turtle with a sharp ridge along its back whose powerful jaws are capable of inflicting a serious wound. Apparently it has not yet established a breeding population in California. The Common Slider or Red-eared Slider, *Pseudemys* (= *Trachemys*) *scripta*, resembles the native pond turtle, but the slider has a red line on each side of its face. Breeding populations of this turtle have become established at a variety of localities in California. The Painted Turtle, *Chrysemys picta*, sometimes available in pet stores, also resembles the Western Pond Turtle. Although this species is sometimes found in the wild in California, breeding populations apparently have not become established.

The other turtle is the Spiny Softshell, *Trionyx spiniferus*, a species introduced into the lower Colorado River. This is a pancake-shaped turtle up to a foot (30 cm) in length with a long protrusible neck. One of these turtles may be seen floating along with the current, with only its head above water. They have a long, narrow, flat-tipped nose with two large nostrils at the tip. In quiet backwaters, they will bury themselves in the mud. From time to time, in order to breathe, they extend their long necks to break the surface. They feed on all sorts of slow-moving aquatic animals.

12

The Coastline

CLIMATE AND GEOGRAPHY

California's coastline is about 1100 miles (1760 km) long. This great range of latitude causes the climate to vary considerably along the coast from north to south. From Crescent City to San Diego the range of average annual precipitation is from about 80 inches (200 cm) to 10 inches (25 cm). On the other hand, the proximity of the ocean means that air temperatures are not extreme. At the coast, freezing is rare, and the temperature rarely exceeds 100°F (38°C). At San Francisco, September temperature averages 62°F (17°C), and January temperature averages 51°F (9°C).

Ocean water along the California coast is generally cold. Off the northern California coast, winter water temperature is usually around 50°F (10°C). In its journey southward it warms about 7° to 8°F (3–4°C). During summer it is only 8 to 10°F (5–6°C) warmer. Cold ocean water causes frequent fog, and relative humidity remains high most of the time. Plants water themselves with fog drip, and evaporation rates are low. Along the coast, plant communities range from moist Mixed Evergreen Forest in the north to dry Coastal Sage Scrub in the south.

The shape of California's coastline is a product of geologic activity and erosion (fig. 12.1). California has an emergent coastline. Most of the rocks distributed along the coast were formerly on the ocean floor. North of San Francisco, coastal rocks are mostly Franciscan sediments 100 to 150 million years of age. South of San Francisco, most of the rocks are sediments no older than about 60 million years. Most of these sedimentary rocks are relatively soft, and the action of the surf has cut into them, forming flat benches backed by sea cliffs. Uplift of the shoreline has elevated these wave-cut benches into a series of terraces. Vegetation of these terraces is discussed in chapter 7.

At various points the cliffs are broken by river mouths, which are usually blocked by a sand bar or spit, forming a region of quiet water influenced by the interplay of marine and fresh water. These are estuaries or coastal lagoons. Most of these river mouths are relatively narrow, typical of an emergent coastline. San Francisco Bay, however, has a different shape. It was caused by downcutting of large rivers during a period of lower sea level, presumably hundreds of thousands of years ago, during the Pleistocene. Elevated sea level since then has drowned the old river mouths, forming the bay. To the north of San Francisco, Tomales Bay is another drowned river mouth, but it is a zone of subsidence that occurs where the San Andreas fault passes out to sea.

Where the coastline is formed of hard rocks such as granitics or basalts, the land is more resistant to erosion, and rocky headlands jut into the Pacific. At the base of these headlands, tide pools, visible at low tide, abound in marine life. Between the

FIGURE 12.1   Surf at San Clemente Island. Dynamics of ocean water and geologic activities are responsible for the shape of California's coastline. Note the wave-cut terraces in the background.

rocky headlands are beaches and coves of various sizes. Sands for these beaches are carried to the ocean by rivers and deposited along the shore by the action of waves.

The most powerful force of erosion along the coast is wave action. Waves are generated by winds associated with storm fronts. Most of these storms form over the north Pacific; therefore most waves hit the coast from the northwest. In much the same manner as a pool ball bounces off a cushion, waves bounce off the coastline. Waves arriving from the northwest are reflected southwest. This action carries sand off the beach in a southwest direction. The next wave carries it back toward the coast in a southeast direction. The flow is always southward, forming a "river of sand" that migrates down the coast. This southerly flow of water, known as the longshore current, is just outside the surf line. It carries sand southward until it reaches a submarine canyon, where the sand is drained off to the ocean floor. If the source of new sand is interrupted by dams on the rivers, beaches will continue to erode and become smaller each year. Furthermore, construction of seawalls to protect coastal buildings directs the energy of waves to nonprotected stretches of beach, increasing erosion there.

As waves move into shallow water, friction with the ocean floor causes them to slow down. Where the depth of the water is about half the distance between the waves (wavelength), the wave becomes steeper, finally breaking when its height is 1.3 times higher than the depth. The energy of the wave is directed forward as the water rushes up the beach. This is known as the swash. Water that flows back again is called the backwash.

FIGURE 12.2   The energy of waves is directed by the bending of waves to all sides of a rocky headland.

Where waves strike the coast at an angle, they are bent in the process so that they tend to become oriented parallel to the coastline. Where rocky headlands project into the surf, wave energy tends to become concentrated on all sides of it, causing the headland to erode (fig. 12.2). Softer rocks erode first, resulting in typical coastal formations such as arches and stacks. A stack is a small, steep-sided rock island that may be the remains of a collapsed arch. Regardless of their hardness, all of these rock formations are doomed to become victims of the energy of wave action.

In coves or recessed areas, energy of the waves is intercepted so that sand accumulates and beaches form. The result is that the coastline is being straightened. Rocky headlands erode while the beaches between them become larger. In other areas the longshore current carries sand away from the beach and deposits it at the mouths of bays, parallel to the coast. These are known as bay-mouth bars, and they help to shelter the bays from the action of surf. The sand spit at Morro Bay is a good example. Farther south, the sand spit known as the Newport Peninsula was also formed this way. It is a large bay-mouth bar, behind which is Newport Harbor.

Human-constructed artificial barriers such as jetties and breakwaters also interfere with the energy of the waves, causing sand to accumulate on the "downstream" side. Marinas up and down the coast must constantly be dredged, or their entrances would become so filled with sand they would not be navigable.

Summer storms tend to come from the south. At this time the waves strike the coast from a different angle. As a result south-facing beaches become eroded in summer while north-facing beaches fill with sand—the reverse of the winter pattern.

Winter waves tend to be larger because winter storms are more severe. These waves carry sand away from the beach to create offshore bars. The beach becomes narrow, and a steep berm is formed. During summer, smaller waves pick up sand grains and move them toward the shore. Water sinks through the sand, depositing the suspended grains on the beach. The usual result is a wide beach that slopes gradually toward the water.

TIDES

Of all the physical phenomena associated with the seashore, none is more interesting and more misunderstood than the tides. It is the combination of surf and tides that makes the intertidal zone one of the harshest environments on earth. Because of tides, organisms in the intertidal zone are covered part of the time and exposed part of the time.

The cause of tides is the gravitational pull of the sun and moon. Even though the moon is much smaller than the sun, its influence on tides is greater, because it is much closer to the earth than is the sun.

Tides are not the same on all parts of the earth. The magnitude and duration of the tides vary with latitude, the shape of the coastline, and the season. In some regions there is only one high tide and one low tide each day. Most regions, however, experience two high and two low tides per day. On the Atlantic side of North America, the high and low tides each day are approximately equal. In California, there are two high tides and two low tides each day, but they are quite different in extent (fig. 12.3).

The greatest tidal extremes are associated with shallow water and narrow inlets. On the Pacific Coast of North America, the greatest extremes in tides occur in the upper reaches of Puget Sound, Washington, and Cook Inlet, Alaska. In these areas the difference between high and low tides is 15 to 20 feet (5–7 m). Along most of the California coast, daily tidal ranges of 10 to 15 feet (3–5 m) are considered maximal.

Because the sun and moon are not always in the same positions with respect to the earth, tides also fluctuate on a monthly and seasonal basis. When the sun, moon, and earth are in a line, as they are during a new moon or full moon, the gravitational pull on the water becomes additive, causing a greater extreme between high and low tides. These tides are called spring tides (fig. 12.4). The word *spring* in this case means "upwelling" and refers to the extreme upwelling of the seawater at high tide. In contrast, during a half-moon, the moon and sun are at right angles. The effect of these bodies pulling against each other reduces the difference between high and low tides. These are known as neap tides. The word *neap* means "scarce."

In addition, orbits are elliptical, so the distance of the sun or moon from the earth is not always the same. The moon varies in distance from the earth by about 15,000 miles (24,000 km). Its closest position, known as perigee, occurs about twice each month. The farthest position, known as apogee, also occurs twice each month. If perigee occurs during a spring tide, the effect is compounded so that the high tide

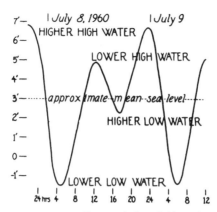

FIGURE 12.3   Characteristics of tide at San Francisco. (From: J. W. Hedgpeth, *Introduction to Seashore Life of the San Francisco Bay Region and the Coast of Northern California*. Berkeley: University of California Press, 1962.)

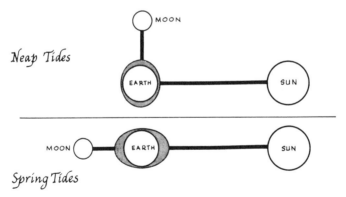

FIGURE 12.4   Spatial arrangements of earth, sun, and moon at neap tide and spring tide. Darkened area indicates relative depth of seawater at various points on the earth. The point of view is directly above one of the earth's poles. (From S. Hinton. *Seashore Life of Southern California*. Berkeley: University of California Press, 1987.)

is about 40% higher. On the same day, the low tide will be correspondingly lower. This combination of events occurs only periodically, but it can be predicted. These are the days of extremely low tide when thousands of people go to the beach to view intertidal life. Finally, the earth is closest to the sun in June and December. High and low tides during those months are the most extreme of the year.

FIGURE 12.5   Six summer days during a typical spring tide series (top) and a typical neap tide series (bottom). Note that the lower low tides of summer occur in the very early morning; in winter they are in the afternoon. (From S. Hinton. *Seashore Life of Southern California.* Berkeley: University of California Press, 1987.)

All of these relationships are also influenced by the seasons (fig. 12.5). Because the earth is inclined on its axis, in the northern hemisphere the North Pole tilts toward the sun in summer. This means that the highest high tide occurs during daylight in the summer. Conversely, in winter, the lowest low tide occurs during daylight hours. Putting all these effects together, the lowest low tide each year occurs during the day in December. This low tide is the best time to view life in the intertidal zone.

MARINE TERRACES

The staircase shape to the California coastline is the product of coastal uplift and changing sea level. Fossil assemblages in sediments on these terraces tell us a great deal about climate and ocean temperatures during various glacial and interglacial episodes. By comparing the terrace sediments with those deposited in the Ventura and Los Angeles basins, we can get a picture of these changes since the late Pliocene, 2 to 4 million years ago. The basin sediments are particularly notable because they appear to be the thickest in the world. Depositions in the Los Angeles basin are up to 5200 feet (1800 m) thick. Comparable sediments in the Ventura area reach a thickness of approximately 4900 feet (1600 m).

The fossil remains in these embayments are primarily foraminifera and ostracods, planktonic forms indicating that moderately deep water once covered the basins. Present-day distributions of comparable micro-organisms indicate that depths of water over these basins probably reached about 600 feet (180 m). Other comparative data of the fossil remains indicate that the minimum temperature of the sea off the California coast during the late Pliocene was at least 3°F (2°C) warmer than it is today.

The Pleistocene terraces of southern California lie at various elevations up to 1200 feet (350 m) above the present sea level. These terraces have been intensively studied in three basic areas: San Diego, Los Angeles, and Ventura. The fossiliferous strata of these terraces yield primarily intertidal and shallow-water echinoderms, molluscs, and crustacea, in addition to a few shallow-water planktonic forms such as foraminifera and ostracods.

The upper terraces are the oldest, dating from the middle Pleistocene and representing an interglacial episode. These upper terraces contain primarily a warm-water fauna, and as one samples progressively lower, younger terraces, a trend toward cooler waters is indicated. The lowest, most recent terraces are characterized by a cold-water fauna of northern affinities quite similar to the fauna of today.

INTERTIDAL COMMUNITIES

The region where the land and sea overlap is known as the intertidal or littoral zone. This region, influenced by the daily ebb and flow of tides, is one of the best examples of edge effect in the world. The diversity of species and habitats within 10 vertical feet is greater in the intertidal zone than in any other habitat on earth. This is because the area retains characteristics of both ocean and terrestrial habitats; hence it contains organisms associated with both regions.

There are three major habitats influenced by the tides: beaches, rocky headlands, and estuaries. Because the substratum is always shifting, beaches are the most hostile of the three habitats. On beaches where the action of surf has carried away the sand, cobbles or shingles may roll and slide with every wave. Very few living organisms can tolerate this environment. Where there is abundant sand, however, there may be an assortment of creatures that tolerate or even require the shifting of sand.

Sandy Beaches

Sands of beaches are derived primarily from weathering of rocks in the mountains. The sand is delivered to the ocean by rivers and carried southward by the action of waves and currents. Additional materials are added to beaches by erosion of shoreline cliffs. The bulk of material in beach sand is quartz, a hard, insoluble mineral sorted into particles that usually range between 0.06 and 2 mm in size. Particle size determines water-holding capacity of the beach, a feature that has a profound influence on the nature of the creatures that live there. Sands that remain soft are the most habitable for organisms.

Food for sand-dwelling organisms comes primarily from planktonic or detrital particles suspended in seawater. Another important source of food is organic molecules that adhere to the sand particles themselves. A third source of food for beach dwellers is broken-up kelp and other debris washed up on the beach by high tides or storms. Of course, beach-dwelling organisms also eat each other.

One of the most common animals of sandy beaches is the Pacific Mole Crab or Western Sand Crab, *Emerita analoga* (fig. 12.6A). These crustaceans, about 1 inch (25 mm) in length, are shaped like small flattened eggs. Their small appendages can be used for swimming or digging. Mole crabs move up and down the beach in the surf line, feeding on detritus and plankton. Every time a wave recedes, they burrow backward into the soupy sand, so they are seldom seen. People wading in the surf

FIGURE 12.6   Some animals of sandy beaches. *A*. Pacific Mole Crab, *Emerita analoga*. B. Lugworm, *Arenicola brasiliensis*. (Illustrations from S. Hinton. *Seashore Life of Southern California*. Berkeley: University of California Press, 1987.)

may feel them as a tingling sensation on their bare feet. Between molts, when the carapace is soft, mole crabs are prized bait for surf fishermen.

Among the filter-feeding inhabitants of sandy beaches are several varieties of clams. When the tide is in, these organisms pass a current of water through their bodies and extract small organisms and particulate organic matter from the water. The Pacific Razor Clam, *Siliqua patula*, one of the most common of these clams, is narrow and elongated, about 3 inches (75 mm) in length. In a manner similar to mole crabs, they move in and out with the tides. They are surprisingly motile, fast-digging organisms. During the lowest of spring tides, many people search the low-tide line for these clams, which are considered among the finest of delicacies.

Occurring south of Monterey is a large, thick-shelled clam known as the Pismo Clam, *Tivela stultorum*. These are inhabitants of the zone just outside the surf line. They are not particularly tasty, but their large size makes them sought after. On the lowest winter tide of the year, thousands of people visit Pismo Beach and dig up the clams with shovels and pitchforks. The beach here is very flat, and on this day of the lowest of low tides, hundreds of yards (meters) of beach that are usually underwater become exposed, allowing clams to be dug up on the shore. This is not the only beach where Pismo Clams occur, but it is the most famous. In southern California, Huntington Beach is a good place to find Pismo Clams. For reasons not well understood, the abundance of these large clams seems to be declining. This may be the result of overharvesting by humans or squashing by off-road vehicles. The resurgence of Sea Otters also has been blamed.

Bloodworms (*Glycera* spp.) and lugworms (*Arenicola* spp.) (fig. 12.6B) also oc-cur on sandy beaches. These segmented worms (Annelida) feed like earthworms on beaches with fine sand. They ingest sand, feeding on the suspended organic material and passing the undigestible portion through their bodies. These worms, belonging to the group known as polychaete worms, have small bristly paddles on their sides. They are usually about 1 inch (25 mm) long, although in some habitats they may be much larger. The bright red color of these worms comes from hemoglobin, the same pigment that gives vertebrate blood its color. Similar to vertebrate blood, the pigment is used to carry oxygen, an important adaptation that helps them survive in the sand when the tide is out. At this time they feed actively near the surface of the sand. When the tide is in, they retreat to deeper sand so that they will not be carried away by the surf. These worms are known to penetrate the beach sands to a depth of 18 inches (45 cm).

Larger polychaete worms, up to 1 foot (30 cm) in length, are active predators. When the tide is in, they emerge from the sand to prey upon other sand dwellers. They have a pair of curved jaws that resemble the fangs of a spider. There are several such species, but among the most common are the clam worms (*Nereis* spp.)

On the beach, at the upper tide line, deposits of kelp and associated organisms are commonly washed ashore. A number of scavengers live among these piles of rotting kelp. One of the most common of these is the California Beach Flea or Beach Hopper, *Orchestoidea californiana*, an amphipod crustacean up to 1 inch (25 mm) in length. Usually they spend daylight hours in burrows under the decaying kelp, and after dark they come out by the thousands to feed on kelp and other detritus. In southern California, sunbathers may be pestered by small Beach Hoppers. People lying on the beach near piles of kelp often find them hopping on their legs.

Isopod crustaceans also occur on beaches. These creeping, tank-shaped crustaceans, related to sowbugs, prefer to eat meat. One form, known as Harford's Greedy Isopod, *Cirolana harfordi*, occurs in swarms large enough to clean the skeleton of a dead fish in a matter of hours.

Perhaps the most conspicuous of the beach dwellers are the kelp flies (*Fucellia, Coelopa,* etc.). Larvae of these flies, known as maggots, can be seen in decaying piles of seaweed. Adults are small black flies that rise in swarms when people walk near the kelp.

Higher up on the beach, usually on drier sands, predatory tiger beetles (Cicindelidae) occur. These elongate beetles occur in swarms and run along the beach feeding on other beach dwellers. They occur most commonly on beaches where there are not many people. In general, insects are not very common near the sea, but tiger beetles come closer to seawater than most insects. Distribution of tiger beetles on beaches of the world is an interesting problem in biogeography, because, theoretically, they are unable to disperse for long distances over seawater. Perhaps they get from beach to beach by riding logs or other debris.

One of the most interesting inhabitants of sandy beaches is a fish that lays its eggs on land! This is the California Grunion, *Leuresthes tenuis*. This member of the silversides family (Atherinidae) is a sardine-sized fish about 8 inches (20 cm) in length. What do grunion have in common with human females? Their reproductive cycles are keyed to phases of the moon; they have a lunar biorhythm. California Grunion occur from San Francisco south, but they are seldom seen north of Morro Bay. In the spring of the year, on nights following the full moon, grunion migrate by the thousands to beaches. Females burrow tail first into the soupy sand at the upper limits of high-tide swash. Males wrap their bodies around the females and release sperm into the burrows as the females lay their eggs. Fertilized eggs incubate in the wet sand. Two weeks later, during the new moon, tides once again rise high on the beach. At this time, in the dark of the moon, the eggs hatch, and the tiny fish swim out to sea under the cover of darkness.

Dates of the high tides and the grunion runs are listed in most coastal newspapers and in a number of free publications. On nights of predicted runs, hordes of people swarm to beaches where grunion are known to spawn. Grunion do not always behave according to schedule, but if they do, people catch them with their hands (a fishing license is required). Many people enjoy eating them, but unfortunately for the grunion, most people are there for the beach party; often, whatever grunion are caught wind up fertilizing the roses.

Among predators of sandy beaches are various species of birds. Included here are gulls and long-billed shorebirds such as Willets (*Catoptrophorus semipalmatus*), Marbled Godwits (*Limosa fedoa*), and Sanderlings (*Calidris alba*). They feed on the creatures mentioned in the preceding paragraphs. Because they are also common inhabitants of estuaries, these birds will be discussed in more detail later.

Rocky Headlands

A profound example of edge effect, the rocky intertidal region of the ocean is one of the most diverse habitats in the world. In spite of its harshness, many authorities believe that most higher animals evolved in the intertidal region and tide pools of rocky headlands. Representatives of every major group (phylum) of animals are found in this region.

The rocky intertidal region can be divided into five distinctive zones, based on the length of time that organisms are out of water. From upper to lower, these are known as the splash zone, upper intertidal zone, middle intertidal zone, lower intertidal zone, and subtidal zone (fig. 12.7). Each zone has its own combination of stresses, including wave shock, exposure, temperature extremes, and predators. Adaptations for these stresses are diverse (table 12.1). Each zone has its characteristic organisms that are conspicuous at low tide. Although there is some controversy over the precise boundaries of each zone or the organisms that inhabit each, the zones do occur in distinct bands on the rocks. Reasons for this zonation represent some of the most interesting concepts in ecology.

Splash Zone. The source of water in the splash zone is that which splashes up on the rocks as the surf crashes against the shoreline. This is primarily a terrestrial community that is wetted by surf spray during high tide. Photosynthetic organisms in this zone are drought-tolerant, crustose forms such as blue-green algae (cyanobacteria) and black-colored lichens. This is an extremely harsh habitat, subject to prolonged drying every time the tide is out. Animals in this region either hide in cracks during daylight hours or take refuge in shallow tide pools. Not many species of animals can tolerate such conditions. Most common among the dwellers in the cracks is an isopod crustacean 1 inch (25 mm) long known as a rock louse, *Ligia* spp. (fig. 12.8). A rock louse is seldom seen because it spends daylight hours in hiding, seldom venturing out before dark. It feeds on attached algae or kelp that is deposited on rocks by the surf. Biologists have studied these small animals to gain a better understanding of innate biological clocks. Rock lice exhibit a circadian (daily) rhythm in which they change color. They are dark during daylight hours and lighter at night.

FIGURE 12.7 Zonation in the rocky intertidal region. (Drawing by Thomas Trooien.)

TABLE 12.1 Some Examples of Adaptations to Stresses of the Rocky Intertidal Region

Stress	Adaptation	Example
Wave shock	Adherent threads	Mussels
	Stick tightly	Chitons, limpets
	Conical shape	Barnacles, limpets
	Flexible stalks	Goose barnacle, kelps
	Hide in cracks	Crabs
	Motility	Periwinkles
Dehydration	Motility	Starfish
	Operculum	Turban shells
	Stick tightly	Abalone, limpets
	Seal openings	Barnacles
	Valved shells	Mussels
Temperature extremes	Motility	Crabs
	Evaporative cooling	Mussels
	Tolerance	Barnacles
	Nocturnal behavior	Rock lice
Salinity extremes	Tolerance	Periwinkles
	Motility	Crabs
Feeding	Filter feeding	Mussels, barnacles
	Grazing	Chitons, limpets
	Detritus feeding	Sea hares, crabs
	Absorption of DOM	Sea urchins
	Predation	Octopi, starfish
Predation	Hard shells	Barnacles, mussels
	Motility	Crabs
	Toxins	Nudibranchs, kelps
	Protective coloration	Tidepool sculpin
Competition	Aggression	Crabs, octopi
	Rapid growth	Barnacles
	Opportunistic larval establishment	Mussels, barnacles
	Large numbers of offspring	Sea urchins, barnacles
	Good dispersal	Planktonic larvae

In the shallow tide pools, the most common animals are small snails known as periwinkles, *Littorina* spp. There are several species of these snails, but they share an ability to tolerate exposure. When the tide goes out, they find refuge in cracks or gather in shallow tide pools, where they continue feeding. If it becomes too dry, they retreat into their shells, sealing the entrance with circular bit of shell known as an operculum. When the tide is in, they creep about on the rocks, grazing on attached algae. These small snails are especially suited to life in the splash zone. They can

FIGURE 12.8   Rock louse, *Ligia* sp., a typical animal of the splash zone.

breathe in or out of water, and they can tolerate submersion in fresh water, a common occurrence in the rainy northwest.

One of the hazards of life in the intertidal zone is the awesome power of a crashing wave. Snails are equipped to stick tightly to the rock and resist the force of most waves. Even so, they may be knocked off their perches and carried by the backwash into deeper water. Periwinkles have an interesting set of reflexes that brings them back to their normal habitat in the upper intertidal or splash zone. When they are underwater, they respond negatively to gravity. This instinct, known as a negative geotaxis, causes them to crawl along rocks upward toward the surface. If the snail crawls into a crack, when it is right-side up it has a negative reaction to light. If it is upside down, it has a positive reaction to light. These instincts are known as positive and negative phototaxes. The result is that cracks pose no problem. A snail crawls into the crack and back out again, always moving upward. Once the snail emerges from the water it knows it is "home." As long as it remains moist, it will move only to feed.

Upper Intertidal Zone.   The upper intertidal zone is covered by nearly every high tide and exposed by most low tides. This area is characterized by attached green algae (Chlorophyta) such as sea felt (*Enteromorpha* spp.) and sea lettuce (*Ulva* spp.). These algae are found in intertidal zones all over the world, and in California they are quite similar in appearance. Sea felt is thin and fragile, and sea lettuce is usually larger, up to 4 inches (10 cm) in length, with a wavy margin. These forms of algae are heavily grazed upon by the animals of the rocky intertidal zone. Sea lettuce gets its name from the fact that humans gather it for food. Dried sea lettuce, supposedly rich in vitamins and minerals, is sold under the name of Iceland Sea Grass or Green Laver.

Most animals of the upper intertidal zone are grazers and filter feeders. Periwinkles will move into this zone to feed, but more common grazers are chitons, and limpets, which are flattened marine snails (Gastropoda).

There are many species of limpets in the rocky intertidal zone. Limpets are circular when viewed from the top (fig. 12.9A), but a side view shows that the shell is in the form of a flattened cone. This is an ideal shape to disperse the energy of wave shock. They stick tightly to the rocks, which helps to hold them in place. During low tide this shape also helps to seal water under the edge of the shell. Studies of these grazers show that they too have instinctive patterns of behavior. They feed when the tide is in, but they have a "home" depression to which they return to wait out the low tide. Limpets follow a slime trail back to the same depression from which they started. They must return in time to settle down tightly before the tide goes out. Their internal clock causes them to move away from home when the tide comes in and toward home when the tide starts to go back out.

Chitons (fig. 12.9B) belong to a group of molluscs known as the Polyplacophora, a word that means that they bear many plates. It specifically refers to their hinged shell, which is made up of eight plates. The advantage to the hinged shell is that they are able to bend as they move over irregularities on the rock. Furthermore, if one becomes dislodged, it can roll up to protect its vulnerable underside from drying or predators.

Filter feeders of the upper intertidal zone consist mostly of small barnacles (*Chthamalus* spp.) (fig. 12.9C). There is confusion concerning the common names for these barnacles, but the name "buckshot barnacles" seems to suit them as well as any. These are small crustaceans that live in a volcano-shaped shell. When the tide is in, they feed with a featherlike hind appendage. When the tide goes out, the shell, made of several plates, contracts to seal in the water. In the upper intertidal zone, they may be so common as to coat the rocks in a nearly solid band of gray volcanoes about $1/4$ inch (6 mm) high. Of all the species of barnacles, these are able to tolerate desiccation for the longest period of time. The upper limit of these barnacles is also heavily influenced by the activities of predatory birds such as oystercatchers.

At the lower margin of this zone is a belt of larger barnacles known as acorn barnacles (*Balanus* spp.) (fig. 12.9D), usually about 1 inch (25 mm) in height. They do not tolerate desiccation as well as buckshot barnacles, so they are unable to grow higher on the rocks. On the other hand, they grow faster and larger than buckshot barnacles and can pry the smaller species off the rocks by growing under them. This type of zonation in barnacle species is found all over the world.

Hundreds of snails may occur in tide pools of the upper intertidal zone. These include the periwinkles mentioned earlier, but there are also other species. One common type is known as the Black Turban Shell, *Tegula funebralis* (fig. 12.9E). When the tide is in, turban shells move about, grazing on algae. When the tide is out, they retreat to the tide pools.

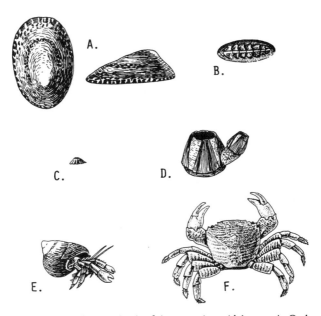

FIGURE 12.9 Some animals of the upper intertidal zone. *A*. Owl Limpet, *Lottia gigantea*. *B*. Troglodyte Chiton, *Nuttalina fluxa*. *C*. Buckshot Barnacle, *Chthamalus* sp. *D*. Red-striped Acorn Barnacle, *Megabalanus californicus*. *E*. Hairy Hermit Crab, *Pagurus hirsutiusculus*, in the shell of a Black Turban Shell, *Tegula funebralis*. *F*. Striped Shore Crab, *Pachygrapsus crassipes*. (Illustrations from: S. Hinton. *Seashore Life of Southern California*. Berkeley: University of California Press, 1987.)

A person peering into these upper tide pools will note that many of the turban shells appear empty. Also, it may be a surprise to see some of these shells lurching along in a most un-snail-like fashion. Closer inspection will reveal that the shell is actually inhabited by a small crab known as a hermit crab. The most common of these is the Hairy Hermit Crab, *Pagurus hirsutiusculus* (fig. 12.9E). These crabs commonly occupy empty turban shells, although they will use any hollow container of appropriate size, perhaps even a discarded lipstick tube or a film can. In southern California, these crabs are seldom over 1 inch (25 mm) in length, but to the north they may reach lengths of 4 inches (10 cm). As they grow, they must find a larger container. Life for a hermit crab includes incessant scavengings, either for food or for a home with the proper fit.

The most conspicuous crab inhabiting theses upper tide pools is the Striped Shore Crab, *Pachygrapsus crassipes* (fig. 12.9F). Many children delight in chasing these squarish, flattened crabs with big claws. The flattened shape of these crabs is ideal for clinging in a shelter to resist wave shock. For the most part, they are nocturnal, and they seek shelter in cracks during the daytime. In the tide pools, however, any bit of food—animal or vegetable—that becomes available will lure them out of hiding. Battles between rival crabs are common, and usually the larger crab wins.

Middle Intertidal Zone.   The middle intertidal zone is uncovered by many low tides, but not all of them, and it is covered by every high tide. This is a zone of filter-feeding animals and highly resilient attached algae, including small kelps or brown algae (Phaeophyta). Principal among these are rockweeds (*Pelvetia, Pelvetiopsis, Fucus, Hesperophycus*) (fig. 12.10). These are small kelps, seldom over 4 inches (10 cm) in height, that grow in clumps in exposed rocky areas.

Sea Palm, *Postelsia palmaeformis*, is one of the most conspicuous organisms of this zone from Morro Bay northward. This distinctive kelp looks like a palm tree about 2 feet (60 cm) tall. It is an annual species that is torn loose by the surf during fall and winter. Each year, about February, a new forest of Sea Palms grows on bare surfaces produced by disturbance. In this sense, it competes with other attached organisms, particularly mussels. This yearly turnover and regrowth makes this one of the most productive ecosystems in the world. Many people consider Sea Palm a delicacy. The stipe and blades may be washed in fresh water, steamed, and eaten with lemon juice and soy sauce. Some people make sweet pickles from the stipes.

The most conspicuous animals of this zone are the mussels (*Mytilus* spp.), which are bivalve molluscs (Pelecypoda). They are black-colored clams that adhere to the rocks by strong tendrils known as byssal threads. When the tide is in, they feed on plankton and perhaps dissolved organic matter by passing a current of water through their bodies. When the tide is out, they close up in order to prevent dehydration. If they become exposed on hot days, they may remain partially open so that evaporation of water from the inside will help to cool them.

Throughout California, there are two species of mussels. The smaller Bay Mussel, *Mytilus edulis*, tends to be more resistant to desiccation; hence it most commonly occurs on the upper fringes of the mussel beds. The larger mussel is the California Mussel, *Mytilus californianus* (fig. 12.11A). This mussel dominates in regions of stronger wave shock. The byssal threads of the Bay Mussel are thinner, which makes them less firmly attached to the rocks. In protected areas, however, the Bay Mussel dominates. Bay Mussels are better able to tolerate quiet water because they are motile. They can grow new byssal threads and detach the old ones, which enables them to move upward out of sedimentation that might clog their filter-feeding system. These adaptations also suggest seasonal changes in dominance within the same "wads" of mussels. During periods of quiet surf, usually in the summer, Bay Mussels are more common because they are able to move to the outer edges of the mussel clumps. During winter, when the pounding of the surf is more severe, Bay Mussels get carried away, and the California Mussels, with their stronger byssal threads, prevail.

Mussels are common intertidal organisms throughout the world and are important in the diets of many nations. Because they grow so rapidly, mussels are one of the world's most important cultured sea foods, and in many nations they may be the most important cultured source of protein. In Spain they are grown abundantly on floating rafts. In this way, kept full-time underwater, mussels feed continuously and

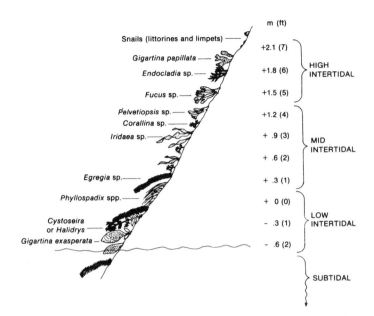

Snails (littorines and limpets)

Gigartina papillata

Endocladia sp.

Fucus sp.

Pelvetiopsis sp.

Corallina sp.

Iridaea sp.

Egregia sp.

Phyllospadix spp.

Cystoseira or Halidrys

Gigartina exasperata

m (ft)

+2.1 (7)

+1.8 (6)   HIGH INTERTIDAL

+1.5 (5)

+1.2 (4)

+ .9 (3)   MID INTERTIDAL

+ .6 (2)

+ .3 (1)

+ 0 (0)   LOW INTERTIDAL

- .3 (1)

- .6 (2)

SUBTIDAL

FIGURE 12.10 Vertical zonation of some common seaweeds in the rocky intertidal region. (From E.Y. Dawson and M.S. Foster. *Seashore Plants of California*. Berkeley: University of California Press, 1982.)

grow rapidly. Where they are not cultured, they are knocked from the rocks with a chisel. Where such harvesting is legal in California, mussels have been known to provide an impromptu beach meal. First, they should be allowed to feed in clean seawater so that grit may be cleared from their bodies. Then, if they are steamed until they open, dipped in garlic butter, and served with hot french bread and cold white wine, they will provide a memorable feast. In some parts of California, however, many mussel beds are now threatened by overharvesting. This is a consequence of the large number of immigrants from nations that routinely thrive on intertidal life. This problem is particularly severe in many of the coastal marine life refuges, where any form of harvest is illegal.

An animal that commonly occurs in mixed colonies with the mussels are Goose Barnacles or Leaf Barnacles, *Pollicipes polymerus* (fig. 12.11B) which occur on flexible stalks. The arrangement of the enclosing plates resembles a goose in profile. In Europe there is an ancient legend concerning the Goose Barnacle. In the North Atlantic, along the west coast of Europe, there is a bird known as the Barnacle Goose, *Branta leucopsis*. It resembles the Canada Goose, *Branta canadensis*, of North America. As the story goes, the leaves of certain trees fall into the sea and become barnacles. After a time the barnacles fall off rocks, logs, or ships' timbers and become Barnacle Geese. Furthermore, in the thirteenth century, Irish priests believed that Barnacle Geese arose from Goose Barnacles. Thus they were considered seafood, not fowl, and were eaten during lent. Pope Innocent III was not convinced and issued a decree in 1215

FIGURE 12.11   Some animals of the middle intertidal zone. *A*. California Mussels, *Mytilus californianus*.

FIGURE 12.11 *(continued)*   Some animals of the middle intertidal zone. *B*. Goose Barnacles, *Pollicipes polymerus*.

that forbade the eating of Barnacle Geese during Lent. Meanwhile, a prominent rabbi in France concluded that if Barnacle Geese arose from Goose Barnacles, Jews couldn't eat them because they were shellfish, which were forbidden under religious dietary laws.

An interesting predatory bird frequents the rocky intertidal region. It is known as the Black Oystercatcher, *Haematopus bachmani*. Because it is a mobile animal, it cannot truly be considered a member of any particular intertidal zone; but because it feeds primarily in mussel beds, it should be mentioned here. These are not common birds where humans are abundant, but if one approaches inaccessible rocky shores by boat, these interesting birds may be observed at work. These are bizarre-looking birds that appear as if they might have been assembled from spare parts. They are completely black except for pink legs and a bright red bill. The long bill, which is compressed laterally, is used to open mussels. With a swift peck they open a mussel and pluck out the meat. Oystercatchers also feed heavily on juvenile mussels or other sedentary prey species, such as barnacles. Their activity, along with that of gulls and other predatory birds, is very important to the formation of bare areas that are constantly being recolonized.

Lower Intertidal Zone.   The lower intertidal zone is exposed only by the lowest of low tides, the spring tides. Its upper margin is considered to be the average sea level, the line from which the height of a tide is measured. A low tide that drops below this line is called a minus tide. During a 6-foot tide, this line would be 6 feet underwater.

This zone is characterized by a number of kelps, such as the Feather Boa Kelp, *Egregia menziesii*, and farther north, the Sugar Wrack, *Laminaria saccharina*. Also found here are interesting seed plants known as Eel Grass (*Zostera marina*) and surfgrasses (*Phyllospadix* spp.). Plants in this family (*Zosteraceae*) are unique in that they are terrestrial plants adapted to living underwater. These plants actually have roots and flowers. Eel Grass is usually associated with quiet water, as in bays, but surfgrasses are the conspicuous, bright green plants that seem to form meadows when they become exposed by the low tides. Usually the roots are anchored in the sand, but tough, fibrous, rootlike stems (rhizomes) may become anchored to solid rock. Surfgrasses produce millions of filamentous pollen grains that are shed into the water. These microscopic slimy threads become entangled with the stigmas of flowers on female plants. These stigmas produce a sticky secretion that adheres like glue to the pollen and holds it in place in the surf. The bond does not form with pollen of the wrong species. This specificity prevents hybridization when different kinds of surfgrass pollen are shed simultaneously into the surf.

Most of the animals of the lower intertidal zone take refuge in or attach to these plants. Included here are many species of worms, snails, and limpets. The "spiny-skinned" animals (Echinodermata) are a purely marine phylum. They are unique among animals in that they circulate seawater through their bodies. Perhaps the most familiar of these animals are the sea stars or starfishes (Asteroidea). The most common California sea star is the Ochre Starfish (*Pisaster ochraceus*) (fig. 12.12A). It can be seen clinging to rocks by means of hundreds of small hydraulic suction cups known as tube feet. In southern California, this was once one of the most conspicuous animals at low tide, but over the years curious children and collectors of memorabilia have decimated the population. These days, particularly in southern California, starfishes seldom are exposed by low tide. Their usual habit is to migrate during high tide into the middle intertidal zone in order to feed on mussels or acorn barnacles and retreat before the tide goes out.

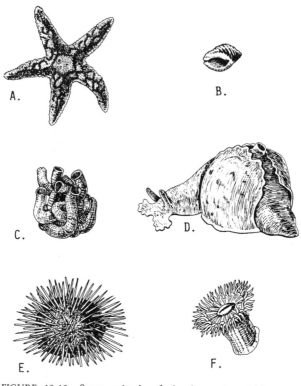

FIGURE 12.12   Some animals of the lower intertidal zone.
A. Ochre Starfish, *Pisaster ochraceus*. B. Rock Thais, *Nucella
emarginata*. C. Scaly Tube Snail, *Serpulorbis squamigerus*. D. Brown
Sea Hare, *Aplysia californica*. E. Red Sea Urchin, *Strongylocentrotus
franciscanus*. F. Solitary Green Anemone, *Anthopleura xanthogrammica*. (Illustrations from S. Hinton. *Seashore Life of Southern California*. Berkeley: University of California Press, 1987.)

Different species and/or sizes of sea stars feed on different kinds of prey. For
example, the lower limit of the mussel bed is regulated by starfish predation. The
regulating factor is the length of time it takes for a starfish to digest the flesh of a
mussel, which is dictated by the feeding style of the starfish. When a starfish feeds,
it everts its stomach and inserts it between the mussel's shells, through the small
openings the mussel uses to siphon water. Digestive juices break down the mussel's
soft body parts, and the starfish draws back its stomach to complete the process. The
starfish attempts to move onto the mussel bed during high tide, feed, and move back
before the tide exposes it. The length of time it takes to complete this procedure is
the critical factor that enables mussels to dominate the middle intertidal zone.

A group of predatory snails of the lower intertidal zone includes the unicorns and
dogwinkles. The Emarginate Dogwinkle or Rock Thais, *Nucella* (= *Thais*) *emarginata*

(fig. 12.12B), is about 1 ¹/₂ inches (37 mm) in length. These snails have a rasplike drill that they use to make a hole in another shelled animal, such as a mussel or limpet. Prey species such as periwinkles or turbans have an unusual escape mechanism: They crawl on top of the Emarginate Dogwinkle so they cannot be eaten. During the larval stage, these dogwinkles are cannibalistic; larvae eat each other within the egg capsules. Another name for this group of snails is purple snails. It does not refer to the color of the shell, which is white to pale brown, but to a purple dye that may be extracted from the flesh.

Filter-feeding animals of the lower intertidal zone are not particularly common because much of the area is covered by kelps. In protected areas, out of the crash of surf, however, honey-combed masses of tubes may be found that belong to polychaete worms known as Sand-castle Worms, *Phragmatopoma californica*. These worms possess an operculum so that they may close the entrances to the tubes when the tide is out. They form the tubes by cementing together many particles of sand. These tubes should not be confused with those of Scaly Tube Snails, *Serpulorbis squamigerus* (fig. 12.12C), limy tubes about ¹/₄ inch in diameter that are laid out on rocks like toothpaste in coiled piles. These tubes actually belong to a true snail that has taken up a filter-feeding way of life. Tubes of the snails are also common in the middle tide zone.

Grazers in the lower intertidal zone feed primarily on the kelp. These animals are seldom seen out of water. During the low spring tides they are found either in tide pools of the lower intertidal zone or in the subtidal zone. Studying tide pools of the lower intertidal zone provides a glimpse of what goes on when the tide is in, and also what the subtidal zone is like.

The Brown Sea Hare, *Aplysia californica* (fig. 12.12D), is a sluglike mollusc. It is brownish purple with two longitudinal folds along its back. It may be up to 15 inches (35 cm) long and weigh 15 pounds (6.8 kg). These creatures creep snail-like along the bottom of tide pools, grazing on attached kelp or bits of kelp that have broken off and sunk to the bottom. When a Brown Sea Hare is disturbed, it emits a cloud of deep purple ink. This cloud can allow it to escape by obscuring the vision of, or at least distracting, a predator.

Other grazers in this zone include three species of abalone (*Haliotis*), which are actually large, flattened snails (Gastropoda). A close look will reveal that the shell is spiraled but flat like a cinnamon roll. A number of open holes in the shell carry away wastes from the animal. The edible part, which brings a high price in gourmet restaurants, is the large muscular foot. The three species are named by color: black, green, and red. Black Abalone, *Haliotis cracherodii*, is the most commonly seen. Small ones occur in the lower intertidal zone, where they graze on various kinds of algae, including kelps. Individuals of this species are seldom over 6 inches (15 cm) in diameter, and they have five to nine open holes. Green Abalone, *H. fulgens*, is larger. It averages about 8 inches (20 cm) in diameter and has five to seven open holes that are slightly elevated from the shell. It is less common than Black Abalone in the intertidal zone, but it is fairly common in the subtidal zone. Red Abalone, *H. rufescens*, occurs in the deepest water, up to 500 feet (150 m) in depth. With individuals up to 11 inches (28 cm) in diameter, it is the most important from a commerical point of view. It has only three to four open holes that are raised from the shell in small tubes. The Red Abalone is rarely found in the intertidal zone.

Tide pools of the lower intertidal zone are often coated with red algae (Rhodophyta) known as coralline algae (*Corallina* spp.). These algae are short, seldom over 4 inches (10 cm) high, and resemble coarse, pinkish lace. The coarse texture is provided by a coating of calcium carbonate secreted by the plant. This hard coating is a deterrent to grazing by most herbivores.

Sea urchins and sand dollars (Echinoidea) are in the same phylum as the starfishes (Echinodermata). The Common Sand Dollar, *Dendraster excentricus*, is a species that occurs in sand outside the surf line or on sand flats in protected bays. It is seldom seen alive by vistors to the beach. When alive, they are covered by a ruglike mat of soft spines, but when they are dead and washed up on the beach, usually the spines are gone, and all that is left is the flattened calcareous skeleton or test. The off-center flowerlike pattern on the back is formed by holes that are penetrated by tube feet.

California has two common species of sea urchin in the intertidal zone. The smaller, Purple Sea Urchin, *Strongylocentrotus purpuratus*, is more common. The Red Sea Urchin, *S. franciscanus* (fig. 12.12E), may have a body 5 inches (13 cm) in diameter, with the spines extending beyond that. These animals resemble pincushions with long, movable spines. Careful inspection of sea urchins will reveal long, flexible tube feet between the spines. If a sea urchin is turned over, it can right itself in minutes using its tube feet. Purple Sea Urchins rest in depressions that they enlarge by abrasion from their spines and gnawing. This is a mechanism to help protect them from wave shock.

Sea urchins are grazers and scavengers. They have five jaws that form a structure known as Aristotle's lantern, which they use to gnaw on kelp or carrion. Gnawing of sea urchins on the holdfast that anchors a kelp can cause the kelp to be carried away by the surf. Predators that keep sea urchins under control therefore help to maintain kelp beds.

Fresh water is lethal to sea urchins. Following heavy storms, when the intertidal zone becomes flooded by fresh water, mortality in Purple Sea Urchins exceeding 90% has been recorded. When a sea urchin dies, its internal skeleton (test) and mouthparts may remain for many years. The skeleton resembles a hollow pincushion.

In recent years, a market for sea urchin gonads has developed. Between 1970, when the industry began, and 1987 the harvest grew to over 45 million pounds (21 million kg) annually. Those of the Red Sea Urchin are more valuable. This product is sold as "uni" or "frutta del mare" and is considered a delicacy in Japan, Italian markets, and some American sushi bars. It brings such a high price that it is now profitable to harvest sea urchins, remove the gonads—a mere fraction of the total body mass—and discard the rest. The present abundance of sea urchins near sewer outfalls makes this a profitable venture. However, if the "normal" population density returns, or if overfishing decimates them, as is likely in northern California, where over half of the 1987 harvest took place, this industry may be nipped in its infancy.

In the bottoms of tide pools or on lower cliff faces, rocks may be found with holes and tunnels burrowed in them. These tunnels, up to 1 inch (25 cm) in diameter, are carved by boring clams known as piddocks. There are several species in this family of clams (Pholadidae). They are separated by size and the hardness of the substratum into which they can burrow. The Flap-tipped Piddock, *Penitella penita*, usually occurs in shale or sandstone, but it has been reported to bore into concrete. Its shell is about 3 inches (7 cm) in length. The Scale-sided Piddock, *Parapholas californica*, is about 6 inches (15 cm) long. It burrows into hard clay, shale, or sandstone. This species may be an important cause of erosion in the intertidal zones.

The Rough Piddock, *Zirfaea pilsbryi*, usually bores into heavy clay or mud. Its shell reaches a length of 5 inches (13 cm). One reseacher observed its boring movements in a glass tube. Its foot, which is modified into a sucker, holds on to the clay while the shell is moved up and down and slightly rotated. Thirty-two turning movements, over 70 minutes of time, were required to make a single complete revolution. After a revolution, the direction was usually reversed. Most piddocks quit boring when their burrows are complete, but the Rough Piddock remains active throughout its life of seven to eight years.

A person searching beneath rocks in the tide pools will discover other forms of animal life. Brittle stars or serpent stars (Ophiuroidea) are starfish without tube feet that travel by moving their serpentlike arms. They feed on fine particulate organic matter that collects between sand grains. Sea Bats, *Patiria miniata*, are small red starfish that have a webbing between their arms. They feed in typical starfish fashion on small mussels and barnacles. Careful inspection of the grooves lined with tube feet on the underside of these animals will reveal the presence of a small polychaete worm, *Ophiodromus pugettensis*. This worm lives on the "table scraps" left over by the feeding of the starfish. It benefits from the starfish, but does not harm it. This type of symbiosis is known as commensalism.

Flatworms (Platyhelminthes) are primitive animals that have a saclike digestive cavity. There is but one opening. Many members of this group are parasitic, including flukes and tapeworms. Under rocks in the lower tide pools are free-living flatworms known as planarians. They creep about on their ciliated bellies looking more like gray shadows than animals. Lacking a circulatory system, they have a flattened body form that enables them to get oxygen and nutrients to their cells by simple diffusion. A pair of light receptors on the head enables them to tell when it is day or night. At night they creep over the rocks feeding on detritus, and during the day they remain under the rocks. There are two common species. The Common Flatworm, *Notoplana acticola*, looks like a one-way sign, sort of a fat arrow. These forms are seldom over 1/2 inch (12 mm) in length. The other type, known as the White Flatworm, *Pseudoceros luteus*, is roughly circular and may be up to 1 1/2 inches (37 mm) in length. This form is able to swim gracefully with lateral undulations of its body, looking like a miniature bat ray.

Among the most conspicuous members of these tide pools are the sea anemones (*Anthozoa*). These are in the phylum of hollow-bodied animals (Coelenterata or Cnidaria) that includes jellyfishes and corals. The body plan of these animals is a two-layered bag with a single opening into the digestive cavity. A ring of tentacles around the mouth gives them a flowerlike appearance. The tentacles bear tiny sting cells known as nematocysts. Any small object that touches the tentacles is instantly pierced by toxic barbs. The tentacles fold toward the mouth, and cilia carry the object inward until it drops into the mouth. Digestion is rapid, and undigestible parts are burped up in a surprisingly short time. These are opportunistic predators. They lie in wait with their tentacles open wide, catching materials that drop in or small organisms that carelessly walk across them. Among the food items that might drop in are pieces of mussel or barnacle that, during high tide, escape from a sloppy eater in the mussel bed above. The largest of the anemones is known as the Green Anemone, *Anthopleura xanthogrammica* (fig. 12.12F). It may be up to 10 inches (25 cm) in diameter, although half that size is more usual. This species is bright green due to the presence in the tissues of a single-celled alga that is photosynthetic. It uses the anemone for support and protection but apparently contributes nothing to the anemone. This is another form of commensalism.

Among the carnivores of these lower tide pools is a group of sluglike molluscs known as nudibranchs. These are shell-less snails with exposed gills; the name *nudibranch* means "naked gills." Nudibranchs are often brightly colored, but most are smaller than 2 inches (50 cm) in length, so they are seldom conspicuous. One interesting species, *Phidiana* (= *Hermissenda*) *crassicornis*, is white with bright blue lines on the center of its back. This species feeds on sea anemones and their relatives. Sting cells are ingested intact and are translocated to the tips of the exposed gills, technically known as cerata, where they provide protection for the nudibranch. Once again, it may be seen that a brightly colored animal need not fear predators.

The largest predator of these lower tide pools is the Two-spotted Octopus, *Octopus bimaculatus*. It may be up to 3 feet (1 m) across, but it is more likely about half that size. An octopus grasps its prey with its tentacles and immobilizes it with its venomous saliva. The saliva may be emitted into the water, in which case it acts as an anesthetic, relaxing the prey. Crabs are trapped and eaten in this way. An octopus can also drill a hole into an abalone shell with a file-like radula and inject the venom. The Two-spotted Octopus is capable of producing a painful bite when grabbed by a human, but apparently this is a rare occurrence. The octopus is famous for its ability to change color instantly, a trait that enables it to match its background perfectly while it lies in wait for unwary prey. In the tide pools it usually remains out of sight under an overhanging ledge, but even in the open it is difficult to see.

Octopus is edible and is considered a delicacy when properly prepared. To catch one, some people pour bleach in the water of a tide pool to bring the octopus out of hiding. This is an illegal practice. It causes great harm to all the animals in the intertidal system.

Fishes of the lower tide pools are usually kelplike in appearance and are colored to remain nearly invisible. Most common is the Woolly or Tidepool Sculpin, *Clinocottus analis*, sometimes known as a Tidepool Johnnie. These fish remain motionless on the bottom most of the time. When they move, they often crawl with their large pectoral fins. When they swim, it is in a short burst. They feed primarily on detritus that accumulates in the tide pools.

Superficially similar to the Woolly Sculpin is the California Klingfish, *Gobiesox rhessodon*. This little fish has an adhesive sucker on its underside so that it can cling upside down under rocks of the low tide zone. Among the kelps, a diligent observer may notice the Spotted Kelpfish, *Gibbonsia elegans*. This is an elongated, kelp-colored fish with a long dorsal fin running almost to its tail and a prominent eyelike spot above and behind the gill cover (operculum). This shy little fish so resembles the kelp in which it hides that it seldom is seen. The Rockpool Blenny, *Hypsoblennius gilberti*, and its relative the Bay Blenny, *Hypsoblennius gentilis*, resemble the kelpfishes, but they are rounded rather than flattened in cross section. They have a short, stubby nose and a long, continuous dorsal fin. They are common in the lower intertidal zone, but they are seldom seen because they also hide in the kelp.

A unique eel-like fish of the rocky intertidal is the Monkeyface Prickleback or Monkeyface-eel, *Cebidichthys violaceus*. This is a member of the prickleback family, which includes the Rock Prickleback or Rock-eel, *Xiphister mucosus*, an algae eater sometimes confused by skindivers with the California Moray, *Gymnothorax mordax* (fig. 12.13F). What makes the Monkeyface Prickleback unique is that it is an air breather. When the tide is out, through a mechanism that is not understood, it can absorb oxygen from the air. These fish can reach 30 inches (90 cm) in length, and large specimens have been known to survive for 24 hours out of water.

The most conspicuous fishes of the lower tide pools are juveniles of those that characterize the subtidal zone. Most common of these is the Opaleye, *Girella nigricans*, which gets its name from the opalescent blue color of its eyes. In the tide pools Opaleyes move about in active schools. They are easily identified by their dark color and distinctive white spot on each side of the dorsal fin. They remain tide-pool residents until they grow to about 2 inches (5 cm) in length, after which they move offshore to become members of the kelp forests. Adults reach a length of 15 inches (40 cm). These are primarily herbivorous fishes, although they will take detritus.

The Garibaldi, *Hypsypops rubicundus* (fig. 12.13A), is the official state saltwater fish. Juveniles are sometimes seen in tide pools, particularly in the spring and early summer. Garibaldis are in the tropical damselfish family (Pomacentridae). As juveniles, these fish are a bright reddish orange with very brilliant blue spots. As adults they are brilliant orange without the blue color, although there may be some blue on the edges of the fins. It is illegal to harm or capture them at any age. Adults reach about 1 foot (30 cm) in length. They are seldom seen in tide pools, but they are so common offshore that from any of a number of high cliffs they may be seen as glints of gold in the water. Goldfish Point in La Jolla gets its name from this phenomenon. The bright orange color is an advertisement to another fish that it is in for a fight if it tries to invade the Garibaldi's territory, which is usually an offshore rock crevice or cave. The name *Garibaldi* is probably in reference to a loose-fitting red garment by that name that was popular in the 1890s. The garment was named for Giuseppe Garibaldi, an Italian patriot who wore such a shirt as a uniform.

Subtidal Zone.   Offshore, beyond the influence of tides is a zone where wave surge carries away fine sediments, leaving a rocky or sandy bottom. Anchored to rocks or sand by large rootlike holdfasts are huge kelps that grow in water up to 100 feet (30 m) deep. In suitable areas there are forests of these kelps. Because of their flexible

FIGURE 12.13   Some fishes of the kelp beds. *A*. Garibaldi, *Hypsypops rubicundus*. *B*. Senorita, *Oxyjulis californica*. *C*. Cabezon, *Scorpaenichthys marmoratus*. *D*. California Sheephead, *Pimelometopon pulchrum*. *E*. Wolf-eel, *Anarrhichthys ocellatus*. *F*. California Moray, *Gymnothorax mordax*. (Illustrations *A*, *B*, and *E* from J. E. Fitch and R. J. Lavenberg. *Tidepool and Nearshore Fishes of California*. Berkeley: University of California Press, 1975. Illustrations *C* and *D* from J. E. Fitch and R. J. Lavenberg. *California Marine Food and Game Fishes*. Berkeley: University of California Press, 1971. Illustration *F* from S. Hinton. *Seashore Life of Southern California*. Berkeley: University of California Press, 1987.)

nature, kelps play an important role in moderating wave action. This dispersal of wave energy helps to protect beaches from erosion.

In southern California the most common kelp is known as the Giant Bladder Kelp, *Macrocystis pyrifera*. This is the largest of all known species of algae. Individual plants have been recorded at up to 200 feet (60 m) in length. Furthermore, it is the fastest-growing plant known. Individual fronds can grow over 14 inches (35 cm) per day. Long intertwined stipes of giant kelp extend to the surface, where a canopy of wrinkled leaflike blades is kept floating by gas bladders located at the base of each blade.

On the outer fringe of kelp beds in southern California is another giant kelp, Elk Kelp, *Pelagophycus porra*. It has a single very long stipe that terminates at the surface with a gas bladder that may be 6 inches (15 cm) in diameter. The bladder bears antlerlike branches that form huge membranous blades. If storms break the slender stipe, the bladder will float away and eventually the blades will break off, leaving only the huge bladder and a portion of the stipe. Years ago Spanish seamen recognized the appearance of these bulbs at sea as a sign they were approaching land. The Spanish called these bulbs *porra*, which means "club" in reference to the appearance of the bulb attached to a short section of stipe.

From about Pismo Beach northward, Bull Kelp, *Nereocystis luetkeana*, becomes the dominant seaweed. This massive species has a long, hollow, hoselike stipe up to 115 feet (35 m) long that ends in a single gas bladder. Above the bladder, long, flat, straplike blades up to 3 feet (1 m) in length extend into the water. As unlikely as it may seem, this is an annual species, attaining its enormous size in one year. Bull Kelp was an important food item for Pacific Indians, who also made musical instruments from the hollow stipes and bladders. For example, a trumpet can be made with a section of stipe and half a bladder.

Kelp beds provide a variety of habitats for animals. More than 750 species of fish and invertebrates live in these kelp forests. There are more than 150 species of fishes along the California coast, and nearly all of them can be found at one time or another in the kelp beds. They are attracted there because of the food. About 15 to 20 species are regularly found in kelp beds, where they feed on invertebrates and each other. Small fishes such as Topsmelt, *Atherinops affinis*, use the kelp for refuge, feeding largely on plankton. These fishes, similar in appearance to grunion, are also in the silversides family (Atherinidae).

Many fish species swim about among the stipes. Among these are Kelp Bass, *Paralabrax clathratus*, and the brightly colored Garabaldi, mentioned earlier. Also in the damselfish family (Pomacentridae) is the Blacksmith, *Chromis punctipinnis*, a blunt-nosed fish about the same size as the Garibaldi. It is blue-black with black spots on its upper surface and dorsal fin. Blacksmiths swim in swarming schools at the upper surface of the kelp beds. Their upturned mouths are useful for feeding at the surface. Blacksmiths often occur with brightly colored Senoritas, *Oxyjulis californica* (fig. 12.13B). These are members of the large, mostly tropical wrasse family (Labridae). Senoritas are long, thin fishes up to 10 inches (25 cm) in length. They are bright yellow with a black tail. These are the "cleaners" of the kelp beds, another example of commensalism. Senoritas pick parasites off other fishes, particularly the Blacksmiths and Garibaldis. Their bright color is an advertisement. Because their feeding activity is beneficial, other fishes seldom prey on them. In fact, customers may wait in line to be cleaned.

Another conspicuous member of the wrasse family is the California Sheephead, *Pimelometopon pulchrum* (fig. 12.13D). Typical of many wrasses, the sheephead has large, doglike teeth that are used to feed on starfish, sea urchins, lobsters, crabs, and many varieties of molluscs. When the tide is in, the California Sheephead is a major predator in the intertidal zone. Lobster fishermen often comment that a sheephead will enter a lobster trap and destroy the catch. A male California Sheephead is a brightly colored fish with a black head and tail. The chin is bright white, and the midbody is brick red. Young fish are females and are reddish brown all over. When they reach the age of seven to eight years, they change sexes. Females become males.

The most common fishes of the California coast are in the scorpionfish or rockfish family (Scorpaenidae). Many of these forage on the bottom. Of particular interest in this niche is the California Scorpionfish, *Scorpaena guttata*. California Scorpionfish are common in lower tide pools, where they lie motionless, concealed by their color, waiting for prey. Scorpionfish get their name from their venomous spines. All their median fins are equipped with venom to discourage predators. Fishermen who grab a scorpionfish without taking care to avoid the fins may receive a painful sting. Different people react with different degrees of severity, but most describe a deep, numbing pain and a sensation of heat. Swelling may be extensive. Much to the dismay of lobster fishermen, scorpionfish also invade lobster traps.

The Cabezon, *Scorpaenichthys marmoratus* (fig. 12.13C), superficially resembles the California Scorpionfish, and both fishes occur in the same habitat. The Cabezon, however, is smooth-skinned, and the California Scorpionfish is scaly. The Cabezon is in the sculpin family (Cottidae). Although the California Scorpionfish is commonly called a sculpin, it is not in the sculpin family. Moreover, the scientific name for the Cabezon means "scorpionfish." No wonder there is confusion!

In Spanish, *cabezon* means "big head." Food of the Cabezon includes almost any animal of the right size that moves. They are considered to be important predators of abalones. The Cabezon moves in and out with the tides, migrating from kelp beds to the intertidal zone when the tide is in. It is not uncommon for a Cabezon to become trapped in a lower tide pool when the tide is out. The Cabezon is capable of changing color to mimic its surroundings. It lies in crevices, where its mottled color makes it nearly invisible.

Also found on the bottom, among the stipes, is the California Moray, *Gymnothorax mordax* (fig. 12.13F). It ranges from the Santa Barbara area south to Baja California. In spite of its large size—specimens up to 5 feet (1.5 m) have been reported—this eel-like fish is well adapted for swimming among tangled kelp stipes or wriggling into cracks and hollows in the rocks. Morays spend daylight hours in the rocks, and they forage for crabs, shrimps, and lobsters among the kelps during the night. Among divers, morays have a reputation for being aggressive. It is true that morays will bite divers, and the bite may require stitches, but the moray does not attack in an unprovoked manner. A moray protects its territory in the rocks. Usually it remains in its crevice with only its head and jaws, armed with large teeth, visible at the entrance. A diver feeling about in the cracks for lobsters who unwittingly puts his or her hand in the home of a moray is almost certain to receive a painful bite.

From about Point Conception northward, the Wolf-eel, *Anarrichthys ocellatus* (fig. 12.13E), a California Moray look-alike, occurs in shallow rocky areas. It seems to replace the California Moray in northern waters. South of Point Conception to San Diego County, this fish occurs farther offshore in deeper, colder water. This fish is not really an eel but is a member of the wolf-fish family (Anarhichadidae), closely related to the blennies. The Wolf-eel is the only member of this family that occurs in the eastern Pacific Ocean. It is an example of parallel evolution. The Wolf-eel has moray-like habits and a similar body shape. It eats mostly crabs, sea urchins, snails, and abalone. It differs from the California Moray by having large eyelike spots all over its body. In addition, the nose of the Wolf-eel is blunter (like that of a large blenny), and its eye is larger and higher on its head.

Among the invertebrates that inhabit the subtidal zone, none is more important commercially than the lobster. Lobsters are found in kelp forests, reefs, and tide pools from Point Conception southward. The California Spiny Lobster, *Panulirus interruptus*, lacks the large pincers of the Atlantic lobsters. It is not defenseless, however, possessing spines on its antennae and body. Grabbing a lobster bare-handed may cause the antennae to be sawed across the wrist of the captor. Furthermore, the captive lobster will slap its tail back and forth vigorously, causing sawteeth on the lower margin of the abdomen to cut like a mechanical hedge clipper. Lobsters have been captured up to 3 feet (1 m) in length and at weights of almost 30 pounds (14 kg). Such monsters appear to be a thing of the past, however. In many areas, intensive fishing seems to crop them rapidly as they reach legal size.

Lobsters move by walking. They can move in any direction in this manner. When they are in a hurry, however, they swim backward with rapid flips of their muscular tail. Lobsters feed on practically anything; they are omnivorous scavengers. They feed on dead or living plants and animals and are particularly important as predators of sea urchins. In turn, they are fed on by fishes and octopi.

A number of species of crabs also characterze the subtidal zone. California's largest crab, the Sheep Crab, *Loxorhynchus grandis*, lives at the bottom of kelp beds, where it feeds on attached invertebrates or carrion. This member of the spider crab family (Majidae) may attain a leg spread of 38 inches (96 cm). Similar to the Masking Crab, *Loxorhynchus crispatus*, with which it may coexist, a young Sheep Crab camouflages itself by covering its back with a variety of living invertebrates and algae. An adult Sheep Crab has very few enemies; therefore large specimens are not decorated with camouflage.

Sea cucumbers (Holothuroidea) are in the phylum that includes starfish and sea urchins (Echinodermata). In southern California, the Common Sea Cucumber, *Parastichopus californicus*, is an orange, pickle-shaped member of the subtidal community. In northern California, two species may be encountered. A large orange species, *Cucamaria miniata*, is found subtidally. Small black cucumbers, *C. curata*, about 1 inch (25 mm) long, occur in the mussel beds. A sea cucumber maintains its body shape by filling itself with seawater. This is known as a hydrostatic skeleton. Its tube feet are reduced to a ring of tentacles around the mouth that are used to gather detritus. Sea cucumbers move around on the floor of kelp beds, where they feed heavily on broken pieces of kelp. They do not have many enemies, but when disturbed they eviscerate themselves, expelling most of their internal organs through the anus. Presumably, this habit is so disgusting that a would-be predator moves off in revulsion. A new set of internal organs can be regenerated in about six weeks.

California's kelp forests are constantly changing. The abundance of kelp itself has undergone a dramatic decrease. In southern California, this decrease has been so profound that it is considered by many to be an ecological disaster. In many areas, the absence of kelp has contributed to beach erosion; without the kelp beds to absorb some of the wave energy, the surf pounds on the beach without interference and washes away the sand. Furthermore, loss of kelp causes the loss of all the associated animal species.

Doubtless, an assortment of factors contributes to the decline in the abundance of kelp. Loss of kelp up and down the coast has been attributed in part to increases in temperature associated with periodic El Niño conditions. Warming of coastal waters occurred in the 1950s, 1960s, 1980s, and 1990s. Each time there was an associated loss of kelp.

The influence of temperature is not understood thoroughly, but it has been demonstrated that the giant kelps (*Macrocystis* spp.) cannot survive long if water temperature exceeds 58°F (14.5°C). During an El Niño episode, a water temperature of 70°F (20°C) or higher is common. Furthermore, in areas where seawater is used to cool electrical power plants, the temperature near the outflow often is warmer than that tolerated by many kelp communities. For example, near the outflow of the nuclear power plant at San Onofre, the temperature commonly exceeds 70°F (20°C). Nuclear power plants produce a great deal of heat. They require more water for cooling than fossil fuel plants; consequently, they emit more heat to the sea.

Another factor associated with loss of kelp is the increase in number of sea urchins in the subtidal zone, particularly in the vicinity of sewer outfalls. Their mode of feeding, which includes scraping of the holdfast or stipe of the kelp, increases the amount of kelp that gets carried away by the surf. It appears that grazing by sea urchins has kept the kelp from returning long after the warming effect of an El Niño episode subsides.

Feeding of sea urchins has been studied thoroughly. In addition to grazing, sea urchins are able to absorb dissolved organic matter (DOM) from seawater. The additional load of such water-soluble nutrients in the vicinity of sewer outfalls encourages the growth of the sea urchin population, which in turn increases grazing pressure on the kelp.

The natural order of things should encourage an increase in sea urchin predators. Two of the primary predators of sea urchins, California Spiny Lobsters and Sea Otters, *Enhydra lutris*, are victims of human interference. Lobsters cannot be counted on to limit the number of sea urchins because of the near-complete cropping of legal-sized lobsters by commercial fishermen. The Sea Otter, which will be discussed later, was all but eliminated by the 1800s, a victim of fur hunters. Today Sea Otters range regularly from about Pismo Beach north to Santa Cruz, and often to Año Nuevo.

Humans also must be considered predators of sea urchins. The industry that harvests sea urchins for their edible gonads is having an impact on sea urchin populations. How this industry will fare in the face of intensive cropping, and whether the kelp will return, remains to be seen. What is certain is that species composition and abundance of California's kelp forests has changed over the years. Factors influencing these changes seem to be a complex of natural environmental changes influenced by the activities of humans.

Causes of Intertidal Zonation

A combination of abiotic and biotic factors is responsible for intertidal zonation. Certain generalizations may be made, however. Upward distribution of most species is regulated by their tolerance for physical factors such as heat, light, and desiccation. Lower limits tend to be established by biological interactions such as predation and competition. Distribution on outer, more exposed sites is limited by wave shock or colonization by larvae. The opportunity for larvae to become established is directly related to the abundance of organisms. Appropriate bare space must be available, and larvae must be able to reach the site. In protected areas, accumulation of sediment also becomes a problem.

The effect of these interactions is that drought- and/or heat-tolerant species such as periwinkles and buckshot barnacles occur in the upper intertidal zone. They are kept from inhabiting lower zones because of competition with larger or faster-growing species such as acorn barnacles and limpets. Similarly, mussels inhabit the middle tide zone. Their upward establishment is restricted by tolerance for desiccation, and their lower distribution is controlled by starfish predation. Within mussel beds, two species are segregated by their respective abilities to tolerate wave shock or sedimentation. If an offshore reef intercepts larvae, mussels or barnacles may be less common than one would expect, and other species may seem unusually common. Similarly, juvenile rockfishes (Scorpaenidae) in offshore kelp beds prey on the larvae of intertidal invertebrates. One study in Monterey Bay found that predation by juvenile rockfishes reduced recruitment of barnacles to one–fiftieth of the level in the absence of fish.

Predatory birds, particularly oystercatchers, are also important in limiting the upward distribution of organisms such as barnacles and mussels. In some areas, cropping of attached intertidal animals is so complete that the oystercatchers become a major factor contributing to the bare space necessary for colonization of new organisms.

Distribution of algae is regulated by the same sorts of constraints. Most photosynthesis takes place while the tide is in; therefore different varieties of algae are sorted into distributional belts based on their abilities to tolerate heat and desiccation as well as depth of water.

Water is a very effective filter for light. Different wavelengths of light penetrate to different depths. Shorter wavelengths, such as blues and violets, penetrate more deeply. Longer wavelengths, such as reds and oranges, are eliminated near the surface. Different pigments within plants are associated with the absorption of different wavelengths. Chlorophyll absorbs red and blue light most effectively. Obviously, in deep water the red light cannot be used effectively by plants. The result of this complex of factors is that different kinds of aquatic plants live at different depths. They have different assortments of pigments with which they optimize light for photosynthesis at their respective depths. Green algae are the most similar to land plants and grow in shallow water. Kelps are brown algae, and they grow in deeper water. Holdfasts may be quite deep, but photosynthesis in brown algae seldom occurs below 50 feet (15 m). Red algae grow in the deepest water, up to 100 feet (30 m) deep. The red pigment reflects red light and absorbs the other colors, but at the depth where they grow there is no red light. They must photosynthesize only with the deeply penetrating blue light. Red algae are effectively black where they grow. This also may be an adaptation to conceal them from herbivores in the dim light.

Red algae that grow in deep water include agarweeds (*Gelidium* spp., *Pterocladia* spp.). These algae are sources of agar, a gelatin used as a culture medium for microorganisms and for making casts such as dental impressions. Because they live in deep water, where there is a limited amount of illumination, they do not grow rapidly. Consequently, harvesting red algae has limited promise as an economic enterprise in California. Most of our agar is imported from Japan.

Many seaweeds have defenses to prevent them from being eaten. For example, coralline algae are covered with calcareous material that makes them hard to eat. Chemical defenses are also used. One of the most interesting is that the gas bladder of Bull Kelp contains about 10% carbon monoxide. Furthermore, most kelps are poor food items because they contain toxic tannins and phenols. Another interesting adaptation may be seen in the subtidal kelp *Desmarestia*. This plant has small bubbles (vacuoles) of sulfuric or malic acid within its tissues. These acids can dissolve the calcareous teeth of sea urchins.

Succession is another feature that influences which organisms may be seen at any time. Disturbances cause bare areas, and the sequence in which organisms reappear is an example of succession. A typical situation is a large object such as a floating log being bashed against the rocks during a storm. The impact could clean the rocks locally of organisms such as mussels. Reestablishment of mussels and Goose Barnacles would take about a year. Early successional stages would include filamentous and sheetlike green algae. These are heavily grazed by limpets and crabs, but they are soon followed by forms that resist grazing, such as crustose and coralline algae with their calcareous coatings. Replacement of these forms may be accomplished by acorn barnacles, which physically pry off the algae as they grow. Mussels and Goose Barnacles eventually overtop the acorn barnacles. If the water is too deep, predators such as starfish and dogwinkles will soon eliminate the mussels and Goose Barnacles. In the long run they will be replaced by thick, leathery or coarsely branched kelps such as Sea Palms and rockweeds. An interesting characteristic of sewer outfalls is that they tend to keep the intertidal zone in a juvenile state, in which the dominant life forms include mostly filamentous and sheetlike green algae, or calcareous crustose and coralline algae.

There are also seasonal changes in the organisms that inhabit the intertidal zone, particularly the algae. As might be expected, the early successional species dominate in summer and fall, but they are far less common in winter. These are primarily annual forms. They have a rapid turnover, typical of early successional species in any habitat. Perennial species such as surfgrasses and kelps dominate during winter. Although there is also some variation in animal species, on a seasonal basis it is not obvious. There is a slight increase of attached animals, such as barnacles, in the spring. This coincides with their reproductive cycles and probably reflects attempts to colonize bare areas.

Differences in the distribution of animals up and down the coast seem to be primarily a function of water temperature. Most species of the intertidal zone are widespread, occurring all along the coast. For those that show a difference in distribution, it seems that Monterey Bay is a breaking point. Many northern species go no farther south, and many southern species go no farther north than that point. A second, less pronounced breaking point is at Point Conception, north of Santa Barbara. This is where the coastline makes a dramatic change in direction. South of Point Conception the coast is nearly on an east–west line, and there is a tendency of some northern species of intertidal fishes to move into colder, deeper water offshore.

Because of the overlap between northern and southern species, there is greater diversity south of Monterey, especially around Palos Verdes. This pattern seems to be reflected in the distribution of marine algae as well, with the greatest diversity occurring in the red algae (Rhodophyta).

Intertidal Productivity

To a large degree, nutrients in the intertidal zone come from outside sources. A major source of nutrients (nitrates and phosphates) is outwelling from rivers and estuaries. Estuaries are among the most productive ecosystems in the world, and a major portion of their nutrients is exported to the sea and carried southward by the longshore current.

Another source of nutrients is upwelling from the deep ocean. The major beneficiary of these nutrients is the oceanic ecosystem at the edge of the continental shelf. In southern California this upwelling occurs from about 55 to 125 miles (90–200 km) offshore. Also, this upwelling in southern California tends to occur in late summer and autumn when winds blow offshore. North of Point Conception a different kind of upwelling occurs. During summer months, associated with a persistent high pressure system over the north Pacific, there is a prevailing wind that blows southward along the coast. Because wind in the northern hemisphere tends to turn to the right, this effectively blows surface water away from the coast, causing an upwelling of cold water near shore.

Upwellings, estuaries, and the rocky intertidal region are highly productive areas. Photosynthesis in upwellings and estuaries fixes about 6000 grams of carbon per square meter per year. Kelp of the intertidal zone fix over twice that. One particular species, the Sugar Wrack and related members of the genus *Laminaria* produce about 90% of the food for the intertidal ecosystem in California.

Studies of primary production in Sea Palms indicate that the intertidal region is one of the most productive ecosystems on the planet, producing more biomass per year than a tropical forest. A grove of Sea Palms fixes about 32 pounds of carbon per square yard of surface per year (14.6 kg/m^2/yr). To explain such productivity, theories are being developed to incorporate the energy of waves into photosynthetic output. There seem to be three interrelated factors. Moving water enhances nutrient exchange. Also, by keeping the kelp in constant motion, it maximizes the amount of light that can shine on each frond. Third, wave energy constantly knocks organisms off the rocks, providing vacant surfaces for establishment and growth of new organisms. The sum of these effects is that total growth and photosynthesis are optimized.

The extreme diversity of the rocky intertidal region is also due to these forces. The number and size of niches available for colonization are proportionate to the amount of disturbance by waves and predators. A notion of ecosystem dynamics is developing that relates high-energy flow to diversity.

Even though growth of kelp blades is quite fast, the blades seldom seem to get any longer. This is because the tip of a kelp blade wears away as fast as it grows. Of the total amount of biomass produced by kelp, only about 11% is eaten by herbivores. Sea urchins are the most common of these, and they are sloppy eaters. As a result, about 4% of the biomass escapes the herbivores and winds up as bits and pieces that become particulate detritus. Sea hares and sea cucumbers eat the detritus. By far, the greatest amount of nutrient, amounting to 71% of the biomass, winds up as dissolved organic matter (DOM) in the seawater. It appears that seawater of the intertidal zone is a dilute broth of organic matter. Most of this water-soluble material gets there by direct release from growing plants. Some of it is released by natural cell breakdown due to abrasion and erosion, and some of it is a product of decay.

The significance of all this dissolved organic matter is unknown. Plankton can benefit from it, but plankton in the intertidal zone are not a major part of the ecosystem. Perhaps filter feeders such as mussels also absorb DOM. Mussels are known to be among the most productive, fastest-growing animals in the world. Sea urchins can absorb DOM directly from the water, but a full 42% of it leaks back as more dissolved organic matter. The implication is fascinating. Sea urchins absorb DOM and leak DOM, which seems very inefficient. Because it is inefficient, it forces us to search for some advantage to being leaky. Possibly, the loss of organic matter by the urchins is balanced by absorption of different materials. Another possibility is that properties of membranes that allow absorption of organic matter during a food shortage may result in a natural loss of organic matter when food is abundant. All of these possibilities await substantiation.

Marine Mammals

Mammals are air-breathing, fur-bearing animals. Because marine mammals have interacted with humans along the California coast for over two centuries, and because they are conspicuous, they deserve special mention. Seals and sea lions range out to sea to feed, but they return to the land to reproduce. They therefore can be considered members of both the intertidal and oceanic zones. The Sea Otter, however, is a legitimate permanent resident of the subtidal zone.

The Sea Otter, *Enhydra lutra* (fig. 12.14), is in the weasel family (Mustelidae). Males, slightly larger than females, reach lengths of over 4 feet (120 cm), including the 10- to 12-inch (25–30 cm) tail. Large males have been recorded up to 86 pounds (39 kg). Average weights are from 44 to 64 pounds (20–29 kg).

FIGURE 12.14   Sea Otter, *Enhydra lutris*. Not only is the thick fur important for insulation, but it traps air that provides for buoyancy. A Sea Otter floats on its back with its feet out of the water. This behavior helps to prevent loss of body heat from the nearly furless parts of the appendages.

Sea Otters live in a cold environment. In spite of the insulating qualities of their fur, Sea Otters must eat a remarkable amount of food to keep warm. They consume about 25% of their body weight each day, and this appetite is the basis for a new controversy. Shellfish fishermen fear that the Sea Otter will put them out of business.

These comical animals are truly a delight to watch. They float on their backs in the kelp beds and seem to feed constantly. Their preferred food items are sea urchins, crabs, and abalone. In sandy beach areas they also eat clams. They swim to the bottom, where they use a rock to dislodge their prey. Back at the surface they swim on their backs with the rock on their chest. They use this rock to crack the shells.

The history of Sea Otters in California is closely tied to the activities of humans. At one time, otters ranged in a continuous arc from Japan to Baja California. Biologists estimate that 200 years ago the California herd numbered about 20,000. By the turn of the twentieth century hunters had reduced the otter herd to perhaps 14 animals living near Point Sur. Hunting was outlawed in 1911 by the Fur Seal Treaty with Russia, Japan, and Great Britain. In 1913 Sea Otters were further protected in California by state law.

The species was feared extinct in California until a group of about 100 was "re-discovered" in 1938 during construction of Highway 1 along the coast. In 1941 a California Sea Otter Game Refuge was established, and in 1959 it was enlarged to include the area from the mouth of the Carmel River south to the mouth of Santa Rosa Creek near Cambria. Sea Otters responded to protection, and by 1976 the Sea Otter herd had increased to an estimated 1700 individuals. In 1977 the federal government listed the Sea Otter as a threatened species and outlawed the use by commercial fishermen of gill nets in shallow coastal water. Nevertheless, the herd has failed to expand significantly since the 1970s. Carrying capacity may have been reached, or perhaps there is a problem with incidental catches in gill nets set near Sea Otter habitat.

In recent years there has been a dramatic increase in offshore drilling and tanker transport of oil along the California coast. Experts fear that an oil spill could threaten the Sea Otter herd because insulating and buoyancy properties of Sea Otter fur are lost if the animal is soiled with oil. Authorities propose that, as a buffer against catastrophe, a portion of the herd be translocated to a second locality. To reduce economic impact to a minimum, the U.S. Fish and Wildlife Service has proposed translocating about 250 otters to San Nicolas Island, about 80 miles off the southern California coast. Commercial fishermen countered that about 11% of Santa Barbara's abalone and lobster catch comes from San Nicolas Island, and that introduction of the Sea Otter would certainly put them out of business. As evidence, they implicated the Sea Otter in the disappearance of the Pismo Clam south of the present refuge. Some biologists responded to that claim by explaining that the extermination of Sea Otters from the area had kept the abalone, lobster, and clam populations artificially large, and that commercial fishermen were lucky to have had it so good. In August 1987, U.S. Fish and Wildlife officials released 22 Sea Otters at San Nicolas Island. Success of the new colony was not good. Some of the animals tried to return to the mainland population, and others died. Attempts will continue to establish a viable population on San Nicolas Island, and its impact on shellfish will be monitored closely. Controversy will continue, but in this case it appears that public opinion will favor cute, cuddly Sea Otters over slimy snail meat.

There are six species of seals and sea lions along the California coast. There are two families of these marine mammals. Superficially they resemble each other, but they are easy to tell apart if a person knows what to look for. Earless seals or true seals (Phocidae) have no visible external ears. Eared seals (Otariidae), including sea lions, have small, visible external ears. Furthermore, earless seals swim in a fishlike fashion, with a side-to-side motion of the torso and hind flippers. Eared seals swim with a birdlike flapping of their front flippers and steer with their hind flippers. When these animals are on land, anatomical differences associated with these two modes of swimming are obvious. Earless seals have small, clawed front flippers. On land their hind flippers project backward, so they move themselves by lurching wormlike on their bellies. Eared seals have large, winglike front flippers, and they can bring their hind flippers forward to support their weight. On land they walk on all fours with a side-to-side swinging motion.

Earless Seals include hair seals and elephant seals. Worldwide, there are seven species of hair seals (*Phoca*). In general, these are the animals with white babies that are born on ice in polar latitudes. They have received worldwide attention because of the demand for their fine white fur, which leads to the seal babies being clubbed to death while they are on the ice. The local Harbor Seal, *Phoca vitulina* (figs. 12.15, 12.16A), is the only member of the group that routinely does not have babies with white fur. The white hair is lost either in the uterus or shortly after birth. The Harbor Seal has not escaped notoriety. There has been some talk that the feeding of Harbor Seals is

FIGURE 12.15   Juvenile Harbor Seal, *Phoca vitulina*.

a threat to commercial fisheries. In northern latitudes, Harbor Seals feed heavily on small fishes. In California waters they also feed on octopus.

Biologists estimate that there are about 18,000 to 20,000 Harbor Seals in California. Harbor Seals are so named because they frequently are observed in protected inlets, bays, or river mouths. They seem not to like human disturbance, and they will flee to the water when approached by a boat. Harbor Seals also haul out on rocks or reefs or in waterline caves, where they may feel secure. Males and females are similar in appearance. They are mottled with numerous small black and white spots, and their color darkens considerably when they are wet. Males are slightly larger, up to 6 feet (2 m) in length and weighing up to 300 pounds (136 kg).

Unlike other seals and sea lions, Harbor Seals seem not to have an elaborate social structure, nor are there breeding harems. They are sometimes described as monogamous, but they are actually promiscuous. Males will mate with any female in heat, and females may mate with more than one male. There is some evidence of a dominance hierarchy among males, but the male will defend the female only if she has not yet mated. Mating usually takes place in the water, and the female is left to fend for herself after copulation is accomplished. A female gives birth to a single pup in the spring, between February and May. Young are precocial. They are able to swim as soon as they are born, and they nurse for only about four weeks.

Harbor Seals are well adapted for diving. Similar to other seals, they exhale before diving and can remain submerged up to 23 minutes. By exhaling before they dive, they carry only a small amount of air below. In this way they can dive deeply, to depths of 1000 feet (300 m), and surface rapidly without experiencing the bends.

FIGURE 12.16   Some California seals and sea lions.
A. Harbor Seal, *Phoca vitulina:* mother and pup. B.
Northern Elephant Seal, *Mirounga angustirostris:* bull,
cows, and pup. Note that the earless seals (*A* and *B*)
have no external ears, and their hind flippers project
backward.

("The bends" is a name for nitrogen bubbles that appear in the blood of humans
when they come to the surface too quickly after breathing compressed air.) Oxygen
is stored in the seal's blood and tissues. Blood volume is large, and when they dive,
the spleen and liver are capable of storing the oxygenated blood. While they are
underwater their heart rate drops from about 55 to 15 beats per minute. In the
absence of oxygen they accumulate lactic acid. While diving, they triple the amount
of lactic acid in their blood. When they surface and breathe again, they metabolize
this lactic acid rapidly in their heart, lungs, and brain.

The Northern Elephant Seal, *Mirounga angustirostris* (fig. 12.16B), is the largest
seal in the Northern Hemisphere. A large male may attain a length of 16 feet (5 m)
and weigh up to 5000 pounds (2200 kg). Females are about two-thirds the size of
males. Adult males may be distinguished by their bizarre foot-long (30-cm) snout,
which they use as a resonating chamber to amplify their vocalizations.

C.

D.

FIGURE 12.16 (*continued*)   Some California seals and
sea lions. *C.* California Sea Lion, *Zalophus californianus*: bull, cows, and pups. *D.* Northern Fur Seal,
Callorhinus ursinus: bull, cows, and pup. The eared
seals (*C* and *D*) have external ear flaps (pinnae), and
their hind flippers can be brought forward to support
their bodies when they are on land. (Illustrations by
Jacqueline Schonewald from R. T. Orr and C. Helm.
Marine Mammals of California. Berkeley: University
of California Press, 1989.)

The former distribution of the Northern Elephant Seal was from Baja California to Point Reyes, north of San Francisco. Because of their valuable blubber, they were hunted nearly to extinction. One 16-foot male reportedly would yield 245 gallons (925 l) of precious oil, which was used as a lamp fuel. By 1892 the population was estimated to number less than 100 individuals. Hunting stopped in the late 1800s, when the animals had become so scarce that it required too much effort to locate them. Petroleum products were also beginning to replace seal oil as fuel for lamps. Hunting of these animals was prohibited by the 1911 Fur Seal Treaty.

In 1930 a small colony of Northern Elephant Seals was discovered on Guadalupe Island, 157 miles (252 km) from the Baja California mainland. From that group of seals, the population has made a remarkable recovery. At the present time the population is estimated at more than 90,000 individuals, and it is still increasing. Now they reproduce on the mainland at Año Nuevo near Santa Cruz, and they are reproducing as far north as the Point Reyes Peninsula. Favorite viewing points include Año Nuevo and the Farallon Islands, near San Francisco.

Elephant seals practice a type of polygamy known as polygyny, in which males keep a harem. Males engage in fierce battles to establish dominance and maintain access to females. Facing each other on land or in shallow water (fig. 12.17), they raise their chests, throw back their heads, and make loud clapping noises with their snouts extended into their open mouths. If such a threat doesn't settle the matter, they press against each other chest to chest and lash downward at each other's neck with their upper canine teeth. The neck and chest of the males is covered with thick, scarred skin, which is presumably the result of many such encounters and also helps to protect them during a fight. Once dominance is established, a male inseminates a harem of 10 to 100 females. Subdominant males tend to remain on the periphery of a breeding colony (rookery). Sometimes a subdominant male will accomplish copulation with one of the females, but about 85% of the females are fertilized by only 4% of the males. Nevertheless, the contribution of the sneak males is important for maintaining variation in the population.

Rookeries or breeding colonies begin to form in December, and mating and childbirth take place during winter. Some authorities contend that the only limiting factor on these huge mammals is available space on the beach for childbirth. Females appear on the beach first. As soon as males arrive, the fights begin. Once a harem is formed, the male will defend access to a female whether it is in water or on the land. Males defend access to females, not the space they occupy on land. Throughout most of the winter months, elephant seals remain in or near the rookeries. During this time they molt, or they haul out on the beach, where they spend most of their time sleeping.

The value of basking and sleeping by the large mammals is subject to some debate. Studies of their physiological state during basking show that heartbeat and breathing rates diminish considerably, and body temperature drops 10° to 15°F (5–9°C). The value of this behavior seems to be conservation of energy. For every 16°F (10°C) drop in body temperature, metabolic rate is cut in half. Other studies imply that basking by elephant seals is necessary to stimulate hair growth during this period of molting. One theory states that basking warms the skin, enhancing blood flow

FIGURE 12.17 Male Northern Elephant Seals, *Mirounga angustirostris*, battling for dominance.

to the surface necessary for growth of new hair. Although the fur probably plays a minimal role in keeping these animals warm, it must have some value. The animal's most effective insulation is the thick layer of subcutaneous blubber.

The growth rate of young Northern Elephant Seals is remarkably rapid. At birth they are not much larger than Harbor Seal pups. They require nursing for about four weeks, and during this time they drink about a gallon (4 l) of milk a day. The milk is very rich, containing about 45% fat. In comparison, cow's milk is only about 4% fat, and the fat content of human milk is slightly lower. During the first few weeks of life, pups remain on the beach. Later they enter the water from time to time. Once the pups are weaned, mother-child interactions are minimal. By this time the pup has become remarkably fat and usually has quadrupled its weight.

Where Northern Elephant Seals go after they leave the rookery is not well understood. They are known to travel great distances. Young animals, three to four months old, are known to migrate from Guadalupe Island to San Miguel Island of the Channel Island group, a distance of nearly 600 miles (950 km). Some stragglers have been recorded as far north as Prince of Wales Island in southeast Alaska, 1800 miles (3000 km) north of their northernmost breeding ground.

Apparently, Northern Elephant Seal herds disperse to spend most of their time at sea. During spring and summer, they are constantly at sea. Females equipped with recording instruments were found to spend up to 90% of their time underwater during the time they are at sea, an interval that averages 72 days. Little is known of their food habits, but based on their behavior in very deep water, it appears that they feed on squid and other organisms that inhabit the oceanic zone at the lower reaches of light penetration. They have very large eyes, which implies that they see well in the dim light of deep water. They are capable of diving deeply and remaining underwater up to 45 minutes. Individuals equipped with recording devices have been found to dive routinely to depths in excess of 3000 feet (900 m), and one dive to an estimated depth of at least 4125 feet (1289 m) has been reported.

The California Sea Lion, *Zalophus californianus* (fig. 12.16C), is the most common eared seal on the California coast. These are the trained "seals" that perform in the circus. The name *sea lion* refers to the breeding and social behavior, in which males fight for dominance and keep a harem of females. Moreover, in some species of sea lions the dominant male has a large, thick mane of yellowish hair on his neck and chest, somewhat like a male African Lion. Male sea lions primarily maintain a territory on land, which they will fight to keep clear of subdominant males. Dominant males are conspicuously larger than females, attaining a length of 8 feet (2.5 m) and a weight of 600 pounds (280 kg). Females grow to a length of 6 feet (2 m), but they seldom weigh more than 200 pounds (90 kg). Adult males, with their huge chest and large head, may appear quite regal as they maintain a position on a high perch amidst a harem of 10 to 20 females and juveniles. Adults are tan when dry but are dark brown to black when wet.

California Sea Lions are not as well insulated as seals or Sea Otters. They have neither thick fur nor a thick layer of blubber. Consequently, they tend to remain in tropical and subtropical areas of the world. Subspecies of the California Sea Lion also occur in Japan and the Galapagos Islands, but distribution of the species does not occur northward beyond Vancouver Island in British Columbia. About 90% of the California subspecies population breed on San Nicolas and San Miguel, the outermost of the southern California Channel Islands. Even though they do not have the insulation of seals, their high metabolic rate apparently more than compensates. Their body temperature is not known to fall when they are basking. In fact, it appears that they are more concerned about keeping cool. On warm days they frequently wet themselves in tide pools or roll in wet sand, which increases evaporative cooling. After a period of exercise in the water, they float on their sides with one front and one hind flipper out of the water, which also assists in evaporative cooling. Where the water is cold, sea lions apparently are able to reduce heat loss by holding dry flippers out of the water. Fur seals also do this, and sometimes they grasp together their front and hind flippers in a position that reminded old sailors of a jug handle. Thus the behavior became known as "jugging."

Breeding aggregations of California Sea Lions begin in May. Unlike elephant seals, sea lions breed and give birth in the spring. Similar to elephant seals, mating and birth take place on land. Pups nurse for about four months on milk that is nearly 16% fat. Each female knows her own pup and keeps track of it by its odor and vocalizations. At first, newborn pups have black pelage, which may enhance heat absorption on land. By the end of the first year, the hair takes on the tan color of the adult. After the breeding season, about mid-August, California Sea Lions disperse up and down the coast from their rookeries. There is some evidence that males tend to go northward and females southward. During this time they appear along the coast singly or in small groups.

Sea lions are thought to feed primarily at night. They have been observed to dive to a depth of over 900 feet (300 m), although they probably feed closer to the surface than most of the earless seals. Their eyes are relatively large, which suggests that they use vision to locate prey. In addition, movement and sounds of prey are detected by their whiskers (vibrisae) as vibrations in the water. Experiments have indicated that their whiskers are about 10,000 times more sensitive than their ears. They prey upon schooling animals such as anchovies, squid, and shrimps. Estimates of the amount of food eaten per day vary from 2 to 30 pounds (1–14 kg). A 600-pound (280-kg) sea lion in a New York Zoo was fed nearly 100 pounds (45 kg) of fish each week. Doubtless, this sea lion was relatively inactive and required less food than a free-ranging animal at sea.

A peculiar feature of sea lions is that many have been found with rocks in their stomachs. One specimen in a zoo had 69 pounds (31 kg) of stones in its stomach! Theories of the function of these stones vary considerably. It has been suggested that they are used as a ballast or to suppress appetite. It also has been suggested that the stones aid in breaking up fish bones, or at least in their defecation. Perhaps the stones help to grind up the parasitic worms that often plague sea lions. Whatever the case, the sea lions are stone swallowers.

The actual number of sea lions along the California coast is subject to some controversy. Estimates of the total number vary from about 50,000 to 150,000. Since the late 1970s, consistently conducted population surveys seem to have produced reliable estimates of population numbers. According to personnel at the National Marine Fisheries Service, as of 1988 the total number of California Sea Lions in the United States was around 85,000 and was increasing by about 3% per year.

There also has been an increase in the number of documented shark attacks on humans. Of particular concern are deaths caused by attacks of the Great White Shark, *Carcharodon carcharias*. The cause of this increase is not understood, but some authorities relate it to the resurgence of the marine mammal populations, particularly sea lions. Other authorities relate the attacks to the increased number of surfers riding small surfboards, the silhouette of which from beneath might resemble a sea lion.

Interactions between sea lions and fishermen have been controversial in California since the early 1920s. The population was provided protection by the state in the 1930s and by the federal government in 1972, with passage of the Marine Mammal Protection Act. Increasing numbers of sea lions and fishermen have resulted in an increasing number of conflicts. Commercial fishermen can obtain a permit allowing them to take measures to protect their gear and catch, including killing. Sportfishermen were not permitted to take such steps, but in 1986 the federal government began permitting operators of sportfishing boats to use nonlethal harassment to keep sea lions away from the fishing lines of passengers. Various government agencies are cooperating in studies to devise methods to reduce interactions between sea lions and fishermen.

The Northern Sea Lion or Steller's Sea Lion, *Eumetopias jubatus*, occurs from San Miguel Island northward. This is a large, tawny sea lion whose range overlaps that of the California Sea Lion as far north as Vancouver Island. Most frequently, Northern Sea Lions occupy remote, rocky coasts, so they are not conspicuous to humans. They can be observed, however, at Sea Lion Caves in Oregon or at Año Nuevo Island off the central California coast. Sometimes they may be observed at Seal Rocks by the Golden Gate.

Populations of these sea lions have diminished off the southern California coast since the 1930s. Data are inconclusive, but during the late 1920s they were apparently more common than California Sea Lions. The cause of the decline is not well understood, but it may be related to a gradual warming of the water. Other possible causes include competition from expanding populations of California Sea Lions and the effects of pesticides such as DDT. By 1976 the population at the Channel Islands, particularly San Miguel, had dropped to about 50 animals, and it has not recovered significantly since. The Channel Islands represent the southernmost portion of the range, and large-scale fluctuations are not uncommon at the periphery of an animal's range. On the Farallon Islands, mortality of Northern Sea Lion pups has increased markedly. By 1982, two-thirds of the pups were dying. Perhaps slight changes in the environment or food supply stress them in the southern portion of their range. There are about 1600 individuals in northern California. Over the total range, including most of the northern Pacific, there are about 250,000 of these majestic animals, although that number seems to be declining, too.

The male (bull) Northern Sea Lion may reach a length of 13 feet (4 m) and a weight of 2000 pounds (900 kg), over twice the size of a male California Sea Lion. A female Northern Sea Lion is about the size of a California Sea Lion male. Social behavior of the Northern Sea Lion is similar to that of the California Sea Lion. They can dive to a depth of 600 feet (190 m), and they feed on items such as squid and herring.

The other two species of eared seals that occur off California are known as fur seals. Northern Fur Seals, *Callorhinus ursinus* (fig. 12.16D), are primarily winter visitors, although a small colony is present year-round on the Channel Islands. Most of the time Northern Fur Seals are seen in small groups in the open ocean 10 to 50 miles (16–80 km) offshore. They can be distinguished from sea lions by their short gray nose, long flippers, and thick fur. These southern migrants are usually females and juveniles. Males tend to remain in northern waters. Major breeding rookeries are on the Pribilof Islands in the Bering Sea. Adults return each year to their place of birth, and their round-trip migrations of 6000 miles (9600 km) are among the longest of any mammal species. Similar to other fur-bearing mammals, they were hunted almost out of existence for their high-quality fur. Fur seal treaties enabled them to rebound.

In the 1960s, a breeding colony of Northern Fur Seals was discovered on San Miguel Island. By the 1980s that number had risen to almost 4000 animals. Winter sightings at sea indicate that at least some animals are not migrating to the Arctic. Archeological excavations indicate that Northern Fur Seals historically occurred on the Channel Islands, so perhaps this resurgence is part of normal population fluctuations.

The Guadalupe Fur Seal, *Arctocephalus townsendi*, originally inhabited a range that extended from Monterey Bay to the Revillagigedo Islands of Mexico. The northernmost rookeries were likely on San Miguel Island. These seals also resemble sea lions, but they can be distinguished by their long, collie-like muzzle; long, narrow flippers; and thick, dark fur. They were hunted ruthlessly for their fur, and by 1895 they were thought to be extinct. In 1926 a few were reported on Guadalupe Island off Baja California, and in 1928, two males from this group were collected for the San Diego Zoo. They died in captivity, and the species was once again thought to be extinct. In 1949 a single lone male was reported on San Nicolas Island, but it was not until 1954 that a small breeding colony, 14 animals in a cave, was once again discovered on Guadalupe Island. Since that time, their numbers have grown to over 1600, and their range appears once again to be expanding northward. Lone males have been observed as far north as San Miguel Island.

It was not the fur treaties that protected Guadalupe Fur Seals. They were saved because of their rarity, which by the turn of the century made it unprofitable to hunt for them. Guadalupe Fur Seals were provided protection in 1928, when Guadalupe Island was designated a nature preserve by Mexico. Hunting was banned by Mexico in 1966, and the species was afforded protection by the United States with the passage of the Marine Mammal Protection Act in 1972. Additional protection was provided in 1985, when the species was listed as threatened by the federal government. Recovery was also facilitated by the seals' habit of hauling out in dark, inaccessible caves. Perhaps continued protection will enable them once again to reestablish a breeding population on the Channel Islands.

Regarding the conflict between humans and marine mammals, what humans think of the animals seems to depend on whether or not they are attempting to make a living from the harvesting of marine life. Many would like to see marine mammals harvested for their fur, blubber, or meat. Others would like to reduce their numbers because they compete with humans for fish, clams, abalone, or lobsters. There is no question that unregulated hunting seriously decimated the number of marine mammals, and that since they have been provided protection, their numbers have increased. If they eventually become so abundant that they interfere with the natural order of things, it is possible that they could be hunted in a regulated way, as are terrestrial game animals such as deer. Critics of this idea contend that the economic gain or loss associated with seals, sea lions, and Sea Otters is trivial compared to the good they do as top-order carnivores in the coastal ecosystem. Another benefit, which is often overlooked, is that these animals, by feeding in deep water and returning to the surface to eliminate wastes, actually perform an important service in bringing nutrients upward. Ecological equilibrium in the ocean benefits all of mankind. Killing Sea Otters, seals, and sea lions for the economic protection of a few hundred fishermen makes very little sense.

Estuaries

An estuary is a place where fresh water mixes with seawater. This occurs where a river flows into a bay. In California the origin of such a bay is usually associated with a barrier beach bar, a sandspit formed by the longshore current. The type of bay formed by a drowned river mouth is less common in California because, for the most part, the coastline here is rising rather than subsiding. San Francisco Bay is a notable example of a drowned river mouth. Tomales and Bolinas Bays, along the San Andreas fault near Point Reyes, are drowned rift valleys.

Estuaries are productive ecosystems, but there is not a great diversity of habitats. As a result, there is not as large a number of species as there is in the rocky intertidal zone, but the number of individuals of each species is enormous. What diversity there is is another manifestation of edge effect. There is a boundary between the land and water, and there is also a boundary between fresh water and seawater that moves back and forth with the tides.

Fresh water is lighter than seawater, so it flows over the top of seawater in the estuary. Because of coriolis force, fresh water also tends to flow closer to the coast on the north side (the right side) of the estuary. A wedge of water where salinity changes rapidly from fresh to seawater (0.0% to 3.5% TDS), moves back and forth with the tides. Free-swimming organisms will remain in the region that suits them best, but organisms in the mud may be subjected to dramatic changes in salinity as this wedge of water passes over them. It appears that a critical region for organisms occurs where the salinity varies from 0.05% to 0.08%. Upstream from that region, freshwater species increase in number, and below that region there is an increase in numbers of marine species. Surprisingly few species occur at the region of transition.

The consequence of this variation is that estuaries are characterized by four primary communities: Freshwater Marsh, Salt Marsh, Mud Flats, and Open Water. The Freshwater Marsh was discussed in chapter 10. Attention here will be directed to the other three habitats.

Salt Marsh.   As in the Freshwater Marsh, there are bands of vegetation in the Salt Marsh based on the amount of submergence tolerated by the plants. Among the rooted macrophytes, the plant that occurs farthest into seawater is Eel Grass, *Zostera marina*. Eel Grass grows from the low-tide level to depths of about 20 feet (6 m). This is the same species that grows with surfgrasses in the rocky intertidal zone. However, it tends to be more filamentous in appearance in estuaries.

The emergent plant that grows farthest into seawater is Cord Grass, *Spartina foliosa* (fig. 12.18). This is a plant up to 3 feet (1 m) in height that may be half submerged. It spreads through the salty mud by means of buried runners (rhizomes). Cord Grass grows like rice in a paddy, and it is able to tolerate its harsh habitat by means of several important adaptations. Cord Grass stems are hollow and air-filled, a feature that enables oxygen to reach submerged roots. Also, similar to many salt-tolerant plants (halophytes), Cord Grass is equipped with salt glands to excrete excess salts. It is also interesting to note that Cord Grass is one of the very few cool-climate plants that has C_4 photosynthesis. This type of high-efficiency photosynthesis occurs in desert halophytes such as saltbushes that must photosynthesize and excrete salts in

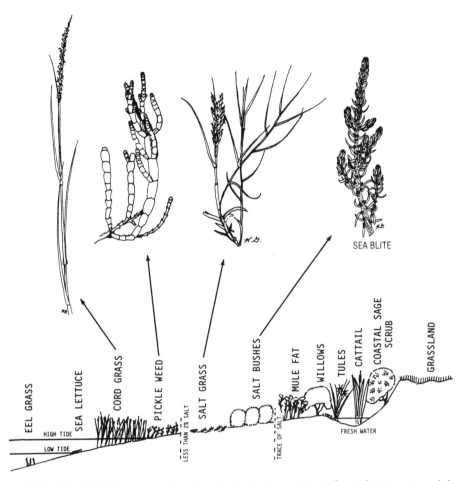

FIGURE 12.18 Salt Marsh zones. (Drawings by Karlin Grunau Marsh from *The Mountains and the Wetlands,* Orange County Land Environment Series, no. 2, 1975.)

a hot, dry climate. In order for this plant to cope with drought stress, it is probably important that it be able to photosynthesize with stomates partly closed, and this is enhanced by high-energy C_4 photosynthesis. Cord Grass is also equipped with nitrogen-fixing bacteria in its roots; therefore its foliage is an important source of protein for the marsh ecosystem.

Cord Grass is the greatest contributor to the high productivity of an estuary ecosystem, although it does not make its contribution in the expected way. Very few organisms are equipped to eat the salty foliage. Cord Grass adds to the ecosystem through detritus. Root systems trap sediment and detritus. Micro-organisms consume the detritus and contribute to the dissolved organic matter that enters the water. Worms and snails feed directly on the detritus, and nutrients enter the estuary food web. Fishes and birds feed on the snails and worms, and nitrogenous wastes of the animals return to the system to complete the cyle. When the tide goes out, soluble nutrients are carried out to sea. It is this outwelling that contributes nutrients to sandy beaches and the rocky intertidal region.

Inland from the Cord Grass is a belt of succulent plants. Of these, the pickle-weeds and glassworts (*Salicornia* spp.) are the most common. Roots of pickleweeds are covered by seawater only during the highest tides, a habitat similar to the Alkali Sink community discussed in the chapter on deserts. A pickleweed absorbs water and salt. The salty water is stored in its tissues, which helps to maintain a favorable flow of water into the plant even though it is rooted in salty soil. The plant is leafless. Its stem resembles a series of small green pickles. The section at the tip of the stem becomes filled with salt and drops off, recycling the salt back into the ecosystem.

Associated with the pickleweeds may be other halophytes such as Salt Grass, *Distichlis spicata*, and salt-tolerant shrubs such as Sea Blite, *Suaeda californica*. Similar to plants in the desert, these shrubs excrete salt upon their leaves through salt glands. Because salt marshes are among our most endangered habitats, they have their share of endangered species. The Salt-marsh Bird's-beak, *Cordylanthus maritimus*, is a paintbrush-like species in the figwort family (Scrophulariaceae) that is federally listed as endangered.

Diversity in the Salt Marsh is maintained by environmental perturbations such as freshwater flooding and tidal flushing. Plant productivity is high, and growth of new plants is rapid. Detritus enriches the muds. Dense root systems trap the detritus and mud, which allows more nutrients to accumulate. A natural catastrophe such as a flood may scour an area, and the cycle of regeneration repeats itself. Some people call this a "build-and-tear" ecosystem.

Animals are not numerous in Salt Marshes. The kinds of animals vary from aquatic to terrestrial, but no type is particularly conspicuous. In the water there is a variety of immature and adult aquatic invertebrates, including arthropods, worms, and snails. When the tide comes in, fishes such as the California Killifish, *Fundulus parvipinnis* (fig. 11.19), move among submerged stems and feed on detritus and invertebrates. The Bay Pipefish, *Syngnathus leptorhynchus* (fig. 11.24), hides in the Eel Grass, feeding on small crustaceans. Also when the tide is in, burrowing detritus feeders and filter feeders, many of which are worms, go to work. Among these are polychaete worms similar to those that live on sandy beaches (fig. 12.6B). Filter-feeding tube worms build their tubes of cemented sand grains, fitted together as precisely as the rocks in a stone wall. This is remarkable considering that the tubes are composed of very fine particles and are only one grain thick. One worm in captivity was observed to require two months to build only 3/4 inch (19 mm) of tube. Each tube is the life work of its resident.

There are few terrestrial animals in a Salt Marsh. The vegetation is not very nutritious, so few organisms eat it. Apparently, grasshoppers are able to tolerate a diet of Salt Marsh vegetation, but most of the animals that live in a Salt Marsh feed upon seeds or the aquatic animals.

The largest Salt Marsh in the state occurs in San Francisco Bay. In this marsh there is an endemic mammal, the Salt-marsh Harvest Mouse, *Reithrodontomys raviventris*. This mouse builds its nest in the vegetation in a birdlike manner. It is nocturnal, coming out at night to feed on seeds. Even though this small mouse has a high metabolic rate, it is able to conserve energy by huddling in its insulated nest. Salt-marsh Harvest Mice are truly unique in their ability to survive on seawater. Because Salt Marshes are endangered habitats, it should be no surprise that the Salt-marsh Harvest Mouse is listed by the federal government as an endangered species. Due to the filling and diking of various portions of San Francisco Bay, the range of this unique mouse has declined to a small population on a few isolated islands in the remaining marshland.

There are very few resident bird species in Salt Marshes. Of the five species and subspecies that nest here, four are listed as threatened or endangered by the California Department of Fish and Game. Three of these are in the rail family (Rallidae). These are narrow, slab-sided birds that move through marsh vegetation without disturbing it. The expression "skinny as a rail" refers to the appearance of a rail in front view. The only rail that is not threatened is the Sora, *Porzana carolina* (pl. 14G), which is equally at home in a freshwater marsh.

Clapper Rails, *Rallus longirostris*, are the largest of these rails. They are more often heard than seen, and their distinctive call is the basis for their name. It is a series of 10 or more sharp "kek, kek, kek" noises that sound a bit like clapping. They resemble chickens with a short, upturned tail and light rump. They are active at dawn and dusk, feeding on insects and other invertebrates. At this time they may venture onto Mud Flats to feed.

Three subspecies of Clapper Rail in California are listed as endangered. The two that inhabit coastal Salt Marshes are the California Clapper Rail, *R. longirostris obsoletus*, which occurs from San Francisco north, and the Light-footed Clapper Rail, *R. longirostris levipes*, which occurs from Santa Barbara south. The third variety, the Yuma Clapper Rail, *R. longirostris yumanensis*, frequents Freshwater Marshes in the southwest deserts. All three of these forms are victims of habitat destruction, including damming, diking, draining, pollution, and predation by introduced Black Rats, *Rattus rattus*. In spite of protection, it appears that the Light-footed Clapper Rail is in serious trouble. It was listed as endangered in 1970, and in 1974 the California Department of Fish and Game estimated that there were from 500 to 750 birds left. By 1986 only 143 pairs of the birds were left, and five marshes within its range contained none.

The other threatened rail that occurs in Salt Marshes is a sparrow-sized bird known as the California Black Rail, *Laterallus jamaicensis*. It is small and secretive; therefore it is seldom seen by humans. Black rails also range into Freshwater Marshes at several inland localities. They have been observed in the San Joaquin and Imperial valleys.

Belding's Savannah Sparrow, *Passerculus sandwichensis beldingi*, is also listed as endangered. This is a dark-colored, heavily striped sparrow that occurs most commonly in the pickleweed habitat from southern California to Baja California. It feeds primarily on seeds but will take insects when they are available. This bird is unique among the songbirds of California because it can drink seawater.

The fifth resident bird of the Salt Marshes is the Marsh Wren, *Cistothorus palustris*, a fairly common bird in marshes throughout the United States. It is a small, long-billed bird with a distinctive white eye stripe. It is secretive, but during the breeding season it will sing day and night, uttering a series of loud, rapid notes and rattles. It moves about incessantly, feeding on insects it gleans from the vegetation.

Of migratory birds that spend time in marshes, none is more at home than the American Bittern, *Botaurus lentiginosus*. This member of the heron family (Ardeidae) has a brown and yellow streaked breast. During daylight hours, bitterns usually remain motionless with their beaks pointed straight up. The streaking on the breast provides perfect protective coloration. They also have been reported to sway back and forth when the wind blows and remain still when the wind quits. Bitterns are most active at dusk or during moonlight. They feed on snails, frogs, fish, and even small mammals if they can get them. The sound of a courting American Bittern on a spring moonlit night has been described as a "thunder pump." Males make an outrageous booming sound accompanied by an inflated breast and peculiar posturing. American Bitterns seldom breed in southern California, but this mating ritual may be observed farther north.

Another bird that spends most of its time in the marshes is the Northern Harrier, *Circus cyaneus*. This raptor was formerly known as the Marsh Hawk, in reference to its preference for this habitat. These hawks are most easily recognized by their light-colored rump and habit of flying low over the marsh. They seldom soar in the typical hawklike manner. Northern Harriers are not restricted to Salt Marshes. They occur in a variety of open habitats, including agricultural fields, and they have even moved into desert areas where agriculture is important. Their numbers have increased since the banning of DDT.

Most birds seen from time to time in the marshes are merely using the marsh for a temporary refuge or resting place. For example, during high tide it is very common for birds that feed on the Mud Flats to wait in the marshes for the tide to go out.

Mud Flats.   When the tide is in, Mud Flats are covered with water. At this time a variety of creatures become active, feeding on the surface of the mud or emerging from their tubes to feed on small planktonic organisms. When the tide is out, many kinds of birds venture onto the mud to feed.

Various kinds of algae grow on the surface of the mud, but this is not the primary food for the Mud Flat community. The contribution of these algae is greatest during spring and summer, when long day length enables more photosynthesis to occur. The primary food is detritus. Of secondary importance is the food provided by plankton or that which is in the water as dissolved organic matter.

A variety of animals inhabit tubes and burrows in the mud. Most famous of these is the Innkeeper, *Urechis caupo* (fig. 12.19A), a specialized worm. Some authorities classify it as a type of segmented worm (Annelida), but others put it in its own phylum, Echiuroidea. These large, tube-dwelling worms are unsegmented as adults,

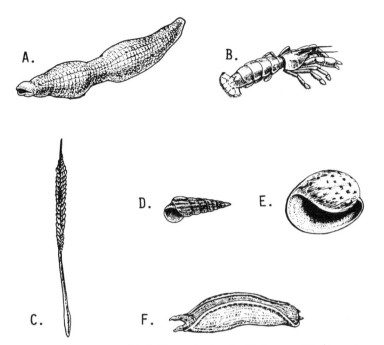

FIGURE 12.19 Some Mud Flat animals. *A.* Innkeeper, *Urechis caupo.*
B. California Ghost Shrimp, *Callianassa affinis. C.* Slender Sea Pen, *Stylatula
elongata. D.* California Horn Shell, *Cerithidea californica. E.* Cloudy Bubble
Snail, *Bulla gouldiana. F.* Bay Sea Hare, *Navanax inermis.* (Illustrations from
S. Hinton. *Seashore Life of Southern California.* Berkeley: University of Cali-
fornia Press, 1987.)

which is part of the reason to classify them differently. The Innkeeper lives in a U-
shaped burrow with two entrances up to 3 feet (1 m) apart. Inside the burrow the
animal constructs a funnel-shaped slime net that traps detritus and plankton. When
it feeds, the Innkeeper crawls forward, eating the net and the material trapped in
it. The name *Innkeeper* refers to cohabitation of the burrow by other animals, such as
worms, crabs, and fishes, which may eat the Innkeeper's "table scraps," another form
of commensalism. One of the best-known cohabitants is the Arrow Goby, *Clevelandia
ios.* This 2-inch (5-cm) fish uses the burrow primarily as a refuge. It forages on the
surface of the mud and retreats to the burrow when danger is near. As many as five
gobies may be found at a single time in an Innkeeper's burrow.

Also common in the mud is a variety of shrimps. Among these is the California
Ghost Shrimp, *Callianassa affinis* (fig. 12.19B). When the tide is in, these shrimps
propel through their burrows a current of water, from which they extract plankton
and detritus. The digging of these animals is important to the community because
it helps to overturn and oxygenate the mud.

Another interesting mud dweller is the Slender Sea Pen, *Stylatula elongata*
(fig. 12.19C). This is a coral-like animal in the group that includes jellyfish and

sea anemones (Coelentrata or Cnidaria). The Slender Sea Pen is about 10 inches (25 cm) long and is constructed around a central limy axis above which are leaflike structures that bear sting cells. When the tide is in, these animals elongate their bodies, expand the "leaves," and proceed to feed on plankton. When the tide is out, they retreat into the central axis, leaving an inch or two (25–50 mm) of the central stalk above the mud. Among the oddities of this animal is its ability to produce light. When disturbed, it gives off flashes of light that move in waves along the body.

A variety of clams occurs in the mud. These are among the most common filter feeders. The largest of these is the Geoduck (pronounced "gooey-duck"), *Panopea generosa*, of the northern California bays. Shells of this species commonly exceed 8 inches (12 cm) in length and may weigh up to 12 pounds (5.5 kg). The Geoduck lives in a semipermanent burrow up to 3 feet (1 m) in depth. A disturbance such as a person walking on the mud causes the clam to withdraw its siphon, expelling a jet of water. This enables the clam hunter to locate the animal. The difficulty of extracting a Geoduck from its burrow is legendary, leading to the notion that this clam possesses enormous willpower. In fact, it simply is not possible to pull one from its burrow by its siphon. If a person wants a Geoduck, he must dig it out. Geoduck hunters leave the Mud Flats looking as if they were bombed.

Clams that occur in the muds of estuaries have been harvested as food for many years. It is unfortunate that the concentration of toxic metals such as lead and mercury has been increasing in association with urbanization. In southern California, the concentration of these metals is so high that it is no longer advisable to eat shellfish harvested from bays and estuaries.

A variety of snails and slugs occurs on the surface of the mud. From San Francisco southward, the most common snail is the California Horn Shell, *Cerithidea californica* (fig. 12.19D). These snails have elongate, spiral-shaped shells over 1 inch (25 cm) in length. These snails are so common that at low tide the surface of the mud appears bumpy. When the tide is in, they move about feeding on detritus, and many birds feed on them. Of special interest is that the California Horn Snail serves as an alternative host for many parasitic flatworms, such as the bird liver flukes (Microphallidae). The fluke life cycle also involves the California Killifish. Birds get the parasites by eating the fish and then pass them back to the mud with their feces.

Another common snail is the Cloudy Bubble Snail, *Bulla gouldiana* (fig. 12.19E). This predatory snail is a shelled member of the same group that includes sea hares. It has a thin, fragile shell about 2 inches (5 cm) in length. When it is active, its soft parts extend over the shell, partially concealing it. It is too large to retreat completely into its shell. The mucous layer that normally covers this snail picks up small particles of sand and mud, which helps to conceal it when the tide is out. The Channeled Dog Whelk, *Nassarius fossatus*, is another common snail of the Mud Flats. This snail is a scavenger, locating food by its odor.

The Bay Sea Hare or Sea Slug, *Navanax inermis* (fig. 12.19F), is a large snail that occurs far out on the mud and is seldom exposed by low tide. This sea hare ranges up to 6 inches (15 cm) in length. It is a strikingly colored animal with yellow and blue dots on a brown background. Unlike its cousin of the rocky intertidal zone, it commonly feeds on other snails.

A variety of crabs occur on sandy bottoms, outside the direct influence of tides. Perhaps the best-known of these is the large edible crab or Dungeness Crab, *Cancer magister*. This species is most common in northern waters, where there is an important crab-trapping industry. In California south of Monterey Bay it does not occur in sufficient numbers to be commercially valuable. These large crabs are most abundant on sandy bottoms or in good growths of Eel Grass, where they commonly feed on clams. There is a sandy bar about 30 to 60 feet (9–18 m) deep outside of the Golden Gate where these crabs have been harvested commercially for many years. The decline in numbers of this formerly abundant species has been related to a variety of factors, including pollution and the introduction of aggressive crab species native to the Atlantic.

The most conspicuous animals of the mud flats are the birds. Most are migratory shore birds that spend the spring and summer months feeding and reproducing in northern latitudes, where the long photoperiod provides abundant food. During winter months, these birds migrate southward by the thousands to productive habitats such as estuaries. There may seem to be too many birds to be fed in one habitat, particularly where there is not an abundance of conspicuous prey species. However, careful inspection will show that these birds are equipped with bills of different shapes and lengths, and with legs of different lengths, a means of niche partitioning. Different birds wade in different depths of water, and the different shape and length of each bill enables different birds to probe the mud for different food items.

One strategy is to wade in shallow water and feed on fish. This is the strategy practiced by members of the heron family (Ardeidae). The largest of these birds is the Great Blue Heron, *Ardea herodias* (pl. 14E), which stands about 4 feet (120 cm) tall and has a 6-foot (2-m) wingspan. They often stand motionless and spear fish quickly with their long bill. When the tide is in, they retreat to the marsh. In the early 1900s, Great Blue Herons were hunted for their long blue-gray plumes, and their numbers diminished radically. Since the hunting ceased, they recovered remarkably, and now they are one of the most common wetland birds.

The Great Blue Heron is sometimes called a crane, but true cranes are rare along the coast, although Sandhill Cranes, *Grus canadensis*, may be observed at some inland aquatic habitats. Herons fly with their necks pulled back, and cranes fly with their necks outstretched. The expression "to crane one's neck" refers to the way a crane flies. Juvenile Great Blue Herons disperse widely in summer, occurring from the coast to the desert, wherever there are fish to eat. They are even observed in habitats away from wetlands. It is not uncommon to see a Great Blue Heron in a pasture, presumably hunting mice. This is the bird for which many places were named. For example, Crane Flat in Yosemite National Park was named for the occasional presence there of the Great Blue Heron. John Muir mentioned seeing the "blue crane" there.

Egrets are also in the heron family. There are three kinds in California, all of which are white. The largest is the Great or Common Egret, *Casmerodius albus*, a bird nearly as large as the Great Blue Heron. It can be distinguished from other egrets by its large size and yellow bill. The Snowy Egret, *Egretta thula* (pl. 14F) is smaller, but it is nearly 3 feet (1 m) tall. The Snowy Egret has a black bill and black legs. In the adult, the feet are bright yellow. Apparently, the Snowy Egret uses its yellow toes to lure curious fishes. Snowy Egrets can be seen wading in the shallows, pushing their feet ahead of them, stirring the sediments and attracting small fishes to come take a look. The smallest egret is the Cattle Egret, *Bubulcus ibis*, an Old World species that has become naturalized in North America. They are most commonly seen in pastures or agricultural regions, where they feed on insects. They are also common on the Channel Islands. Cattle Egrets have a yellow bill, and their legs are yellowish to pinkish. Herons and egrets also have been common at the Salton Sea, but, as mentioned in chapter 11, in recent years the U.S. Fish and Wildlife Service has documented a precipitous decline in numbers. For unknown reasons, the number of active nests declined from over 1700 in 1987 to only 19 in 1990. Pesticides and heavy metals are implicated.

A strategy practiced by various shorebirds is walking or wading at the water's edge to feed on organisms that live in the mud. Depending on the length and shape of their bills, they feed on different organisms. Among the most diverse of these birds are those in the sandpiper family (Scolopacidae). Curlews and Whimbrels are mottled, brown birds with very long, downcurved bills. The Long-billed Curlew, *Numenius americanus* (pl. 14D), is the largest of the shorebirds, nearly 2 feet (60 cm) in length. Its downcurved bill may be 8 inches (20 cm) in length. The Long-billed Curlew walks along the shore probing deeply into the mud. One of its favorite foods is ghost shrimp. The Whimbrel, *Numenius phaeopus*, is slightly smaller and can be distinguished by its shorter bill and dark head stripes. It feeds in a similar way, but on different food.

The Marbled Godwit, *Limosa fedoa*, is similar to the Whimbrel in size and appearance, except that its bill turns up at the end. Also, the bill is dark at the tip and pinkish at the base. In mixed flocks with the godwits and curlews occur various other sandpipers in assorted sizes. The smallest is the Least Sandpiper, *Calidris minutilla*. Its total length is only about 6 inches (15 cm). Sandpipers are most conspicuous in flocks feeding just above the water's edge. Sanderlings, *Calidris alba*, are common where there is surf. They run back and forth in front of the swash and backwash. Characteristic of many sandpipers, when they fly, they call to each other with loud peeps. Some people call all sandpipers "peeps."

Also included in the sandpiper group are Dunlins (*Calidris alpina*), Red Knots (*Calidris canutus*), Surfbirds (*Aphriza virgata*), snipes (*Gallinago* spp.), yellowlegs (*Tringa* spp.), phalaropes (*Phalaropus* spp.), tattlers (*Heteroscelus* spp.), turnstones (*Arenaria* spp.), dowitchers (*Limnodromus* spp.), and Willets (*Catoptrophorus semipalmatus*). There is no point in describing all of these, but a few additional comments are in order. Turnstones feed as their name suggests: they flip over stones to feed on organisms that take refuge there. They are also quite common on rocky shores where there is surf. Dowitchers usually feed while wading. They are known as "sewing machine birds" because their heads move up and down rapidly as they walk along probing into the mud. Willets are among the most common shorebirds. They are medium-sized, about 15 inches (38 cm) in length, and are gray with a dark bill. The most distinctive feature about their color are the white wing patches, known as flash marks, that show when they fly. White patches in the wings occur in other shorebirds too, but they are most distinctive in the Willets. If a predator were to attempt to grab a single Willet from a flock, the mass of confusion caused by the sudden appearance of all the white flash marks is enough to enable the entire flock to escape.

Similar to the members of the sandpiper family are birds in the plover family (Charadriidae), the most distinctive of which are the Semipalmated Plover, *Charadrius semipalmatus,* and the Killdeer, *C. vociferus.* Compared to many other shorebirds, these are short-legged and short-necked. Both of these birds have distinctive dark neckbands; the Semipalmated Plover has one, and the Killdeer has two. The loud call of the Killdeer sounds like "kill-dee," which is the basis for its name. It is a very common bird in all kinds of wetlands, from the beach to mountain meadows. A Killdeer makes its nest on the ground. The eggs are protectively colored, but certain predators, such as foxes and Coyotes, attempt to prey on eggs, babies, or nesting adults. The adult is famous for a broken-wing act, designed to fool the predator into thinking the bird is hurt. The limping bird is actually leading the predator away from its nest.

Birds of the avocet family (Recurvirostridae) are characterized by a narrow bill and long legs. The American Avocet, *Recurvirostra americana* (fig. 12.20), is easily recognized by its distinctive black, narrow, upturned bill. In winter plumage it is a gray bird with distinctive black and white wings. Breeding adults in spring and summer have a rusty-colored head and neck. Adults are about 18 inches (45 cm) in length. These birds are very much at home on the Mud Flats, where they are among the most common birds. They walk all over the mud or in shallow water, feeding by sweeping their bills from side to side.

Related to the American Avocet is the Black-necked Stilt, *Himantopus mexicanus* (fig. 12.20). This bird is distinctly bicolored—black above, including its neck, and white beneath. It has bright red legs. These birds are common in a variety of wetland habitats, particularly marshes. They usually feed while wading.

During low tide, out on the mud, American Avocets are joined by a few other common birds. Among these, no bird is more conspicuous than the American Coot or Mud Hen, *Fulica americana* (pl. 14H). This bird looks like a black duck, but it is a short-legged member of the rail family. It differs from a duck by having a relatively short, white bill that extends to its forehead. Also, instead of a web connecting its toes, a coot has flattened, lobed toes that aid in swimming and walking on soft mud. The bird's feet are conspicuously large, and as it walks about on the mud it makes a sucking sound. American Coots make their nests of Cord Grass or other reeds that float when the tide is in. They are common in all quiet-water habitats. Many people view them as pests because they may be the only water bird in the area, and they are aggressive. This is particularly true in the artificial lakes and ponds on golf courses, or in "planned" communities that include a pond or lake. Coot feces are a source

FIGURE 12.20   American Avocet, *Recurvirostra americana,* and Black-necked Stilt, *Himantopus mex-icanus.* These two birds, in the same family, have differently shaped bills, indicating that they are adapted for different feeding modes.

of eutrophication, causing these ponds and lakes to turn green or emit foul odors. Various schemes to exterminate coots from these areas have been attempted, to no avail.

The Northern Shoveler, *Anas clypeata,* is a duck that may be seen walking about on the mud or in shallow water. These may be distinguished from other ducks by their large, spoon-shaped bills. No other duck has a bill that is larger than its head. Females are a mottled brown, and males have a green head and buff-colored sides. They are distinctive, but no more so than when they wander across the mud with their necks extended, sloshing their bills back and forth in the mud.

There are many kinds of ducks (Anatidae) in a typical estuary, and it is unnecessary to describe them all. There are two basic kinds of ducks: dabblers, also known as bay ducks, and diving ducks. Dabblers consume algae, detritus, and snails. Even though some authorities would call them birds of open water, they are more correctly birds of mud flats. They feed in shallow water by tipping tail-up in order to reach the bottom. Some of them also walk out on the mud when the tide is out. Dabblers differ from diving ducks in their ability to become airborne. Dabblers can spring directly into the air, but diving ducks have to run along the surface of the water for some distance in order to reach sufficient speed to fly.

Dabblers (*Anas* spp.) include Northern Shovelers, Gadwalls (*Anas strepera*), Northern Pintails (*Anas acuta*), and Mallards (*Anas platyrhynchos*), as well as several types of teals and wigeons. The Northern Pintail is the most common duck in the state, but the Mallard is probably the most familiar. The long, pointed tail is the distinguishing feature of the Northern Pintail. The Mallard resembles the Northern Shoveler in that the male has a green head. However, the Mallard's bill is much smaller, and it is yellow. Male Mallards have a buff-colored breast, whereas on the Northern Shoveler, the buff color is on the side. Mallards also have orange feet. Mixed in with flocks of Mallards may be domestic ducks that have gone wild—in other words, feral ducks. These white ducks are European in origin, but they will hybridize with Mallards. The result is that along with typical Mallards there may be hybrid ducks with a variety of color patterns, from white to blotched.

Open Water.   The Open Water habitat is characterized by a typical aquatic food chain. Nutrients are absorbed by phytoplankton, which are fed upon by zooplankton. Plankton are fed upon by filter-feeding or top-feeding fishes such as Topsmelt, Striped Mullet, and perhaps California Killifish. These fishes in turn may be fed upon by marine mammals, predatory fishes, or predatory birds. The birds are the most conspicuous.

Birds may hunt from a floating position, or they may dive into the water from the air. Of those that float, most numerous are the ducks. Diving ducks spend most of their time on the water. They dive to feed on fishes, crustaceans, and various kinds of aquatic larvae. These ducks are good swimmers, but they are awkward on land. Many species have their legs placed well back on their bodies so that locomotion on land is nearly impossible. Among common ducks that dive for food are Canvasbacks (*Aythya valisineria*), Redheads (*Aythya americana*), Ring-necked Ducks (*Aythya collaris*), Buffleheads (*Bucephala albeola*), and Ruddy Ducks (*Oxyura jamaicensis*) (pl. 14B), as well as several kinds of scoters (*Melanitta* spp.), scaups (*Aythya* spp.), and mergansers (*Mergus* spp.).

Scaups, Buffleheads, and Ruddy Ducks often form mixed flocks floating on the water. They are similar in profile—small, chunky ducks with short necks. Scaups have iridescent feathers on the head that, depending on the light, range from purple to green. Buffleheads have a large white patch on each side of the head. Male Ruddy Ducks also have white cheeks, but they are not apt to be confused with any other type of duck. Ruddy Ducks float with their stiff tail feathers pointing upward. In good light during the breeding season, it can be seen that males are brownish red and have a bright blue bill.

Scoters are thick-billed ducks with very large nostrils. They seem more at home fishing and diving outside the surf line than they do in bays, but some species are fairly common in bays or inland waters. California has three kinds of scoters. The Surf Scoter, *Melanitta perspicillata*, has the widest distribution, but the Black Scoter, *Melanitta nigra*, may be locally common during winter. Males are black with an orange bill. The Surf Scoter may be distinguised by white patches on its forehead and the back of its neck.

Mergansers are fish-eating ducks. Unlike typical ducks, they have long, thin, serrated bills, ideal for grasping prey. There are three kinds of mergansers in California, but the one most common in estuaries is the Red-breasted Merganser, *Mergus serrator*. This is another green-headed duck, but its shaggy double crest, white neck ring, and thin bill should distinguish it from any other type of duck. As in many other ducks, females are brown.

Geese are also in the duck family, but they are larger than ducks and have very thick bills. Geese are winter visitors in wetlands all over the state. Migrating flocks of geese are recognizable by their familiar V formation. The most common species is the Canada Goose, *Branta canadensis*. It can be recognized by its large size, up to 45 inches (114 cm) in length, and its distinctive coloration. Both males and females are pale-breasted and have a black neck and head with a broad white ring across the chin. Canada Geese commonly feed in grasslands and cultivated fields along with domestic livestock.

Geese that are occasionally observed in estuaries include the White-fronted Goose, *Anser albifrons*, and the Snow Goose, *Chen caerulescens*. The Snow Goose is a large white bird with pink feet. In California, they tend to occur inland rather than along the coast. They winter in the wildlife refuges of the Great Central Valley in northern California or in the Salton Sea area.

It is possible to confuse Snow Geese with American White Pelicans, *Pelecanus erythrorhynchos,* when they are in flight. Both are white with black wing tips. Pelicans, however, are much larger, and their massive bills are usually visible from a distance. With wings spanning more than 8 feet (2.8 m) , they are the second largest birds in North America. American White Pelicans also overwinter at the Clear Lake National Wildlife Refuge or the Salton Sea, but they are much more common to the east. Like the herons and egrets, numbers of American White Pelicans at the Salton Sea are declining. From 40,000 birds in January 1987, the number had dropped to 650 as of January 1991. A similar decline was documented for the Clear Lake National Wildlife Refuge. On the other hand, the number of locations, from the deserts to the coast, where overwintering American White Pelicans have been documented has increased markedly. Perhaps pollution at their traditional wintering sites, such as the Salton Sea, has caused the flocks to disperse. Again, pesticides and heavy metals are implicated as well as selenium and boron. They are classified as a species of special concern by the California Department of Fish and Game.

California's typical coastal pelican is the Brown Pelican, *Pelecanus occidentalis* (pl. 14C). Females are uniformly brown, and males have a white head that becomes yellow during the breeding season. A pelican's large size and enormous bill are easy features to recognize and should keep it from being confused with other birds. Brown Pelicans dive into the water from the air, capturing fish in their pouch. The size of the pouch enables them to feed on fairly large fishes such as Striped Mullet. The crash dive of a Brown Pelican is a thing to behold. It looks so awkward that it is difficult to believe they don't get hurt. A pelican seems to stop short as it hits the surface because the bill becomes distended by the water and acts like a parachute. In contrast to the awkward-looking dive, the graceful flight of pelicans as they glide in formation, inches above a wave, is one of the most beautiful sights a beach walker can experience.

Brown Pelicans nest on the islands off southern California and Baja California. They were severely threatened by DDT in the 1960s, and subsequently the species was listed as endangered. In 1971, at the height of their decline, 552 pairs of birds nested on Anacapa Island. Only one bird hatched that year. Not only did DDT interfere with egg production, but the eggs that were laid had thin shells. A large bird such as a pelican crushes a thin-shelled egg when it sits on it.

After the banning of DDT, Brown Pelicans from Mexico began to move into California, and by the late 1980s the population had recovered remarkably. In 1985, about 6500 newborn pelicans survived on Anacapa Island, and over 4000 fledged in 1986 and 1987. The remarkable recovery of this species has led some authorities to recommend that its listing be downgraded from endangered to threatened. On the other hand, it has been pointed out that about 85% of California's Brown Pelicans nest on the Coronado Islands, about 6 miles (10 km) from the coast near Tijuana, Mexico. In that area, beyond the jurisdiction of the U.S. Fish and Wildlife Service, pelican and gull eggs are gathered for human consumption. Without protection from "eggers" in Baja California, the population in the United States probably would not be as safe as it appears.

Cormorants are similar to pelicans in that they have webbed feet with four toes and a membranous pouch under their beak. The cormorant's beak, however, is much shorter. There are three kinds of cormorant along the coast, but only two are common. These are large black birds with a visible hook on the tip of the beak. When they swim or perch, they are easily recognized by their beaks, which are pointed upward at an angle. The membranous pouch of the Double-crested Cormorant, *Phalacrocorax auritus*, is orange, whereas that of Brandt's Cormorant, *Phalacrocorax penicillatus*, is blue. Cormorants hunt while swimming. They dive and chase fish. Because they spend so much time underwater, they often stand on a perch with their wings outspread. Not only does this help to warm them, but it dries their wing feathers as well. Unlike most aquatic birds, cormorants have no oil gland with which to waterproof their feathers.

Grebes (Podicipedidae) also hunt while swimming. There are five different species of grebes in California's estuaries, four of which are small. In winter plumage they are all rather similar in appearance, with short, rounded bodies and short tails. Even though they seem ducklike, the bill and feet are nothing like those of a duck. Grebes have a slender pointed beak, which they use to catch small fish, crustaceans, and various kinds of larvae. Their feet are not webbed but have flattened, lobed toes similar to those of an American Coot. Their feet are much smaller than those of a coot, however, and unlike a coot they are very awkward on land. The state's largest grebe is the Western Grebe, *Aechmophorus occidentalis*, which is about 2 feet (60 cm) long. This is a black bird with a long white neck and throat. It has a thin yellow bill and red eyes. These are common winter vistors in estuaries. When they dive, they remain underwater for several minutes. It is difficult to believe that they can hold their breath so long or swim so far underwater.

Loons resemble large grebes, but they are in a different family (Gaviidae). Loons are almost 3 feet (90 cm) long. They ride low in the water and have short necks.

Unlike most birds, they have dense bones, and this added weight enables them to dive easily. They have been caught in fishermen's nets 200 feet (60 m) below the surface. In California, loons are usually seen in winter plumage. At this time they resemble the Western Grebe, but they are not as dark, and the neck is considerably shorter. There are three kinds of loons that may occur in California's waters, but the Common Loon, *Gavia immer*, is most likely to be seen. Loons breed in the north. The yodeling call of the male loon is usually uttered at night and is the sound that many people identify with the north woods. Loons are usually silent throughout the winter, but their unusual cry may be heard in the spring before they migrate northward.

Mergansers, cormorants, grebes, and loons hunt in a similar manner, but the species have different bill sizes and can swim to different depths. In this way, they partition their food supplies and reduce competition.

The most conspicuous birds of the California coast are the gulls and their allies (Laridae). For the most part these are fish eaters, but their scavenging habit is well known. In many coastal areas, large flocks migrate back and forth every day from the estuary to the dump. During winter, all along the California coast, flocks of mixed species may be observed. Gull species may be distinguished from each other by the color of their bills and legs, as well as differences in plumage. In the spring, most gull species migrate northward to reproduce, but the Western Gull, *Larus occidentalis*, remains to nest along the California coast. It can be recognized by its dark gray wings and pinkish feet. A variant of this species that often occurs during winter at the Salton Sea is known as the Yellow-footed Gull, *Larus livens*. As its name implies, it has yellow legs. It breeds in the Gulf of California.

During winter, the two most common gulls of estuaries are the Ring-billed Gull, *Larus delawarensis*, and the California Gull, *Larus californicus*. Ring-billed Gulls have a black ring around their bill, light gray wings with black wing tips, and yellow feet. California Gulls look like Ring-billed Gulls except that they lack the black ring and have a red spot on the lower part of the beak. For breeding, Ring-billed and California Gulls migrate to various lakes of the Great Basin in the United States and Canada. The California Gull has a breeding population at Mono Lake, where it has been threatened in recent years by lowering of the water level. Diversions of water to Los Angeles have caused the lake to become so low that the island on which the gulls were breeding became connected to the mainland. Coyotes and other predators walked onto the island and ate the eggs and baby gulls. A series of court battles between environmentalists and the Los Angeles Department of Water and Power has established that enough water must be allowed to enter Mono Lake so that the island remains an island.

The California Gull has been immortalized in Salt Lake City. A statue there commemorates an incident in which a flock of California Gulls arrived in time to consume a swarm of Mormon Crickets, *Anabrus simplex*, that threatened the Mormon settlers' first crop.

Terns are in the same family as gulls, and many of them look like forked-tail gulls. Most terns can be distinguished from gulls because they fly with their beaks aimed downward; gulls fly with their beaks straight out. Terns feed on fish that they spot from the air. Unlike the behavior of pelicans, their dive into the water is very graceful. Often, terns hover over the water before dropping on their prey, and in this respect they resemble kites and kingfishers. Three kinds of terns might be seen along the coast. The most common is probably Forster's Tern, *Sterna forsteri* (pl. 14A). In winter plumage, it is pale gray with a black eye stripe. In breeding plumage, the top of the head is black, and the bill and feet are red.

The only bird in the area with which Forster's Tern could be confused is the Least Tern. The Least Tern, however, is only about 9 inches (22 cm) long. It is another endangered species. Its problem is that it nests in small colonies in an endangered habitat, that is, open sand, at the highest point before dune vegetation begins. The loss of beach dunes to recreation and development will be discussed later.

Perhaps the most spectacular bird of Open Water is the Osprey, *Pandion haliaetus* (fig. 12.21), a fish-eating hawk. From beneath it appears to be all white, but it is dark brown on the top. It has a white head with a conspicuous dark eyestripe. Ospreys are fun to watch as they fly over the water, plunging feet-first to grasp fish in their talons. When they fly back to a perch to feed, they turn the fish in their feet so that it aims head-first into the wind. They construct large nests made of sticks, usually in trees or on top of poles.

Formerly these birds were conspicuous all along the coast and around lakes in northern California. Like other raptors, they experienced a serious decline in association with the widespread use of DDT. They are making an important recovery. Recently, for example, an Osprey constructed a nest on the shoreline of Mono Lake for the first time in known history. This is a strange place for an Osprey nest, for Mono Lake is fishless; the birds would have to feed elsewhere. Another interesting incident occurred in Newport Harbor, where an Osprey constructed a nest in the mast of a sailboat. The owner objected, so the Department of Fish and Game erected a tall post nearby and moved the Osprey nest there. The birds abandoned it. They knew where they wanted to live!

Estuaries are among our most threatened habitats. Originally there were about 300,000 acres (120,000 ha) of coastal marshes. Due to filling and development, about 80% of it is gone. San Francisco Bay contains about 90% of California's remaining Salt Marsh habitat. The remaining 10% is made up of about 25 Salt Marshes scattered between Oregon and Mexico. Even though San Francisco Bay is the state's largest Salt Marsh, 60% of it also has been lost. By the early 1960s, filling had reduced the bay from 780 to 550 square miles (2000 to 1400 km^2). Of what remains, the Suisun Marsh, at 87,000 acres (34,800 ha) is the largest Salt Marsh in the United States. It was preserved through the Suisun Marsh Preservation Act. It and the Bay Conservation and Development Act of 1969 are models of what grassroots efforts can bring about.

North of San Francisco, the largest Salt Marsh was formerly in Humboldt Bay. Draining and filling nearly destroyed it, but a grassroots movement among Arcata's citizens produced a remarkable turnaround. Today there are 94 acres (40 ha) of wetlands, fed largely by sewer effluent. By trapping and utilizing various organic mate-

FIGURE 12.21   Osprey, *Pandion haliaetus,* a fish-eating hawk.

rials and nutrients, marsh plants such as cattails act as a "natural" sewage treatment facility, and wildlife have returned.

In southern California, wetlands have fared more poorly. South of Morro Bay, 90% of this habitat has been destroyed. Of what remains, the largest area is in Upper Newport Bay. Of the Salt Marsh in Newport Bay, 740 acres (296 ha) is administered by the California Department of Fish and Game as an ecological preserve—this is another example of grassroots preservation efforts.

Loss of wetland habitats has taken its toll on wildlife. For example, there has been a 50% decline in California's waterfowl population just since the 1970s. Some birds, such as the Fulvous Whistling-duck, *Dendrocygna bicolor* (fig. 12.22A), and the Hooded Merganser, *Lophodytes cucullatus* (fig. 12.22B), were never common, but now they are rare. This loss is exacerbated by the fact that some 40,000 birds die each year from diseases. Some of these diseases, such as waterfowl botulism and avian cholera, have been recognized in California for over 100 years. On the other hand, duck virus enteritis was introduced from Europe with domestic waterfowl and has been known to occur in the United States only since 1967. Crowding of birds on dwindling habitat, particularly where they must share resources with domesticated waterfowl, could lead to devastating outbreaks of this deadly viral infection.

FIGURE 12.22   Rare ducks of California wetlands. *A*. Fulvous Whistling-duck, *Dendrocygna bicolor*. *B*. Hooded Merganser, *Lophodytes cucullatus*. (Drawings by Gene Christman from H. L. Cogswell. *Water Birds of California*. Berkeley: University of California Press, 1977.)

In addition to these infectious diseases, there are deaths associated with pollutants such as selenium, lead, or boron. Lead poisoning takes the greatest toll and results from shotgun pellets ingested by the bird while sifting marsh mud for food or grit. Some authorities contend that 80,000 to 150,000 birds die of lead poisoning in California every year, but Department of Fish and Game personnel claim that the correct number is closer to 6000 deaths per year. Whatever is the correct number, the combination of habitat loss and disease has had a severe impact on waterfowl in the state.

Reconstruction and reclamation attempts have restored viable wetland habitats in Elkhorn Slough near Monterey and Bolsa Chica near Huntington Beach. At Elkhorn Slough (fig. 12.23), over 3000 acres (1225 ha) of marshland and adjacent habitats consisting of federal, state, and private holdings have been preserved and are under protection. The Bolsa Chica reserve represents the largest marshland reconstruction project ever undertaken. In 1984 the California Coastal Commission authorized 915 acres (370 ha) for Salt Marsh restoration.

Even though sanctuaries and ecological preserves have been established to protect the state's remaining estuaries, they are still threatened by water diversions and pollution. Water diversions are a problem principally for San Francisco Bay. At the present time, diversion of fresh water from the Sacramento–San Joaquin delta has robbed San Francisco Bay of at least half of its freshwater input, increasing salinity and allowing intrusion of salt water into surrounding wetlands and farmland. Various proposals to divert a large portion of the Sacramento River around the delta (fig. 11.8) are perceived as major threats to water quality in the bay.

In spite of the 1972 ban on DDT, the pesticide is still being found in mussels, clams, and fishes. In 1985 levels of pesticides found in Elkhorn Slough prompted the Monterey County Health Department to declare a "health advisory," suggesting that visitors not eat shellfish from the slough. Similarly, in Newport Bay in 1985,

FIGURE 12.23   Elkhorn Slough, a restored wetland in Monterey County. (Photo by Diana J. Cosand.)

concentrations of DDT in sediment in San Diego Creek were 17 times higher than ever recorded before. A health advisory was posted there as well. Red Shiners (*Notropis lutrensis*) taken in San Diego Creek contained DDT residues 9 times higher than the limit set by the National Academy of Sciences. The same fish contained toxaphene, another illegal pesticide, in concentrations that were 30 times the academy's limit. In the bay itself, concentrations of DDT in mussels were the highest ever recorded in salt water. A concentration of 2.9 ppm was recorded at one undisclosed Orange County locality. That value is nearly three times more than the level of 1.0 ppm considered allowable by the state Department of Health Services. DDT has been found in mussels as far out as the Channel Islands.

In Santa Monica Bay, White Croaker (Tom Cod), *Genyonemus lineatus*, was reported with the highest concentrations of DDT ever recorded in a saltwater fish. Concentrations in the liver of this species ranged up to 624 ppm. Other bottom-dwelling fish showed similar high concentrations of DDT. As far south as Dana Point, fish livers were reported to contain 11.1 ppm DDT. In 1985 it also was reported that levels of DDT 3 to 10 times higher than the national average were found in the blood of Los Angeles residents that frequently ate fish caught in Santa Monica Bay. Furthermore, DDT and PCB residues were found in at least eight varieties of fish purchased in local markets. Many markets in the area no longer carry locally caught fish because of concerns over bay contamination. A dolphin found dead at Huntington Beach in 1983 had 1970 ppm DDT in its blubber. Since that time, dolphins have been found with concentrations of PCBs up to 6900 ppm.

What is the source of this DDT? It is not certain, but storm drains have been implicated. Also, the DDT could be still in the ecosystem from the period of heavy use prior to 1972, when its use was legal. A Los Angeles chemical factory that manuractured DDT seemed to be the primary source; its effluent made it to Santa Monica Bay via the sewer system. The effluent from this factory may have carried to the bay the DDT that is now showing up in the fishes. Another possibility is that DDT is still being used illegally; it is still legal in Mexico. Or it may be accumulating from use of a legal pesticide known as Dicofol, which contains about 10% DDT.

DDT is not the only toxin endangering California wildlife. PCB, a known carcinogen, behaves similarly to DDT: it is concentrated in fatty tissues and therefore becomes magnified as it moves up the food chain. PCBs are used to disperse heat in electrical transformers and hydraulic systems. Its use is illegal except in closed systems. Nevertheless, the third highest levels of PCBs in the state were found in mussels on the Lido Peninsula in Newport Bay. The source of PCBs in the environment is unknown, but boatyards and landfill dumps have been implicated. In fact, a plume of underground tainted water from the Coyote Canyon dump has been detected by groundwater geologists. The tainted water heads underground from the landfill toward Newport Bay. Anything discarded in the dump, including all sorts of toxic household wastes, could end up in the groundwater, and then in the bay.

Another possible source of these materials is runoff from the terrestrial environment. This runoff is augmented by agriculture, and it increases during rainstorms. It has been estimated that about 12,000 pounds of nitrate fertilizers flow daily into upper Newport Bay. The source of these nitrates is agricultural runoff from crops grown on nearby ranches and from Orange County wholesale nurseries. This nutrient-rich runoff is a contributary factor to eutrophication, but it is not a health problem. The discovery, however, provides measurable proof that a large component of the chemicals in the bay come from terrestrial sources. It supports the hypothesis that the primary source of lead and other heavy metals found in bay shellfish is runoff from the land.

Studies in Huntington Harbor, near Bolsa Chica, found the highest levels of toxic manganese recorded anywhere in California. Likewise, lead and zinc concentrations in the mussels there were higher than the amounts found in 90% of the state's waterways. In Huntington Harbor, the source of the chemicals was found to be ordinary storm drains that carry runoff from inland.

Studies of Mole Crab populations along the Orange County coastline revealed four to five times the normal concentrations of nickel, zinc, manganese, and iron in their tissues. It was also determined that only 5% of the females bore viable egg masses. When these crabs were removed from the area and raised under controlled conditions in the laboratory, their normal reproductive capacity returned.

These observations have been verified in San Francisco Bay. Regional water quality officials in the bay area estimate that two-thirds of the heavy metals in San Francisco Bay flow in with the rain. As evidence of the ecologic consequence of this pollution, the Department of Fish and Game has noted the disappearance of wildlife, including crabs, birds, and fishes such as Striped Bass, *Morone saxatilis*. Furthermore, in the bay area it has been estimated that storm drains carry into the bay about 500,000 gallons of oil and grease per year. This is the equivalent of a mid-sized oil spill. Some of this comes from leaky underground fuel tanks. Add to this what might be released by oil refineries that discharge their wastes into the bay. In 1988, 365,000 gallons (1,372,400 l) of crude oil escaped from a refinery near Martinez and invaded a portion of the Suisun Marsh.

Last but not least of the problems is the discharge from sewage-processing plants. Estimates of contamination by sewer discharge are based on the number of intestinal microorganisms such as coliform or enterococcal bacteria found in a sample of water. Santa Monica Bay is one of the worst areas. The Hyperion sewage-processing plant is badly overloaded, dumping about 425 million gallons of sewage per day into the bay—nearly half of the sewage produced by all of southern California. This amount of liquid could fill the Los Angeles Coliseum and the Rose Bowl each day. Of this volume of water, as of 1988 over three-fourths had not received secondary treatment. The federal Clean Water Act of 1972 requires secondary treatment of all sewage discharged into navigable waters. However, the city applied for and was granted a "temporary" exemption on the basis that its discharge was not degrading the environment! In 1988 the city was fined $10,000 for a 24 million–gallon spill that dumped untreated wastewater into the bay. Following that, water rationing measures were imposed in Los Angeles, largely to reduce the volume of water entering the sewer system.

At the point of an outflow is a degraded zone occupied by very few organisms. Of extreme abundance here are reddish worms that resemble earthworms. These are segmented worms (Annelida, Polychaeta) known as *Capitella capitata*. They are scavengers that possess hemoglobin, a feature enabling them to store oxygen so that they can tolerate the anaerobic mud and hydrogen sulfide (H_2S) produced by anaerobic bacteria. In ever-widening circles around the outflow, some of the 75 kinds of life that normally dwell on the ocean floor gradually appear. Is this outfall a source of DDT and PCBs? This cannot be proved, but in Santa Monica Bay it is in the general area in which the high concentrations of these chemicals are found in fish livers.

One proposed solution to this pollution was carrying sewage farther out to sea. Consider what happened at Morro Bay in 1983, when the sewer outfall was extended to 4000 feet (1220 m) offshore. The sewage was no longer chlorinated and, as it turned out, was being carried back into the bay. Water in the bay carried 5 to 10 times the allowable amount of coliform bacteria, and oysters carried 1000 times the allowable limit. The health department closed the bay to commercial shellfishing. Morro Bay is the fourth largest commercial shellfish area in the state. Shellfishermen were forced to quit harvesting or to transport their catch to tanks of purified water for cleansing. The cost of chlorinating the water again was estimated at $10,000 to $15,000 per year, and the city refused to do it.

The problem of sewer outfalls is not limited to bays and estuaries, but it is heightened there. South of the Los Angeles area, Orange County was also plagued by a series of sewage spills. In the early 1990s various beaches were closed to swimmers an average of 14 days per month. All up and down the California coast, cities dump their sewage at sea. The increase in organic matter has contributed to an increase in sea urchins which has caused the decrease in kelp forests described earlier. In 1986, as part of the revamped Clean Water Act, Congress passed an amendment calling for construction of a sewer outfall that would dump processed sludge 8 miles (13 km) out to sea off Huntington Beach. The bill was vetoed by President Reagan because it was too expensive, not because of any environmental concerns. What becomes of the project remains to be seen, but hooking a sewage dumping project to the Clean Water Act requires some stretching of definitions. It is analogous to putting a taller smokestack on a polluting steel mill. Instead of reducing pollution, export it.

COASTAL STRAND

Coastal Strand is a terrestrial community of sandy beaches and dunes, the pioneer community of the coastline. It occurs where there is no sea cliff. Here, the ever-present winds stack up sand carried to the area by a nearby river. Water-holding capacity of the sand is low, and accumulation of sea salts (sodium chloride) is high. This is a stressful environment for plants. Those that beome established here have long taproots and are commonly prostrate and succulent. The long taproot enables them to reach water deep in the soil. Succulence enables them to cope with the salty soil in a manner similar to that used by plants of the Salt Marsh. By storing water in their tissues, plants are able to dilute the concentration of salts. Many common plants here are related to desert plants. Among these are Beach Sagewort, *Artemisia pycnocephala* (a sagebrush); Seacliff or Dune Buckwheat, *Eriogonum parvifolium*; and Beach Ragweed or Beach-bur, *Ambrosia chamissonis*, which is related to the desert Bur-sage. These low shrubs of the dunes have silvery herbage and grow in loose mats up to 10 feet (3 m) across.

Members of the ice plant family (Aizoaceae) occur on the beaches of the southern Coast Ranges and down to Baja California. These succulent plants are native to Africa, but they have colonized beaches here to the degree that they are among the most common species. One species is the familiar succulent ground cover often called Hottentot Fig, *Carpobrotus* (= *Mesembryanthemum*) *edulis* (fig. 12.24B). It has been used to stabilize slopes in all forms of landscaping. The other ice plant is a succulent annual with tiny water-filled blisters on its leaves. Its scientific name, *Mesembryanthemum crystallinum* (fig. 12.24A), refers to the crystal-like appearance of the blisters, which apparently are related to the plant's attempt to excrete salts. Also found on these southern sand dunes are plants related to those found on desert dunes, such as the Red Sand Verbena, *Abronia maritima*. Similar to the desert Sand Verbena, this viney species covers many dune areas. During spring many clusters of reddish violet flowers form a colorful carpet on the dunes. Another species with desert relatives, the Beach Evening Primrose, *Camissonia cheiranthifolia* (fig. 12.24D), is a prostrate evening primrose that bears bright yellow, four-petaled flowers. The flowers grow on long wiry stems that radiate from a central rosette. It is a conspicuous species all along the California coast.

FIGURE 12.24 Some plants of the Coastal Strand. *A*. Ice Plant, *Mesembryanthemum crystallinum*.

FIGURE 12.24 (*continued*) Some plants of the Coastal Strand. *B*. Beach Morning Glory, *Calystegia soldanella*, mixed with Hottentot Fig, *Carpobrotus edulis*.

Many of the coastal species differ from their desert relatives by being perennial as opposed to ephemeral. The constant overcast along the coast limits light intensity so much that it is nearly impossible for annual plants to complete a life cycle in a single year. A true desert plant that occurs on dunes is a root parasite, *Pholisma arenarium* (fig. 12.24C). This low-growing species is a relative of the plant known as Sand Food, which was discussed along with desert sand dunes. Unlike Sand Food, which resembles a small bagel, this sand plant is more like a mushroom in appearance. Close inspection will show that it bears many small flowers on its rounded upper surface.

FIGURE 12.24 (*continued*)   Some plants of the Coastal Strand. *C*. Pholisma, *Pholisma arenarium*.

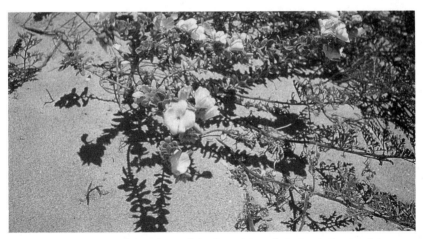

FIGURE 12.24 (*continued*)   Some plants of the Coastal Strand. *D*. Beach Evening Primrose, *Camissonia cheirianthifolia*.

Perhaps the most spectacular flower of the beach dunes is Beach Morning Glory, *Calystegia soldanella* (fig. 12.24B). This species is a geophyte, returning each year from deep-seated, fleshy rootstock. It is not an annual, even though it may appear so. It produces a large rose to purple flower that looks like a typical morning glory, but it is not a vine. It is common on beaches from Washington to San Diego.

Native Dune Grass, *Elymus mollis*, was formerly common from Monterey County north to Alaska. Unfortunately, it is being replaced by an introduced grass known as

European Beachgrass, *Ammophila arenaria*. The native grass reproduces vegetatively and by seed. The European grass reproduces mainly by vegetative means, but more rapidly than the native form. It spreads by means of underground stems (rhizomes) that can be broken up by ocean waves and dispersed to new localities. It grows so fast that it is more effective at stabilizing sand than is the native species. The result is a wall of grass tussocks near the shoreline that blocks the introduction of new sand. Starving a dune field of new sand leads to rapid degradation of the entire ecosystem.

A dune field is a food-poor ecosystem. Consequently, the most common animals are insects. Of the vertebrate animals, there are a few lizards and small birds that visit the area. Most of the predators are birds such as Kestrels (Sparrow Hawks) and Red-tailed Hawks. The sandspit at Morro Bay is one of the few places in the state where a person can still see Peregrine Falcons. They nest on nearby Morro Rock.

The endangered Least Tern, *Sterna albifrons* (fig. 12.25), is a member of the gull family (Laridae). It nests on open sand, just below the zone where dune vegetation occurs. In order to protect the Least Tern, government employees have erected small fences around the bird's nesting areas. At Bolsa Chica, near Huntington Beach, a wetlands has been reconstructed. The area has been off limits to development, largely to protect a breeding colony of Least Terns.

An interesting irony at Bolsa Chica involves Red Foxes, *Vulpes fulva*, which were introduced at the nearby Seal Beach Naval Weapons Station. They have found refuge at Bolsa Chica and have been implicated in the demise of a colony of Light-footed Clapper Rails at Seal Beach and a group of fledgling Least Terns at Bolsa Chica. Under criticism from environmentalists, the Navy began a trapping program to remove the nonnative foxes. Between 1986 and 1989, 250 of the animals were trapped and removed. As is often the case, the Navy experienced difficulty finding new homes for these animals and aroused the ire of animal rights activists at the same time. In 1989 a permit to shoot the foxes was granted to the Navy. Another interesting situation with Red Foxes occurred at Point Mugu. Coyotes, *Canis latrans*, were reintroduced in the 1980s and seemed to chase out the Red Foxes. (Generally, Coyotes do not prey on birds.) After three years, not a single Red Fox could be located, and 100 Least Tern chicks fledged in a single year.

The Snowy Plover, *Charadrius alexandrinus*, is another bird that nests on the dunes, and it too has experienced a serious decline in numbers. It also nests to a small degree on the shores of alkaline lakes such as Mono Lake, and some have adapted to nesting on dikes constructed for salt evaporation ponds. This change in behavior may be its salvation.

Interesting symbiotic relationships between plants and their pollinators occur in dunes. For example, at Morro Bay, the Beach Primrose is pollinated only by bumble-bees (*Bombus* spp.). Consistent, strong winds pose a problem for pollinators. It takes a great deal of energy to fly in such an environment. Large, powerful bumblebees apparently are able to cope with this problem by flying into the wind as they approach each flower. Because the wiry stems of Beach Primrose are flexible, the wind causes flowers to be oriented downwind. Also, because the flowers are so close to the ground,

FIGURE 12.25   The Least Tern, *Sterna albifrons*, an endangered species that nests on the Coastal Strand. (Drawing by Gene Christman from H. L. Cogswell. *Water Birds of California*. Berkeley: University of California Press, 1977.)

the bumblebees are able to fly low where wind intensity is reduced. Here the Beach Primrose and bumblebee are able to thrive and reproduce by mutual cooperation.

Tiny blue butterflies (*Euphilotes* spp.) are found in many dune areas. These are diminutive but beautiful butterflies that occur in association with beach buckwheats. Buckwheats are their preferred nectar sources, and the larvae feed inside the flowers. Different species of these butterflies are associated with buckwheats in other habitats, but along the coast, and in association with extreme habitat destruction, several subspecies occur today at only a few localities. Five of California's federally listed endangered species are blue butterflies. The most restricted is the El Segundo Blue Butterfly, *Euphilotes* (= *Shijimiaeoides*) *battoides allyni*, which occurs only in the dunes west of the Los Angeles International Airport. The reason this area has not been developed is that a clear space is required for overflying aircraft. The dunes formerly covered the Coastal Strand from Playa Del Rey to San Pedro. All that is left are about 300 acres (120 ha) that the Los Angeles Department of Airports wanted to convert to a 27-hole golf course. The Palos Verdes Blue Butterfly, *Glaucopsyche lygdamus palosverdesensis*, was lost forever when its habitat was bulldozed for a baseball diamond.

Sand dunes are one of California's most disturbed communities. There are few natural dune systems left. All have been invaded by introduced plants, and most have been altered by sandmining, highway construction, military and recreation activities, and urbanization. Probably the least disturbed area is the Lanphere-Christensen Dunes in Humboldt County. Here the Samoa Peninsula forms a barrier between the Pacific Ocean and Humboldt Bay. These dunes were protected by the Lanphere and Christensen families until 1974, when the land was donated to the Nature Conservancy. Since then, more land has been purchased so that over 200 acres (80 ha) are now administered jointly by the Nature Conservancy and Humboldt State University. This is one of the few places in California where a dune field ecosystem can be studied in a nearly natural state.

Another, much smaller natural dune field may be observed at Morro Beach State Park, where a sandspit forms a barrier enclosing Morro Bay, the last natural estuary in California. This sandspit, about 4 miles (7 km) long, is the only place in southern California where a dune field can be observed in a seminatural state, and where the forces of nature are allowed to continue shaping the land.

The largest field of coastal dunes occurs south of Pismo Beach. Here, near the small town of Guadalupe, there is an 18-square-mile (32-km²) ecoystem of dunes and lakes. The area was designated a National Natural Landmark in 1980 by the secretary of the Department of the Interior. Huge dunes along the coast have impounded 10 freshwater lakes (fig. 11.7). This type of landform was formerly a bay separated from the ocean by a sandspit, much like the Morro Bay sandspit today. The area is a treasure of restricted species; the California Native Plant Society lists at least 18 species as rare or endangered, or of very limited distribution, in these dunes. One of the species, the Nipomo Mesa Lupine, *Lupinus nipomensis* (fig. 12.26), had been reduced to six known plants.

Up until 1982, when the state park system took stewardship of 3000 acres (1200 ha), hundreds if not thousands of people on any weekend would drive over the dunes in various forms of all-terrain vehicles. The Nature Conservancy manages a 567-acre (229-ha) parcel just south of the Santa Maria River that protects the rare La Graciosa Thistle, *Cirsium loncholepis*; Surf Thistle, *Cirsium rhothophilum*; and Dune Indian Paintbrush, *Castilleja mollis*. Of importance to the dunes is that these species, particularly Surf Thistle, help to stabilize the system, preventing loss of sand. Off-road vehicles disrupt the sand, causing it to move out from the root systems of the plants. This in turn allows the sand to be blown away. Areas occupied by sensitive species were marked and fenced, but a few inconsiderate people showed no respect for these organisms and drove wantonly through the restricted areas. Since state park acquisition in 1982, the dunes at Oso Flaco Lake have been closed to off-road vehicles, and camping along the beach has been prohibited. Off-road vehicle activity has been brought partially under control by better enforcement and fencing. An agenda for restoration of damaged areas has been implemented, including an ambitious plan to rid the area of European Beachgrass.

In Orange County, a remnant of a large dune field is still present on the Newport Peninsula near the town of Balboa. Formerly, the entire peninsula was a large sandspit similar to that at Morro Bay. In this region, development is set well back from the surf. Between the houses and the ocean is a small dune field occupied mostly by ice plants. But among the introduced species native species may still be found, such as Beach Primrose, Beach Morning Glory, and Beach Ragweed.

On the north coast, the interior portion of the dune fields is occupied by an interesting forest of conifers. Where the sand has become somewhat stabilized, Shore Pine, *Pinus contorta contorta* (fig. 12.27), becomes established. This is a pioneer species

FIGURE 12.26 Nipomo Mesa Lupine, *Lupinus nipomensis*. (Drawing by Bonnie K. Walters from D. R. Walters and B. K. Walters. "Natural History of the Nipomo Mesa Lupine," *Crossosoma* 15 (3,4), 1989.)

FIGURE 12.27 Shore Pine, *Pinus contorta contorta*.

that is notable as a close relative of the pioneer in mountain meadows, the Lodgepole Pine, *Pinus contorta murrayana*. Similar to the Lodgepole Pine, needles occur in clumps of two. Although the cones resemble those of the Lodgepole in size and appearance, they often remain closed and on the tree for many years. Also, they tend to be visibly asymmetrical, curling backward along the stem.

These Shore Pines are distributed as far south as Mendocino County. To the north, however, they are associated with coastal communities such as dunes and bogs as far north as Alaska. In association with the pines are other species of northern affinity such as Sitka Spruce, *Picea sitchensis*; Grand Fir, *Abies grandis*; and Western Hemlock, *Tsuga heterophylla*. These north coastal trees were discussed in chapters 6 and 7. They reach their southernmost distribution along the north coast of California, where they depend on the moisture from fog drip. One of the best examples of this assemblage of species is preserved in the Lanphere-Christensen dune field of Humboldt County.

ISLANDS

From a good vantage point on a clear day, California's islands are visible from the mainland (fig. 12.28). They vary in size and distance from the mainland, but most of them are not far offshore. The California islands are continental islands as opposed to oceanic islands. Oceanic islands occur far out to sea, and most of them are volcanic in origin and were never attached to the mainland.

Calfornia's islands can be divided into three groups (fig. 12.29). To the north are the Farallon Islands and Año Nuevo. These are very small islands near the central California coast that are best known for their populations of marine mammals and birds.

Off the southern California coast are the Channel Islands. They can be divided into two groups. The northern Channel Islands lie on an east–west line, roughly parallel to the coast south of Santa Barbara. These islands are mountaintops that project above water. In a sense they represent a westward extension of the Santa Monica Mountains. These are the islands that most Californians think of as the Channel Islands. From east to west the islands are Anacapa, Santa Cruz, Santa Rosa, and San Miguel.

The southern Channel Islands lie west of Los Angeles and Orange counties. They consist of four islands in a diamond pattern. Santa Catalina is the closest to the mainland, and San Nicolas is farthest away. Santa Barbara Island, the smallest of the Channel Islands, lies to the north. To the south is San Clemente Island.

A small island group known as Los Coronados lies south of San Diego. These islands actually belong to Mexico, but they are close enough that they should be mentioned here. Farther south, off Baja California, are a number of other interesting islands. These will be discussed where their animal or plant life is relevant to distributions on the California islands.

Examination of a fault map (fig. 8.3) will reveal that many of the islands are separated from each other by major fault systems. With our present knowledge of plate tectonics, it is apparent that the islands have not always been located in their present positions, nor have they always been arranged in the pattern we see today. The islands

FIGURE 12.28 Santa Catalina Island, as seen from the San Joaquin Hills, Orange County. Laguna Beach in left center.

originated much farther to the south, and they have been carried to their present latitudes by right-lateral offset along California's rifted borderland. These are extant terranes that have not yet become attached to the mainland, and because southern California no longer has a subducting margin, they probably will remain detached.

The islands are geologically complex. Most of the rock materials exposed on the surface are various kinds of sediments, illustrating that the regions formerly were underwater. The northern Channel Islands include a granitic component similar to the Transverse Ranges, which means that they were parallel to the coast during formation of the Southern California batholith. Santa Catalina and San Clemente islands contain a fair amount of Franciscan rock, which was formed in association with the subduction trench. Layered on top of the others are many types of volcanic rock deposited from about 16 to 12 million years ago (Miocene). Paleomagnetic data in these rocks indicate that the islands have been translocated northward, and the nothern Channel Islands have been rotated clockwise at least 75°. Santa Catalina also has a large component of "young" granite of about the same age as the volcanics.

The northward drift of these islands is established by a number of other geologic features (fig. 12.30). For example, present-day Poway Creek lies east of Torrey Pines State Reserve, in San Diego County. The alluvial outwash from this creek, when it was a much larger stream, contributed to a large underwater fan about 40 million years ago. This fan has been formed into a distictive conglomerate rock that can be found on San Miguel Island, which is now over 100 miles (160 km) north of Poway

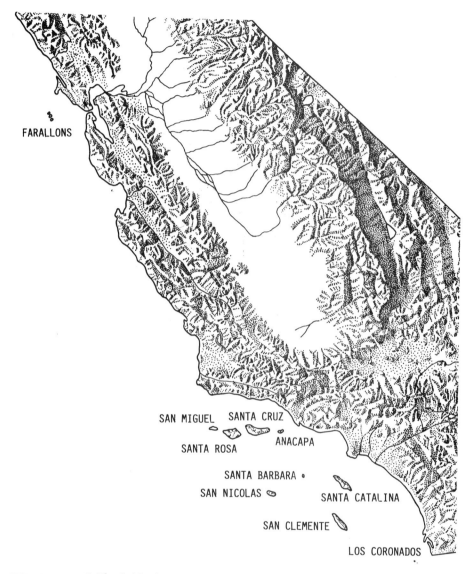

FIGURE 12.29   California islands.

Creek. Pebbles in the conglomerate may have a source as far south as Sonora, Mexico. This is a logical possibility, because at that time southern California west of the San Andreas fault was still attached to mainland Mexico. Rivers that began in what is now Sonora, Mexico, could have flowed directly westward into the Pacific Ocean. Poway Creek has been moved northward about 200 miles (320 km) and San Miguel an additional 100 miles (160 km). Poway gravels are also found on Santa Rosa and San Nicolas islands, but not on Santa Cruz, Santa Catalina, or San Clemente islands.

FIGURE 12.30   Reconstructed Eocene paleogeography showing the positions of islands, the Eocene shoreline, and the deposition of Poway river gravels. (After Howell and others, 1974. From S. M. Rowland. "Geology of Santa Catalina Island," *California Geology* 37(11): 239–251, 1984.)

It is further noteworthy that the present Santa Cruz Island is a composite terrane. This means that it was formed by the fusion of two formerly separate terranes. A fault running down the center of Santa Cruz Island is marked by the central valley of the island today.

It also significant that San Clemente and Santa Catalina were a great deal larger than they are today. Landslide materials including Franciscan rocks such as Catalina schist formed distinctive deposits known today as the San Onofre Breccia. This breccia was formed underwater, but the source was a very large island, the remains of which is probably Santa Catalina. It is possible that about 25 million years ago a series of earthquakes caused the landslides that later became cemented into the breccia. This distinctive rock is found today on Santa Cruz Island, Santa Rosa Island, Anacapa Island, Santa Catalina Island, and various points on the mainland from Point Mugu south to Oceanside (fig. 8.8). The actual shoreline at the time was inland, about where the Santa Ana Mountains lie today; therefore, the eastern edge of the former island probably lay about where the mainland coastline occurs today.

Island Endemics

The implication of plate tectonics on the distribution of sedentary animals such as salamanders has been discussed frequently throughout this book. If unique salamanders
were found on these islands, it would add credence to the hypothesis that distribution
of specialized forms on the mainland may be related to populations on former islands
that became attached to California by accretion of extant terranes that carried their
plants and animals with them.

The Farallon Islands are the northernmost of California's islands, but they are
composed of only 211 acres (85 ha) of land (table 12.2). Nevertheless, 12 species of
sea bird nest there, and the largest sea bird rookery south of Alaska is there. There are
only 36 species of plants on the islands, 13 native and 23 introduced. The dominant
plant is the Farallon Weed or Maritime Goldfields, *Lasthenia maritima*. This relative of
the common Coast Goldfields, *L. californica*, is in the sunflower family (Asteraceae). It
grows on the islands in mats over 1 foot (40 cm) thick. When it blooms, its flowers
occur in great profusion, turning the landscape yellow.

There is a population of Arboreal Salamanders, *Aneides lugubris* (fig. 7.25), on
the Farallon Islands. These are the salamanders frequently associated with oak trees,
although there are no native oaks on the Farallons. Throughout most of its range the
salamander is characterized by small yellow spots. On the islands the salamanders
show a pattern of large spots that also typify the forms in the Gabilan Range east
of Monterey. The Farallon Islands and the Gabilan Range are both west of the San
Andreas fault. The Farallons are pure weathered granite, and the Gabilans also contain
much granite. It has been postulated that the Gabilans and Farallons were once part
of a long peninsula. It is apparent that the Gabilan Range was once an island, too.
Whether or not the Farallons were ever large enough to have remained continuously
above sea level is subject to some conjecture. It is possible that the salamanders were
carried to the island on a log raft, or it may be that these wave-lashed outcrops are
all that remains of a former large land mass. Small-spotted members of this species
are also found on Santa Catalina Island, but they have not been studied thoroughly
enough to determine how different they are from mainland forms.

The most sedentary of all California salamanders, the slender salamanders (*Batrachoseps* spp.), are found on some of the southern islands (fig. 7.24). On Santa Catalina
and Los Coronados the Garden Slender Salamander, *B. pacificus major*, may be found.
It is also found on Todos Santos Island near Ensenada. At the present time it is assigned to the same subspecies that occurs on the adjacent mainland. To date, however,
electrophoretic studies that could establish differentiation have not been published.
A different subspecies, the Channel Islands Slender Salamander, *B. pacificus pacificus*,
occurs on the four northern Channel Islands. These also have been assigned to the
same subspecies that occurs on the adjacent mainland. Analysis of these island forms
using electrophoresis, however, shows that the island forms differ enough to indicate
that they have been separated from the mainland forms by at least 4 million years. It
is of special interest that Santa Cruz Island, which is composed of two terranes, has
two kinds of slender salamander! The Black-bellied Slender Salamander, *B. nigriventris*,

TABLE 12.2 A Comparison of California's Islands

	Area, mi² (km²)		Elevation, ft (m)	Distance to Mainland, mi (km)		Native Species and Subspecies of Plants[a]		Amphibians	Reptiles	Resident Birds[a]	Mammals[a]
Northern California Islands											
Farallons	0.5	(1.4)	385 (109)	20	(33)	13	(1)	1			
Año Nuevo	0.02	(0.05)	60 (18)	0.3	(0.5)						
Northern Channel Islands											
San Miguel	14	(37)	830 (253)	26	(42)	190		1	2	15	3 (2)
Santa Rosa	84	(217)	1560 (475)	27	(44)	340	(3)	2	2	25	4 (3)
Santa Cruz	96	(249)	2470 (753)	19	(30)	420	(7)	3	6	37 (1)	10 (4)
Anacapa	1.1	(2.9)	930 (283)	13	(20)	70		1	2	14	3 (2)
Southern Channel Islands											
Santa Barbara	1.0	(2.6)	635 (194)	38	(61)	40	(1)		1	6	2 (1)
San Nicolas	22	(58)	910 (277)	61	(98)	120	(2)		2	11 (1)	4 (2)
Santa Catalina	75	(194)	2125 (648)	20	(32)	375	(3)	3	8	34	9 (5)
San Clemente	56	(145)	1965 (599)	49	(79)	233	(11)		2	24	6 (2)

[a] The number of endemic species is indicated in parentheses.

also occurs on Santa Cruz Island. It too is believed to have diverged from its mainland counterpart at least 4 million years ago.

It is tempting to search for alternative explanations for the presence of these salamanders on islands. Amphibians are unable to swim in salt water, so any hypothesis that involves dispersal from the mainland must involve some sort of rafting. It is entirely possible that sedentary salamanders might float across on a piece of wood or debris washed out by heavy rains. This explanation might apply particularly to the presence of the Arboreal Salamanders on the islands. However, it is difficult to believe that slender salamanders, which usually occur under rocks and logs, could reach so many islands in that manner. Nevertheless, it is interesting that in 1955 a live Black-tailed Jack Rabbit, *Lepus californicus*, was found floating on a kelp raft near San Clemente Island, 39 miles (62 km) from the California mainland.

It is often speculated that land bridges once connected California islands to the mainland. These land bridges presumably were formed during periods of low sea level, when a great deal of the earth's water was tied up in the polar ice caps. Lowering of sea level most certainly connected Mexico's Todos Santos to the mainland, and perhaps the Coronados, but it seems highly unlikely that Santa Catalina was ever attached to the southern California mainland. If it were, it would have been attached a long time ago and a good deal farther south—most likely at a latitude presently corresponding to mainland Mexico.

An argument rages over whether the northern Channel Islands were ever connected to the mainland. Maximum lowering of sea level occurred about 18,000 years ago, at which time the four northern Channel Islands were most likely a single large island. The channel between this island and the mainland simply was too deep for the two to be connected, however. During the lowest possible sea level, the gap between the mainland and the island would have been at least 4.4 miles (7 km) in width.

Interesting evidence supporting the premise that the Channel Islands were connected to the mainland is that fossils of a pygmy elephant known as the Exiled Mammoth, *Mammuthus exilis*, have been found on Santa Cruz, Santa Rosa, and San Miguel islands. Supporters of the land bridge hypothesis contend that it is not possible for an elephant, no matter how small, to reach an island by any means other than walking. Critics point out that Indian elephants (*Elephas maximus*) are good swimmers, and that a 4 1/2-mile (7-km) swim would not be out of the question. Furthermore, there are fossil remains of elephants, most of which were dwarfed, on at least 10 islands in the Mediterranean Sea.

Of special interest in the biogeography of California's islands is the presence of the Island Night Lizard, *Xantusia riversiana* (fig. 12.31), on three islands. Dense populations of these lizards are found on San Clemente, San Nicolas, and Santa Barbara islands. Electrophoretic studies show that these are clearly the most divergent of all the vertebrates on the islands. They differ enough from their mainland relatives that some authorities have placed them in a different genus (*Klauberina*).

Similar to salamanders, Island Night Lizards spend most of their time under rocks or in cracks. They are without question sedentary. Mark-and-recapture studies on San

FIGURE 12.31   Two color patterns of the Island Night Lizard, *Xantusia riversiana*, on San Clemente Island.

FIGURE 12.31 (*continued*)   Two color patterns of the Island Night Lizard, *Xantusia riversiana*, on San Clemente Island.

Clemente Island show that over a period of years, lizards are frequently recaptured under the same rock. Average home ranges are about 10 feet (3 m), and the greatest distance a marked lizard is known to have moved is 30 feet (10 m). The density of these lizards on San Clemente Island is truly remarkable. Studies indicate that there are over 3500 lizards per acre (1450/ha), amounting to a biomass of 55 to 85 pounds per acre (10–16 kg/ha). This high biomass is maintained by a lack of competitors and predators.

Mainland relatives of this lizard include the Desert Night Lizard, *X. vigilis*, and the Granite Night Lizard, *X. henshawi*. Desert Night Lizards are commonly found in association with *Yucca* plants, and Granite Night Lizards are found in cracks in rocks in the Peninsular Ranges. A fossil night lizard is also represented in the San Diego area in sediments determined to be at least 40 million years of age. These fossils are similar to but not the same as the island form.

Electrophoretic studies suggest that the island form has been separated from its mainland relatives for at least 10 to 15 million years. The two mainland forms appear to have diverged from each other about 7 million years ago. Correlating the electrophoretic data with the age of the fossils leads to speculation that the Island Night Lizards have been separated from the mainland forms for 10 to 40 million years. They may have been island dwellers all that time.

The night lizard family (Xantusiidae) is distributed similarly to other animals that seem to have been translocated on extant terranes. Members of this family occur in Cuba, tropical Middle America, and the arid southwest. The Island Night Lizard may have evolved on San Clemente Island and ridden to its present locality from a former position attached to mainland Mexico. There is no evidence that San Clemente Island was ever completely submerged, and the time period of tens of millions of years is appropriate for this type of transport.

The other two islands on which the Island Night Lizard occurs are not high enough to have remained above sea level. It is therefore believed that these lizards were somehow transported to the other islands sometime in the last million years. Electrophoretic studies substantiate this idea, because there is very little difference among the lizards of the different islands. This transport would require rafting of some sort. A problem with this hypothesis is that the currents seem to move the wrong way for anything to disperse passively northward. Another hypothesis is that the lizards were carried as pets by Indians that inhabited the islands. This, of course, does not explain why the lizards are not found on all the islands.

The presence of the Island Fox, *Urocyon littoralis* (fig. 12.32), on several islands also has been explained as an example of transport by Indians. These small foxes are relatives of the Gray Fox, *U. cinereoargenteus*, which occurs on the mainland. Island Foxes occur on the six largest islands: San Miguel, Santa Rosa, Santa Cruz, San Nicolas, Santa Catalina, and San Clemente. Each island is considered to have its own subspecies, which implies that the foxes have been isolated on the islands for quite some time. It may be that the Island Fox is more closely allied to three small species of foxes that occur in Yucatan, Mexico, and in Guatemala. If this is the case, the Island Fox may represent another example of the distribution pattern noted for the Island Night Lizard. The fact that Island Foxes have differentiated more than any other island mammals supports the idea they may have been isolated longer than we think.

If Indians did carry foxes around as pets, it would have been a long time ago. However, differences in the subspecies might be less significant than we think. Dif-

FIGURE 12.32   Island Fox, *Urocyon littoralis,* on San Clemente Island.

ferences involve mainly size and color. Such differences are known to evolve rapidly, and these changes are typical of animals and plants on all sorts of ecological islands.

Studies of DNA in the chromosomes of living foxes can reveal degrees of similarity. Greater differences would imply that the populations have been separated for longer periods of time. All island foxes are significantly different from the mainland Gray Fox, and the degrees of differentiation among the island forms suggest that they arrived on the northern islands first. Foxes on San Clemente and San Nicolas are most closely related to the foxes on the northern island of San Miguel. The foxes on Santa Catalina appear to be an amalgamation and were likely the consequence of the mixing of genetic strains from several of the other islands. There is nothing in these data to dectract from the theory that the transport of the foxes occurred by humans.

The oldest fossil fox on the northern Channel Islands is from deposits dated at approximately 16,000 years. The fact that this fox was smaller than the mainland form implies that foxes arrived prior to 16,000 years ago. The earliest dates for human habitation in southern California are not clear-cut, but most authorities agree that about 10,000 years ago humans were well established here. A fire pit on Santa Rosa Island has been dated at 30,000 years, one of the oldest dates attributed to human habitation in North America. It is also difficult to determine exactly when the last period of high sea level occurred. At best guess, it can be stated that sometime during the last 500,000 years, water was high enough to cover all the islands except San Clemente, Santa Catalina, Santa Cruz, and Santa Rosa. The sea reached its lowest point some 18,000 to 20,000 years ago, and humans could very likely have been here then. Unfortunately, traces of human populations along the sea shore would have been obliterated by the rising sea. Whatever the time sequence, species differentiation on islands that were submerged had to occur in the last half-million years.

Most birds on the California Islands are similar to their mainland relatives. Some differentiation has occured on the subspecies level, but not to the degree typical of other vertebrates. This, of course, is complicated by the fact that birds are highly mobile. Of the birds that have become differentiated, the Santa Cruz Island Jay, *Aphelocoma insularis*, is the most notable. This jay differs from the Scrub Jay, its mainland counterpart, by being bluer, larger, and having a different call. The island subspecies sounds like a Scrub Jay with laryngitis.

Animals of the intertidal zone are similar in most respects to their mainland counterparts. The differences that occur primarily are associated with differences in water temperature, a function of the major currents. For example, animals on the outermost islands, San Nicolas and San Miguel, show affinities with northern California species. Those on the southernmost islands, San Clemente and Santa Catalina, show more affinity to mainland species in the San Diego area.

An analysis of marine algae shows a similar grouping of species. Most species are widespread in distribution, but of those that are more localized, outer-island species resemble those of the northern coast, and the southern-island species resemble species of the southern coast. The greatest diversity occurs in the red algae (Rhodophyta). As mentioned previously, the great diversity of types that occurs in southern California appears to be a function of overlap in the distribution of northern and southern species.

Native terrestrial vegetation of the islands consists mostly of species associated with Coastal Sage Scrub. The larger islands also contain some Chaparral and Oak Woodland. Prior to deliberate fire suppression, Coastal Grassland was a very important community on the islands. It was burned year after year by Indians, who depended heavily for food on seeds of wildflowers that followed the fires.

The infestation of nonnative weeds has taken its toll on the islands as well as the mainland. Of the 353 species of plants known to occur in the Channel Islands National Park, 20% are nonnative. Most of these are weeds of Mediterranean origin, but species of Australian eucalyptus have also become naturalized. Nowhere is this more conspicuous than on Santa Catalina Island, where about 90% of the nonnative trees are eucalyptus. Ironically, those trees are now threatened by infestations of an Australian longhorn boring beetle.

The number of native species on each island is roughly proportionate to the size of the island. The overwhelming majority of native plants on the islands are the same as those on the mainland; the number of endemics is small. Of the endemics, there are two kinds: those that occur only on islands but may appear on more than one, and those that occur on only one island. Of the latter type, only San Clemente has more than 10 species. Altogether, the California islands are home to between 90 and 100 island endemics.

The largest number of island endemics are leaf succulents known as live-forevers (*Dudleya* spp.). Nine species are restricted in distribution to islands. These are drought-tolerant members of the Coastal Sage Scrub community. Other groups of Coastal Sage Scrub that have diversified on islands are buckwheats (*Eriogonum* spp.) and locoweeds (*Astragalus* spp.). Locoweeds, members of the pea family (Fabaceae), are important as nitrogen fixers.

One of the most attractive island endemics is a mallow (Malvaceae) known as Malva Rosa, *Lavatera assurgentiflora* (fig. 12.33A), a drought-deciduous shrub with large, dark green, palmately lobed leaves. It may grow to tree size if it gets abundant rainfall. The flowers are strikingly beautiful, containing five violet to lavender petals with light stripes. These shrubs were originally found only on San Clemente, Santa Catalina, San Miguel, and Anacapa islands. They have been planted on the other islands and at various localities on the mainland. They are a very attractive shrub for landscapes along the coast. Unfortunately, due to grazing by goats and sheep, the species is becoming rare on the islands. Bush mallows also occur on some islands, but they have become so rare that the Santa Cruz Island Bush Mallow, *Malacothamnus fasciculatus nesioticus*, and the San Clemente Island Bush Mallow, *M. clementinus*, are listed as endangered. There are at least 20 endangered or threatened species on the islands.

Another distinctive shrub, in the sunflower family (Asteraceae), is the Giant Coreopsis, *Coreopsis gigantea* (fig. 12.33B). This shrub has succulent stems and large, finely divided leaves borne in tufts on the ends of the stems. It is another drought-deciduous species. In bloom, each shrub is covered with many large yellow sunflowers. These plants are so common that whole hillsides turn yellow. Giant Coreopsis is also found on the mainland at a few localities, but it is considered a typical island species, occurring on all the islands north of Santa Catalina.

A rather distinctive tree in the rose family (Rosaceae) that is found only on islands is Catalina Ironwood, *Lyonothamnus floribundus*. There are two subspecies on the islands. *L. floribundus aspleniifolius* (fig. 12.33C) has a fernlike appearance with pinnate leaves and occurs on Santa Rosa, Santa Cruz, and San Clemente islands. *L. floribundus floribundus* occurs only on Santa Catalina. Its lance-shaped leaves are about 4 inches (10 cm) long, and the leaf margins may be smooth or variously incised. These are both attractive trees, with red shaggy bark, shiny green foliage, and clusters of white flowers. This is another ideal plant for southern California landscapes.

A tree that many people associate with Santa Catalina Island is the Catalina Cherry, *Prunus lyoni*. Cherry Cove, a popular mooring on the east side of the island, is named in its honor. Catalina Cherry is related to the common chaparral shrub Holly-leaved Cherry, *Prunus ilicifolia*. Groves of Catalina Cherry also occur in canyons on San Clemente, Santa Cruz, and Santa Rosa islands. Individual trees may be up to 50 feet (15 m) in height. The large red cherries appear in the fall and are delicious, but they have a very large poisonous seed. These cherries are an important autumn food for animals on the islands. They swallow the seed whole without releasing its load of cyanide. Indians ate the seeds, too, but they leached out the cyanide in the same way they leached the tannins from acorns.

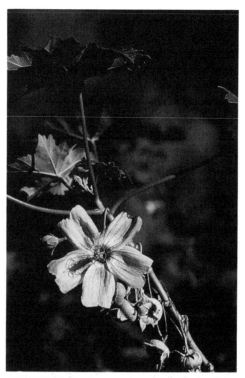

FIGURE 12.33 Some unique or endemic plants of the Channel Islands. *A*. Malva Rosa, *Lavatera assurgentiflora*, on Santa Cruz Island.

FIGURE 12.33 (*continued*) Some unique or endemic plants of the Channel Islands. *B*. Giant Coreopsis, *Coreopsis gigantea*, on Santa Cruz Island.

FIGURE 12.33 (*continued*) Some unique or endemic plants of the Channel Islands. *C.* San Clemente Ironweed, *Lyonothamnus floribundus aspleniifolius.*

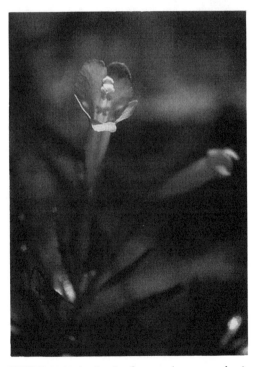

FIGURE 12.33 (*continued*) Some unique or endemic plants of the Channel Islands. *D.* Island Monkeyflower, *Mimulus flemingii*, on Santa Cruz Island.

FIGURE 12.33 (*continued*)   Some unique or endemic plants of the Channel Islands. *E*. Island Live Oak, *Quercus tomentella,* on San Clemente Island.

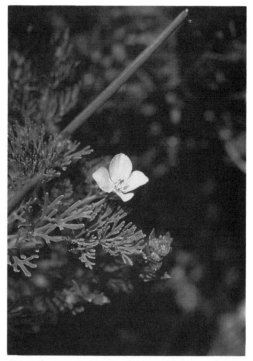

FIGURE 12.33 (*continued*)   Some unique or endemic plants of the Channel Islands. *F.* Island Poppy, *Eschscholzia ramosa*.

It has been mentioned many times throughout this book that California is the center of diversity for pines and oaks. It is only fitting, therefore, that its islands are characterized by distinctive oaks and pines. Interior Live Oak, *Quercus wislizenii*, occurs on Santa Cruz Island as a low-growing shrub. Blue Oak, *Quercus douglasii*, occurs in a few groves on Santa Cruz and Santa Catalina islands, and a few specimens of Canyon Live Oak, *Quercus chrysolepis*, and Valley Oak, *Quercus lobata*, also occur on those islands.

Two oaks are associated specifically with the islands. Island Live Oak, *Quercus tomentella* (fig. 12.33E), is a tree of north-facing slopes and canyons. It grows on Santa Cruz, Santa Rosa, Santa Catalina, and San Clemente islands. Young twigs on this species are conspicuously hairy. Leaves are oblong, 2 to 3 inches (50–75 mm) long, with smooth margins. The underside of the leaf is also hairy.

Another insular oak is known as *Quercus macdonaldii*. This tree grows in similar locations as Island Live Oak, but it is not found on San Clemente Island. It also has hairy twigs, and the underside of the leaves is faintly hairy. It differs from Island Live Oak by having two to four bristle-tipped lobes on each leaf. As unlikely as it may seem, this species is believed to have arisen by hybridization between Valley Oak and California Scrub Oak. The latter is widely distributed on these islands today, but Valley Oaks are limited and must have been far more common in the past. *Quercus macdonaldii* appears to enjoy limited distribution on the mainland as well, growing in isolated localities as far south as Morro Canyon in Crystal Cove State Park, Orange County. The trees in Crystal Cove State Park are considered by some authorities to be the southernmost specimens of Valley Oak, and not Macdonald Oak.

The presence of Torrey Pine, *Pinus torreyana* (fig. 8.56), on Santa Rosa Island is particularly interesting. This large-coned, long-needled species occurs only on the mainland near Del Mar and on Santa Rosa Island. This may be the smallest distribution of any pine species in the world. The island population is characterized by larger cones. The possibility that this may be more southerly in origin is discussed in chapter 8.

Among the closed-cone pines, two or three species have island populations. Bishop Pine, *Pinus muricata* (fig. 7.17), has the widest distribution, occurring on upper coastal terraces from Humboldt County to Santa Barbara County, and on Santa Cruz Island. It is also found on Cedros Island off Baja California. A close relative of this pine is the Santa Cruz Island Pine, *Pinus remorata*, which occurs on Santa Cruz and Santa Rosa islands as well as on the mainland near Lompoc. Many authorities do not recognize this as a distinct species. Its cones grow straight out rather than curling down along the branch. The Monterey Pine, *Pinus radiata*, occurs naturally at three locations near Monterey and also on Guadalupe Island (fig. 7.18), a true oceanic island 157 miles (252 km) off the Baja California coast. This volcanic island seems never to have been connected to the mainland, so all plants and animals must have arrived there by overwater dispersal. How these trees arrived at this remote island is subject to much debate. Also the subject of debate is which of the closed-cone pines actually inhabits Guadalupe and Cedros islands. Some authorities describe them both as varieties of Bishop Pine; others contend they are both types of Monterey Pine. It also has been stated that both species are on both islands.

Distribution of closed-cone pines on islands is discussed more thoroughly in chapter 7. It should be remembered, however, that they require fire for their cones to open, and they are dependent on fog drip for adequate moisture. They are also associated with depauperate soils such as acidified sandstones, serpentinites, and diatomites. On the islands where fire has been suppressed, many of the trees are dying of old age, and there is very little regeneration.

Principles of Island Biology

Animals and plants that inhabit islands are often relics of former widespread distributions, and because they evolve in isolation; they are often specialized. Most of the endemics mentioned here share both of these characteristics.

Another feature of island organisms is that they are often distinctly different in size from their mainland counterparts. The Island Fox, for example, is smaller than the mainland form. Of special interest in this respect is the fossil dwarf mammoth found on Santa Cruz, Santa Rosa, and San Miguel islands. The rationale for dwarfism is that islands have a limited food supply. A population of small animals, requiring less food, should do better where food is scarce.

If limited food is a problem, how can it be rationalized that island animals are sometimes much larger than their mainland counterparts? On California's islands most mammals are larger than their mainland relatives. Examples are the Big-eared Harvest Mouse (*Reithrodontomys megalotis catalinae*), Deer Mice (*Peromyscus maniculatus*), the Island Ground Squirrel (*Spermophilus beecheyi nesioticus*), and the Spotted Skunk (*Spilogale putorius*). Larger size is also illustrated in the Island Night Lizard. An explanation often used for gigantism on islands is that all available ecological niches may not be occupied. It is more difficult for large species to become dispersed to islands; therefore smaller species arrive and take over the vacant niches, and in time, a small species becomes larger. The Island Night Lizard might be an example. On the mainland, night lizards are insect eaters. On islands, they eat a more varied diet, including animal and plant material. In the absence of competition from a larger omnivore, perhaps the Island Night Lizard has moved into that niche.

Gigantism on islands might also be related to a shift in life history strategy. If resources are scarce but relatively stable, the emphasis should be on survival of existing individuals rather than on the reproduction of more individuals. Animals that fit this model tend to be long-lived and large and to have poor dispersal and low reproductive rates. This is the opposite of the pioneers most likely to colonize the island in the first place. Hence, island animals seem to be larger than their mainland counterparts.

Plants also show size changes on islands. The Giant Coreopsis is large on islands, and so is the Catalina Cherry. The Interior Live Oak is smaller, as are many annual wildflowers, such as the Island Poppy, *Eschscholzia ramosa* (fig. 12.33F). It also has been observed that island plants have larger leaves than their counterparts on the mainland.

From comparisons of chaparral species on the mainland with those on Santa Cruz Island, it was determined that leaves were indeed larger on the island. Comparison of variables such as precipitation, average temperature, temperature extremes, and wind velocity showed no significant differences. The island had greater cloud cover and, to a degree, deeper soils. The conclusion was that plants on the island experience lower water stress, so their leaves grow larger.

Island animals and plants also seem to lose their mobility, which is coincident with the life history strategy that causes them to be larger. The dispersal mechanism that brought them to the island might become a disadvantage once a population is established. Island plants and animals do not want to be carried away from the island. Birds become flightless, and some animals become sedentary. Plants lose their mechanisms for wind dispersal. Plumes on seeds disappear, and seeds become larger.

In the absence of heavy predation, animals lose their fear, and plants lose some of their protective mechanisms, such as toxins and spines. Perhaps the larger leaves and seeds observed are also related to reduced herbivory. As long as leaves are not being preyed on by herbivores, it is more efficient to grow one set of large leaves rather than to keep replacing smaller ones.

Larger islands and islands close to the mainland tend to have more species. This concept is verified by the relative numbers of species on California's islands. The concept of a filter is also illustrated by our islands. A filter implies that in a series of islands extending in a line away from the mainland, the number of species decreases from island to island as function of distance from the mainland. With the exception of the Anacapas, which are small, the number of species diminishes from Santa Cruz to Santa Rosa to San Miguel.

A very important concept in island biology is that once an island becomes saturated, the total number of species tends to remain the same. Even though species composition may be different at a later date, the number of extinctions should equal the numbers of colonizations. Although this is not always verifiable from comparing animals such as mammals that have limited ability to cross water barriers, those that are good dispersers fit the pattern well. Data on numbers and types of breeding land birds on the California islands, collected from 1917 to 1968, indicated that in nearly every case the total number of species remained stable, with the extinctions equal to the colonizations.

Comparison of the total number of species on an island with those in an equivalent area on the mainland usually reveals that saturation on the island occurs with fewer species. There are probably several reasons for this phenomenon. First of all, species that require large ranges are automatically selected against. Second, a defined area on the mainland includes many species that are on the fringe of their preferred habitats, and that are more common in adjacent areas. These two types of species are seldom found on islands. Perhaps of greatest importance is that the total diversity of habitats on an island tends to be reduced.

An interesting experiment in island biology is being confirmed by observations in mainland national parks. Because of a variety of disturbances on the outsides of parks, they tend to become ecologic islands that experience an overall loss of species with time. As might be expected, this "faunal collapse" is greatest in the small parks. A study of national parks of similar age in the United States and Canada shows that a number of mammal species has declined in direct proportion to the size of the park. Lassen Volcanic National Park in California, only 164 square miles (420 km^2) in total area, has lost 43% of its mammal species since 1910. The provincial parks in Alberta and British Columbia, including Kootenay, Banff, Jasper, and Yoho, with conterminus boundaries, function as one large park with 8000 square miles (20,500 km^2) of territory. In that large area there has not been a single extirpation since 1903. Parks of intermediate size, such as Yosemite and Sequoia–Kings Canyon, have lost 25% and 23% of their mammal species, respectively, since their establishment in the 1890s.

Introduced Animals

The devastation that can be wreaked by nonnative animals is nowhere more apparent than on islands. Most of the problem occurs with the introduction of large herbivores. Island plants evolved in the absence of large herbivores, so many of them have no defenses. Without large carnivores, the herbivores overpopulate in a short time. Introduced herbivores that are left unattended on an island soon strip it of most of its native vegetation.

Goats, *Capra hircus* (fig. 12.34A) seem to do the most damage. They will eat practically anything. Goats were introduced to Santa Catalina in 1827, and they are still there. The only thing that has kept them from denuding the entire island is a series of fences that has kept them localized. Nevertheless, 48 native species have been lost on Santa Catalina.

Fencing could have helped San Clemente Island, too, but attempts to control the goats came too late. The Navy owns and operates San Clemente Island. They use it for target practice and as a missile-tracking station. Goats have made the island a wasteland (fig. 12.34B). The native vegetation that has survived in reasonable health includes cactus, and shrubs that are in canyons with walls too steep to climb. The native oaks are pruned flat on their undersides, and no seedlings are allowed to grow more than 1 inch (25 mm) or so before they are nibbled off.

Because of the presence of plants and animals protected by the Endangered Species Act, the Navy took action to reduce or eliminate the goats on San Clemente Island. They announced a plan to shoot the goats systematically, but an animal rights group succeeded repeatedly in stopping the shooting program. At one time there were close to 15,000 goats on the island. Over a period of several years, various efforts to round them up alive reduced the numbers to perhaps 1500. The herds were transplanted to a variety of localities in the continental United States. In 1986 the animal rights group, at the Navy's expense, was allowed to drop nets on the goats from helicopters. The goats were transferred to the mainland, where they were put up for adoption. However, the same problem faced the goat adoption program that hampered the Burro adoption program in the desert: not enough people wanted goats. Nevertheless, nearly 900 goats were removed from the island and put up for adoption. Obviously, the

FIGURE 12.34   Goats and their damage on San Clemente Island. *A*. Goats, *Capra hircus*.

FIGURE 12.34 (*continued*)   Goats and their damage on San Clemente Island. *B*. Denuded landscape.

problem is not solved, because all the goats were not removed. As of 1991 the Navy was still working to remove the remaining animals. Efforts have been rewarded by obvious signs of recovery.

Sheep, *Ovis aries*, are nearly as bad as goats. San Miguel, San Nicolas, and Santa Cruz islands have had sheep on them since the 1800s. San Nicolas may have been hit the hardest. By 1890 there were more than 30,000 sheep on San Nicolas Island. They ate off the native vegetation, and by 1930 the island was already in bad shape. In 1933 the Navy acquired the island and built a weather station. The last sheep rancher left the island in 1941, when his lease expired. At that time there was very little vegetation left. In an effort to reduce further erosion, the Navy applied fertilizer and grass seed from an airplane. Today, all sheep have been removed, and nonnative grasses are all that remain. At this point, San Nicolas is a good candidate for observations on natural island colonization.

San Miguel is nearly as bleak as San Nicolas. It was denuded, and topsoil has blown away, exposing interesting limestone concretions on old tree roots. This fossil forest is one of the bizarre attractions on this bleak island. With the removal of the sheep, San Miguel is beginning to show signs of recovery.

Santa Cruz Island has had sheep since the 1850s. All regions above a fence line showed damage from grazing, and very little native vegetation within reach of a sheep was left. All shrubs were pruned on the underside as high as a sheep could reach. When sheep are present, seedlings are not able to get established, and the native plants eventually die of old age. Fortunately, Santa Cruz Island is managed today by a combination of the Nature Conservancy and the National Park Service. The Nature Conservancy added fences, and between 1983 and 1986 they removed over 20,000 sheep. The recovery of Santa Cruz Island looks very promising. Including subspecies, there are 600 kinds of plants on Santa Cruz. Ironwood seedlings are reappearing, and Silver Deerweed, *Lotus argophyllus niveus*, once on the brink of extinction, is flourishing. The live-forevers *Dudleya greenei* and *D. nesiotica*, once confined to steep cliff faces, are expanding their ranges.

Cattle, *Bos taurus*, also have been herded on Santa Rosa, Santa Cruz, and Santa Catalina. There are only small herds left on Santa Catalina and Santa Cruz. Santa Rosa Island still has a major cattle herd that shares resources with introduced Mule Deer, *Odocoileus hemionus*, and Wapiti (Roosevelt Elk), *Cervus elaphus*. The elk and deer are not native, but their presence there is controlled by hunting. The goal is to keep the two herds limited to about 700 animals each, although the elk herd now numbers about 1000.

The elk on Santa Rosa Island grow to uncommonly large size. Half of the 16 trophy Roosevelt Elk listed in the Safari Club International's record book were shot on Santa Rosa Island. Is this another example of island gigantism? The Santa Rosa ranch is privately owned, and hunters pay $6000 for the five-day privilege of shooting a six-by-six elk (i.e., with six points on each antler).

A most unlikely introduced herbivore is the Bison (American Buffalo), *Bison bison* (fig. 12.35A). There are about 500 of them today on Santa Catalina Island. That population is also controlled. They were introduced there in 1924 during the filming of a silent movie, *The Vanishing American*. From the original 14 animals released, the herd has grown significantly, to the detriment of native vegetation. It is true, however, that at the present time Bison graze primarily on introduced grasses. The dramatic difference between the damage produced by goats and Bison can be seen where the two herds graze on opposites sides of a fence (fig. 12.35B). The side where goats live is chewed off clear to the soil.

A secondary influence of Bison on Santa Catalina is the appearance of Brown-headed Cowbirds, *Molothrus ater*. Flocks of these birds follow Bison herds and feed

FIGURE 12.35   Bison and their damage on Santa Catalina Island. *A*. Bison, *Bison bison*.

FIGURE 12.35 (*continued*)   Bison and their damage on Santa Catalina Island. *B*. Fence line showing the effect of overgrazing: Bison graze on the left of the fence, and goats graze on the right.

on their droppings. Unfortunately, these are nest parasites that lay their eggs in the nests of various native songbirds on the island. This problem in the Sierra Nevada is discussed in chapter 4. It remains to be seen what will happen to the abundance of native birds on the island.

Santa Barbara Island, the smallest of the Channel Islands, has suffered from farming, sheep ranching, and the introduction of feral rabbits. The European Rabbit, *Oryctolagus cuniculus*, was introduced about 1915 by a farmer, and apparently reintroduced by the Navy in 1942. The rabbits flourished, and native vegetation was seriously damaged. From 1979 through 1981, the National Park Service removed the rabbits, and native vegetation is recovering. The endemic Santa Barbara Live-forever, *Dudleya traskiae*, once thought to be extinct, is expanding its range again. The European Rabbit still inhabits the Farallon Islands.

Perhaps the most serious threat to the native island biota is the presence of introduced Wild Boars or Feral Hogs, *Sus scrofa* (fig. 12.36A). This is the same species as the domesticated hog. They are abundant on San Clemente, Santa Cruz, and Santa Rosa islands. Pigs are omnivorous. They don't see well, but they use their excellent sense of smell to locate various underground roots, tubers, and bulbs. To find these carbohydrate-rich storage organs, pigs turn over the soil, uprooting whatever is on the surface. Among their favorite foods are the bulbs of Blue Dicks, *Dichelostemma capitatum*, and mariposa lilies (*Calochortus* spp.). After a group of pigs has moved through an area, it looks as if it had been rototilled. Large areas of bare earth are the result (fig. 12.36B). When it rains, the disturbed topsoil is carried away, and patches remain bare for many years.

To human visitors on islands, it also is important to realize that a boar hog is one of the most dangerous animals one could encounter. If cornered, they are ferocious. Their large canine teeth project upward as tusks. Although wild males may have shorter tusks than their domesticated counterparts, the arrangement remains useful for digging, as well as for waylaying an opponent.

Not many carnivores become introduced to islands, because they are not good to eat. The introduction of herbivores was a deliberate action to provide a source of food for humans. The early introductions of goats were done to provide fresh meat for sailors. Introductions of cattle and sheep, of course, were done to capitalize on the availability of unfenced range, free of predators. Pigs were introduced to provide food, and also for sport hunting.

Introductions of these animals have not been limited to islands. It is simply that islands are more susceptible to overcrowding. Pigs, goats, sheep, and other herbivores also roam free on various parts of the mainland, particularly in the Coast Ranges. Natural predators such as Mountain Lions help to control them. The problem of feral pigs was also discussed in the section on Oak Woodland in chapter 7.

The carnivores that have been introduced to islands are principally escaped pets. Feral dogs seem to have been more of a problem in the past. One of the limiting factors for sheep on San Nicolas Island was the pack of dogs left over from the Indian days. It didn't take long, however, for the sheep herders to remove all the dogs.

FIGURE 12.36   Wild Boars and their damage on San Clemente Island. *A.* Wild Boar, *Sus scrofa*.

FIGURE 12.36 (*continued*)   Wild Boars and their damage on San Clemente Island. *B.* Bare spots caused by pigs uprooting the vegetation.

An interesting situation occurred on Cedros Island, off Baja California. This is a large, steep island that is one of the least disturbed of the islands along the Pacific coast. There was a population of native deer, and there were introduced goats. Apparently, the deer were able to thrive on the island without overpopulation, and a pack of wild dogs kept the goats under control.

Feral cats abound on many islands. The presence of these cats is a problem for native rodents, but they seem to survive somehow. Possibly it is because the rodents take refuge in cactus patches. However, these cats tend to keep introduced rats and mice under control, too.

Epilogue

California is a marvelous place, with a greater range of landforms, a greater variety of habitats, and more kinds of plants and animals than any area of equivalent size in North America. Similarly, there are more endemic plants and animals here than anywhere in the United States. When Europeans first arrived in California, it was a scene of unparalleled, almost unimaginable, natural richness. Unfortunately, this richness coupled with the region's pleasant Mediterranean climate soon attracted an unprecedented number of people, and humanity has encroached upon the landscape to such a degree that California is the state with the greatest number of endangered species.

Nevertheless, California still has the greatest amount of open space and roadless terrain in the lower 48 states, and an increasingly devoted group of citizens attempting to protect it. These people have won great victories, but many Californians still fail to appreciate the intricacy and beauty of the natural order of things, and that human activities are capable of spoiling it all.

Humans are merely one of the living organisms in the system, but unlike other organisms, they are capable of thinking and analyzing. Those who choose not to think about natural treasures have already altered the face of California forever. This book is dedicated to an attitude that is essential if future generations are to enjoy and appreciate California's natural beauty and diversity. It is also dedicated to the thoughtful people who are willing to work together to preserve the natural order of things and restore the land from damage that thoughtless development has brought.

Selected References

GENERAL REFERENCES

Airola, D. A., and T. C. Messick. 1987. *Sliding toward Extinction: The State of California's Natural Heritage*. Prepared at the request of the California Senate Committee on Natural Resources and Wildlife. Commissioned by the California Nature Conservancy. Prepared by Jones and Stokes Associates, Sacramento.

Anderson, B. R. 1975. *Weather in the West*. Palo Alto: American West.

Bakker, E. 1984. *An Island Called California*. Berkeley: University of California Press.

Betancourt, J. L., T. R Van Devender, and P. S. Martin. 1990. *Packrat Middens: The Last 40,000 Years of Biotic Change*. Tucson: University of Arizona Press.

Brewer, W. H. 1966. *Up and Down California,* 3rd ed. Berkeley: University of California Press.

Brown, J. H., and A. C. Gibson. 1983. *Biogeography*. St. Louis: C. V. Mosby.

Buckman, H. O., and N. C. Brady. 1974. *The Nature and Properties of Soils*. New York: Macmillan.

Colinvaux, P. 1978. *Why Big Fierce Animals Are Rare*. Princeton: Princeton University Press.

Dasmann, R. F. 1965. *The Destruction of California*. New York: Macmillian.

———. 1981. *California's Changing Environment*. Cincinnati: Boyd & Fraser.

Dott, R. H., Jr., and R. L. Batten. 1981. *Evolution of the Earth*. New York: McGraw-Hill.

Felton, E. L. 1965. *California's Many Climates*. Palo Alto: Pacific Books.

Hunt, C. B. 1967. *Physiography of the United States*. San Francisco: W. H. Freeman.

Miller, G. T. 1988. *Living in the Environment*. Belmont: Wadsworth.

Ricklefs, R. E. 1979. *Ecology*. New York: Chiron Press.

Sloan, E. 1952. *Eric Sloan's Weather Book*. Hudson, N.Y.: Hawthorn Books.

Smith, R. L. 1991. *Ecology and Field Biology*. New York: Harper & Row.

Vessel, M. F., and H. H. Wong. 1987. *Natural History of Vacant Lots*. California Natural History Guides, no. 50. Berkeley: University of California Press.

Whitaker, R. H. 1970. *Communities and Ecosystems*. New York: Macmillian.

GEOLOGY

Alt, D. D., and D. W. Hyndman. 1975. *Roadside Geology of Northern California*. Missoula, Mont.: Mountain Press.

Cooper, J. D., R. H. Miller, and J. Patterson. 1986. *A Trip through Time: Principles of Historical Geology*. Columbus, Ohio: Charles E. Merrill.

Ernst, W. G. 1981. *The Geotectonic Development of California*. Englewood Cliffs, N.J.: Prentice-Hall.

Hill, M. 1984. *California Landscape: Origin and Evolution*. California Natural History Guides, no. 48. Berkeley: University of California Press.

Iacopi, R. 1964. *Earthquake Country*. Menlo Park, Calif.: Lane.

Norris, R. M., and R. W. Webb. 1990. *Geology of California*. New York: John Wiley & Sons.

Oakeshott, G. B. 1978. *California's Changing Landscapes*. New York: McGraw-Hill.

Sharp, R. P. 1972. *Geology Field Guide to Southern California*. Dubuque, Iowa: Kendall/Hunt.

PLANTS

Abrams, L., and R. S. Ferriso 1923–60. *Illustrated Flora of the Pacific States*. 4 vols. Stanford: Stanford University Press.

Axelrod, D. I. 1976. *History of the Coniferous Forests, California and Nevada*. University of California Publications in Botany, no. 70.

Barbour, M. G., J. H. Burk, and W. D. Pitts. 1987. *Terrestrial Plant Ecology*. Menlo Park, Calif.: Benjamin/Cummings.

Barbour, M. G., and J. Major. 1988. *Terrestrial Vegetation of California*, new exp. ed. California Native Plant Society Special Publication no. 9.

Benson, L. 1982. *The Cacti of the United States and Canada*. Stanford: Stanford University Press.

Brown, D. E. 1982. "Biotic Communities of the American Southwest—United States and Mexico" (Special Issue), *Desert Plants* 4 (1–4).

Chabot, B. F., and H. A. Mooney. 1985. *Physiological Ecology of North American Plant Communities*. New York: Chapman and Hall.

Clarke, C. B. 1977. *Edible and Useful Plants of California*. California Natural History Guides, no. 41. Berkeley: University of California Press.

Crampton, B. 1974. *Grasses in California*. California Natural History Guides, no. 33. Berkeley: University of California Press.

Elias, T. S. 1987. *Conservation and Management of Rare and Endangered Plants*. California Native Plant Society.

———. 1980. *The Complete Trees of North America*. New York: Van Nostrand Reinhold.

Griffin, J. R., and W. B. Critchfield. 1976. *The Distribution of Forest Trees in California*. USDA, Forest Service Research Paper PSW-82.

Grillos, S. J. 1966. *Ferns and Fern Allies of California*. California Natural History Guides, no. 16. Berkeley: University of California Press.

McMinn, H. E. 1964. *An Illustrated Manual of California Shrubs*. Berkeley: University of California Press.

McMinn, H. E., E. Maino, and H. W. Shepherd. 1963. *Pacific Coast Trees*. Berkeley: University of California Press.

Munz, P. A. 1961. *California Spring Wildflowers*. Berkeley: University of California Press.

Munz, P. A., and D. D. Keck. 1968. *A California Flora: With Supplement*. Berkeley: University of California Press.

Niehaus, T. F., and C. L. Ripper. 1976. *Field Guide to Pacific States Wildflowers*. Boston: Houghton Mifflin.

Orr, R. T., and D. B. Orr. 1979. *Mushrooms of Western North America*. California Natural History Guides, no. 42. Berkeley: University of California Press.

Ornduff, R. 1974. *Introduction to California Plant Life*. California Natural History Guides, no. 35. Berkeley: University of California Press.

Plumb, T. R. 1980. *Proceedings of the Symposium on the Ecology, Management, and Utilization of California Oaks*. U.S. Forest Service, Pacific Southwest Forest and Range Experiment Station General Technical Report PSW-44.

Raven, P. H., and D. I. Axelrod. 1978. *Origins and Relationships of the California Flora*. University of California Publications in Botany, no. 72.

Smith, Jr., J. P. and R. York. 1988. *Inventory of Rare and Endangered Vascular Plants of California*. California Native Plant Society Special Publication no. 1.

Spellenberg, R. 1979. *The Audubon Society Field Guide of North America Wildflowers (Western Region)*. New York: Alfred A. Knopf.

Spurr, S. 1964. *Forest Ecology*. New York: Ronald Press.

Standiford, R. B. 1991. *Proceedings of the Symposium on Oak Woodlands and Hardwood Rangeland Management*. U.S. Forest Service, Pacific Southwest Forest and Range Experiment Station General Technical Report PSW-126.

Sudworth, G. B. 1908 (Dover reprint published 1968). *Forest Trees of the Pacific Slope*. USDA, Forest Service.

Warner, R. E., and K. M. Hendrix, eds. 1984. *California Riparian Systems: Ecology, Conservation, and Productive Management*. Berkeley: University of California Press.

ANIMALS

Banks, C. R., R. W. McDiarmid, and A. L. Gardner. 1987. *Checklist of Vertebrates of the United States, the U.S. Territories, and Canada*. U.S. Department of the Interior, Fish and Wildlife Service, Resource Publication 166.

Behler, J. L. 1979. *The Audubon Society Field Guide to North American Reptiles and Amphibians*. New York: Alfred A. Knopf.

Bennett, R. S. 1983. *Field Guide to the Birds of North America*. Washington, D.C.: National Geographic Society.

Borrer, D. J., and R. E. White. 1970. *Field Guide to the Insects of America North of Mexico*. Boston: Houghton Mifflin.

Dasmann, R. F. 1964. *Wildlife Biology*. New York: John Wiley & Sons.

Garth, J. S., and J. W. Tilden. 1986. *California Butterflies*. California Natural History Guides, no. 51. Berkeley: University of California Press.

Hall, E. R. 1981. *Mammals of North America*. New York: John Wiley & Sons.

Ingles, L. G. 1965. *Mammals of the Pacific States*. Stanford: Stanford University Press.

Jameson, E. W., Jr., and H. J. Peeters. 1988. *California Mammals*. California Natural History Guides, no. 52. Berkeley: University of California Press.

Jennings, M. R. 1987. *Annotated Check List of the Amphibians and Reptiles of California*. Southwestern Herpetologists Society Special Publication no. 3.

Klauber, L. M. 1982. *Rattlesnakes,* abr. ed. Berkeley: University of California Press.

Merritt, R. W., and K. W. Cummings. 1978. *An Introduction to the Aquatic Insects of North America*. Dubuque, Iowa: Kendall/Hunt.

Pearse, V., J. Pearse, M. Buchsbaum, and R. Buchsbaum. 1987. *Living Invertebrates*. Palo Alto: Blackwell Scientific Publications; and Pacific Grove, Calif.: Boxwood Press.

Peterson, R. T. 1990. *A Field Guide to Western Birds*. Boston: Houghton Mifflin.

Powell, J. A., and C. L. Hogue. 1979. *California Insects*. California Natural History Guides, no. 44. Berkeley: University of California Press.

Robbins, C. S., B. Brunn, and H. S. Zim. 1966. *Birds of North America*. New York: Golden Press.

Robins, C. R., et al. 1980. *A List of Common and Scientific Names of Fishes from the United States and Canada*. American Fisheries Society Special Publication no. 12.

Small, A. 1975. *The Birds of California*. New York: Collier Books.

Smith, A. C. 1961. *Western Butterflies*. Menlo Park, Calif.: Lane.

Stebbins, R. C. 1954. *Amphibians and Reptiles of Western North America*. New York: McGraw-Hill.

———. 1966. *Field Guide to Western Reptiles and Amphibians*. Boston: Houghton Mifflin.

———. 1972. *California Amphibians and Reptiles*. California Natural History Guides, no. 31. Berkeley: University of California Press.

Steinhart, P. 1990. *California's Wild Heritage: Threatened and Endangered Animals in the Golden State*. San Francisco: Sierra Club Books.

Tilden, J. W., and A. C. Smith. 1986. *Field Guide to Western Butterflies*. Boston: Houghton Mifflin.

Udvardy, M. D. F. 1977. *The Audubon Society Field Guide to North American Birds (Western Region)*. New York: Alfred A. Knopf.

Whitaker, J. O. 1980. *The Audubon Society Field Guide to North American Mammals*. New York: Alfred A. Knopf.

SIERRA NEVADA

Arno, S. 1973. *Discovering Sierra Trees*. Yosemite Natural History Association, Sequoia Natural History Association.

Beedy, E. C., and S. L. Granholm. 1985. *Discovering Sierra Birds*. Yosemite Natural History Association, Sequoia Natural History Association.

Browning, P. 1986. *Place Names of the Sierra Nevada*. Berkeley: Wilderness Press.

Gaines, D. 1988. *Birds of Yosemite and the East Slope*. Lee Vining, Calif.: Artemisia Press.

Grater, R. K. 1978. *Discovering Sierra Mammals*. Yosemite Natural History Association, Sequoia Natural History Association.

Harvey, H. T., H. S. Shellhammer, and R. E. Stecker. 1980. *Giant Sequoia Ecology*. U.S. Department of the Interior, National Park Service.

Hill, M. 1975. *Geology of the Sierra Nevada*. California Natural History Guides, no. 37. Berkeley: University of California Press.

Horn, E. L. 1976. *Wildflowers 3: The Sierra Nevada*. Beaverton, Ore.: Touchstone Press.

Huber, N. K. 1987. *Geologic Story of Yosemite National Park*. U.S. Department of the Interior, Geological Survey Bulletin 1595.

Huning, J. B. 1978. *Hot Dry Wet Cold and Windy: A Weather Primer for the National Parks of the Sierra Nevada*. Yosemite Natural History Association, Sequoia Natural History Association.

Hutchinson, J. L., and G. L. Stebbins. 1986. *A Flora of the Wright's Lake Area*. Pollock Pines, Calif.: Judy L. Hutchinson.

Jenkins, O. P. 1948. *Geologic Guidebook Along Highway 49: Sierran Gold Belt, the Mother Lode Country*. California Department of Natural Resources, Division of Mines, Bulletin 141.

Johnston, V. R. 1970. *Sierra Nevada*. Boston: Houghton Mifflin.

Morgenson, D. C. 1975. *Yosemite Wildflower Trails*. Yosemite Natural History Association.

Muir, J. 1961. *The Mountains of California*. Garden City, N.Y.: Doubleday.

Munz, P. A. 1963. *California Mountain Wildflowers*. Berkeley: University of California Press.

Niehaus, T. F. 1974. *Sierra Wildflowers*. California Natural History Guides, no. 32. Berkeley: University of California Press.

Peterson, P. V., and P. V. Peterson, Jr. 1975. *Native Trees of the Sierra Nevada*. California Natural History Guides, no. 36. Berkeley: University of California Press.

Smith, G. S. 1976. *Mammoth Lakes Sierra*. Palo Alto: Genny Smith Books.

Stebbins, C. A., and R. C. Stebbins. 1974. *Birds of Yosemite National Park*. Yosemite Natural History Association.

Stocking, S. K., and J. A. Rockwell. 1969. *Wildflowers of Sequoia and Kings Canyon National Parks*. Sequoia Natural History Association.

Storer, T. I., and R. Usinger. 1963. *Sierra Nevada Natural History*. Berkeley: University of California Press.

Sumner, L., and J. S. Dixon. 1953. *Birds and Mammals of the Sierra Nevada*. Berkeley: University of California Press.

Thomas, J. H., and D. R. Parnell. 1974. *Native Shrubs of the Sierra Nevada*. California Natural History Guides, no. 34. Berkeley: University of California Press.

Verner, J., and A. S. Boss. 1980. *California Wildlife and Their Habitats: Western Sierra Nevada*. USDA, Forest Service, Pacific Southwest Forest and Range Experimentation Station, General Technical Report PSW-37.

Weeden, N. F. 1986. *A Sierra Nevada Flora*. Berkeley: Wilderness Press.

Whitney, S. 1979. *A Sierra Club Naturalist's Guide to the Sierra Nevada*. San Francisco: Sierra Club Books.

MOUNTAINTOPS

Arno, S. F., and R. P. Hammerly. 1984. *Timberline, Mountain and Arctic Forest Frontiers*. Seattle: The Mountaineers.

Hall, C. A., Jr. 1991. *Natural History of the White-Inyo Range, Eastern California*. Berkeley: University of California Press.

Lanner, R. M. 1981. *The Piñon Pine*. Reno: University of Nevada Press.

Lloyd, R. M., and R. S. Mitchell. 1973. *A Flora of the White Mountains, California and Nevada*. Berkeley: University of California Press.

Marchand, P. J. 1991. *Life in the Cold: An Introduction to Winter Ecology*. Hanover: University Press of New England.

Zwinger, A. H., and B. E. Willard. 1972. *Land above the Trees: A Guide to American Alpine Tundra*. New York: Harper & Row.

PACIFIC NORTHWEST

Ferlatte, W. J. 1974. *A Flora of the Trinity Alps of Northern California*. Berkeley: University of California Press.

Gillett, G. W., J. T. Howell, and H. Leschke. 1961. *A Flora of Lassen Volcanic Park, California*. University of San Francisco Press. (Reprinted from the *Wasmann Journal of Biology*.)

Wallace, D. R. 1983. *The Klamath Knot: Explorations of Myth and Evolution*. San Francisco: Sierra Club Books.

Whitney, S. 1989. *A Sierra Club Naturalist's Guide to the Pacific Northwest*. San Francisco: Sierra Club Books.

COAST RANGES

Becking, R. W. 1982. *Pocket Flora of the Redwood Forest*. Covelo, Calif.: Island Press.

Bowen, O. E. 1959. *Rocks and Minerals of the San Francisco Bay Region*. California Natural History Guides, no. 5. Berkeley: University of California Press.

Bowerman, M. L. 1944. *The Flowering Plants and Ferns of Mount Diablo, California*. Gillick Press.

Cooney-Lazaneo, M. B., K. Lyons, and H. King. 1981. *Plants of Big Basin Redwoods State Park and the Coastal Mountains of Northern California*. Missoula, Mont.: Mountain Press.

Evans, J. G. 1988. *Natural History of the Point Reyes Peninsula*. Point Reyes, Calif.: Point Reyes National Seashore Association.

Ferris, R. S. 1968. *Native Shrubs of the San Francisco Bay Region*. California Natural History Guides, no. 24. Berkeley: University of California Press.

Gilliam, H. 1962. *Weather of San Francisco Bay Region*. California Natural History Guides, no. 6. Berkeley: University of California Press.

Hoover, R. F., 1970. *The Vascular Plants of San Luis Obispo County, California*. Berkeley: University of California Press.

Howard, A. D. 1979. *Geologic History of Middle California*. California Natural History Guides, no. 43. Berkeley: University of California Press.

Howell, J. T. 1970. *Marin Flora*. Berkeley: University of California Press.

Jenkins, O. P. 1951. *Geologic Guidebook of the San Francisco Bay Counties.* California Division of Mines and Geology, Bulletin 141.

Metcalf, W. 1959. *Native Trees of the San Francisco Bay Region.* California Natural History Guides, no. 4. Berkeley: University of California Press.

Peattie, B. 1946. *The Pacific Coast Ranges.* New York: Vanguard Press.

Sharsmith, H. K. 1945. "The Flora of the Mount Hamilton Range of California," *American Midland Naturalist,* September.

———. 1965. *Spring Wildflowers of the San Francisco Bay Region.* California Natural History Guides, no. 11. Berkeley: University of California Press.

Sholars, R. E. 1982. *The Pygmy Forest and Associated Plant Communities of Coastal Mendocino County, California.* Mendocino: Black Bear Press.

Smith, A. C. 1959. *Introduction to the Natural History of the San Francisco Bay Region.* California Natural History Guides, no. 1. Berkeley: University of California Press.

Smith, C. F. 1976. *A Flora of the Santa Barbara Region.* Santa Barbara Museum of Natural History.

Thomas, J. H. 1961. *Flora of the Santa Cruz Mountains of California.* Stanford: Stanford University Press.

CISMONTANE SOUTHERN CALIFORNIA

Ancinec, D. G., K. W. Radford, and R. Schwenkmeyer. 1985. *Natural History of Southern California.* Palo Alto, Calif.: Peek Publications.

Bailey, H. P. 1966. *Weather of Southern California.* California Natural History Guides, no. 17. Berkeley: University of California Press.

Beauchamp, R. M. 1986. *A Flora of San Diego County, California.* National City, Calif.: Sweetwater River Press.

Belzer, T. J. 1984. *Roadside Plants of Southern California.* Missoula, Mont.: Mountain Press.

Booth, E. S. 1968. *Mammals of Southern California.* California Natural History Guides, no. 21. Berkeley: University of California Press.

Bowler, P., and S. Brown, eds. 1987. *California Oak Heritage Conservation Conference.* Irvine, Calif.: Sea and Sage Audubon Society.

Clarke, H. 1989. *An Introduction to Southern California Birds.* Missoula, Mont.: Mountain Press.

Dale, N. 1986. *Flowering Plants: The Santa Monica Mountains, Coastal and Chaparral Regions of Southern California.* Santa Barbara, Calif.: Capra Press.

De Lisle, H. D., et al. 1986. *The Distribution and Present Status of the Herpetofauna of the Santa Monica Mountains.* Southwestern Herpetologists Society Special Publication no. 2.

Garrett, K., and J. Dunn. 1981. *Birds of Southern California.* Los Angeles Audubon Society.

Jaeger, E., and A. C. Smith. 1966. *Introduction to the Natural History of Southern California.* California Natural History Guides, no. 13. Berkeley: University of California Press.

Lathrop, E. W., and R. F. Thorne. 1985. *A Flora of the Santa Rosa Plateau.* Southern California Botanists Special Publication no. 1.

Latting, J., ed. 1976. *Plant Communities of Southern California.* California Native Plant Society Special Publication no. 1.

Lenz, L. W., and J. Dourley. 1981. *California Native Trees & Shrubs for Garden & Environmental Use in Southern California.* Claremont, Calif.: Rancho Santa Ana Botanic Garden.

Munz, P. A. 1974. *A Flora of Southern California.* Berkeley: University of California Press.

Perry, B. 1981. *Trees and Shrubs for Dry California Landscapes.* San Dimas, Calif.: Land Design.

Peterson, P. V. 1966. *Native Trees of Southern California.* California Natural History Guides, no. 14. Berkeley: University of California Press.

Raven, P. H. 1966. *Native Shrubs of Southern California*, California Natural History Guides, no. 15. Berkeley: University of California Press.

Raven, P. H., H. J. Thompson, and B. A. Prigge. 1986. *Flora of the Santa Monica Mountains, California.* Southern California Botanists Special Publication no. 2.

Schoenherr, A. A. 1976. *The Herpetofauna of the San Gabriel Mountains.* Southwestern Herpetologist's Society Special Publication no. 1.

Schoenherr, A. A., ed. 1990. *Endangered Plant Communities of Southern California.* Southern California Botanists Special Publication no. 3.

Thomas, B. 1981. *Life in the Chaparral.* Anaheim: Wildlife and You.

DESERTS

Benson, L. 1969. *Native Cacti of California.* Stanford: Stanford University Press.

Benson, L., and R. A. Darrow. 1981. *Trees and Shrubs of the Southwest Deserts.* Tucson: University of Arizona Press.

Brown, G. W., Jr. 1974. *Desert Biology,* 2 vols. New York: Academic Press.

Cloudsley-Thompson, J. L., and M. J. Chadwick. 1964. *Life in Deserts.* Philadelphia: Dufour Editions.

Cornett, J. W. 1987. *Wildlife of the North American Deserts.* Palm Springs: Nature Trails Press.

Cowles, R. B., and E. S. Bakker. 1977. *Desert Journal.* Berkeley: University of California Press.

Dawson, E. Y. 1966. *Cacti of California.* California Natural History Guides, no. 18. Berkeley: University of California Press.

DeDecker, M. 1984. *Flora of the Northern Mojave Desert, California.* California Native Plant Society Special Publication no. 7.

Dodge, N. N. 1952. *Poisonous Dwellers of the Desert.* Popular Series, no. 3. Globe, Ariz.: Southwestern Monuments Assn.

Foster, L. 1987. *Adventuring in the California Desert.* San Francisco: Sierra Club Books.

Hunt, C. B. 1975. *Death Valley: Geology, Ecology, and Archaeology.* Berkeley: University of California Press.

Jaeger, E. 1933. *The California Deserts.* Stanford: Stanford University Press.

———. 1967. *Desert Wildflowers.* Stanford: Stanford University Press.

———. 1950. *Our Desert Neighbors.* Stanford: Stanford University Press.

Kirk, R. 1973. *Desert, The American Southwest.* Boston: Houghton Mifflin.

Larson, P. 1977. *A Sierra Club Naturalist's Guide to The Deserts of the Southwest.* San Francisco: Sierra Club Books.

Louw, G. N., and M. K. Seeley. 1982. *Ecology of Desert Organisms.* New York: Longman.

Mabry, T. J., and J. H. Hunziker, and D. R. Difeo, Jr. 1977. *Creosote Bush.* New York: John Wiley & Sons.

Miller, A. H., and R. C. Stebbins. 1964. *The Lives of Desert Animals in Joshua Tree National Monument.* Berkeley: University of California Press.

Monson, G., and L. Sumner. 1980. *The Desert Bighorn.* Tucson: University of Arizona Press.

Munz, P. A. 1962 *California Desert Wildflowers.* Berkeley: University of California Press.

Pianka, E. R. 1986. *Ecology and Natural History of Desert Lizards.* Princeton: Princeton University Press.

Reimold, R. J., and W. H. Queen. 1974. *Ecology of Halophytes.* New York: Academic Press.

Schmidt-Nielsen, K. 1964. *Desert Animals: Physiological Problems of Heat and Water.* London: Oxford University Press.

Simpson, B. B. 1977. *Mesquite*. New York: John Wiley & Sons.

Smith, G., ed. 1978. *Deepest Valley: Guide to Owens Valley and Its Mountain Lakes, Roadsides, and Trails*, Rev. ed. Los Altos, Calif.: William Kaufman.

Stein, B. A., and S. F. Warrick. 1979. *Granite Mountains Resource Survey*. University of California–Santa Cruz Environmental Field Program, Publication no. 1.

Stone, R. D., and V. A. Sumida. 1983. *The Kingston Range of California: A Resource Survey*. University of California–Santa Cruz Environmental Field Program, Publication no. 10.

Zabriskie, J. G. 1979. *Plants of Deep Canyon and the Central Coachella Valley, California*. University of California–Riverside, Philip L. Boyd Deep Canyon Desert Research Center.

GREAT CENTRAL VALLEY

Jain, S. 1976. *Vernal Pools: Their Ecology and Conservation*. University of California–Davis, Institute of Ecology, Publication no. 9.

Mason, H. L. 1957. *A Flora of the Marshes of California*. Berkeley: University of California Press.

Sampson, A. W., and B. S. Jesperson. 1963. *California Range Brushlands and Browse Plants*. Division of Agricultural Sciences, Manual 33.

Sands, A. 1977. *Riparian Forests in California*. University of California–Davis Institute of Ecology, Special Publication no. 15.

Twisselman, E. 1967. *A Flora of Kern County*. San Francisco: University of San Francisco.

INLAND WATERS

Cole, G. A. 1983. *Textbook of Limnology*. St. Louis: C. V. Mosby.

Frey, D. G. 1963. *Limnology in North America*. Madison: University of Wisconsin Press.

Goldman, C. R., and A. J. Horne. 1983. *Limnology*. New York: McGraw-Hill.

Macan, T. T. 1974. *Freshwater Ecology*. New York: Halstead Press.

McGinnis, S. M. 1984. *Freshwater Fishes of California*. Berkeley: University of California Press.

Minckley, W. K., and J. E. Deacon, eds. 1991. *Battle Against Extinction: Native Fish Management in the American West*. Tucson: University of Arizona Press.

Moyle, P. B. 1976. *Inland Fishes of California*. Berkeley: University of California Press.

Naiman, R. J., and D. L. Soltz, eds. 1981. *Fishes in North American Deserts*. New York: Wiley-Interscience.

Palmer, T. 1982. *Stanislaus: The Struggle for a River*. Berkeley: University of California Press.

Pennack, R. W. 1953. *Fresh-Water Invertebrates of the United States*. New York: Ronald Press.

Reisner, M. 1986. *Cadillac Desert: The American West and Its Disappearing Water*. New York: Viking Press.

Rinne, J. N., and W. L. Minckley. 1991. *Native Fishes of Arid Lands: A Dwindling Resource of the Desert Southwest*. U.S. Forest Service, Rocky Mountain Forest and Range Experiment Station Technical Report RM-206.

Soltz, D. L., and R. J. Naiman. 1978. *The Natural History of Native Fishes in the Death Valley System*. Natural History Museum of Los Angeles County.

Usinger, R. L. 1956. *Aquatic Insects of California*. Berkeley: University of California Press.

Whitton, B. A. 1975. *River Ecology*. Berkeley: University of California Press.

Winkler, D. W. 1977. *An Ecological Study of Mono Lake, California*. University of California–Davis Institute of Ecology, Publication no. 12.

COASTLINE

Abbot, I. A., and G. J. Hollenberg. 1976. *Marine Algae of California*. Stanford: Stanford University Press.

Barbour, M., et al. 1973. *Coastline Ecology: Bodega Head*. Berkeley: University of California Press.

Baxter, J. L. 1960. *Inshore Fishes of California*. California Department of Fish and Game.

Bostic, D. L. 1975. *A Natural History Guide to the Pacific Coast and North Central Baja California and Adjacent Islands*. Vista, Calif.: Biological Educational Expeditions.

Brandon, J. L., and F. J. Rokop. 1985. *Life between the Tides*. San Diego: American Southwest.

California Coastal Commission. 1987. *California Coastal Resource Guide*. Berkeley: University of California Press.

Carefoot, T. 1977. *Pacific Seashores: A Guide to Intertidal Ecology*. Seattle: University of Washington Press.

Carlquist, S. 1965. *Island Life*. Garden City, N.Y.: Natural History Press.

Chapman, V. J. 1974. *Salt Marshes and Salt Deserts of the World*. Von J. Cramer.

Cogswell, H. L. 1977. *Water Birds of California*. California Natural History Guides, no. 40. Berkeley: University of California Press.

Daily, M. 1987. *California's Channel Islands: 1001 Questions Answered*. Santa Barbara: McNally & Loftin.

Dawson, E. Y., and M. S. Foster. *Seashore Plants of California*. California Natural History Guides, no. 47. Berkeley: University of California Press.

Ferren, W. R. 1985. *Carpinteria Salt Marsh*. University of California–Santa Barbara Department of Biological Sciences, the Herbarium, Publication no. 4.

Fitch, J. E., and R. J. Lavenberg. 1971. *California Marine Food and Game Fishes*. California Natural History Guides, no. 28. Berkeley: University of California Press.

———. 1975. *Tidepool and Nearshore Fishes of California*. California Natural History Guides, no. 38. Berkeley: University of California Press.

Hedgpeth, J. W. 1962. *Introduction to Seashore Life of the San Francisco Bay Region and the Coast of Northern California*. California Natural History Guides, no. 9. Berkeley: University of California Press.

Hinton, S. 1987. *Seashore Life of Southern California*. California Natural History Guides, no. 26. Berkeley: University of California Press.

Kozloff, E. N. 1983. *Seashore Life of the Northern Pacific Coast*. Seattle: University of Washington Press.

Lerman, M. 1986. *Marine Biology: Environment, Diversity, and Ecology*. Menlo Park, Calif.: Benjamin/Cummings.

Levinton, J. S. 1982. *Marine Ecology*. Englewood Cliffs, N.J.: Prentice-Hall.

Light, S. F., et al. 1975. *Intertidal Invertebrates of the Central California Coast*. Berkeley: University of California Press.

McConnaughey, B. H. 1978. *Introduction to Marine Biology*. St. Louis: C. V. Mosby.

Moore, P. G., and R. Seed. 1986. *The Ecology of Rocky Shores*. New York: Columbia University Press.

Morris, R. H., D. P. Abbott, and E. C. Haderlie. 1980. *Intertidal Invertebrates of California*. Stanford: Stanford University Press.

Munz, P. A. 1964. *Shore Wildflowers of California, Oregon, and Washington*. Berkeley: University of California Press.

North, W. 1976. *Underwater California*. California Natural History Guides, no. 39. Berkeley: University of California Press.

Orr, R. T., and C. Helm. 1989. *Marine Mammals of California*. California Natural History Guides, no. 29. Berkeley: University of California Press.

Philbrick, R. N. 1967. *Proceedings of the Symposium on the Biology of the California Islands*. Santa Barbara Botanic Gardens.

Power, D. M. 1980. *The California Islands*. Santa Barbara Museum of Natural History.

Ricketts, E. F., J. Calvin, and J. W. Hedgpeth. 1968. *Between Pacific Tides*. Stanford: Stanford University Press.

Riedman, M. 1990. *The Pinnipeds: Seals, Sea Lions, and Walruses*. Berkeley: University of California Press.

Sumich, J. L. 1976. *Biology of Marine Life*. Dubuque, Iowa: Wm. C. Brown.

Tierney, R. J., et al. 1966. *Exploring Tidepool Life*. Berkeley: Berkeley-Tidepool Associates.

Zedler, Z. B. 1982. *The Ecology of Southern California Coastal Salt Marshes: A Community Profile*. U.S. Fish and Wildlife Service, Biological Services Program, FWS/OBS-81/54.

Index

Cascade Province, 170
biotic zonation of, 247–49
geology of, 234–36
Cash crops, 540
Cashew family, 359, 388
Casmerodius albus, 679–80
Cassia armata, 441
Cassiope mertensiana, 199
Castilleja, 200, 281, 347
mollis, 698
Castle Lake, 240
Castor canadensis, 533, 562–63
Catadromous species, 604, 612
Catalina Cherry, 711, 716
Cataract, 570
Catclaw Acacia, 467
Cathartes aura, 307, 544, 545
Catharus guttatus, 147
Cathedral Peak, 89
Cation-ratio dating, 426
Catkins, 154
Catoptrophorus semipalmatus, 636,
680–81
Catostomus fumeiventris, 592, 598
luxatus, 598
microps, 592, 598
occidentalis, 592, 598
platyrhynchus, 592, 598
rimiculus, 598
santaanae, 592, 598
snyderi, 598
tahoensis, 592, 598
Cattails, 527, 528
Cattle, 720
Cattle Egret, 680
Cattle Spinach, 447
Caverns, 83, 560
Mitchell, 14, 560, *pl. 11B*
Ceanothus
Cropleaf, 274
Desert, 358, 359
Hairy, 344
Hoary, 352
Hoaryleaf, 344, 358
Monterey, 274
Otay, 400
see also California lilacs
Ceanothus, 29
Ceanothus crassifolius, 344
cuneatus, 120, 125, 242
dentatus, 274
greggii, 358
integerrimus, 126
jepsonii, 278
leucodermis, 344–46
oliganthus, 344
otayensis, 400
rigidis, 274
Cebidichthyes violaceus, 651

Cedars, 292
Alaska, 5, 245
Incense, 108, 109, 110, 134, 241, 247, 249,
278, 287, 354, 387, 404
Port Orford, 241, 245, 250
Salt, 480–81
Cedros Island, 291
Cell death, 168–69
Cell division, 439
Cellular respiration, 21, 28, 32, 110, 153, 169,
439
Cenozoic Era, 58, 59, 68, 232
Centipedes, 503
Central Valley Project, 16
Century Plant, 413, 453, 460–62
Desert, 360
Cephalanthus occidentalis, 528
Cercidium floridum, 415, 465
microphyllum, 465
Cercis occidentalis, 97, 270
Cercocarpus, 29
Cercocarpus betuloides, 350
ledifolius, 180, 358
Cerithidea californica, 677, 678
Cerro Gordo Mine, 424
Cervus elaphus, 720
elaphus nelsoni, 258
elaphus roosevelti, 258
elaphus nannodes, 524, 550
Ceryle alcyon, 166, *pl. 13G*
Chaetura vauxi, 252
Chagoopa Plateau, 91
Chalcedon, 163
Chalk Lettuce, 338
Chamaea fasciata, 375
Chamaebatia foliolosa, 123
Chamaecyparis lawsoniana, 241
nootkatensis, 245
Chamise, 99, 100, 273, 341, 342–43, 347
Channeled Dog Whelk, 678
Channel Islands, 8, 314, 326, 700
Channelization, 541
Chaoborus astictopus, 585
Chaparral, 7, 9, 29, 99, 264, 313, 328; *see also*
Scrub communities
animals of, 362–87
Ceanothus, 345
Chamise, 342–44
Desert, 329–60
and fire, 341–47
Lower, 329, 339–50
Maritime, 273–76
Manzanita, 350
Productivity in, 361–62
Red Shanks, 352
Scrub Oak, 347
Soft, 328; *see also* Coastal Sage Scrub
Upper, 329, 350–57
Chaparral Broom, 282, 336